HANDBOOK OF MONETARY ECONOMICS

VOLUME II

HANDBOOKS IN ECONOMICS

8

Series Editors

KENNETH J. ARROW
MICHAEL D. INTRILIGATOR

NORTH-HOLLAND
AMSTERDAM · NEW YORK · OXFORD · TOKYO

HANDBOOK OF MONETARY ECONOMICS

VOLUME II

Edited by

BENJAMIN M. FRIEDMAN
Harvard University

and

FRANK H. HAHN
Cambridge University

1990

NORTH-HOLLAND
AMSTERDAM · NEW YORK · OXFORD · TOKYO

ELSEVIER SCIENCE PUBLISHERS B.V.
Sara Burgerhartstraat 25
P.O. Box 211, 1000 AE Amsterdam, The Netherlands

Distributors for the United States and Canada:
ELSEVIER SCIENCE PUBLISHING COMPANY INC.
655 Avenue of the Americas
New York, N.Y. 10010, U.S.A.

Library of Congress Cataloging-in-Publication Data

Handbook of monetary economics / edited by Benjamin M. Friedman and
    Frank H. Hahn.
        p.   cm. -- (Handbooks in economics; 8)
    Includes bibliographical references.
    ISBN 0-444-88027-5 (set). -- ISBN 0-444-88025-9 (v. I). -- ISBN
0-444-88026-7 (v. II)
    1. Money. 2. Monetary policy.   I. Friedman, Benjamin M.
II. Hahn, Frank.   III. Series: Handbooks in economics ; bk. 8.
    HG221.H24   1990
332.4--dc20   90-6983
                                                                     CIP

ISBN for this set: 0 444 88027 5
ISBN for this volume: 0 444 88026 7

PRINTED IN THE NETHERLANDS

325872

INTRODUCTION TO THE SERIES

The aim of the *Handbooks in Economics* series is to produce Handbooks for various branches of economics, each of which is a definitive source, reference, and teaching supplement for use by professional researchers and advanced graduate students. Each Handbook provides self-contained surveys of the current state of a branch of economics in the form of chapters prepared by leading specialists on various aspects of this branch of economics. These surveys summarize not only received results but also newer developments, from recent journal articles and discussion papers. Some original material is also included, but the main goal is to provide comprehensive and accessible surveys. The Handbooks are intended to provide not only useful reference volumes for professional collections but also possible supplementary readings for advanced courses for graduate students in economics.

KENNETH J. ARROW and MICHAEL D. INTRILIGATOR

CONTENTS OF THE HANDBOOK*

* Detailed contents of this volume (Volume I of the Handbook) may be found on p. xxi.

VOLUME II

PART 6 – MONEY, OTHER ASSETS, AND ECONOMIC ACTIVITY

PART 7 – MONEY, INFLATION, AND WELFARE

PART 8 – MONETARY POLICY

PREFACE TO THE HANDBOOK

Monetary economics has always represented a symbiosis, albeit at times an uncomfortable one, between a priori theorizing and the development and exploitation of empirical evidence. Formal theory describing an economy with money, and perhaps other financial instruments as well, has its clear antecedents in the more general structures of utility maximization and economic equilibrium. Just as clearly, this theory has steered decades of empirical research in the field. In the other direction, quantitative analysis of such fundamentals as the relationship between money and prices (for example, Smith, Tooke, Thornton) antedated anything remotely recognizable as modern economic theory. Indeed, the very existence of money itself is not a missing link for which analysis of formal models has cried out in order to connect otherwise loose conceptual strands, but – quite to the contrary – an institutional datum, the incorporation of which has proved either naggingly untidy or endlessly challenging, depending on one's point of view. The interaction here between theory and evidence has been very much a two-way street.

Yet a further influence that has significantly complicated the development of monetary economics is the direct relevance of so many of the behavioral questions at issue for the conduct of actual public policies. Which policy framework is optimal under any particular set of circumstances, or which policy action is optimal in any specific situation within a given overall framework, not only depends importantly on theoretical presumptions but often turns on comparisons among identifiable quantitative magnitudes. As a result, it is difficult if not impossible to separate either theoretical or empirical work in monetary economics from the evaluation (explicit or otherwise) of actual policies carried out in the past or, correspondingly, judgments about potential future policies.

Because of this fundamental two-way interaction between the theoretical and the empirical aspects of monetary economics, together with the relationship of both to matters of public policy, any organization of material comprehensively spanning the subject is bound to be arbitrary. We have arranged the 23 surveys commissioned for this Handbook in a way that we think reflects some of the most important logical divisions within the field. No single way of organizing this material, however – especially a linear sequencing, as publication in book form requires – can fully encompass interrelationships as rich, and among lines of thinking as diverse, as is the case in monetary economics. Different

Handbook of Monetary Economics, Volume II, Edited by B.M. Friedman and F.H. Hahn
© *Elsevier Science Publishers B.V., 1990*

arrangements are in some ways equally plausible, and we could just as well have chosen any of several potential alternatives.

It is important to recognize at the very outset that monetary theory has to contend with the handicap that it is not easily accommodated within the most complete and general theory of equilibrium which we have. It has been recognized for a long time, and many chapters in this Handbook refer to it, that at the very heart of any satisfactory theory there will have to be an account of transaction costs and of "missing markets". Monetary theory cannot proceed in the elegant manner of Arrow and Debreu, which collapses the future into the present, nor can it ignore the actual process of exchange. These are the facts of the situation, and they have the consequence of launching the monetary economist on journeys where no generally agreed upon axiomatic guideposts are available. This in turn has two further consequences: the assumptions that monetary economists make often attempt to encapsulate empirical regularities rather than axioms, and the subsequent theorizing has not often attained the definiteness one would like.

While a "high" monetary theory is, at best, incomplete at present, it is not obvious that this is widely felt to be a serious matter. Much of monetary theory and econometrics is macroeconomics, and the aim is to build (simple) models which can be estimated. Such models are often based on "the representative agent" who behaves very much as in a microeconomic textbook. This construct often allows one to sidestep problems of multiple equilibria or, for instance, the distribution of money balances. But there clearly is a tension between this manner of proceeding and the recognition that, for instance, money is a means of exchange between agents differently situated, with different preferences and possibly different beliefs. This tension is even more readily apparent if the model is to encompass borrowing and lending, or the trading of debts, neither of which can strictly occur in an economy made up only of "representative" agents. The reader will find some of these tensions reflected, repeatedly, in the present volume.

We decided to start this Handbook with "fundamentals" which are of concern to those who study the transition from an Arrow–Debreu economy to one in which an intrinsically worthless means of exchange has value. The chapters by Ostroy and Starr (Chapter 1) and by Duffie (Chapter 3) study this question. The first of these concerns the transaction role of money and so takes explicit note of transaction costs. It is interesting to realize that what appears so simple, and for so long has been taken as so simple, is not so at all but requires all the wit of a theorist. Duffie, also paying attention to transaction costs, achieves a satisfactory integration of money into general equilibrium theory. It goes beyond the shortcuts of the assumed "money in advance" requirement. There are still assumptions here which one would wish to relax, but the chapter goes a long way toward providing the required understanding.

The other chapter in Part I, by Hahn (Chapter 2), is not so much concerned with foundations of general equilibrium theory with money, but with one consequence of allowing explicitly for transaction costs: the "flexibility" or "liquidity" property of assets. In an economy with transaction costs, which has trading at all dates, uncertainties may be resolved or reduced as time proceeds, and the optimum plan would then allow for the probability that asset composition should be changed.

But of course it may be argued that general equilibrium theory is itself open to sufficient empirical objections as to make it doubtful that modifying it to allow for money is a profitable strategy. For instance, the theory neglects strategic interactions of agents as well as the more familiar possibilities of imperfect competition. Moreover, it is essentially a long-run equilibrium theory. Benassy (Chapter 4) gives an account of what has come to be known as "non-Walrasian equilibrium" theory, to which he has made many contributions. He shows how such a theory may form a foundation for macroeconomics. The reader will note that it is useful to recognize that equilibrium must be defined relatively to the environment in which agents operate, and that it is a mistake to think of the models Benassy discusses as "disequilibrium" models.

Shubik (Chapter 5) gives an account of his research into a game-theoretic approach to monetary theory. For some readers these will be unfamiliar waters. But we have learned in recent years that game theory is a promising route to a theory of institutions, and it is these that will have to be understood before monetary theory has been properly formulated. Shubik's chapter discusses the main lines such theorizing can take.

As we have already noted, the problems of "fundamentals" need to be understood and, one hopes, resolved. They arise whether one is concerned with macroeconomic theory or, indeed, with empirical investigation. Both have a need to "simplify", but in each case it is important that one knows what it is that is being simplified. On the other hand it is possible that investigating how the presence of money and other financial instruments modifies simple models which we already know well may itself be a route along which new insights can be gained.

The contributions in Part III are just of this type. Orphanides and Solow (Chapter 6) undertake a thorough and exhaustive study of canonical growth models modified by the presence of money. They critically examine earlier work in this direction, and they pay particular attention to the investment decision when there is an alternative asset to which savings can be directed. As elsewhere in this Handbook, the reader will find that paying attention to the existence of money in an economy matters.

In recent years the overlapping generations (O.G.) model has come to play a large part in macroeconomic theorizing. Brock (Chapter 7) modifies it to allow for transaction costs. This is a desirable modification, since in many O.G. models money has no recognizable purpose other than being the (often the only) means of transferring consumption from one period to the next. Brock's chapter is thus an advance on what we have, and exactly the right move to bring genuine monetary phenomena into the orbit of the model. Here too the analysis goes deeper than merely postulating a "money in advance" constraint.

It is worth remarking that O.G. models are both more robust and more interesting than is sometimes believed, at least at the abstract level. Of course the postulate of two-period lives is highly unrealistic. On the other hand, it is difficult to think of a *qualitative* conclusion of these models – for example, the existence of many equilibrium paths, or of sunspot paths – that is plausibly at risk from more realistic life times. At first sight one might think this false, since infinitely lived agents who with perfect foresight plan their optimal future must obey a transversality requirement. The latter, it might then be thought, will preclude "disagreeable" paths for the economy. But recent research has shown this not to be the case when agents discount the future sufficiently highly.[1] On the other hand, infinitely lived agents may make a difference to the "indeterminacy" results of standard O.G. models. There may then be a difference in qualitative conclusions as one passes from finitely to infinitely lived agents. It takes, however, a peculiar perception of the world to regard the latter as the more "realistic" approach. In general, economies with finitely lived agents who discount the future are unlikely to be grossly mal-analyzed in O.G. models with two-period lives.

In parallel with such "fundamental" analyses of why money exists and under what circumstances it will be valued, investigation of the empirical and institutional facts of the demand for and supply of money has also made recognizeable advances in recent years. As Goldfeld and Sichel (Chapter 8) show, the main "event" in this regard has been the collapse of previously long-standing empirical regularities relating familiar measures of money to aggregate income and prices over time. Although their chapter documents this phenomenon only for the case of the United States, research along the lines of that which they summarize has amply shown that conventional money demand functions have suffered similarly in other countries as well.[2] As their chapter shows, there is no lack of potential explanations for the breakdown of these prior relationships, and so there is at least room for cautious optimism that, in the future, "normalcy" (if a stable money demand function is that) may be restored. But it is also possible that that may not occur or, if it does, that it may not be for some substantial time. Along the way, investigation of competing hypotheses about just why all this has happened is a potentially rich source of new insights.

[1]See Boldrin and Montruchio (1986).
[2]See, for example, Fair (1987).

The other two chapters in Part IV, by Brunner and Meltzer (Chapter 9) and by Modigliani and Papademos (Chapter 10), lay out these authors' conceptions of how money demand interacts with money supply in a setting that explicitly includes the important institution of a banking system.[3] As a result, the analysis distinguishes "inside" from "outside" money. In addition, both sets of authors further enrich the institutional setting by distinguishing debt (or "credit") from either money or capital. Brunner and Meltzer's analysis provides the basis for the emphasis on the monetary base which has characterized many of their contributions over the years, an emphasis that has by now influenced the practical conduct of monetary policy in many countries. Modigliani and Papademos focus even more directly on the working of the banking system itself and its implications for the money supply process.

Although much of monetary economics not surprisingly concentrates on the role of money per se, it is also important to recognize that actual economies (unlike many O.G. models) have more assets than just money. Willingness to hold money itself therefore represents, in part, a decision not to hold wealth in other forms. At the same time, conditions determined by the interaction of money supply and money demand can also influence the terms on which other assets will be held, terms that in turn potentially affect macroeconomic outcomes in any of a variety of familiar ways. The three chapters in Part V address several important features of the pricing of non-money assets that have also played important roles in monetary economics.

Merton (Chapter 11) systematically lays out in a general form the theory of pricing of speculative assets in a frictionless continuous-time setting, which his own work, along with that of Samuelson and others, has developed.[4] The theory in this form has long been the central workhorse of "finance", as a distinct field of economic inquiry. But an important development in recent years, which is still ongoing, is the erosion of any recognizable barrier between financial economics and monetary economics.[5]

The other two chapters in Part V use more specialized apparatus, based on a discrete-time framework, to focus on specific aspects of asset pricing that have traditionally been important to empirical monetary economics. Intertemporal aspects of asset pricing – what makes the subject interesting, really – are at the heart of both. Singleton (Chapter 12) reviews not only the empirical evidence bearing on asset pricing behavior per se (and presents the results of new tests) but also the connections that the literature in this area has drawn between asset pricing and macroeconomic behavior in explicitly dynamic settings. Shiller's

---

[3]Our friend and colleague Karl Brunner co-authored this chapter with Allan Meltzer, but died before the Handbook went to print. We take this opportunity to express our admiration for Karl's outstanding contribution to monetary economics, and our sorrow at his passing.

[4]Merton's chapter is an expanded and updated version of his contribution to the *Handbook of Mathematical Economics* (1981), edited by Arrow and Intrilligator.

[5]See, for example, the discussion in Fischer and Merton (1984).

chapter (Chapter 13), including McCulloch's data for the United States which we hope will be useful to many researchers in the field, consolidates and interprets the literature of the term structure of interest rates. While this subject may at first seem somewhat specialized, the term structure has long been a central issue in monetary economics because of the need to bridge the gap between asset returns that are at least proximately (and, in most models, in the short run) subject to direct influence by the central bank – primarily short-term interest rates – and the long-term asset prices and yields that are typically more important in theories of how what happens in financial asset markets influences non-financial economic activity.

But how *do* the prices and yields determined in the asset markets affect the nonfinancial economy? This question, which moves monetary economics to the center of macroeconomics, is the focus of all four chapters in Part VI. Abel (Chapter 14) adopts a partial equilibrium approach, reviewing the literature of consumption and investment, and surveying both theoretical developments and empirical results. Blanchard (Chapter 15) assumes a general equilibrium perspective, and therefore frames the issue as the specific question of whether changes in the quantity of money or its growth rate affect real output (Is money non-neutral?) and, if so, why. Both Abel's chapter and Blanchard's leave the reader with a strong sense of the ultimately empirical nature of monetary economics as a field of study. While it is straightforward to state, in the abstract, hypotheses about what determines consumption and/or investment, and likewise to advance theories about whether money is neutral and why, these chapters show that comparative evaluation of competing theories in this area is also, in the end, largely an empirical matter.

Although it is often merely implicit, an aspect of economic behavior that underlies much of what monetary economics has to say about how money affects spending and output is that credit markets are imperfect. For example, Abel's review of the modern consumption literature makes clear the importance of any constraints that arise from consumers' not being able to borrow at the same interest rate at which they can lend – in some cases, being unable to borrow at all – and hence having to base consumption spending in part on the flow of current income. The same phenomenon is also relevant to investment behavior (as well as in the field of "corporate finance").[6] Jaffee and Stiglitz (Chapter 16) show how "credit rationing" can arise, not just temporarily when lending rates adjust slowly, but as a consequence of profit-maximizing lenders' equilibrium response to adverse selection and incentive effects due to information imperfections and asymmetries. It is worth pointing out explicitly that, here again, a phenomenon that has played an important part in monetary economics but would be difficult if not impossible to rationalize in a world

---

[6]See, for example, the "pecking order" hypothesis advanced by Myers and Majluf (1984).

populated only by "representative agents", is fully consistent with standard norms of economic theorizing in a more general setting. Jaffee and Stiglitz also review the empirical evidence bearing on effects of credit rationing on spending and output.

Whether or not credit markets are perfect also bears importantly on questions of fiscal policy. Haliassos and Tobin (Chapter 17) review the issues that have dominated the discussion of fiscal effects on non-financial economic activity. Along with the Barro–Ricardo "debt neutrality" hypothesis, according to which debt-for-taxes substitutions do not affect spending, Haliossos and Tobin also address whether money is "superneutral" in the sense that real variables in the steady state are invariant with respect to the growth rate of money, and whether debt-for-money substitutions ("open market operations") affect real behavior. In each case they first show the conditions under which the kind of policy action in question would leave all real variables unchanged, and then evaluate the theoretical and empirical plausibility of these conditions.

Regardless of whether money does or does not affect output in either the short or the long run, money and monetary policy are still of prime interest to economists on account of their consequences for prices – a subject about which, at least at the qualitative level, disagreement like that surrounding the effect of money on output is strikingly absent. The three contributions in Part VII focus on the relationship between money and inflation, importantly including implications for economic welfare. McCallum's chapter (Chapter 18) is a broad survey of theoretical models and empirical evidence on this subject, encompassing both steady-state relationships and the co-movements of money and prices (and output) over the business cycle. McCallum also reviews the growing literature that provides a different perspective on inflation via a positive analysis of the behavior of monetary policy.

For many macroeconomic theories, the cost of inflation is the induced economizing in money balances and hence the induced increase in transaction costs. On the face of it, however, this (except perhaps in hyperinflation) seems too small a cost to explain the belief that inflation is ever enemy number one. Driffil, Mizon and Ulph (Chapter 19) consider, both theoretically and empirically, this and other possible costs – most importantly, the possibility that higher inflation necessarily implies greater uncertainty about inflation and/or greater variability of relative prices, and hence an erosion of the price system's ability to allocate resources efficiently. Like so much else in economics, it will be found that the subject requires more sophisticated treatment than it usually receives from politicians and bankers.

The subject of inflation is also related to what, since Milton Friedman, has been called the theory of the optimum quantity of money. Woodford (Chapter 20) provides a very detailed and sophisticated analysis of this problem. For instance, it has been held that rising price levels, by leading agents to hold less money in their portfolios, would lead in steady states to a higher capital–labor ratio than would otherwise be the case. Hence, it was argued, the rise in output per capita would have to be taken into account in a judgment of the welfare effects of inflation. Woodford shows this view to be mistaken. Indeed, his chapter's range is so wide and his arguments so meticulous that it is likely that his will become the standard account of this matter.

As we have been at some pains to emphasize, in monetary economics the connections between research on economic behavior and implications for economic policy are sufficiently pervasive that most of the chapters in this Handbook bear on matters of monetary policy, either implicitly or directly, despite the fact that their principal focus lies elsewhere. Even so, no collection of essays attempting to survey the field could be complete without a straightforward examination of some of the major issues surrounding the conduct of actual monetary policy. The Handbook therefore concludes with three contributions that do just that.

The chapters by Fischer (Chapter 21) and by Friedman (Chapter 22) mostly take up aspects of monetary policy that arise in the context of monetary policy for a single (closed) economy. Although Fischer discusses the gold standard, his interest in it here is not as a means of regulating exchange rates among countries' currencies but as a way of resolving, for any one country, the age-old dilemma of rules versus discretion (which, of course, also pervades many other aspects of decision-making, both public and private). As he shows, recent advances, based in part on game-theoretic concepts, have done much to clarify long-standing views as well as to open new roads for analysis. Friedman takes the discussion closer to the actual practice of monetary policy by addressing the nuts-and-bolts question of how the central bank operates: How should it evaluate the merits of alternative policy instruments? And should it use any target(s) intermediate between its policy instrument and the intended macroeconomic outcomes? As is so often the case, while the way of framing these questions is fundamentally shaped by underlying theoretical constructs, the answers, for any given country at any given time, turn on magnitudes that can only be determined empirically.

Finally, Dornbusch and Giovannini (Chapter 23) broaden the discussion by introducing the entire range of considerations that become relevant when the economy whose monetary policy is in question is interacting, in non-trivial ways, with others. At the most basic level, placing the economy in an explicitly international setting relaxes one constraint (its spending must equal its output) and introduces one extra variable to be determined (the price of its money in terms of foreign currency). But the immediate implication of a gap between aggregate spending and output (for any one economy) is a capital inflow or outflow, which over time accumulates into a stock of assets or liabilities with further consequences for behavior in both financial and real markets. At this stage, as Dornbusch and Giovannini aptly show both theoretically and empirically, the economics of monetary policy becomes inseparable from open-economy macroeconomics – a fitting place for this Handbook to conclude.

BENJAMIN M. FRIEDMAN
Harvard University

FRANK H. HAHN
Cambridge University

References

Boldrin, M. and L. Montrucchio (1986) 'On the indeterminacy of capital accumulation paths', *Journal of Economic Theory*, 40: 26–39.

Fair, R.C. (1987) 'International evidence on the demand for money', *Review of Economics and Statistics*, 69: 473–480.

Fischer, S. and R.C. Merton (1984) 'Macroeconomics and finance: The role of the stock market', *Carnegie-Rochester Conference Series on Public Policy*, 21: 57–108.

Myers, S.C. and N.S. Majluf (1984) 'Corporate financing and investment decisions when firms have information that investors do not have', *Journal of Financial Economics*, 13: 187–221.

CONTENTS OF VOLUME II

PART 7 – MONEY, INFLATION, AND WELFARE

PART 6

MONEY, OTHER ASSETS, AND ECONOMIC ACTIVITY

Chapter 14

CONSUMPTION AND INVESTMENT

ANDREW B. ABEL*

University of Pennsylvania and NBER

Contents

*I thank Benjamin Friedman, David Wilcox and Stephen Zeldes for their detailed comments on earlier drafts of this chapter.

Handbook of Monetary Economics, Volume II, Edited by B.M. Friedman and F.H. Hahn
© *Elsevier Science Publishers B.V., 1990*

1. Introduction

Consumption and investment expenditure together account for 80 percent of GNP in the United States and for a similarly large percentage of GNP in other major economies.[1] This chapter analyzes the behavior of consumption and investment focusing on the response of these components of spending to changes in income and to changes in assets markets. I have tried to present the material in this chapter so that it will be useful both to Keynesian macroeconomists and to new classical macroeconomists. To a Keynesian economist, the organizing principle of the chapter can be viewed as the development of private domestic behavioral relations underlying the IS schedule. In particular, I have stressed the effects of income and interest rates on consumption and investment. Although a new classical economist would not find it helpful to think of this chapter in terms of the IS curve, he or she could view the separate treatments of consumption and investment as developing, within an intertemporal optimization framework, the behavior of different economic actors.

This chapter is, by design, partial equilibrium in nature. What is missing is the endogenous determination of income and interest rates. A Keynesian economist would close the model and determine income and interest rates by adding an LM schedule, but the LM schedule is covered elsewhere in this Handbook. A new classical economist would specify a production function and then would allow prices and interest rates to adjust to clear all markets. With the exception of a brief discussion of the implications of general equilibrium for testing the permanent income hypothesis, this chapter does not touch upon general equilibrium considerations.

In keeping with the partial equilibrium focus of this chapter, I will first discuss the determinants of consumption and then I will discuss investment. Since the 1950s, economic models of consumption behavior have explicitly recognized that in making consumption decisions, consumers take account of their lifetime resources rather than simply their current income. Both the life-cycle model of Modigliani and Brumberg (1954) and Ando and Modigliani (1963) and the permanent income model of Friedman (1957) are based on the notion that consumers prefer smooth streams of consumption over time. Access to capital markets allows consumers to choose a sequence of consumption over time that is smoother than the sequence of income. In Subsection 2.1 I show that if income in every period is deterministic, then for a consumer with

---

[1] The ratio of private consumption to GNP and the ratio of gross fixed investment to GNP for the period 1980–85 are: United States: 64.3 percent and 15.7 percent; U.K.: 60.1 percent and 16.8 percent; Germany: 57.0 percent and 20.8 percent; Japan (1980–84): 59.0 percent and 27.8 percent.

access to perfect capital markets, there would be no relation between income and contemporaneous consumption. However, if income follows a stochastic process, then there is, in general, a positive contemporaneous correlation between consumption and income. Subsection 2.2 analyzes the relation between consumption and income and discusses several empirical tests of the permanent income hypothesis.[2]

The simple permanent income model discussed in Section 2 is applicable to the consumption of non-durable goods and services. However, the model is not applicable to consumers' expenditures on durable goods. Because durable goods produce services to consumers over several periods, these goods are consumed over several periods. Because the expenditure on a durable good usually takes place in one period, it is important to distinguish the consumption of durable goods from the expenditure on these goods. From the viewpoint of the individual consumer, what matters is the flow of consumption services from durable goods. From the viewpoint of the macroeconomic determination of aggregate income, expenditure on durable goods is important. Section 3 enriches the permanent income model to incorporate durable goods as well as non-durable goods and services into the decision problems of individual consumers.

The theoretical analysis of consumer expenditure in Sections 2 and 3 is based on the assumption that consumers have access to perfect capital markets and can borrow or lend at an exogenous rate of interest. However, a substantial fraction of consumers is unable to consume as much as predicted by the permanent income model because they cannot borrow as much as they would like at the prevailing interest rate. Consumers who would like to increase their current borrowing in order to increase current consumption are said to be liquidity constrained. The importance of liquidity constraints from the viewpoint of macroeconomics is that the relation between consumption and contemporaneous income is generally different for liquidity constrained consumers than it is for consumers who do not face binding liquidity constraints. The implication of liquidity constraints for the relation between consumption and income is discussed in Section 4.

In analyzing the relation between income and consumption in the first three sections of the chapter, the rate of return on wealth is assumed to be constant. However, there are important links between asset markets and consumption behavior. In particular, the level of consumption depends on the consumer's wealth, and the intertemporal pattern of consumption depends on the rate of return on assets. Section 5 presents a formal model of consumption by an infinitely-lived consumer who faces a stochastic rate of return on wealth. This

---

[2]For a complementary survey of the recent consumption literature that focuses on the joint stochastic behavior of consumption and income, see Hall (1989).

model produces a simple relation between consumption and wealth and allows us to distinguish the effects of ex post changes in the rate of return from changes in the ex ante rate of return.

Although the statement that consumption depends on the consumer's level of wealth is not controversial, there is still wide-ranging disagreement about what constitutes the wealth of a consumer. In particular, should a consumer's holding of government bonds be counted as net wealth? An equivalent question in a different guise is whether a bond-financed cut in lump-sum taxes has an effect on consumption. At first glance it would appear that consumers who received a tax cut would view themselves as having an increase in lifetime disposable resources and would increase their consumption accordingly. However, because the government must eventually pay interest on the newly issued bonds and repay the principal, the bond-financed tax cut implies that future taxes will be increased. Indeed, the increase in future taxes will have a present value equal to the current tax cut, and thus, it is argued by some economists, there will be no response of consumption to a change in tax policy. In Section 6 this argument, which is known as the Ricardian Equivalence Theorem, will be presented and critically evaluated.

The discussion of capital investment begins in Section 7 with the Jorgensonian neoclassical theory of investment. This theory explicitly treats the demand for capital as a derived demand by starting with the firm's production function and demand curve. The demand curve and production function are used to obtain a relation between a firm's cash flow and its contemporaneous stock of fixed capital (plant and equipment). The firm's demand for fixed capital is set at a level that equates the marginal product of capital with the user cost of capital in production over a certain period of time. The neoclassical theory of investment predicts that a firm's demand for capital will be positively related to the firm's level of output and will be negatively related to the user cost of capital. A more restricted model which corresponds to a special case of the neoclassical model is the accelerator model, in which the demand for capital is proportional to the level of output but is independent of the user cost. The accelerator model and the more general neoclassical model are discussed in Subsection 7.1.

An alternative theory of investment behavior by firms is the q theory. Tobin (1969) defined q to be the ratio of the market value of a firm to the replacement cost of the firm. This ratio is meant to measure the value of fixed capital relative to its cost. The greater is this ratio, the greater would be the incentive to acquire the capital and hence the greater would be the rate of investment. Because the value of the firm is measured using data from equity and bond markets, the link between asset markets and investment expenditure is quite explicit. Although Tobin's presentation of the q theory did not explicitly model the firms' production function and demand curve, it is possible to start with the demand curve and the production function and then derive the q theory as the result of intertemporal maximization by firms. A formal derivation of the q theory, and the link between the formal model and Tobin's q, is presented in Subsection 7.2.

The corporate tax environment – in particular, the corporate tax rate, the investment tax credit, and the schedule of depreciation allowances – has a potentially important impact on capital investment decisions. Although the effects of these aspects of the tax code on investment are important in their own right, from the viewpoint of monetary economics the most interesting feature of the taxation of capital income and expenditure is the interaction of inflation, taxes and investment. This interaction is briefly discussed in Section 8.

The models of investment analyzed in Sections 7 and 8 do not take explicit account of uncertainty facing firms. The decision to present deterministic models in these sections reflects two considerations: First, as a matter of expositional clarity, the deterministic models are much simpler than the stochastic models. Second, and more importantly, is that, in contrast to models of consumption, state-of-the-art models of investment behavior do not rely critically on the stochastic nature of the decision problem facing firms. Nevertheless, a brief discussion of the impact of uncertainty is presented in Section 9.

In addition to investment in plant and equipment, firms also invest in inventories. Inventory behavior has been a particularly puzzling component of aggregate demand. It would appear that just as consumers with concave utility functions would want to have smooth time profiles of consumption, firms with convex cost functions would want to have smooth time profiles of production. Inventories provide firms with a means to have smooth production in the face of fluctuating sales. However, it does not appear that firms actually take advantage of inventory accumulation and decumulation to smooth out production relative to sales. Section 10 discusses this apparent contradiction in the simple production smoothing model as well as possible explanations.

2. Consumption

The life-cycle and permanent income hypotheses, which are the major theories of consumption behavior, each relate the consumption of a consumer to his lifetime income rather than to his contemporaneous income. The underlying choice-theoretic framework is that a consumer has an intertemporal utility function that depends on consumption in every period of life. The consumer maximizes utility subject to single lifetime budget constraint. There is no static, or period-by-period, budget constraint that requires consumption in a period to equal the income in that period.[3] Indeed, in the absence of uncertainty, the life-cycle and permanent income hypotheses both predict that there will be no relation between consumption and contemporaneous income. However, the introduction of uncertainty will generally induce a positive relation between consumption and contemporaneous income.

To develop the implications of the permanent income model, consider the decision problem facing an individual consumer at time t. Let y_{t+j} denote the consumer's after-tax labor income at time $t + j$, for $j = 0, 1, 2, \ldots$. It is convenient to assume that the consumer lives forever. Strictly speaking, this assumption is consistent with the permanent income hypothesis but is inconsistent with the life-cycle hypothesis. One of the major implications of the life-cycle hypothesis is that saving is done by consumers when they are working to provide for consumption when they are retired. This implication will not be captured in a model in which the consumer lives, and earns income, forever. However, for the purpose of examining the cyclical relation between consumption and contemporaneous income, it is simply not important whether the consumer has a finite horizon.[4] Let c_{t+j} denote the consumption of the consumer in period $t + j$ and let W_t denote the wealth of the consumer at the beginning of period t before earning interest. The rate of return on wealth carried from period $t - 1$ to period t is r_t. The accumulation of wealth is described by

$$W_{t+1} = (1 + r_t)W_t + y_t - c_t . \tag{1}$$

Equation (1) describes the evolution of the consumer's wealth over time but, by itself, does not constrain behavior. There is nothing in equation (1) that prevents the consumer from borrowing to finance arbitrarily large consumption. An additional constraint is needed. If the consumer has a finite lifetime, with period T being the last period of his life, then one could impose the constraint $W_{T+1} \geq 0$, which states that the consumer cannot die in debt. Under an infinite horizon, the appropriate constraint is:

$$\lim_{j \to \infty} \{(1 + r_t)(1 + r_{t+1})(1 + r_{t+2}) \ldots (1 + r_{t+j})\}^{-1} W_{t+j+1} \geq 0 .$$

The intertemporal utility function of the consumer is assumed to be additive-

---

[3] In the presence of binding liquidity constraints, which are discussed in Section 4, the consumer will face a sequence of period-by-period budget constraints.

[4] The wealth effects associated with changes in the timing of lump-sum taxes and the validity of the Ricardian Equivalence Theorem discussed below depend critically on whether the horizon of an individual consumer is finite or infinite. Poterba and Summers (1987) argue that empirically the distinction between infinite horizons and finite horizons has a small effect on the impact of tax policy.

ly separable over time.[5] Let $u(c_{t+j})$ denote the utility of consumption in period $t+j$. The period utility function $u(\cdot)$ is assumed to be strictly increasing and strictly concave. As of the beginning of period t the consumer maximizes the intertemporal utility function:

$$U_t = E_t\left\{\sum_{j=0}^{\infty} (1+\rho)^{-j}u(c_{t+j})\right\},\tag{2}$$

where ρ is the rate of time preference and where $E_t\{\cdot\}$ denotes the expectation conditional on information available at the beginning of period t. This available information includes the realization of current income y_t and the current rate of return on wealth r_t.

It is now straightforward to derive the first-order condition characterizing optimal consumption behavior:

$$u'(c_t) = (1+\rho)^{-1}E_t\{(1+r_{t+1})u'(c_{t+1})\}.\tag{3}$$

To interpret (3) consider a reduction in c_t of one unit accompanied by a one unit increase in the wealth carried into period $t+1$. The additional unit of wealth carried into period $t+1$ produces an additional $1+r_{t+1}$ units of disposable resources in period $t+1$ which can be consumed in period $t+1$ without affecting any future opportunities of the consumer. In evaluating whether this potential intertemporal rearrangement of consumption is a good idea, the consumer compares $u'(c_t)$, which is the loss in utility from the unit reduction in c_t, with

$$(1+\rho)^{-1}E_t\{(1+r_{t+1})u'(c_{t+1})\},$$

which is the expected discounted gain in utility from the increase of $(1+r_{t+1})$ in c_{t+1}. If the utility loss associated with a unit reduction in c_t is smaller than the expected discounted utility gain from the increase in period $t+1$ consumption, then the consumer can increase expected utility by reducing c_t. Alternatively, if the utility loss associated with a unit reduction in c_t is greater than the expected discounted utility gain from the increase in period $t+1$ consumption, then the consumer can increase expected utility by increasing c_t. Optimality requires that neither an increase nor a decrease in c_t can lead to higher expected utility, which is implied by equation (3).

Now suppose that the rate of return on wealth is perfectly predictable one period in advance; more precisely, suppose that r_{t+1} is in the information set at

---

[5]For examples of non-time-separable utility functions, see Hayashi (1985b) and Eichenbaum, Hansen and Singleton (1986).

time t. This assumption holds, for example, if the real interest rate r_t is constant over time. Empirically, if the length of a period is taken to be a calendar quarter and if r_t is the real return on 90-day Treasury bills, then the assumption that r_t is perfectly predictable one period in advance may be a reasonable approximation.[6] Alternatively, if r_t is the one-period holding return on common stocks, then the assumption that r_t is perfectly predictable one period in advance is clearly inappropriate. Nevertheless, I make this assumption to understand some of the implications of the first-order condition in equation (3). Observe that equation (3) can be rewritten as:

$$u'(c_{t+1}) = [(1 + \rho)/(1 + r_{t+1})]u'(c_t) + e_{t+1}, \tag{4}$$

where e_{t+1} is an unpredictable random variable. More precisely, $E_t\{e_{t+1}\} = 0$. Equation (4) is particularly useful for understanding the stochastic implications of the permanent income hypothesis. Before examining the stochastic implications of (4), I will first discuss the implications of intertemporal utility maximization in the absence of uncertainty.

2.1. Deterministic income

In the absence of uncertainty the random disturbance e_{t+1} in (4) is identically equal to zero. In this case, equation (4) implies that the marginal utility of consumption grows (or falls) at a rate equal to $(\rho - r_{t+1})/(1 + r_{t+1})$. Thus, if the rate of return r_{t+1} exceeds the discount rate ρ, then the marginal utility falls over time which implies that consumption rises over time. That is, if the reward to postponing consumption (r_{t+1}) exceeds the impatience cost of waiting (ρ), then the consumer will choose to have lower consumption today than in the future. Alternatively, if the rate of return on saving is less than the rate of time preference, then the consumer will choose to have higher consumption today than in the future.

Now make the stronger assumption that the rate of return r_t is a constant, and furthermore that r_t is equal to the rate of time preference ρ. It follows immediately from (4) that if $r_t = \rho$ and if e_{t+1} is identically zero, then consumption is constant over time. The level of consumption will be the maximum permanently sustainable flow of consumption, which Friedman (1957) has called permanent income. Note that if the consumer always consumes an amount equal to the net return on his or her wealth (appropriately defined, as below, to include human as well as non-human wealth), then

---

[6] Although the nominal rate of return on 90-day T-bills is perfectly predictable, the rate of inflation cannot be predicted perfectly, so the real rate of return cannot be predicted perfectly.

his or her total wealth will remain constant over time. Any attempt to permanently consume more than the return on wealth will not be sustainable. Thus permanent income is equal to the real rate of return on total wealth multiplied by total wealth.

To calculate the level of permanent income, it is necessary to calculate human wealth. In the absence of uncertainty, and in the presence of a real interest rate which is constant and equal to ρ, human wealth is simply the present value of current and future labor income,[7] which I will denote as H_t^*. More precisely,

$$H_t^* = \frac{1}{1+r} \sum_{j=0}^{\infty} (1+r)^{-j} y_{t+j} .$$

(5)

The factor $1/(1+r)$ appears in front of the summation because, consistent with the definition of non-human wealth, I am defining human wealth in period t to be calculated prior to earning the rate of return r in that period. The implication of this definition is that if income is always equal to some constant, say y_0, then human wealth would be equal to y_0/r. In this case, the return to human wealth would be y_0 so that in the absence of non-human wealth, permanent income would be equal to y_0.

In the presence of non-human wealth, permanent income, y_t^{P*}, is equal to the return on human plus non-human wealth so that

$$y_t^{P*} = r(W_t + H_t^*) .$$

(6)

Recall that with $r = \rho$, consumption is constant over time. The invariance of consumption over time holds even if labor income is (deterministically) time-varying. Thus, for an individual living in a world without uncertainty, there would be no relation between consumption and contemporaneous income over time. However, in a cross-section of individuals with different levels of permanent income, there would be a positive cross-sectional relation between consumption and permanent income. From the viewpoint of macroeconomics and stabilization policy, it is the time-series co-movement of consumption and contemporaneous income which is of interest. Since there would be no systematic co-movement of consumption and contemporaneous income for a consumer in a deterministic environment, it is necessary to shift attention to a stochastic environment.

---

[7]Flavin (1981) pointed out that Sargent (1978) erroneously defined permanent income as the present value of disposable income. However, because disposable income includes the return on wealth, this concept involves double counting.

2.2. Stochastic income

In the presence of income uncertainty the definition of permanent income needs to be modified somewhat. Although current non-human wealth W_t and current after-tax labor income y_t are each known at the beginning of period t, future labor income is uncertain at the beginning of period t. Therefore, human wealth as defined in (5) is not observable to the individual consumer at time t. In the presence of uncertainty, the expression on the right-hand side of (5) will be called the ex post human wealth and the expression on the right-hand side of (6) will be called ex post permanent income at time t. An individual consumer in period t must choose consumption in period t prior to observing the ex post permanent income.

Let $H_t \equiv E_t\{H_t^*\}$ denote ex ante human wealth in period t and let $y_t^P \equiv E_t\{y_t^{P*}\}$ denote ex ante permanent income in period t. Taking the conditional expectation of each side of (6) yields:

$$y_t^P = r(W_t + H_t) . \tag{7}$$

Suppose that the consumer sets consumption in period t equal to ex ante permanent income y_t^P so that

$$c_t = y_t^P = r(W_t + H_t) . \tag{8}$$

Strictly speaking, it is not generally optimal to set consumption equal to permanent income as in (8). The uncertainty associated with future income flows may generate precautionary saving which would imply that an intertemporally optimizing consumer would choose to consume less than permanent income as defined here.[8] However, if the utility function $u(\cdot)$ is quadratic, which implies that the third derivative of $u(\cdot)$ is identically equal to zero, then the certainty equivalence principle implies that it is indeed optimal to set consumption equal to permanent income, as defined in (6). I will ignore the complications associated with a non-zero third derivative of $u(\cdot)$, and proceed as if optimal consumption is equal to permanent income in (6).

Before proceeding to study the response of consumption to income for a fairly general stochastic process for income, I first derive a consumption function for a simple special case. Suppose that y_t evolves according to the

---

[8]See Drèze and Modigliani (1972), Kimball (1986), and Zeldes (1989) for discussions of precautionary saving. Recently, Caballero (1987) has derived the solution to the consumer's optimization problem under uncertainty with a constant absolute risk aversion utility function. He has argued that precautionary saving behavior can explain the excess sensitivity and excess smoothness phenomena discussed below.

first-order autoregressive process:

$$y_t - \bar{y} = a_1(y_{t-1} - \bar{y}) + u_t, \tag{9}$$

where $0 \le a_1 < 1$, $E_{t-1}\{u_t\} = 0$, and $\bar{y}$ is the unconditional expected value of y_t. In this case, $E_t\{y_{t+j}\} = \bar{y} + a_1^j(y_t - \bar{y})$ so that using the definition of permanent income in (5) and (6) it can be shown that consumption is:

$$c_t = rW_t + [r/(1 + r - a_1)]y_t + [(1 - a_1)/(1 + r - a_1)]\bar{y}. \tag{10}$$

Equation (10) relates consumption to wealth and contemporaneous income and thus resembles a traditional aggregate consumption function.[9] Note that the coefficients on y_t and $\bar{y}$ are each positive and they sum to one. Thus, ignoring wealth W_t, consumption would be a weighted average of current income and the unconditional average value of income. The weight on current income is an increasing function of a_1 which measures the persistence of deviations in income. Although (10) may not appear at first glance to be a forward-looking consumption function, it does take account of forecasts of future income. It turns out that for a first-order autoregressive process, y_t contains all information that is known about future deviations of income from $\bar{y}$.

For a more general stochastic process on y_t, I will not derive a consumption function relating consumption to wealth and current and past income. Instead I will focus on the relation between fluctuations in consumption and fluctuations in income.

To study the fluctuations in consumption, recall that consumption, c_t, is equal to contemporaneous (ex ante) permanent income y_t^P. Therefore, fluctuations in consumption will be identical to fluctuations in permanent income. If the rate of return on wealth is constant, then all fluctuations in permanent income are due to fluctuations in human wealth; specifically, fluctuations in permanent income are due to revisions in expectations about future labor income. It follows immediately from the definition of human wealth (5) and

---

[9]See, for example, Ando and Modigliani (1963) and Modigliani (1975). In the formulation presented in equation (10), a one dollar increase in current wealth leads to an r dollar increase in current consumption. This result depends on the assumption that the consumer has an infinite horizon. Alternatively, under the life-cycle model, which assumes that the consumer has a finite horizon, the consumer consumes some of the principal in addition to the interest on his wealth. In this case, the coefficient on wealth is larger than the real interest rate r. Empirically, Ando and Modigliani (1963) estimated this coefficient to be in the range from 0.04 to 0.10 for a sample of U.S. data; in examining Italian data, Modigliani (1975) estimated the coefficient on wealth to be roughly in the range from 0.06 to 0.09.

the fact that $E_t\{E_{t+1}\{y_{t+j}\}\} = E_t\{y_{t+j}\}$, $j = 1, 2, 3, \ldots$, that

$$H_t = \frac{1}{1+r} [y_t + E_t\{H_{t+1}\}] . \tag{11}$$

Adding non-human wealth to both sides of (11) yields:

$$W_t + H_t = \frac{1}{1+r} [(1+r)W_t + y_t + E_t\{H_{t+1}\}] . \tag{12}$$

Now multiply both sides of (12) by $(1 + r)$ and use the wealth accumulation equation (1) to replace $(1 + r)W_t + y_t$ by $c_t + W_{t+1}$ to obtain:

$$(1 + r)[W_t + H_t] = c_t + W_{t+1} + E_t\{H_{t+1}\} . \tag{13}$$

Equation (13) was derived simply by manipulating the definition of human wealth and using the wealth accumulation equation; it does not embody any behavioral assumptions. Now suppose that consumption is equal to permanent income and use (8) and (13) to obtain:

$$r(W_t + H_t) = r(W_{t+1} + E_t\{H_{t+1}\}) . \tag{14}$$

Equation (14) indicates that if consumption is equal to permanent income, then permanent income is not expected to change. Equivalently, any change in permanent income and consumption between period t and period $t + 1$ must be unanticipated from the viewpoint of period t. The underlying economic reason for this result, of course, is that if the return on wealth is equal to the rate of time preference, the individual optimally plans to have constant consumption over his life. Indeed, using the definition of permanent income in (8), and using the fact that $E_t\{H_{t+1}\} = E_t\{E_{t+1}\{H_{t+1}\}\}$ yields:

$$c_t = y_t^P = E_t\{y_{t+1}^P\} = E_t\{c_{t+1}\} . \tag{15}$$

Thus, the conditional forecast of c_{t+1} based on information available in period t is equal to c_t. That is, consumption follows a random walk.[10] This important and powerful insight was first noted and tested by Hall (1978).[11]

It follows immediately from (15) and the permanent income hypothesis in

[10]The observation that consumption follows a random walk is based on the first-order condition (3). If the utility function $u(c_t)$ is quadratic and if the interest rate is equal to ρ, then (3) can be written as $\phi_0 - \phi_1 c_t = E_t\{\phi_0 - \phi_1 c_{t+1}\}$, which implies that $E_t\{c_{t+1}\} = c_t$.

[11]See Hall (1989) for an excellent survey of the literature that tests and interprets the random walk hypothesis.

(8) that

$$c_{t+1} - c_t = y_{t+1}^P - E_t\{y_{t+1}^P\} . \tag{16}$$

The change in consumption from one period to the next is equal to the innovation, i.e. the unanticipated change, in permanent income.

In order to calculate the changes in permanent income and consumption, it is necessary to specify the stochastic process for after-tax labor income. The simplest stochastic environment to analyze is one in which after-tax labor income is stochastic but the rate of return on wealth r_t is constant. Let r denote the constant value of r_t. Suppose that y_t evolves according to a univariate autoregressive process:

$$y_t - \bar{y} = a(L)(y_t - \bar{y}) + u_t , \tag{17}$$

where $a(L)$ is a polynomial in the positive powers of the lag operator L, and the innovation u_t is a random disturbance with the property that $E_t\{u_{t+1}\} = 0$. For example, if y_t follows the first-order autoregressive process $y_t - \bar{y} = a_1(y_{t-1} - \bar{y}) + u_t$, then the polynomial $a(L)$ is simply $a_1 L$. It is sometimes more convenient to work with the moving average representation of the income process:

$$y_t - \bar{y} = b(L)u_t , \tag{18}$$

where $b(L)$ is a polynomial in the non-negative powers of the lag operator L. It follows from inspection of (17) and (18) that $b(L) = (1 - a(L))^{-1}$. The effect on future income y_{t+j} of a one unit innovation in y_t is b_j so that

$$E_{t+1}\{y_{t+1+j}\} - E_t\{y_{t+1+j}\} = b_j u_{t+1} . \tag{19}$$

Using the definitions of ex post and ex ante permanent income yields an expression that relates the innovation in permanent income to the innovation in after-tax labor income:

$$y_{t+1}^P - E_t\{y_{t+1}^P\} = r/(1 + r) \sum_{j=0}^{\infty} (1 + r)^{-j}[E_{t+1}\{y_{t+1+j}\} - E_t\{y_{t+1+j}\}] . \tag{20}$$

Equation (20) states that the revision in expected permanent income is equal to the present value of revisions in expectations of y_{t+j}, $j = 1, 2, 3, \ldots$. Substituting (19) into (20) and recalling that $b(L)$ is the polynomial in the non-negative powers of L, the expression for the innovation in permanent income in (20) can be written more succinctly as:

$$y_{t+1}^{P} - E_t\{y_{t+1}^{P}\} = (r/(1+r))b(1/(1+r))u_{t+1} . \tag{21}$$

Equation (21) relates the innovation in permanent income to the innovation in current after-tax income.[12] It is perhaps easiest to interpret (21) and its implications in the special case of a first-order autoregressive process. In this case the coefficients b_i are equal to a^i for $i = 0, 1, 2, \ldots$ so that equation (21) and equation (16) together imply that

$$c_{t+1} - c_t = r/(1 + r - a_1)u_{t+1} . \tag{22}$$

Equation (22) relates consumption to the contemporaneous innovation in income. Interpreting the response of consumption to the contemporaneous innovation in income as the marginal propensity to consume (MPC), equation (22) implies that the MPC is equal to $r/(1 + r - a_1)$. The size of the marginal propensity to consume plays a crucial role in Keynesian models of aggregate demand. Equation (22) illustrates that the value of the MPC depends on the nature of the stochastic process of income as stressed by Friedman (1957). If income is serially uncorrelated, then $a_1 = 0$ and the MPC is equal to $r/(1 + r)$. The average annual real rate of return in the United States is, depending on the asset, somewhere between zero and perhaps 7 percent.[13] This suggests that if annual income is serially uncorrelated, then the MPC is quite small, ranging roughly from zero to 0.07.

The MPC is an increasing function of the parameter a_1, which is the first-order serial correlation coefficient of a first-order univariate autoregressive process for income. In fact, income – more precisely aggregate income – tends to be very highly serially correlated. Note that if income follows a random walk, then $a_1 = 1$ and the MPC is equal to one. The reason for a unitary MPC in the case of a random walk is that any innovation in income is expected to be permanent. That is, a one dollar innovation in income at time t raises the forecast of income at all future dates by one dollar and hence raises the expectation of permanently sustainable consumption by one dollar.

The relation between consumption and income that is predicted by the permanent income hypothesis serves as a basis for econometrically testing this hypothesis. Flavin (1981) examined the joint behavior of consumption and

---

[12]The factor $(r/(1+r))b(1/(1+r))$ on the right-hand side of (21) is equal to $(r/(1+r))(1 - a(1/(1+r)))^{-1}$. Note that if y_t is stationary, then this factor is positive. However, it is not necessarily less than one, even if y_t is stationary.

[13]Mehra and Prescott (1985) report that in the United States over the period from 1889 to 1978 the average real rate of return on short-term bonds is 0.80 percent per year and the average real rate of return on equity is 6.98 percent per year.

income and concluded that consumption displays excessive sensitivity to the anticipated change in contemporaneous income. Of course, this conclusion depends on the estimated stochastic process for income. More recently, Deaton (1986) and Campbell and Mankiw (1987) have suggested that income has a random walk component so that, for example, a positive innovation to income raises the forecasts of future income into the indefinite future. Deaton (1986) and Campbell and Deaton (1987) have estimated the stochastic process for income including a random walk component and have argued that permanent income is more variable than current income because changes in labor income are positively serially correlated. Therefore, if consumption is equal to permanent income, then consumption should be more variable than current income. Deaton and Campbell and Deaton calculate, based on the estimated time-series process for income, the degree to which the variance of consumption should exceed the variance of current income. They conclude that consumption is "too smooth".[14] At first glance Flavin's finding of excess sensitivity of consumption to income appears to be contradicted by Campbell and Deaton's finding that consumption responds too little to innovations in income. Campbell and Deaton resolve this apparent contradiction by observing that Flavin's result concerns the relation between consumption and the anticipated change in income, whereas their excess smoothness result concerns the relation between consumption and the contemporaneous innovation to the income process. When Campbell and Deaton examine the relation between consumption and anticipated changes in income, they also find excess sensitivity. In addition, they present an analytic argument that "there is no contradiction between excess sensitivity and excess smoothness; they are the same phenomenon" (p. 33).

The tests of the permanent income hypothesis based on the time-series properties of income and consumption maintain the assumption that the rate of interest used to discount future cash flows is constant. This seemingly innocuous assumption has important implications for the interpretation of tests of permanent income hypothesis. Michener (1984) developed a simple stochastic general equilibrium model in which the interest rate is endogenously determined. He showed that even if consumers maximize the expected value of a standard time-separable utility function, the stochastic process for aggregate consumption can fail to satisfy the properties discussed above. Although Michener's model includes production and capital accumulation, his point can be made more simply, and more starkly, by considering an endowment economy in which each (identical) consumer receives an endowment y_t of the

---

[14]West (1987) models the income process with a random walk component and develops a variance bounds test of the permanent income model. He also finds that consumption is too smooth relative to income.

homogeneous perishable good. In equilibrium, aggregate consumption (per capita), c_t, will be equal to aggregate income, y_t, and hence aggregate consumption would inherit the time-series properties of aggregate income. In this situation, consumption and income would have equal variances so that comparisons of the variances of these series would be uninformative. Also, if the change in income were forecastable, the change in consumption would be forecastable, which violates one of the implications of the permanent income hypothesis. The lesson from Michener's analysis is that the tests of the permanent income hypothesis discussed above maintain several auxiliary assumptions in addition to the hypothesis that consumers maximize an intertemporal utility function subject to a budget constraint and subject to available information about future income. Therefore, rejections of the permanent income hypothesis based on the time-series properties of consumption and income can be interpreted as rejecting specific formulations of the permanent income hypothesis but do not necessarily reject the hypothesis of intertemporal utility maximization under uncertainty.

3. Consumer durables

The discussion so far has proceeded under the assumption that there is a homogeneous consumption good. While this assumption is intended to be only a simplifying abstraction, one must ask what sorts of important or interesting differences among goods are masked by this assumption. The major heterogeneity among goods that is recognized in the literature on consumption is the distinction between durable goods and non-durable goods. In fact, expenditure on durable goods and consumption of non-durable goods (and services) have quite different cyclical behavior. Durable goods expenditures display much more volatility over the business cycle than do non-durable goods and services. More precisely, the percentage variation in durables expenditures is much greater than the percentage variation in non-durables consumption. However, the level of expenditure on durables is much smaller than the level of expenditures on non-durables. In fact, it is this difference in the average level of expenditures on durables and non-durables that accounts for the difference in the percentage variation. The variation in the absolute level of durables expenditures is smaller than the variation in the absolute level of non-durable expenditures.[15]

---

[15]Startz (1987) reports that "the standard deviation of deviations from trend for durables is large (60 dollars), about one-half the size of that for nondurables" (p. 2). Mankiw (1982) uses lagged information to forecast durables expenditure and non-durables consumption. He finds that the standard deviations of the forecast errors are roughly equal (13.1 for durables vs. 13.2 for non-durables).

In analyzing the behavior of consumer durables, it is important to distinguish between expenditure on consumer durables, which I will denote x_t, and the consumption of the services of durables, which I will denote by d_t. I will assume that the flow of consumption services from durables during period t, d_t, is proportional to the stock of durables held at the beginning of period t, D_t, plus the durables acquired during period t, x_t. In particular, suppose that

$$d_t = \psi(D_t + x_t) . \tag{23}$$

Although the concept of the consumption of the flow of services from the durable good is important for some purposes, it is the level of expenditure on durable goods which is important for the determination of aggregate demand.

It is useful to introduce the concept of the user cost of durables. To simplify the analysis, suppose that the relative price of durables and non-durables remains fixed over time. Let μ denote the price of durables in terms of non-durables. In the absence of relative price changes, there are two components to the user cost of the durable: forgone interest and depreciation. By holding a unit of a durable rather than interest-earning wealth, the consumer forgoes interest of $r\mu$ per period, where r is the real interest rate. In addition, if the durable depreciates at a rate δ per period, then depreciation imposes a cost of $\delta\mu$ per period to the owner of the durable. Therefore the user cost of a durable is $(r + \delta)\mu$.

The introduction of durables implies that the consumer holds two assets: interest-earning wealth and durables. Previously, W_t was defined to be the non-human wealth of a consumer at the beginning of period t. Now W_t is to be interpreted as the interest-earning wealth, or equivalently, as the non-human wealth of the consumer minus the value of the consumer's stock of durable goods. The budget constraint in (1) must be amended to:

$$W_{t+1} = (1 + r_t)W_t + y_t - c_t - x_t , \tag{24}$$

where c_t is now interpreted as the consumption of non-durables. Recalling that δ is the depreciation rate per period of the durable leads to the following relation between the stock of the durable and expenditures on the durable:

$$D_{t+1} = (1 - \delta)(D_t + x_t) . \tag{25}$$

In order to motivate expenditure on durables as well as non-durables, the utility function must be augmented to include services from durables as well as from non-durables. Let $u(c_t, d_t)$ be the utility function in period t. The consumer will allocate spending in period t between the purchase of non-durables and the rental of durables. The optimal allocation will equate the marginal rate of substitution with the rental price. Writing the utility function as $u(c_t, \psi(D_t + x_t))$ makes clear that the marginal rate of substitution between non-durables and durable goods is $\psi u_d / u_c$ where u_d is the derivative of $u(c, d)$ with respect to durable services and u_c is the derivative of $u(c, d)$ with respect to non-durables. Setting this marginal rate of substitution equal to the rental price of durables yields:

$$\psi u_d / u_c = (r + \delta)\mu .$$

(26)

For simplicity, suppose that the period utility function has the following Cobb–Douglas specification:

$$u(c_t, d_t) = c_t^{1-\alpha} d_t^{\alpha} .$$

(27)

In this case, the consumer will allocate a fraction $1 - \alpha$ of his or her consumption basket to non-durables, c_t, and a fraction α to the rental of services of durables, $(r + \delta)\mu(D_t + x_t)$. Therefore,

$$D_t + x_t = \frac{1}{(r + \delta)\mu} \cdot \frac{\alpha}{1 - \alpha} \cdot c_t .$$

(28)

Substituting (28) into (25) yields:

$$D_{t+1} = (1 - \delta) \frac{1}{(r + \delta)\mu} \frac{\alpha}{1 - \alpha} c_t .$$

(29)

To obtain the relation between expenditures on durables and expenditures on non-durables, substitute (29) into (25) to obtain:

$$x_t = \kappa \{ c_t - (1 - \delta)c_{t-1} \} ,$$

(30a)

where

$$\kappa = [1 / (r + \delta)\mu][\alpha / (1 - \alpha)] .$$

(30b)

Equation (30a) can be used to determine the response of expenditures on durables to an innovation in income. It follows immediately from (30a) that in response to an innovation in income, the marginal propensity to spend on durables is equal to κ times the marginal propensity to consume non-durables. Let $\sigma_t(x)$ denote the standard deviation of the one-period forecast error of x_t, conditional on information known at the end of period $t - 1$; similarly, let $\sigma_t(c)$ denote the standard deviation of the one-period forecast error of c_t, conditional on information known at the end of period $t-1$. It follows immediately from (30a) that

$$\sigma_t(x) = \kappa\sigma_t(c) . \tag{31}$$

The parameter κ measures the cyclical volatility of expenditures on durables relative to the cyclical volatility of non-durables consumption. In principle, κ can be either greater or less than one so that the cyclical variability of durables expenditures can exceed or fall short of the cyclical variability of non-durables consumption. However, the theory predicts that the *relative* variability of durables expenditure must exceed the *relative* variability of non-durables consumption. To derive this implication of the theory, first observe from (30a) that if x_t and c_t are stationary, then

$$\bar{x} = \kappa\delta\bar{c} , \tag{32}$$

where $\bar{x}$ is the average value of x and $\bar{c}$ is the average of c. Then divide (31) by (32) to obtain $\sigma_t(x)/\bar{x} = (1/\delta)\sigma_t(c)/\bar{c}$. Therefore, since δ is less than one, this simple extension of the permanent income model to include consumer durables as well as non-durables explains the fact that the percentage volatility of durables expenditures exceeds that of non-durable consumption.

Equation (32) can be used to get an estimate of the parameter κ using data on the rate of depreciation and the average levels of expenditures on durables and non-durables. Using the figures for average durables expenditure and average non-durables consumption reported in Startz (1987, p. 2) yields a value of $\bar{x}/\bar{c}$ equal to 12.2 percent. Therefore, the factor κ is equal to $0.122/\delta$. Bernanke (1985, p. 53) reports a depreciation rate for consumer durables of 0.0506 per quarter. Therefore, for quarterly data, the value of κ is 2.41. This value of κ appears to be substantially larger than is reflected in consumer spending. It implies, counterfactually, that $\sigma_t(x)$ should be larger than $\sigma_t(c)$. Also recall from (30) that κ is equal to the ratio of the effect of an income innovation on durables expenditure to the effect of an income innovation on non-durables consumption. Bernanke (1985, p. 57) estimates this ratio to be 0.775. The fact that the calculated value of κ appears to overstate the cyclical variability of durables expenditures may reflect that the model derived above has ignored costs of adjusting the stock of durables [see Bernanke (1985)] and has ignored implications of irreversibility discussed below.

Equation (30a) can be used to analyze the serial correlation of expenditure on consumer durables. The contrast between the predicted serial correlation of durables expenditure and non-durables consumption is particularly striking in the case in which durables are perfectly durable. Formally, durables are perfectly durable when the rate of depreciation, δ, is equal to zero. In this case, equation (30a) implies that x_t is proportional to $c_t - c_{t-1}$, the change in non-durables consumption. Under the permanent income hypothesis the change in non-durables consumption is completely unpredictable, and thus expenditure on durables cannot be predicted. Equivalently, $E_{t-1}\{x_t\} = 0$. Therefore, in the absence of depreciation, expenditure on durables follows a white noise process but expenditure on non-durables follows a random walk.

It is also worth noting that if the rate of depreciation is equal to one, so that durables are completely non-durable, then equation (30a) states that x_t is proportional to c_t. That is, x_t and c_t both follow a random walk, as should be expected because in this case "durables" are non-durable.

The analysis above suggests that the serial correlation of expenditures on durables is an increasing function of the rate of depreciation. In fact, expenditures on durables are highly serially correlated.[16] If the large degree of serial correlation is to be consistent with the model outlined above, then the rate of depreciation would probably have to be implausibly large. Alternative explanations for the high degree of serial correlation would point to departures from the simple model. Two such departures are liquidity constraints, to be discussed later, and irreversibility of durables expenditures.

The term "irreversibility" of durables expenditures is meant to capture the notion that an individual who tries to sell a used consumer durable generally receives a price that is lower than the value of the remaining durables services evaluated at the market price for new durables. In the extreme case of complete irreversibility, the consumer cannot obtain any resources by selling a used durable good. To see the effects of irreversibility, consider a small unanticipated decrease in the consumer's income. Under perfect reversibility, the consumer should reduce consumption of both durables services and non-durables. However, if the resale price of the durable is low, then the consumer may choose not to sell any of the durable, but instead may reduce non-durable consumption or interest-earning wealth by more than in the optimal plan under complete reversibility. If income continues to be unexpectedly low for a few periods, then the consumer may have to sell off some of the durable in order to avoid a large decline in non-durables consumption. The date at which it becomes optimal to sell some of the durable depends on the level of the consumer's other wealth. With a higher level of wealth, the consumer can wait longer before selling some of the non-durable. Although this discussion has focused on the response to a decrease in income, the consumer will display a conservative response to an increase in income because of the possibility of a future decline in income. At the level of the individual consumer, the effect of the introduction of irreversibility is to reduce the

---

[16]Lam (1986) reports that, except for motor vehicles, most categories of consumer durables expenditures "are well characterized by a first-order process of coefficient around 0.95" (p. 12). The first-order autocorrelation of new cars is 0.770.

marginal propensity to purchase durables in response to an increase in income. As for the behavior of aggregate expenditure on durables, Lam (1986) has used simulation techniques to show that if there is cross-sectional variation in household wealth, then irreversibility will induce a high degree of serial correlation in aggregate durables expenditures.

4. Liquidity constraints

The permanent income hypothesis presented above is based on the assumption that an individual consumer can borrow and lend at the same interest rate, and furthermore that the consumer can borrow or lend any amount subject to the lifetime budget constraint described above. An important departure from this assumption is the possibility that the consumer may face a liquidity constraint. Broadly interpreted, the term liquidity constraint is meant to capture the notion that an individual is not able to borrow any amount he or she chooses at an interest rate equal to the rate he or she earns on financial wealth. The departure from the assumption of perfect capital markets may take any of several forms. For instance, the individual may be able to borrow any amount he or she chooses at a fixed interest rate but this rate exceeds the rate of return on financial assets. In this case the intertemporal budget constraint of the individual is piecewise linear, with a kink occurring at a point where current consumption is equal to current income plus liquid financial wealth. An extreme example of this type of liquidity constraint, which corresponds to an infinite borrowing rate, is the case in which the consumer is simply unable to borrow. Alternatively, the capital market imperfection may manifest itself in the form of an interest rate on borrowing that rises with the level of the consumer's borrowing.[17] For the sake of simplicity, I will use the term liquidity constraint to refer to a situation in which the consumer is unable to borrow at all.

Liquidity constraints have important implications for the relation between consumption and contemporaneous income.[18] A consumer who is currently liquidity constrained would like to increase current consumption but is unable to do so because he or she cannot borrow. If the consumer's income turns out to be one dollar higher, then it is both feasible and desirable to increase current consumption by one dollar. Alternatively, if income turns out to be one dollar lower, then the consumer is forced to reduce consumption by one dollar. Thus, for a consumer currently facing a binding liquidity constraint, the

---

[17]See Stiglitz and Weiss (1981) for a discussion of credit rationing.

[18]In addition, liquidity constraints have important implications for the effects of tax policy. See Hayashi (1985c) and Yotsuzuka (1987) for a discussion of the implications of liquidity constraints for the Ricardian Equivalence Theorem.

marginal propensity to consume out of current disposable income is equal to one. Even if the consumer does not face a binding liquidity constraint in the current period, the prospect of a binding liquidity constraint in the future would affect the current marginal propensity to consume.[19]

Although liquidity constraints have strong implications for the marginal propensitiy to consume, they may be difficult to detect in aggregate data. The reason for this difficulty is that under the permanent income hypothesis, the marginal propensity to consume depends on the stochastic properties of income. Since aggregate income is highly serially correlated, and indeed may even be a random walk, the permanent income hypothesis predicts an MPC of about one even in the absence of liquidity constraints. Thus, an MPC near unity could result from either a binding liquidity constraint or highly serially correlated income.

Evidence of binding liquidity constraints has been found in econometric analyses of panel data. Hall and Mishkin (1982) analyzed expenditures on food in the Panel Study of Income Dynamics and concluded that about 20 percent of the households in their sample of U.S. households were liquidity constrained. Hayashi (1985a) and Zeldes (1989a) used data on individual household wealth and found that households with large amounts of liquid assets appeared to adhere to the permanent income hypothesis but households with small liquid wealth appeared to behave as if liquidity-constrained. The importance of liquidity constraints from the viewpoint of the cyclical relation between consumption and income is that the MPC of constrained households is equal to one. Thus, if the MPC implied by the permanent income hypothesis is less than one and is less than the apparent MPC in the data, one might appeal to liquidity constraints to explain the "excess sensitivity" of consumption. Alternatively, if income has a unit root and if the changes in income are as persistent as estimated by Campbell and Deaton (1987), then one might appeal to liquidity constraints to explain excess smoothness.

5. Interest rate and wealth effects on consumption

The response of consumption to changes in after-tax labor income y_t were analyzed above in a model in which consumers take account of stochastic variation in y_t in optimally reaching consumption decisions. Ideally, to analyze the response of consumption to changes in the rate of interest or to changes in the value of wealth, one would like to develop a model of a consumer

---

[19]For example, suppose that $\rho = r = 0$ and the consumer does not currently (in period t) face a binding liquidity constraint. If the consumer will face a binding liquidity constraint in period $t + N$, then the marginal propensity to consume out of a one-time addition to wealth in period t is $1/(N + 1)$.

maximizing an intertemporal utility function subject to random variation in the rate of return as well as random variation in labor income. Unfortunately, it is difficult to develop a simple model with a closed-form solution for a consumer facing both labor income uncertainty and rate of return uncertainty. To analyze the response of consumption to changes in the rate of return on wealth, I will present a simple model in which the only source of income is the return on non-human wealth.

Suppose that the consumer has no labor income so that the wealth accumulation equation (1) can be written as:

$$W_{t+1} = (1 + r_t)W_t - c_t ,$$ (33)

where the real rate of return on wealth is now treated as a random variable. For analytic simplicity suppose that the random rate of return r_t is identically and independently distributed over time. The consumer attempts to maximize the time-separable utility function in (2). The maximum attainable value of U_t depends only on the consumer's available resources in period t, $(1 + r_t)W_t$. Let the function $V((1 + r_t)W_t)$ denote the maximum attainable value of U_t in (2) and note that

$$V((1 + r_t)W_t) = \max u(c_t) + (1/(1 + \rho))E_t\{V((1 + r_{t+1})W_{t+1})\} .$$ (34)

The function $V(\cdot)$ cannot be specified independently. It is a solution to the functional equation in (34).

In general the functional equation in (34) is difficult to solve, but in the case of isoelastic utility a solution can be derived in a straightforward manner.[20] Suppose that the utility function $u(c)$ has the isoelastic form $u(c) = c^{1-\gamma}/(1 - \gamma)$, where $\gamma > 0$ is the (constant) coefficient of relative risk aversion. In this case the intertemporal utility function in (2) is homothetic so that the income expansion path relating consumption at various dates is a straight line through the origin. Thus, changes in $(1 + r_t)W_t$ induce an equiproportionate change in c_t. A solution to the functional equation is:[21]

$$V((1 + r_t)W_t) = A((1 + r_t)W_t)^{1-\gamma}/(1 - \gamma) ,$$ (35)

where A is a coefficient to be determined later. To solve the consumer's

---

[20]Samuelson (1969) derives the solution for this finite-horizon version of this problem using backward induction.

[21]The functional equation (34) has a continuum of solutions of the form:

$$V((1 + r_t)W_t) = A((1 + r_t)W_t)^{1-\gamma}/(1 - \gamma) + \phi(1 + \rho)^t ,$$

where ϕ is an arbitrary constant. The solution in (35) sets ϕ equal to zero.

optimization problem, consider a reduction in c_t of one unit and an accompanying increase of one unit in W_{t+1}. The reduction in c_t will reduce current utility on the right-hand side of (34) by $u'(c_t)$ and the increase in W_{t+1} will increase the expected present value of next period's utility on the right-hand side of (34) by $(1/(1 + \rho))E_t\{(1 + r_{t+1})V'((1 + r_{t+1})W_{t+1})\}$. At the optimum, the net effect on the consumer's utility will be zero, and hence consumption will be at the optimal level when

$$u'(c_t) = (1/(1 + \rho))E_t\{(1 + r_{t+1})V'((1 + r_{t+1})W_{t+1})\} . \tag{36}$$

Using the isoelastic specification for $u(\cdot)$ and using (35), equation (36) can be written as:

$$(c_t)^{-\gamma} = (A/(1 + \rho))E_t\{(1 + r_{t+1})^{1-\gamma}\}((1 + r_t)W_t - c_t)^{-\gamma} . \tag{37}$$

Now raise both sides of (37) to the $-1/\gamma$ power to obtain:

$$c_t = G(1 + r_t)W_t , \tag{38a}$$

where

$$G = \{1 + [(A/(1 + \rho))E_t\{(1 + r_{t+1})^{1-\gamma}\}]^{1/\gamma}\}^{-1} . \tag{38b}$$

Substituting the optimal consumption rule (38a) into (34) and using the definition of G in (38b) implies, after some manipulation, that

$$A = G^{-\gamma} . \tag{39}$$

Finally, substituting (39) into (38b) yields:

$$G = 1 - [E_t\{(1 + r_{t+1})^{1-\gamma}\}/(1 + \rho)]^{1/\gamma} . \tag{40}$$

Observe from (38a) that G is the marginal ($=$ average) propensity to consume out of available resources. I have now derived the optimal consumption rule of a consumer who faces a stochastic rate of return on wealth. It follows immediately from (38a) that consumption is proportional to the contemporaneous value of wealth including the current return to capital. Note, in particular, that consumption in period t is an increasing function of the ex post rate of return r_t.

This model allows us to distinguish the effects of changes in the ex ante probability distribution of the rate of return from changes in the ex post rate of return. From the point of view of period t, the ex ante information about the stochastic rate of return r_{t+1} is summarized by the factor $[E_t\{(1 + r_{t+1})^{1-\gamma}\}]^{1/\gamma}$

in the marginal propensity to consume out of wealth, G. Note first that if γ is equal to one, in which case the utility function $u(\cdot)$ is logarithmic, then $G = 1 - [1/(1 + \rho)]$. Thus, under logarithmic utility, consumption, c_t, is invariant to the ex ante distribution of the rate of return. The reason for this invariance is that the income and substitution effects associated with an increase in the prospective rate of return offset one another exactly. An increase in the prospective interest rate has a positive income effect because the consumer is assumed to be a net lender rather than a net borrower (i.e. $W_t > 0$). The substitution effect of a higher prospective interest rate is to make current consumption more expensive relative to future consumption and thus to reduce current consumption. The income and substitution effects are in opposite directions, and for the case of logarithmic utility, they are of equal magnitude. If the utility function $u(\cdot)$ displays less curvature than the logarithmic function, i.e. if $\gamma < 1$, then the substitution effect is strengthened; if the rate of return, r_{t+1}, is non-stochastic, then consumption, c_t, would be a decreasing function of r_{t+1}. Alternatively, if the utility function is more curved than the logarithmic function, ($\gamma > 1$), then the substitution effect is diminished; if the rate of return, r_{t+1}, is non-stochastic, consumption, c_t, would be an increasing function of r_{t+1}.

I have shown that consumption, c_t, increases in response to an increase in the ex post interest rate r_t, but may rise, fall, or remain unchanged in response to a given change in the ex ante distribution of the rate of return r_{t+1}. The difference in the effects of ex post and ex ante interest rates is that the ex post interest has only an income effect associated with it, whereas a change in the ex ante interest rate has both an income effect and a substitution effect. In particular, if, at the beginning of period t, the consumer sees that the realized value of the interest rate r_t is higher than expected, then the consumer is wealthier than expected and therefore increases consumption. The interest rate r_t represents the consumer's terms of trade between periods $t - 1$ and period t; because r_t does not affect the terms of trade between period t and any future period, there is no substitution effect on c_t. By contrast, if in period t the value of r_{t+1} is seen to increase, then the terms of trade between period t and period $t + 1$ are altered, thereby inducing a substitution effect in addition to the income effect.

The magnitude of the response of consumption to changes in the expected rate of interest can be measured by the intertemporal elasticity of substitution. Under the isoelastic utility function, $u(c) = c^{1-\gamma}/(1 - \gamma)$, the intertemporal elasticity of substitution is equal to $1/\gamma$. This result can be derived by substituting $u'(c) = c^{-\gamma}$ into the first-order condition (3) and rearranging to obtain:

$$\ln c_{t+1}/c_t = -(1/\gamma)\ln(1 + \rho) + (1/\gamma)\ln(1 + r_{t+1}) - (1/\gamma)\ln \eta_{t+1}, \qquad (41)$$

where η_{t+1} is a positive random variable and $E_t\{\eta_{t+1}\} = 1$. Recalling that $1 + r_{t+1}$ is the relative price of consumption in periods t and $t + 1$, it is clear from (41) that a 1 percent change in the relative price of c_{t+1} and c_t induces a $1/\gamma$ percent change in c_{t+1}/c_t. Thus, the intertemporal elasticity of substitution is equal to $1/\gamma$. Using monthly data and measuring the rate of return on wealth by the value-weighted aggregate return on stocks on the New York Stock Exchange, Hansen and Singleton (1983) estimated γ to be between zero and two.

The formal analysis of the effect of the interest rate is based on the assumption that all of the consumer's disposable resources come from return on wealth. In particular, after-tax labor income is ignored. To the extent that there will be positive flows of after-tax labor income in the future, an increase in the ex ante interest rate would have a smaller income effect, or possibly even a negative income effect. Intuitively, an increase in the prospective rate of return would reduce the present value of future labor income and thus would reduce the current value of human wealth. Indeed, if the consumer's current non-human wealth and current income are sufficiently low compared to his future earnings, the consumer may be a net borrower rather than a net lender (i.e. W_t may be negative). In this case, an increase in the interest rate would have a negative income effect; both the income effect and the substitution effect would tend to reduce consumption in response to an increase in the interest rate.[22]

6. Government bonds and Ricardian equivalence

Having shown that consumption is an increasing function of non-human wealth, the next task is to examine whether government bonds are to be included in wealth. To see why this is an interesting question consider the effects of a $100 cut in current lump-sum tax revenues that the government finances by issuing $100 of bonds. It was pointed out by Ricardo (1911), and later modeled formally by Barro (1974), that under certain conditions forward-looking consumers would not change their consumption at all in response to this tax change. The reason is that consumers recognize that the government will have to increase taxes in the future to repay the principal and interest on

---

[22]Using a simulation model, Summers (1981b) finds that the reduction in human wealth that accompanies an increase in the interest rate is quantitatively substantial. In addition, he finds that the interest elasticity of saving is quite substantial (roughly in the range from 1 to 3) and that this interest elasticity is not very sensitive to the parameter γ. Estimates of this elasticity based on consumption and rate of return data are generally much smaller [Boskin's (1978) estimate of 0.4 for the interest elasticity of saving is at the high end of the range], but Summers attributes much of the difference to the fact that these other studies hold wealth constant, whereas he takes account of the negative impact of higher interest rates on human wealth.

the newly-issued bonds. Because of the need to increase taxes in the future, the opportunity set of the representative consumer is unaltered by this policy. The consumer can achieve exactly the same path of current and future consumption by increasing current saving by $100, and by holding this additional saving in the form of government bonds. The consumer can hold these bonds in his portfolio earning interest until future taxes are increased to pay the interest and principal on the bonds. The future tax increases will be exactly equal in value to the principal and interest earned by the consumer. Therefore, the consumer can support the same path of consumption as initially planned. Furthermore, since the tax change is in a lump-sum tax, there will be no change in relative prices. Therefore, it is both feasible and optimal for the consumer to maintain the same consumption and portfolio decisions (except for increasing the holding of government bonds) as before the tax change. This invariance of private spending to changes in the timing of lump-sum taxes has been dubbed "The Ricardian Equivalence Theorem" by Buchanan (1976). It is worth noting that although Ricardo stated the basic argument, he cautioned against taking the argument seriously as a description of the actual impact of debt financed tax cuts, claiming that such a system tends to discourage saving [Ricardo (1911, pp. 162–163)].

To analyze the question of whether government bonds are net wealth, suppose that the interest rate is constant and use the expression for permanent income implied by (5) and (6) to obtain:

$$c_t = r\left[W_t + (1/(1+r)) \sum_{j=0}^{\infty} \{(1+r)^{-j} E_t\{y_{t+j}\}\} \right]. \tag{42}$$

Now distinguish government bonds, B_t, from the rest of the consumer's non-human wealth, K_t, so that

$$W_t = K_t + B_t. \tag{43}$$

It is also convenient to separate after-tax labor income into pre-tax labor income y_{Lt} and taxes T_t so that

$$y_t = y_{Lt} - T_t. \tag{44}$$

Substituting (43) and (44) into the consumption function (42) yields:

$$c_t = r\left[K_t + (1/(1+r)) \sum_{j=0}^{\infty} \{(1+r)^{-j} E_t\{y_{Lt+j}\}\} \right]$$
$$- r\left[(1/(1+r)) \sum_{j=0}^{\infty} \{(1+r)^{-j} E_t\{T_{t+j}\}\} - B_t \right]. \tag{45}$$

The Ricardo–Barro insight is that the government's budget constraint implies that the present value of tax revenues must equal the sum of the current government debt outstanding plus the present value of government expenditure on goods and services. Thus, the second line of (45), which is the excess of the present value of current and future tax revenues over the value of currently outstanding government bonds, is equal to the present value of current plus future government spending. Therefore, debt-financed changes in taxes that leave the path of government spending unchanged have no effect on consumption. To make the point starkly, suppose that government spending on goods and services is always equal to zero so that the second line of (45) is equal to zero. In this case, the consumption function is simply:

$$c_t = r\left[K_t + (1/(1 + r)) \sum_{j=0}^{\infty} \{(1 + r)^{-j} E_t\{y_{Lt+j}\} \right].$$ (46)

Inspection of (42) and (46) sheds light on the question of whether government bonds should be treated as part of net wealth in an economy in which the Ricardian Equivalence Theorem holds. It follows from (42) that if the income variable is net of taxes, then the wealth variable should include government bonds. Alternatively, if the income variable is pre-tax labor income, then it follows from (46) that the wealth variable should not include government bonds as net wealth. In addition, if there is government spending, then (45) implies that the present value of government spending should appear as an additional explanatory variable along with pre-tax labor income and K_t.

The above discussion has proceeded under the assumption that the Ricardian Equivalence Theorem holds. There is a large theoretical literature that explores many reasons why the Ricardian Equivalence Theorem may not hold. I will mention only three reasons why the impact of actual tax policy may not be accurately described by the Ricardian Equivalence Theorem. First, the argument underlying the Ricardian Equivalence Theorem requires the taxes to be non-distortionary taxes. However, virtually all taxes are distortionary taxes in that they affect the relative price of some economic activity. In addition to non-distortionary taxes, the Ricardian Equivalence Theorem relies on the assumption of forward-looking intertemporally optimizing consumers who do not face binding constraints on the intertemporal allocation of consumption. The Ricardian Equivalence Theorem will fail to hold if consumers lack the foresight to take account of the implications for future taxes of current fiscal policy.

A third source of departure from the Ricardian Equivalence Theorem may arise if consumers face binding constraints on the intertemporal allocation of consumption. One such binding constraint is a binding liquidity constraint as discussed above in Section 4. Consumers who face currently binding liquidity constraints will reduce their current consumption by an amount equal to the current increase in taxes, if the constraint on their borrowing does not change when taxes are changed. It is possible to construct models in which the borrowing constraint endogenously adjusts with tax changes in a way that leaves current consumption unchanged. However, whether the borrowing constraint endogenously adjusts in a manner to maintain Ricardian Equivalence depends on the rationale for liquidity constraints and on the extent of communication among lenders.[23]

An alternative type of constraint on the intertemporal allocation of consumption that violates the Ricardian Equivalence Theorem is a binding constraint on the intergenerational allocation of consumption. If current taxes are reduced, and if the implied future tax increase is levied on future generations, then the current recipients of the tax reduction would increase their consumption unless they have operative altruistic bequest motives. In particular, current consumption will be increased under any of the following sets of assumptions: (1) consumers do not have bequest motives; (2) the bequest motive is a function of the size of the bequest; and (3) the bequest motive is of the altruistic form, but is not strong enough to induce the consumer to leave a positive bequest.[24]

There is also a large empirical literature that attempts to test whether the Ricardian Equivalence Theorem accurately describes the impact of tax policy in actual economies. There are many papers which support each side of this question. This literature can be read as supporting the Ricardian Equivalence Theorem [see, for example, Seater (1985)] or as rejecting it [see, for example, Bernheim (1987)]. More importantly, the critical question is not whether the Ricardian Equivalence Theorem is literally true; the critical question is whether there are quantitatively substantial departures from Ricardian Equivalence and, if so, what is the magnitude of these departures. This last question remains unanswered.

7. Investment

In addition to consumption expenditure, the other major component of private spending is business investment, which includes inventory investment as well as fixed investment in plant and equipment. The discussion below will analyze the sources of fluctuations in investment with particular attention to the effects of interest rates, asset prices, inflation, and aggregate demand. Ideally, a theory of investment fluctuations should be developed in a stochastic environment just

---

[23]See Hayashi (1985c) and Yotsuzuka (1987).
[24]See Weil (1987) and Abel (1987).

as the consumption function presented above was based on utility-maximizing consumers facing uncertain streams of exogenous income. Although the literature does contain formal models of investment under uncertainty,[25] and also contains the econometric implementation of models of investment under uncertainty,[26] it has not developed and tested a set of stochastic implications with the sharpness of the stochastic implications of the permanent income hypothesis. Therefore, I will develop the basic models of investment under the assumption of certainty; the effects of uncertainty will be briefly discussed later. Of the several popular models of fixed investment, I will limit attention to three models: the accelerator model, the neoclassical model, and the q-theory model.[27]

7.1. The neoclassical model and the accelerator

The demand for productive capital is a derived demand by firms. I will begin by considering the investment and employment decision of a firm in a deterministic environment without taxes. For analytic tractability and clarity, the model will be set in continuous time. Let K_t be the stock of capital at time t, let L_t be the amount of labor employed at time t, and let I_t be the firm's gross investment at time t. Let $Y(K_t, L_t)$ be the real revenue function of the firm and assume that it is concave. This function embodies the firm's production function and the demand curve it faces. For a price-taking firm $Y(K_t, L_t)$ is simply the output of the firm multiplied by the real price of its output. At the level of the aggregate economy, $Y(K_t, L_t)$ is to be interpreted as the aggregate real revenue function, which depends on aggregate demand. The net real cash flow at time t, X_t, is:

$$X_t = Y(K_t, L_t) - w_t L_t - p_t I_t - c(I_t, K_t), \tag{47}$$

where p_t is the real price of investment goods and w_t is the real wage rate. The final term in the expression for cash flow in (47), $c(I_t, K_t)$, requires further explanation. This function represents the cost of adjusting the capital stock. This cost is in addition to the price of investment goods. The adjustment cost function is meant to capture the notion that if the capital stock is to be increased by a given increment, it is more costly to achieve this increase rapidly rather than slowly. This idea was formalized by Eisner and Strotz (1963) and

---

[25]See, for example, Lucas and Prescott (1971), Hartman (1972), and Abel (1985).
[26]See, for example, Pindyck and Rotemberg (1983) and Bernanke (1983).
[27]See Bischoff (1971) and Clark (1979) for comparison of the empirical performance of alternative investment models. Nickell (1978) provides an excellent comprehensive treatment of several models of investment and many issues related to investment behavior.

was used later by Lucas (1967), Gould (1968), Treadway (1969), Mussa (1977), Abel (1980, 1982), Yoshikawa (1980), and Hayashi (1982). The adjustment cost function is non-negative and is convex in the rate of investment I_t. It is convenient to think of the adjustment cost function as representing installation costs. With this interpretation, p_t can be called the price of uninstalled capital, and $p_t + c_I(I_t, K_t)$ is the marginal cost of new installed capital. Although the neoclassical and accelerator models ignore costs of adjustment, I introduce adjustment costs at this point to develop a unifying framework that will include the q theory of investment to be developed in the next subsection.

The firm attempts to maximize the present value of its net cash flow over an infinite horizon. Let r_t be the instantaneous real rate of interest at time t and define $R(t, s) = \exp[-\int_t^s r_v \, dv]$ to be the discount factor that discounts real cash flows at date s back to date t. Let V_t be the value of the firm at time t and observe that

$$V_t = \max \int_t^\infty X_s R(t, s) \, ds .$$ (48)

In the maximization on the right-hand side of (48) the firm can choose the path of employment, L_s, and the path of gross investment, I_s, for $s \geq t$. The level of the capital stock at time t, K_t, is treated as an initial condition. The change in the capital stock, i.e. net investment, is equal to gross investment less depreciation. Assuming that capital depreciates at a constant proportional rate h, the evolution of the capital stock is given by

$$\dot{K}_t = I_t - hK_t ,$$ (49)

where a dot over a variable denotes the derivative of that variable with respect to time.

The firm chooses the paths of employment and investment to perform the maximization in (48) subject to the dynamic constraint in (49) and the condition that K_t is given. To solve this maximization problem define:

$$H_t = X_t + q_t \dot{K}_t ,$$ (50)

where q_t is the shadow price of a unit of installed capital. The determination of q_t will be discussed further below. Interpreting q_t as the shadow price of capital, the term $q_t \dot{K}_t$ is the value of the net increment to the capital stock, $\dot{K}_t$. Thus, the right-hand side of (50) can be viewed as the value accruing to the firm's employment and investment activities at time t. These activities produce real cash flow at the rate X_t and increase the capital stock by an amount worth $q_t \dot{K}_t$. Technically, H_t is the "current value Hamiltonian".

To solve the firm's maximization problem, employment and investment must be chosen to maximize H_t. Substituting (47) and (49) into (50) yields:

$$H_t = Y(K_t, L_t) - w_t L_t - p_t I_t - c(I_t, K_t) + q_t(I_t - hK_t) . \tag{51}$$

Differentiating H_t with respect to L_t and I_t, respectively, and setting the derivatives equal to zero, yields:

$$Y_L(K_t, L_t) = w_t , \tag{52a}$$

$$c_I(I_t, K_t) = q_t - p_t . \tag{52b}$$

Equation (52a) simply states that the firm hires labor to the point at which the marginal revenue product of labor is equal to the wage rate. Equation (52b) states that the firm chooses a rate of investment such that the marginal cost, which is equal to the price of the investment good, p_t, plus the marginal adjustment cost, $c_I(I_t, K_t)$, is equal to the value of an additional unit of installed capital, q_t.[28] This equation has important implications to which I will return later.

In addition to choosing I_t and L_t to maximize H_t, the solution to the firm's intertemporal maximization problem in (48) requires that the shadow price, q_t, obey the relation $\dot{q}_t - r_t q_t = -\partial H_t / \partial K_t$. Using (51) this relation can be written as:

$$\dot{q}_t = (r_t + h)q_t - Y_K(K_t, L_t) + c_K(I_t, K_t) . \tag{53}$$

Although equation (53) may appear to be merely a technical condition for optimality, it has important economic interpretations. As a step toward interpreting (53), observe that it is a differential equation and that the stationary solution of this differential equation is:

$$q_t = \int_t^\infty [Y_K(K_s, L_s) - c_K(I_s, K_s)]R(t, s) \, e^{-h(s-t)} \, ds . \tag{54}$$

Equation (54) states that the shadow price of capital is equal to the present discounted value of the stream of marginal cash flow attributable to a unit of capital installed at time t. At each future date s, the marginal cash flow consists of two components: (1) $Y_K(K_s, L_s)$ is the extra revenue attributable to an

---

[28] This analysis ignores any non-negativity constraint on gross investment; instead I have assumed that it is possible for individual firms to remove capital goods and sell them subject to an adjustment cost. See Sargent (1980) for an analysis that explicitly incorporates a non-negativity constraint on gross investment in a discrete-time model. Bertola (1987) analyzes the implications of the non-negativity constraint in a continuous-time model.

additional unit of capital at time s; (2) $-c_K(I_s, K_s)$ is the reduction in the adjustment cost made possible by an additional unit of installed capital. The (instantaneous) rate at which marginal cash flows at date s are discounted is equal to $r_s + h$ rather than simply r_s because a unit of capital depreciates at rate h. Thus, if a unit of capital is installed at time t, then at some future time s, only a fraction $e^{-h(s-t)}$ of the unit of capital remains.

A second interpretation of (53) is based on viewing the shadow price q_t as if it were the price at which a marginal unit of installed capital could be bought or sold. With this interpretation in mind, consider the decisions of whether to invest in an additional unit of installed capital at a cost of q_t, or alternatively to invest the q_t units of numeraire in a financial asset paying a rate of return r_t. If the capital investment decision is optimal, then the firm should be indifferent between these two alternative uses of q_t units of the numeraire, which implies that the rate of return on capital investment is equal to r_t. The return to capital investment consists of four components: (1) a unit of capital increases revenue by $Y_K(K_t, L_t)$; (2) a unit of capital reduces the adjustment cost by $-c_K(I_t, K_t)$; (3) capital depreciates at rate h so that the value of the capital lost to depreciation is hq_t; and (4) the price of capital changes at the rate $\dot{q}_t$ which represents a capital gain if $\dot{q}_t$ is positive and a capital loss if $\dot{q}_t$ is negative. Adding together the four components of the return to capital, and then dividing by the shadow price of capital to express the return as a rate of return, yields $[Y_K(K_t, L_t) - c_K(I_t, K_t) - hq_t + \dot{q}_t]/q_t$. Equation (53) simply states that this rate of return is equal to r_t.

A third, related, interpretation of equation (53) involves the concept of the user cost (sometimes called the rental cost) of capital derived by Jorgenson (1963). The rental cost interpretation is facilitated by again viewing the shadow price q_t as the price at which a unit of capital can be bought or sold. Consider someone who owns a unit of capital that will be rented to someone else for use. The owner of the capital will charge a rental cost u_t such that the rate of return from renting the capital is equal to r_t, which is the rate of return available on financial assets. The owner's return consists of the rental cost u_t plus the capital gain $\dot{q}_t$ less the value of the physical depreciation $q_t h$. Therefore, the owner's rate of return is $[u_t + \dot{q}_t - hq_t]/q_t$. Setting this rate of return equal to r_t yields:

$$u_t = (r_t + h)q_t - \dot{q}_t. \tag{55}$$

Equation (55) is the analogue of the Jorgensonian user cost of capital, except that in place of the shadow price, q_t, Jorgenson uses the price of the investment good, p_t. The reason for this difference is that Jorgenson ignores the adjustment cost function, or equivalently, assumes that $c(I_t, K_t)$ is identically zero. Under this assumption, equation (52b) indicates that q_t is equal to p_t so that the user cost in (55) is identical to the Jorgensonian user cost in this case.

The definition of the user cost in (55) can be used to rewrite equation (53) as

$$Y_K(K_t, L_t) - c_K(I_t, K_t) = u_t \,. \tag{56}$$

Equation (56) states that at each instant of time the marginal cash flow of an additional unit of capital is equal to the user cost, u_t. Except for the fact that Jorgenson's formulation does not have an adjustment cost function, so that $c_K(I_t, K_t)$ is identically zero, this relation is the same as Jorgenson's condition which states that the marginal product of capital is equal to the user cost of capital.

For the purpose of expositional clarity, I will assume that the adjustment cost function has the following form:

$$c(I_t, K_t) \equiv g(I_t - hK_t) \,, \tag{57}$$

where $g(\cdot) \geq 0$, $g(0) = 0$, $g'(0) = 0$, and $g''(\cdot) > 0$. The adjustment cost function specified in (57) is a non-negative convex function of the rate of net investment. When the rate of net investment is zero, the adjustment cost is assumed to be zero.[29]

Now suppose that the price of investment goods, p_t, the real wage rate, w_t, and the real interest rate, r_t, are constant and consider the steady state in which both the capital stock, K_t, and the shadow price of capital, q_t, are constant. When the capital stock is constant, $I_t = hK_t$, so that it follows from the specification of the adjustment cost function in (57) that the adjustment cost is equal to zero. In addition, the partial derivatives, c_I and c_K, are each equal to zero. The fact that c_I is equal to zero implies, using (52b), that the shadow price, q_t, is constant and equal to the price of investment goods, p_t. Because q_t is equal to p_t, it follows from the definition of the user cost in (55) that

$$u_t = (r + h)p_t \,. \tag{58}$$

Finally, recall that the partial derivative, c_K, is equal to zero in the steady state so that (56) implies that

$$Y_K(K_t, L_t) = u_t \,. \tag{59}$$

Equations (58) and (59) correspond to the user cost of capital and the

---

[29]Gould (1968), Treadway (1969), and Abel (1985) express the adjustment cost function as a function of gross investment. Expressing the adjustment cost function as a function of net investment implies that in the long run, when $\dot{K} = 0$, the value of capital, q_t, is equal to its replacement cost, p_t, as argued by Tobin (1969).

desired capital stock derived by Jorgenson under the condition that the price of investment goods, p_t, is constant. The desired capital stock is determined from (59). To illustrate Jorgenson's derivation, as well as the Eisner–Nadiri (1968, 1970) criticism of Jorgenson's derivation, suppose that the revenue function is constant returns to scale in K_t and L_t and displays a constant elasticity of substitution between K_t and L_t. In particular, suppose that

$$Y(K, L) = A[mK^{-\phi} + (1-m)L^{-\phi}]^{-1/\phi}, \tag{60}$$

where $A > 0$, $0 < m < 1$, and $\phi > -1$. The revenue function in (60) describes the revenue function of a competitive firm with a constant elasticity of substitution production function. It can be shown that the elasticity of substitution, σ, is equal to $1/(1+\phi)$ and that the marginal revenue product of capital is:

$$Y_K(K, L) = [m/A^{\phi}][Y/K]^{1/\sigma}. \tag{61}$$

Recalling from (59) that the marginal revenue product of capital is set equal to the user cost, u_t, (61) can be rearranged to yield:

$$K = [m/A^{\phi}]^{\sigma}Yu^{-\sigma}. \tag{62}$$

Equation (62) expresses the steady-state capital stock, K, as a function of the real revenue of the firm and the user cost of capital. Of course, the revenue of the firm is a decision variable of the firm, so (62) cannot properly be regarded as a relation expressing the steady-state capital stock as a function of exogenous variables. It is more appropriately regarded as a relation among endogenous variables in the steady state.

The neoclassical investment model developed by Jorgenson is based on a special case of (62). In particular, Jorgenson assumed that the revenue function is Cobb–Douglas, which in terms of (62) implies that the elasticity of substitution, σ, is equal to one. In this case, the steady-state capital stock, K, is proportional to revenue, Y, and is inversely proportional to the user cost, u.

Jorgenson's derivation of the investment equation proceeded in two steps. The first step was the derivation of a "desired capital stock", which corresponds to the steady-state capital stock in (62) with σ equal to one. The second step is the determination of the rate at which the firm's capital stock approaches its desired level. Rather than specifying a particular dynamic adjustment mechanism, such as an adjustment cost function, in the firm's optimization problem, Jorgenson assumed that there is some exogenous mechanism that determines the rate at which the gap between the desired capital stock and the actual capital stock is closed. In particular, Jorgenson specified the investment equation as:

$$I_t = \left\{ \sum_{i=0}^{n} \omega_i [K^*_{t-i} - K^*_{t-1-i}] \right\} + hK_t \,, \tag{63}$$

where K^*_t is the desired capital stock at time t.

Observe that a strong implication of Jorgenson's assumption of a unitary elasticity of substitution between K and L is that the desired capital stock depends only on the ratio of revenue to the user cost of capital. Jorgenson exploits this fact in his estimation by constraining the response of investment to revenue to be the same (proportionately, except for sign) as the response to the user cost. However, Eisner and Nadiri have claimed that this procedure may overstate the response of investment to cost of capital changes because the elasticity of substitution is less than one. When the elasticity of substitution is not equal to one, then it follows from (62) that the elasticity of the desired capital stock with respect to real revenue Y is still unity but the elasticity of the desired capital stock with respect to the user cost is equal to $-\sigma$. With an elasticity of substitution less than one, the magnitude of the response of investment to the user cost will be smaller than the response to revenue. Therefore, constraining the responses to be of equal (percentage) magnitude, as Jorgenson does, will tend to overstate the response of investment to the user cost. Eisner and Nadiri (1968, p. 381) argue that the elasticity of substitution is nearer zero than unity, but Jorgenson and Stephenson (1969) claim that empirical evidence supports a unitary elasticity.

There is another reason to expect the response of investment to the user cost to differ from the response to output or revenue. In discussing the elasticity of substitution between capital and labor, it is important to distinguish the ex ante elasticity of substitution from the ex post elasticity of substitution. More specifically, before a piece of capital is built and put into place, there may be a substantial degree of substitutability between capital and labor. However, after the capital is put in place, there may be very limited, or even zero, substitutability between capital and labor. An extreme version of this notion is the putty–clay hypothesis: ex ante, capital is malleable like putty and the firm can choose the capital–labor ratio; ex post, capital is not malleable, like clay, and there is no substitutability between capital and labor. Under the putty–clay hypothesis, we might expect to see larger and more rapid responses to changes in output than to changes in the user cost. For example, an increase in output may lead to an increase in the desired capital stock, as described above in equation (62). However, a fall in the user cost would lead to a smaller response of the desired capital stock than in (62). The reason is that a fall in the user cost leads to an increase in the desired capital–labor ratio, but under the putty–clay hypothesis the capital–labor ratio on existing capital is immutable. Thus, newly installed capital will be less labor intensive, but the old capital will not be replaced with labor-saving capital until the old capital becomes uneconomical.

An even more extreme limitation on capital labor substitutability gives rise to the accelerator model of investment. In particular, suppose that there is no substitutability either ex ante or ex post. In terms of the expression for the desired capital stock in (62), suppose that the elasticity of substitution, σ, is equal to zero. In this case, the desired capital stock in (62) is simply proportional to revenue. Investment in this case would be a distributed lag function of changes in the level of revenue:

$$I_t = \left\{ \sum_{i=0}^{n} \omega_i [Y_{t-i} - Y_{t-1-i}] \right\} + hK_t . \qquad (64)$$

The accelerator model (64) is a special case of the neoclassical investment model (63) in which the user cost of capital is ignored.[30] Although some studies find significant effects of the user cost,[31] it is part of the "folk wisdom" that user cost effects on investment are harder to estimate in the data than are accelerator or output effects. Perhaps one reason for the difficulty of finding user cost effects is the problem of simultaneity. If there is an exogenous increase in the real interest rate, then the user cost would increase and investment would decrease. However, if for some reason there were an upward shift in the investment function [for example, Keynesian "animal spirits" (Keynes (1936, pp. 161–163))], then investment would increase and would put upward pressure on the real interest rate. Thus, as a consequence of the upward shift in the investment function, both investment and the user cost would increase. If data contain both exogenous increases in the real interest rate and exogenous shifts in the investment function, then the predicted negative relation between user cost and investment might be masked by the positive relation between user cost and investment in response to exogenous shifts in the investment function.

It should be noted that simultaneity of the sort discussed above would tend to exaggerate, rather than diminish or reverse, the estimated accelerator effects. An exogenous upward shift in the investment function would increase investment, which would increase output. This positive relation between investment and output reinforces the positive relation due to the accelerator effect discussed above. Finally, it should be noted that although simultaneity problems can be alleviated by the use of instrumental variables, the resulting estimates are only as good as the instruments.

---

[30] See Eisner (1978) for an excellent comprehensive treatment of the accelerator model using the McGraw-Hill Publishing Co. capital expenditure surveys from 1956 to 1969.
[31] See Feldstein (1982), for example.

An additional complication in estimating the effect of the user cost is the question of whether to use a short-term or long-term interest rate in measuring the cost of capital. Traditionally, the long-term interest rate is viewed as the appropriate rate, but Hall (1977) argues that "as a matter of theory, what belongs in the service price of capital is a short-run interest rate, though the issue of short versus long rates is unlikely to be resolved empirically" (p. 100). Hall's point that the user cost depends on the short rate rather than the long rate is illustrated by equation (55). In the absence of adjustment costs, q_t is equal to the price of investment goods, p_t, and the expression for the user cost of capital in (55) yields the Jorgensonian user cost, $u_t = (r_t + h)p_t - \dot{p}_t$. The interest rate in this expression is the instantaneous real rate of interest.

While it is true that the user cost is related to the contemporaneous instantaneous interest rate, one must avoid the temptation to say that investment depends on the short-term interest rate rather than the long-term interest rate. Hall's argument that the short-term rate is the appropriate interest rate was based on a model without adjustment costs in which the "firm faces an open choice about the scheduling of investment" (p. 74). However, the essence of adjustment costs is to interfere with "the open choice about the scheduling of investment". In the presence of costs of adjustment, the scheduling of investment affects the cost of investment. In this case, investment is necessarily forward-looking and depends on the present value of the stream of marginal products accruing to a newly-installed unit of capital. Observing that the real interest rate prevailing from date t to date s is $[R(t, s)]^{-1} - 1$, equation (54) implies that q_t, and a fortiori investment, depends on the entire term structure of real interest rates. To make this point more sharply, consider the response of investment to an instantaneously-lived increase in r_t and, alternatively, the response of investment to a permanent increase in the interest rate. An instantaneous increase in r_t will have no effect on $R(t, s)$ and will have no effect on q_t or investment at time t. By contrast, a permanent increase in the instantaneous interest rate would reduce the stream of discount factors, $R(t, s)$, and would reduce q_t and investment. In the presence of adjustment costs, investment depends on the entire term structure of interest rates.

Although there is no consensus about the magnitude of the response of investment to changes in interest rates, the analysis above offers some guidance on the size of this effect. Suppose that the relevant real rate of interest is equal to 4 percent per year and the rate of depreciation is equal to 6 percent per year, which is an appropriate depreciation rate for structures. Now consider the effect of a 1 percentage point decrease in the real interest rate (from 4 to 3 percent per year). It follows immediately from the expression for the user cost in (58) that this decrease in the real interest rate decreases the user cost of capital by 10 percent. Under a Cobb–Douglas production function, this 10 percent decrease in the user cost increases the desired stock of capital by 10 percent. In the long run, the rate of investment would rise by 10 percent in order to maintain the capital stock at its higher level. In the short run, the rate of investment would increase by even more than 10 percent in order to increase the capital stock to its new desired level. The magnitude of the increase in the rate of investment in the short run depends, of course, on how rapidly the new desired capital stock is achieved.

The 10 percent increase in the desired capital stock in response to a 1 percentage point decrease in the real interest rate may overstate the response of the desired aggregate capital stock for three reasons. First, as emphasized by Eisner and Nadiri (1968), the elasticity of substitution between capital and labor may be substantially less than one. Recalling that this elasticity of substitution is denoted by σ, it follows immediately from (62) that the response of the desired capital stock to this 1 percentage point decrease in the real interest rate is equal to (10σ) percent. Thus, if $\sigma = 0.1$, the desired capital stock rises by only 1 percent in response to a 1 percentage point fall in the real interest rate. Second, the depreciation rate of 6 percent per year may be a reasonable rate for structures, but the depreciation rate for equipment is about 16 percent per year. Thus, for equipment a decrease in the real interest rate from 4 to 3 percent reduces the user cost of capital by only 5 percent rather than the 10 percent calculated for structures.[32] Third, the real rate of interest used by firms in capital budgeting decisions is generally a risk-adjusted rate of return such as a weighted average of the after-tax interest rate on debt and the expected rate of return on equity.[33] Feldstein (1982) calculates the cost of funds annually for the period 1954–1977. Although this real cost of funds is about 4 percent for the first half of this sample, it is higher than 4 percent throughout the second half of the sample and reached a value of 7.2 percent in 1977. A 1 percentage point increase in the real cost of funds has a smaller impact on the user cost of capital if the cost of capital starts from a higher value.

7.2. The q theory

The neoclassical model and the accelerator model were each derived above by using the steady-state capital stock as the desired level of the capital stock and then positing some sort of adjustment mechanism of the actual capital stock toward its desired level. An alternative approach is provided by a model that

---

[32] Hall and Jorgenson (1967) estimate the depreciation rates for broadly defined capital aggregates using the so-called Bulletin *F* lifetimes from the Department of the Treasury. They present the following (annual) depreciation rates: manufacturing equipment: 0.1471; manufacturing structures: 0.0625; non-farm, non-manufacturing equipment: 0.1923; non-farm, non-manufacturing structures: 0.0694.

[33] See Auerbach (1979a) for a derivation of the weighted-average cost of capital.

incorporates adjustment costs as well as the price of investment goods directly into the maximization problem and then derives the optimal rate of investment at each point of time. In addition to determining the optimal rate of investment, this model makes explicit the dynamic response of investment to permanent and temporary changes in the firm's economic environment and to anticipated as well as unanticipated changes. Furthermore, the adjustment cost model can be used to provide formal underpinnings to the q theory of investment introduced by Tobin (1969).

Tobins' q theory of investment formalizes a notion of Keynes (1936, p. 151) that the incentive to build new capital depends on the market value of the capital relative to the cost of constructing the capital. If an additional unit of installed capital would raise the market value of the firm by more than the cost of acquiring the capital and putting it in place, then a value maximizing firm should acquire it and put it in place.[34] The greater the amount by which the value of the capital exceeds its cost the greater is the incentive to invest. To capture this notion in an observable quantitative measure, Tobin defined the variable q to be the ratio of the market value of a firm to the replacement cost of its capital stock. He then argued that investment is an increasing function of q. A major advantage of Tobin's q is that it relies on securities markets to value the prospects of the firm.

Before discussing the q theory of investment more formally, it is worthwhile to digress briefly to discuss a related model in which the rate of investment depends on the market valuation of capital. Foley and Sidrauski (1970) developed a two-sector model of the economy in which there is a concave production possibilities frontier relating the aggregate output of the consumption good and the aggregate output of the capital good. In a competitive economy, resources are allocated to these two sectors depending on the relative prices of these two goods. More precisely, the production of new capital goods is an increasing function of the price of capital goods relative to the price of consumption goods. In the Foley–Sidrauski model, the price of capital is determined endogenously in securities markets in which three assets – money, bonds, and capital – are traded. The price of capital is determined to equilibrate the demand for capital with the existing supply of capital. This price then determines the flow of new capital goods production. Although the formal model is different from the q theory, in both the Foley–Sidrauski model and the q theory, the rate of investment is an increasing function of the price of capital goods which is determined in asset markets.

A version of the q theory of investment can be derived from the adjustment

---

[34]This argument depends on the assumption that capital investment is reversible. If investment is irreversible, then firms may optimally forgo some projects whose present value exceeds their cost. See McDonald and Siegel (1986).

cost model of investment presented above. For the sake of continuity of exposition, suppose that the adjustment cost function is as specified in (57) so that the marginal cost of investment is $c_I(I_t, K_t) = g'(I_t - hK_t)$. Using this form of the marginal adjustment cost function in the first-order condition for the optimal rate of investment, (52b), yields:

$$I_t = G(q_t - p_t) + hK_t ,$$ (65)

where $G(\cdot) = g'^{-1}(\cdot)$ so that $G' > 0$ and $G(0) = 0$. Equation (65) expresses the rate of investment as an increasing function of the shadow price of installed capital, q_t. Note that in the steady state, with $\dot{K}_t = 0$, the rate of gross investment, I_t, is equal to depreciation, hK_t; the shadow price of a unit of capital, q_t, is equal to the price of investment goods, p_t. The latter result ($q_t = p_t$ in the steady state) is a consequence of specifying the adjustment cost function such that the marginal adjustment cost, $c_I(I, K)$, is equal to zero when net investment is equal to zero. Alternatively, if the adjustment cost function is specified so that the marginal cost of investment is equal to zero when gross investment is equal to zero, then in the steady state q_t would exceed p_t by the marginal cost of replacement investment, hK_t.

The investment equation in (65) is related to Tobin's q theory of investment. To understand the relation between (65) and Tobin's q theory of investment, it is important to distinguish "average q", which will be denoted as q^A, from "marginal q", which will be denoted as q^M. Tobin defines q to be the ratio of the average value of the capital stock, V_t/K_t, to the price of a unit of capital, p_t. Thus, Tobin's q is q^A where

$$q_t^A = V_t/(p_t K_t)$$ (66)

and where V_t is the value of the firm at time t. Alternatively, marginal q, q^M, is the ratio of the marginal value of an additional unit of installed capital, dV_t/dK_t, to the price of a unit of capital, p_t. Therefore,

$$q_t^M = (dV_t/dK_t)/p_t .$$ (67)

Observe that the numerator of q_t^M, dV_t/dK_t, is equal to the shadow price, q_t. Therefore, (65) and (67) imply that

$$I_t = G((q_t^M - 1)p_t) + hK_t .$$ (68)

A natural question is whether there are conditions under which average q and marginal q are equal to each other. The answer can be obtained using the following proposition, which is a generalization of a result due to Hayashi

(1982). Suppose that the revenue function, $Y(K, L)$, is linearly homogeneous in K and L, the adjustment cost function is linearly homogeneous in I and K, and that p_s, w_s, and $R(t, s)$ are exogenous to the firm. Then the value of the firm, V_t, is proportional to the stock of capital, K_t. Under these conditions, it follows that dV_t/dK_t is equal to V_t/K_t; thus, (66) and (67) imply that average q is equal to marginal q in this case.

The equality of average q and marginal q holds more generally than under the conditions stated above. It holds even if the interest rate is stochastic. It also holds if the cash flow, X_t, is subject to random multiplicative shocks. The key assumption about the behavior of cash flow is that it is a linearly homogeneous function of the three variables K, L, and I.

The use of Tobin's q to explain investment provides an attractive link between asset markets and investment activity. In particular, stock and bond markets are relied upon to value the firm's capital stock, thereby relieving the economist from having to calculate the relevant expected present value of future cash flows. Unfortunately, investment equations based on Tobin's q are not free of difficulty. Typically, estimated equations relating investment to Tobin's q leave a large unexplained serially correlated residual.[35] In addition, lagged values of Tobin's q often enter significantly as explanators of investment, which contradicts the simple adjustment cost model described above. Finally, other variables such as output and capacity utilization have additional explanatory power in investment equations with q. This finding contradicts the notion that all information that is relevant to the valuation of capital and to the investment decision is captured by the market value of the firm.

There are several possible explanations for the departures of empirically estimated investment equations from the simple predictions of the theory. First, average q and marginal q may display different movements. For example, consider a firm that has a large amount of energy-intensive capital. If the price of energy rises dramatically, then the value of the firm would fall as the quasi-rents available on existing energy-intensive capital would fall. However, the firm may undertake substantial investment in energy-saving capital. Therefore, an observer of this firm would see a drop in average q coinciding with an increase in investment. This example makes clear that heterogeneity of capital can potentially destroy the relation between average q and investment. As for marginal q, it is important to distinguish the marginal q, or shadow price, for the different types of capital. In the example above, the marginal q of energy-intensive capital is reduced and the marginal q of energy-saving capital is increased by the rise in the price of energy.

The fact that lagged values of q are found to be significant explanators of investment is perhaps suggestive of the importance of delivery lags in the

---

[35]See von Furstenberg (1977), Summers (1981a), and Blanchard and Wyplosz (1981).

investment process. For many types of capital, especially structures, there may be a substantial delay between the date on which it is decided to the acquire and install new capital and the date at which the capital expenditures are actually made.[36] The existence of delivery lags complicates the relation between investment and q. If, for example, there is a two-period delay between the decision to invest and the capital expenditure, then capital expenditure in period t should be related to the forecast in period $t-2$ of the value of capital in period t, i.e. $E_{t-2}\{q_t\}$. However, the variable which appears significantly in investment equations is lagged q, i.e. q_{t-2}, rather than the lagged expectation of q. To the extent that q_{t-2} is a predictor of q_t, it may serve as a proxy for $E_{t-2}\{q_t\}$.

The q theory of investment is based on the notion that all relevant information is captured in the market valuation of the firm, and therefore other variables such as cash flow, profit, or capacity utilization should have no additional predictive power for investment. The fact that cash flow or profit often have significant additional predictive power is consistent with there being different costs of internal and external funds or with firms having limited ability to finance investment by raising funds in capital markets. The underlying economic reasons for, and implications of, these capital market imperfections remain an open question.[37]

8. Corporate taxes and inflation

The incentive to invest is influenced by the corporate tax environment in general, and by the interaction of corporate taxes and inflation in particular. The three aspects of the corporate tax code that have been analyzed most widely in the context of investment are the corporate tax rate, the depreciation allowance, and the investment tax credit.[38] Let τ be the tax rate assessed on corporate profits. Taxable corporate profits are calculated as revenues less wages, depreciation allowances, and adjustment costs. For simplicity, I will assume that adjustment costs are expensed, which is consistent with treating adjustment costs as forgone output or revenue. Let $D(x)$ be the depreciation allowance for an asset of age x that cost one dollar when new. Then, following Hall and Jorgenson (1967), let $z = \int_0^\infty D(x) e^{-ix} \, dx$ be the present value of depreciation deductions over the life of the asset, where i is the nominal

---

[36]Abel and Blanchard (1988) have found that for non-electrical machinery and fabricated metals there is an average delivery lag of 2 quarters, and for electrical machinery the average lag is 3 quarters. For structures, the average lags range from 3 to 8 quarters.

[37]See Fazzari, Hubbard and Petersen (1987).

[38]See Hall and Jorgenson (1967), Feldstein (1982), Abel (1982), Taylor (1982), and Auerbach (1983).

interest rate. Finally, let k be the rate of the investment tax credit so that for each dollar spent on investment goods, the firm receives a rebate of k dollars.[39] Thus, the net cost to the firm of a dollar of investment goods is $(1 - k - \tau z)$.[40]

Now define X^*_t to be the excess of after-tax real revenues over real wages, adjustment costs, and the real net price of investment goods at time t:

$$X^*_t = (1 - \tau)[Y(K_t, L_t) - c(I_t, K_t) - w_t L_t] - (1 - k - \tau z)p_t I_t \,. \qquad (69)$$

In the absence of taxes, X^*_t would be equal to the cash flow X_t in (47). The maximization problem of the firm is equivalent to maximizing the present value of the stream of X^*_t.[41] This maximization problem can be solved using the same procedure as presented earlier in the absence of taxes. The current value Hamiltonian, which is analogous to (51), is:

$$
\begin{aligned}
H^*_t = {} & (1 - \tau)[Y(K_t, L_t) - c(I_t, K_t) - w_t L_t] - (1 - k - \tau z)p_t I_t \\
& + q^*_t(I_t - hK_t) \,.
\end{aligned} \qquad (70)
$$

Differentiating the current value Hamiltonian with respect to L_t and setting the derivative equal to zero yields the condition that labor is hired until the marginal revenue product of labor is equal to the wage rate [equation (52a)]. Differentiating (70) with respect to the rate of investment, I_t, yields the analogue of (52b):

$$(1 - \tau)c_I(I_t, K_t) = q^*_t - (1 - k - \tau z)p_t \,. \qquad (71)$$

The shadow price q^*_t must obey the relation $\dot{q}^*_t - r_t q^*_t = -\partial H^*_t / \partial K_t$, which implies the following analogue of (53):

$$\dot{q}^*_t = (r_t + h)q^*_t - (1 - \tau)[Y_K(K_t, L_t) - c_K(I_t, K_t)] \,. \qquad (72)$$

The stationary solution to the differential equation in (72) is:

$$q^*_t = \int_t^\infty \{(1 - \tau)[Y_K(K_s, L_s) - c_K(I_s, K_s)]R(t, s)\, e^{-h(s-t)}\, ds\} \,. \qquad (73)$$

[39] The Tax Reform Act of 1986 eliminated the investment tax credit in the United States.

[40] Under the Long Amendment, which was in effect in 1962 and 1963, the basis for depreciation allowances was reduced by the investment tax credit, and the net price of investment goods was $(1 - k)(1 - \tau z)$. The expression in the text is appropriate for the period after the repeal of the Long Amendment.

[41] The present value of X^*_s is not equal to the present value of cash flow because it ignores the depreciation allowances on capital installed before date t. Because the cash flows associated with these deductions are predetermined at time t, they can be ignored in the maximization problem at time t.

Equation (73) states that the shadow price, q_t^*, is equal to the present value of the stream of after-tax marginal products of capital.

Before deriving the investment equation, I will first describe the steady state in which $I_t = hK_t$ and $\dot{q}_t^* = 0$. It follows immediately from (72) that if $\dot{q}_t^*$ is equal to zero, then the shadow price, q_t^*, is equal to the present value of the stream of constant after-tax marginal cash flows accruing to capital:

$$q_t^* = (1 - \tau)(Y_K - c_K)/(r + h) . \tag{74}$$

Now suppose that the adjustment cost function has the specification in (57) so that the marginal adjustment cost, c_I, is equal to zero in the steady state. In this case, the first-order condition is (71) implies that, in the steady state, the shadow price of capital is equal to the tax-adjusted price of investment goods:

$$q_t^* = (1 - k - \tau z)p_t . \tag{75}$$

Next set the right-hand side of (74), which is the present value of after-tax marginal cash flow, equal to the right-hand side of (75), which is the tax-adjusted price of capital, to obtain:

$$Y_K - c_K = T(r + h)p_t , \tag{76a}$$

where

$$T \equiv (1 - k - \tau z)/(1 - \tau) . \tag{76b}$$

The right-hand side of (76a) is equal to the tax-adjusted user cost of capital derived by Hall and Jorgenson (1967). The factor T is a tax-adjustment factor; when T is equal to one, as it would be in the absence of taxes, then the user cost is identical to the steady-state user cost presented above in (58).

To obtain a simple investment equation in the presence of corporate taxes, suppose that the adjustment cost function is independent of the capital stock, i.e. $c_K \equiv 0$. In this case, the first-order condition in (71) can be rewritten as:

$$I_t = H\left(\frac{q_t^*}{1 - \tau} - Tp_t\right), \tag{77}$$

where $H(\cdot) = c_I^{-1}(\cdot, \cdot)$ is an increasing function. The behavior of the investment equation (77) can be easily examined under the assumption that the revenue function is linearly homogeneous in K and L. The linear homogeneity of $Y(K, L)$ implies that when cash flow is maximized with respect to labor, L_t, the maximized value of $Y(K_t, L_t) - w_t L_t$ is equal to $\theta(w_t)K_t$, where $\theta(w_t)$ is a positive but decreasing function of the real wage rate, w_t. Therefore, when the firm follows an optimal employment policy, we obtain:

$$Y_K(K, L) = \theta(w) , \tag{78}$$

so that the marginal revenue product of capital is positive and decreasing in the real wage rate. Recalling that c_K is identically equal to zero, the shadow price of capital can be easily calculated from (73) to be

$$q_t^* = \int_t^\infty \{(1 - \tau)\theta(w_s)R(t, s)\, e^{-h(s-t)}\} \, ds . \tag{79}$$

It follows immediately from (79) that $q_t^*/(1 - \tau)$ is independent of the tax rate, τ. The effect of the tax code is captured by the tax adjustment factor, T, and inspection of (77) reveals immediately that the rate of investment is a decreasing function of T. Therefore, investment is an increasing function of the investment tax credit, k, and is also an increasing function of the present value of depreciation deductions, z.

Now consider the effects on investment of changes in real and nominal interest rates. In the neoclassical model, an increase in the real rate of interest raises the user cost of capital and hence reduces the desired capital stock and investment. It would appear that changes in the nominal interest rate would not affect the user cost unless they were accompanied by changes in the real interest rate. However, the U.S. tax code contains an important inflation non-neutrality, which gives nominal interest rates an effect on investment over and above the effect of real interest rates. Depreciation allowances are based on the nominal historical cost of a piece of capital rather than on its replacement cost. Thus, inflation reduces the real value of future depreciation deductions so that an increase in inflation reduces z, the present value of real depreciation deductions. An alternative, but equivalent, explanation for the negative relation between inflation and z is that the depreciation deductions represent a stream of nominal flows and can be discounted by a nominal interest rate. If the (expected and actual) rate of inflation rises without any change in the real interest rate, then the nominal interest rate also arises, so that the present value of the unchanged stream of nominal flows is reduced. The reduction in z increases the tax adjustment parameter, T, and thus tends to reduce the rate of investment. In addition, inflation in the presence of historical cost depreciation may distort the choice among different types of capital with different useful lives and different depreciation allowance schedules.[42] An increase in the rate of inflation can either increase or decrease

---

[42]See Auerbach (1979b), Kopcke (1981), and Abel (1981).

the degree of durability of capital chosen by firms, depending on the nominal interest rate and the rate of depreciation.[43]

9. Uncertainty

The investment behavior of firms has been derived above in the absence of uncertainty. It seems intuitively plausible that the desirability of investment projects would depend on the risk associated with the project and, furthermore, one might suspect that an increase in risk would reduce the rate of investment. However, much of the existing analytic work on investment under uncertainty does not support the notion that greater uncertainty inhibits investment. Hartman (1972) and Abel (1985) have shown that an increase in the variance of the output price or in the variance of the price of variable factors will induce a competitive firm to increase its rate of investment. Pazner and Razin (1974) have shown that an increase in interest rate uncertainty also induces the firm to increase its rate of investment. The argument underlying these results can be illustrated using the expression for q_t^* in (79) which was derived under the assumption that the revenue function is linearly homogeneous in K and L. This equation would apply to a competitive firm with a constant returns to scale production function. It can be shown that the marginal revenue product of capital, $\theta(w_s)$, is a convex function of w_s. Therefore, if the variance of w_s is increased while its expected value is held constant, then Jensen's inequality implies that the expected value of $\theta(w_s)$ increases. This increase in the expected value of $\theta(w_s)$ implies that the expected present value of marginal revenue products of capital increases and thus the optimal rate of investment increases. Similarly, it can be shown that $R(t, s)$ is a convex function of future instantaneous rates of interest, r_v, for $v > t$, and hence an increase in the variance of interest rates will also increase investment.

Recently, Zeira (1987) has developed a model of a monopolistic firm that is uncertain both about its own capacity and about the demand curve it faces. In this particular model, increased price uncertainty will reduce investment.

It should be noted that in all of the above-mentioned works on investment under uncertainty, the firm is modelled as risk-neutral. More precisely, the firm is assumed to maximize the expected present value of cash flow. It seems that future work could usefully model risk-averse managers and/or could model the covariance of the firm's returns with the market portfolio.

---

[43]Feldstein (1982) analyzes other inflation non-neutralities such as the fact that nominal interest payments, rather than real interest payments, are tax deductible.

10. Inventories

Up to this point, the discussion of investment has focused on fixed investment. In addition to fixed investment, firms invest in inventories. Although the average value of inventory investment, i.e. the average change in the stock of inventories, is quite small relative to the average level of fixed investment, the volatility of inventory investment is quite large.[44] Rather than develop a formal analytic model of inventory behavior, I will simply discuss some of the major issues. The first step is to explain why firms hold inventories. Two reasons that have been studied are: (a) For technological reasons, there is a lag between the beginning of production and the sale of a good. To the extent that the production process takes time, there will be an inventory of goods in process. To the extent that there is a delay between the completion of production and the sale of the good, there is a finished goods inventory. (b) Even if it were possible to make production always equal to the contemporaneous value of sales, so that there might be no need to hold inventories, cost-minimizing firms may choose to hold inventories as a means of avoiding large fluctuations in production in the face of large fluctuations in sales. This "production smoothing" motive for holding inventories would arise if the marginal cost of production were an increasing function of the level of production. In this case, the cost-minimizing scheduling of any level of average production requires minimizing fluctuations in production.

The production smoothing model of inventories has a striking resemblance to the permanent income model of consumption, which could be described as a model of consumption smoothing. Indeed, some of the lessons from the permanent income model could be carried over to the production smoothing model of inventories. For example, if all changes in a firm's sales were perfectly forecastable, then the production smoothing model would predict that the firm would maintain a smooth profile of production in the face of variations in its sales. Only unanticipated changes in sales would lead firms to alter production. The macroeconomic implication of this observation is that an anticipated increase in final demand, arising from (say) government spending, would not affect GNP because the firm would meet the extra demand by selling out of inventory. The increase in government spending would be exactly offset by negative inventory investment. Alternatively, if the increase in government spending were unanticipated, then the firm would presumably revise its production plans and raise production somewhat.

The production smoothing model of inventories has the implication that the

---

[44]Blinder (1981) reports that declines in inventory investment account for 70 percent of the peak-to-trough decline in real GNP during recessions. During the period 1959:1 to 1979:4 changes in inventory investment accounted for 37 percent of the variance of changes in GNP.

variance of production should be less than or equal to the variance of sales. However, Blinder (1986) and West (1986) argue convincingly that the data on production and sales contradict this implication of the theory. There are a few potential explanations of the apparent production "counter-smoothing" in the data. A simple but unsatisfying explanation is that shocks to the production function or to the cost of inputs lead firms to vary their production even in the face of unchanging demand. An alternative explanation is that an unantici-pated increase in sales implies that future sales will be even higher. If the average level of expected future sales increases by more than the current increase in sales, then a firm facing increasing marginal costs of production would respond by increasing production by more than the current increase in sales. Hence, the variance of production responses to sales shocks would exceed the variance of sales shocks.[45] Thus, for example, an unanticipated increase in government purchases of goods would lead firms to increase production by an even greater amount, thereby increasing inventory invest-ment. Thus, the initial sales innovation has a magnified effect on GNP.

A third explanation of production counter-smoothing is that firms have a desired level of inventories that depends on the stochastic distribution of sales.[46] An unanticipated increase in sales would deplete inventories by an equal amount. In order to restore inventories to the originally desired level, production would have to increase by an amount equal to the unanticipated increase in sales. If, in addition, the unanticipated increase in sales leads the firm to revise upward its forecast of future sales, the desired level of inven-tories would increase. In order to reach the new, higher, desired level of inventories, the firm would have to increase production by even more than the increase in sales. Again, the production response to an innovation in inven-tories magnifies the effect on GNP.

In addition to depending on sales expectations, inventory investment may depend on the behavior of interest rates. The reason for the dependence of inventory investment on interest rates is similar to the reason that fixed investment should depend on interest rates. Specifically, the interest rate measures the opportunity cost of holding inventories rather than interest-earning assets. An increase in the real interest rate should lead to a decrease in the desired holding of inventories. However, as in the case of business fixed investment, it has been difficult to detect the effect of interest rates on inventory investment econometrically. Recently, Irvine (1981) and Akhtar (1983) have reported statistically significant negative responses of inventory investment to increases in short-term interest rates. Specifically, Akhtar finds

---

[45]See Blinder (1986) and Kahn (1987).
[46]See Feldstein and Auerbach (1976). Kahn (1987) motivates the desired level of inventories by explicitly considering stockout costs.

that a 1 percentage point rise in the short-term nominal interest rate would reduce aggregate inventory investment by about \$2 billion; a 1 percentage point increase in the expected rate of inflation leads to an increase in inventory investment of about \$0.8 billion.

11. Concluding remarks

Although the last decade has seen tremendous progress in understanding the stochastic behavior of consumption, many questions still remain. As mentioned earlier in this chapter, recent evidence suggests that labor income is characterized by a unit root, and the presence of a unit root has important implications for consumption behavior. Whether it is ultimately determined that the trend in labor income is stochastic, as suggested by the evidence on a unit root, or is deterministic, there still remains the question of whether consumers think of the trend as being stochastic or deterministic in making consumption decisions. The formal analysis of the permanent income model employs the assumption of rational expectations which implies that consumers know whether the trend is stochastic or deterministic; however, it must be recognized that the assumption of rational expectations is simply an assumption. Whether it will prove fruitful to explore alternative assumptions about the expectations of consumers is an open question.

Other important questions about consumption behavior remain for policy-makers. For instance, are there quantitatively important departures from the Ricardian Equivalence Theorem? If so, what is the source of these departures and is there scope for tax policy to achieve alternative allocations of consumption that might be preferred according to some criterion? Another unresolved question relevant for policy involves the interest elasticity of saving. If this elasticity could be reliably estimated, then there would be scope for fiscal policy to increase the level of saving by somehow subsidizing the rate of return on saving.

The empirical performance of investment equations could also benefit from future advances. Many capital goods are indivisible and take a long time to build. The indivisibility of these goods and the delivery lags associated with capital continue to pose challenges to the theory of investment and its empirical implementation.

Another area of open research questions involves the cost of capital and its relation to investment. The theory of corporate finance is still working toward an understanding of the financing decisions of firms and an appropriate concept of the cost of capital. Further developments in this theory may help to clarify the role of risk in affecting the cost of capital and the investment decisions of firms.

References

Abel, A.B. (1980) 'Empirical investment equations: An integrative framework', in: K. Brunner and A.H. Meltzer, eds., *On the state of macroeconomics*, Vol. 12 of the Carnegie-Rochester Conference Series on Public Policy, a Supplementary Series to the *Journal of Monetary Economics* (1980) 39–91.

Abel, A.B. (1981) 'Taxes, inflation and the durability of capital', *Journal of Political Economy*, 89: 548–560.

Abel, A.B. (1982) 'Dynamic effects of permanent and temporary tax policies in a q model of investment', *Journal of Monetary Economics* 9: 353–373.

Abel, A.B. (1985) 'A stochastic model of investment, marginal q, and the market value of the firm', *International Economic Review* 26: 305–322.

Abel, A.B. (1987) 'Operative gift and bequest motives', *American Economic Review*, 77: 1037–1047.

Abel, A.B. and O.J. Blanchard (1988) 'Investment and sales: Some empirical evidence', in: W.A. Barnett, E.R. Berndt and H. White, eds., *Dynamic econometric modeling*. Cambridge: Cambridge University Press, pp. 269–296.

Akhtar, M.A. (1983) 'Effects of interest rates and inflation on aggregate inventory investment in the United States', *American Economic Review*, 73: 319–328.

Ando, A. and F. Modigliani (1963) 'The "life-cycle" hypothesis of saving: Aggregate implications and tests', *American Economic Review*, 53: 55–84.

Auerbach, A.J. (1979a) 'Wealth maximization and the cost of capital', *Quarterly Journal of Economics*, 93: 433–446.

Auerbach, A.J. (1979b) 'Inflation and the choice of asset life', *Journal of Political Economy*, 87: 621–638.

Auerbach, A.J. (1983) *The taxation of capital income*. Cambridge, Mass.: Harvard University Press.

Barro, R.J. (1974) 'Are government bonds net wealth?', *Journal of Policical Economy*, 82: 1095–1117.

Bernanke, B.S. (1983) 'The determinants of investment: Another look', *American Economic Review, Papers and Proceedings*, 73: 71–75.

Bernanke, B.S. (1985) 'Adjustment costs, durables, and aggregate consumption', *Journal of Monetary Economics*, 15: 41–68.

Bernheim, B.D. (1987) 'Ricardian Equivalence: An evaluation of theory and evidence', in: S. Fischer, ed., *Macroeconomics annual*, Vol. II. Cambridge, Mass.: M.I.T. Press.

Bertola, G. (1987) 'Irreversible investment', M.I.T., mimeo.

Bischoff, C.W. (1971) 'Business investment in the 1970's: A comparison of models', *Brookings Papers on Economic Activity*, 1: 13–58.

Blanchard, O.J. and C. Wyplosz (1981) 'An empirical structural model of aggregate demand', *Journal of Monetary Economics*, 7: 1–28.

Blinder, A.S. (1981) 'Inventories and the structure of macro models', *American Economic Review Papers and Proceedings*, May: 11–16.

Blinder, A.S. (1986) 'Can the production smoothing model of inventory behavior be saved?', *Quarterly Journal of Economics*, 101: 431–453.

Boskin, M.J. (1978) 'Taxation, saving and the rate of interest', *Journal of Political Economy*, 86: S3–S27.

Buchanan, J.M. (1976) 'Barro on the Ricardian Equivalence Theorem,' *Journal of Political Economy*, 84: 337–342.

Caballero, R.J. (1987) 'Consumption and precautionary savings: Empirical implications', M.I.T., mimeo.

Campbell, J. and A. Deaton (1987) 'Is consumption too smooth?', Princeton University, mimeo.

Campbell, J. and N.G. Mankiw (1987) 'Are output fluctuations transitory?', *Quarterly Journal of Economics*, 102: 857–880.

Clark, P.K. (1979) 'Investment in the 1970's: Theory, performance, and prediction', *Brookings Papers on Economic Activity*, 1: 73–113.

Deaton, A. (1986) 'Life-cycle models of consumption: Is the evidence consistent with the theory?', National Bureau of Economic Research, Working Paper 1910.

Drèze, J. and F. Modigliani (1972) 'Consumption decisions under uncertainty', *Journal of Economic Theory*, 5: 308–335.

Eichenbaum, M. S., L. P. Hansen and K.J. Singleton (1986) 'A time series analysis of representative agent models of consumption and leisure under uncertainty', National Bureau of Economic Research, Working Paper, 1981.

Eisner, R. (1978) *Factors in business investment*. Cambridge, Mass.: Ballinger.

Eisner, R. and M.I. Nadiri (1968) 'Investment behavior and neo-classical theory', *Review of Economics and Statistics*, 50: 369–382.

Eisner, R. and M.I. Nadiri (1970) 'Neoclassical theory of investment behavior: A comment', *Review of Economics and Statistics*, 52: 216–222.

Eisner, R. and R.H. Strotz (1963) 'Determinants of business investment', in: *Impacts of monetary policy*, compiled by the Commission on Money and Credit. Englewood Cliffs: Prentice-Hall.

Fazzari, S., R.G. Hubbard and B. Petersen (1987) 'Financing constraints and corporate investment', Northwestern University, mimeo.

Feldstein, M.S. (1982) 'Inflation, tax rules and investment: Some econometric evidence', *Econometrica*, 50: 825–862.

Feldstein, M.S. and A.J. Auerbach (1976) 'Inventory behavior in durable goods manufacturing: The target adjustment model', *Brookings Papers on Economic Activity*, 2: 351–396.

Flavin, M. (1981) 'The adjustment of consumption to changing expectations about future income', *Journal of Political Economy*, 89: 974–1009.

Foley, D. and M. Sidrauski (1970) 'Portfolio choice, investment and growth', *American Economic Review*, 60: 44–63.

Friedman, M. (1957) *A theory of the consumption function*. Princeton: Princeton University Press.

Gould, J.P. (1968) 'Adjustment costs in the theory of investment of the firm', *Review of Economic Studies*, 35: 47–55.

Hall, R.E. (1977) 'Investment, interest rates and the effects of stabilization policies', *Brookings Papers on Economic Activity*, 1: 61–103.

Hall, R.E. (1978) 'Stochastic implications of the life cycle–permanent income hypothesis: Theory and evidence', *Journal of Political Economy*, 86: 971–987.

Hall, R.E. (1989) 'Consumption', in: R.J. Barro, ed., *Handbook of modern business cycle theory*. Cambridge, Mass.: Harvard University Press, pp. 153–177.

Hall, R.E. and F.S. Mishkin (1982) 'The sensitivity of consumption to transitory income: Estimates from panel data on households', *Econometrica*, 50: 461–481.

Hall, R.E. and D.W. Jorgenson (1967) 'Tax policy and investment behavior', *American Economic Review*, 57: 391–414.

Hansen, L.P. and K.J. Singleton (1983) 'Stochastic consumption, risk aversion, and the temporal behavior of asset returns', *Journal of Political Economy*, 91: 249–265.

Hartman, R. (1972) 'The effects of price and cost uncertainty on investment', *Journal of Economic Theory*, 5: 258–266.

Hayashi, F. (1982) 'Tobin's marginal and average q: A neoclassical interpretation', *Econometrica*, 50: 213–224.

Hayashi, F. (1985a) 'The effect of liquidity constraints on consumption: A cross-sectional analysis', *Quarterly Journal of Economics*, 100: 183–206.

Hayashi, F. (1985b) 'The permanent income hypothesis and consumption durability: Analysis based on Japanese panel data', *Quarterly Journal of Economics*, 100: 1083–1113.

Hayashi, F. (1985c) 'Tests of liquidity constraints: A critical survey', National Bureau of Economic Research, Working Paper 1720.

Irvine, O.F., Jr. (1981) 'Retail inventory investment and the cost of capital,' *American Economic Review*, 71: 633–648.

Jorgenson, D.W. (1963) 'Capital theory and investment behavior', *American Economic Review*, Papers and Proceedings, 53: 247–259.

Jorgenson, D.W. and J.A. Stephenson (1969) 'Issues in the development of the neoclassical theory of investment behavior', *Review of Economics and Statistics*, 51: 346–353.

Kahn, J.A. (1987) 'Inventories and the volatility of production', *American Economic Review*, 77: 667–679.

Keynes, J.M. (1936) *The general theory of employment, interest and money*. The Macmillian Press Ltd.

Kimball, M.S. (1986) 'Precautionary saving and the marginal propensity to consume', Harvard University, mimeo.

Kopcke, R.W. (1981) 'Inflation, corporate income taxation, and the demand for capital assets', *Journal of Political Economy*, 89: 122–131.

Lam, P.-S. (1986) 'Two essays on consumer durable expenditures', Ph.D. Dissertation, Harvard University.

Lucas, R.E., Jr. (1967) 'Adjustment costs and the theory of supply', *Journal of Political Economy*, 75: 321–343.

Lucas, R.E., Jr. and E.C. Prescott (1971) 'Investment under uncertainty', *Econometrica*, 39: 659–681.

Mankiw, N.G. (1982) 'Hall's consumption hypothesis, and durable goods', *Journal of Monetary Economics*, 10: 417–425.

McDonald, R. and D. Siegel (1986) 'The value of waiting to invest', *Quarterly Journal of Economics*, 101: 707–727.

Mehra, R. and E.C. Prescott (1985) 'The equity premium: A puzzle', *Journal of Monetary Economics*, 15: 145–161.

Michener, R. (1984) 'Permanent income in general equilibrium', *Journal of Monetary Economics*, 13: 297–305.

Modigliani, F. (1975) 'The life cycle hypothesis of saving twenty years later', in: M. Parkin, ed., *Contemporary issues in economics*. Manchester: Manchester University Press.

Modigliani, F. and R. Brumberg (1954) 'Utility analysis and the consumption function: An interpretation of cross-section data', in: K. Kurihara, ed., *Post-Keynesian economics*. Rutgers University Press, pp. 388–436.

Mussa, M. (1977), 'External and internal adjustment costs and the theory of aggregate and firm investment', *Economica*, 47: 163–178.

Nickell, S.J. (1978) *The investment decision of firms*. Oxford: Cambridge University Press, 1978.

Pazner, E.A. and A. Razin (1974) 'A model of investment under interest rate uncertainty', *International Economic Review*, 15: 798–802.

Pindyck, R. and J. Rotemberg (1983) 'Dynamic factor demands and the effects of energy price shocks', *American Economic Review*, 73: 1066–1079.

Poterba, J.M. and L.H. Summers (1987) 'Finite lifetimes and the effects of budget deficits on national saving', *Journal of Monetary Economics*, 20: 369–391.

Ricardo, D. (1911) *The principles of political economy and taxation*. London: J.M. Dent and Sons Ltd. (last reprinted 1960).

Samuelson, P.A. (1969) 'Lifetime portfolio selection by dynamic stochastic programming', *Review of Economics and Statistics*, 51: 239–246.

Sargent, T.J. (1978) 'Rational expectations, econometric exogeneity, and consumption', *Journal of Political Economy*, 86: 673–700.

Sargent, T.J. (1980) ' "Tobin's *q*" and the rate of investment in general equilibrium', in: K. Brunner and A.H. Meltzer, eds., *On the state of macroeconomics*, Vol. 12 of the Carnegie-Rochester Conference Series on Public Policy, a Supplementary Series to the *Journal of Monetary Economics* (1980).

Seater, J.J. (1985) 'Does government debt matter? A review', *Journal of Monetary Economics*, 16: 121–131.

Startz, R. (1987) 'The stochastic behavior of durable and nondurable consumption', University of Washington, mimeo.

Stiglitz, J.E. and A. Weiss (1981) 'Credit rationing in markets with imperfect information', *American Economic Review*, 71: 393–410.

Summers, L.H. (1981a) 'Taxation and corporate investment: A *q*-theory approach', *Brookings Papers on Economic Activity*, 1: 67–127.

Summers, L.H. (1981b) 'Capital taxation and accumulation in a life cycle growth model', *American Economic Review*, 71: 533–544.

Taylor, J.B. (1982) 'The Swedish investment funds system as a stabilization rule', *Brookings Papers on Economic Activity*, 1: 57–99.

Treadway, A.B. (1969) 'On rational entrepreneurial behavior and the demand for investment', *Review of Economic Studies*, 36: 227–239.

Tobin, J. (1969) 'A general equilibrium approach to monetary theory', *Journal of Money, Credit and Banking*, 1: 15–29.

von Furstenberg, G.M. (1977) 'Corporate investment: Does market valuation matter in the aggregate?', *Brookings Papers on Economic Activity*, 2: 347–397.

Weil, P. (1987) ' "Love thy children": Reflections on the Barro debt neutrality theorem', *Journal of Monetary Economics* 19: 377–391.

West, K.D. (1986) 'A variance bounds test of the linear quadratic inventory model', *Journal of Political Economy*, 94: 374–401.

West, K.D. (1987) 'The insensitivity of consumption to news about income', National Bureau of Economic Research, Working Paper 2252.

Yoshikawa, H. (1980) 'On the "q" theory of investment', *American Economic Review*, 70: 739–743.

Yotsuzuka, T. (1987) 'Ricardian equivalence in the presence of capital market imperfections', *Journal of Monetary Economics*, 20: 411–436.

Zeira, J. (1987) 'Investment as a process of search', *Journal of Political Economy*, 95: 204–210.

Zeldes, S.P. (1989a) 'Consumption and liquidity constraints: An empirical investigation', *Journal of Political Economy*, 97: 305–346.

Zeldes, S.P. (1989b) 'Optimal consumption with stochastic income: Deviations from certainty equivalence', *Quarterly Journal of Economics*, 104: 275–298.

Chapter 15

WHY DOES MONEY AFFECT OUTPUT? A SURVEY

OLIVIER JEAN BLANCHARD*

Massachusetts Institute of Technology and NBER

Contents

*I thank the HSF for financial support. I thank Larry Ball, Stan Fischer, Ben Friedman, Herschel Grossman, Ben McCallum, Greg Mankiw, Danny Quah, David Romer, Julio Rotemberg, and Larry Summers for many helpful discussions and suggestions.

Handbook of Monetary Economics, Volume II, Edited by B.M. Friedman and F.H. Hahn
© *Elsevier Science Publishers B.V., 1990*

0. Introduction

Much of the research on economic fluctuations has focused on the effects of nominal money on output. This is not because money is the major source of movements in output; it is not. Rather, it is because economic theory does not lead us to expect such effects. Indeed, it holds that, with flexible prices, money should be approximately neutral, with changes in nominal money being reflected in nominal prices rather than in output.

Of course we know that, even with competitive markets, full information and flexible prices, the neutrality proposition is only an approximation. Any anticipated change in nominal money must lead to anticipated changes in the price level, and thus introduce a wedge between the opportunity cost of holding money and the cost of capital; in all cases this will affect utility and, in most cases, is likely to affect capital accumulation as well [see Fischer (1979) and Chapter 6 by Orphanides and Solow in this Handbook]. Even unanticipated changes, if they are the result of open market operations, are likely to be non-neutral: open market transactions will usually involve some but not all holders of money and have distribution effects [see Rotemberg (1984) and Grossman and Weiss (1983)]. But, except for the effects of steady inflation which may be substantial (especially when the non-neutrality of the tax system is taken into account), these effects are mere intellectual curiosities; they can account neither for the size nor for the shape of the effect of money on output which we shall review below. For that reason, most of the research has taken as given that prices do not adjust fully and instantaneously to nominal money and focused on the reasons for and implications of imperfect price adjustment. This will also be the approach of this survey.

From Keynes to the mid 1970s, most researchers had shared a common framework, the so-called neoclassical synthesis. Changes in money led to changes in aggregate demand. Because nominal wages and prices adjusted slowly to changes in employment and output, changes in nominal money led to sustained changes in real money and in output. Within that framework, research had proceeded on each of the components, the "transmission mechanism" of money to aggregate demand on the one hand and the "wage–price mechanism" on the other. By the early 1970s, research on the wage–price mechanism had a strongly empirical and a theoretical bent, which was to lead to a serious crisis. While the counter revolution of the 1970s was partly triggered by events, its success was due to the weakness of the theoretical foundations of the dominant approach. A brief description of the evolution of thought from Keynes to the early 1970s is given in Section 1, which then goes on to review the facts, both on the relation of money and output, and on the joint behavior of prices, wages and employment. It concludes that the research on the wage–price mechanism had its facts mostly right, and that the crisis was one of theory, rather than one of empirical adequacy. The rest of the survey is devoted to the reconstruction effort.

The initial strategy was to go back to a model with perfect competition, thus avoiding the theoretical muddle in which previous research had fallen, but to relax the assumption of perfect information. The initial model built by Lucas showed how, with imperfect information, nominal money could affect output. Subsequent research, focusing on intertemporal decisions by firms and households, has examined how money shocks could have both large and persistent effects on output. This direction of research is analyzed in Section 2. Partly because of its own dynamics and partly because of mixed empirical success, this research program has moved away from studying the effects of nominal money and is now focused on the effects of real, productivity, taste or fiscal shocks.

By contrast, much of the recent research on the real effects of nominal money has been based on imperfect competition. While it has been labeled Keynesian, it often bears only a distant resemblance to the earlier models, and certainly does not yet constitute a unified whole. Recent developments are presented in Sections 3 and 4.

Section 3 starts by presenting the models built in the late 1970s by Fischer and Taylor, which showed that one could introduce rational expectations in models with nominal wage and price setting and still get long-lasting effects of nominal money on output. These models made an important point and have become workhorses in the field. Nevertheless, they begged important questions, indeed the same questions which had not been answered by earlier research on the "wage–price mechanism". Long-lasting effects of money on output in the Taylor model, for example, require that two conditions be satisfied. The first is that the elasticity of the desired real wage with respect to movements in employment be small; we can think of this as "real wage rigidity". The second is that, in addition, nominal wages be preset for some period of time; we can think of that as "nominal wage rigidity". Why both types of rigidity are present is not answered in the model. Research has examined the two issues in parallel. The rest of Section 3 reviews the research on real rigidities, on why fluctuations in the demand for goods lead to movements in output with little movement in markups of prices over wages, and why fluctuations in the demand for labor lead to movements in employment with little movement in real wages.

Section 4 describes research on nominal rigidities. It starts with the "menu cost" argument, which holds that, under imperfect competition, and in response to a change in aggregate demand, the private return to each price-setter from adjusting his price is smaller than the social return. The argument is important for two reasons: first, it implies that small menu costs may lead to nominal rigidities and large output effects; second, it implies that the welfare effects of nominal rigidities arising from small menu costs may be large. The argument is, however, a static one, looking at the effect of a one-time change in aggregate demand, starting with identical prices. Subsequent research has shown that the argument does not extend straightforwardly to a dynamic context. Individual price rigidity may or may not lead to aggregate price rigidity, depending on the specific nature of price rules and the interaction between price-setters. The relation between welfare effects and menu costs is also much less clear cut than in the static context. The second half of Section 4 reviews the current state of play.

Section 5 questions three implicit assumptions of the previous analysis. The first is that prices are set in nominal terms. The first part of Section 5 looks at the scope for indexation or other monetary reforms to automatically decrease or eliminate the effects of money on output. The second is that more price flexibility reduces the effect of money on output and the size of undesired output fluctuations. But, ever since Fisher and Keynes, we have known that more price flexibility may in fact be destabilizing, through its effect on real interest rates and through the redistribution of claims in the economy. This is discussed in the second part of the section. The third is that the economy, left to itself, eventually returns to its natural level of unemployment. Recent analysis suggests that this may not always be the case. If that analysis is correct, even short-lived nominal rigidities may lead to permanent effects of nominal money, or of aggregate demand shocks in general, on output and employment.

Section 6 concludes.

1. From Keynes to the early 1970s

1.1. From Keynes to the neoclassical synthesis

Keynes' explanation in the "General Theory" of the effects of nominal money on output was based on two main assumptions. He accepted the classical principle that employment could only increase if real wages decreased. But he added the assumption that, because workers focused mostly about nominal wages, nominal wages were more rigid, "sticky" (the word appears to be Keynes') than prices. An increase in money would then lead to an increase in prices, a reduction in real wages and an increase in output.

It will be convenient to use throughout a simple log-linear structure to point out the major differences between models. As the focus is on aggregate supply, I shall for the most part use a simple – indeed simplisitic – representation of aggregate demand, expressing output demand only as a function of real money balances, without any dynamics. I shall also ignore unimportant constants so as not to clutter the notation. The aggregate demand–aggregate supply framework corresponding to the General Theory can then be expressed as:

$$y = a(m - p), \quad a > 0, \tag{1.1}$$

$$y = b(w - p), \quad b < 0, \tag{1.2}$$

$$w = w^*, \tag{1.3}$$

where y is the log of real output, and m, p and w the (logarithms of) nominal money, nominal prices and nominal wages, respectively. If nominal wages are fixed at level w^*, increases in m increase both output and the price level. Aggregate demand increases with real money balances, and aggregate supply increases with the decrease in the real wage.[1]

This model is a familiar one and has made it to the textbooks up to this day. It was, however, discarded by macroeconomists soon after the General Theory as it quickly became clear that it was in contradiction with the facts. Dunlop (1938) showed that, for the United Kingdom, real wages were, if anything, procyclical, an assumption difficult to reconcile with decreasing returns to labor and marginal cost pricing.[2] He also showed, using informal evidence, that unions often cared explicitly about the cost of living and suggested that the assumption that workers cared more about nominal than real wages may not be appropriate. These findings led most economists, including Keynes himself (1939), to conclude that a more drastic departure from classical theory was needed and that price-setting in particular could only be understood by appealing to imperfect competition.

This task was however not taken up by macroeconomists working within the "neoclassical synthesis", the consensus view of macroeconomics which emerged in the 1950s and 1960s and within which most of the major developments of post-war macroeconomics took place. The main achievement of the synthesis was to give solid theoretical foundations to many of the decisions taken by individuals and firms, such as consumption or investment. But price and wage decisions were left out and few formal attempts were made to link them explicitly to, for example, bargaining models in the labor market or imperfect competition in the goods market. The prevailing mode of thinking about prices and wages was in terms of tatonnement, with prices and wages adjusting to excess demand or supply in their respective markets, along the

---

[1] There is obviously more to Keynes (as always . . .) than this simplistic characterization. We shall return to some other aspects later in the chapter.

[2] Tarshis (1939), who is often credited with the same observation, showed instead that for the United States there was a negative correlation between changes in manhours and changes in real wages.

lines of the dynamic process of adjustment studied by Samuelson in his "Foundations" (1947).

In retrospect there are probably two main reasons why the neoclassical synthesis did not take up the task. The first is that it was hard, and the marginal return to other explorations was higher. The second was the providential role played by the discovery of the "Phillips curve" relation between the rate of change of nominal wages and unemployment [Phillips (1958)]: the existence of a reliable empirical relation made less urgent the need for better microeconomic underpinnings of price adjustments. Because the facts seemed to be clear and progress on the theoretical front difficult, most of the research on wage and price behavior was, until the early 1970s, characterized by its strong empirical bent and a rather eclectic use of microeconomic justifications.

1.2. The wage–price mechanism as of the early 1970s

By the early 1970s there was a wide consensus as to the main empirical characteristics of the "wage–price mechanism". This consensus, summarized in a survey paper by Tobin (1972) [see also the survey by Santomero and Seater (1978)] was roughly the following.

Prices were markups over unit costs at standard rates of output and capacity utilization; they did not seem to respond to demand movements. The response to changes in input prices was quick, so that prices played a passive role in the adjustment of the price level to changes in nominal money; they reflected wage increases quickly and fully.

Wages were explained by the "augmented" Phillips curve. After its transplantation into the United States by Samuelson and Solow (1960), the Phillips curve specification, augmented to allow for an effect of price inflation, had had an excellent track record in the 1960s. The rate of change of nominal wages was a function of the level of unemployment and of current and past price inflation. The question of whether the sum of coefficients on past inflation was equal to one was treated as an empirical issue, to be settled by the data. By the early 1970s the consensus was that, while it had increased over time, the coefficient was still less than one, although not significantly so [Gordon (1972)]. This implied the existence of a long-term trade-off between inflation and unemployment.

In terms of our log-linear model, the wage–price mechanism summarized by Tobin, can be written as:

$$y = a(m - p),$$ (1.1)

$$p = w,$$ (1.4)

$$w - w(-1) = b(p(-1) - p(-2)) + cy, \quad 0 < b < 1, c > 0.$$ (1.5)

Equation (1.1) is aggregate demand. Equation (1.4) is the price equation and embodies the assumption of quick passthrough of wage costs and no effect of demand. Equation (1.5) is the wage equation, giving wage inflation as a function of lagged price inflation and output, used as a proxy for unemployment.[3] This system reduces to a second-order difference equation in p. If a is positive, the equation is stable, possibly with complex roots. An increase in the level of money leads to an increase in output; output returns to normal over time, with or without oscillations. The model shares with the earlier Keynes' model the fact that aggregate demand determines output in the short run. In contrast to the earlier model, however, the real wage remains the same throughout; this is the result of markup pricing by firms, as characterized in equation (1.4).

The wage–price blocks of the large macroeconometric models built in the early 1970s were similar in structure to equations (1.4) and (1.5), with the implication that movements in money led to a slow adjustment of prices and wages, a long-lasting effect on output and little or no movement in the real wage along the way.

1.3. The counter-revolution: The theoretical attack

It was clear even then that while the wage–price mechanism appeared to fit the facts successfully, its components were at sharp variance with standard neoclassical theory. In the price equation, whether the lack of effects of demand on the markup of prices over labor costs was due to flat marginal cost, or to a squeeze in profit margins as output increased, was not resolved [see Nordhaus (1972) for a critical analysis of those price equations]. In the wage equation, letting the data decide whether the coefficient on inflation was equal to one was in contrast with, for example, the sophisticated derivation of the appropriate user cost under inflation in the investment literature. It was also not clear why unemployment affected the rate of change of wages independently of their level. While consistent with a tatonnement assumption that wages moved as a function of excess supply, measured by unemployment, it was in contradiction with the idea that, at least in the long run, there should be a relation between the level of the real wage and the level of labor supply.

These problems were clearer to some than to others. Two important contributions had questioned the possibility of a long-run trade-off on a priori grounds. Both Phelps (1967) and Friedman (1968) had argued that there could only be one equilibrium rate of unemployment, i.e. the "natural" rate, and

---

[3]For simplicity, I shall assume throughout the models presented in this chapter the existence of a linear relation between the logarithm of output, the logarithm of employment and the level of unemployment. I shall therefore use them interchangeably, as I do in equation (1.5).

that there was no permanent trade-off between unemployment and inflation; unemployment could only remain below its natural rate if inflation accelerated. This "accelerationist hypothesis" was further refined in an influential book by Phelps (1970) which explored how models of search in the labor and goods markets could or could not explain wage and price behavior as embodied in the wage–price mechanism.

The proximate cause of the crisis, however, was the introduction of rational expectations. Together with the natural rate hypothesis, it implied that unemployment could only be associated with unexpected inflation, thus with unexpected demand movements. Furthermore, it was shown first by Sargent (1971) and then by Lucas (1976) in his celebrated critique that the natural rate–rational expectations hypothesis could be true while the sum of coefficients on inflation in the Phillips curve, which had been the subject of so much attention, was less than one. Their argument was the following. Suppose that the true Phillips curve had the following form:

$$w - w(-1) = (\mathrm{E}p - p(-1)) + cy ,$$

where E denotes the expectation of the price level based on past information, so that wage inflation depended on expected price inflation with a coefficient of one. Assume also that price inflation followed a first-order autoregressive process:

$$p - p(-1) = \rho(p(-1) - p(-2)) + e .$$

Then, if workers had rational expectations and formed expectations of inflation based on past inflation, the observed Phillips curve would be:

$$w - w(-1) = \rho(p(-1) - p(-2)) + cy .$$

As long as ρ was less than one, the Phillips curve would appear to imply a long-run trade-off when in fact there was none. A change in the inflation process, coming for example from an attempt by the government to lower unemployment, would lead to a change in ρ and a change in the coefficient on lagged inflation in the Phillips curve. The trade-off would vanish as the government tried to exploit it.

The critique implied that the theoretical issue of whether there was a long-run trade-off could not be settled simply by looking at the sum of coefficients on lagged inflation. But the influence of the critique went far beyond that. It had in particular the effect of focusing attention on the underlying microeconomic underpinnings of the wage–price mechanism, and many found them lacking. What has happened since the mid-1970s is best

described as a return to basics (sometimes very basics), a search for theoretically consistent explanations of the movement of nominal wages and prices.

1.4. The counter-revolution: The facts

The above account emphasizes the crisis in theory. Some have emphasized the
empirical failure of the wage–price mechanism. In a polemical article, Lucas
and Sargent (1978) conclude to "an empirical failure on a grand scale". This is
a considerable overstatement. It is true that the estimated coefficient on lagged
inflation kept rising with inflation, and that the estimated equations initially
failed to predict the inflationary effects of the oil shocks of 1974–75, but once
the coefficient on lagged inflation was increased, and the price equation was
respecified so as to allow for materials costs, the equations were once again on
track and have performed decently since then [see Englander and Los (1983)
for example]. This decent empirical performance should come as no surprise
and may be seen as the result of the rather atheoretical approach to the data
which we described earlier.

Indeed, while macroeconomists have been working on rebuilding theoretical
foundations, the wage–price component of empirical macroeconometric models has not changed much since the early 1970s. Major modifications have been
the elimination of the long-run trade-off and the introduction of exchange
rates, affecting the price behavior of sectors exposed to foreign competition,
and introducing a wedge between producers' prices and consumer prices. Table
15.1 gives the results of a dynamic simulation of the 1985 version of the DRI

Table 15.1
Effects of a 1 percent permanent increase in M1 in the DRI model

Quarters / Effects on:	4	8	12	16	20	24
Real GNP	0.7	1.4	0.8	−0.5	−1.1	−0.8
WPI	0.7	1.4	1.7	1.6	1.6	1.6
PGNP	0.0	0.4	1.0	1.3	1.4	1.3
CPI	0.1	0.4	0.7	1.0	1.2	1.3
AHE	0.1	0.5	1.0	1.3	1.4	1.3
M1/PGNP	1.0	0.6	0.0	−0.3	−0.4	−0.3
AHE/WPI	−0.6	−0.9	−0.6	−0.3	−0.3	−0.3
AHE/PGNP	0.1	0.1	0.0	0.0	0.0	0.0
AHE/CPI	0.0	0.1	0.3	0.3	0.2	0.0

Source: DRI Model, 1985.
All variables measured as percentage deviations from initial path.
GNP = real gross national product; WPI = wholesale price index; PGNP = price deflator for GNP;
CPI = consumer price index; AHE = average hourly earnings in manufacturing.

model. An increase in money of 1 percent increases GNP for about 3 to 4 years; it takes many more years for output to return to normal, and only after long and slightly damped oscillations. The behavior of the real wage depends very much on which price deflator is used. The real wage in terms of the GNP deflator varies with output. The real wage in terms of the CPI moves very little, increasing slightly before it returns to normal.

That empirical macroeconometric models have not changed suggests that, whether or not their structural interpretation of the data is appropriate, they capture accurately the important cross-correlations present in those data. In what follows, I review the empirical evidence on the effects of money on output. That evidence can be divided into direct reduced-form evidence on the relation between money and output, and evidence on each of the components of the wage–price mechanism.

1.4.1. Reduced-form evidence on money and output

That money had a strong impact on output was the major theme of Friedman and Schwartz (1963). Relying on evidence from the period 1867–1960, and in particular on a study of turning points in money and output, they concluded that there was a strong and stable relation between money, nominal and real income, with the causality often running from money to economic activity. Much of the research on reduced-form evidence since then has taken the same approach, but relied on formal econometric methods instead. To see what can be learned from such an approach, suppose that output is affected by money and other variables according to the reduced-form relation:

$$y = \sum a_i y_{-i} + \sum b_i m_{-i} + \sum x_{-i} c_i + e , \qquad (1.6)$$

where y is some measure of output, such as the logarithm of GNP, m a measure of nominal money, such as the logarithm of M1, x a vector of other variables, such as fiscal policy or exports, and e is serially uncorrelated. Sums run from 1 to n for y, from 0 or 1 to k for m and x.

When will estimation of this equation by ordinary least squares give unbiased estimates of the effects of nominal money on output? Two conditions are required. The first is that all right-hand-side variables be uncorrelated with the current innovation in output, e. The second is that, if current money or x are not included, their true coefficients be equal to zero.[4]

---

[4]These conditions are regularly rediscovered. They were emphasized in the discussion of the St. Louis model, and more recently when economists tried to understand what could or could not be learned from causality tests [see Cooley and LeRoy (1985)].

Causality tests were first introduced by Sims (1972) to characterize the dynamic interactions between money and output. Bivariate causality tests are based on equations such as (1.6), but allowing for no other variables than y and m, and excluding current m. When applied to the relation between money and output, they typically have found that the estimated a_1's and b_1's imply a strong dynamic response of y to m. [The dynamic response of y to m is given by the coefficients of $(1 - a(L))^{-1} b(L)$, where $a(L)$ and $b(L)$ are the lag polynomials in (1.6).] A typical response pattern, from Sargent (1976) is given on the left-hand side of Table 15.2. It shows a response of unemployment to M1 peaking after 5 quarters and becoming negative after 11 quarters. Many bivariate causality tests have been run, using different empirical counterparts for the quantity variable and for money, different periods and sampling intervals, and different treatments of non-stationarity in m and y. The effect of money usually has been found to be significant, although the level of significance depends on the method of detrending (stochastic or deterministic) [Stock and Watson (1987)]. Eichenbaum and Singleton (1986), for example, using first differences of log GNP and second differences of log M1, and monthly data from 1949 to 1983, find the effect of money on output to be barely significant.

Given our discussion above, it is clear that the conditions under which this estimated dynamic response is the true dynamic response are unlikely to be met. First, there are surely other variables than money which affect output and are correlated with money. Second, it is quite likely that current money is affected by e, innovations in output. It may even be that lagged money is correlated with the current innovation in output. This will be the case if the central bank has information about future output beyond what can be learned

Table 15.2
Reduced-form dynamic effects of money on output

Quarters	Unemployment[a]	Effects of a 1% permanent increase in nominal money on:	
		Output[b]	
		Anticipated	Unanticipated
0	0.0	1.3	2.0
2	−0.3	1.9	2.3
4	−0.4	1.8	2.2
6	−0.3	1.3	2.0
8	−0.2	0.7	1.6
12	0.0	−0.4	0.5
16	0.1	−0.6	−0.4
20	0.1	−0.1	−0.3

[a]From Sargent (1976, table 1, line 1).
[b]From Mishkin (1983, table 6.5).

from the history of money and output; in this case lagged money will help predict output even if it does not affect it [this is the stochastic extension of the "Post hoc, ergo propter hoc" argument made by Tobin (1970)].[5] This simultaneity problem may be less serious for some components of money than for others. King and Plosser (1984), using annual data from 1953 to 1978, find a weaker and shorter effect of high powered money than of M1. A possible interpretation is that the strong effect of M1 on output found by others comes in fact partly from the reaction of inside money to output.

Multivariate causality tests, i.e. tests in which variables other than y and m are allowed on the right-hand side of (1.6), have also been implemented. Sims (1980) in particular has found that when short nominal interest rates are added to nominal money in (1.6), money no longer has a significant effect on output. What this means is, however, unclear and open to many interpretations; McCallum (1983a) has shown that these results would arise if, for example, the Federal Reserve used money to peg interest rates.

Another line of research has looked at the effects of money while more explicitly controlling for the presence of other variables, the x variables in (1.5). The first attempt was made by Andersen and Jordan (1970) in the St. Louis model. More recently, work by Barro (1977) has spurred a new set of estimates. Barro ran an equation similar to (1.6), allowing for the presence of a time trend and a proxy for exogenous government spending in x. He also decomposed money growth into two components, one "unanticipated", obtained as the residual from a forecasting equation including lagged money and other variables, and one "anticipated" and equal to the forecast value. Using annual data for the period 1946 to 1976, he concluded that the hypothesis that only the unanticipated component affected output could not be rejected, and that this unanticipated component affected output for up to three years. In Barro (1978), this approach was extended to look at the joint response of output and prices, and in Barro and Rush (1980) the same approach was used on quarterly data. The data have been re-examined by Mishkin (1983) who, using quarterly data for 1954–1976 and longer lag structures, concludes that both the unanticipated and the anticipated components have a long-lasting effect on output. The dynamic response of output to an "anticipated" and an "unanticipated" permanent change in money, from Mishkin, is given on the right-hand side of Table 15.2. Both components of money have large and long-lasting effects on output. It is clear, however, that while this approach is more careful about the inclusion of other variables than money in (1.6), the interpretation of the dynamic response as structural still depends on the

---

[5]These problems of economic interpretation of causality tests were pointed out by Sims; users of causality tests have not always resisted the temptation to make unwarranted inferences.

maintained assumption of zero correlation between the innovation in output and current and lagged money, anticipated or unanticipated.[6]

The decomposition of money between anticipated and unanticipated components has also been questioned. Sargent (1976) has pointed out that, if expectations of money were based only on past money, there would be infinitely many ways of decomposing a distributed lag of money as the sum of two distributed lags in anticipated and unanticipated money. Identification depends on the presence of explanatory variables other than money in the equation for money, and may therefore be weak. Fischer (1980) has also noted that the data are unlikely to be able to distinguish between Barro's specification and a specification in which output depends on anticipated money and unanticipated money *n* periods – rather than one period – ahead. The two specifications have, however, drastically different policy implications.

Poterba, Rotemberg and Summers (1986) have adopted an indirect approach to testing nominal rigidities that avoids this simultaneity problem by looking not at the effects of money but at the effects of shifts between direct and indirect taxation. In the absence of nominal rigidities, it should not matter which side of the market a tax is collected on. In the presence of nominal rigidities, it may, however, affect the price level and output: if, for example, nominal wages are fixed, the shift from direct taxation to a value added tax will increase the price level and decrease output. To the extent that changes in taxation are more exogenous than money, this avoids some of the problems mentioned above. Their analysis of the empirical evidence leads them to conclude that there are substantial nominal rigidities, both in the United States and the United Kingdom.

Reduced-form evidence thus suggests a strong relation between money and output. Part of it may be due to the effect of output on money. Part of it surely is not. The event studies provided by the U.K. and U.S. disinflations of the early 1980s, in addition to those described by Friedman and Schwartz, strongly support the view that monetary policy affects output.

1.4.2. Evidence on the components of the wage–price mechanism

It would take us too far afield to review the empirical work on wage and price behavior in any detail (we shall discuss some of it in relation to specific theoretical developments later on). But, in the spirit of the general skepticism

---

[6]It is interesting to note the qualitative similarity of the dynamic responses in Table 15.2 to those in Table 15.1, obtained from the DRI model. Reduced-form estimates are, however, larger than those obtained from simulations of structural models. This was already noted and discussed in the context of the St. Louis model. Potential explanations involve the bias in reduced-form estimation discussed above, or the neglect of some transmission channels in structural models.

that has permeated macroeconometrics since the mid-1970s, research has proceeded to see whether the stylized facts on which the wage–price mechanism was based were actually present in the data.

The first stylized fact was the lack of response of the markup of prices on wages to movements in output or, put another way, the lack of a negative correlation between real product wages and employment, as would be expected if the economy moved along a stable demand for labor. Sargent (1978) suggested that the presence of costs of adjustment for employment implied a more complex dynamic relation between real wages and employment and could be consistent with little contemporaneous negative correlation between the two. His attempt to explain the data in this way was, however, not very successful. Later research along the same lines has confirmed that there is no clear correlation at any lag between product wages and employment in the United States, but has shown the existence of a negative correlation between lagged real wages and employment in some other industrialized countries [see Bruno and Sachs (1984) and Geary and Kennan (1982)]. Bils (1985), using U.S. panel data on individual workers, concludes that the real consumption wage is procyclical.

The other main stylized fact was the Phillips curve, a relation between wage changes, past price changes and unemployment. Causality tests have consistently shown that lagged employment does not Granger cause real wages [Sargent (1978), Neftci (1978)]. While this has been taken as evidence against the Phillips curve, it does not look at the same set of correlations; the Phillips curve is a relation between nominal wage inflation, lagged inflation and current as well as lagged employment, not necessarily between actual real wages and lagged employment. If the economy had both a Phillips curve and markup pricing, for example, there would be no relation between real wages – which are constant – and employment.

Looking at reduced-form evidence on wages, prices and employment, I have asked whether an econometrician who ignored the existence of the wage–price mechanism described by Tobin could find it in U.S. data [Blanchard (1986b)]. To do so, I wrote down a structural model, with a wage, a price and an aggregate demand equation, and then derived and estimated the unconstrained reduced form. I then asked what structural price, wage and aggregate demand equations were consistent with the reduced-form evidence and concluded that the reduced-form evidence was roughly consistent with the existence of the structural wage–price mechanism described by Tobin.

1.5. The reconstruction effort

To summarize, the crisis of the 1970s arose not because the wage–price mechanism was in contradiction with the facts, but because its explanation of the facts was at variance with theory. Thus, the reconstruction effort has been largely theoretical. It is part of a much larger enterprise affecting all of macroeconomics, and it interacts with it. For example, if we think of contracts under asymmetric information as being an important factor in labor markets, then the price level is a potential signal and the study of why nominal wages are not fully indexed should start from there. Or if we think of imperfect competition as being important in goods markets, this may explain why, as price may exceed marginal cost most of the time, firms may be willing to accommodate increases in demand at a given price. We shall touch on those other developments only to the extent that they are relevant to the issue at hand.

Research has taken two radically different directions.

The first has explored whether the stylized facts could be reconciled with a more standard neoclassical model. Thus, it has worked under the maintained "as if" assumption of perfect competition in all markets but relaxed the assumption of full information. It has focused both on the impact effects of disturbances such as money and on the channels for persistence. I shall refer to this approach as the "imperfect information" approach and review it in the next section.

The second has explored instead whether the many leads and insights of the earlier literature could be made more rigorous and could form the basis for a theoretically consistent explanation of the effects of money on output and of the wage–price mechanism. I shall refer to that approach as the "imperfect competition" approach and study it in Sections 3 and 4.

While the two approaches differ in their philosophy, they share two common methodological precepts. The first is that any explanation for the effects of money on output should hold even under rational expectations. Nearly all of the research has indeed assumed rational expectations as a working hypothesis. The second, which we shall not focus on, is that fluctuations should be analyzed using the Frisch–Slutzky impulse-propagation framework in which fluctuations are thought of as the result of stochastic impulses affecting variables through a propagation mechanism;[7] this approach, which is consistent with time-series methods, has allowed a better integration of macroeconomic theory and econometric methods; this integration is perhaps as important a development as the substantive results described below.

---

[7]Because linear stochastic processes are easier to deal with, work on non-linear dynamic systems, which had been popular earlier, has dwindled. There has, however, been recently renewed interest in non-linear deterministic systems which can generate rich dynamics or even dynamics similar to those of stochastic processes [see, for example, Grandmont (1985)]. There are few results to date using this approach on the issues studied in this chapter.

2. Imperfect information

Models of search, developed initially by macroeconomists to explain the various aspects of the wage-price mechanism, had shown the importance and the potential of relaxing the assumption that markets were cleared by a fully informed auctioneer [see the introduction by Phelps to his volume (1970)]. This had two main implications. First, because of imperfect information on the part of buyers and sellers, whoever set a price was likely to have at least transient monopoly or monopsony power. Markets could no longer be viewed as competitive. Second, if individuals had limited information, there was the potential for aggregate nominal shocks to affect output. The reason was sketched by Phelps. Individuals and firms faced both individual and aggregate shocks. Because they had limited information, they could not distinguish accurately between the two. Even if they had wanted to react only to individual shocks, they ended up reacting also to aggregate shocks such as changes in nominal money. Nominal money therefore could affect output.

Developing general equilibrium models with optimal price-setting under imperfect information proved difficult, however, and, early on, the choice was made to examine the implications of imperfect information while maintaining the assumption of pefect competition in all markets. This was an important choice, making for more tractable models at the cost of eliminating important issues. The first macroeconomic models along those lines were developed by Lucas.

2.1. The Lucas model[8]

Lucas (1972) constructed a macroeconomic model with optimizing agents, decentralized markets and imperfect information. A streamlined version was given in Lucas (1973) and has the following structure:

$$y = a(m - p) , \tag{2.1}$$

$$p_i = p + e_i, \quad i = 1, \ldots, n , \tag{2.2}$$

$$y_i = b(p_i - E_i p) . \tag{2.3}$$

No distinction is made between workers and firms. Output is produced by n firms, indexed by i, each operating as a price-taker in its own market. Equation

---

[8]See Lucas (1972) and (1973).

(2.1) is aggregate demand. Equation (2.2) gives the price facing each firm, p_i; p_i differs from the price level p by a random variable e_i, which reflects movements in relative demands across markets. The e_i are uncorrelated across firms and are white noise. The supply of each firm is given by equation (2.3); $E_i p$ is the expectation of the price level by firm i, based on its observation of p_i. Firms react only to perceived relative price changes.

When firms observe a high value of p_i, this may reflect either a high value of m, or a high value of e_i, or both. This leads them to revise upwards their expectation p, according to $E_i p = Em + k(p_i - Em)$, where Em is the expectation of m (and p) they held before observing p_i. The parameter k depends on the relative variances of unanticipated money and of the shock e_i, and is between zero and one. Replacing in (2.3) gives $y_i = b(1 - k)(p_i - Em)$. The higher the nominal price it observes, the higher its conditional expectation of a relative price shock e_i, the higher the supply of firm i. Aggregating over firms gives an aggregate supply curve:

$$y = b(1 - k)(p - Em) \,. \tag{2.4}$$

Solving (2.3) and (2.4) gives:

$$p = d\,Em + (1 - d)m \,,$$

where $d = b(1 - k)/(a + b(1 - k))$, and

$$y = ad(m - Em) \,. \tag{2.5}$$

Imperfect information leads therefore to an effect of unanticipated money on output. This is because firms partly misperceive money shocks for relative price shocks. The counterpart is that firms partly misperceive relative price shocks for money shocks and thus underreact to those; this, however, has no macroeconomic implications.

The Lucas (1972) and (1973) models showed how, under market clearing and imperfect information, unanticipated money could affect output. Neither, however, showed why money could have lasting effects on output,[9] nor did they try to explain the specific behavior of firms versus workers, wages versus prices. Those issues were taken up by subsequent research.

---

[9]While the (1973) model includes lagged output in the supply equation, leading to lasting effects of unanticipated money on output, it is, as Lucas indicated, an assumption without justification within the model.

2.2. Impulse and propagation mechanisms

2.2.1. Intertemporal substitution

The mechanism through which money had a positive effect on output in the Lucas model raised two questions. The first was asked by Lucas himself: How could misperceptions about money have such large effects on supply? The second was raised most explicitly by Friedman (1978): Why was it that suppliers rather than buyers were the ones who misperceived prices? If the information structure was such that suppliers observed prices accurately, but that buyers were misled in thinking that a high price meant in part a high relative price, would this not lead to a decrease in demand and an output contraction instead?

The answer to the first question had already been suggested by Lucas and Rapping (1969) who had focused on workers and labor supply. Perceived permanent changes in the real wage were unlikely to lead to large supply responses, because of conflicting income and substitution effects. Perceived temporary changes, however, had mainly substitution effects and could lead to large responses. More generally and more formally, the relevant intertemporal relative price to a supplier i was $(P_i/P)/(1 + r^e)(P_i^e/P^e)$, the ratio of his perceived relative price (the real wage for workers) to his expected relative price discounted by the expected real interest rate. If, when suppliers observed an increase in their price, they inferred that it was partly due to a favorable shift in demand, and if they did not expect these shifts in demand to be permanent, they would then respond to nominal shocks by increasing supply.

The issues raised by the second question were analyzed by Barro who, in a series of papers, constructed models allowing for intertemporal substitution and misperceptions on both the supply and the demand side. A general equilibrium model where money is the only asset so that the real interest rate is the negative of the rate of inflation and the relevant relative price is simply P_i/P_i^e was developed in Barro (1976); it was extended in Barro (1981) to allow for other assets than money and to deal with the endogeneity of the real interest rate. These models show how intertemporal substitution and specific information structures can deliver positive effects of money on output; they do not, however, make a convincing case for the specific information structure and set of structural coefficients which deliver such positive effects.

2.2.2. Persistence

The second issue was how the initial misperception could have long-lasting effects on output and employment. Two types of channels were later identified.

First, if the initial misperception led firms or workers to change a state variable, a variable which affected their decisions in subsequent periods, the initial impulse would have lasting effects. Lucas (1975) emphasized the role of capital in creating persistence. If misperceptions led first to both sell and invest more, the higher capital stock would later on lead to a higher profit-maximizing level of output. Output would be higher until firms decreased their capital back to equilibrium. While capital accumulation appears to be an unlikely channel for cyclical persistence, similar effects, but working through inventories or through employment in the presence of costs of adjustment, were characterized by Blinder and Fischer (1981) and Sargent (1979), respectively. Howitt (1986) has recently show that persistence also emerges from an explicit search model of the labor market, where persistence arises from costs of changing employment.

Another channel for persistence was identified by Taylor (1975) and Lucas (1975): if direct information about nominal shocks was not available, even ex post, large permanent changes in money could be misperceived for relative price changes for a long time, during which they would have an effect on output.

Those extensions still imply that only unanticipated changes in nominal money matter, but their effects on output can now be long lasting. There is, however, an obvious tension between the factors needed to get large impulses and those needed to get persistence. Strong intertemporal substitution, for example, leads to a strong response of labor supply to misperceptions, but through the accumulation of wealth also leads to lower labor supply later and to negative serial correlation of output in response to shocks. Costs of adjustment, on the other hand, lead to more persistence, but to smaller initial effects of shocks.

2.2.3. Policy implications

Most of the models above share the same policy implications. These were first pointed out by Lucas (1973), Sargent (1973) and Sargent and Wallace (1975). Anticipated money had no effect. Unanticipated money could in general affect output but, if the monetary authority had no more information than the public, this effect was unlikely to improve welfare. If the policy-maker had no more information than the public, unanticipated monetary movements would be uncorrelated with other shocks, increasing noise and making signal extraction more difficult for individuals and firms, decreasing the allocative efficiency of the price system. If the policy-maker had more information, money could then obviously be used to offset other shocks and improve welfare but an equally efficient way of achieving the same outcome would then be simply to make information available to the public. These conclusions have been slightly qualified since. Weiss (1980) and King (1982) have shown that policy rules based on public information can sometimes affect the outcome by changing the information content of observable prices. Other examples have been constructed of economies with other distortions in which additional noise can be welfare improving. These qualifications not withstanding, the role of monetary policy is drastically reduced from the role it can play under the standard wage–price mechanism.

2.3. Empirical evidence

2.3.1. Reduced-form evidence: Money, output and the price level

The most striking implication of imperfect information models, and the most at variance with previous beliefs, is that anticipated money does not matter. The evidence on the relation between money and output has been re-examined by Barro in a series of articles (1977, 1978, 1980) which we have already briefly described. Dividing money into two components – unanticipated and anticipated money – Barro concluded that he could not reject the hypothesis that anticipated money did not affect output. Further work by Mishkin (1983) has shown, however, that anticipated money also affects output, although by less than unanticipated money. These results were shown in Table 15.2.

While money stock figures are published with little delay, they are subsequently revised. A literal interpretation of imperfect information models suggests that only the unperceived component of money, i.e. the difference between the final revision and the initial announcement, should affect economic activity. This was tested by Barro and Hercowitz (1980) and Boschen and Grossman (1982) and decisively rejected; this, however, is a rejection only of an extreme and absurd version of imperfect information models.

Another implication of most – although not all – imperfect information models is that money affects output through price level surprises. An equation relating output movements to unanticipated price level movements was first run by Sargent (1976) who found only weak evidence in favor of such an effect. Fair (1979) found instead, by extending the sample period to include the 1970s, a positive correlation between unemployment and price level innovations! These results have been challenged by Gray and Spencer (1984) who argue that whether the correlation between price level and output innovations is positive or negative depends on whether supply or demand shocks dominate the sample. Specifying unemployment as a function of price level surprises, energy price surprises and proxies for frictional unemployment, they find that price level surprises have a significant effect on unemployment. Using annual data, they find the following relation between unemployment and unanticipated price level movements:

$$u = -0.4(p - E(p| -1)) - 1.4(p - E(p| -2)) - 0.8(p - E(p| -3))$$
$$+ \text{(supply factors)},$$

where u is the unemployment rate, and $E(p| -i)$ is the expectation of the (logarithm of the) price level at time t based on information available at time $t - i$.[10] Note that this relation can be rewritten as a price–price Phillips curve, namely as

$$p = -0.4u + (0.1E(p| -1) + 0.6E(p| -2) + 0.3E(p| -3))$$
$$+ \text{(supply factors)}.$$

What Gray and Spencer have thus shown is that the set of correlations traditionally summarized by the Phillips curve can also be given an alternative interpretation, an interpretation more consistent with the imperfect information approach.[11] More generally, one may conclude from a reading of the research on reduced-form evidence that the co-movements of output, prices and money are consistent with the view that unanticipated money has weaker effects on the price level and stronger effects on output than anticipated money.[12]

2.3.2. *Intertemporal substitution, the real wage, labor supply and consumption*

While most imperfect information models share the same reduced-form implications for output and prices, they differ in their implications as to the relation between real wages and employment, which depends crucially on the source of disturbances and the information structure. If firms perceive prices and wages accurately, money shocks must lead to movements along the labor demand of firms and are likely to imply a negative correlation of real wages and employment. But if instead workers perceive wages and prices accurately, movements take place along labor supply, with a likely positive correlation between real wages and employment. In all cases, however, intertemporal

---

[10]The presence of lagged expectations is easier to justify in a contract model, such as those studied in the next section, than in an imperfect information model. Gray and Spencer derive their specification from such a contract model.

[11]The presence of lagged expectations is, however, easier to justify in the context of models with nominal rigidities reviewed in the next section.

[12]See, however, the discussion of identification of unanticipated versus anticipated money in the previous section.

substitution by workers in response to correctly or incorrectly perceived opportunities must be an essential part of the model. Thus, intertemporal substitution has been subject to exhaustive econometric examination.

If variations in individual wages largely exceed aggregate variations, misperception of current real wages because of incorrect perceptions of the price level, while essential to explain aggregate fluctuations, may be a minor issue for individual workers.[13] Thus, even if aggregate fluctuations are due to imperfect information, panel data on real wages and employment can still be used to estimate the elasticity of substitution. If individuals are formalized as intertemporal utility maximizers with additively separable utility in consumption and leisure, there are two ways in which the elasticity of substitution can be estimated. The first is to look at the effects of changes in wages on hours worked, controlling for total wealth. The other is to estimate the static first-order condition which gives a relation between consumption, leisure and the real wage. Empirical evidence using both approaches is reviewed by Ashenfelter (1984) [see also Altonji (1986)]. Most of the evidence points to a small positive elasticity, surely insufficient to explain the fluctuations in aggregate employment.

Mankiw, Rotemberg and Summers (1985) have examined the joint behavior of aggregate consumption, employment and real wages to see whether consumption and employment could be explained as the result of optimal intertemporal choice by a "representative" individual. This approach implicitly assumes that workers can observe actual real wages and have common expectations about the future. They show that the joint behavior of aggregate employment, consumption and real wages is inconsistent with such assumptions. The reason why is a simple and important one: business cycles are characterized by co-movements in consumption and employment, or equivalently by opposite movements in consumption and leisure. If utility is additively separable in time, this can only be explained by large procyclical movements in the aggregate real wage [this point is further developed by Barro and King (1984)] which, however, are not present in the data. Attempts to reconcile the behavior of the real wage, consumption and leisure by allowing for non-time separability in utility have not been successful [Eichenbaum, Hansen and Singleton (1988)]. There appear to be only two ways to reconcile the data with large intertemporal substitution effects: the first is that business cycle fluctuations are largely the result of taste shocks, taste shifts between consumption and leisure. The other is that the real wage is not equal to the marginal rate of substitution between leisure and consumption: this would be the case if labor

---

[13]The fact that business cycle fluctuations are small compared to fluctuations in individual fortunes was stressed by Lucas (1977).

contracts provided insurance through real wages.[14] In this latter case, the marginal rate of substitution should still be equal to the marginal product of labor; thus, intertemporal substitution may still be testable.

2.3.3. Current developments

Research on macroeconomic models with imperfect information has dwindled in the 1980s. Many of its proponents have moved on to develop real business cycles models, models in which money and misperceptions play little or no role and where shocks come instead from either government spending [Barro (1986)], or tastes and technology [see, for example, Prescott (1986)]. In those models the correlation between money and output is explained by reverse causality; money may precede movements in output if, for example, it is an input in production and production takes time [King and Plosser (1984), Eichenbaum and Singleton (1986)]. There are probably two reasons for this shift in focus.

The first is that, as the emphasis has shifted more and more to intertemporal choice, it has proven convenient to work with explicit representative agent models in which cycles are formalized as the result of equilibrium with intertemporally maximizing identical firms and identical individuals. These models have complex dynamics even in the absence of money and imperfect information. The focus on real business cycles may then be justified as a tractable and necessary first step.

The other reason arises from the mixed empirical success of the imperfect information–money shocks approach. Focusing on other types of shocks may help reconcile the behavior of quantities and prices. Allowing for taste shocks, for example, may help explain the opposite movements in consumption and leisure in the face of little movement in real wages. It is too early to tell whether this approach will be more successful [see Summers (1987) for a negative forecast]. But it surely falls outside the scope of this chapter.

3. Imperfect competition

For those who believed that the wage–price mechanism was generally sound despite its weak theoretical foundations, the immediate task was to explore how it could accommodate rational expectations. Two important papers, by Fischer (1977a) and by Taylor (1980), developed models which embodied

---

[14]We describe briefly the implications of such contracts in the next section.

nominal rigidities and rational expectations, and which implied a role for policy in general and for monetary policy in particular. The section starts with them. While these models answered the immediate challenge, they did not, however, dispose of most of the earlier theoretical objections to the wage–price mechanism. Much of the research since has attempted to put price and wage determination on more solid foundations. This is reviewed in this and the next section.

3.1. Price and wage setting, and the effects of money on output

3.1.1. The Fischer model

Fischer (1977a) introduced the following model:[15]

$$y = (m - p) + u \, , \tag{3.1}$$

$$y = -(w - p) \, , \tag{3.2}$$

$$w = E(p| - 1) \, . \tag{3.3}$$

Equation (3.1) is aggregate demand, with, for convenience, unit elasticity of output with respect to money balances. u is a non-policy demand disturbance. Equation (3.2) is output supply, obtained from profit maximization, with, again for convenience, the assumption of unit elasticity of output supply with respect to the wage.[16] The important equation is (3.3) which says that nominal wages are preset at the beginning of the period, on the basis of available information so as to achieve, in expectation, a constant real wage and constant employment. The information available when the nominal wage is set includes lagged but not current values of m and u.

Solving for w under rational expectations and replacing gives:[17]

$$y = (1/2)[(m - E(m| - 1)) + (u - E(u| - 1))]$$

---

[15]A closely related model was presented at the same time by Phelps and Taylor (1977). It is interesting to note that Phelps, in presenting his model, thought of it as a natural extension of the work presented in the Phelps volume, in particular of the work on the implications of imperfect information on price-setting. In that sense, both the imperfect information and imperfect competition approaches trace back to the same origin.

[16]Fischer introduces also a supply disturbance, v; in the presence of such a disturbance, workers cannot in general choose nominal wages so as to achieve both constant expected real wages and constant expected employment. I do not want to deal with those issues here and put v equal to 0. I return to those issues when I study indexation below.

[17]For the mechanics of solving linear models with rational expectations, see Taylor (1986b).

Thus, demand and money shocks affect output only to the extent that they are unanticipated; the reduced-form relation is very similar to that of the Lucas model. But the channel is the same as in Keynes: as prices are flexible but nominal wages fixed within the period, demand shocks increase prices, decrease real wages and increase output.

In this first model, if policy-makers cannot act more often and do not have more information than wage-setters, there is no role for policy to stabilize output. But this is no longer true when nominal wages are set for periods of time longer than the time between policy decisions. This is shown in the second model presented by Fischer. In that model, at the beginning of each period, half of the labor force now presets its nominal wages for two periods: the current and the next. Each nominal wage is again set so as to achieve a constant expected real wage in each of the two periods. The model becomes:

$$y = (m - p) + u , \tag{3.1}$$

$$y = -(1/2)[(w - p) + (w(-1) - p)] , \tag{3.2'}$$

$$w = E(p| - 1) , \qquad w(-1) = E(p| - 1) . \tag{3.3}$$

Equation (3.2') gives the wage relevant to firms. It is a weighted average of the nominal wages currently in existence. The first, which applies to half of the labor force, is the wage chosen for this period at the beginning of this period; the second is that chosen for this period at the beginning of the previous period. They are denoted w and $w(-1)$, respectively. Equation (3.3) states that each of these two nominal wages is in turn equal to the expectation of the current price level based on information available as of the time the wage was set: wages are set so as to achieve, in expected value, a constant real wage. Solving for output under rational expectations gives:

$$y = (1/2)[(1/3)(m - E(m| - 1) + (2/3)(m - E(m| - 2)]$$
$$+ (1/2)[(1/3)(u - E(u| - 1) + (2/3)(u - E(u| - 2)] .$$

Output movements still depend only on unanticipated money and demand shocks. But unanticipated money is now equal to money minus a weighted average of money anticipated as of this and the previous period. This has two implications. The first is that the effects of money on output last for two periods. The second is that monetary policy based only on information available at the beginning of the period can decrease output fluctuations. To see this, assume, for example, that u follows a random walk, say $u = u(-1) + v$, where v is white. Then, if money were constant, output would follow:

$$y = (1/2)[v + (2/3)v(-1)].$$

If, instead, monetary policy follows the rule $m = -(2/3)v(-1)$, output follows $y = (1/2)v$ and has smaller variance. The reason why money works is simple: in response to unexpected demand disturbances this period, nominal wage-setters would like to readjust their nominal wages for next period. Half of them cannot, but the monetary authority can by adjusting money for next period, which cancels the effect of the unexpected demand disturbance on next period's price level.

An implication of this result is that if an optimal feedback rule is used for money, the variance of output does not increase with the number of periods during which nominal wages is fixed. Thus, activist monetary policy can offset the effects of multiperiod predetermination of wages. The model makes a strong case for activist policy.

3.1.2. The Taylor model

Following an earlier paper by Akerlof (1969), Taylor (1980) introduced a model similar in most respects to the two-period staggered wage-setting model of Fischer but with one important difference: wages were not only pre-determined, but were *fixed* for two periods, i.e. set at the same nominal level for those two periods.[18] A simpler version was presented by Taylor (1979) and has the following structure:

$$y = (m - p),$$ (3.4)

$$p = (1/2)(w + w(-1)),$$ (3.5)

$$w = (1/2)[p + E(p(+1)|-1)] + (1/2)a[E(y|-1) + E(y(+1)|-1)].$$ (3.6)

Equation (3.4) gives aggregate demand. We do not allow here for shocks other than nominal money.

---

[18]The two other differences are unimportant. In Fischer, firms operate under decreasing returns and workers desire a constant real wage. In Taylor, firms operate under constant returns to scale and workers' desired real wage is an increasing function of employment. Thus, in Fischer, output appears in the price equation, but not in the wage equation. In Taylor, output appears in the wage equation, but not in the price equation. As long as labor supply and labor demand are not both infinitely elastic with respect to the wage, whether output appears in one or in the other or in both equations does not affect the qualitative effects of money on output. It does affect, however, the qualitative effects of money on real wages. In Taylor, real wages are constant; in Fischer, they are countercyclical.

Each period, half of the labor force chooses a nominal wage for the current and the next period; this wage is denoted w. Thus, in the current period, half of the labor force is paid w, and half is paid $w(-1)$. Equation (3.5) gives the price level as a weighted average of these two wages. The markup of prices over wages is assumed not to depend on the level of output.

Equation (3.6) gives w, the wage chosen this period for the current and the next period. If workers could choose their nominal wage each period it would be an increasing function of the price level, with unit elasticity, and of output (employment), with elasticity a. As they preset their nominal wage for two periods, the nominal wage w depends on the price level and on output this period and expected for the next. Money is assumed to be known only after wages have been set and is therefore not in the information set when w is chosen.

Replacing p and $E(p(+1)|-1)$ from (3.5) in (3.6) and reorganizing:

$$w = (1/2)[w(-1) + E(w(+1)|-1)] + a[E(y|-1) + E(y(+1)|-1)].$$
$$(3.7)$$

This suggests an alternative interpretation of wage behavior. Workers care about relative wages and thus about $w(-1)$ and $E(w(+1)|-1)$, the wages paid to the other half of the labor force this period and next. This is the interpretation given by Taylor.[19]

To solve this model under rational expectations, it is easier to specify a process for m. If m follows a random walk, for example, the solution is given by:

$$w = kw(-1) + (1-k)m(-1),$$

$$p = (1/2)(w + w(-1)),$$

$$y = (m - p),$$

where $k = (1 - \sqrt{a})/(1 + \sqrt{a}) < 1$.

Consider the dynamic effects of an unanticipated increase in money. Because wages are set before money is observed, money has no effect on wages or prices in the current period and thus has a full effect on output. Over time, however, nominal wages adjust and so does the price level. Output returns to equilibrium over time at an exponential rate. The smaller the parameter a,

---

[19]It is sometimes argued that the Taylor model depends on the assumption that workers care directly about their wages in comparison to other wages, an assumption which is thought by some to be unattractive. As the first presentation of the model in the text should make clear, this is not the case.

which measures the effect of labor market conditions on wages, the closer is k to one and the longer lasting the real effects of money.

These results differ from those of Fischer in one important way: the effects of money last for much longer than the time during which each nominal wage is fixed. The intuition behind this result is that, as shown in (3.7), staggering implies that workers care indirectly about relative wages. If the effect of labor market conditions is weak, workers choose a nominal wage w close to the existing wage $w(-1)$; nominal wages and thus the price level adjust slowly to equilibrium.[20]

3.1.3. The issues

While the models of Fischer and Taylor showed that rational expectations could be introduced in the "wage–price mechanism", could generate long-lasting effects of nominal money, and leave a role for policy, they left many issues unanswered. Taking the Taylor model as an example, that model raises two sets of issues.

Long-lasting real effects of money require k to be close to unity. This in turn requires a, the elasticity of the (target) real wage with respect to employment, to be small. Taylor assumes that the markup is insensitive to movements in output but, if we were to relax this assumption and allow the markup to be a function of demand, say with elasticity equal to b, a parallel condition would emerge: long-lasting real effects of nominal money would require b to be small as well.

More generally, a necessary condition for persistent real effects of money is the presence of *real rigidities*. Put another way, which is more intuitive but slightly misleading, *long-lasting effects of money require flat supply curves for goods and labor*.[21] The issue is then to reconcile such required small values of a and b with the presumption that, ruling out strong intertemporal substitution effects, the elasticity of labor supply with respect to wages is likely to be small, and with the presumption that, if capital is fixed in the short run, marginal cost is upward sloping. I discuss this first set of issues in the next subsection.

Real rigidities are a necessary but not a sufficient condition for persistence: if wages and prices adjusted continuously, money would still be neutral, independently of the values of a and b. In the Taylor model the two elements, the

---

[20]Although we do not show it here, this wage-setting structure also implies that anticipated money affects output.

[21]The way in which this is misleading is that if, for example, a price is set by a monopolist, or a wage determined as a result of bargaining between a firm and a union, there is no such thing as a supply curve. There is, however, a relation between prices and output, or wages and employment, which is traced out by shifting demand, which can be thought of as an implicit supply curve.

nominal rigidities which imply non-neutrality of money, are preset nominal wages and staggered wage decisions. But this raises a second set of issues. If the reason why wages are set only at discrete intervals of time is the presence of costs of changing wages, can such costs, which are likely to be small, explain the fluctuations in output we actually observe? If wage-setters are free to choose the timing of their decisions, is staggering an equilibrium? If nominal wage-setting and staggering are the result of optimal wage-setting by individuals or firms, does this not imply that fluctuations in output are optimal, when account is taken of the costs of adjusting wages? I discuss those issues in the following section.

3.2. Real rigidities

I review here research on the behavior of the goods and labor markets from a narrow angle, namely by asking: Can models of the goods market explain why, in response to shifts in demand, the adjustment falls mostly on quantities and not on prices, given wages? Can models of the labor market similarly explain why shifts in the demand for labor fall mostly on employment and not on wages, given prices?[22]

3.2.1. The goods market

Research on the goods market has focused on the implications of imperfect competition. Imperfect competition per se does not imply price rigidity: it is well known that the price rule followed by a monopolist in response to multiplicative shifts in isoelastic demand is the same, up to a constant reflecting monopoly power, as the supply curve which would follow from competitive behavior with the same technology. But if technologies differ under perfect and imperfect competition, or if the degree of monopoly power varies with the level of demand, imperfect competition may then lead to more price rigidity.

If imperfect competition leads firms to have more capital at a given level of demand than would be the case under perfect competition, marginal cost may be flat over a larger range of output: this may arise if entry leads firms with monopoly power to dissipate profit [Hall (1986)] through excess capacity, or if excess capacity serves as a barrier to entry [Fudenberg and Tirole (1983)]. Is marginal cost flat at normal levels of production? This is doubtful. While labor productivity is procyclical, the proportion of overtime labor, of labor paid time and a half, is strongly procyclical. If firms had cheaper means of increasing

---

[22]I have made no attempt to give a complete bibliography of the work presented in this subsection. Many of the references are themselves surveys and serve that function.

production, they would not use overtime. Bils (1985), pursuing this line of reasoning, concludes that marginal cost is upward sloping in most industries, so that this does not appear to be the explanation for real price rigidity.

The monopolist example above assumes that the degree of monopoly power, which in that example is only a function of the elasticity of demand, is constant. But, if monopoly power is countercyclical, an increase in demand will lead to lower markups of prices over marginal costs, thus to less movement in the markup than in marginal cost. This may be the case if the elasticity of demand increases with the level of demand, so that monopoly power is lower in booms [see Stiglitz (1984) for a review of such cases]. It can also be the case if the sustainable degree of collusion is lower when demand is high [Rotemberg and Saloner (1986a)].

Many stories do not, however, make a theory of price rigidity. They also suggest that price rigidity should vary across markets, in particular as a function of market structure. The evidence is mixed, however, with some evidence that markups are more cyclical in concentrated industries [Domowitz, Hubbard and Petersen (1986)]. A more radical departure from standard price-setting has been developed by Okun (1981) who suggests that, in all customer markets, customers develop a notion of fairness. If price changes are perceived as unfair, a firm may actually lose profit by increasing prices in response to increases in demand. While there is evidence that fairness plays an important role in goods markets [Kahneman et al. (1986)], the issue becomes that of what in turn determines fairness.

3.2.2. The labor market

If we believe that intertemporal substitution in labor supply is not of major relevance for macroeconomic fluctuations, and that the elasticity of labor supply with respect to permanent changes in the real wage is small, the fact that shifts in demand for labor appear to fall mostly on employment rather than on wages is puzzling. It also suggests that a radical departure from perfect competition is needed. Research on real wage rigidity has explored three different directions.

The first has been the implication of the presence of unions. Again, the presence of a union does not necessarily imply more real rigidity than in a competitive labor market [see the surveys by Oswald (1985) and Farber (1986)]. But it may: McDonald and Solow (1981), concentrating on the case of bilateral monopoly between a firm and a union, have shown that if in response to shifts in demand both sides decide to share gains from trade "fairly", the outcome will usually be one of large employment fluctuations and small real wage fluctuations.

Large parts of the labor market are neither unionized nor under threat of unionization. Another direction of research has explored the scope and the implications of implicit contracts between workers and firms. Initially, the implications of insurance by risk-neutral firms to risk-averse workers were seen as providing a potential explanation for real wage rigidities and large employment fluctuations. It was soon realized, however, that while this could explain real wage rigidity, it implied, absent income effects from insurance, exactly the same employment pattern than under perfect competition and thus could not, if individual labor supply was inelastic, explain large employment fluctuations [see Azariadis (1979)]. The theory of implicit contracts was then extended to allow for asymmetric information between workers and firms. The employment characteristics of optimal contracts under asymmetric information depend very much on the relative degrees of risk aversion of firms and workers and on the information structure. There does not, at this stage, appear to be good reasons to think that they will, in general, lead to larger employment fluctuations than full information contracts [see the survey by Stiglitz (1986)]. Hart and Holmstrom (1986) discuss also the potential role of such contracts in explaining macroeconomic fluctuations.

The last direction of research has focused on "efficiency wage" models, models in which the wage may directly affect the marginal product of labor. One possible reason, emphasized by Akerlof (1982), and closely related to the customer market argument of Okun discussed above, is simply that workers form wage norms and sharply decrease their effort if wages go below the norm. As in the case of fairness, the issue is again here that of what determines those norms, given that they clearly evolve over time, increasing, for example, as productivity increases. Other models which do not rely on interpersonal comparisons of utility have also been developed [see the surveys of Yellen (1984) and Katz (1986) of the theoretical and empirical evidence]. If, for example, effort can only be imperfectly monitored, it may be optimal for a firm to pay a wage above the market: it is then costly for a worker to be caught shirking and fired, and workers may then choose the optimal amount of effort.

To see what efficiency wage theories may imply for the issue at hand, consider the following example from Solow (1979). Suppose that profit for a firm is given by $aF(e(W)L) - WL$, where L is the number of workers and e is the effort per worker. Effort is assumed to be an increasing function of the real wage W. The firm chooses L and W so that the first-order conditions are:

$$e'(W)W/e(W) = 1 , \qquad (3.8)$$

$$e(W)aF'(e(W)L) = W . \qquad (3.9)$$

The real wage chosen by the firm is given by (3.8) and is such that the elasticity of effort with respect to the wage is equal to one. Equation (3.9) in turn determines employment.

In this example there is complete real wage rigidity. A shift in a, which can be interpreted as a shift in the relative price facing the firm, has no effect on the real wage paid by the firm and falls fully on employment. The model assumes, however, that effort depends only on the absolute level of the real wage. Suppose that effort depends instead positively on the wage paid by the firm relative to the aggregate wage, and positively on unemployment, as is the case in the shirking model. In that case the condition corresponding to (3.7) then gives the relative wage as a function of unemployment. In equilibrium, all wages must be the same; this in turn determines a relation between the real wage and unemployment. In the model of Shapiro and Stiglitz (1984), workers have a reservation wage below which they do not work and above which they supply one unit of labor, so that, absent efficiency wage considerations, aggregate labor supply has an inverted L shape. With efficiency wages, this labor supply locus is replaced by a smooth increasing equilibrium relation between wages and employment. Thus, an economy which, absent efficiency wages, operated at full employment with shifts in demand translating only into changes in wages, will, with efficiency wages, experience movements in both wages and employment. Employment fluctuations will be larger, and wage fluctuations smaller, under efficiency wages than under perfect competition.

4. Imperfect competition (continued)

4.1. Nominal rigidities: The static case

An old but vague Keynesian theme, starting with Keynes' own explanation of nominal wage rigidity, is that of coordination problems. The argument is the following: to be neutral, a decrease in money requires a proportional decrease in all nominal prices, leaving all relative prices the same. But if price-setters do not want to change relative prices, none of them will want to decrease his price first. The outcome will be nominal rigidity, or at best slow adjustment of nominal prices.

The argument is clearly right in the extreme case in which price-setters want to keep relative prices constant, in the case of complete real price rigidities. A change in nominal money, at given prices, changes real balances, output and employment, but does not lead any price-setter to change his price given others. The analogy with Daylight Saving Time in the United States, introduced by Friedman (1953) to make the case for flexible exchange rates, is revealing. While it may be socially desirable to change the hours during which stores are open in winter, this will not happen without explicit coordination of decisions, as each store wants to keep the same hours as other stores. A change in the clock achieves the result without need for coordination. Woglom (1982) develops an economic model with the same structure. The economy is composed of monopolists who face kinked demand curves. This leads them not to want to change their relative price in response to changes in demand; this in turn leads to nominal rigidities and non-neutrality of money.

But the argument, at least in this simple form, does not hold when the relative price chosen by each price-setter is an increasing function of the output he produces. In this case an increase in nominal money, which increases demand and output, leads all price-setters to attempt to increase their relative price; as this is impossible, all nominal prices increase until real money balances are back to equilibrium. The initial argument holds, however, in slightly modified form; its structure has recently been clarified and I now present it.

4.1.1. Nominal rigidities, pecuniary externalities and menu costs

The argument requires some deviation from perfect competition and its specific form depends on the specific deviation. I present it here in a simple general equilibrium model with monopolistic competition, which follows Mankiw (1985), Kiyotaki (1985), Ng (1986) and is extended in Blanchard and Kiyotaki (1987). Akerlof and Yellen (1985) have developed a closely related argument, but in a model with efficiency wages in the labor market and imperfect competition in the goods market.

The economy is composed of n workers–producers, $i = 1, \ldots, n$, selling differentiated products, but otherwise identical. The demand facing producer i is a decreasing function of his relative price (P_i/P) and an increasing function of aggregate real money balances (M/P). Each producer also faces an upward-sloping marginal cost function, which reflects increasing marginal disutility of work and/or decreasing returns to scale in production. Marginal cost, demand and marginal revenue functions facing producer i are drawn in Figure 15.1. Demand and marginal revenue are drawn for an arbitrary level of aggregate real money balances.

The profit-maximizing level of output for producer i is given by the intersection of marginal cost and marginal revenue, with the associated price being given by the demand curve, point A. In symmetric equilibrium, all prices must be the same, so that $P_i/P = 1$. This in turn determines the equilibrium level of real money balances and the price level.

If each producer acted competitively instead, the equilibrium would be at the intersection of marginal cost and demand. In symmetric equilibrium, P_i/P would still be equal to one, so that the equilibrium would be at point B instead. This in turn implies that, as the demand curve must go through B, the equilibrium real money balances would be higher under perfect competition, the price level lower. Note that, as all producers have the same degree of monopoly power, monopoly power has no effect on the relative price of

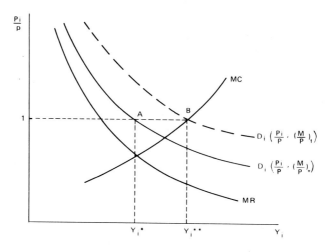

Y_i^* : monopolistically competitive equilibrium output

Y_i^{**} : Competitive equilibrium output

Figure 15.1

produced goods. Monopolistic competition affects instead the relative price of goods in terms of money, i.e. the price level, which is higher than under competition. Welfare, measured by consumer and producer surplus,[23] is higher under perfect competition.

The informal argument can now be formalized and proceeds in two steps.

(1) Associated with the monopolistically competitive equilibrium is a pecuniary externality.

A decrease in an individual producer's nominal price has two effects. First it increases the demand for that producer's good; second, by decreasing (slightly) the price level, it increases real money balances, increasing demand and output of all other producers. In equilibrium, prices are such that the first effect on profit is equal to zero to a first order: each producer has no incentive to change his price. But, because output is initially below its socially optimal level under monopolistic competition, the second effect leads to an increase in welfare.

Put another way – which will be convenient below – a small proportional decrease in all nominal prices, a decrease in the price level, would increase output and have a first-order positive effect on welfare. But, no individual producer has an incentive to decrease his own price given other prices since he would experience a second-order loss in profit.

---

[23]In Blanchard and Kiyotaki, marginal utility of income is constant and the sum of consumer and producer surplus for a representative market is indeed the appropriate measure of welfare.

(2) In the presence of small costs of changing prices, "menu costs", the pecuniary externality implies nominal price rigidity.

Instead of a small decrease in the price level given nominal money, consider a small increase in nominal money given the price level. Output and welfare increase to a first order; but each producer has a second-order incentive to increase his price. Absent menu costs, the economy would return to the initial level of output with higher prices. Small menu costs, i.e. second-order costs but larger than the loss in profit associated with not changing the price, will, however, prevent this adjustment. If they do, nominal prices will not adjust and the change in nominal money will affect output and have first-order effects on welfare.

To summarize, imperfect competition implies that, in response to an increase in nominal money, the incentive to adjust relative prices may be weak. Small costs of changing prices will prevent adjustment of relative prices, thus of nominal prices, leading to an increase in aggregate demand. Because price initially exceeds marginal cost, firms will willingly increase output even if they do not adjust prices. Output will go up and so will welfare.

4.1.2. Extensions: *The role of structural parameters; multiple equilibria*

Two more sets of results can be derived from this simple framework.

(1) The first relates the size of menu costs needed to prevent adjustment of prices to the parameters of demand and cost. Second-order menu costs are sufficient to imply real effects of small changes in nominal money. But, with respect to larger changes in nominal money, the size of the menu costs required to prevent adjustment depends on the characteristics of technology and market structure.

If marginal cost were constant, a condition which implicitly requires both constant marginal disutility of work and constant returns in production, no price-setter would want to change his relative price and nominal prices would remain unchanged even in the absence of menu costs. By continuity, as long as marginal cost is fairly flat, small menu costs can prevent adjustment of prices. But, if the disutility of work is a strongly increasing function of the level of work – an assumption which would imply an inelastic labor supply in a competitive labor market – the menu costs required to prevent price adjustment become implausibly large. This shows the limits of the menu cost argument and the need to construct models which combine menu costs with real rigidities. This has been, for example, the approach followed by Akerlof and Yellen (1985) who develop a model with efficiency wages in the labor market, and monopolistic competition and menu costs in the goods markets. Their version of efficiency wages, which is the same as that in equations (3.8) and (3.9), delivers movements in employment with no change in the real wage.

As long as there is unemployment, this implies that the labor market behaves as if labor supply were infinitely elastic at the prevailing wage. Thus, as long as firms operate under close to constant returns to scale, monopolistic competition and menu costs in price-setting easily deliver nominal rigidity of both prices and wages, and real effects of nominal money.

The other main parameter in the model above is the elasticity of substitution between goods, which determines the elasticity of demand with respect to relative prices. The higher this elasticity, the higher the opportunity cost of not adjusting relative prices and thus the higher the menu costs required to prevent adjustment of prices. Rotemberg and Saloner (1986b) use this argument to explain why prices appear to be more rigid under monopoly than under duopoly in which each firm perceives a more elastic demand curve.

(2) What has been shown above was that if menu costs were large enough, there was an equilibrium with unchanged nominal prices. What has not been shown is that this was the only equilibrium. Whether or not it is depends on the interactions between prices. The argument has been formalized by Ball and Romer (1987b) and Rotemberg (1987) and has the following structure.

A change in the price level has two effects on the nominal price that an individual price-setter wants to set. Other things equal, an increase in the price level leads to a proportional increase in the desired nominal individual price. But, at the same time, an increase in the price level decreases real money balances, shifting inwards the demand curve faced by the price-setter, and leading him to decrease his desired relative price. The net effect is in general ambiguous, depending on the strength of the effect of real money on aggregate demand and on the degree of substitution between goods. In the – more likely – case where the substitution effect dominates, an increase in the price level increases the desired individual nominal price; following Cooper and John (1985), this case can be called the case of "strategic complementarity".[24]

Assuming strategic complementarity and the presence of menu costs, consider the effects of an increase in nominal money. The incentive for a given price-setter to adjust his price is clearly stronger the larger the proportion of other price-setters who adjust theirs. This suggests that for some values of the menu costs, there may be two equilibria: one in which all price-setters adjust, making it optimal for each price-setter to adjust, and one in which no one adjusts, making it optimal for each price-setter not to adjust. The papers by Ball and Romer and by Rotemberg show that this is indeed the case. This potential multiplicity of equilibria is more than a curiosum. It appears in some guise in many of the dynamic extensions of the static model which we describe below.

[24]Cooper and John (1985) have looked at the characteristics of equilibria in games such as this one where the action of one player depends positively on the actions of other players, a condition they call "strategic complementarity". They show that many "Keynesian" models exhibit such a characteristic and that those games exhibit "multiplier effects" and may have multiple equilibria.

4.1.3. From statics to dynamics: The issues

The menu cost argument points to an important externality in price-setting. Before it can be used to conclude that macroeconomic fluctuations are in part the result of such an externality, two sets of questions must, however, be answered.

(1) The menu cost argument, as we have presented it, assumes that all prices are initially equal and set optimally. In a dynamic economy and in the presence of menu costs, such a degenerate price distribution is unlikely to prevail. But if prices are initially not all equal or optimal to start with, it is no longer obvious that even a small change in nominal money will leave all prices unaffected. It is no longer obvious that money will have large effects on output.

(2) Even if nominal money has large effects on output, it must be the case that money is sometimes unanticipatedly high, sometimes unanticipatedly low. When money is high, output increases and so does welfare to a first order. When money is low, output decreases and so does welfare, again to a first order. These welfare effects would appear to cancel out to a first order. It is therefore no longer obvious that, even if menu costs lead to large output fluctuations, the welfare loss of those fluctuations largely exceeds the menu costs which generate them. This point is developed by Ball and Romer (1987a) in the context of the static model above, but assuming money to be a random variable.

I now review what we know about the answers to those two questions in dynamic models. It turns out that the answers depend very much on the specific form of nominal rigidities and on the specific price rules used by price-setters. I start by reviewing what we know about the effects of money if price-setters use either time-dependent or state-dependent rules. I end the section by discussing what rules are likely to be chosen, and the nature of actual price and wage rules.

4.2. Time-dependent rules and the effects of money on output

The simplest time-dependent rules are rules in which the time between price decisions is fixed.[25] As the Fischer and Taylor models show, time-dependent rules do generate non-neutrality. As the difference between the two models also shows, an important issue, if prices are fixed – rather than predetermined – between price decisions, is whether those decisions are synchronized or staggered. Staggering leads to longer lasting effects of nominal

---

[25]This, however, is not necessary. An example of a time rule with random time between price decisions is given below.

money on output. Research has thus proceeded in two directions. The first has studied the determination of the time structure of price decisions. The second has studied the implications of alternative staggering structures, taking staggering as given. While the first logically precedes the second, it is only recently that research has focused on the first.

4.2.1. Implications of alternative staggering structures

Research on the implications of wage staggering has focused on the implications of staggering for monetary policy, in particular for disinflationary policies. Phelps (1979) had shown that if wage-setting was characterized by staggering and rational expectations, there was in principle, and in sharp contrast to the implications of the standard Phillips curve, a path of disinflation consistent with no output loss. Taylor (1983) has extended this analysis by computing the actual path of disinflation consistent with no recession given the actual staggering structure of wage-setting in the United States. The path needed to decrease inflation from 10 to 3 percent at no output loss has interesting characteristics: inflation goes from 10 to 9.9 percent in the first year, from 9.9 to 8.7 percent in the second, and from 8.7 to 3.6 percent in the third. The very slow initial decrease is needed because past wage decisions, which were taken before the change in money growth, have to be accommodated. But this slow initial decrease raises obvious issues of credibility, as little happens in the first two years after the change in policy. These issues have been studied by Fischer (1985) and are analyzed at more length in his Chapter 21 in this Handbook. Fischer (1984) has extended the analysis to the open economy to study the implications of the changes in real exchange rates implied by monetary contraction. While the analyses of Taylor and Fischer are based on the assumption that staggering is unaffected by changes in monetary policy, and are thus subject to the Lucas critique, empirical studies of the 1979–82 U.S. disinflation suggest that there was indeed little change in aggregate wage behavior during the period [Englander and Los (1983)].

I have studied the implications of staggering of price decisions. While most prices change more often than wages, I have shown [Blanchard (1983)] that if output is produced through a chain of production, with price decisions being taken at different times at different production steps, there can be substantial price level inertia even if each price-setter takes price decisions very often. U.S. empirical evidence [Blanchard (1987)] shows this effect to be important: I find that, while prices adjust fast to input prices and wages at the disaggregated level, interaction between price decisions implies substantial aggregate price inertia. I conclude that price level inertia in the United States comes as much from staggering of price decisions as from staggering of wage decisions. I have also studied [Blanchard (1986a)] the implications of wage and price staggering, showing that, even under rational expectations, such staggering generates a wage–price spiral, as well as cost push and demand pull inflation, ideas which had been emphasized in earlier work on inflation.

All staggering structures have in common that, after an increase in nominal money which increases demand, price- and wage-setters attempt to increase, or at least to maintain, relative prices and wages. Along the path of adjustment, there are oscillations but no systematic movement in relative prices and real wages. Implications of staggering for the variability of relative prices have been drawn and examined by Taylor (1981) in particular.

All the above papers assume that price decisions are taken for fixed periods of time and that the cost of changing prices is independent of the size of the change. Two alternative formalizations have also been explored. Calvo (1982) has built a model with a continuum of price-setters and in which the probability of a given price-setter changing his price at any point in time is constant. Together, these two assumptions imply that a constant proportion of prices change at any point in time, and give a very convenient continuous time specification of aggregate price dynamics. Rotemberg (1982) has developed and estimated a model of monopolistic competition with quadratic costs of adjustment of nominal prices, so that the cost varies with the size of the change.[26] Most of the above papers focus on the effects of price-setting rather than on the relation between money and aggregate demand. Svensson (1986) attempts to integrate the two strands of recent research on money demand on the one hand, and on price-setting by monopolistic competitors on the other.

4.2.2. Determination of the time structure of decisions

The research reviewed above takes the structure of staggering as given. The other direction of research has been to see whether such a structure can indeed arise as an equilibrium if each price-setter is free to choose both the length of time between price changes and the timing of his decisions in relation to others.

The question has been studied by Parkin (1986), Ball (1986a) and Ball and Romer (1986) in models similar to the model of monopolistic competition sketched above. Their argument has the following structure.[27]

Suppose that nominal money follows a given stochastic process and that each

---

[26]Julio Rotemberg has pointed out to me that, despite their different motivations, his and Calvo's model have the same dynamics. This can be seen as a justification for using the quadratic cost formalization as a convenient "as if" approach.

[27]The three models differ in various ways. The first two assume that prices are predetermined between price decisions (à la Fischer). The third assumes that prices are fixed between price decisions (à la Taylor). Parkin assumes that money follows a feedback rule while the other two papers take money as exogenous.

price-setter takes price decisions at fixed intervals of time, say – by defining the period appropriately – every two periods. Each producer still has the choice between taking decisions at the same time as the others, say at even times, or at a different time, at odd times. It is clear that symmetric staggering is an equilibrium: if exactly half of the price-setters take decisions at odd times and half at even times, the stochastic environment faced by a price-setter is the same whether he takes decisions at even or odd times and he is therefore indifferent to timing.[28] But one can ask whether this staggered equilibrium is stable. Whether, for example, if the economy is characterized initially by asymmetric staggering and if individual price-setters are allowed to change their timing, the economy will converge to the staggered equilibrium.

The answer turns out to depend on whether the strategic complementarity condition described earlier is satisfied or not; whether an increase in the price level increases or decreases the nominal price that an individual price-setter wants to set. In the more likely case where an increase in the price level increases desired individual prices, staggering cannot be stable. The intuition for this result is simple. Suppose that initially a larger proportion of price-setters change prices at even than at odd times, so that the price level moves more on average at even than at odd times. A price-setter who was initially taking decisions at odd times has an incentive to move so as to take decisions with the majority of price-setters. The stable equilibrium is one in which all price decisions are taken at even times. In the less likely case where an increase in the price level decreases individual nominal prices, staggering can be stable but this hardly provides a convincing explanation for the general presence of staggering in the economy.

The introduction of stochastic idiosyncratic shocks does not make staggering more likely. With respect to idiosyncratic shocks, choosing odd or even timing is irrelevant, so that, if strategic complementarity holds, price-setters still have an incentive to move with others and staggering is not a stable equilibrium. If, however, idiosyncratic shocks have a deterministic, "seasonal" component, and if, for example, some firms experience shocks mostly at odd times, some mostly at even times, staggering can then be an equilibrium, with each firm choosing its natural timing habitat.[29] This will be the case if idiosyncratic shocks are large, or if the strategic complementarity effect is weak. This is explored by Ball and Romer (1986) who also analyze the welfare properties of the

---

[28]This assumes that the price-setter is small compared to the economy, so that in considering whether to change his price at even or odd times, he takes the stochastic process followed by the price level as given. Fethke and Policano (1984) have studied the properties of the equilibrium when the number of price-setters is small.

[29]An example may be that of grocery stores which change prices with new deliveries. Prices will then change as the delivery truck goes from store to store, leading to staggering.

equilibrium. The empirical importance of such shocks seems however limited, and insufficient to provide a general explanation of staggering.

Two other ideas have been explored. The first, pursued by Ball and Cecchetti (1987), is that, in the presence of imperfect information, price decisions carry some information and it may be optimal for a price-setter to wait for the information before deciding on his own price. The question is, however, whether an equilibrium will exist in such a context. If each price-setter prefers to make decisions just after the others, it is not clear that an equilibrium exists, at least not an equilibrium with fixed timing of price decisions. The second, explored by Maskin and Tirole (1986), is that staggering may change the nature of the game played by price-setters and allow price-setters to achieve a more collusive sustainable outcome. Both of these approaches have implications which go far beyond staggering. Imperfect information reintroduces some of the channels studied in Section 2. Maskin and Tirole show that games with staggered decisions may generate outcomes which resemble, for example, those obtained with kinked demand curves. This last example shows that further progress requires a better integration of the theories of real and nominal rigidities.

It may well be that trying to generate staggering given fixed timing of individual price changes is the wrong strategy. After all, it is plausible that if price-setters experience different histories of shocks, they will naturally change prices at different times. This, however, points to state- rather than time-dependent rules, rules in which the decision to change prices is a function of the state. I now examine the aggregate implications of such rules.

4.3. State-dependent rules and the effects of money on output

The simplest state-dependent rules are *Ss* rules which, in our context, imply that the nominal price is readjusted whenever the difference between the actual price and a target price exceeds some fixed threshold value. *Ss* rules are optimal only under restrictive assumptions; because they are analytically convenient, research has usually proceeded under those restrictive assumptions, or simply assumed the use of *Ss* rules as convenient if suboptimal rules.

The optimal *Ss* rule for a monopolist facing random walk fluctuations in demand was characterized by Barro (1972) under the assumption of no inflation. Sheshinski and Weiss (1977, 1983) derived instead optimal *Ss* rules in the presence of deterministic or stochastic inflation and no demand uncertainty[30]. Benabou (1986a) has extended their analysis to the case where goods are

---

[30]A mistake in Sheshinski and Weiss (1983) is corrected in Caplin and Sheshinski (1987).

storable, showing that, even in the absence of uncertainty, firms may resort to randomized strategies to avoid price speculation in anticipation of price changes.

The important question, for our purposes, is that of the aggregate implications of Ss rules. These rules, with their implication that the length of time between individual price changes is random, seem to have the potential to explain staggering and thus price level inertia. Rotemberg (1983) and Caplin and Spulber (1987) have shown, however, that this is not necessarily the case. In their paper, Caplin and Spulber derive the aggregate behavior of prices and output in response to changes in nominal money when individual price-setters follow Ss rules. A simplified version of their argument is the following.[31]

Suppose that there are n price-setters. The (log of the) nominal price p_i^* that each price-setter would choose in the absence of costs of changing prices is only a function of nominal money and an idiosyncratic shock. Furthermore, p_i^* is assumed to be a non-decreasing function of time (i.e. there is enough average money growth that even if there is an adverse idiosyncratic shock, p_i^* does not decrease).

There are fixed costs of changing prices, which lead each price-setter to adjust the actual nominal price p_i according to the following Ss rule: when the deviation $p_i^* - p_i$ exceeds a threshold value S, p_i is readjusted so that the deviation is equal to s.

Caplin and Spulber then show that:

(1) For a given price-setter, the deviation $(p_i^* - p_i)$ is uniformly distributed between S and s. That is, if we observe $(p_i^* - p_i)$ at a point in time, we are as likely to observe any value of the deviation between S and s. Furthermore, as long as the idiosyncratic shocks are not perfectly correlated, the distribution of deviations $(p_i^* - p_i)$ across price-setters is also joint uniform: $(p_i^* - p_i)$ and $(p_j^* - p_j)$ are uncorrelated for all i and j. Together, these propositions imply that price decisions will, on average, be uniformly staggered. While this would appear to provide foundations for slow adjustment of the price level to changes in nominal money, the next proposition shows just the opposite to be true.

(2) Changes in nominal money lead on average to proportional increases in the price level. Figure 15.2 provides the intuition for this result. Assuming that there are four prices in the economy and that the distribution of deviations is uniform between $[s = -1, S = +2]$, the initial distribution is characterized in the first column of Figure 15.2. An increase in nominal money of 1 increases all target prices by 1; one price is adjusted and the new distribution is given in the second column, which is obviously identical to the first. Although only one price has increased, it has increased by four times as much as it would have,

---

[31]The formal model they develop does not have idiosyncratic shocks.

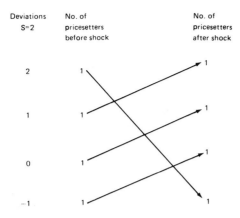

Figure 15.2. The Caplin–Spulber neutrality result.

absent costs of adjustment. Thus, the price level increases by as much as nominal money.

This result shows that menu costs do not necessarily imply non-neutrality of money. All that is needed for this result to obtain is that the distribution of deviations be uniformly staggered. It applies, for example if desired prices depend on the price level, real money balances and relative demand shocks. Benabou (1986b) constructs a general equilibrium model where consumers search optimally given the dispersion of prices implied by Ss pricing by firms and in which Ss rules are optimal given the search behavior of consumers. In his model as well, money is neutral.

The neutrality result in the above example follows from the fact that while only one out of four prices is readjusted, it adjusts by four times the size of the change in nominal money. More formally, the size of the price adjustment is equal to the support of the distribution of deviations. This is not, however, a characteristic of all Ss rules and thus not all Ss rules imply neutrality.

An example will show why. In Caplin and Spulber the desired nominal price increases through time. The firm just needs one threshold value, such that when the actual price is too low, it is readjusted upwards. Suppose instead that the average inflation rate is zero so that the desired nominal price increases or decreases through time, with equal probability. The firm then needs a rule with both an upper and a lower threshold [such as in Barro (1972)]. Under such a rule, the price is readjusted whenever it becomes too low or too high. Aggregation of such rules is difficult and no general result is available; changes in money do not, however, lead in general to contemporaneous proportional adjustment in the price level. An example is given in Figure 15.3. Assume that

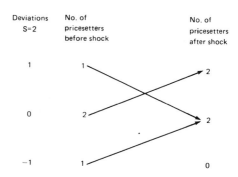

Figure 15.3. An example of non-neutrality.

there are four prices, which are readjusted to equal the target price whenever the deviation between actual and target price exceeds 1 in absolute value. Under such a rule price deviations are most likely to be at the return point, 0, than at −1 and +1 [see, for example, Barro (1972)], so that in Figure 15.3 two price deviations are assumed initially equal to zero, one to −1 and one to +1. An increase in nominal money of 1, assumed to increase all target prices by 1, leads to the readjustment of one price by 2, and to an increase in the price level of 1/2 only.

Whether aggregation of such Ss rules can explain long-lasting effects of money remains to be seen. An interesting implication of this line of research is that the higher the average rate of inflation, the closer Ss rules will be to the one-sided rules assumed by Caplin and Spulber, the more neutral money will be.[32]

4.4. Time- or state-dependent rules?

To summarize: the static menu cost argument is an important insight. It does not, however, extend straightforwardly to the dynamic case. With time-dependent rules, menu costs generate real effects of nominal money; a complete analysis of the relation of welfare effects to menu costs remains, however, to be done. With state-dependent rules, money may still be neutral. This raises two further issues.

The first is that of the type of rule price-setters are likely to adopt. Why would price- and wage-setters ever use time- rather than state-dependent rules?

[32]This is true, however, only under the maintained assumption of fixed values for S and s. For general stochastic processes for money, fixed Ss rules are dominated by rules in which S and s are also functions of the state. Tsiddon (1987) has shown that under such more general rules, a decrease in money growth, rather than being neutral, would instead be initially contractionary.

One simple possibility is that the state is costly to observe or verify; in that case, it may be optimal to collect information and revise the price at fixed intervals, with the interval determined by the characteristics of the process determining the underlying target price. This may explain why labor contracts, in which agreement on the state may be costly, are negotiated at fixed intervals of time. In general, the optimal rule is likely to be both state and time dependent. What the implications of such rules will be remains to be seen. Non-neutrality of money is likely, but little else can be said.

The other issue is empirical. What type of rule do price- and wage-setters actually use? The answer is far from clear. Labor contracts are signed for fixed periods of time, and while nominal wages are not fixed for the duration of contracts, cost of living adjustments are usually both state and time dependent. Many more prices are changed in January in the United States than would be expected from a uniform distribution,[33] which suggests some time dependence. Evidence on individual prices suggests that prices are adjusted faster in periods of higher inflation [Cecchetti (1986) on newspapers]; this, however, is consistent with time-dependent rules, where the length of time between price decisions is a function of the underlying parameters of the economy and thus changes over time. Evidence on individual price-setting within manufacturing is also provided by Carlton (1986) who re-examines the Kindahl and Stigler data base. This re-examination does not lead to a simple characterization of price changes or of price rules.

Finally, I have reviewed in this section only the research dealing specifically with foundations of price-setting; in that research, the dynamics of output in response to shocks arise mainly or exclusively from price- and wage-setting. This is in sharp contrast to the research summarized in Section 2 and to the channels for persistence emphasized there, such as costs of adjustment in employment, inventory and capital accumulation. The contrast is much too sharp. Price- and wage-setting equations such as those in Taylor have been integrated in larger models with richer dynamics, and used to look at many macroeconomic issues. Taylor (1986a), for example, has constructed a medium size multi-country model with staggering of wage decisions. He uses the model to analyze the effects of monetary policy on the United States and the rest of the world and contrasts his results with those of traditional models. Reviewing those applications would, however, take us too far afield.

5. Indexation and other issues

In this section I study three issues. The first is that of indexation and monetary reforms designed to make prices more flexible. The second is the possibility,

---

[33]I owe this fact to Julio Rotemberg.

raised by Keynes in the context of the effects of deflation, that price flexibility, far from being stabilizing, may in fact exacerbate output fluctuations. The third is the possibility that changes in nominal money may not be neutral, even in the long run.

5.1. Indexation and monetary reforms

The analysis of the previous sections suggests that changes in the price-setting process, which allowed prices to adjust more quickly to other prices, would be desirable. One such change is indexation which, at least in principle, makes prices or wages adjust quickly to changes in the price level.

5.1.1. Wage indexation

The debate about the effects of wage indexation on fluctuations was formalized in papers by Fischer (1977b) and Gray (1976). Gray's model has a structure similar to that of the early Keynesian model;

$$y = (m - p) , \tag{5.1}$$

$$y = -(w - p) - u , \tag{5.2}$$

$$w = kp + (1 - k)Ep . \tag{5.3}$$

Equation (5.1) gives aggregate demand. Equation (5.2) gives labor demand under perfect competition, and allows for a supply or productivity shock, u, with expected value $Eu = 0$. Equation (5.3) gives the wage-setting rule, with the degree of indexation being equal to k, which is between zero (no indexation) and one (full indexation). The solution to those equations, under rational expectations, is:

$$y = ((1 - a)/(2 - k))(m - Em) - (1/(2 - k))u . \tag{5.4}$$

With no indexation, both nominal and real shocks affect output. Real shocks, however, as they increase the price level, lead to a lower real wage, partly attenuating the effect of the shock on output. Full indexation protects the economy from nominal shocks but exacerbates the effects of real shocks as the real wage is fixed. Thus, Fischer and Gray argued, full indexation is not optimal in an economy with both real and nominal shocks;[34] Gray proceeded

---

[34]The relevant distinction is between demand and supply shocks. Here, the only demand shocks are nominal shocks.

to derive the socially optimal degree of indexation as a function of the variances of both sources of shocks.

The Fischer–Gray analysis has been extended in two main directions. The first has allowed for more sources of shocks, such as external shocks for an open economy; the second has looked at the properties of alternative indexation schemes, such as whether wages should be indexed to the CPI or to the GNP deflator, or to nominal income [see, for example, Aizenman and Frenkel (1985)].

The simple Fischer–Gray model implies that full indexation leads to complete nominal and price flexibility. But actual indexation clauses index the nominal wage not to the current price level but rather to the lagged price level. As a result, they do not remove all nominal rigidities. The implications of actual indexation formulas were sketched in Fischer (1977b) and have been studied by Simonsen (1983); his conclusion is that actual indexation may in fact make disinflation harder and more costly in terms of output loss. The model above also assumes that the only source of nominal rigidities is wage-setting. If price rigidities are important, as I have argued earlier, eliminating wage rigidities may still leave large real effects of nominal money. For both of those reasons, economies with different degrees of indexation are likely to have, at least a given average rate of inflation, more similar behavior than is implied by the simple Gray–Fischer model.[35]

Just as in the case of nominal price-setting and staggering, we must ask: Is the form of indexation rules and the degree of indexation which arise from individual decisions socially optimal? I examined the question in Blanchard (1979) under the assumption of competitive goods markets. I assumed that each contract faced a fixed cost to indexing on the price level, and a further fixed cost to indexing in addition to the real shock. I then asked whether, if private contracts decided to index only on the price level, this decision and the degree of indexation they chose were socially optimal. The answer was that they were. This assumes, however, that the costs of collecting information and designing indexation rules are private costs. If part of those costs can be shared by firms and is therefore a public good, it may then be that indexation to more than just the price level, although not an equilibrium, would be socially optimal. Ball (1986b) has extended the analysis to monopolistically competitive goods markets.

5.1.2. Generalized indexation and monetary reforms

If wage indexation decreases the real effects of nominal money, why not introduce general indexation? Various such schemes, which we can equivalent-

---

[35]Note the use of "at a given average rate of inflation". It may well be that wage indexation, because it changes the trade-offs faced by policy makers, leads to higher inflation. This is discussed in Chapter 21 of this Handbook.

ly think of as monetary reforms, have been suggested, and I briefly review the issues involved.

General indexation presents a conceptual problem that wage indexation does not. One can think of general indexation as a change in the numeraire, with all prices being set in terms of the price level instead of in dollars. But if all prices are freely set in terms of the price level, only by coincidence will the average of those prices be in turn equal to the price level. Thus, general indexation schemes have considered the use of either one good or a small basket of goods as numeraire.

To see what such indexation may achieve, the analogy with Daylight Saving Time is again useful. Suppose that all stores, instead of announcing opening hours with reference to the clock, use a Sears and Roebuck standard, announcing, for example, they will open at the same hours as Sears and Roebuck. It is clear that this solves the coordination problems discussed in Section 3. If it is desirable to change opening hours in winter, all that is needed is for Sears and Roebuck to change its opening hours in winter, and it will do so, as it knows that other firms will change hours simultaneously. In the same way, general indexation allows for changes in the price level without changes in relative prices.

The argument, however, raises further questions: Why is it better for the economy to have one price-setter setting the price level given money than for the monetary authority to set money given the price level? Or, in the context of the Sears and Roebuck example, what is it that Sears and Roebuck can do that the state could not do before by changing the clock in winter? It is because the set of incentives facing the price-setter are different from those facing the monetary authority? Those questions must be answered before we understand the gains of monetary reform over more active monetary policy in the present system.

5.2. Destabilizing price flexibility

Another line of work has questioned whether price flexibility is indeed stabilizing. It is true that under complete and instantaneous adjustment of prices, money has no effect on output.[36] It has been argued, however, that the relation between price flexibility and real effects of money is in fact not monotone and that, given the existing degree of flexibility, more flexibility may increase rather than decrease output fluctuations. This is because aggregate demand, instead of depending only on real money balances as we have assumed until now, depends also on the rate of inflation.

---

[36]Except for the channels mentioned in the Introduction.

The argument dates back at least to Irving Fisher and is part of Keynes' argument for why, even if nominal wages were flexible, this would not be enough to maintain full employment. Keynes was mostly concerned with the effects of deflation in response to unemployment. While deflation led to a lower price level, increasing real money balances and lowering nominal interest rates, its direct – price changes – effect was however contractionary. It increased the real interest rate given the nominal rate (an effect now known as the Mundell effect) and led to transfers of wealth from debtors to creditors, increasing bankruptcies and disrupting credit markets. Both Fisher and Keynes thought that those direct effects might well offset the indirect effect through the lower price level, and Keynes saw this as a strong argument in favor of relying on expansionary monetary policy rather than deflation to avoid recessions. This argument was formalized by Tobin (1975) who concluded that it could indeed be that deflation led to increases in the real rate and could lead to more rather than less unemployment.

The issue has been recently re-examined under rational expectations by Driskill and Sheffrin (1986), DeLong and Summers (1986) and Chadha (1986), using the Taylor model but expanding the specification of aggregate demand to allow for price change as well as price level effects [see also McCallum (1983b)]. Their aggregate demand specification is the reduced form of an ISLM specification, with the real interest rate in the IS equation and the nominal rate in the LM equation and has the form:

$$y = b(\mathrm{E}(p(+1)|0) - p) + c(m - p) , \quad b, c > 0 . \tag{5.5}$$

DeLong and Summers then characterize the dynamic effects of money on output when money follows the first-order process $m = rm(-1) + e$.[37] They compute the steady-state variance of output as a function of both the elasticity of desired real wages to output [the coefficient a in equation (3.5)] and the length of time during which each wage is set. They conclude that, in most cases and for most plausible parameters, increased price flexibility – defined as an increase in a, or a decrease in contract length – is likely to increase the steady-state variance. Their result is, however, quite different from the earlier Tobin result. In all cases they find the steady-state variance to be finite; equivalently, in no case do they find that increased price flexibility may actually lead to an explosive path for output. The increase in output variance comes from an increased short-run reaction to nominal shocks: in response to an increase in money, increased price flexibility has more effect on expected inflation than on the current price level, leading to a sharper initial decline in the real interest rate.

---

[37]They actually look at the effects of IS shocks, assuming that the nominal money supply responds to the nominal interest rate. Their equation can, however, be reinterpreted as in the text.

DeLong and Summers also show that although increased flexibility ultimately leads to smaller real effects, this happens at degrees of flexibility far in excess of those we observe. The conclusion one should draw is probably that of Keynes, namely that price flexibility may not be a very good substitute for activist monetary policy.

5.3. Hysteresis and long-run neutrality

All the models we have seen impose long-run neutrality of money as a maintained assumption. This is very much a matter of faith, based on theoretical considerations rather than on empirical evidence.

Blanchard and Summers (1986), examining the evidence from both the current prolonged European recession and the prewar U.S. and U.K. depressions, were led to question this maintained assumption. We found that, in all three cases, high unemployment had, after a while, little or no effect on disinflation. Put another way, it appeared that equilibrium unemployment had eventually adjusted to actual unemployment. This has led us to explore the possibility that equilibrium unemployment may be affected for long periods of time by the history of actual unemployment.

We have explored in particular the implications of membership considerations in the determination of wages. To see what they imply, we can again start with a Fischer-like model, assuming that a union sets the nominal wage before money is realized[38] and that employment is chosen by firms after the realization of money. Assuming that the union chooses the nominal wage so as to achieve, in expected value, employment of its members, and solving the model gives a relation between employment n, membership n^*, and nominal money of the form:

$$n = n^* + a(m - \mathrm{E}(m| - 1)) , \qquad (5.6)$$

where a is a coefficient which depends on the parameters in the aggregate demand and labor demand equations.[39] Employment deviates from membership to the extent that unanticipated money differs from zero. The crucial issue is that of what determines membership in the union. If n^* is fixed over time, then the dynamics of the model are similar to those of the one-period Fischer model. But, if n^* depends on the past history of employment, and if, for

---

[38] In Blanchard and Summers (1986) we use a model with monopolistic competition and many unions. This difference is unimportant for the issues discussed in the text.

[39] The derivation is as in Section 3, with two minor differences. The equation gives employment rather than output, and n^*, which was constant and thus put in the constant term in Section 3, is now treated explicitly.

example, unions tend to represent mostly the currently employed, then the dynamics are very different. If, to take an extreme case, the union represents only the currently employed, $n^* = n(-1)$ so that employment follows:

$$n = n(-1) + (1/2)(m - E(m| - 1)) .\tag{5.7}$$

In that case, unanticipated changes in nominal money have *permanent* effects on employment. The reason is a simple one: after a negative surprise, for example, the workers who are fired are no longer represented and there is no tendency for employment to go back to its previous value.

The model generates hysteresis: the steady state of the economy depends on its path, and unemployment does not return to any fixed equilibrium value. But its conclusions are too strong: unemployed workers must always exert some direct or indirect influence on wage-setting, so that over time unemployment returns to an equilibrium value. What the model points out is that, because of the dynamics of labor supply, the adjustment may be very slow. In that case, the real effects of money do not come from prolonged price and wage rigidity. In the above model nominal wage rigidity lasts only for one period but the effects of money last forever.

6. Conclusion

Considerable progress has been made in the last ten years on why money affects output. Some of it has come from clarifying old and fuzzy ideas, such as that of coordination problems, and in clarifying the respective roles of expectations, of nominal and real rigidities. A lot of it has come from running into dead ends, such as the failure to explain the joint price and output responses to money in "as if" competitive models, or the failure of individual nominal rigidities to generate aggregate price inertia under simple Ss rules.

Where should research go from here? I believe that research on real rigidities is the most urgent. It is a general feature of goods markets that fluctuations in demand lead mostly to movements in output rather than in markups, and of labor markets that fluctuations in the demand for labor lead mostly to movements in employment rather than in real wages. Given these features, a very small amount of nominal rigidity will lead to long-lasting effects of nominal money on output. Indeed, as was shown in Section 4, if all suppliers were happy to supply more at the same relative price, there would be no need for nominal rigidities: as no price-setter desired to change his relative price, nominal prices would not move in response to changes in nominal money. While many reasons have been given (and reviewed in Section 3) for why we observe such real rigidities, the sheer number of unrelated explanations is distressing. One cannot help but think that there might be some general explanation. While "fairness" and "norms" pretend to give such a general explanation, they remain at this stage vague and untestable ideas.

Work on nominal rigidities is also important. But in counterpoint to the previous paragraph, the amount of nominal rigidities may well have been overemphasized. In recent empirical work [Blanchard (1987)] I have found that in the post-war United States, the adjustment of nominal wages, and of prices to wages, is more than two-thirds over within a year. Such lags may not be very difficult to explain, as a result of short lengths of time between changes in individual wages and prices, together with staggering. Work on time- and state-dependent rules and on the equilibrium time structure of price decisions is just beginning and is important and exciting.

References

Aizenman, J. and J. Frenkel (1985) 'Supply shocks, wage indexation and monetary accommodation', NBER Working Paper 1609.

Akerlof, G. (1969) 'Relative wages and the rate of inflation', *Quarterly Journal of Economics*, 83: 353–374.

Akerlof, G. (1982) 'Labor contracts as partial gift exchange', *Quarterly Journal of Economics*, 87: 543–569.

Akerlof, G. and J. Yellen (1985) 'A near-rational model of the business cycle, with wage and price inertia', *Quarterly Journal of Economics*, Supplement 100: 823–838.

Altonji, J. (1986) 'Intertemporal substitution in labor supply: Evidence from micro data', *Journal of Political Economy*, 94: S176–S213.

Andersen, L. and J. Jordan (1970) 'The Saint Louis model', Federal Reserve Bank of Saint Louis.

Ashenfelter, O. (1984) 'Macroeconomic analyses of labor supply and microeconomic analyses of labor supply', Carnegie Rochester Conference Volume.

Azariadis, C. (1979) 'Implicit Contracts and Related Topics', in: Z. Ernstein, ed., *The economics of the labour market*. London: Her Majesty's Stationery Office.

Ball, L. (1986a) 'Externalities from contract length', NYU, mimeo.

Ball, L. (1986b) 'Is equilibrium indexation efficient?' NYU, mimeo.

Ball, L. and D. Romer (1986) 'The equilibrium and optimal timing of price changes', NYU, mimeo.

Ball, L. and S. Cecchetti (1987) 'Imperfect information and staggered price setting', NBER Working Paper 2201.

Ball, L. and D. Romer (1987a) 'Are prices too sticky?', NBER Working Paper 2171.

Ball, L. and D. Romer (1987b) 'Sticky prices as coordination failures', NYU, mimeo.

Barro, R. (1972) 'A theory of monopolistic price adjustment', *Review of Economic Studies*, 34: 17–26.

Barro, R. (1976) 'Rational expectations and the role of monetary policy', *Journal of Monetary Economics*, 2: 1–23.

Barro, R. (1977) 'Unanticipated money growth and unemployment in the United States', *American Economic Review*, 67: 101–115.

Barro, R. (1978) 'Unanticipated money growth, output and the price level in the United States', *Journal of Political Economy*, 86: 549–580.

Barro, R. and M. Rush (1980) 'Unanticipated money and economic activity', in: S. Fischer, ed., *Rational expectations and economic policy*. Chicago: University of Chicago and NBER, pp. 23–48.

Barro, R. (1981) 'The equilibrium approach to business cycles', in: R. Barro, ed., *Money, expectations and business cycles*. New York: Academic Press.

Barro, R. (1986) 'Government spending, interest rates, prices and budget deficits in the United Kingdom, 1701–1918', University of Rochester, mimeo.

Barro, R. and Z. Hercowitz (1980) 'Money stock revisions and unanticipated money growth', *Journal of Monetary Economics*, 6: 257–267.

Barro, R. and R. King (1984) 'Time separable preferences and intertemporal substitution models of the business cycle', *Quarterly Journal of Economics*, 99: 817–840.

Benabou, R. (1986a) 'Optimal price dynamics and speculation with a storable good', chapter 1, Ph.D. Thesis, M.I.T.

Benabou, R. (1986b) 'Searchers, price setters, and inflation', Chapter 2, Ph.D. Thesis, M.I.T.

Bils, M. (1985) 'Essays on the cyclical behavior of price and marginal cost', Ph.D. Thesis, M.I.T.

Blanchard, O. (1979) 'Wage indexing rules and the behavior of the economy', *Journal of Political Economy*, 87: 798–816.

Blanchard, O. (1983) 'Price asynchronization and price level inertia', in: R. Dornbusch and M.H. Simonsen, eds., *Inflation, debt and indexation*. Cambridge, Mass.: M.I.T. Press, p. 3–24.

Blanchard, O. (1986a) 'The wage price spiral', *Quarterly Journal of Economics* 101: 543–565.

Blanchard, O. (1986b) 'Empirical structural evidence on wages, prices and employment in the US', M.I.T., mimeo.

Blanchard, O. (1987) 'Individual and aggregate price adjustment: Empirical evidence', *Brookings Papers on Economic Activity*, 1: 57–122.

Blanchard, O. and N. Kiyotaki (1987) 'Monopolistic competition and the effects of aggregate demand', *American Economic Review*, 77: 647–666.

Blanchard, O. and L. Summers (1986) 'Hysteresis and European unemployment', *NBER Macroeconomics Annual*, 1: 15–89.

Blinder, A. and S. Fischer (1981) 'Inventories, rational expectations and the business cycles', *Journal of Monetary Economics*, 8: 277–304.

Boschen, H. and H. Grossman (1982) 'Test of equilibrium macroeconomics using contemporaneous monetary data', *Journal of Monetary Economics*, 10: 309–333.

Bruno, M. and J. Sachs (1984) *Economics of worldwide stagflation*. Harvard University Press.

Bryant, J. (1983) 'A simple rational expectations Keynes-type model', *Quarterly Journal of Economics*, 98: 525–528.

Calvo, G. (1982) 'On the microfoundations of staggered nominal contracts: A first approximation', Columbia University, mimeo.

Caplin, A. and D. Spulber (1987) 'Menu costs and the neutrality of money', *Quarterly Journal of Economics*, 102: 703–726.

Carlton, D. (1988) 'The rigidity of prices', *American Economic Review*, 76: 637–658.

Cecchetti, S. (1986) 'The frequency of price adjustment: A study of the newsstand prices of magazines 1953 to 1979', *Journal of Econometrics*, 31: 255–274.

Chadha, B. (1986) 'Is increased price inflexibility stabilizing? Some analytical results', Columbia University, mimeo.

Cooley T. and S. LeRoy (1985) 'Atheoretical macroeconometrics: A critique', *Journal of Monetary Economics*, 16: 283–309.

Cooper, R. and A. John (1985) 'Coordinating coordination failures in Keynesian models', Cowles Foundation, 745, mimeo.

DeLong, J.B. and L. Summers (1986) 'Is increased price flexibility stabilizing?', *American Economic Review*, 76: 1031–1044.

Diamond, P. (1982) 'Aggregate demand management in search equilibrium', *Journal of Political Economy*, 90: 881–894.

Domowitz, I., G. Hubbard and B. Petersen (1986) 'Business cycles and the relationship between concentration and price cost margins', *Rand Journal*, 17: 1–17.

Driskill, R. and S. Sheffrin (1986) 'Is price flexibility destabilizing?', *American Economic Review*, 76: 802–807.

Dunlop, J.T. (1938) 'The movements of real and money wage rates', *Economic Journal*, 48: 413–434.

Eichenbaum, M. and K. Singleton (1986) 'Do equilibrium real business cycle theories explain post-war business cycles?', in S. Fischer, ed., *NBER macroeconomics annual*, Vol. 1. Cambridge, Mass.: M.I.T. Press, pp. 91–134.

Eichenbaum, M., L. Hansen and K. Singleton (1988) 'A time series analysis of representative agent models of consumption and leisure', *Quarterly Journal of Economics*, 51–78.

Englander, S. and C. Los (1963) 'The stability of the Phillips curve and its implications for the 1980's', Federal Reserve Bank of New York, mimeo.

Fair, R. (1979) 'An analysis of the accuracy of four macroeconometric models', *Journal of Political Economy*, 87: 701–718.

Farber, H. (1986) 'The analysis of union behavior', in: O. Ashenfelter and R. Layard, eds., *Handbook of labor economics*. Amsterdam: North-Holland.

Fethke, G. and A. Policano (1984) 'Wage contingencies, the pattern of negotiation and aggregate implications of alternative contract structures', *Journal of Monetary Economics*, 14: 151–171.

Fethke, G. and A. Policano (1986) 'Will wage setters ever stagger decisions?', *Quarterly Journal of Economics*, 101: 867–877.

Fischer, S. (1977a) 'Long term contracts, rational expectations, and the optimal money supply rule', *Journal of Political Economy*, 85: 163–190.

Fischer, S. (1977b) 'Wage indexation and macroeconomic stability', in: *Stabilization of the domestic and international economy*. Carnegie Rochester Conference, Vol. 5, 101–147.

Fischer, S. (1979) 'Anticipations and the nonneutrality of money', *Journal of Political Economy*, 87: 225–252.

Fischer, S. (1980) 'On activist monetary policy with rational expectations', in: S. Fischer, ed., *Rational expectations and economic policy*. Chicago: NBER and University of Chicago Press, pp. 211–248.

Fischer, S. (1984) 'Real balances, the exchange rate and indexation: Real variables in disinflation', NBER Working Paper 1497.

Fischer, S. (1985) 'Contracts, credibility and disinflation', in: Argy and Nevile, eds., *Unemployment: Theory, experience and policy making*. London: Allen and Unwin, pp. 39–59.

Friedman, B. (1978) 'Comment on "After Keynesian Macroeconomics", by Robert E. Lucas and Thomas Sargent', in: *After the Phillips curve*, Conference Series, Vol 19. Federal Reserve Bank of Boston, pp. 73–80.

Friedman, M. (1953) 'The case for flexible exchange rates', in: *Essays in positive economics*. Chicago: University of Chicago Press, pp. 157–203.

Friedman, M. (1968) 'The role of monetary policy', *American Economic Review*, 58: 1–17.

Friedman, M. and A. Schwartz (1963) *A monetary history of the United States, 1867–1960*. Princeton University Press.

Fudenberg, D. and J. Tirole (1983) 'Capital as a commitment: Strategic investment to deter mobility', *Journal of Economic Theory*, 31: 227–250.

Geary, P. and J. Kennan (1982) 'The employment real wage relationship: An international study', *Journal of Political Economy*, 90: 854–871.

Gordon, (1972) 'Wage price controls and the shifting Phillips curve', *Brookings Papers on Economic Activity*, 2: 385–421.

Grandmont, J.M. (1985) 'On endogenous competitive business cycles', *Econometrica*, 53: 995–1046.

Gray, J.A. (1976) 'Wage indexation: A macroeconomic approach', *Journal of Monetary Economics*, 2: 221–235.

Gray, J.A. and D. Spencer (1984) 'The role of price prediction errors in a natural rate model: Some new evidence', mimeo.

Grossman, S. and L. Weiss (1983) 'A transactions based model of the monetary transmission mechanism', *American Economic Review*, 73: 871–880.

Hall, R. (1986) 'Market structure and macroeconomic fluctuations', *Brookings Papers on Economic Activity*, 2: 285–338.

Hart, O. (1982) 'A model of imperfect competition with Keynesian features', *Quarterly Journal of Economics*, 97: 109–138.

Hart, O. and B. Holmstrom (1986) 'The theory of contracts', M.I.T. Working Paper 418.

Howitt, P. (1986) 'Business cycles with costly search and recruiting', mimeo.

Kahneman, D., J. Knetsch and R. Thaler (1986) 'Fairness as a constraint on profit: Seeking entitlements in the market', *American Economic Review*, 76: 728–741.

Katz, L. (1986) 'Efficiency wage theories: A partial evaluation', *NBER macroeconomics annual*, 1: 235–290.

Keynes, J.M. (1935) *The general theory of employment, interest and money.* The Macmillan Press Ltd.

Keynes, J.M. (1939) 'Relative movements in real wages and output', *Economic Journal*: 34–51.

King, R. (1982) 'Monetary policy and the information content of prices', *Journal of Political Economy*, 90: 247–279.

King, R. and C. Plosser (1984) 'Money, credit and prices in a real business cycle', *American Economic Review*, 74: 363–380.

Kiyotaki, N. (1985) 'Macroeconomics of monopolistic competition', Ph.D. Thesis, Harvard.

Lucas, R.E. (1972) 'Expectations and the neutrality of money', *Journal of Economic Theory*, 4: 103–124.

Lucas, R.E. (1973) 'Some international evidence on output–inflation tradeoffs', *American Economic Review*, 63: 326–334.

Lucas, R.E. (1975) 'An equilibrium model of the business cycle', *Journal of Political Economy*, 83: 1113–1144.

Lucas, R.E. (1976) 'Econometric policy evaluation: A critique', in: K. Brunner and A. Meltzer, eds., *The Phillips curve and labor markets.* Carnegie Rochester Conference Volume 1, pp. 19–46.

Lucas, R.E. (1977) 'Understanding business cycles', in: K. Brunner and A. Meltzer, eds., *Stabilization of the domestic and international economy.* pp. 7–29.

Lucas, R.E. and L. Rapping (1969) 'Real wages, employment and inflation', *Journal of Political Economy*, 77: 721–754.

Lucas, R.E. and T. Sargent (1978) 'After Keynesian economics', in: *After the Phillips curve: Persistence of high inflation and high unemployment.* Federal Reserve Bank of Boston.

McCallum, B. (1983a) 'A reconsideration of Sims' evidence concerning monetarism', *Economic Letters*, 13: 167–171.

McCallum, B. (1983b) 'The liquidity trap and the Pigou effect: A dynamic analysis with rational expectations', *Economica*, 50: 395–405.

McDonald, I. and R. Solow (1981) 'Wage bargaining and employment', *American Economic Review*, 71: 896–908.

Mankiw, G. (1985) 'Small menu costs and large business cycles: A macroeconomic model of monopoly', *Quarterly Journal of Economics*, 100: 529–539.

Mankiw, G., J. Rotemberg and L. Summers (1985) 'Intertemporal substitution in macroeconomics', *Quarterly Journal of Economics*, 100: 225–253.

Maskin, E. and J. Tirole (1986) 'Dynamics of oligopoly, Part III: Price competition', M.I.T., mimeo.

Mishkin, F. (1983) *A rational expectations approach to macroeconometrics.* Chicago: NBER and the University of Chicago Press.

Neftci, S. (1978) 'A time series analysis of the real wages–employment relationship', *Journal of Political Economy*, 86: 281–291.

Ng, Y.-K. (1986) *Mesoeconomics.* Brighton: Harvester Press.

Nordhaus, W. (1972) 'Recent developments in price dynamics', in: O. Eckstein, ed., *The econometrics of price determination.* Board of Governors of the Federal Reserve System, pp. 16–49.

Okun, A. (1981) *Prices and quantities: A macroeconomic analysis.* Washington: The Brookings Institution.

Oswald, A. (1985) 'The economic theory of trade unions: An introductory survey', *Scandinavian Journal of Economics*, 87: 160–193.

Parkin, M. (1986) 'The output–inflation trade off when prices are costly to change', *Journal of Political Economy*, 94: 200–224.

Phelps, E. (1967) 'Phillips curves, expectations of inflation and optimal unemployment over time', *Economica*, 34: 254–281.

Phelps, E. (1970) *Microeconomic foundations of employment and inflation theory.* New York: Norton.

Phelps, E. (1979) 'Disinflation without recession: Adaptive guideposts and monetary policy',

Weltwirtschaftliches Archiv, 100, *pp*. 239–265. Reprinted in: E. Phelps, *Employment and inflation*, Vol. 1. New York: Academic Press, pp. 239–265.

Phelps, E. and J. Taylor (1977) 'Stabilizing powers of monetary policy under rational expectations', *Journal of Political Economy*, 85: 163–190.

Phillips. A.W. (1958) 'The relation between unemployment and the rate of change of money wages in the United Kingdom, 1861–1957', *Economica*, 25: 283–299.

Poterba, J., J. Rotemberg and L. Summers (1986) 'A tax based test of nominal rigidities', *American Economic Review*, 76: 659–675.

Prescott, E. (1986) 'Theory ahead of business cycle measurement', Federal Reserve Bank of Minneapolis, Staff Report 102.

Rotemberg, J. (1982) 'Monopolistic price adjustment and aggregate output', *Review of Economic Studies*, 44: 517–531.

Rotemberg, J. (1983) 'Aggregate consequences of fixed costs of price adjustment', *American Economic Review*, 73: 343–346.

Rotemberg, J. (1984) 'A monetary equilibrium model with transaction costs', *Journal of Political Economy*, 92: 40–58.

Rotemberg, J. (1987) 'The new Keynesian microeconomic foundations', *NBER macroeconomics annual*, pp. 69–114.

Rotemberg, J. and G. Saloner (1986a) 'A supergame theoretic model of price wars during booms' *American Economic Review*, 76: 390–407.

Rotemberg, J. and G. Saloner (1986b) 'The rigidity of prices under monopoly and duopoly', M.I.T. Working Paper 414.

Samuelson, P. (1947) *Foundations of economic analysis*. Harvard University Press.

Samuelson, P. and R. Solow (1960) 'Analytical aspects of anti inflation policy', *American Economic Review*, 5: 177–194.

Santomero, A. and J. Seater (1978) 'The inflation unemployment trade off: A critique of the literature', *Journal of Economic Literature*, 16: 499–544.

Sargent, T. (1971) 'A note on the "Accelerationist Controversy" ', *Journal of Money, Credit and Banking*, 3: 721–725.

Sargent, T. (1973) 'Rational expectations, the real rate of interest, and the natural rate of unemployment', *Brookings Papers on Economic Activity*, 2: 429–472.

Sargent, T. (1976) 'A classical macroeconometric model for the United States', *Journal of Political Economy*, 87: 207–237.

Sargent, T. (1978) 'Estimation of demand schedules under rational expectations', *Journal of Political Economy*, 86: 1009–1044.

Sargent, T. (1979) *Macroeconomic theory*. New York: Academic Press.

Sargent, T. and N. Wallace (1975) ' "Rational expectations", the optimal monetary instrument and the optimal money supply rule', *Journal of Political Economy*, 83: 241–254.

Shapiro, C. and J. Stiglitz (1984) 'Equilibrium unemployment as a worker discipline device', *American Economic Review*, 74: 433–444.

Sheshinski, E. and Y. Weiss (1977) 'Inflation and costs of price adjustment', *Review of Economic Studies*, 44: 287–303.

Sheshinski, E. and Y. Weiss (1983) 'Optimum pricing policy under stochastic inflation', *Review of Economic Studies*, 50: 513–529.

Simonsen, M.H. (1983) 'Indexation: Current theory and the Brazilian experience', in: R. Dornbusch and M.H. Simonsen, eds., *Inflation, debt and indexation*. Cambridge, Mass.: M.I.T. Press, pp. 99–132.

Sims, C. (1972) 'Money, income and causality', *American Economic Review*, 62: 540–542.

Sims, C. (1980) 'Comparison of interwar and postwar business cycles: Monetarism reconsidered', *American Economic Review*, 70: 250–257.

Solow, R. (1979) 'Another possible source of wage stickiness', *Journal of Macroeconomics*, 1: 79–82.

Startz, R. (1986) 'Monopolistic competition as a foundation for Keynesian macroeconomic models', University of Washington, mimeo.

Stiglitz, J. (1984) 'Price rigidities and market structure', *American Economic Review*, 74: 350–355.

Stiglitz, J. (1986) 'Theories of wage rigidity', in: J.L. Butkiewicz et al., eds., *Keynes' economic legacy: Contemporary economic theories*. New York: Praeger.

Stock, J. and M. Watson (1987) 'Interpreting the evidence on the money income causality', NBER Working Paper 2228.

Summers, L. (1987) 'Some skeptical observations on real business cycle theory', Fed. of Minneapolis.

Svensson, L. (1986) 'Sticky goods prices, flexible asset prices, monopolistic competition, and monetary policy', *Review of Economic Studies*, 53: 385–405.

Tarshis, L. (1939) 'Changes in real and money wages', *Economic Journal*: 150–154.

Taylor, J. (1975) 'Monetary policy during a transition to rational expectations', *Journal of Political Economy*, 83: 1009–1022.

Taylor, J. (1979) 'Staggered price setting in a macro model', *American Economic Review*, 69: 108–113.

Taylor, J. (1980) 'Aggregate dynamics and staggered contracts', *Journal of Political Economy*, 88: 1–24.

Taylor, J. (1981) 'On the relation between the variability of inflation and the average inflation rate', *Carnegie Rochester Conference Series on Public Policy*, 15: 57–86.

Taylor, J. (1983) 'Union wage settlements', *American Economic Review*, 73: 981–993.

Taylor, J. (1986a) 'The treatment of expectations in large multicountry econometric models', in: *Empirical macroeconomics for interdependent economies: Where do we stand?*. Washington: Brookings Institution.

Taylor, J. (1986b) 'New econometric techniques for macroeconomic policy evaluation', in: Z. Griliches and M. Intriligator, eds., *Handbook of econometrics*. Amsterdam: North-Holland.

Tobin, J. (1970) 'Post hoc ergo propter hoc', *Quarterly Journal of Economics*, 84: 310–317.

Tobin, J. (1972) 'The wage price mechanism: Overview of the Conference', in: O. Eckstein, ed., *The econometrics of price determination*. Board of Governors of the Federal Reserve System, pp. 5–15.

Tobin, J. (1975) 'Keynesian models of recession and depression', *American Economic Review*, 65: 195–202.

Tsiddon, D. (1987) 'On the stubbornness of sticky prices', Columbia University, mimeo.

Weiss, L. (1980) 'The role for active monetary policy in a rational expectations model', *Journal of Political Economy*, 88: 221–233.

Wright, R. (1986) 'Job search and cyclical unemployment', *Journal of Political Economy*, 94: 38–55.

Woglom, G. (1982) 'Underemployment equilibria with rational expectations', *Quarterly Journal of Economics*, 97: 89–108.

Yellen, J. (1984) 'Efficiency wage models of unemployment', *American Economic Review*, 74: 200–205.

Chapter 16

CREDIT RATIONING

DWIGHT JAFFEE

Princeton University

JOSEPH STIGLITZ

Stanford University

Contents

Handbook of Monetary Economics, Volume II, Edited by B.M. Friedman and F.H. Hahn
© *Elsevier Science Publishers B.V., 1990*

1. Introduction

Credit markets differ from standard markets (for chairs, tables, and pencils) in two important respects. First, standard markets, which are the focus of classical competitive theory, involve a number of agents who are buying and selling a *homogeneous commodity*. Second, in standard markets, the delivery of a commodity by a seller and payment for the commodity by a buyer occur *simultaneously*.

In contrast, credit (in money or goods) received today by an individual or firm is exchanged for a *promise* of repayment (in money or goods) in the future. But one person's promise is not as good as another – promises are frequently broken – and there may be no objective way to determine the likelihood that the promise will be kept.[1] After all, for most *entrepreneurial* investment, the project is sui generis. The need for credit is evidence of change: those who control existing resources, or have claims on current wealth, are not necessarily those best situated to use these resources. They thus transfer control over their resources to others, in return for a promise.

The analysis of credit allocation can go astray in trying to apply the standard supply and demand model, which, as well as it may work for the market for chairs, is not totally appropriate for the market for promises. If credit markets were like standard markets, then interest rates would be the "prices" that equate the demand and supply for credit. However, an excess demand for credit is common – applications for credit are frequently not satisfied. As a result, the demand for credit may exceed the supply at the market interest rate. Credit markets deviate from the standard model because the interest rate indicates only what the individual promises to repay, not what he will actually repay (which means that the interest rate is not the only dimension of a credit contract).

In the United States, a complicated, decentralized, and interrelated set of financial markets, institutions, and instruments has evolved to provide credit. Our discussion of credit rationing will focus on one set of these instruments – loan contracts – where the promised repayments are fixed amounts. At the other extreme, equity securities are promises to repay a given fraction of a firm's profits. A spectrum of securities, including convertible bonds and preferred shares, exists between loans and equity. Each of these securities provides for the exchange of a current resource for a future promise. In our

---

[1]Moral hazard and adverse selection – special types of behavior we will describe later – may affect the likelihood of loan repayment.

discussion we shall uncover a number of "problems" with the loan market. While some of these problems are addressed by other instruments, these other instruments have their own problems (although we will only be able to discuss these further problems briefly in the space available).

The issue of the allocation of credit has profound implications at both the micro and macro levels. At the micro level, in the absence of a credit market, those with resources would have to invest the resources themselves, possibly receiving a lower return than could be obtained by others. When credit is allocated poorly, poor investment projects are undertaken, and the nation's resources are squandered. Credit markets, of course, do exist, but they may not function well – or at least they may not function as would a standard market – in allocating credit. The special nature of credit markets is most evident in the case of credit rationing, where borrowers are denied credit even though they are willing to pay the market interest rate (or more), while apparently similar borrowers do obtain credit.

At the macro level, changes in credit allocations are one likely source for the fluctuations which have marked capitalist economies over the past two centuries. For example, the disruption of bank lending during the early 1930s may have created, or at least greatly extended, the Great Depression of the 1930s. The availability of credit may also be an effective instrument for monetary policy. One example is that the Federal Reserve often provides liquidity when the financial system is disrupted, such as after the stock market crash of 1987. Another example is that the Federal Reserve has used credit crunches – enforced credit rationing – to slow down an overheating economy.

2. Basic notions

Our discussion of credit rationing in Section 3 relies on certain features of loan contracts and loan markets that make the standard demand and supply model inapplicable and that give rise to credit rationing phenomena. This section provides background about these special features.

2.1. Uncertainty

Differences between promised and actual repayments on loans are the result of *uncertainty* concerning the borrower's ability (or willingness) to make the repayments when they are due. This creates the risk of borrower default. Some aspects of uncertainty may be treated with the standard model, as illustrated by the capital asset pricing model or other models where there is a fixed and known probability of default.[2] Therefore, default risk is a necessary condition, but not a sufficient condition, for the standard model to be inapplicable.

Given that borrowers and lenders may have differential access to information concerning a project's risk, they may form different appraisals of the risk. We refer to *symmetric information* as the case in which borrowers and lenders have equal access to all available information. The opposite case – which we will call generically *imperfect information* – has many possibilities. *Asymmetrical information*, where the borrower knows the expected return and risk of his project, whereas the lender knows only the expected return and risk of the average project in the economy, is a particularly important case.

Uncertainty regarding consumer and (risky) government loans can be described with the same format used for firms, although, of course, the underlying sources of uncertainty are different. For individuals, future income prospects and demographic factors (children in college) illustrate the type of factors that determine repayment prospects. For governments, the willingness to repay may matter as much as the ability to repay; we discuss this special aspect of loan markets further below.

The response of both lenders and borrowers to uncertainty is determined in part by the extent of their risk aversion. Lenders may use credit rationing to reduce default risk, so credit rationing is more likely when lenders have a higher degree of risk aversion. However, we will assume that lenders are risk neutral, since we want to investigate other factors that may be sufficient to create credit rationing. To simplify matters, we will also generally assume that borrowers are risk neutral.[3]

The role of uncertainty is readily evident in loan markets where firms borrow to finance risky investment projects. We will often use a simple, but instructive, framework – where each investment project has precisely two possible outcomes – to illustrate the effects of uncertainty. We will denote the uncertain outcomes as X, with X^a the larger "good" outcome and X^b the lower "bad" outcome $(X^a > X^b)$. The probabilities P^a and P^b indicate the likelihood of each outcome (with $P^a + P^b = 1$). The expected value X^e $(= P^a X^a + P^b X^b)$ is the central tendency of the outcomes. Several important properties of this framework are worth highlighting.

(1) The economy may contain an array of projects with varying risks and expected returns. The risk of each project can be measured by the difference between X^a and X^b. The comparison of projects is further simplified by

[2]In particular, the standard model may be applicable to credit markets which issue and trade securities that are free of default risk. For example, U.S. Treasury securities are free of default risk because the taxation and money printing powers of the Federal government guarantee repayment. However, other risks, such as inflation risk, apply even to Treasury securities.

[3]There may be less credit rationing when borrowers are more risk averse, but only because risk-averse borrowers may not even apply for risky loans.

assuming a *mean preserving spread* – that all projects (all possible $\{X^a, X^b\}$ combinations) have the same expected value X^e [Rothschild and Stiglitz (1971)].

(2) If each firm has one project, then risk is determined at the level of the firm. If a firm has a portfolio of possible projects, then the evaluation of a firm's risk requires the further identification of which project(s) it carries out.

(3) Although we use the two discrete outcomes model for its analytic convenience, most of our results carry over when projects outcomes are described by a continuous distribution. For such cases, the probabilities associated with the continuous set of outcomes are given by a density function $f(X)$.

2.2. *Loan contracts*

Uncertainty is important in loan markets because it determines the likelihood of default (a broken promise for repayment). Loan contracts specify the amount borrowed B, and the interest rate r, so that the promised repayment is the fixed amount $(1 + r)B$. As a basic case, we will consider a one-period model in which the borrower repays the loan fully when the outcome X exceeds the repayment amount $(1 + r)B$, and the borrower defaults when the outcome X is less than $(1 + r)B$. We will also consider multi-period models in which more complex loan contracts may be used and where further negotiations may occur after the project outcome is known.

Default on a loan contract creates a conflict between the borrower and the lender. In past eras, lenders relied on debtor's prisons and physical punishment to enforce loan contracts or to punish default. Now, in the case of default, at least for the organized loan markets, lenders have to accept the principle of *limited liability* – a lender's only recourse is to try to claim the assets of the borrower. Specifically, when default occurs and there is only a single lender, we assume that the lender receives the realized outcome X. We comment later on the complications introduced by the costs of bankruptcy proceedings and by the existence of more than one creditor.

Limited liability and the uncertainty of project outcomes jointly determine the actual repayment received by the lender. There are three basic cases, depending on the size of the contracted repayment $(1 + r)B$ relative to the size of the two possible outcomes. If the contracted repayment $(1 + r)B$ is less than the bad outcome X^b, then the lender always receives the contracted repayment. If the contracted repayment $(1 + r)B$ exceeds the good outcome X^a, then the borrower always defaults, and the expected repayment equals the expected outcome of the project X^e.

The main case of interest occurs when the loan repayment falls between the two possible outcomes, that is when $X^b < (1 + r)B < X^a$. The expected repayment is then $P^a(1 + r)B + P^bX^b$, reflecting repayment of the contracted amount $(1 + r)B$ when the good outcome occurs (with probability P^a) and repayment of the available proceeds X^b when the bad outcome occurs (with probability P^b).

Two fundamental features of loan contracts are illustrated by this result. First, the *expected repayment rises as the loan rate rises*, since the promised repayment $(1 + r)B$ rises as the loan rate rises. Second, the *expected repayment falls as uncertainty rises*, since the expected repayment is reduced by a lower value for the bad outcome, but is unaffected by a higher value for the good outcome [at most, the borrower pays back $(1 + r)B$]. Once a specific investment project is chosen and the loan rate is set, the borrower and lender participate in a zero-sum game, with the borrower keeping that part of the outcome not repaid to the lender. Consequently, other things the same, lenders prefer safer projects and higher loan rates, while borrowers prefer just the opposite.

Loan contracts also include terms – called non-price terms – which constrain the borrower in order to reduce the likelihood of default. Collateral is among the most important of these. Collateral consists of financial and tangible capital assets that are pledged by the borrower to guarantee at least partial, if not complete, loan repayment. If a loan defaults, then the collateral is used to supplement the proceeds available to the lender (up to the repayment amount). In the extreme case of a fully collateralized loan, the collateral value is sufficient to cover any possible shortfall in loan repayment. In practice, even highly collateralized loans do not generally warrant interest rates as low as the rates on Treasury securities. We will look at some of the reasons for this, including that the value of the collateral may be uncertain and that there may be transactions costs associated with liquidating it.[4] As a result, collateral may reduce, but generally does not eliminate, the risk of default.

2.3. The classification of borrowers

Given that the expected repayment depends on the risk character of a project, it is natural for lenders to classify borrowers on the basis of their risk. Under an efficient classification system, riskier borrowers are charged higher interest rates to account for their higher likelihood of default. Banks, for example, use a schedule of quoted interest rates, with the safest borrowers charged the prime rate and riskier borrowers quoted a premium over the prime rate. A premium above prime reflects a higher likelihood of default.

---

[4]Indeed, in the absence of these problems, the borrower could sell the collateral instead of borrowing.

Borrower classification – based on risk screening – is a main function of the banking system. After appraising the risk of a firm, a bank has a basis for setting the loan interest rate and making the loan. Alternatively, another lender can make the loan, with the bank selling its "screening" service in the form of a guarantee against default.[5] However, competitors may free ride on screening information when it is publicly released. Also, the credibility of bank screening is reduced to the extent that bank funds are not at risk with respect to the outcome. Therefore, for these and other reasons, banks generally integrate their screening and lending activities.

Since a borrower's classification determines the interest rate charged, the efficiency of credit allocation in the economy is dependent on the accuracy of the classification system [see Jaffee and Modigliani (1969) and Stiglitz and Weiss (1981)]. With our decentralized system of banking, competition among suppliers of credit works to eliminate systematic misclassifications. For example, if a firm is classified as excessively risky by one lender, competitive lenders may offer a lower interest rate. However, owing to the intrinsically subjective nature of risk evaluations and judgments, competition in the market for loans is not likely to be as "perfect" as competition in the market, say, for chairs. Even in insurance markets, where actuarial data are available to measure risk, significant variations are sometimes observed in the premia charged for the same risk. All the more so, competition in loan markets will not always eliminate errors in borrower classifications.

Competition is also limited by "customer relationships" between lenders and borrowers. These relationships tend to be exclusive (the borrower has a single lender), both at a moment in time and over time. The market is, to use Okun's terminology, a customer market, not an auction market. The following comments refer to some of the loan market features that create a need for exclusive relationships between borrowers and lenders. The first three points refer to exclusivity at a point in time and the last three to exclusivity over time.

(1) Since the costs of information for determining the likelihood of default are predominantly sunk costs, there is an economy of scale in funneling all of a firm's credit needs through one lender. For similar reasons, lenders tend to specialize in making loans to particular industries. As a result, there is a tendency toward natural monopoly – not in banking as a whole, but in the supply of credit to a particular person, firm, or industry.[6]

(2) Borrowers have an incentive to take actions that raise the probability of default, as when a firm with several investment projects chooses the most risky

---

[5]For example, the World Bank is starting to separate its screening and lending functions by establishing an insurance firm to guarantee loans, thus enabling countries to raise funds directly in world capital markets.

[6]Risk aversion and other arguments for diversification work in the opposite direction. Large banks, however, can make large loans and still obtain the benefits of diversification. See Stiglitz (1985).

one (because it provides the highest expected return). A lender can respond by placing restrictive clauses in a loan contract, but the borrower's actions may not be fully foreseen and costs may arise in later renegotiating such clauses. Alternatively, lenders can influence the borrower's incentives, without directly monitoring the borrower's actions, by controlling the size of the loan and related terms of the loan contract. The returns from controlling the size of the loan, however, may accrue to all of the firm's lenders, which leads to the next point.

(3) Several important *public good* problems are associated with any classification of creditors. These problems arise when events occur which provide the creditors, as a class, with some discretion over the actions of the firm. For instance, many loan contracts contain a clause that states that the loan is in default if any loan of the borrower is in default. This clause ensures that the lender can maintain control of the collateral and can represent his interests in the event of a reorganization of the borrowing firm. These public good problems become paramount when bankruptcy occurs and the majority of the creditors of any class must agree to any settlement. By the same token, monitoring the firm's activities, to ensure that these adverse contingencies do not arise, is a public good, the return on which accrues, at least to some extent, to all creditors [Stiglitz (1985)]. In brief, there is a natural incentive to concentrate the sources of credit.

(4) Continuing relationships provide cost savings for lenders who make a sequence of loans to the same borrower, since information obtained at one date may also be used to assess risk at a later date. These cost savings are also important for lines of credit, which are the basis for many business, credit card, and consumer loans.[7] In these cases, continuing customer relationships provide the current lender a distinct advantage over competitors in assessing the current riskiness of its customers.

(5) As a result of the information provided by a long-term customer relationship, competitors may fear that winning away a customer means that the previous lender learned of adverse developments. This illustrates clearly why Akerlof's (1970) "lemons" principle is an important factor in loan markets.

(6) Finally, the threat of termination of credit acts as an important incentive device to encourage the firm to undertake safer actions this period [Stiglitz and Weiss (1983)]. It is sensible that these "moral hazard" problems can be better handled when there are exclusive relationships [see Arnott and Stiglitz (1985)].

Exclusivity arrangements limit, but do not eliminate, competition. When a

---

[7]Credit lines allow loans to be contracted on a forward basis. A credit line may serve an insurance purpose: either protecting the borrower against an unexpected change in credit rating (if the loan rate is fixed relative to the prime rate) or, less commonly, against a change in the level of interest rates (if the specific level of the loan rate is fixed).

new borrower enters the market, for example, there will be competition to become that firm's supplier of credit. Competition is limited, however, to the extent that the costs of gathering information are sunk costs. So, given the amount of ex ante competition, there will be less ex post competition. Hence, a misclassification of a borrower's risk category may not be easily corrected through competition.

2.4. The sources of loanable funds: Banks and bank deposits

Lenders obviously need funds to make loans, so the cost and availability of loanable funds necessarily interacts with loan market activity. We will adopt the descriptive shorthand of referring to lenders as "banks", and their sources of loanable funds as safe "deposits". However, the following points indicate how the analysis generally applies to all types of lenders.

(1) *Bank lending is typical of most lending.* Although bank loans are the dominant form of credit in many countries, capital market instruments, such as bonds, are also used for credit transactions. Capital markets and loan markets share similar problems, and solve many of them in comparable ways, as the following examples illustrate:

(a) The underwriting process for new risky bonds is intensive in gathering information concerning the borower's credit worthiness, and the likelihood of default is reflected in the rate of return required by investors.[8]

(b) Credit ratings are used to classify risk level (although the screening and lending functions tend to be separated more in capital market transactions than in lending transactions).

(c) Restrictive covenants in corporate bond contracts are comparable to non-price terms in loan contracts, both reflecting attempts by lenders to control the extent of default risk.[9]

(d) Only the low-risk bonds issued by the U.S. Treasury and AAA corporations trade in standard demand and supply markets.

(2) *Bank deposits can be treated as safe securities.* For simplicity, we treat deposits – the source of loanable funds – as though they were free of default risk. This is actually the case with respect to bank deposits insured by federal deposit insurance. Even without such insurance, depositors generally receive the fixed return promised by a bank because banks hold diversified portfolios

---

[8]The links between bank loan markets and the capital markets are further increased by the new process of "securitization" in which banks package portfolios of their loans for sale in the capital markets.

[9]Myers (1977) has emphasized the importance of restrictive corporate bond covenants for understanding the financing behavior of corporations (including why the Modigliani–Miller theorem may fail to hold).

of loans and their capital and loan loss reserves provide a further tier of protection.[10]

(3) *The banking industry is competitive.* This assumption applies to free entry into the banking system as a whole, even though each bank is likely to maintain exclusivity in its customer relationships. Until 1980, bank competition in the United States was limited by Regulation Q deposit rate ceilings and by various restrictions on bank charters, mergers, statewide branching, and interstate banking. However, deregulation legislation and related developments have now removed most of the reasons for expecting bank markets to be less (or more) competitive than say the market for chairs. Consequently, free entry and zero expected profits are our maintained assumption, but imperfect competition is considered where it may be relevant.

Competition causes expected bank profits to be zero, so banks pass through their expected earnings on loans (net of operating costs) to depositors as interest payments. Even though deposit rates equal expected loan returns, an additional relationship is required to determine the common *level* for the two rates. One possibility is to use the market-clearing condition of the Walrasian demand and supply model – that the demand for loans (by borrowers) equals the supply of deposits (by depositors) – to determine the equilibrium level of the two rates.

Another possibility, developed below in Section 3, is that special features of loan markets cause loan rates to be *endogenously* determined below the Walrasian market-clearing level. To illustrate how this might work, without going too far ahead, let us suppose that a binding *usury ceiling* exogenously restricts loan rates below their Walrasian equilibrium level.[11] Competition will force expected bank profits to be zero, so deposit rates must settle at the same low level as the usury ceiling (default risk aside). As a result, there will be an excess demand for loans – a simple example of credit rationing.

Imperfect competition in deposit and loan markets does not fundamentally change the situation. If the special features of loans are ignored, then following the standard model of *monopoly*, banks will maximize their profits by equating the marginal cost of deposits with the marginal expected return on loans, while satisfying all loan demand. On the other hand, if the special features of loans cause loan rates to be quoted at a level lower than the monopoly level, then a continuing state of excess demand may exist, just as in the competitive case.

---

[10] The recent experience of S and L's, however, suggests that in the absence of deposit insurance, the reserves and capital may not suffice to protect depositors. The losses that depositors suffer as a result of bank runs raise a different issue – bank liquidity – as discussed by Diamond and Dybvig (1983).

[11] Although the ecclesiastical sources of usury ceilings have presumably long passed, similar ceilings still exist in many states in the United States as part of consumer protection laws for unsecured consumer and credit card loans.

Banks may also internally connect loans to deposits when the external markets for these securities function imperfectly. *Compensating balance requirements*, for example, are a contractual arrangement whereby a borrower or a holder of a line of credit is required to maintain a specified level of deposits in the bank. This arrangement can be interpreted as a "time-sharing" plan, whereby a firm receives the right to borrow from time to time as part of its compensation for maintaining deposits in the bank. Such arrangements may allow banks to equilibrate the supply of deposits and the demand for loans even when Regulation Q deposit ceilings and usury loan ceilings constrain the market levels of interest rates. Banks may also use these arrangements to monitor a firm's financial condition by observing the patterns and trends in its deposit balances.

In summary, loan and deposit markets involve three different interest rates: (1) the *quoted loan rate* determines the amount that borrowers promise to repay; (2) the *expected return* on a loan is the quoted rate adjusted for the lender's expected loss if default occurs; and (3) the *deposit rate* is the rate paid to depositors to raise loanable funds. Under competition, the deposit rate determines the expected return a bank must earn on each loan. That is, a bank determines the quoted rate for each loan so that it earns the required return; or, if this is not possible, the bank will not make the loan.

2.5. Definitions of credit rationing

Credit rationing is broadly defined as a situation in which there exists an excess demand for loans because quoted loan rates are below the Walrasian market-clearing level. There are a number of different types of credit rationing depending on how excess demand is defined, on whether the excess demand is temporary or continuing, and most importantly, on the factors that cause the loan rate to be depressed. Given the number of possible variations, definitions of credit rationing have often been a source of confusion in the literature. For this reason, we list here several common definitions of credit rationing and remark on the extent to which they are or are not relevant to the issues we address.

(1) *Interest rate (or price) rationing*. A borrower may receive a loan of a smaller size than desired at a given loan rate. To obtain a larger loan, the borrower has to pay a higher rate.

Remark. This describes standard price rationing and is not relevant to our discussion of credit rationing. Of course, it is sensible that a borrower has to pay a higher rate on a larger loan since the probability of default tends to be higher on a larger loan. In contrast, it is striking that a large part of the literature for monetary economics and corporate finance assumes that there exists a market in which people or firms can borrow as much as they like at a fixed rate of interest [see Stigler (1967) and Stiglitz (1970)].

(2) *Divergent views rationing.* Some individuals cannot borrow at the interest rate they consider appropriate based on what they perceive to be their probability of default.

Remark. Although lenders relative to borrowers may commonly have more pessimistic appraisals of default risk, this is also not the focus of our analysis of credit rationing.[12] For example, if the Treasury bond rate is 8 percent, the fact that most firms are "excluded" from the market for 8 percent loans simply reflects the market's judgment that loans to these firms are risky. From this perspective, a borrower's perception of his risk is mainly relevant as a factor determining his demand for credit.

There is an analogous kind of rationing in labor markets: there may be an excess supply of those willing to be president of General Motors at the going market wage, but (at least in the neoclassic story) the reason that the president of GM receives such a high wage is that he has "more efficiency units": he is equivalent to, say, 100 ordinary laborers. A person who could only supply 50 efficiency units (even working 24 hours a day) would thereby be excluded from the market for GM president.

(3) *Redlining.* Given the risk classification, a lender will refuse to grant credit to a borrower when the lender cannot obtain its required return at any interest rate. Moreover, loans which are viable at one required rate of return (as determined by the deposit rate) may no longer be viable when the required return rises. (The term redlining originally referred to the cross-hatched maps used by urban mortgage lenders to designate neighborhoods in which they would not lend. Our use of the term does not imply any type of discriminatory behavior.)

Remark. The possibility of redlining is easily illustrated in an extreme example where the borrower's project has a single outcome X^m. If the required return is δ, then a loan in excess of $B^* = X^m/(1 + \delta)$ clearly cannot yield the required return, so the firm will be rationed out of the market. The same result can apply to the expected return on a loan when there are various possible project outcomes.

In a similar fashion, a firm, which received a loan when the supply of deposits was high and the deposit rate was low, may be rationed when the supply of deposits shifts and the deposit rate rises. This happens because a "promise" to pay a higher rate on a loan may not translate fully (or even at all) into a higher expected return for the lender. For these firms the availability of credit (the supply of deposits) – not the quoted loan rate – determines whether

---

[12]Divergent views on loan repayments are common because they refer to the fulfillment of a promise, not to an actuarial event such as whether or not it will rain.

they can borrow. These firms would feel they are being rationed out of the market.[13]

(4) *Pure credit rationing.* There may be instances in which some individuals obtain loans, while *apparently identical individuals*, who are willing to borrow at precisely the same terms, do not.

Remark. This is the purest form of credit rationing, and we show below how it may arise when there is imperfect information. When it does arise, changes in the availability of credit, not changes in the interest rate, *may* determine the extent of borrowing.

We also show that redlining (type 3 credit rationing) may be nearly indistinguishable from pure credit rationing (type 4) when lenders classify borrowers into a large number of groups so that each group has a small number of borrowers. In this case, borrowers in a redlined group may have *nearly* the same features as the borrowers in a group that does obtain loans.

2.6. The earlier credit rationing literature: Brief review

The literature on credit rationing can be conveniently separated into two parts: an earlier literature based on various loan market imperfections; and a current literature based on imperfect information. Imperfect information was suggested as a factor in loan markets by Akerlof (1970) and Rothschild and Stiglitz (1971), and was first applied in a model of credit rationing by Jaffee and Russell (1976). We briefly review the earlier literature in this subsection before turning to the current imperfect information theories.

The earliest references to credit rationing pertain to usury ceilings [Smith (1776)] and to the English banking and currency controversies of the nineteenth century [Viner (1937)]. Modern references to credit rationing begin with Keynes' discussion of an "unsatisfied fringe of borrowers" in his *Treatise on Money* (1930, I: pp. 212–213; II: pp. 364–367):

> So far, however, as bank loans are concerned, lending does not – in Great Britain at least – take place according to the principles of a perfect market. There is apt to be an unsatisfied fringe of borrowers, the size of which can be expanded or contracted, so that banks can influence the volume of investment by expanding or contracting the volume or their loans, without there being necessarily any change in the level of bank-rate, in the demand-

---

[13]It has been debated whether redlining should be called credit rationing since, in the market's judgment, redlined borrowers cannot provide the bank its required rate of return (in an expected value sense). These borrowers are "rationed" out of the market in the same way that an individual who cannot afford a \$200 000 automobile is rationed out of the car market because the lender does not believe that the auto loan will be repaid.

schedule of borrowers, or in the volume of lending otherwise than through the banks. This phenomenon is capable, when it exists, of having great practical importance.

Keynes did not actively pursue this notion in his later work, but it became part of the "availability doctrine", or "new view", of monetary control at the Federal Reserve in the United States following World War II. The availability doctrine was primarily macroeconomic in its outlook (we consider it later in this regard), but it started a microeconomic literature concerned with the theoretical underpinnings of credit rationing behavior.[14]

2.6.1. The risk of default as the basis of credit rationing

Hodgman (1960) was among the first to consider the risk of default as the reason a rational bank might not raise its quoted loan rate even though it faces an excess demand for loans. Hodgman's model looked at a risk-neutral bank that is making a one-period loan to a firm. The firm's investment project provides possible outcomes X, bounded by $k < X < K$, with the probability density function $f[X]$. The contracted repayment equals $(1 + r)B$, based on the loan B and the lending rate r. If default occurs, the bank receives the available proceeds X.

The bank is assumed to obtain its funds in a perfect deposit market at the constant interest rate δ. For the single borrower, the bank's expected profits Φ are then written:

$$\Phi = \int_{k}^{(1+r)B} Xf[X]\,\mathrm{d}X + \int_{(1+r)B}^{K} (1 + r)Bf[X]\,\mathrm{d}X - (1 + \delta)B . \qquad (2.1)$$

The first term accounts for the bank's income X when there is default $(X < (1 + r)B)$, the second term for the income $(1 + r)B$ when the loan is repaid in full, and the third term for the bank's cost of funds $(1 + \delta)B$. The bank's decision variables are the quoted loan rate r and the size of the loan B.

This formulation can be used to derive the bank's loan offer curve for the borrower, showing the size of the loan offered B for each loan rate r. Under competition, the offer curve is simply the zero profit locus of contracts for which the bank's expected profit Φ is zero. The loan offer curve, as illustrated in Figure 16.1, has three basic properties:

(1) It is a horizontal line at the deposit rate δ over the range of small loan sizes where the loan is risk-free $(B < k/(1 + \delta))$.

---

[14]This literature has been surveyed in Lindbeck (1962), Jaffee (1971), Koskela (1976, 1979), and Baltensperger (1978).

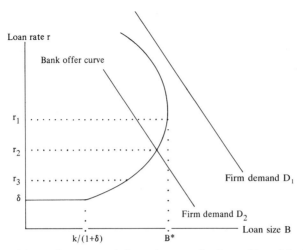

Figure 16.1. A bank loan offer curve and alternative cases for the position of the borrowing firm's demand curve.

(2) It has a positive slope over the range where the probability of default rises with the size of the loan, as higher loan rates compensate the bank for the higher likelihood of default on larger loans.

(3) There may be a maximum loan size B^* beyond which the offer curve becomes backward bending. Otherwise, were the loan rate r and the size of the loan B to rise together over the full range, at some point the contracted repayment $(1+r)B$ would equal the firm's best possible outcome K and default would be certain.

Freimer and Gordon (1965) used the loan offer curve construction to develop a redlining theory of credit rationing. Their point was that the size of the loan demanded by an individual borrower could exceed the size of the loan offered at any interest rate, as illustrated by demand curve D_1 in Figure 16.1.[15] Hence, the size of the loan demanded might exceed the maximum size of the loan the lender was willing to offer. The model, however, did not carefully delineate between the information available to the borrower and to the lender, so that the type of credit rationing was unclear. These issues are clarified by the theories of credit rationing discussed in Section 3 that focus on imperfect information.

Rationing is eliminated when the demand curve intersects the offer curve, as illustrated by the demand curve D_2 in Figure 16.1. In this case, the loan

---

[15]This assumes the offer curve is the locus of contracts with zero expected profits. Freimer and Gordon, in fact, assume the lender is a monopolist making all or nothing loan offers, but similar considerations apply. In particular, along the loan offer curve, the probability of default approaches 1 as the loan rate approaches infinity.

demanded and the loan offered are equal at the market-clearing rate r_2, so credit rationing – in terms of the size of loan – will occur only if the quoted rate loan is maintained below r_2. Several alternative approaches were taken to motivate why quoted loan rates might be maintained below the market-clearing level. However, as we will now see, they are all based on exogenous institutional factors.

2.6.2. Borrower classification

The credit rationing theory of Jaffee and Modigliani (1969) used the fact that banks classify borrowing firms into a small number of groups based on objective factors such as industry affiliation and firm size. Each bank determines a single interest rate for each group, even though the firms within a group may be diverse with respect to risk and the amount of their loan demand. Banks deal with the diversity by rationing those firms within the group which have a loan demand that exceeds the loan offer.

The demand curve D_2 in Figure 16.1 can be interpreted as applying to a particular firm in the group for which r_3 is the group loan rate. Jaffee and Modigliani demonstrate that even when the group loan rate is selected to maximize bank profits (over the group), some firms in the group are necessarily in the situation illustrated. These firms, in other words, face credit rationing because the bank recognizes that they have above average demand or above average risk – so the size of the loan offered to these firms is smaller than the size they demand. A firm might prefer to pay a higher interest rate to obtain a larger loan, but this would conflict with the purpose of the classification scheme, namely to simplify rate-setting with just one rate for each group.

2.6.3. Customer relationships

In a related approach, Hodgman (1963) and Kane and Malkiel (1965) used customer relationships to motivate why banks set loan rates below the market-clearing level of r_2. These models assumed that firms provide banks with deposits on a continuing basis and in return the firms receive a priority status for their loans. A priority status for loans is valuable precisely because banks maintain loan rates below the market-clearing level. Consequently, the model implies an equilibrium in which banks set loan rates below the market-clearing level, and then give priority to borrowers with established bank relationships.[16]

The main shortcoming of these earlier formulations of the customer relationship theory is that they fail to explain why bank competition for deposits and loans does not cause deposit and loan rates to reach market-clearing levels.

---

[16]A similar mechanism may occur in labor markets when firms pay wages above the market-clearing level, and then use the threat of dismissal to discipline workers [see Shapiro and Stiglitz (1984)].

Federal deposit rate ceilings used to provide one explanation for why deposit rates might be constrained, but bank deregulation has now eliminated these ceilings. In contrast, the theories of credit rationing discussed in the next section show that imperfect information provides a consistent explanation of why loan rates might be maintained below the market-clearing level and why customer relationships remain so important.

As another variant of the customer relationship, Fried and Howitt (1980) provided an implicit contract theory of credit rationing in which banks provide firms with loan rate guarantees as part of risk-sharing arrangements. The implicit contract notion, adopted from labor economics, is a generalization of the customer relationship. Fried and Howitt applied the concept to cases where firms acquired protection against unexpected increases in their borrowing costs, and they showed that what may appear as credit rationing can result as long as it is costly to break contracts. The theory is subject, however, to the same objections raised with regard to implicit contracts as a theory of unemployment in labor markets.[17]

In summary, the theories reviewed in this section adopt the special characteristics of loan markets – such as the likelihood of default, the use of borrower classification schemes by banks, and the exclusive customer relationships that arise between banks and borrowers – to motivate why banks set loan rates below the market-clearing level and then use credit rationing to balance the demand and supply of credit. There is little doubt that these are important features of loan markets and are part of the credit rationing process. However, the theories fail to explain the origins of the features as an integrated part of their models. In contrast, we now turn to theories based on imperfect information, which consistently explain both credit rationing and the special characteristics of loan markets.

3. Credit markets with imperfect information[18]

In this section we present the basic argument for why there may be credit rationing in markets with imperfect information. In Figure 16.2 we have

[17]Implicit contracts do not provide a complete theory of rigid wage rates (or interest rates) because the allocative role of the wage rate depends on the shadow price of labor for the marginal worker, and this price may still be variable. See, for example, Stiglitz (1986).

[18]Large parts of this section are based on Stiglitz and Weiss (1981). The model with incentives effects was independently analyzed by Keaton (1979). Recent surveys of the literature are provided by Baltensperger and Devinney (1985) and Clemenz (1986).

The fact that markets in which there is imperfect information may be characterized by non-market-clearing equilibria was noted in Stiglitz (1976a). In labor markets, models generating these unemployment equilibria are referred to as efficiency wage models, as a result of the close affinity of these models with those in which wages affected labor quality because of nutritional effects [Leibenstein (1957), Mirrlees (1975a, 1975b), and Stiglitz (1976b)]. For recent surveys, see Stiglitz (1987) and Yellen (1984).

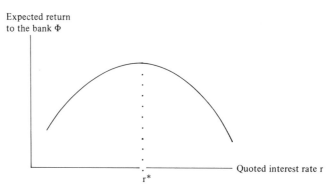

Figure 16.2. The quoted interest rate r^* maximizes the expected return to the bank.

plotted the expected return earned on a loan as a function of the *quoted* (or *promised*) interest rate. Raising the rate of interest charged does not result in a proportionate increase in the receipts of the lender, because the probability of default may rise. Indeed, if the probability of default rises enough, the return to the lender may actually decrease, as depicted in the figure. We denote the quoted rate at which the lender's expected return is maximized as r^*. No bank will ever charge more than r^*.

To see how credit rationing – a situation where there is an excess demand for credit – may persist, recall the standard argument for market clearing. There it is argued that if the demand for credit exceeds the supply of credit, lenders will raise the rate of interest charged, which will increase the supply and decrease the demand, until market clearing is restored. But at r^*, no bank has an incentive to raise its interest rate, because doing so only *reduces* the return it receives. This is why the Walrasian (market-clearing) interest rate may not be the equilibrium interest rate. Indeed, whenever the Walrasian interest rate occurs at a level in excess of r^*, the market equilibrium is characterized by credit rationing: each bank would find it in its interest to lower the interest rate to r^*, even though the demand for credit exceeds the supply.[19]

Therefore, to obtain credit rationing, it is only required that the expected (certainty equivalent) return received by the lender does not increase monotonically with the rate of interest charged.[20] There are two basic reasons why the relationship between the interest rate charged and expected receipts may not be monotonic: adverse selection effects and adverse incentive effects. These are now discussed in turn.

---

[19]With multiple Walrasian equilibria, if there is any Walrasian equilibrium with r in excess of r^*, then there exists a credit rationing equilibrium, though there may also exist another market-clearing equilibrium.

[20]That is, if there is ever a region of non-monotonicity, there is some supply of credit (funds) function such that the Walrasian equilibrium lies in the downward-sloping portion of the curve. In this case, there will be credit rationing.

3.1. Adverse selection effects

As the interest rate is increased, the mix of applicants changes adversely; safe potential borrowers drop out of the market. This is the *adverse selection effect*. Stiglitz and Weiss (1981) suggested several reasons why there might be an adverse selection effect.

They couched their analysis in terms of a specific example, where the bank (lender) had categorized potential borrowers by the mean return on their investment projects. For simplicity, all investment projects were assumed to be of the same size, and there was no collateral.[21] The return to the lender is

$$\Phi = \min\{(1 + r), X/B\} \ ,$$

where X is the return to the project, and B is the size of the loan. That is the lender either receives the promised amount, or the firm goes into bankruptcy. They ignored bankruptcy costs, and assumed that the returns in the event of bankruptcy would be divided among the lenders. In Figure 16.3 we plot the return received by the lender as a function of the return on the project, X. It is a concave function. On the other hand, the return to the borrower is

$$\pi = \max\{0, X - (1 + r)B\} \ .$$

Because of limited liability, the lowest return he obtains is zero (the return function can be modified by collateral as we indicated earlier). This is a convex function. The analysis then has three steps:

(1) Because of the convexity of the firm's profit function, borrowers whose

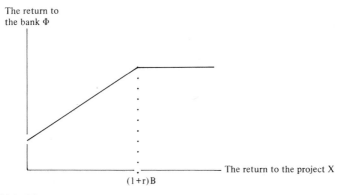

Figure 16.3. The return to the bank is a concave function of the return on the project.

[21]We will later remove both of these assumptions.

return is riskier (in the mean-preserving sense) have a higher expected profit. We denote the riskiness of a project (firm) by θ, with higher θ representing greater riskiness. If (risk-neutral) borrowers have to put up a fixed amount of equity of their own, e_0, then a project will be undertaken if

$$E\pi > e_0(1 + \delta).$$

Since the expected profit depends on a project's risk, there exists a risk level $\bar{\theta}$ such that firms with $\theta > \bar{\theta}$ undertake the investment, while others do not. We plot $E\pi - (e_0(1 + \delta))$ as a function of θ in Figure 16.4.

(2) An increase in the quoted rate r reduces the expected profits for all borrowers. This downward shift in the $E\pi$ curve means that the critical value of θ is higher, so fewer firms will demand loans. Moreover, it is the safest firms – those with the lowest value of θ – which drop out of the market. This is the adverse selection effect.

(3) The negative effect on the lender's expected return can now easily be seen. Because of the concavity of the lender's return function, the expected return to the lender is smaller with higher θ; this follows immediately given our assumption that all projects in the given category have the same expected return. If the expected return to the borrower for high-risk projects is higher, then the expected return to the lender must be lower. Thus, the total expected return – averaged over all applications for loans – may either increase or decrease when the interest rate r is increased. There is a positive direct effect, but a negative adverse selection effect, as the best risks (those with the lowest θ) drop out of the market.

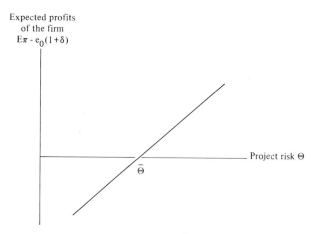

Figure 16.4. Only firms with projects at risk level $\bar{\theta}$ or higher will carry out their projects.

The fact that the adverse selection effect can easily outweigh the direct effect can be seen most easily in an example with just two groups in the population, groups a and b, with each group having two possible outcomes. The unsuccessful outcome for both groups is a return of 0. The successful outcome for the groups are X^a and X^b and the probabilities of success are P^a and P^b, respectively. We further assume that

$$X^a < X^b \quad \text{and} \quad P^a > P^b, \quad \text{with} \quad P^a X^a = P^b X^b,$$

so that the mean returns are equal but group a is safer and group b is riskier. We also set the loan size B equal to 1. Thus, if the good group a represent a proportion Γ of the total population, and all individuals apply for loans, the mean gross return to the lender is

$$(1 + r)\bar{P}, \quad \text{where} \quad \bar{P} = \Gamma P^a + (1 - \Gamma)P^b,$$

while if only the high-risk individuals apply, the mean gross return is

$$(1 + r)P^b.$$

There is a critical interest rate, r^*, at which the safer borrowers stop applying. Thus, the return to the bank declines precipitously at r^*, as illustrated in Figure 16.5.

An adverse selection effect arises because a higher loan rate affects the safer borrowers – who anticipate they will always repay the loan – more than it does the riskier borrowers – who will recognize that the loan rate does not matter in situations where they have to default on the loan. (At the extreme, an individual who was fairly sure he would not pay back the loan fully would be

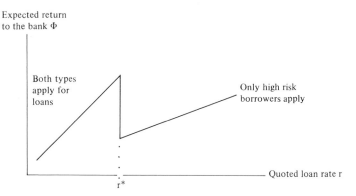

Figure 16.5. The determination of the optimal loan rate.

almost indifferent to the promised rate of interest.) Thus, raising the loan rate r adversely affects safer borrowers more than riskier borrowers.

The argument that a higher loan rate creates an adverse selection effect may become even more cogent in a competitive setting, in which loan applicants apply to several different banks. If one bank then raises its quoted loan rate, it knows that only those borrowers who have been refused loans at all other banks will accept its loans. If the bank is not confident about its judgment of the riskiness of the loan applicant, the fact that other banks have rejected the given applicant conveys a lot of information. When the given bank is quoting precisely the same rate as all other banks, then the same information is not conveyed when a borrowers accepts a loan.[22]

3.2. Adverse incentive effects

As the interest rate is increased, applicants undertake riskier projects. We call this the *adverse incentive effect*. Of course, lenders could try to control directly the actions of borrowers, but unfortunately, monitoring is costly and never perfect. Thus, lenders must resort to *indirect control* mechanisms. That is, lenders know that the behavior of a borrower is affected by the terms of the contract, including the interest rate. This is the basis of a key result of Stiglitz and Weiss that we will now demonstrate – that the risk-taking of borrowers rises as the interest rate they are charged rises.

This is seen most simply in the case of a firm with two techniques, a and b, which are described exactly as were the two projects in the previous subsection, the only difference being that they now reside within a single firm. The net expected return to the firm from undertaking project $i(= a$ or b) is $P^i(X^i - (1 + r)B)$, which declines with r.

We plot the return in Figure 16.6, where the slope of the expected return function is $-P^iB$. The return on the safer project a decreases more with an increase in the interest rate because the safer project is more likely to have to pay the promised rate. The firm undertakes the project with the highest expected return; from the figure, it is apparent that for $r < r^*$, the firm undertakes the safer project; for $r > r^*$, the riskier one. [The gross return to the bank if the firm undertakes project i is $(1 + r)P^i - B$, with the safer project

---

[22]This argument is weaker, at least for small changes in interest rates charged, in the context of the customer markets discussed in earlier sections. On the other hand, a bank which suddenly charged a rate in excess of that charged by other banks would suffer a loss of reputation, and accordingly might find it more difficult to recruit borrowers.

A bank may deal with this problem by conditioning the extension of its loan to the provision of matching credit by some other bank. This is another illustration of the public good aspect of loan markets.

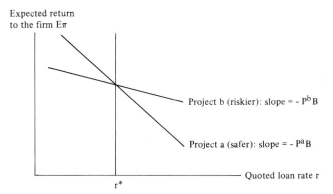

Figure 16.6. The safer project is chosen at loan rates below r^*, the riskier project at loan rates above r^*.

undertaken if $r < r^*$. Thus, there will be a precipitous decline in the bank's return at $r = r^*$, similar to that illustrated in Figure 16.5.]

3.3. Credit rationing with many groups

When there are many groups in the population (distinguished in whatever manner), quoted rates will be set for each group to make the expected return on loans in each group equal to the deposit rate. In competitive equilibrium, all loans must have the same expected return, this rate representing the cost of deposits. Thus, we can divide the groups into three types, as illustrated in Figure 16.7.

Type 1 borrowers are completely denied credit – they are "redlined" (credit

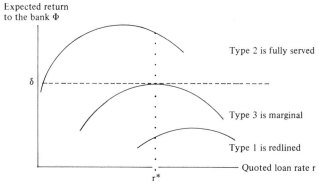

Figure 16.7. Credit rationing status of different borrower groups.

rationing definition 3) because there is no interest rate at which the lender's expected return reaches the required return.

Type 2 borrowers are fully served because banks actively compete to make them loans. That is, the expected return on their loans (which equals the deposit rate) is less than the maximum expected return a bank could earn with a higher quoted rate.

Type 3 borrowers are the *marginal group*. They are rationed in the strongest sense of the term (credit rationing definition 4): some members of this group received credit, while other, apparently identical members (in terms of observable characteristics), are denied credit. Banks obtain the required return from members of this critical, marginal group by charging them the interest rate which maximizes the expected return.

Reduced credit availability always has its first impact on the marginal group: more of these borrowers become rationed, while the interest rate charged borrowers in this group may not change at all (the expected return is already maximized). Moreover, a sufficiently large reduction in credit availability will be reflected as a change in the marginal group. In this case, the interest rate will be adjusted, the old marginal group will be totally excluded from loans, and the new marginal group will be partially excluded from loans.

Riley (1987) has suggested that the credit rationing of the marginal group is significant only when the number of groups is small. His point is that, as the number of groups increases, the number of borrowers in the marginal group falls, so the extent of this credit rationing falls. In the limit, the marginal group would consist of just one borrower.

Stiglitz and Weiss (1987b) have responded that redlining (credit rationing definition 3) and pure credit rationing (credit rationing definition 4) may be nearly indistinguishable when there is a continuum of groups. This happens because there are groups just above the marginal group who are not rationed and groups just below the marginal group who are redlined. The characteristics of these two groups will converge when there is a continuum of groups. Consequently, the situation is effectively one of pure credit rationing, namely that among groups of (nearly) indistinguishable borrowers some are credit rationed and some are not. The extent of this kind of "nearly" pure rationing may not diminish as the number of types increases.[23]

3.4. Some comparative statics of credit rationing

Changes in uncertainty have an ambiguous effect on the quoted loan rate. For example, as the economy goes into a recession, it is plausible that the expected

---

[23]Stiglitz and Weiss (1987b) also point out that there are many natural extensions of their basic model in which credit rationing occurs at several, or even all, contracts. An example of such a model with collateral is discussed in Subsection 4.3 below.

return falls, given the quoted interest rate; but there is no a priori reason to believe that the quoted interest rate at which the expected return is maximized will either increase or decrease, as illustrated in Figure 16.8.

Consider first the incentives model. The curve relating a bank's expected return to its quoted interest rate can be derived from a more fundamental curve, which relates the probability of default to the quoted interest rate. It is more convenient to depict the bankruptcy probability as a function of $1/1 + r$; for the slope of this curve is just $P/(1/1 + r) = P(1 + r)$, the expected return. Hence, the bank's optimal interest rate is that interest rate at which the slope of a line from the origin to the curve is maximized. An increase in uncertainty (associated with a move into a recession) may be thought of as shifting this curve upwards; at each r there is a higher probability of bankruptcy. But there is no easy way of seeing whether the interest rate at which the slope is maximized is likely to increase or decrease.

We illustrate this with the case where there are only two types of activities, the safer (a) and the riskier (b). The critical interest rate, where the expected return to the borrower is the same if he undertakes either project a or b, is

$$1 + r^* = [P^a X^a - P^b X^b]/[P^a - P^b] . \tag{3.1}$$

If as the economy goes into a recession, the probability of success of both safer and riskier projects is reduced proportionately, then there is no change in the quoted rate of interest, in spite of the reduction in the expected return to loans. All of the adjustments must occur then through loan availability. On the other hand, if, as the economy goes into a recession, risky projects have their success probabilities reduced more than proportionately, then the quoted rate of interest will increase in a recession,[24] in spite of the fact that the demand for

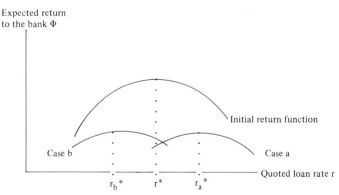

Figure 16.8. In a recession, the expected return function shifts down, but the optimal loan rate may increase (case a) or decrease (case b).

[24]Define $\tau = P^a/P^b$. Then we can rewrite equation (3.1) as $1 + r^* = [\tau X^a - X^b]/[\tau - 1]$. Differentiating with respect to τ, we obtain $dr^*/d\tau = -[X^a - X^b]/[\tau - 1]^2 > 0$.

loans has decreased: it is easier to discourage borrowers from undertaking riskier loans when the threat of bankruptcy is greater.[25]

Similar results obtain when adverse selection effects are the reason for credit rationing. Again, consider the two-group case. The critical interest rate at which the safe borrowers drop out may increase or decrease in a recession. The greater uncertainty associated with any project means that, at a fixed expected return for the project, the expected return to the firm has increased; but the expected return to any project is also likely to decrease in a recession.

3.5. A consumer loan model

Jaffee and Russell (1976) developed a model of credit rationing that applies many of these same concepts to a *consumer* loan market. The basic structure is a simple two-period model in which each consumer receives current income Y_1 and future income Y_2, and has current consumption C_1 and future consumption C_2. A loan B is taken out to increase current consumption and is repaid with interest (at the rate r) from the income received during the future period. The resulting consumption pattern is then

$$C_1 = Y_1 + B ,$$
$$C_2 = Y_2 - (1 + r)B .$$

The basic model assumes that all consumers have the same income and consumption preferences. Consequently, all consumers have the same loan demand, which is assumed to be negatively related to the interest rate.

A "moral hazard" is introduced by the fact that consumer i will default on his loan if his cost of default Z_i is less than the loan repayment $(1 + r)B$. The cost of default is interpreted broadly to include the lost access to further credit, the social stigma, and similar factors. The cost of default is assumed to vary over the population: some consumers have high Z_i values, so they tend to repay their loans (they are "honest" borrowers); while other consumers have lower Z_i values, so they may intend to default. Banks, however, cannot identify the consumers who are likely to default. In fact, consumers who intend to default will act exactly as their honest counterparts so as not to identify their true character.

Loans are made through a competitive banking industry with access to deposits at the constant rate δ. If a bank knows that Γ percent of its borrowers

---

[25]All of these results extend to the more general model, described below, where there is collateral, and multiple forms of loan contracts offered by firms [Stiglitz and Weiss (1987a)].

will repay their loans, then its profit function is

$$\Phi = \Gamma(1 + r)B - (1 + \delta)B \ .$$

Given that competition forces bank profits to be zero, the equilibrium value for the loan rate r^* will be such that

$$1 + r^* = (1 + \delta)/\Gamma \ .$$

This shows that the loan rate factor $(1 + r)$ exceeds the cost of funds factor $(1 + \delta)$ by an amount $1/\Gamma$ that compensates the bank for the borrowers that default. Loans are made in the size demanded by honest borrowers at the loan rate r^*. This is a "pooling" contract since all borrowers are offered the same, single contract.

The honest borrowers have an incentive to create a separate loan pool because they are subsidizing the dishonest borrowers by the amount that the contract rate r^* exceeds the cost of deposits δ. However, the dishonest borrowers always mimic the actions of the honest borrowers. Therefore, the best the honest borrowers can do is to adopt a pooling contract that has a smaller size than their loan demand at r^*. Even though this contract still pools honest and dishonest borrowers, fewer borrowers default, so the loan rate is lower. It is easily demonstrated that the honest borrowers are better off in this case.[26]

4. Extensions of the basic theory

In the preceding section we explained why an increase in the interest rate might have adverse selection and incentive effects, so that lenders might choose not to increase the interest rate charged, even when there is an excess demand for credit. The basic theory has been extended in a number of different directions to respond to criticism of the simpler versions of the theory and to apply the basic theory in different institutional settings.

4.1. Enforcement problems

In some important contexts – international lending – legal recourse in the event of a default is limited. In other contexts, legal recourse simply has very high

---

[26]If the market allows only a single contract, then this pooling contract represents an equilibrium. Otherwise, the concept of equilibrium depends on whether an informed or uninformed agent has to act first.

costs. In these situations, a debt contract – a promise to pay in the future – is enforced only if the borrower faces costs of default that exceed the benefits of default. Eaton and Gersovitz (1981) have focused on the fact that borrowers lose their reputation for repaying if they default.[27] Access to the capital market has a value, say M, because borrowing can be used to smooth consumption; in the absence of borrowing and lending an individual (or country) must adopt more expensive ways to smooth consumption. The benefit of repudiating a debt is D when the debt has a value of D (assuming the debt is a perpetuity which promises to pay \$1 a year, and the interest rate is r and is expected to remain there). Thus, repudiation will occur if $D > M$. Since lenders know this, they will restrict loans to M, i.e. there will be credit rationing. If there is uncertainty about the future rate of interest or the value of M, then the initial level of lending will be set so that there is some probability of default. An increase in the degree of variability should lead to a reduction in the maximum amount that lenders will be willing to lend.[28]

In other contexts, a default simply results in a period during which the borrower must search out a new source of lending. Then the penalty for default is, of course, much smaller [Allen (1983)].

4.2. Enforcement problems in multiple period models

While the meaning of default is clear in simple two-period models, it is not clear in multi-period models. That is, the lender may have an incentive to postpone a default by extending additional credit to the borrower. Thus, for a default to occur there must in effect be complicity between the lender and the borrower: the lender must refuse to continue to extend further credit on terms which the borrower finds acceptable. Indeed, given that real costs are associated with default (the costs of bankruptcy or corporate reorganizations), there should be mutually agreeable arrangements that avoid default [Eaton, Gersovitz, and Stiglitz (1986)]. On this basis, it is remarkable that the number of defaults is so high.

Two explanations suggest themselves. First, an effective threat of cutting off credit may have important incentive effects on borrower behavior, causing borrowers to undertake less risky projects, thus reducing the likelihood that

---

[27]They construct a simple model in which the by now familiar perfect equilibrium entails the firm repaying the loan.

[28]This analysis implies that loans to less developed countries (LDCs) may not be viable (in the absence of trade or similar sanctions). In principle, an LDC should borrow funds when the marginal productivity of its capital is high, and repay the funds to the developed economy later. But the LDC may not have incentive at the future date to repay its loan: access to future credit, by assumption, is no longer important. If lenders anticipate this, they may not lend initially.

the economic circumstances will occur under which default is contemplated [Stiglitz and Weiss (1983)]. But how can the threat of cutting off credit be made convincing? And even if one bank cuts off credit, why would not other banks provide the credit? There are two possible explanations. Stiglitz and Weiss provide a model in which banks earn profits on their initial loans; they take a loss on the continuation of the loan contract, but they do so because the contractual arrangement with the borrower allows them to cut off credit when the default circumstances occur. As a result, when credit has been terminated by one lender, no other lender would be willing to lend to the individual. Seniority provisions in debt contracts, as well as the information-theoretic concerns discussed earlier in this chapter, reinforce the conclusion that there may be high costs imposed on the borrower by the termination of his relationship with his lender.

Second, reputation models provide a different set of explanations. Reputations affect firm behavior in two ways. First, they provide the rationale for the enforcement of implicit contracts, such as the continuation of the customer relationship between a bank and a borrower. Secondly, they provide an explanation for why, given that there is imperfect information, a bank may sometimes force bankruptcy on a borrower who is technically in default, even though a renegotiated agreement might appear to be a Pareto improvement. The bank knows that if customers come to believe that such renegotiations will occur, they will undertake riskier actions, making it necessary to undertake these renegotiations, and thus the banks' expected profits will be lowered.[29] [Eaton (1986) has addressed the question of how bank reputations can be maintained in circumstances in which the owner-managers of banks are finitely lived. He argues that an asset is created which can be transferred to the next generation. The firm's current owner has an incentive to maintain this asset, the firm's reputation.]

However, the possibility of mutually agreeable renegotiations which avoid reorganization/bankruptcy costs must be taken into account. For as Stiglitz (1972) pointed out, there is always a conflict of interest in the presence of bankruptcy between the interests of debtors and of shareholders. So long as control remains vested in the shareholders, they may take actions which,

---

[29]The Eaton–Gersovitz model is effectively a reputation model in which a borrower repays his loan to protect his reputation. Indeed, to our knowledge their paper provided one of the first theoretical models of reputation (in which maintaining a reputation constituted a perfect equilibrium). Subsequent more formal developments in reputation models have surprisingly failed to cite their pioneering work.

Shapiro (1983) has provided an alternative theory of reputations in which reputations are based on simple extrapolations of past behavior. In the context of highly complex environments, in which the characteristics of the agents vary greatly and are hard to ascertain and there may not be common knowledge concerning the "game" which the agents are supposed to be playing, Shapiro's behavioristic model may provide more insights into the nature of the reputation mechanism than the game theoretic models.

though increasing the value of their shares, decrease the value of debt. The amount of this activity may increase the "closer" the firm is to bankruptcy; this explains loan contract provisions which enable control of the firm to switch to debtors when events occur that significantly increase the probability of the firm being unable to meet its debt obligations, even though it currently is meeting them. (Eastern Airlines went technically into default when it failed to obtain wage concessions from its unions.)

4.3. Collateral, loan size, and non-price rationing

A continuing criticism leveled against credit rationing theories is that it may be possible to adjust other terms of the loan contract to eliminate the credit rationing. Two contract terms in particular – collateral and loan size – deserve attention.

4.3.1. Collateral

Several articles have suggested that credit rationing disappears when a bank can set collateral requirements and interest rates simultaneously. The argument is that the bank could offer a set of self-selecting contracts [Rothschild and Stiglitz (1971)] that would fully reveal the risk character of each borrower; in this case, credit rationing would not occur. For example, if the market consisted of just two types of borrowers – good risks and bad risks – then the good risks might choose a contract with a lower interest rate and higher collateral requirement (because it is unlikely they will default and lose their collateral), while the bad risks might choose a contract with a higher interest rate and a lower collateral requirement (because there is a higher probability they will default and lose their collateral). As a result, if the *only* informational imperfection concerned which borrowers were good risks and which bad, then the bank could design contracts that reveal this information, and credit rationing would not occur.

The fact that banks never have perfect information concerning the characteristics of their borrowers suggests what is wrong (or irrelevant) about this argument: the conclusion holds only if individuals differ in just one dimension (say wealth), so that a simple set of contracts can completely separate and identify the different groups.[30] but if the groups differ in two dimensions (risk aversion and wealth), then a perfect separation cannot be made with {interest

---

[30]Even then there may exist problems when there are a large number of groups. Under monopoly, there may be partial pooling [see Mirrlees (1971), Stiglitz (1977), and a large subsequent literature analyzing conditions under which the relevant functions are differentiable], while under competition, there never exists an equilibrium.

rate, collateral} contracts. Of course, if individuals differ in just two dimensions, then it might still be possible to find a more complicated contract that would perfectly identify the different groups. But so long as the dimensionality of the space of borrower characteristics is larger than the dimensionality of the space of contracts, it seems unlikely that perfect information can be obtained.[31]

Stiglitz and Weiss (1981) showed that while increasing collateral requirements have a positive incentive effect, they could have a negative selection effect. They argued that even if all individuals in society had the same utility functions, wealthier individuals will, in general, be willing to take greater risks (based on decreasing absolute risk aversion). Moreover, among those with large amounts of wealth, there is likely to be a larger proportion of risk-takers: individuals who gambled, and by chance won. Thus, as a result of such adverse selection effects, it may not be desirable to require collateral to the point where credit rationing is eliminated.

Stiglitz and Weiss (1986, 1987b) have also examined a model in which adverse selection and incentive effects are both present, and in which interest rates and collateral requirements are both used. They find that the equilibrium may take on different forms:

(1) There may be a pooling equilibrium with credit rationing in which both types of borrowers (high-risk and low-risk) adopt the same contract; collateral is not increased, since doing so would have adverse selection effects; interest rates are not increased, since doing so would have adverse incentive effects.

(2) Alternatively, equilibrium may be characterized by multiple contracts, with credit rationing on each one. Some rich individuals who undertake risky projects may have to accept low collateral, high interest rate contracts because they do not receive high collateral, low interest rate contracts. The fraction of those of each type at the low collateral contract is determined endogenously in such a way to ensure that the expected return on a low collateral contract exactly equals the expected return on a high collateral contract.

Since a loan application has no cost in the model, the extent of credit rationing on different contracts does not serve as a screening device. However, the role of rationing as a screening device can be examined using straightforward adaptations of similar models in the context of labor markets [Nalebuff and Stiglitz (1983)].

---

[31]Some of the papers that attempted to show that collateral requirements can eliminate credit rationing did so by developing examples in which credit rationing does not occur. However, Stiglitz and Weiss (1981) had pointed out earlier that credit rationing would occur *only if* the adverse selection effect outweighed the direct effect of an increase in the interest rate. Thus, creating an example to show that credit rationing does not occur is an exercise directed at an irrelevant question; they would have to show that credit rationing does not arise in any "plausible" model. See, for instance, Bestor (1985).

4.3.2. Smaller loans

It has also been suggested that banks can substitute smaller loans for credit rationing. To the extent that there are projects of fixed (or optimal) investment scale, reducing loan size simply forces borrowers to put up more of their own equity, and the effects of this are analogous to those just described for collateral.[32]

But even when there are no non-concavities in the production technology, the nature of the credit relationship may cause banks to avoid making loans that are "too small". Loan size is an attribute of the loan contract which affects borrower behavior; by reducing loan size, borrowers may take actions which actually reduce the expected return to the lender (when appropriate account of further "forced loans" are taken into account) [see Stiglitz and Weiss (1981)]. For example, in a multi-period context, borrowers always are in a position to return to the lender to ask for further funds; a refusal to lend further funds may then jeopardize the amounts already lent out.[33]

4.4. Issues of efficiency and welfare

There are several basic results regarding the welfare aspects of equilibrium with credit rationing:

(a) A market equilibrium with credit rationing (as in other cases in which markets are characterized by imperfect information and incomplete markets) is not Pareto efficient in general, even when account is taken of the costs of information.[34]

(b) Pareto efficiency may well entail credit rationing (in other words, market clearing is not, in general, an attribute of efficient markets in the presence of imperfect information).

(c) When credit rationing occurs in markets, there are systematic biases *against* undertaking projects which maximize expected returns.

Although our analysis has focused on competitive markets, informational costs are likely to result in imperfect competition among banks (particularly ex post, after the customer relations have been initiated). Credit rationing may (will) characterize imperfectly competitive lending markets as well as competitive lending markets.

---

[32]Indeed, in some simple versions of the credit rationing model, increasing equity requirements and increasing collateral requirements are equivalent.

[33]This is the point we have emphasized earlier in our discussion of lending with enforcement problems. It was originally noted in an important paper by Hellwig (1977) and in Stiglitz and Weiss (1981).

[34]They are, to use the fashionable phrase, not constrained Pareto efficient. See Greenwald and Stiglitz (1986a) and Stiglitz and Weiss (1981, 1983).

5. Macroeconomic aspects of credit rationing

The macroeconomic ramifications of credit rationing have been a focus of attention at least since the development of the Availability Doctrine at the end of World War II. At that time, there was pessimism regarding the effectiveness of monetary policy for two reasons:

(a) real expenditures were thought to be relatively unresponsive to interest rates; and

(b) the Federal Reserve was under pressure to maintain stable (and low) interest rates.[35]

In this context, Roosa (1951) and others at the Federal Reserve developed the Availability Doctrine, according to which monetary policy could still affect real expenditures through a credit rationing channel. The Availability Doctrine relied on three steps.

(1) Federal Reserve open market sales of Treasury securities would cause banks to reallocate their portfolios from loans to Treasury securities.[36]

(2) Banks would tend to reduce the quantity of loans through credit rationing, not by raising loan interest rates.

(3) As credit rationing rose, rationed firms would face a rising shadow price for credit, causing their investment activity to fall, even though market interest rates were quite stable.[37]

We have seen in the previous sections how a theory of credit rationing has developed that is consistent with the first two steps. We will now look at research that has focused on step 3 – the macroeconomic effects of credit rationing, particularly with regard to the fixed-capital investment of firms and the housing investment and consumption expenditures of households.

5.1. Market interest rates and the shadow price of credit

The connection between credit rationing and capital investment is illustrated in Figure 16.9. The economy is initially at point E_0, where the quantity of loans Q_0 is supplied by the banks (based on their supply curve S_0) at the loan interest rate r_0. There is credit rationing here because the demand for loans (based on

---

[35]An important record of these views is provided in testimony provided by economists and the Federal Reserve before the Joint Economic Committee (1952), the Patman Hearings.

[36]Lindbeck's (1962) survey of the Availability Doctrine discusses a variety of factors that cause this shift.

[37]Modigliani (1963) particularly emphasized the shadow price of credit as the mechanism that transmitted the impact of credit rationing from the loan markets to the real markets. The idea that monetary policy was asymmetrical in its effect – you cannot push on a string – also was emphasized in the Availability Doctrine.

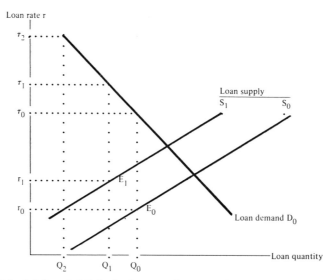

Figure 16.9. A leftward shift in the loan supply curve raises the shadow price of loans.

demand curve D_0) exceeds Q_0. The shadow price of credit, τ_0, is determined
on the demand curve D_0 by the loan quantity Q_0.

Now suppose that Federal Reserve action causes the supply curve of loans to
shift to the left, to curve S_1. This establishes a new equilibrium at a point such
as E_1, with a lower loan quantity Q_1, a higher loan interest rate r_1, and a
higher shadow price of credit τ_1. Moreover, the *less* the loan rate rises, the
more the shadow price of credit rises. For example, if the loan rate were to
remain unchanged at the level r_0 – which the credit rationing theory in Section
3 indicates is quite possible – then the loan quantity falls to Q_2 and the shadow
price of credit rises to τ_2.

The actual pattern of real interest rates in the U.S. economy since 1952 is
shown in Figure 16.10. The real interest rate is measured by the 6 to 9 month
commercial paper rate minus the inflation rate for the Consumer Price Index.
Three distinct periods are evident.

(1) From 1952 to the early 1970s the real interest remained in a narrow band
centered on 2 percent. (William McChesney Martin was Chairman of the Fed
for most of this period.)

(2) During most of the 1970s the real interest was negative, usually about
−1 percent. (Arthur Burns was Chairman of the Fed.)

(3) During most of the 1980s the real interest rate was positive, sometimes
above 5 percent. (Paul Volcker was Chairman of the Fed.)

In the absence of credit rationing, the (before-tax) cost of capital to firms is
determined by the real interest rate. The cost of capital for a new capital

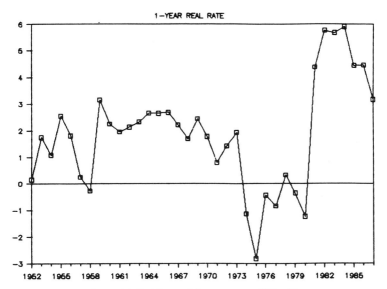

Figure 16.10. The real interest rate: 1952–87.

investment that is initiated each year and that provides a return of an equal amount of output at the end of each of the following 5 years is illustrated in Figure 16.11.[38] The cost of capital smooths out the year-to-year fluctuations in the real interest rate, so that over the 20-year period ending in the early 1970s, the cost of capital was virtually constant at 2 percent. After that, the cost of capital first fell and then rose in a smooth fashion.

The variations in the cost of capital can be contrasted with the variations in real, fixed, non-residential capital investment that occurred over the same period of time, as illustrated in Figure 16.12. This figure shows that the annual percentage change in the amount of real investment was often in the range between −2 and +10 percent. The amount of variation in capital investment appears to be about the same in the period prior to the early 1970s and the period after that time.

The implication of Figures 16.11 and 16.12 is that variations in the cost of capital appear prima facie to be implausible as a major source of the observed fluctuations in capital investment.[39] That is, a theory of capital investment cannot be based on a constant – which the cost of capital roughly represented

---

[38]For example, the capital investment in 1952 provides 1 unit of output at the end of each year from 1952 to 1956. The cost of capital is the constant annual rate that creates the same present value for this investment as the actual real rates shown in Figure 16.10.

[39]The point would be made even stronger by using an *after-tax* cost of capital to the extent that the tax rates applicable to capital investment are reduced when capital investment is low.

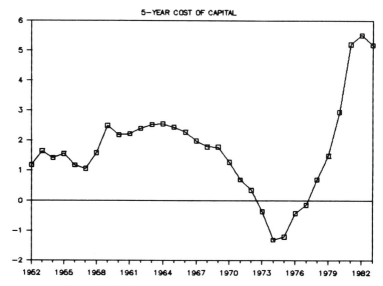

Figure 16.11. The cost of capital on 5-year investments.

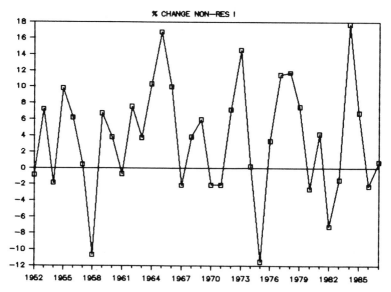

Figure 16.12. Annual percentage change in fixed non-residential investment.

throughout the 1950s and 1960s. Other factors, including credit rationing, must therefore account for the observed range of variation in capital investment. We will now evaluate credit rationing as a factor that may affect capital investment.

5.2. Cyclical changes in credit rationing

In our earlier discussion we analyzed the comparative statics of the credit rationing model, with a particular focus on how interest rates would be affected by changes in mean returns, uncertainty, and the availability of credit. The analysis was, however, static, and a full cyclical analysis requires a more explicitly dynamic model, yet to be formulated. Here, we offer three observations.

We began by discussing why the conventional "auction-market" analysis for chairs and tables is inappropriate for the market for loans. An analogy may be useful. Some might find it appealing for American universities to auction the space in each incoming class to the highest bidders. After all, the individuals are presumably well informed concerning their own abilities – they *know* how hard they had to work to obtain the A – and might be the best judges of the expected value added of, say, a Harvard education. Also, the losses created by bad judgments would be borne by the individuals who over (or under) bid. Standard efficiency arguments would thus seem to call for such auctions.[40]

However, none of the major private universities uses an auction system. Presumably it is *not* believed that individuals are good judges of their own ability. One reason might be that an auction system would have a systematic bias; individuals who are over-confident (individuals that many of us as teachers find particularly objectionable to instruct) would be over-represented. Rational expectations arguments might well counter that, were these individuals to live the 9 lives of a cat, but with memory of only the *return* to learning, not the learning itself, crossing over from life to life, they would not make these mistakes. However, modern Western ideology has cast skepticism on views of repeated reincarnations, which makes a theory of resource allocation based on that premise particularly problematical. Accordingly, it is not surprising that non-price rationing systems have persisted at all of the major private universities, in spite of the eminence of the economists on their faculty and the ready availability of advice on how to improve the efficiency of resource allocations.

Similar arguments hold for credit markets, with particular force in changing environments. We argued earlier that credit is used when there is a discrepancy between the availability of current resources and judgments concerning the

---

[40]Problems caused by lack of resources could presumably be rectified by loan programs.

returns on potential uses of resources. But are individual judgments to be trusted? Assume that interest rates were the only dimension of loan contracts that individuals cared about. In undertaking projects, individuals compare the expected returns with the expected interest payments. An individual who, when confronted with a high current (short-term) interest rate, believes that future interest rates are going to go down, may be willing to undertake a project; while another individual, with an equally good project, who believes that future interest rates are going to remain the same, will not. The bank does not want to select among alternative borrowers on the basis of their projections of future interest rates; it wishes to discriminate on the basis of the quality of the project. But willingness to borrow (at any interest rate) may be affected as much by the borrowers' optimism concerning future interest rates, prices, and wages as it is by the "real" characteristics of the project. The price system would work no better in allocating capital resources than it would in allocating scarce places in our major private universities.

The second observation is that the response of real expenditures to credit rationing can follow a variety of dynamic patterns.

(1) Expenditures may respond with variable lags depending on the initial liquidity of the spending units and on their willingness to use this liquidity.

(2) The anticipation of future credit rationing may have current effects, even when there is no credit rationing at present. Thus, the impact of credit rationing cannot be assessed just by looking at those periods in which there is direct evidence for its presence.

(3) There will be further multiplier effects of the initial changes in spending induced by credit rationing.

The third observation is that the loan interest rate is not necessarily a good measure of monetary tightness. For example, as we showed in the discussion of the comparative statics of credit rationing in Subsection 3.4, the quoted loan rate and the expected return on loans may even change in opposite directions.

5.3. The measurement of credit rationing

A major pitfall in evaluating the effect of credit rationing on capital investment is that the amount of credit rationing in the economy at a given time is not readily measured. In principle, the amount of credit rationing could be measured as the demand for credit minus the supply of credit. However, we generally only observe the quantity of credit that is transacted (or that is outstanding), not the amount that is demanded or supplied. This is illustrated in Figure 16.13 for the interest rate r_0, at which the quantity that is transacted might possibly correspond to the supply curve (at Q_s), to the demand curve (at Q_d), or to any quantity in between, depending on how the difference between

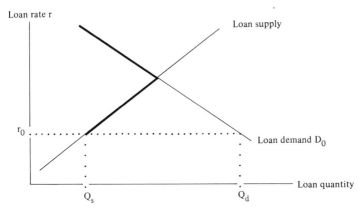

Figure 16.13. The observed loan quantity is the minimum of loan demand and loan supply.

demand and supply is allocated. Whatever the specific case, if demand and supply are not directly observed, then the amount of credit rationing is not directly observed.

Nevertheless, Fair and Jaffee (1972) developed a basic technique for estimating the demand and supply curves for a market that may be in disequilibrium. They assumed that transactions are voluntary, in the sense that the quantity transacted Q_t must be the minimum of demand and supply:

$$Q_t = \min\{Q_d, Q_s\} \,.$$

In this case, only the darkened portions of the demand and supply curves in Figure 16.13 would actually be observed. But it is still possible to obtain maximum likelihood estimates of the demand and supply curves, and therefore of the amount of credit rationing. Indeed, a large literature now exists for estimating markets in disequilibrium, including applications to loan markets.[41]

There have also been attempts to measure credit rationing with proxy variables and survey techniques: Jaffee and Modigliani (1969) developed a proxy measure of bank credit rationing based on the percentage of banks loan that are granted to low-risk firms; and the Federal Reserve carries out a quarterly survey of the terms of bank lending that refers to availability of credit [see Harris (1974) and Jaffee (1971)]. Although disequilibrium estimation, proxy variables, and surveys all generally confirm that banks use non-price rationing, these techniques do not directly provide evidence of the impact of

[41] The theory of disequilibrium estimation is developed in Maddala (1983) and Goldfeld and Quandt (1975). Specific applications to loan markets are discussed by Bowden (1978), Laffont and Garcia (1977), and Sealey (1979).

credit rationing on real expenditures. We will now consider the evidence regarding different classes of investment and consumption spending.

5.4. Fixed capital investment of business firms

The neoclassical theory of capital investment focuses on changes in the cost of capital as a key variable determining changes in investment demand [Hall and Jorgenson (1967), Eisner and Nadiri (1968), Bischoff (1971), and Clark (1979)]. Consistent with the Modigliani–Miller theory, the theory assumes that firms can borrow whatever funds they need to carry out their desired capital investment. In contrast, if credit rationing limits a firm's access to external finance, then the firm's liquidity and internally generated cash flow may determine how much of its investment demand is realized as actual capital investment [Meyer and Kuh (1957)]. Furthermore, credit rationing would have a larger impact on firms that have a higher ratio of investment demand to internally generated cash flow.

The relationship of capital investment to internal cash flow is the focus of recent research by Fazzari, Hubbard and Petersen (F-H-P) (1988). They extend a q theory of investment to include imperfections in loan and equity markets that may cause firms to be credit constrained. Their empirical analysis compares the investment behavior of classes of firms that vary in the extent of their need for, and access to, external finance, based on panel data (from the Value Line database) for individual manufacturing firms.

The F-H-P analysis shows that the investment expenditures of certain firms display "excess sensitivity" to variations in their cash flow. In response to lower interest rates or other factors that raise investment demand, the increase in the investment expenditures of these firms is closely tied to the amount of their internally generated cash flow. By implication, these firms do not have substantial and continuing access to external financing.

F-H-P identify the firms that are hampered by inadequate access to external finance as firms that retain most of their earnings – they pay little or no dividends. Although the earnings retention rate is an endogenous variable for firms, and therefore it is not an ideal basis for classifying them, the F-H-P data indicate that these firms are also distinctive as being fast growing, relatively small, and highly profitable.

All of the firms studied by F-H-P are relatively large – even their group of small firms had an average capital stock of $347 million in 1984 (in 1982 prices). This means that about 80 percent of all manufacturing firms in the United State are smaller than the F-H-P group of small firms. Since the sensitivity to internal cashflow is presumably greater for smaller firms, this reinforces the F-H-P conclusion that the investment expenditures of many firms may be limited by the amount of their cash flow.

On the other hand, the firms studied by F-H-P also represent about 85 percent of the total assets held by manufacturing firms. This highly skewed distribution of firms by size suggests that the contribution of smaller firms to aggregate investment may be limited. That is, even though credit rationing may have a significant impact on the investment spending of smaller firms, these firms might account for only a small part of the fluctuations in aggregate investment. Additionally, if the large firms that dominate the statistics for aggregate investment are rationed by banks, they might still have access to non-bank capital markets for equity and debt or to other sources of funds. We will now consider some of the reasons that raising funds in the capital markets may not substitute for bank credit.

5.5. Credit substitutes for bank loans

For credit rationing to be effective in reducing investment, firms must be unable to raise capital in other ways, or the (marginal) cost of raising capital in other ways must be higher than the cost of borrowing. Equity capital represents an obvious alternative to bank loans for this purpose. Also, trade credit – loans from one firm to another – may provide firms with an alternative source of working capital. We will now look at these in turn.

5.5.1. Equity capital as a substitute for bank credit

For (the manager of) a firm, equity has the distinct advantage that since there is no fixed commitment to repay, there is no bankruptcy risk. Equity has, however, three problems:

(a) *Monitoring.* Equities represent promises to pay shareholders a given fraction of the firm's profits. But it may be difficult for shareholders to monitor what the profits are. Or the firm's managers may divert a large fraction of the firm's returns to their own uses. Alternative control mechanisms (voting, takeovers) have only limited efficacy, partially because of free-rider problems and the costliness of information. (The benefits associated with monitoring accrue to all shareholders.)

(b) *Signalling* (adverse selection effects). Issuing equities may provide an adverse signal to the market. If firms were risk neutral (and there were no costs of bankruptcy), the owners of the firm would only be willing to sell a share of a firm whose actuarial value is say, $X, for a price which equalled or exceeded $X: so there would not exist a market for equities.[42] With bankruptcy costs/manager risk aversion, there are gains from the issue of equities, but

---

[42] This is an application of the standard Akerlof (1970) lemons model to equities.

there will be a significant signalling effect, with only the worst firms (within any category of firms) issuing equity.[43,44]

(c) *Agency* (adverse incentive effects). The costs of monitoring managers' activities imply that managers may have a wide discretion. This discretion is limited by a large supply of outstanding debt in two ways. First, if managers wish to avoid bankruptcy, then the necessity of meeting these fixed obligations alters their actions. Second, and perhaps more importantly, banks (lenders) monitor the actions of the firm directly, paying particular attention to actions which adversely impact the likelihood that the loan will be repaid. They have an effective threat – cutting off credit and demanding the repayment of outstanding loans – not available to those who supply equity funds. This means that effective control of managers is exercised as much by lenders as it is by shareholders.[45]

As a result of these factors, firms may be reluctant to raise capital by issuing new equities, even (or particularly) when they are credit constrained. Greenwald and Stiglitz (1986a, 1986b) refer to this as an equity constrained firm; although firms have the option of issuing equity, the cost of doing so is so high that they act as if they cannot do so. (Clearly, for large enough perturbations to their environment, the constraint will no longer be binding.)

For many purposes the whole set of financial constraints is relevant; that is, as a result of informational asymmetries, funds inside the firm are less expensive than outside funds, whether obtained in the form of equity or in the form of debt. Raising funds provides a signal, and outsiders' judgments, at least in some cases, are likely to be more pessimistic concerning the firm's prospects than insiders' judgments (or, in any case, less confident). Thus, what the outsider expects to get may be less than the insider thinks he has promised to give.[46] (Even in rational expectations models with risk neutrality, where those who pay more than the market expects them to pay are exactly offset by those who pay less, the informational asymmetries have real effects not only on

---

[43]This is demonstrated in the theoretical models of Stiglitz (1982), Greenwald, Stiglitz and Weiss (1984) and Myers and Majluf (1984). Empirical confirmation is provided by Asquith and Mullins (1986).

An important aspect of the issue of equities is that they tend not to be issued continuously, but rather in discrete amounts. With few exceptions, firms that enter the equity market do so only infrequently. A dynamic model of equity issue which explains this is provided by Gale and Stiglitz (forthcoming).

[44]Earlier models focused on the incentive of the original owners of the firm to sell their shares. The willingness to do so had an adverse selection effect [Stiglitz (1974, 1982) and Leland and Pyle (1977)]. Ross (1977) has argued that a firm's willingness to issue debt, and thus to incur bankruptcy costs, has a positive signalling effect. In each of these instances, one needs to ask whether there are alternative ways in which the given information can be credibly disclosed without the costs (bankruptcy, lack of diversification, etc.) associated with the choice of financial structure.

[45]This is an old view. For a more modern rendition of the argument, explaining why the free-rider problems which limit the effectiveness of shareholder control do not apply with equal force to lenders, see Stiglitz (1985).

[46]This point was emphasized in Stiglitz (1972).

the allocation of capital, but also on the magnitude of investment; the increase in investment by those who underpay for credit may be less than the decrease in investment by those who overpay.)

5.5.2. Trade credit

Trade credit – loans between firms that are used to finance the purchase of materials and goods in process – represents a way of redistributing credit among firms, which could also serve as a substitute for bank loans [Meltzer (1960), Jaffee (1971), and Duca (1986)]. The idea is that large firms, which are not rationed by banks (or which use debt and equity capital markets), can make loans to smaller firms that cannot obtain bank loans. Trade credit is a major element in the U.S. credit system: trade credit outstanding is almost as large as bank loans to business firms and as corporate bonds.[47]

The price charged for trade credit by a lending firm is generally very high, usually translating to an annual interest rate in excess of 24 percent.[48] This implies that firms that borrow through trade credit have faced credit rationing with respect to bank loans. In addition, most lending firms rarely change their trade credit interest rate, so trade credit outstanding is basically determined by the demand for the credit. (Of course, firms with very low credit ratings may be denied access to trade credit.)

The existence of this trade credit system raises two basic questions:

(1) Why do lending firms extend trade credit, given that the borrowing firms are likely to have been denied credit by banks?

(2) Why are lending firms willing to extend more trade credit when bank credit rationing rises?

Earlier research tried to answer these questions by analyzing trade credit as a sales expense (like advertising) of firms operating in imperfectly competitive markets [Nadiri (1969) and Schwartz and Whitcomb (1980)]. However, a more interesting and complete answer is provided by analyzing trade credit with the same model we used in Section 3 to analyze the lending decisions of banks [see Duca (1986)].

The key point is that trade credit allows for an efficient diffusion of information in the form of risk-sharing arrangements that eliminates elements of moral hazard. The idea is that firms which are selling goods to other firms are likely to have better information about the profit prospects of the buyers than would a bank lending to the same buyers. Trade credit can thus serve as a risk-sharing arrangement between buying and selling firms.

---

[47]According to the Flow of Funds accounts, the outstanding debts of non-financial business firms at the end of 1987 included trade debt of $546 billion, bank loans of $618 billion, and corporate bonds of $790.

[48]For example, a firm may offer a 2 percent discount from its list price if payment is made immediately (within 5 days); otherwise the list price must be paid within 30 days.

The result is that trade credit contracts and bank loan contracts can represent two parts of a *separating equilibrium*: all borrowers first apply for bank loans, and those who do not receive bank loans (due to redlining or to pure credit rationing) then apply for trade credit. Firms that extend trade credit will thus anticipate that their borrowers will have above average credit risk, and therefore they would charge an above average interest rate. Moreover, since the trade credit interest rate mainly represents a premium for the high risk of default, it would not be highly sensitive to the market interest rate.

5.6. Housing investment

Between World War II and 1980, housing investment was often the most volatile component of aggregate expenditures. During most business cycles, housing investment fell during the recession and rose during the boom by more than 50 percent relative to its average level. At the same time, nominal mortgage interest rates tended to be more stable than comparable bond interest rates. Under these circumstances, credit rationing was considered to be a major source of the observed fluctuations in housing investment.[49] Both the risk of default and government regulations were possible sources of this credit rationing.

5.6.1. The risk of default and mortgage credit

Most mortgage lenders try to control the risk of default on mortgages by using two key ratios as their lending criteria.

(1) The *equity ratio* equals the borrower's equity investment in a real estate property divided by the appraised value of the property. Typical equity ratios range from 5 to 25 percent. Lenders charge lower interest rates on loans with higher equity ratios because there is a greater likelihood that the housing collateral will cover the loan amount should the borrower default.

(2) The *income ratio* equals the carrying cost of the property (mortgage interest, property taxes, etc.) divided by the borrower's income. Typical income ratios range from 25 to 35 percent. To satisfy the income ratio criterion, a borrower may have to buy a smaller house or make a larger downpayment. Lenders use an income ratio to supplement the equity ratio because real estate values can fluctuate and the transactions costs of selling a property are substantial.

Credit rationing in the mortgage market is a good example of a situation where the redlining form of rationing merges into pure credit rationing.

---

[49]Jaffee and Rosen (1979) review the earlier housing investment cycles and the research that pointed to credit rationing as a source of these cycles.

Specifically, young, first-time homebuyers often do not have the equity or the income to satisfy even the minimum requirements for the equity and income ratios. Although this appears to be redlining, it occurs because lenders adopt a small number of equity and income ratio categories. If transaction and information costs were lower, then lenders would adopt a larger number of categories, and the rationing would take the form of pure credit rationing, not redlining.[50]

5.6.2. Government regulations and mortgage credit

Until 1980, two sets of government regulations – usury ceilings on mortgage interest rates and Regulation Q ceilings on bank deposit rates – created an additional source of credit rationing in the mortgage market. The Regulation Q ceilings – which set limits on the deposit rates of commercial banks and thrift institutions – created *disintermediation* – an outflow of deposit funds – whenever market interest rates rose above the ceilings. This happened with some frequency during the 1960s and 1970s, with the result that the total amount of lending by banks and thrifts had to be reduced. Credit rationing arises under these circumstances to the extent that lending rates are constrained by the considerations of adverse selection and moral hazard discussed in Section 3.

There were also reasons to expect disintermediation to have a particularly strong impact on the mortgage market, one aspect of which could be credit rationing.

(1) About half of all mortgage lending in the United States is carried out by thrift institutions – savings and loan associations and savings banks. By regulation, these institutions raised most of their funds through deposits that were subject to Regulation Q ceilings and invested most of these funds in mortgages. As a result, an outflow of deposits due to disintermediation had a particularly sharp impact on mortgage lending.

(2) Although large commercial banks had access to sources of funds that were not affected by Regulation Q ceilings, they did not expand their share of the mortgage market significantly. One factor was that most mortgage loans were fixed-rate, long-term contracts, so if these loans were made on the basis of short-term deposits, a loss would result if interest rates rose. Most large banks tried to balance the maturities of their assets and liabilities rather closely, and this limited the amount of their mortgage lending (wisely so, as

---

[50]The amount of mortgage market credit rationing is also offset by the government's FHA and VA mortgage programs. Evidence of credit rationing based on default risk is provided in recent studies by Rosenthal, Duca and Gabriel (1987) and Duca and Rosenthal (1988). The studies indicate that borrowers use more costly or cumbersome VA and FHA mortgages when they are credit constrained in conventional mortgage markets.

evidenced by the huge losses suffered by thrift institutions when interest rates soared in the early 1980s).

(2) Many states had laws – usury ceilings – which set maximum limits on mortgage interest rates. When binding usury ceilings kept mortgage interest rates below the level of rates on other loans or securities, lenders simply stopped making mortgage loans. Furthermore, state legislatures were usually slow to raise the usury ceilings, so the amount of credit rationing tended to rise as market interest rates rose during the 1960s and 1970s.[51]

The situation changed significantly beginning in 1980 when Congressional actions (1) removed the state usury ceilings and (2) phased out all Regulation Q ceilings over a 5-year period. These actions basically eliminated disintermediation and usury ceilings as a source of mortgage market credit rationing.[52] Other related changes in the mortgage market during the 1980s have also tended to reduce the amount of credit rationing:

(a) The facilities for secondary market trading of seasoned mortgages have improved, allowing lenders to separate the activity of making mortgage loans from the activity of holding mortgage loans.

(b) A variety of mortgage pass-through securities (such as GNMAs) and mortgage-backed securities now allow portfolios of mortgages to be packaged for investors in a form comparable to other capital market securities.

(c) Adjustable-rate mortgages have been developed to allow investors with short-term funds to hold mortgages without facing a severe maturity mismatch.

(d) Non-banking firms have entered the mortgage market – for example, General Motors Acceptance Corporation (GMAC) is now one of the largest mortgage lenders in the United States.

5.7. Consumption expenditures

It has been long debated in macroeconomics whether consumption depends on current income – the simple Keynesian theory – or on "wealth" (or the discounted value of future income) – the permanent income and life cycle theories [Tobin and Dolde (1971)]. The existence of credit rationing – called liquidity constraints in the consumption literature – is the factor that distinguishes these

---

[51]As market interest rates rose, banks would first ration more risky borrowers (those with lower equity ratios and therefore higher loan rates). However, there were cases in which the usury ceilings were below even the interest rates that lenders required on very safe mortgage loans.

[52]Congress allowed the states a period in which they could reinstate their usury ceilings by passing new legislation, but no state took this action. Comparable usury ceilings still exist in many states on consumer loans and credit card loans, but the states now tend to change these ceilings more promptly when market interest rates change.

theories. The permanent income/life cycle (PI/LC) theory assumes that consumers face no borrowing constraints and adopt optimal consumption plans based on their current and future income, implying that current income will have only a small effect on current consumption. In contrast, if consumers face borrowing constraints, then consumption expenditures would show "excess sensitivity" with respect to current income (relative to the PI/LC theories).

Empirical testing of these theories has been especially active in recent years, following the lead of Hall (1978) who introduced tests based on the Euler equations (the first-order conditions for the optimal consumption plan). Many issues – concerning specification, econometric methods, and data sources – arise in carrying out these tests. Nevertheless, most studies reject the PI/LC theories – for example, it is estimated that from 15 to 50 percent of consumption expenditures are determined by current income rather than by permanent income.[53] Since it seems that most consumers do face borrowing limits, the failure of the PI/LC theories is often attributed to liquidity constraints.[54]

Liquidity constraints have important implications for macroeconomic policy. For one thing, changes in average tax rates affect consumption spending when there are liquidity constraints, in contrast to the traditional case where marginal tax rates matter. This is relevant because recent tax law changes have focused on marginal rates. For another thing, liquidity constraints may cause Ricardian Equivalence not to hold.

The impact of liquidity constraints on consumption expenditures was vividly illustrated in March 1980 when the Federal Reserve (on the urgent request of President Carter) instituted emergency credit controls that required banks and lenders to limit the amount of new loans, especially to consumers (including credit card loans). As a result, during the second quarter of 1980, consumption expenditures experienced one of the largest quarterly declines on record. Indeed, the effect was so powerful that the Fed rapidly reversed its policy, dismantling the controls by the summer of 1980.[55]

5.8. The role of credit for monetary policy

Credit has been considered to be an important transmission channel for the effects of monetary policy by various economists over most of this century.

---

[53]Recent studies that focus on liquidity constraints include Flavin (1981), Hall and Mishkin (1982), Hayashi (1985a, 1985b), Hubbard and Judd (1986), and Campbell and Mankiw (1987).

[54]See, especially, Hayashi (1985a, 1985b). It is instructive that one of the few firm confirmations of the PI/LC theory – Bernanke (1984) – is based on the demand for automobiles, where credit rationing should not be important because autos provide an exceptionally liquid form of collateral.

[55]For an account of this episode, see Greider (1987), a controversial analysis of Federal Reserve operations, especially for the period beginning in 1979 when Paul Volcker became Chairman of the Board of Governors.

Among others, this "credit" school of monetary policy includes Hawtrey (1919), Roosa (1951), Gurley and Shaw (1960), and Friedman (1981). Their shared view is that variations in the availability of credit can have large effects on real economic activity, both on the aggregate level and on its distribution among sectors and even individual projects. In addition, most would argue that monetary policy should be carried out, or at least measured and evaluated, with regard to its effect on the availability of credit.

The "credit" school is often compared with the "money" or Monetarist school. The two schools differ most fundamentally over the modus operandi of monetary policy – whether it is based on the amount of the money supply, or on the availability of credit. This basic conceptual difference leads to different views regarding the implementation of monetary policy: how it should be measured, when and how it should be used, and what it might accomplish.

However, it is important to recognize that within the structure of the U.S. banking and financial system, the *monetary aggregates* of the respective schools – the money supply versus the credit level – are likely to be highly collinear. That is, a Federal Reserve policy that increases the reserves of the banking system is likely to raise the money supply and the credit level in roughly the same proportion. This occurs because bank assets (consisting mainly of loans and other credit instruments) equal bank liabilities (consisting mainly of deposits that are part of the money supply).

The credit school has had a resurgence in recent years as the result of a number of developments:

(1) As developed in our discussion, there now exists a rigorous theory of credit rationing based on the risk of default when there is imperfect information. This theory explains both why credit availability is likely to be important and why the institutions (banks) and the instruments (loan contracts) are structured as they are. (The Monetarist school, in contrast, assumes basically that capital markets are perfect – and also that government policy can control money substitutes.)

(2) Evidence is accumulating that large changes in the availability of credit certainly create correspondingly large changes in the level of economic activity:

- Bernanke (1983) points to the breakdown of the economy's credit facilities, and not the decline in money, as the monetary source of the Great Depression.
- Wojnilower (1980) argues that the availability of credit, not the cost of money, has been the source of most large changes in the level of real economic activity since World War II.
- Nakamura (1984) discusses the key role of banks in determining whether to force a borrowing firm into bankruptcy.
- The Federal Reserve created a deep recession during 1981, yet the growth rate of the money supply fell very little.

(3) Deregulation and other innovations in the financial system in recent

years have created large and unpredictable changes in the demand for money. A key result is that since 1987, the Federal Reserve has not used the M1 money supply as an operating target for monetary policy. At the same time, Friedman (1981) has shown that a broad measure of credit stands at least on par with money as an instrument that (a) the Federal Reserve can control and (b) forecasts future movements in nominal GNP.

References

Akerlof, G. (1970) 'The market for lemons: Qualitative uncertainty and the market mechanism', *Quarterly Journal of Economics*, 84: 488–500.
Allen, F. (1983) 'Credit rationing and payment incentives', *Review of Economic Studies*, 50: 639–646.
Arnott, R. and J. Stiglitz (1985) 'Labor turnover, wage structure, and moral hazard', *Journal of Labor Economics*, 3: 434–462.
Asquith, P. and D. Mullins (1986) 'Equity issues and offering dilution', *Journal of Financial Economics*, 15: 61–89.
Baltensperger, E. (1978) 'Credit rationing: Issues and question', *Journal of Money, Credit and Banking*, 10: 170–183.
Baltensperger, E. and T. Devinney (1985) 'Credit rationing theory: A survey and synthesis', *Zeitschrift Fur Die Gesamte Staatswissenschaft*, 141: 475–502.
Bernanke, B. (1983) 'Nonmonetary effects of the financial collapse in the propagation of the great depression', *American Economic Review*, 73: 257–276.
Bernanke, B. (1984) 'Permanent income, liquidity, and expenditure on automobiles: Evidence from panel data', *Quarterly Journal of Economics*, 99: 587–616.
Bernanke, B. and M. Gertler (1987), 'Financial fragility and economic performance', Princeton University, mimeo.
Bestor, H. (1985), 'Screening versus rationing in credit markets with imperfect information', *American Economic Review*, 75: 850–855.
Bischoff, C. (1971) 'Business investment in the 1970s: A comparison of models', *Brookings Papers on Economic Activity*, 1971-1: 13–58.
Blinder, A. (1987) 'Credit rationing and effective supply failure', *Economic Journal*, 97: 327–352.
Blinder, A. and J. Stiglitz (1983) 'Money, credit constraints, and economic activity', *American Economic Review*, 73: 297–302.
Bowden, R. (1978) *The econometrics of disequilibrium*. Amsterdam: North-Holland.
Calomiris, C., R. Hubbard and J. Stock (1986) 'The farm debt crisis and public policy', *Brookings Papers on Economic Activity*, 1986-2: 441–479.
Campbell, J. and G. Mankiw (1987) 'Permanent income, current income, and consumption', NBER Working Paper 2436.
Clark, P. (1979) 'Investment in the 1970s: Theory, performance, and prediction', *Brookings Papers on Economic Activity*, 1979-1: 73–113.
Clemenz, G. (1986) *Credit markets with asymmetric information*, Lecture Notes in Economics and Mathematical Systems 272. Berlin: Springer-Verlag.
Diamond, D. and P. Dybvig (1983) 'Bank runs, deposit insurance, and liquidity', *Journal of Political Economy*, 91: 401–419.
Duca, J. (1986) 'Trade credit and credit rationing: A theoretical model', Research Papers in Banking and Financial Economics, Board of Governors of the Federal Reserve System.
Duca, J. and S. Rosenthal (1988) 'Mortgage rationing in the post-disintermediation era: Does FHA make a difference?', Economic Activity Working Paper 83, Board of Governors of the Federal Reserve System.
Eaton, J. (1986) 'Lending with costly enforcement of repayment and potential fraud', *Journal of Banking and Finance*, 10: 281–293.
Eaton, J. and M. Gersovitz (1981) 'Debt and potential repudiations', *Review of Economic Studies*, 48: 289–309.

Eaton, J., M. Gersovitz and J. Stiglitz (1986) 'The pure theory of country risk', *European Economic Review*, 30: 481–515.

Eisner, R. and M. Nadiri (1968) 'Investment behavior and neoclassical theory', *Review of Economics and Statistics*, 50: 369–382.

Fair, R. and D. Jaffee (1972) 'Methods of estimations for markets in disequilibrium', *Econometrica*, 40: 497–514.

Fazzari, S., R. Hubbard and B. Petersen (1988) 'Financing constraints and corporate investment', *Brookings Papers on Economic Activity*, 1988-2: 141–195.

Flavin, M. (1981) 'The adjustment of consumption of changing expectations about future income', *Journal of Political Economy*, 89: 974–1009.

Freimer, M. and M. Gordon (1965) 'Why bankers ration credit', *Quarterly Journal of Economics*, 79: 397–410.

Fried, J. and P. Howitt (1980) 'Credit rationing and implicit contract theory', *Journal of Money, Credit and Banking*, 12: 471–487.

Friedman, B. (1981) 'The roles of money and credit in macroeconomic analysis', Working Paper 831, National Bureau of Economic Research.

Gale, I, and J.E. Stiglitz (forthcoming) 'The informational content of initial public offering', *Journal of Finance*.

Goldfeld, S. and R. Quandt (1975) 'Estimation in a disequilibrium model and the value of information', *Journal of Econometrics*, 3: 325–348.

Greenwald, B. and J. Stiglitz (1986a) 'Money, imperfect information, and economic fluctuations', *Symposium on Monetary Theory*, The Institute of Economics, Academia Sinica, Taipei, Taiwan.

Greenwald, B. and J. Stiglitz (1986b) 'Externalities in economies with imperfect information and incomplete markets', *Quarterly Journal of Economics*, 101: 229–264.

Greenwald, B., J. Stiglitz and A. Weiss (1984) 'Informational imperfections in the capital market and macroeconomic fluctuations', *American Economic Review*, 74: 194–199.

Greider, W. (1987) *Secrets of the temple*. New York: Simon and Schuster.

Gurley, J. and E. Shaw (1960) *Money in a theory of finance*. Washington: The Brookings Institution.

Guttentag, J. (1960) 'Credit availability, interest rates, and monetary policy', *Southern Economic Journal*, 26: 219–228.

Hall, R. (1978) 'Stochastic implications of the life cycle–permanent income hypothesis: Theory and evidence', *Journal of Political Economy*, 86: 971–988.

Hall, R. and D. Jorgenson (1967) 'Tax policy and investment behavior', *American Economic Review*, 74: 194–199.

Hall, R. and F. Mishkin (1982) 'The sensitivity of consumption to transitory income: Estimates from panel data on households', *Econometrica*, 50: 461–482.

Harris, D. (1974) 'Credit rationing at commercial banks', *Journal of Money, Credit and Banking*, 6: 227–240.

Hawtrey, R. (1919) *Currency and credit*. New York: Longmans, Green & Co.

Hayashi, F. (1985a) 'The effect of liquidity constraints on consumption: A cross-sectional analysis', *Quarterly Journal of Economics*, 100: 183–206.

Hayashi, F. (1985b) 'Tests for liquidity constraints: A critical survey', NBER Working Paper 1720.

Hellwig, M. (1977) 'A model of borrowing and lending with bankruptcy', *Econometrica*, 45: 1879–1906.

Hodgman, D. (1960) 'Credit risk and credit rationing', *Quarterly Journal of Economics*, 74: 258–278.

Hodgman, D. (1963) *Commercial bank loan and investment policy*. Champaign-Urbana: Bureau of Economic and Business Research, University of Illinois.

Hubbard, R. and K. Judd (1986) 'Liquidity constraints, fiscal policy, and consumption', *Brookings Papers on Economic Activity*, 1986-1: 1–51.

Jaffee, D. (1971) *Credit rationing and the commercial loan market*. New York: Wiley.

Jaffee, D. and F. Modigliani (1969) 'A theory and test of credit rationing', *American Economic Review*, 59: 850–872.

Jaffe, D, and K. Rosen (1979) 'Mortgage credit availability and residential construction activity', *Brookings Papers on Economic Activity*, 1979–2: 333–386.

Jaffee, D. and T. Russell (1976) 'Imperfect information, uncertainty, and credit rationing', *Quarterly Journal of Economics*, 90: 651–666.

Kane, E. and B. Malkiel (1965) 'Bank portfolio allocation, deposit variability and the availability doctrine', *Quarterly Journal of Economics*, 79: 113–134.

Keaton, W. (1979) *Equilibrium credit rationing*. New York: Garland Publishing Company.

Keynes, J.M. (1930) *A treatise on money*. London.

King, M. (1986) 'Capital market imperfections and the consumption function', *Scandinavian Journal of Economics*, 88: 59–80.

Koskela, E. (1976) *A study of bank behavior and credit rationing*. Helsinki: Academiae Scientarum Fennicae.

Koskela, E. (1979) 'On the theory of rationing equilibrium with special reference to credit markets: A survey', *Zeitschrift fur Nationalokonomie*, 39: 63–82.

Laffont, J. and R. Garcia (1977) 'Disequilibrium econometrics for business loans', *Econometrica*, 45: 1187–1204.

Leibenstein, H. (1957) *Economic backwardness and economic growth*. New York: Wiley.

Leland, H. and D. Pyle (1977) 'Informational asymmetries, financial structure and financial intermediation', *Journal of Finance*, 32: 371–387.

Lindbeck, A. (1962) *The 'new' theory of credit control in the United States*, 2nd edn. Stockholm Economic Studies.

Maddala, G.S. (1983) *Limited-dependent and qualitative variables in econometrics*. Cambridge: Cambridge University Press.

Meltzer, A. (1960), 'Mercantile credit, monetary policy, and the size of firms', *Review of Economics and Statistics*, 42: 429–437.

Meyer, J. and E. Kuh (1957) *The investment decision*. Cambridge, Mass.: Harvard University Press.

Mirrlees, J. (1971) 'An exploration of optimum income taxation', *Review of Economic Studies*, 38: 175–208.

Mirrlees, J. (1975a) 'The theory of moral hazard and observable behavior: Part 1', Working Paper, Nuffield College.

Mirrlees, J. (1975b) 'A pure theory of underdeveloped economies', in: L.A. Reynolds, ed., *Agriculture in development theory*. New Haven: Yale University Press, pp. 84–106.

Modigliani, F. (1963) 'The monetary mechanism and its interaction with real phenomena: A review of recent developments', *Review of Economics and Statistics*, 45: 79–107.

Myers, S. (1977) 'Determinants of corporate borrowing', *Journal of Financial Economics*, 5: 147–175.

Myers, S. and N. Majluf (1984) 'Corporate financing decisions when firms have investment information that investors do not have', *Journal of Financial Economics*, 13: 187–220.

Nakamura, L. (1984) 'Bankruptcy and the informational problems of commercial bank lending', Financial Research Center Memorandum 54, Princeton University.

Nadiri, M. (1969) 'The determinants of trade credit in the U.S. total manufacturing sector', *Econometrica*, 37: 408–423.

Nalebuff, B. and J. Stiglitz (1983) 'Equilibrium unemployment as a worker selection device', Princeton University mimeo.

Patman Hearings (1952) 'Hearings before the Subcommittee on General Credit Control and Debt Management of the Joint Committee on the Economic Report', 82nd Congress, 2nd Session. Washington: Government Printing Office.

Riley, J. (1987) 'Credit rationing: A further remark', *American Economic Review*, 77: 224–227.

Roosa, R. (1951) 'Interest rates and the central bank', in: *Money, trade and economic growth: Essays in honor of John H. Williams*. New York: The Macmillan Company, pp. 270–295.

Rosenthal, S., J. Duca and S. Gabriel (1987) 'Credit rationing and the demand for owner-occupied housing', Economic Activity Working Paper 79, Board of Governors of the Federal Reserve.

Ross, S. (1977) 'The determination of financial structure: The incentive signalling approach', *Bell Journal of Economics*, 8: 23–40.

Rothschild, M. and J. Stiglitz (1971) 'Increasing risk: I. A definition', *Journal of Economic Theory*, 2: 225–243.

Schwartz, R. and D. Whitcomb (1980) 'The trade credit decision', in: J. Bicksler, ed., *Handbook of financial economics*. Amsterdam: North-Holland.

Sealey, C. (1979) 'Credit rationing in the commercial loan market: Estimates of a structural model under conditions of disequilibrium', *Journal of Finance*, 34: 689–702.

Shapiro, C. (1983) 'Premiums for high quality products as returns to reputation', *Quarterly Journal of Economics*, 98: 659–679.

Shapiro, C. and J. Stiglitz (1984) 'Equilibrium unemployment as a worker discipline device', *American Economic Review*, 72: 912–927.

Smith, A. (1776) *The wealth of nations*, Modern Library Edition. New York: Random House.

Smith, B. (1983) 'Limited information, credit rationing, and optimal government lending policy', *American Economic Review*, 73: 305–318.

Stigler, G. (1967) 'Imperfections in the capital market', *Journal of Political Economy*, 85: 287–292.

Stiglitz, J. (1970) 'A consumption oriented theory of the demand for financial assets and the term structure of interest rates', *Review of Economic Studies*, 37: 321–351.

Stiglitz, J. (1972), 'Some aspects of the pure theory of corporate finance: Bankruptcies and take-overs', *Bell Journal of Economics and Management Science*, 3: 458–482.

Stiglitz, J. (1974) 'Incentives and risk sharing in sharecropping', *Review of Economic Studies*, 41: 219–255.

Stiglitz, J. (1976a) 'Prices and queues as screening devices in competitive markets', IMSS Technical Report 212, Stanford University.

Stiglitz, J. (1976b) 'The efficiency wage hypothesis, surplus labour and the distribution of income in LDCs', *Oxford Economic Papers*, 28: 185–207.

Stiglitz, J. (1977) 'Monopoly non-linear pricing and imperfect information: The insurance market', *Review of Economic Studies*, 44: 407–430.

Stiglitz, J. (1982) 'Ownership, control and efficient markets: Some paradoxes in the theory of capital markets', in: K. Boyer and W. Shepherd, eds., *Economic regulation: Essays in honor of James R. Nelson*. Ann Arbor: Michigan State Press, pp. 311–341.

Stiglitz, J. (1985) 'Credit markets and the control of capital', *Journal of Money, Credit and Banking*, 17: 133–152.

Stiglitz, J. (1986) 'Theories of wage rigidities', in: J.L. Butkiewicz, K.J. Kotford and J.B. Miller, eds., *Keynes' economic legacy*. New York: Praeger, pp. 153–206.

Stiglitz, J. (1987) 'The causes and consequences of the dependence of quality on price', *Journal of Economic Literature*, 25: 1–48.

Stiglitz, J. and A. Weiss (1981) 'Credit rationing in markets with imperfect information', *American Economic Review*, 71: 393–410.

Stiglitz, J. and A. Weiss (1983) 'Incentive effects of termination: Applications to the credit and labor markets', *American Economic Review*, 73: 912–927.

Stiglitz, J. and A. Weiss (1986) 'Credit rationing and collateral', in: J. Edwards, J. Franks, C. Mayer and S. Schaefer, eds., *Recent developments in corporate finance*. Cambridge: Cambridge University Press, pp. 101–135.

Stiglitz, J. and A. Weiss (1987a) 'Macro-economic equilibrium and credit rationing', Working Paper 2164, National Bureau of Economic Research.

Stiglitz, J. and A. Weiss (1987b) 'Credit rationing with many borrowers', *American Economic Review*, 77: 228–231.

Tobin, J. and W. Dolde (1971) 'Wealth, liquidity, and consumption', Federal Reserve Bank of Boston, Conference Series No 5.

Viner, J. (1937) *Studies in the theory of international trade*. New York: Harper and Brothers.

Wette, H. (1938) 'Collateral in credit rationing in markets with imperfect information: Note', *American Economic Review*, 73: 442–445.

Wojnilower, A. (1980) 'The central role of credit crunches in recent financial history', *Brookings Papers on Economic Activity*, 1980-2: 277–340.

Yellen, J. (1984) 'Efficiency wage model of unemployment', *American Economic Review*, 74: 200–205.

Chapter 17

THE MACROECONOMICS OF GOVERNMENT FINANCE

MICHAEL HALIASSOS*

University of Maryland

JAMES TOBIN

Cowles Foundation, Yale University

Contents

* Haliassos' research was partially supported by the Graduate Research Board of the University of Maryland, College Park.

Handbook of Monetary Economics, Volume II, Edited by B.M. Friedman and F.H. Hahn
© *Elsevier Science Publishers B.V., 1990*

0. Summary

This chapter is a critical survey of literature on the implications of government financial policy for economic activity. The central question is whether the mode of financing of a given path of real government purchases – by taxes, non-monetary debt issue, or money creation – has real effects, in particular real effects of macroeconomic consequence.

In Section 1, the Introduction, we define the issues with greater detail and precision. We briefly review economists' views, over the past fifty years, of the burden of public debt and the neutrality of money. Section 2 is a review of the 1960s vintage mainstream macroeconomics of fiscal and monetary policies, often called the "neoclassical synthesis". We review its implications for both short-run fluctuations and long-run trends. We include this review because the earlier tradition covers some problems and issues now neglected, because its analyses and results may still have some validity, and because they did set the stage for – one might say they provoked or inspired – the recent literature surveyed in Sections 4–6. The earlier tradition and the recent literature differ in methodology, and in Section 3 we discuss the "microfoundations" methodology that dominates contemporary macroeconomics.

Sections 4–6 are a selective critical survey of recent contributions, theoretical and empirical, designed to summarize the current state of play on the central issues: Section 4, the debt neutrality hypothesis of Robert Barro; Section 5, the effects of financing government expenditures by printing money rather than taxing, monetary superneutrality, and the "Fisher effect" of inflation on interest rates; Section 6, open market operations, and shifts between bond- and money-financing of government expenditures induced by the adoption of financial policies which are unsustainable over the longer run. In each section we first set forth the neutrality theorems purporting to show the irrelevance of the financing choice. Then we discuss articles elaborating or criticizing the theorems. In each case we conclude with a review and evaluation of some empirical tests. We conclude in Section 7 with short summary remarks.

1. Introduction

In the years 1945–1970 fiscal and monetary policies were widely regarded, both by economists and by policy-makers, as important instruments of macro-economic stabilization. Counter-cyclical variation of budget deficits (counting surpluses as negative deficits) was accepted as stabilizing, whether it arose as the passive result of built-in responses of revenues and outlays to economic activity or as the result of active tax and expenditure adjustments. Likewise, reactive counter-cyclical monetary policy was regarded, both by economists and by central bankers, as a useful, even an essential, stabilizer.

Subsequently, considerable disillusionment with "discretionary" policies, scornfully labeled "fine-tuning", swept professional and lay opinion. Government's ability and willingness to offset destabilizing non-policy shocks were questioned, and variability of policy instruments themselves became the favorite culprit for cyclical fluctuations. This shift of sentiment persuaded leading central banks to heed the advice of monetarists to adopt and adhere to money stock targets independent of the state of the economy, although never and nowhere to the degree the monetarist theorists prescribed.

In fiscal policy, the same shift revived the popularity of the norm of annual budget balance. In the United States in 1986 thirty-two state legislatures, the President, and majorities of both Houses of Congress supported a Constitutional Amendment mandating a balanced budget. Many economists now favor binding the central government to a fiscal rule limiting deficits. Others, however, advocate rules limiting the size and growth of government expenditures. Whether public claims on national resources are financed by taxes, by borrowing, or even by printing money is, in their view, of secondary importance.

The neoclassical counter-revolution in macroeconomic theory has lent powerful support to these intellectual trends. The two crucial strands in the New Classical Macroeconomics are *rational expectations* and continuous competitive *market clearing*. They reinforce the trained instincts of economists that unfettered markets yield optimal outcomes, that in particular there are no macroeconomic market failures which government need or can correct. They emphasize expectations of future policies as determinants of private behavior, a point especially important for macroeconomics. The famous "Lucas critique" of macroeconometrics [Lucas (1976)] says that the structures of behavior allegedly detected in econometric models will collapse if governments change policies to try to exploit them. Moreover, rational expectations models limit or obliterate the scope of monetary and other financial policies: if they are systematic, private agents will understand them and, by altering their behavior, undermine them; if they are random, the confusion of the public will make the outcomes inefficiently volatile.

1.1. The central questions

The expenditures of a sovereign central government can be financed by tax receipts, printing money, or borrowing. Does it matter in what proportions these three sources of finance are used to finance a given program of expenditures? Do deficits (excesses of expenditures over tax revenues) affect important macroeconomic variables: real output and its growth, unemployment, prices and inflation rates, nominal and real interest rates? Given the size of a deficit, does it make a difference whether it is covered by money or borrowing? These are the central questions to which this chapter is addressed.

Those questions are most significantly posed on several assumptions: the money is fiat money, inconvertible paper; it is not commodity money; it is not even convertible into gold or foreign currency at a guaranteed rate of exchange. Public borrowing usually takes the form of the government's promises to pay amounts of its money at future dates. Most models assume that the government does not promise to deliver commodities or foreign currencies; its debt is not indexed to money prices of commodities.

In practice, of course, many governments do borrow foreign currencies or index their debts to prices of commodities or foreign currencies in their own moneys. Those means of financing raise quite different issues, easier to analyze if not easier for the borrowing governments to manage.

A closed economy is a convenient assumption for most of the issues and literature of concern in this paper. Financial policies in open economies are specifically treated elsewhere in this Handbook (Dornbusch and Giovannini, Chapter 23).

Not all governments have the tripartite financing choice described above. In some countries there is no internal way to finance deficits other than printing money. Essentially fiscal and monetary policy are the same thing. Deficits create money, and there is no other way to create government (as opposed to bank) money. The literature of economic theory contains many models in which deficits are 100 percent monetized and fiscal and monetary policy are indistinguishable. It also contains models in which government money is the only store of value for the whole society. Land and capital are assumed away. These models not only exclude analysis of non-monetized deficits but also evade the issue of "crowding out", the alleged displacement of capital formation by the absorption of saving in government debt.

Our survey will cover some models of all these varieties. But the most relevant, in our view, allow governments both monetary and non-monetary alternatives to taxes in financing current outlays and allow private savers stores of value other than government obligations.

1.2. Some doctrinal history

The burden of public debt. The major question has long been whether borrowing, rather than taxing, to finance a given program of public expenditures can shift the burden of those expenditures to future generations. Laymen instinctively answer "Yes". For example, President Eisenhower solemnly preached against deficit spending, on behalf of the grandchildren and later descendants of his contemporaries. Among economists, however, the long-standing orthodox view was that internal debt could not shift the burden. "We owe it to ourselves." The resources used for government expenditures, for example war, are in a closed economy with full empolyment necessarily drawn from other *current* uses of resources. The reduction in resources available for current non-government use is the same regardless of the method of financing. Subsequent payments from taxpayers to contemporaneous bondholders redistribute income between members of future generations. But these transfers involve no draft on resources in aggregate, other than the deadweight loss of non-lump-sum taxes. That may have been deferred, but not the full real burden of the expenditures themselves.

This view was stated forcefully by Lerner (1943, 1944) in his theory of *functional finance*. He attacks as myths the balanced-budget norm and the fear that deficits burden future generations. As a Keynesian, he does not take full employment for granted. Given the government's expenditure program, the function of taxation is to control private spending; taxes should be set and varied as necessary to equate spending to full employment output. The debt should be monetized to the degree that will bring about the real interest rate needed to sustain the optimal rate of capital investment. Given the government's expenditure program and the desired rate of capital accumulation, adjustment of taxes will make sure that consumption demand equals the remainder of full employment output.

Lerner saw clearly that fiscal and monetary stimuli are substitutes in demand management. Various mixes of the two policies can achieve full employment. Which mix to choose depends on other objectives, specifically the desired division of output between consumption and investment. Lerner did not see that this degree of freedom in macroeconomic policy undermined his assertion that the burden of government could not be shifted to future generations.

After World War II the theory of the burden of public debt excited lively controversy among economists. See the symposium edited by Ferguson (1964), reviewed by Tobin (1965b). In the symposium and elsewhere, James Buchanan attacked the orthodox "no-shift" view on the ground that deficit spending clearly defers what he regarded as the true burden, compulsory payment of taxes. He argued that lending to the government, in contrast, is voluntary and therefore burdenless.

However, the more successful revision of doctrine was what may be called the *capital stock criterion*. This was the prevailing view of public debt burden among American Keynesian architects of the "neoclassical synthesis" and "neoclassical" growth models in the period 1946–65. Franco Modigliani was a forceful advocate of this criterion, also in the Ferguson volume. Government financial policies can, after all, affect the consumption opportunities of future generations. An important test is whether we would endow our descendants with a smaller or larger stock of capital, public and private, human and non-human, foreign and domestic. The neoclassical synthesis placed great emphasis on the monetary–fiscal policy mix, which Lerner had recognized as important. The criterion is quite consistent with Lerner's strictures on the policy mix. The same short-run path of real output can be achieved with tight money and high deficits or with tight budgets and easy money. The former combination will have higher real interest rates and lower capital accumulation and growth. On a flow basis, the deficit "crowds out" productive investment; on a stock basis, the debt displaces capital in the wealth portfolios of private savers.

The next move in this contest revived the older "no-shift" orthodoxy. Robert Barro's extraordinarily influential article, "Are Government Bonds Net Wealth?" (1974), rejected the theory of consumption and saving behavior underlying the arguments of Modigliani and other mainstream neoclassical Keynesians. According to Barro, private citizens will rationally anticipate the future taxes that any current deficit will impose on themselves or their descendants. The present value of these tax liabilities will be exactly the same as those of the debt instruments issued to finance the deficit. Internalizing the circumstances and utilities of their dynasties, current citizens will regard their net wealth as independent of current taxes and deficits. If their taxes are cut, they will not consume more; they will save the full amount of the tax cuts to enable themselves or their heirs to pay the postponed taxes. Buying the debt instruments themselves would be the perfect hedge. Much of this chapter, especially Section 4, will be devoted to discussion of this doctrine, which Barro called the Ricardian Equivalence Theorem [Ricardo (1817; 1951)].[1]

Debt neutrality, as asserted by the Equivalence Theorem, is to be distinguished from monetary neutrality. The debt burden controversy concerns *real* variations in tax revenues, current and anticipated, balanced by equal and opposite variations in real amounts of net public borrowing (or repayment and lending) at market interest rates. Debt neutrality means that these variations

---

[1]The point was not wholly absent from the previous discussion. For example, in Tobin's review (1965b) of the Ferguson book, he offers a comment which "questions the consumption-saving behavior assumed in the Modigliani notion of the burden. Is it not based on some asymmetrical illusion? Society fools itself into consuming more, thinking that possession of government paper provides for its future. Why don't those who will have to pay taxes to service the debt . . . consider themselves poorer and save more accordingly? This observation threatens not only Modigliani's concept of debt burden but equally the belief that the government can influence investment and growth by varying the fiscal-monetary mix. Indeed it comes dangerously close to denying that any internal financial and monetary arrangements are of any real consequence." Nevertheless, the author goes on to suggest that the government as a financial intermediary can "diminish some of the needs which generate saving", and to claim that the weight of empirical evidence is that "the private income and wealth corresponding to government deficit and debt stimulate consumption".

have no real effects. Monetary neutrality, on the other hand, means that variations in *nominal* quantities of government-issued fiat money have no real effects.

Patinkin (1956) called this ancient orthodoxy the *classical dichotomy*. Nominal variables have nominal effects. They do not alter real quantities. They may change the general price level but they do not affect relative prices. They may alter nominal interest rates but not real rates. The quantity theory of money asserts that variations of money stocks are wholly absorbed in nominal prices. This is what happens when government expenditures are financed by issuing money rather than by taxes. The nominal interest rate on base money is fixed, usually at zero. The public is induced to hold the new money by the price increases that raise the nominal values of income, wealth, and transactions. The conclusion is that only the real size, nature, and distributional impacts of government activities affect the behaviors of economic agents and real outcomes. Debt neutrality takes this conclusion further, excluding the timing of taxes from policies of real consequence.

A quantity-theory proposition stressed by Friedman (1970), for example, is that the consequences of increasing the money stock are the same no matter how it is increased. Printing money to finance deficits has the same effect as printing money to buy back government debt obligations. Critics objected that deficit financing increases private wealth, and therefore private demand for goods and services, more than open market operations of equivalent size. The reason is that in the latter case wealth-owners sell assets to acquire money. But if government bonds are not net wealth, the two ways of increasing money stock are identical in effect, as Friedman asserted.

Wealth effects on real consumption and other demands for goods and services have played an important role in macroeconomic theory. They are the source of the real balance effect, resulting from deviations of price levels from expectations [Pigou (1943, 1947), Patinkin (1948)]. These deviations alter the real values of nominal assets – and debts. Private assets exceed private debts to the extent that government debts do not give rise in private calculations to future tax obligations. Ricardian equivalence confines the real balance effect to monetized government debt. Perhaps it obliterates the effect altogether. Wealth-owners may not regard an increase in their holdings of government money as net wealth if they expect it to be eroded by future inflation. Seignorage in modern times is not literally the sovereign's take from coinage. The government can finance part of its budget by meeting the growth in public demands for its fiat money. These demands grow faster the higher the inflation rate, and the higher the economy's real growth. Seignorage is a kind of tax, alternative to explicit taxation.

The real balance effect came into macroeconomics as an answer to Keynes' contention that the market economy lacked an effective mechanism for restoring full employment, once a demand shock had jarred it out of equilibrium. Keynes challenged neoclassical economists' reliance on nominal price adjustments, on the neoclassical ground that real demand should be independent of nominal prices. In particular, Keynes said workers were incapable of lowering real wages by lowering nominal wages, although lower real wages were essential to remedy unemployment. Latter-day skepticism of the real balance effect strengthens Keynes' challenge. Today's new classical macroeconomists finesse the problem of equilibrating adjustment by assuming continuous equilibrium, to which nominal price developments are irrelevant.

The co-existence of monetary and non-monetary government debt continues to be a source of problems and puzzles in macroeconomic theory. Price changes affect the values of both the same way. Currency always bears zero interest; obligations to pay currency in future pay a variable market-determined rate. How come they differ in yields? The answer is that money provides implicit yields, services in kind, that make up for its lack of explicit return. These non-pecuniary yields, and therefore the explicit yield advantages of debt instruments, depend inversely on the real quantity of money. Recognition of this relationship and of its macroeconomic importance is one of Keynes' major contributions to monetary theory.

The fixed nominal interest on money has another major implication. Neutrality with respect to nominal price levels does not imply neutrality with respect to temporal changes in prices. Those changes – inflations and deflations – alter the real rate of return on money, and possibly on other nominal assets and debts as well. Variations in real interest rates are real events and are likely to have real effects. Since money and other assets are substitutes, albeit imperfect, variations in real rates on money will be transmitted to other assets, nominal and real, at least in the short run. This effect, often bearing the name of Mundell (1963b) or Tobin (1965a), will be discussed in Section 5 below. Models that somehow deny these effects are termed "superneutral".

2. Government finance in traditional macroeconomics

2.1. The IS/LM framework

Although Keynes eloquently stressed the heretical implications of his *General Theory* (1936) for fiscal and monetary policies, he did not actually model them explicitly. Hicks' (1937) algebraic formulation of the Keynesian model proved to be a fruitful and durable framework for macroeconomic policy analysis. Generations of students learned the "IS/LM" calculus of aggregate demand, and it is still the tool of instinctive first recourse of many macroeconomists.

Indeed, it is still the basic framework of macroeconometric models, large and elaborate as they have become because of disaggregations and lags.

Fiscal policy shifts the IS curve, monetary policy the LM curve. What could be simpler? The behavioral and structural parameters on which the effects of the policies on aggregate demand depend are easily discerned: the impotence of monetary policy in the liquidity trap (flat LM) or in the event both investment I and saving S are insensitive to interest rates (vertical IS); the impotence of fiscal policy if money demand is insensitive to interest rates (vertical LM) or if investment or saving or both are perfectly interest-elastic (flat IS); and all the cases in between. The analysis can be extended to derive aggregate real demand as a function of price level, allowing for the effects of prices on real supplies of money and wealth, and this "AD" function can confront an aggregate supply "AS" relation between the same variables.

As was Hicks' original intention, the same apparatus can show the effects of financial policies in the "classical" world of market-sustained full employment. Indeed, IS/LM graphs generally look qualitatively the same when the horizontal axis denotes price level, p, rather than real output, Y. The effects of inflation expectations – Mundell–Tobin effects – can be shown very simply, given the approximation that IS involves the real interest rate but LM the nominal rate.

Early in its life the Hicksian model was extended to open economies [Fleming (1962), Mundell (1963a)] and to the analysis of macro policies with and without international capital mobility and under fixed and floating exchange regimes.

Policy analysis with the framework was not confined to shifts in policy-determined variables; the policy-makers could be modeled as following rules, and the rules built in to IS and LM relations themselves. Welfare judgments among alternative rules would depend on the stochastic environment, for example, as in Poole's classic paper (1970) on the variances and covariances of real demand shocks and financial shocks.

2.2. Fiscal multiplier theory

Keynesian analysis of fiscal policy began with the "multiplier", invented by Kahn (1931) to formalize and quantify the instinctive beliefs of Keynes and others that deficit spending for public works during the Depression would create not only direct jobs but also indirect jobs, probably much more numerous. At the same time, the analysis showed why the chain of spending and job creation was not endless, why the multiplier was finite. Kahn's discovery paved the way for the *General Theory* itself, which could not have been written without the consumption function. Although the original idea of the multiplier referred to increases in government purchases, it was later realized that the same logic applies to private expenditures induced by tax reductions or transfer payments.

The explicit implications of multiplier theory for fiscal policy were developed in the late 1930s and the 1940s, largely by Alvin Hansen and his followers, mainly young colleagues and students at Harvard [Hansen (1941)]. Hansen (1953) was also an exponent of the IS/LM framework. As he realized, the multiplier tells the amount of horizontal shift of the IS curve resulting from a fiscal stimulus or other real demand shock, but this is not the end of the story. In any case, fiscal multiplier theory yielded some important elaborations and clarifications:

(1) Government budgets are partly endogenous. Congresses or parliaments enact tax codes, but the revenues they realize depend on their tax bases, and these vary with the state of the economy. The same is true of some budget outlays, notably entitlements to transfers like unemployment compensation, welfare, and farm subsidies. Legislation specifies rules for determining eligibilities and amounts, but the outlays then are open-ended and depend on the economy.

(2) In consequence, budget deficits are partly endogenous. In practice, they are, for given tax and entitlement codes and given expenditure programs, inversely related to economic activity, i.e. to national product. It is important to distinguish these endogenous variations in deficits (or surpluses) from those arising from exogenous policy changes in the codes and programs. The former have no multiplier consequences; they are already built into the multiplier and into the IS curve. The latter are multiplicands; they do have the consequences described by the multiplier and by shifts of IS. The distinction is the reason for calculating cyclically corrected budget deficits from year to year, eliminating endogenous cyclical variations and isolating programmatic changes. Deficit measures calculated for this purpose have, over a history that goes back to the late 1940s, been dubbed "full employment", or "high employment", or "structural".

(3) Taxes and transfers, as well as earned factor incomes, affect consumption spending. A common assumption has been that consumption and saving both depend positively on after-tax, "disposable" incomes. This implies, given the procyclicality of taxes minus transfers, that the multiplier is smaller the larger are the parameters that link tax liabilities positively, and transfer entitlements negatively, to income. A small multiplier limits fluctuations caused by non-policy shocks, and for that reason the elements of fiscal structure that lead to a small multiplier are called "built-in stabilizers". The same stabilizing structure makes deficits *more* sensitive to macroeconomic conditions.

(4) Not all structural budget changes of equivalent dollar amount have the

same effects on aggregate demand. One reason is that they differ as to "multiplicand". For example, part of a lump-sum tax cut or transfer increase will be saved, so that the multiplicand per dollar will be less than a dollar; in contrast, a dollar government purchase of goods and services increases aggregate demand for national product by a dollar even if no indirect multiplier effects occur. This distinction is the source of the celebrated "balanced-budget multiplier theorem", which says that a fully tax-financed one-dollar increase in government *purchases* raises aggregate demand by one dollar.

2.3. Cumulative effects of deficits

Keynes stated explicitly that his model applied to a short run in which the flow of investment determined by its solution alters negligibly the stock of capital. Indeed, that is his definition of "short run". The IS/LM version has this same limitation. It is necessary because changes in the stock of capital would alter the investment function, perhaps also the saving function and other behavioral relationships, and therefore alter also the equilibrium solution. The same is true of other stocks and flows. Saving accumulates wealth. Government budget deficits add to the stock of public debt. Current deficits on international accounts diminish the nation's net foreign claims.

IS/LM analysis usually ignores these stock-flow identities. Strictly speaking, fiscal multipliers apply to the effects of larger or smaller values of policy instruments, expenditures or tax rates, at an instant of time. No matter how large the deficit, a flow, it cannot change the stock of debt in zero time. Thus, the IS/LM snapshot cannot answer questions about alternative means of financing continuing deficits.

Of course, the LM relation, unlike IS, is equality of demand and supply of a stock, the stock of money. The snapshot model allows this stock to vary, presumably by open market exchanges for other assets, notably government securities. These exchanges, however, take no time and involve no saving or dissaving, although they may alter the value of those assets and of total wealth. Note that the IS/LM model contains a consumption/saving function describing the rate at which the public desires to accumulate wealth. But it contains no function telling in what forms, monetary and non-monetary, the public wishes to accumulate it. The money-demand function tells how, given pre-existing asset stocks as altered by instantaneous open market operations, the public chooses to divide its wealth between money and other assets.

These properties of the short-run Keynesian model were well understood by its architects. But in the 1960s and 1970s a number of critics "discovered" what they called the government budget "restraint" (surely a misnomer) or "constraint", and accused standard short-run macroeconomics of erroneously ignoring it or even violating it [Christ (1968), Currie (1978)]. What they meant but mislabeled is simply the budget flow identity: outlays equal tax revenues plus security issues plus new money creation. No error is involved in confining the analysis to a short enough time period so that the resulting stock changes do not matter. The question is, however, whether the comparative-static solutions of such a snapshot model with respect to policy variations are misleading. In particular, the standard model says that, except for extreme shapes if IS and/or LM, pure fiscal stimulus, i.e. 100 percent bond-financed increases of expenditures or reductions of taxes, raises aggregate demand. The critics said that this conclusion might be reversed as the time period is extended and the deficits raise the stocks of securities relative to those of money. Some econometric equations showed fiscal multipliers dying out and even reversing sign with the passage of time [Anderson and Carlson (1970), Modigliani and Ando (1976)].

It is hard to see how this reversal would occur in an under-employed economy with constant real money supply if the two-asset framework of the IS/LM model is maintained. In that framework, government debt securities and capital are perfect substitutes in portfolios, each bearing "the" real rate of interest, and the portfolio choice between that composite asset and money depends on income, wealth, and the nominal interest rate, as in the money-demand function. Could upward shifts of LM due to the rising stock of government securities, i.e. to rising private wealth, more than offest the upward IS shift and consign the economy to a higher interest rate at lower income? Both of those outcomes would diminish the demand for money. Only an increase in wealth could do the reverse. A decline in income would diminish the demand for wealth; only the rise in real interest could do the reverse. It could achieve the reversal only if it induced portfolio managers to hold more wealth not only in the assets whose yields had increased but also in the other one, money. So the story apparently depends on an unlikely combination of effects.

This technical issue – the permanence or transience of positive effects of pure fiscal stimulus on aggregate demand – inspired formal dynamic analysis. Blinder and Solow (1974) showed how the economy would gravitate to an equilibrium of budget balance: incomes would rise until they generated enough revenue flow to offset the continuing fiscal stimulus, inclusive of the rising debt interest outlays. Tobin and Buiter (1976) obtained essentially the same result, with more elaborate modeling of the effects of wealth and capital stock on saving and investment and of the dynamics and stability conditions of the model.

The upshot of these papers is to maintain over the longer run the conclusion of short-run analysis: pure fiscal policy is expansionary unless the interest elasticity of money demand is zero. However, the endogeneity of interest rates makes budget outlays for debt service endogenous also. Just as in short-run

IS/LM analysis there can be perverse comparative statics – expansionary policies cannot balance the budget except at lower output and interest rates. Just as in short-run analysis, these equilibria are unstable. A surprising conclusion is that the long-run multiplier for fiscal stimulus may well be higher if deficits are not monetized than if they are. The equilibrium interest rate is lower if they are monetized, and it takes less income to raise enough revenues to balance the budget.

These scenarios are meant to extend the calculus of aggregate demand to situations in which stocks are allowed to vary endogenously with the passage of time. To focus on the direction and magnitude of stock effects, the authors assume that output is demand-determined. The scenarios cannot be taken as realistic simulations, because supply limitations and price movements will intervene.

Tobin and Buiter also analyze the full employment case where prices are flexible. Output is supply-determined but varies with the capital stock. The comparative statics of balanced-budget equilibrium says that fiscal stimulus is expansionary and *lowers* interest rates, because it takes more income and thus more capital to generate the necessary revenues. The stability of the equilibrium requires that price expectations adapt fairly quickly to price experience. As the authors noted at the time, the long-run comparative statics of models of this type do not depend on counting government debt as net wealth. The budget-balance condition does the trick. Although these papers assume stationary labor force and productivity, they could be formulated as growth models, where the natural counterpart of budget balance is growth of debt (in real terms) at the economy's natural growth rate. Possibly more serious matters are the assumptions that all non-monetary assets are perfect substitutes, that saving and wealth demand are interest-inelastic, and that stochastic disturbances are absent.

2.4. Dynamics of deficits and debt

Some fifty years ago Roy Harrod in England and Evsey Domar in the United States independently originated modern macroeconomic growth dynamics. Domar (1944) applied his model to the growth of public debt. He saw the importance of comparing the debt interest rate (net of taxes paid on such interest) and the growth rate of output and income. Specifically, assume that enough taxes are levied to pay debt interest but not to pay for all other expenditures. The debt will grow. Will tax rates have to be raised without limit? Yes, if and only if the after-tax interest rate on the government's debt obligations exceeds the growth rate. The insight is important in interpreting the Ricardian Equivalence Theorem. In a growing economy, the "government budget constraint" that rational taxpayers will internalize is not that the public debt cannot grow, not even that it cannot grow indefinitely, but that it cannot grow forever faster than the economy itself.

Thus, interest on the outstanding debt differs significantly from other items in the budget. Interest outlays depend on the size of the debt accumulated in the past, on interest rates, on the degree of monetization, and on the composition of the interest-bearing debt by maturities and other characteristics of securities. Like taxes and transfers, interest expenses are, given prior fiscal history, largely endogenous. However, they do not depend directly on economic activity, but on interest rates as determined by the interactions of the economy, the financial markets, and monetary policy. Legislators have even less control over interest outlays in the short run than over tax revenues and entitlement transfers.

The *nominal* deficit, in dollars per year, is at any moment the rate $\dot{D}$ at which the nominal debt D is growing. Let X be the nominal *primary* deficit, the excess at that moment of the rate per year of expenditures, i.e. purchases and transfers, over the rate of accrual of tax revenues, excluding interest outlays from transfers and excluding tax liabilities on such interest from revenues. The primary deficit is what the deficit would be, other things equal, if there were no outstanding debt. Let i be the average nominal interest rate, after taxes, on non-monetary debt, and let H be the nominal amount of monetary debt, the monetary base. Then the deficit is:

$$\dot{D} = X + i(D - H) . \tag{2.1}$$

This is the deficit as conventionally calculated and debated.

However, there are good economic reasons to prefer other measures. A *real* deficit would convert D, H, and X to real quantities, "deflating" them by a price index, p.

Still another measure would charge as the cost of debt service the real interest rate rather than the nominal rate. Let the real after-tax interest on the non-monetary debt be r, equal to $i - \pi$, where π is the rate of inflation. The real inflation-corrected deficit is:

$$\frac{\partial}{\partial t} (D/p) = \dot{D}/p - \pi D/p = X/p + rD/p - (r + \pi)H/p . \tag{2.2}$$

The logic of this concept is "inflation accounting". The government's primary budget is geared to real programs, which cost more dollars when prices are higher; if the tax law is indexed, either formally or by periodic legislative adjustment, real tax revenues are neutral with respect to prices. The deficit is government dissaving, its claim on the nation's private saving in this sense: the amount of investment and other non-governmental claims on private saving that the government either crowds out (when aggregate supply limits output) or makes unnecessary for the maintenance of aggregate demand (when supply is not a constraint).

Private savers are presumably interested in real wealth and real streams of present and future consumption. If so, they will save extra in dollars to offset depreciation by inflation of their net real holdings of nominal assets, including government debt. They will understand that part of their nominal interest receipts is return of principal rather than income. Eisner (1985) has shown how conventional accounting overstated deficits in inflationary years of the 1970s; inflation accounting converts those deficits into real surpluses. However, saving behavior may not be inflation-neutral in the short run, even if savers eventually adapt.

The logic of inflation accounting can be pushed a step further to allow for real growth of output and income as well as inflation. Suppose that savers are interested in maintaining the ratio of their wealth to their income. Let d, h, and x be the ratios of D, H, and X, respectively, to nominal income pY. Let the growth rate of real income Y be g. Then the growth in the debt/income ratio d is:

$$\frac{\partial}{\partial t}(D/pY) = \dot{d} = \dot{D}/pY - (D/pY)(\pi + g) = x + (r - g)d - (r + \pi)h .$$

(2.3)

The first two terms by themselves say that unless the primary deficit is negative, the debt will grow faster than national income if the net real interest rate on the debt exceeds the growth rate of the economy. The last term is equivalent to a reduction of the primary deficit. It is the seignorage "income" of the government, the interest savings due to its power to print interest-free money. To the extent that this term is augmented by inflation, it represents the "inflation tax". In the United States h is small relative to d, of the order of 10–12 percent. Seignorage on base money is small at low or moderate rates of inflation, but there may be other ways in which inflation collects real tax revenue.

According to equation (2.3), the steady-state value of the ratio is:

$$d^* = (x - (r + \pi)h)/(g - r) .$$

(2.4)

Equation (2.3) itself says that the ratio d will be increasing if the primary deficit x less the seignorage term $(r + \pi)h$ is non-negative and the real interest rate r exceeds the growth rate g. Indeed,

$$\dot{d} = (d - d^*)(r - g) .$$

(2.5)

The steady-state debt/GNP ratio will be unstable, ceteris paribus, if and only if the interest rate on government debt exceeds the growth rate of the economy. A positive d^*, implying positive steady-state deficits, is compatible with $r - g > 0$ provided the primary deficit less seignorage is negative, but any initial deviation from d^* will be magnified.

Crowding out of capital accumulation (in open economies of net claims on the rest of the world as well as domestic capital) is the social cost of deficit finance that does not create its own saving. Suppose that the central bank's monetary policy keeps the economy at full employment with a constant inflation rate. Having no reason to expect future tax increases, consumers buy government debt issues with funds that otherwise would have financed domestic (and foreign) investment. The deficits finance private and public consumption. In a stable scenario ($r < g$) the shift from one steady state to another produces a slow and undramatic reduction in capital and consumption per capita. In an unstable scenario, developments are more spectacular and frightening. To the dynamic of equation (2.5) is added another destabilizing feedback – as capital becomes more and more scarce and its marginal productivity rises, the debt interest rate rises too. Eventually the deficit absorbs all private saving, investment ceases, the capital stock gradually wears out, and equity values plummet. The story [Tobin (1986a)] is meant not as a forecast but as a cautionary tale.

2.5. Multi-asset models

Macroeconomic models, both theoretical and empirical, are aggregative in several dimensions: over agents, time periods, commodities, markets, and assets. Index number problems, essentially insoluble, abound. Mostly we ignore them and try to muddle through. In monetary and financial economics, aggregation of assets is especially problematical. Some theoretical monetary models actually contain only one store of value, "money", thus managing to confuse the theory of money with the theory of saving. Consider the "islands" parables supporting the "Lucas supply curve", in which intertemporal consumption and leisure choices also determine demands for money. Some other models allow only two assets, base money and capital. As observed above, these models can illuminate some points, but their asset menu allows no distinction between fiscal and monetary policies.

The standard IS/LM model distinguishes two assets, money and everything else. The constituents of the second category, capital and non-monetary government obligations, are taken to be perfect substitutes, all bearing essentially the same market interest rate. Because of money's use in transactions and its other characteristics, the other assets are not perfect substitutes for money, whose fixed (usually zero) nominal yield is generally smaller than the yield of alternative holdings. As noted above, this model does allow for distinct treatment of monetary and fiscal policies and shocks.

Nevertheless, it has several shortcomings. Equities in real capital and obligations to pay fixed amounts of money are affected differently by various shocks to inflation, productivity, taxes, and other variables. They are portfolio substitutes, but by no means perfect. Their sources of supply are quite different. A three-asset menu – capital, base money, and government non-monetary debt – allows both monetary and fiscal policies to be more faithfully modeled. Open market operations between money and Treasury obligations, which may be bills maturing tomorrow or next week, are not the same as operations in equity or capital goods markets.

The three-asset model sheds light on the problem of Subsection 2.3. What happens when the stock of non-monetary debt is increased relative to the stocks of base money and capital, as the result of a period of bond-financed deficit spending? In particular, what happens to the rate of return wealth-owners require in order to hold the existing capital stock? If this rate goes down – that is, the prices of equities go up – the increase in stock of government debt is favorable to capital investment and to aggregate demand. If the rate goes up, the growth in debt is contractionary. The answer depends, speaking loosely, on whether money and debt are better substitutes than capital and debt. If so, the outcome is expansionary; if not, contractionary [Tobin (1961, 1963)].

Since government debts are futures contracts in government currency, they might be expected to be close substitutes for currency. This is especially true of Treasury bills maturing tomorrow, next week, or next month. By bank reserve requirements and other legal differentiae, governments seek to reduce the substitutability of money and short bills. Long-term government bonds, while connected to short-term obligations by a chain of maturity substitutions, also share many of the sources of risk of ownership of capital or private equities and bonds. It takes more than a three-asset model to handle the complexities of the situation. Tobin (1963) distinguishes long and short debts and considers the effects of debt management, i.e. variations in the maturity structure of non-monetary government debt.

B. Friedman (1977, 1978) has investigated both theoretically and empirically the basic issue: whether, as he puts it, debt accumulation "crowds in" or "crowds out" private capital formation. His conclusion is that the substitution elasticities are such that debt crowds *in*. This must be understood as a demand-side effect, which will prevail only if unemployed resources are available and the central bank does not contract the money stock.

Multi-asset models can be extended to "inside" assets and debts (deposits and other intermediary liabilities, and private loans and securities). In the process, the money markets and reserve requirements through which central bank operations affect banks, financial markets, and the economy can be explicitly shown.

Banks and other financial intermediaries hold, involuntarily and voluntarily, a considerable amount of public debt, monetary and non-monetary. This enables their depositors, the indirect owners of that debt, to hold more convenient and more liquid assets than the debt itself. A much more important macroeconomic function of financial intermediaries is to monetize or to make more liquid the ownership of private debts, the obligations of businesses, entrepreneurs, home-owners, and consumers. Their investments are financed at lower rates and on easier terms than if they had to be financed directly by conservative savers, who accept intermediary liabilities as close substitutes for government money and securities.

A short-run macro model should be regarded as referring to a slice of time or a finite period, with inputs from the past, modified by the solutions of the model in the present, passed on as data for the immediate future. At each time demands for additional amounts of all the assets are equated to the new supplies. New supplies of equities come from capital investment; new supplies of government bonds and base money, in proportions determined by monetary policy, come from the government deficit; new supplies of foreign-currency assets come from net exports. Rates of return, and output and/or prices as well, adjust to induce wealth-owners to absorb these additional supplies in their portfolios. The sums, both of demands and of supplies, equal the additions to wealth. Equations for inside assets and debts can be added; their net new supplies are zero. The non-government sector can be disaggregated, for example into households, non-financial businesses, various financial intermediaries, and the rest of the world. The model is the natural framework for giving life to the Flow of Funds statistics (published in the United States by the Federal Reserve).

The standard short-run comparative statics experiments can be run. For the most part, the qualitative conclusions of IS/LM stand up, but other questions can be asked and answered. Likewise the model's long-run, steady-state properties can be investigated. For details see Tobin (1982) and B. Friedman (1980).

3. "Microfoundations" and parables

In the last twenty years the traditional macroeconomics of government finance has come under heavy theoretical and empirical fire, especially within the profession. The attackers begin with the strong prior belief that strictly financial policies and institutions cannot have real consequences. Some entertain the hypothesis that even the government's real purchases and activities make no difference, because they simply displace private purchases and activities for which they are perfect substitutes. Otherwise, the government can alter real outcomes by doing real things, including the incentives and disincentives of its taxes, subsidies, and transfers. Given these characteristics, the real economy will be the same whether government outlays are financed by taxing or by borrowing or by printing money.

The philosophy underlying this approach is that government financial policy can do nothing that individuals could not have done on their own. There is no role for government as an intermediary between parties who could not have interacted otherwise; or as a creator of missing markets; or as a risk-pooler across agents subject to different sources of uncertainty; or as an agent with superior information utilizing this advantage to influence the economy in beneficial ways or simply conveying this information to others. Indeed, in most models aspects such as these are regarded as unnecessary complications or as arbitrary frictions. In subsequent sections we review this literature and its critics, both theoretical contributions and empirical findings.

Many contemporary theorists adhere to classical propositions more loyally than their original proponents: money is a veil, which may confuse unwary and myopic observers but does not affect the reality behind. Competitive markets work for the best, allocating resources among alternative uses, among different households and agents, among present and future times, and among possible contingent states of nature. Financial variables, nominal magnitudes, do not enter anyone's utility functions, resource constraints, or production technologies. Government financial interventions in markets can be undone by private agents, and optimizing agents surely will undo any real consequences. The neutrality of real outcomes with respect to nominal and financial disturbances and policies is the central message. The burden of proof, in the contemporary intellectual climate, is on those who would question these renascent classical propositions.

This trend is one facet of the New Classical Macroeconomics, which assumes continuous market-clearing and rational expectations; denies the existence of Keynesian unemployment; denies both the efficacy of and the need for policies of demand stabilization; and explains business fluctuations as optimal intertemporal substitutions in production and consumption.

Much recent literature expounds, tests, and criticizes the newly popular neutrality propositions. By and large, the exponents and the critics share the same methodologies. These involve models with explicit "microfoundations"; that is, they base economy-wide general equilibrium results on the optimizing behaviors of agents interacting in specified markets. However, critics also incorporate institutional constraints, missing markets, market imperfections, informational asymmetries, and externalities. The neutrality of money, the irrelevance of government finance, the ineffectiveness of macro policies, and the optimality of market outcomes are propositions that flow easily from and only from models that approximate or mimic Arrow–Debreu general equilibrium specifications. In these models, commodities are defined not just by their physical characteristics but by the times and contingencies of their deliveries. The microfoundations, the deep parameters, are the preferences of individuals, their endowments of commodities, and the technologies that transform commodity inputs into outputs. When government activities and policies are introduced, the question is whether any of these "deep" parameters are altered. If not, if, in particular, agents' opportunity sets remain the same, the conclusion is that the interventions under study make no real difference. Otherwise, the interventions matter. Many papers, some of which we review below, are variations on this theme.

The common methodology makes this literature, even more than most economic theory, a collection, indeed a battle, of parables. These fables are quite abstract and economically primitive. Each is designed to fit some "stylized" facts, particularly qualitative generalizations from macroeconomic time series. Each is intended to have a *moral* relevant to some realistic institutional observation of the world. The methodology limits the scope and realism of the parables; it is very difficult to draw any "big picture" inferences from this literature.

Walrasian and Arrow–Debreu models, in their full generality, yield important theorems concerning the existence and optimality of competitive market-clearing equilibria. They are silent on the comparative-static effects of exogenous shocks and interventions on individual and aggregate outcomes, even on the signs of those effects. The permissible scope of tastes, endowments, and technologies, especially of their heterogeneity among agents, is too great. Yet those effects are the central agenda of macroeconomics, which has always relied on simplifications and specializations of general equilibrium theory.

How can short cuts be made while adhering to microfoundations methodology? One way is to model the whole economy as a single "representative agent", a Robinson Crusoe. Then society's economic choices are those of a single optimizer, whose tastes and opportunity sets are just microcosmic versions of those of the whole society. It is easy to derive the basic propositions of the "Modigliani–Miller" theorem for government – neutrality, irrelevance, ineffectiveness – from models of this kind. It is hard to see why Robinson Crusoe has a government, or why that projection of himself has different objectives from those of private citizen Crusoe.

The "representative agent" model has other implausible implications: there are plenty of markets and market prices, but no transactions take place. There are, in particular, zero "inside" assets and debts. The problems of coordination emphasized by Keynes and other macroeconomists – between investors and savers, borrowers and lenders, capitalists and workers – are finessed. However, recent literature begins to recognize the shortcomings of this approach and to introduce two or more kinds of agents: rich and poor, liquidity-constrained and liquidity-unconstrained, even-period and odd-period bank customers.

The most usual differentiation among agents in current models is by birth date. The overlapping generations model with two-period lifetimes is heavily used, itself a parable with many instructive morals. Everyone is essentially the same, but in each period old and young coexist and trade. Government has a potential role as an immortal institution somehow embodying a compact among the generations. In contrast, a single representative agent model must make Crusoe himself ageless and immortal if it is to handle the intertemporal allocations – saving and capital accumulation – now properly regarded as central to macroeconomics.

On these allocations there is in principle a big difference between agents with finite horizons (because of mortality, generational selfishness, illiquidity, and/or myopia) and agents with infinite horizons (because of immortality, generational altruism, liquidity, and/or foresight). For the issues of theory and policy at stake, this difference is crucial. Infinite-horizon agents in steady states will typically accumulate wealth to the point at which assets yield returns equal to the agents' constant marginal rates of intertemporal substitution in consumption. Their demand for wealth will be infinitely elastic with respect to asset yields. Finite-horizon agents, on the other hand, will have finite demands for wealth at any rate of return; their savings may or may not respond positively to asset returns, but they will not respond infinitely. The rate of interest is determined by "thrift" *and* (marginal) "productivity" in the finite-horizon case, but by thrift alone in the infinite-horizon case.

One important issue to which the distinction is relevant is that of "superneutrality" in an economy with fiat money. Fiat currency has no intrinsic utility in consumption or production. And – this is crucial – its own yield is exogenously constant, usually zero. A dollar greenback today is a dollar tomorrow and tomorrow. Imagine that the stocks of fiat money and of promises to pay fiat money in future, and indeed the values of all predetermined and exogenous present and future nominal variables, are known. Suppose that all those values are scaled up or down in a common proportion. *Neutrality* means that no real variables – quantities or relative prices or interest rates – are different, while all nominal prices are scaled up or down in that same proportion. The common sense of this conclusion is that no one cares whether the unit of account is a dollar or a dime, and the contrived mental experiment is equivalent to a units change. The theoretical sense is simply that quantities of fiat money and other nominal variables do not enter anyone's utility or production functions.

Superneutrality, on the other hand, relates to a different experiment. All the nominal quantities are scaled up or down, not by a common factor but in proportion to their distance in time from the present, i.e. by $\exp(\pi t)$. It is not obvious that the paths of real variables are invariant to π, which can be identified with the rate of inflation. Such invariance is necessary and sufficient for *superneutrality*. But it certainly cannot be deduced simply from the absence of money illusion, the common sense of *neutrality*. Clearly, at least one real, relative price is immediately altered by the experiment; the real rate of interest on fiat money depends inversely on π. This alteration is bound to have repercussions throughout the system.

Superneutrality is usually defined, most precisely in relation to Solow-type aggregate growth models, as invariance of paths of capital stock and consumption with respect to monetary growth and price inflation. This invariance can arise from infinite elasticities of desired wealth with respect to yields on saving, as described above [Sidrauski (1967)]. Independently of how much capital they accumulate, these consumers will hold quantities of money, in real purchasing power, such that its real return too equals their constant supply-price of saving. The real return on money has two parts, the negative of the inflation rate and the implicit service return of money as means of payment; the latter depends inversely on the size of average real balances held. In Tobin (1965a, 1968, 1982), however, consumer-savers have finite horizons and finite demands for wealth, money and capital compete for room in their portfolios, and higher inflation increases the relative attractiveness of capital. This "Tobin effect" tends to raise capital stock and consumption. Against it is the resource cost (sometimes called "shoeleather cost") of handling transactions with smaller real cash balances, which tends to reduce real incomes, consumption, and desired wealth [see Tobin (1986b)].

4. Financing deficits with non-monetary debt

This section addresses the question of whether a shift from tax finance to bond[2] finance of given real government expenditures on goods and services with unchanged monetary policy absorbs any private saving. If it does not, "debt neutrality" prevails, i.e. investment, aggregate demand, realized income, employment, real interest rates, inflation, and the long-run capital intensity of the economy are not influenced by the choice between tax- and debt-financing. After a brief discussion of crowding out and of the interest sensitivity of saving,

---

[2]For simplicity, we use the term "bond" to refer to all non-monetary government debt of whatever maturity and form. We are not distinguishing bonds from bills or notes.

we investigate the theoretical conditions for debt neutrality. Then we present the implications of relaxing each of these conditions. We conclude with a review of available empirical tests of the debt neutrality proposition.

4.1. Crowding out and the interest elasticity of saving

A bond-financed decrease in taxation may lead to "crowding out" of two kinds: lower investment expenditure *flows*; and a lower desired ratio of the capital *stock* to real GNP in a long-run steady state. There are two main sources of stock and flow crowding out: supply constraints and monetary constraints. In standard discussions, these cause interest rates to rise, thus lowering both investment expenditure and the desired capital stock. For a given tax cut, the extent of crowding out would be smaller, the larger the interest-sensitivity of desired private saving and of the desired wealth-to-income ratio.[3] These are, of course, standard results in traditional IS/LM and growth models.

A recently popular framework for exhibiting interest sensitivity is the two-period life-cycle model in which a representative agent chooses consumption in each period so as to maximize his utility $U(C_1, C_2)$ subject to the constraint that the present discounted value of lifetime consumption is equal to the labor income received in the first period.[4] In this model, saving responds positively (negatively) to the interest rate if the elasticity of substitution between present and future consumption is greater than (less than) one. For a "Cobb–Douglas" utility function, the elasticity of substitution is unity and saving is interest insensitive. The convenience of the Cobb–Douglas specification, the dependence of the sign of response on the choice of utility function, and the failure of a significant number of empirical studies to identify interest-rate effects on desired saving, have created a presumption in favor of postulating interest insensitivity.

The validity of this postulate has been challenged by Boskin (1978) and Summers (1981, 1982). Summers argues that the choice of a Cobb–Douglas utility function does not allow the marginal propensity to consume to depend on after-tax interest rates, and that the use of a two-period model in which all income is received in the first period obscures the negative effects of increases

---

[3]In an open economy, international capital mobility causes foreign capital to flow into the country experiencing the tax cut, resulting in an appreciation of its currency, a fall in net exports, and hence a total or partial displacement of foreign investment by the bond-financed budget deficit.

[4]The life-cycle model is due to Fisher (1930) and to Modigliani and Brumberg (1954). An extensive discussion of the two-period consumption decision can be found in Feldstein and Tsiang (1968).

in interest rates on the present discounted value of lifetime labor income, human wealth. He incorporates both effects by considering a multi-period life-cycle model with an additively separable, constant-elasticity-of-substitution utility function and the constraint that the present value of lifetime consumption equal the sum of assets and of human wealth. Summers reports simulations showing that consumption responds more negatively to the rate of return when the elasticity of substitution is greater. Permanent changes in the after-tax interest rate reduce consumption by more or increase it by less than do transitory changes.

Among empirical studies, Boskin's estimate of an interest elasticity of U.S. saving of 0.4 is widely regarded as too high, and has been criticized by Howrey and Hymans (1978) as being sensitive to the choice of sample period and to arbitrary details of data construction. Summers criticizes statistical estimates of consumption functions for using current disposable income as a proxy for human wealth, for errors in measuring interest rates and expected inflation, and for simultaneity bias. His own estimates, based on first-order conditions of an agent's intertemporal optimization problem, also suggest that the elasticity is quite high. These estimates are derived from an optimization model, and the overidentifying restrictions imposed by the first-order condition are often rejected by the data. Whether the interest elasticity of saving is positive is still an open question, especially in view of the stylized fact of a trendless U.S. wealth-to-GNP ratio over long periods of time despite the upward trend in real rates.

Whether desired saving and wealth-to-income ratios are interest sensitive or not, life-cycle models do not imply infinite interest elasticities. When they are amended to incorporate people's concern for their descendants by allowing the size of bequests to enter the utility function, they still do not imply infinite planning horizons, in contrast to the alternative assumption that the utilities of descendants are what matters. The importance of bequests [as documented, for example, by Kotlikoff and Summers (1981), and Mirer (1979)], is not necessarily inconsistent with crowding out. The choice of how to incorporate the bequest motive is a matter of empirical plausibility.

4.2. The theory of debt neutrality and the optimum debt level

4.2.1. Debt neutrality

In 1974 Robert Barro presented the case for debt neutrality. According to this doctrine, also known as the "Ricardian neutrality" or "Ricardian equivalence" or "tax discounting" hypothesis, a bond-financed tax decrease does not affect agents' consumption demand, despite its effect on contemporaneous disposable income. When the economy is in a short-run, full-employment equilibrium, debt finance affects neither the path of prices nor that of interest rates. Finally, capital intensity in a long-run steady state is similarly unaffected. Clearly, one of the strongest implications of this doctrine is that bond-financed tax decreases and the associated deficits do not lead to any crowding out of private capital formation. Similar conclusions apply to variations of social security taxes, which transfer income between the young and the old.

A striking insight of the theory is that finite lives do not necessarily imply finite planning horizons: if the utility of every generation enters that of its predecessor, every agent incorporates the utility and budget constraints of the whole dynasty of successors into the decision concerning consumption and bequest levels.

A second key element in standard formulations of the theory is the assumption that government will not be able to service the debt by issuing more bonds forever, and that it will, therefore, eventually have to raise taxes. When this is so, it is inappropriate to analyze the effects of the bond-financed tax cuts without considering the implications of the associated future tax liabilities.[5] According to Barro, taxpayers will not alter consumption in response to changes in tax law because they regard them merely as changes in the timing of present and future tax liabilities of unaltered total present value.

While both issues will be dealt with extensively below, it is instructive to include a few comments on the latter one here. Practical macroeconomists and macroeconometricians have long factored into their policy analyses and forecasts consumers' and investors' anticipations of tax changes actually scheduled or under serious political and legislative consideration. An implication of life-cycle or permanent income theories of consumption is that current consumption will respond less to tax changes consumers regard as temporary than to those they regard as permanent. Financial market variables also have been used as indicators of expectations. If crowding out is expected to occur through higher interest rates in future, long-term rates should stand above short rates in the present. If deficits are expected to lead to inflation in future, this too should increase nominal longer-term interest rates.

"Ricardian equivalence" raises two interrelated questions. One is what constraint the government actually is under, or will behave as if it is under. The second is what private taxpayers and other agents believe to be the constraints and policies of the government. What degree of rationality must individuals possess in order to know not only how the economy works under given government policies, but also how policy decisions of the entire sequence of

---

[5]This sensible idea had been noted by Ricardo and by others before Barro, but it is not sufficient by itself to establish the equivalence of taxation and of bond financing. Indeed, Ricardo in 1817 argued against the practice of not repaying government debt accumulated during wars. His reasons were that either people would be fooled into thinking that they are richer or they would try to shift the burden onto others, possibly by emigrating. In either of these two cases, their current real consumption would go up [see Ricardo (1951, esp. pp. 244–249)].

future governments are arrived at? In the absence of any schedule for increasing taxes and in a political and ideological climate against taxation, would a citizen of the United States in the 1980s rationally expect future fiscal corrections?

The first question is easier to tackle analytically. Suppose that the interest rate exceeds the economy's growth rate. Then, if a limitless increase in the public debt relative to national product is to be ruled out, the present value of future tax revenues – discounting by the difference between interest and growth rates – must exceed the similarly discounted present value of expenditures by the amount of the current debt. This can be shown through recursive substitutions into the single-period government budget identity, and it is usually termed the "intertemporal government budget constraint". Although this constraint is incorporated in all standard discussions of debt neutrality, it is also possible for the real after-tax interest rate on bonds to be lower than the rate of growth of real GNP. In this case, the debt-to-GNP ratio is stable and the government can continuously issue new bonds to finance interest payments without ever having to increase taxes.

The argument usually employed in support of debt neutrality is that the condition for a stable steady-state debt-to-GNP ratio conflicts with the Phelps "golden rule" condition for dynamic efficiency. According to that condition, an economy with $g > R$ is overcapitalized in the sense that disinvestment could make consumption per capita higher in at least one year without lowering it in any year.

However, the efficiency condition refers to the net marginal productivity of capital, R. There are two respects in which R is not the same as r, the net interest rate on government debt. One is that the relevant marginal contribution of capital to social product is pre-tax, while the cost of debt service is after-tax. Since the Treasury cannot in fact rely on lump-sum taxes, the after-tax rate is lower. The second is that the marginal product of capital exceeds the interest rate on government debt by a risk premium. In the United States safe debt interest rates have generally been below the economy's growth rate, while mean returns on capital have been above. This is indicated by the fact that gross profits, RK, chronically exceed gross investment, gK [Abel et al. (1986)]. It is, therefore, possible to meet the debt stability condition without violating the dynamic efficiency condition for the economy. However, Ricardian Equivalence depends on the debt interest rate's exceeding the growth rate, and on the public's believing correctly that the government will not allow the ratio of its debt to the economy's output and income to increase without limit.

We now turn to the debt neutrality theorem. Tobin (1980) listed the restrictive conditions necessary for it to hold. A complete set of such conditions is the following:

First, agents are either immortal or, if finitely lived, linked by an unbroken infinite dynastic chain of intergenerational gifts and bequests. This condition is needed for agents to have infinite planning horizons and to be able and willing to undo any government financial policy that would redistribute real income intertemporally.

Second, capital markets are perfect, without liquidity constraints or credit rationing. Thus, private agents can lend and borrow on the same terms as the government, which has no role to play as a financial intermediary.

Third, all taxes, transfers, and subsidies are lump sum. This ensures that their effects on present and future agents are independent of agents' behavior. Hence agents can neutralize them only by compensating changes in their own intergenerational transfers.

Fourth, debt servicing through issuing more debt forever, is infeasible. Future tax increases, equal in present value to today's tax cuts, are required. Therefore, given rational expectations, these increases are foreseen by all living agents. This condition has been discussed above.

Formal proofs of the debt neutrality proposition usually employ an overlapping generations model where the utility of each generation is a function of its own consumptions in the two periods of its life, as well as of the maximum attainable utility level of the subsequent generation (and possibly of the immediately preceding one). It is shown that the effect of a bond-financed tax cut on the budget constraints of each generation can be offset by an appropriate change in voluntary intergenerational transfers. Thus, the maximum attainable utility levels of all generations are unaffected by the deficit, and optimal consumption levels do not change.

The intuitive reason for bond neutrality is that under the set of conditions presented above, the introduction of government bonds does not provide agents with opportunities they did not have under tax financing of government spending. Government bonds are simply a means whereby the current generation can undertake expenditure for which future generations will have to pay through increased taxes. If the optimal sizes of bequests both prior to and after the deficit are interior, then the current generation already had the option of transferring wealth from subsequent generations to itself by reducing the size of its bequest, but did not choose to do so. A similar logic applies to intergenerational gifts, and to retirement of outstanding debt by new taxes.

4.2.2. Tax smoothing and optimal debt

Suppose now that all the conditions necessary for debt neutrality do hold. If the choice between bond- and tax-financing does not entail any of the usually assumed costs (such as shifting the burden of the debt on to future generations and crowding out capital), then what determines the optimal path of government debt for a given path of government expenditures?

In his 1979 paper, Barro considers an economy in which debt neutrality holds, the paths of government spending and of real GNP are given, and (consistent with debt neutrality) the real rate of return on bonds relative to that on private debt is not affected by the amount of government debt outstanding. He assumes that perpetual bond finance is not possible. For a given initial bond stock and present value of government spending, the intertemporal government budget constraint determines the present value of tax revenues. The optimal type and timing of taxation remain to be determined with reference to their social costs.

Having ruled out most of the traditionally assumed costs through the postulate of debt neutrality, Barro postulates costs associated with the collection of government revenues. These costs are assumed to be a function of contemporaneous tax revenue and tax base. Abstracting from the choice of tax composition, the optimal timing of taxes is that which minimizes the present value of the tax collection costs for the present value of taxes dictated by the intertemporal government budget constraint. The solution can be shown to imply a constant (planned) average tax rate. This constancy, along with the given present value of taxes, determines the optimal level of tax revenues at each point in time, and accordingly the path of the government's bonded debt.

Barro shows that if the perceived duration of transitory changes in government spending and in income is constant, a temporary increase in government expenditure should have a positive (but less than one-for-one) effect on the current rate of growth of debt; whereas a temporary increase in the rate of growth of real income should have a negative effect. The debt-to-income ratio would be expected to remain constant on average, but would rise in periods of abnormally low income or high government spending. Expected inflation raises the growth rate of nominal debt by an amount equal to the inflation rate, because the optimal level of taxes is the same as under zero expected inflation, the real rate on bonds is assumed to be unaffected by changes in expected inflation, and the increase in nominal interest payments has to be financed through bonds.

4.3. The conditions for debt neutrality

We now investigate how dependent debt neutrality is on its assumptions by relaxing them one by one.

4.3.1. Infinite horizons and intergenerational transfers

Blanchard (1985) relaxes the assumption of infinitely-lived dynasties. He assumes that each agent is faced with a probability p of dying, constant through the agent's life. Here an agent can be interpreted either as an individual or as a dynasty with probability p of dying out.[6] Insurance markets costlessly eliminate the risk of leaving unanticipated bequests. Agents contract to pay their whole wealth, w, to the insurance company when they die in exchange for receiving pw in every period of life. Negative bequests are prohibited.

Agents are assumed to maximize expected utility of consumption over an infinite horizon with uncertainty only as to the time of death. When the instantaneous utility function is isoelastic,[7] aggregate consumption is a linear function of the sum of aggregate human and non-human wealth. Human wealth is defined as the present value of future after-tax labor income accruing to those currently alive. Under the simplest distributional assumption, that after-tax labor income is equal for all agents at all times, and given the constant probability of death, all agents have the same human wealth. Assume that the number of people who die at each instant is equal to the size of the new cohort born at that instant, so that population is constant. Then[8] aggregate human wealth accumulates at a rate equal to $(r + p)$. The intuitive reason for this key result is that agents discount income available tomorrow relative to income available today not only by the rate of return they could earn on it if it were available today, but also by the probability that they will not be alive so as to receive it.

Now consider a decrease in lump-sum taxes today, accompanied by an increase in taxes of equal present value T periods from now. This present value is calculated using interest rates r faced by the immortal government. Thus, the reallocation of taxes raises human wealth, as calculated by private agents, by an amount equal to the current tax cut times the probability that someone

---

[6]The assumed invariance of the probability of death with age ensures that the propensity to consume out of wealth is the same for people of all ages, despite the fact that their wealth levels may differ. This allows the derivation of an aggregate consumption function for general population structures. One drawback is that it does not capture the varying behavior of agents throughout their lives.

[7]An isoelastic utility function in consumption c is of the form:

$$u(c) = (c^{1-\sigma})/(1 - \sigma), \quad \sigma \neq 1; \quad u(c) = \log c, \quad \sigma = 1.$$

The (constant) elasticity of substitution is equal to $1/\sigma$.

[8]If aggregate human wealth is denoted by H, income by Y, and non-human wealth by W, then in the logarithmic utility case,

$$C = (p + \theta)(H + W), \quad \dot{H} = (r + p)(H - Y), \quad \dot{W} = rW + Y - C.$$

currently alive will have died by the time the future tax increase takes place. The longer taxes are deferred, the larger the effect on human wealth. Given that aggregate consumption is a function of human plus non-human wealth, this reallocation of taxes raises consumption. Debt neutrality fails.

One interpretation of this paper is that debt neutrality fails when agents have finite horizons, since the expected lifetime of an agent at each point in time is $1/p$. As p goes to zero, neutrality is approached as a limiting case. An alternative interpretation is that agents represent dynasties with infinite horizons but with a probability that they end because of exogenous events. It is also possible, however, that the chain of intergenerational transfers is broken because some members decide against further transfers.[9]

Drazen (1978) shows that a key element in determining whether dynasty members decide to break the chain or not is the weight their utility functions attach to the utility of other generations. Consider a utility function for generation i, $U_i = U_i(c_i^1, c_i^2, U_{i+1}^*)$, where c_i^1 and c_i^2 are real consumption levels of generation i in each of its periods of life and U_{i+1}^* is the maximum attainable utility of the next generation. Assume that utility functions do not differ between generations and that real wage income is constant. If bequests are invested at the time they are put aside by the parent, the extra utility that a parent receives from one dollar of consumption when old is exceeded by the utility of his descendant from consumption of $1 + r$ dollars of bequest. If the father weighs the descendant's utility equally to his (i.e. if $\partial U_i / \partial U_{i+1}^* = 1$), then bequests will be positive. If he discounts his descendant's utility by a rate equal to (larger than) the market rate of interest, optimal bequests will be zero (negative). If negative bequests (i.e. indebting your children for your own current consumption) are not allowed, agents will be at a corner solution of zero bequests, and the issue of government bonds will have real effects by allowing agents to shift the burden of their current spending to future generations.[10]

Finally, concern about both parents and descendants can be formalized by postulating that $U_i = U_i(U_{i-1}^*, c_i^1, c_i^2, U_{i+1}^*)$. Then a bequest that raises the descendant's utility also raises the utility of the father. But in doing so, it raises the utility of the descendant further. For bequests not to lead to infinite utility,

---

[9]Blanchard also shows that for a logarithmic utility function, the steady state r is between θ and $\theta + p$, and is an increasing function of θ. The finiteness of horizons discourages capital accumulation, since $r = \theta$ for infinite horizons. If labor income declines through life, this tends to raise the steady-state capital stock, with an ambiguous net effect and the possibility that the steady-state r will be negative (i.e. below the zero natural rate of growth of real GNP). In this case the level of the capital stock exceeds the "golden rule" level and the economy is dynamically inefficient, as in Diamond (1965). Finally, for the class of isoelastic utility functions the lower the elasticity of substitution, $1/\sigma$, the lower the steady-state capital stock.

[10]Considerations such as wage growth, taxation of interest, and population growth (in certain cases) further reduce the likelihood of positive bequests.

at least one generation must discount the utility of the other. If a generation weighs the utility of both adjacent generations sufficiently less than its own, then neither the gift nor the bequest motives will be operative and the introduction of government bonds will have real effects.[11]

Inoperative intergenerational links may exist for other reasons, for example that neither all members of a given generation nor all members of the same dynasty across generations are equal in natural endowments. Laitner (1979) postulates that there is an entire distribution of labor incomes in each generation. He assumes, somewhat artificially, that there is no correlation between the labor income of a family at a point in time and the incomes of its descendants. He then shows that a bond-financed tax cut that is repaid through tax increases T periods from now can affect consumption. This is because the government can always pick a finite T so large that some descendants within $0 < t < T$ have zero bequests with positive probability. Similarly, if the government makes transfers to and later levies taxes on all families (or a random cross-section of them), consumption will rise in a positive percentage of cases even with one-period bonds. This is because some families in each generation (or some generations of the same dynasty) cannot afford to leave bequests.

Not only is the ability of all future dynasty members to leave bequests uncertain, but also one's own ability to do so may not be foreseen at the beginning of one's career. Feldstein (1988) introduces uncertainty as to income in the second half of a parent's working life. Despite the presence of lump-sum taxes and the assumption that bequests are solely motivated by intergenerational altruism, current consumption rises as a result of debt finance (including the introduction of an unfunded social security system). The logic is that if the parent were sure that he would not leave a bequest, any increase in current disposable income arising from a tax cut would be divided between the two periods of his life. Since zero-bequest circumstances have positive probability, the parent will raise his current consumption to some extent. Even when the parent, blessed with good luck late in life, actually makes a bequest, the consumption of the second generation is reduced as a result of the tax cut the parent earlier enjoyed.

Although many of the papers on debt neutrality emphasize intergenerational transfers, most of them do not do full justice to human reproductive biology. Notable exceptions are two papers by Bernheim and Bagwell (1988) and Abel

---

[11]The discussion above assumes that bequests are in the form of non-human capital. Drazen argues that a significant share of bequests is in the form of investment in human capital, namely expenditure on the education of descendants. At least up to a certain level of education, such investment yields a higher rate of return than that on non-human wealth and could be used to enhance the father's own second-period consumption. When the father cannot enforce this liability on his descendant, the introduction of government bonds facilitates the transfer and thus has real effects. The enforceability of loans between parents and offspring would mitigate the importance of such considerations.

and Bernheim (1986). Bernheim and Bagwell (1988) demonstrate that in a properly specified dynastic framework, where everybody is "altruistic" towards members of the same dynasty and where the size of bequests per se is not a source of utility, redistributions of wealth leave everybody's consumption and resource allocation unaffected, prices play no role in resource allocation, and apparently distortionary taxes do not induce any change in individual behavior. Since these implications of the dynastic framework seem completely unrealistic, Bernheim and Bagwell argue that this framework should not be trusted for policy analyses. Debt neutrality is attacked through a reductio ad absurdum.

Specifically, Bernheim and Bagwell point out that when two individuals belonging to different families marry and have children, concern for common grandchildren links their two original families. The fact that these grandchildren also get married and have children means that more families of the current generation are linked by their common concern for those distant descendants, etc. Once it is established that two families of the same generation are linked, we can extend the chain further by moving up or down the family tree. Moreover, dynasties will typically be linked through multiple channels. Everybody is a part of every dynasty.

The authors assume that in each period t there is a chain of operative linkages connecting any two living individuals, where each link consists of a transfer made sometime between periods t and $t + T$, with T an integer. They show that for each sufficiently small perturbation of deficit and tax policies, there exists an equilibrium in which factor prices, labor supplies, consumption, and purchases of physical capital are unaffected by the perturbation. The perturbation simply leads to offsetting private transfers and bond purchases. This is true not only for government financial perturbations, but for *all* exogenous shocks, for example in the natural endowments of different agents. These results survive the introduction of various types of uncertainty and informational asymmetries.

Can a dynastic framework with frictions generate plausible conclusions? Abel and Bernheim (1986) introduce frictions such as (a) the derivation of pleasure directly from the act of giving; (b) the existence of both selfish and altruistic parents combined with incomplete information about others' preferences; and (c) social norms dictating that parents should divide transfers equally among all their children. Their overall conclusion is that frictions tend to make redistributional policies non-neutral, but they lead to paradoxes of other kinds.

As an example, consider case (c). Suppose that no parent is selfish; that the size of transfers is not a direct source of utility; and that parent i receives a transfer. In response to it, he raises his transfers to both his children by the same amount. Now consider the two sets of parents of the spouses of those children. They observe that one of their children is better off and, as a result, increase their consumption and lower their transfer. Because of the social norm, however, this reduction of transfers applies to their other children as well. In turn, the families of the spouses of those other children raise their transfers, etc.

Thus, although exact Ricardian equivalence with respect to policies that affect children equally is maintained here, redistributional policies that affect children differentially are not neutralized by the parents due to egalitarian constraints. It would seem that the Berhneim–Bagwell paradox has been resolved and the Barro theorem rescued from the reductio ad absurdum. The disturbing feature of this setup, however, is that an exogeneous increase in the wealth of any given individual is never Pareto improving, i.e. always makes some people worse off. In view of this paradoxical implication, and of similar implications for other frictions, Abel and Bernheim conclude that such frictions cannot provide Ricardian equivalence with a plausible theoretical foundation.

Gifts and bequests can be viewed not only as manifestations of altruism but also as assets transferring consumption from one period of life to the other. Buiter (1979, 1980) and Carmichael (1982) suggest that, under certain conditions, government bonds are perfect substitutes for gifts and bequests in this role. For example, when gifts to parents are reduced, agents can increase their first-period consumption since they offer less to their parents, and lower their second-period consumption since they receive less from their children. Thus, a bond-financed tax cut that substitutes second- for first-period consumption may be neutralized through an appropriate general adjustment of gift and bequest levels for all generations. This result does not require that taxes be eventually raised to service the debt.[12]

4.3.2. Perfect capital markets?

A second condition for debt neutrality is that there are no capital market imperfections leading to credit rationing. There is now a substantial volume of research on the sources and implications of credit rationing, starting with the seminal paper of Weiss and Stiglitz (1981). As an example, suppose that because certain individuals have relatively bad collateral, they can only borrow at a rate r_H which is higher than that for others, r_L. As recognized by Barro (1974), when a government bond is bought by a low-discount-rate individual and the proceeds and taxes associated with it are both distributed in the same way among the two classes of individuals, the bond is in effect a loan from the

---

[12]An exchange with Burbidge [Burbidge (1983, 1984) and Buiter and Carmichael (1984)] shows that in order for this stronger neutrality proposition to hold, the same type of intergenerational transfer has to be operative both before and after the tax cut, a condition which is difficult to meet for large increases in the amount of debt introduced, since these are likely to induce movement to corners with respect to transfers. When this happens, bonds are not neutral, as argued above. By contrast, Burbidge's formulation yields neutrality even for large additions to the stock of bonds, provided that gifts or bequests exist before the tax cut and that future tax increases are necessary.

low-discount-rate to the high-discount-rate individuals. The net wealth of the low-discount group is unaffected, but that of the other group rises since the rate r_H by which they discount the future tax liabilities is higher than the rate r_L by which those who hold the bonds discount the stream of coupon payments. Thus, one would expect the consumption of the high-discount group to go up in response to the increase in their net wealth.

This idea is imbedded in a formal model of credit rationing by Webb (1981). Webb argues that the government's ability to enforce tax repayments is superior to that of private lenders. There may be a higher default penalty for taxes than for private debts, and tax withholding ensures that the government receives payment before any other payments are made. The rate at which the government borrows and lends is therefore below that offered to individual borrowers in the private capital market. A substitution of government for private debt raises agents' net wealth due to this difference in interest rates. It may even be sufficiently large to bring the total volume of private debt below the critical level required to eliminate the occurrence of default in the private market. Debt neutrality fails.

The relative quantitative importance of finite horizons and of capital market imperfections is addressed in two recent papers. Poterba and Summers (1986) employ a life-cycle simulation model to consider the effects of debt-financed transfers of one dollar to each living person for K years. It is assumed that the debt is never repaid, but beginning in period $K + 1$, the government levies lump-sum taxes on working individuals to meet its interest payments and maintain a target real debt stock, aggregate or per capita. Simulations for a range of parameter values suggest that although deficit policies may transfer substantial tax burdens to future generations, they have only trivial short-run effects on consumption and saving. The intuitive reason is that for all but the oldest consumers, marginal propensities to consume out of wealth are quite small. This conclusion is only strengthened by considering realistic debt repayment periods. When the effects of current deficits are simulated on the basis of alternative scenarios for future deficits, even dramatic changes in deficit paths have only minor effects on consumption and saving.

These results suggest that in the absence of liquidity constraints and myopia, the distinction between overlapping generations and infinite-horizon models may be of little practical importance in evaluating short-run (but not necessarily long-run) effects of deficit policies.

Hubbard and Judd (1986a, 1986b) provide additional support for emphasizing liquidity constraints rather than finite horizons. In one illustration they consider agents with logarithmic utility functions and constant probabilities of death and of experiencing a wage increase from w_1 to w_2. With no capital market imperfections and for plausible parameter values, numerical simulations indicate that the marginal propensity to consume (MPC) out of a five-year tax cut financed with a twenty-year delay, during which time people die at a rate of 2 percent per year, would only be about 0.05. Finite horizons per se are not sufficient to generate sizeable effects on consumption. By contrast, the MPC is more than quadrupled when 20 percent of the work force are liquidity constrained and consume all their wages.[13]

4.3.3. Lump-sum taxation?

The third condition for debt neutrality is that taxes and transfers are lump-sum. It is well known that governments cannot typically rely on such taxes for the bulk of their revenues. It is thus appropriate to check the robustness of the theorem under distortionary taxation. When taxes are not lump-sum, the behavior of descendants can be adjusted so as to reduce the impact of tax increases, and this will be taken into account by the current generation experiencing the tax cut. Specifically, there is no reason for the parents to raise their bequest by the entire present value of future taxes implied by the current budget deficit. They will raise their consumption, knowing that their children will manage to reduce their future tax liabilities.

There has been some research on non-lump-sum taxes when the tax base is uncertain. When the increase in expected future taxes is combined with a current tax cut equal to its present value, the present value of total expected tax payments is unaffected. However, an increase in future income taxation reduces uncertainty surrounding disposable income. When income taxes are levied on descendants of the current generation, this logic implies that there will be downward pressure on bequests and upward pressure on current consumption, to the extent that the size of bequests is influenced by the parents' internalization of risk faced by their descendants. In fact, simulations by Barsky, Mankiw and Zeldes (1986) show that for plausible parameter values, the marginal propensity to consume out of a current tax cut associated with uncertain future tax liabilities is in the neighborhood of values implied by neo-Keynesian models that ignore the future tax liabilities.

4.3.4. Limitless debt?

All of the above conditions deal with whether a substitution of lower taxes and more bonds today for higher taxes in the future affects agents' opportunity sets. The question addressed in our introductory discussion of debt neutrality

---

[13]A liquidity constraint may be regarded as a very short horizon, much shorter than a lifetime. Hubbard and Judd also point to the relevance of the distribution of the tax cut for the effect on the aggregate MPC. In particular, if the tax cut is not uniform but results in greater relative relief for the high-income group, the effect of borrowing constraints on the aggregate MPC out of a temporary tax cut is dampened. This questions the practice of regarding the measured MPC as a good indicator of the proportion of liquidity-constrained individuals in economies with proportional or progressive tax systems.

above was whether bond-financed tax cuts do in fact necessitate future tax increases. This was the subject of the early debate between Barro (1976) and Feldstein (1976), who focused on whether the real after-tax interest rate on bonds is higher or lower than the rate of growth of real GNP.

Some recent research on whether real consumption is affected by tax cuts which are never paid for through higher future taxes has been conducted in a game-theoretic framework. An example is the paper by O'Connell and Zeldes (1987) who take up a suggestion by Gale (1983). Gale interprets Barro's dynastic framework as a game played among successive generations. He shows that this game has a vast multiplicity of equilibria, leaving individual behavior indeterminate. O'Connell and Zeldes look at a refinement of this equilibrium set. They start with an overlapping generations model in which debt neutrality cannot be ruled out with respect to debt that is repaid through higher future taxes. They then ask whether current tax cuts would affect consumption if the government never increases taxes in the future. They find that the set of quasi-steady-state Nash equilibria (i.e. those involving unchanged consumption) is unaffected by this experiment. However, there also exist pairs of equilibria across which government financing produces real effects. The authors present an economy with bequests where debt neutrality fails. This is because under certain conditions dynasties behave as though they value terminal wealth, which in turn depends on the size of government debt. Per capita consumption rises, despite the fact that the set of equilibria is unaffected by financial policy.

4.4. Empirical tests of debt neutrality

There are two main approaches to empirical testing of debt neutrality. One consists of structural estimates of consumption or savings functions or of financial sector behavior, and of tests for the statistical significance of taxes, transfers, government debt, and (sometimes) social security wealth. The other is to utilize the assumption of rational expectations to derive cross-equation restrictions and jointly test debt neutrality along with rational expectations and the assumed model of behavior.

4.4.1. Structural estimation

The older approach is structural estimation. The main implications of the debt neutrality hypothesis for the consumption function are: (i) that for a given path of government purchases, variation of taxes has no effect, i.e. the coefficient on taxes in a consumption or saving function should be zero; (ii) since transfer payments are analogous to tax reductions, the same holds for the coefficient on transfers; (iii) since a change in the stock of bonds does not generate a wealth effect on consumption, its coefficient should also be zero;[14] and (iv) if a proxy for social security wealth is included, its coefficient should also be zero, since according to Barro, households will save enough to compensate future generations for the extra tax burdens required to pay higher social security benefits.

There are two main issues that differentiate papers in this strand. The first is the extent to which they test and correct for simultaneity bias resulting from possibly endogenous right-hand-side regressors, such as income, wealth, taxes, transfers, and social security wealth. The second concerns the proxies used for permanent income and the permanent (as opposed to transitory) levels of policy variables.

Early papers estimating consumption or savings functions without allowing for simultaneity bias include Barro (1978), Kochin (1974), and Tanner (1979), who all find support for debt neutrality. On the other hand, Buiter and Tobin (1978) reach the opposite conclusion.

Feldstein (1982) allows for endogeneity of tax revenues and of income by using the lagged value of taxes and of income as instruments. He uses current GNP and then current personal disposable income as proxies for the corresponding permanent levels of these variables. Results do not favor debt neutrality. Feldstein looks at U.S. data for 1930–77 with the war years 1941–46 omitted. When real per capita GNP is used in a regression with real per capita consumer expenditure as the dependent variable, the hypothesis that the coefficient on taxes is not negative can be rejected at approximately the 20 percent significance level, the coefficient on the debt variable does not support the irrelevance of debt, and that on transfers is significant and positive. However, the coefficient on social security wealth is smaller than its standard error. Results are more strongly against debt neutrality when personal disposable income per capita is used as a proxy for permanent income. Feldstein also finds an insignificant coefficient on the government purchases variable suggesting that government spending does not directly crowd out private consumption by providing a substitute for it.

In a recent paper, Seater and Mariano (1985) estimate specifications similar to those of Barro (1978) and Feldstein (1982) by two-stage least squares with first-order serial correlation correction, in an attempt to remove simultaneity bias. They argue that Feldstein's use of only lagged taxes and income as instruments may not be sufficient, as these instruments may still be correlated with the error due to the high degree of serial correlation in the series for

---

[14]If both the stock of bonds and that of total wealth (including bonds) are entered, then the coefficient on the bond stock should be the negative of that on wealth, so that the total effect of bonds is zero.

income and taxes. They use a variety of instrument sets and for each one they apply Hausman tests to determine which right-hand-side variables are endogenous. They then perform the second-stage regressions using fitted values for these variables which did not pass the Hausman test. Although the endogeneity of regressors is sensitive to the choice of instrument set, the conclusions from the second-stage regressions are fairly robust. For Barro's specification, they find support for tax discounting. When using Feldstein's specification, both taxes and transfers become significant for the periods 1931–40/1947–74, questioning tax discounting. However, in a specification which includes unemployment, taxes become insignificant while transfers remain significant.

In the main body of their paper, Seater and Mariano follow Barro (1983) in speficying consumption as a function of: (i) permanent income; (ii) the cost of government represented by its "permanent" real expenditure on goods and services G^P; (iii) current real government expenditure on goods and services G to capture the possibility that increases in G for given G^P partially substitute for private consumption: and (iv) real after-tax interest rates since they induce intertemporal substitution. They estimate permanent income and permanent government expenditure only from these series' own histories. The regressions they run include separately four "financing" variables, namely real tax collections, real transfers, the real market value of outstanding government debt, and social security wealth. The estimation technique is instrumental variables and the sample is 1929–75. The government financing variables, including transfers, are jointly and individually insignificant, in regressions both for total consumption and for consumption of non-durables.

Kormendi (1983) examines roughly the same period (1930–76) under the assumption that government consumption (defined as the portion of government spending that yields utility to the private sector in the current period) is substitutable for private consumption, in the limit perfectly. This is yet another equivalence, challenging the effectiveness even of variations in government expenditure on goods and services. He derives a private consumption function based on this "consolidated approach". The counterpart of integrating private and government consumption is a "total disposable income" that includes the resource flow both from net private incomes and from taxes, since the latter effectively represent claims to government-provided goods and services. "Government" here means federal, state, and local government. Private consumption is a function of total real NNP, government consumption, wealth, and any discrepancy between the values of foregone private goods or services and those provided by government (which Kormendi calls "government dissipation"). By contrast, the standard permanent-income approach would make consumption a function of personal disposable income (defined as income net of taxes, corporate retained earnings, transfers, and government interest payments on its debt), but not of government consumption. Moreover, the market value of government bonds should not affect consumption under debt neutrality. Thus,

Kormendi obtains a set of testable restrictions, similar to Feldstein's, to differentiate the two approaches.

In his estimation, Kormendi uses current and lagged NNP as proxies for permanent NNP. Looking at differenced U.S. data between 1930 and 1976, he finds support for the "consolidated approach", with a fairly high implied substitutability between government and private consumption. With regard to government bonds, Kormendi's results show that there is less than 5 percent probability that future taxes implied by government debt are less than 90 percent discounted. However, the coefficient on transfers is significantly positive, a result which Kormendi attributes to redistribution of income among classes with different spending propensities.

Kormendi's strong results have been challenged by Barth, Iden and Russek (1986), by Modigliani and Sterling (1986), and recently by Feldstein and Elmendorf (1987). The first paper updates Kormendi's sample through 1983, distinguishes between federal and state–local government debt, and also looks at more recent postwar periods. The results raise some doubts about the robustness of Kormendi's findings. Modigliani and Sterling show that when Kormendi's separate tax, transfer, and government interest variables are combined into a single "net tax" variable, the sum of its distributed lag coefficients is significantly negative in the consumer expenditure equations and is not significantly different from the sum of the lag coefficients on NNP. The government purchases coefficient is statistically insignificant. They also point out that Kormendi's specification does not allow for the relatively long lags required to approximate permanent income, and that his practice of running regressions in first differences is inconsistent with his own estimated autoregressive coefficient, which is below unity.

Feldstein and Elmendorf argue that Kormendi's results are mainly due to the inclusion of the Second World War years. In that period, deficits were run to finance a massive increase in defense spending while rationing, patriotic appeals, and shortages were producing abnormally high saving rates. When they exclude these years, they obtain insignificant effects on private consumption of government purchases, along with significant negative effects of tax receipts.

No clear conclusions on debt neutrality emerge from the articles reporting structural estimations. Results seem quite sensitive to the choice of data, of variables to be included, and to estimation procedures. Kormendi's hypothesis that government purchases replace private consumption to significant degree remains a conjecture which requires further testing.

4.4.2. An alternative to structural estimation

A second set of tests seeks to avoid structural estimation that is subject to misspecification bias. Aschauer (1985) defines effective consumption as the sum of private consumption plus θ times government purchases of goods and services, where θ represents the number of units of private consumption required to yield the same utility as one unit of government goods and services. He shows that the first-order conditions for utility maximization[15] are (i) the intertemporal budget constraint and (ii) a condition involving consumption similar to the one estimated by Feldstein, but with the discounted values of future labor income and government purchases also entering the regression.

The procedure then is to combine this relationship with an assumed process for forecasting current government purchases and derive the cross-equation restrictions implied by the joint hypotheses of rational expectations, debt neutrality, the specific optimization model, and the postulated process for government spending. Aschauer estimates the system by FIML both with and without parameter constraints and carries out a likelihood-ratio test for the restrictions implied by the hypotheses. He finds that the restrictions cannot be rejected at the 10 percent significance level (or lower).

Plosser (1982) considers a model combining the efficient market hypothesis, a simple version of the expectations theory of the term structure,[16] and an assumed moving-average representation of policy variables to derive and test cross-equation restrictions. The first two assumptions ensure that the surprise in the holding return of an n-period bond bought at time t and sold at time $t + 1$ as an $(n - 1)$-period bond is negatively related to the unexpected movement in the current one-period rate, $(R_{1,t+1} - E_t R_{1,t+1})$, and to the revisions in the forecasts of future one-period rates, $(E_{t+1} R_{1,t+j} - E_t R_{1,t+j})$, $j = 2, \ldots, (n - 1)$. He also assumes that the reduced form for the one-period interest rate includes government spending, government debt held by the public, and government debt held by the monetary authority. The vector of exogenous[17] variables, augmented by the error in R_1 which is orthogonal to the policy variable, is assumed to have a moving-average representation. Under those assumptions, the current surprise in holding period returns is a function of the contemporaneous innovations in the exogenous variables (including policy variables) which are orthogonal to the innovations in the other exogenous variables.

Plosser jointly estimates an assumed autoregressive scheme for policy vari-

---

[15]Aschauer assumes that a representative agent maximizes a quadratic utility function with a positive discount rate over an infinite horizon, subject to the constraint that the present value of "effective consumption" is equal to net wealth (excluding government bonds) plus the present discounted value of labor earnings plus (a multiple of) the present value of government expenditure.

[16]See Chapter 13 by Shiller and McCulloch in this Handbook for a discussion of empirical tests of the expectations theory of the term structure.

[17]The assumption that these variables are exogenous can be relaxed with minor changes in the interpretation, as shown by Plosser.

ables with one form of the equation for the innovations in holding returns. The technique is to stack the two equations to form a single regression and estimate it using a non-linear GLS procedure. He uses 1954–78 quarterly U.S. data and finds that the effects of surprises in government financing on nominal rates of return are statistically insignificant, with point estimates of the "wrong" sign. Innovations in government spending, on the other hand, do have significant effects on interest rates. Plosser tentatively attributes those to intertemporal substitutions.[18]

Although this strand of literature provides an interesting alternative to structural estimation, it is also subject to the criticism that the processes assumed to be used by the public in forecasting may contaminate expectational variables with measurement error. This would bias the tests towards finding no impact of policy surprises, thus favoring debt neutrality.

4.4.3. Potential for future research

There is no clear conclusion emerging from the empirical research on debt neutrality. This is disturbing, though not very surprising. Bernheim (1987) points to some of the difficulties: picking the proper measure of debt or deficit; purging regressors of endogeneity by the choice of appropriate instruments; not allowing the limited significance of short-run effects to obscure the potentially considerable significance of long-run effects. Another problem is the distinction between the anticipated and unanticipated components of fiscal variables. Anticipated policy changes in a world without frictions would have little contemporaneous effect when actually implemented, but this does not mean the policies are irrelevant for individual behavior. To make things worse, current private behavior may be mainly a response to what current policy settings imply about future settings, specifically to the debt repayment horizon that taxpayers perceive as likely.

Econometric difficulties notwithstanding, one cannot ignore what must be the best "controlled experiment" for the hypothesis, namely the U.S. tax cuts of the early 1980s. Poterba and Summers (1986), among others, have drawn attention to the fact that private saving has declined while taxes have been cut and enormous chronic deficits have arisen. Their regressions show that when tax collections were reduced by legislation, consumption did increase, despite the fact that tax changes were anticipated. These events have to be explained away before it can be claimed that there is strong empirical support for debt neutrality.

---

[18]The results are unchanged when the assumed information set of agents is augmented to include current and lagged short- and long-term interest rates as predictors of future values of policy variables; and when the processes for policy variables are differenced to eliminate non-stationarity.

5. Financing deficits with money

This section deals with substitutions of money for tax financing. Every dollar of deficit is a dollar increase in the stock of high-powered money. If changes in the rate of monetary growth have no real effects, then money is said to be "superneutral", as in Section 3.

Usually, superneutrality refers to the invariance of the capital stock (or the capital–labor ratio), and of real per capita aggregate consumption with respect to changes in monetary growth. Effects on real (per capita) money holdings are not regarded as violating superneutrality. We present both models focusing on invariance of steady-state equilibrium values of real variables, and those investigating the transition path.

5.1. Superneutrality in the steady state

Tobin (1965a) made a case against monetary superneutrality based on portfolio effects of changes in the rate of monetary growth. A higher rate of nominal money growth is associated with a higher rate of steady-state inflation. Since the nominal interest rate on money is constant, usually at zero, this higher inflation lowers the real rate of return on money and makes it less attractive to hold. When the asset demand for capital depends not only on its own real rate of return, but also on how this rate compares with that on the alternative available assets, higher inflation encourages a portfolio shift away from money and into capital. Thus, money is not superneutral. This is known as the "Tobin effect" or the "Mundell effect".[19]

Increases in inflation may favor capital accumulation, at the expense of real money balances. But they also increase the resources needed to effect any given volume of transactions. These "shoeleather costs", which were not explicitly recognized in Tobin (1965a), should be set against the gains from the portfolio effects in assessing consumption and welfare. Tobin (1986b) shows that there are cases in which it is optimal for the government to raise inflation so as to reap the benefits from increased capital and output, despite the resulting increase in "shoeleather costs".

The Tobin effect is what exponents of superneutrality question. They consider variations in deficits and in monetary growth arising from changes in the size of transfers or taxes for given government purchases of goods and services. Superneutrality is proved by showing that the equilibrium condition

---

[19]Note that when private saving is interest-sensitive, as discussed in Subsection 4.2, the magnitude of the Tobin effect is smaller, because desired saving and the desired wealth-to-income ratio are also lowered.

for the size of the capital stock in the steady state is unaffected by the changes in inflation associated with changes in money-financed deficits.

The classic defense of superneutrality is Sidrauski (1967). He considers a representative individual who maximizes the discounted sum of time-separable utility over an infinite horizon. Instantaneous utility is a function of real consumption and of the flow of services of money, assumed proportional to the real money stock. The agent chooses real consumption, as well as how to divide his saving between the two available assets, money and capital. Saving is the difference between income plus government transfers and consumption. Transfers are in money, in amounts unrelated to individuals' previous holdings. The government does not purchase goods and services, and it finances transfers through money creation at a constant rate. The population grows at a constant rate.

Sidrauski's main result is that the sizes of the long-run capital stock and of real consumption are independent of the rate of monetary growth. The reason is that an infinitely-lived agent will accumulate each asset up to the point where its net yield just compensates for the postponement of consumption. This point is where its marginal product equals the sum of the rate of time preference, the rate of population growth, and the rate of depreciation. The equilibrium condition is not affected by changes in the rate of inflation.

Of course, the opportunity cost of holding cash balances (in terms of foregone consumption) rises with inflation. Since the level of consumption remains unchanged, the increase in the marginal yield of cash balances necessary to re-establish equilibrium is brought about through a reduction in real money holdings. Thus, superneutrality does not extend to the per capita real money stock. Since utility is a positive function of both consumption and real money balances, monetary expansions that raise inflation lead to welfare losses.[20]

In view of the source of Sidrauski's superneutrality result, it is not surprising that superneutrality fails when real money balances affect the net marginal product of capital in terms of consumption. A simple setup is presented in Dornbusch and Frenkel (1973), where it is assumed that output available for consumption is a fraction of production (net of output used to meet capital needs arising from population growth). This fraction is in turn assumed to be increasing with real per capita money holdings. Instantaneous utility is a function only of consumption, and the agent maximizes the discounted sum of utilities over an infinite horizon. Although steady-state equilibrium again requires equality of the net marginal product of capital with the rate of time

[20]Sidrauski is careful to distinguish these steady-state results from short-run effects. He notes that in his model, increases in monetary growth imply increased disposable income and consumption in the short run.

preference, the former now depends on the size of per capita money balances. The new steady state with higher inflation will generally involve both lower per capita money holdings and lower capital stock. This is the opposite of the Tobin effect.

In the same class of models, an earlier paper by Levhari and Patinkin (1968) explicitly incorporates the real money stock in the production function and shows that superneutrality fails. It also shows that when the Golden Rule holds, i.e. the net marginal product of capital equals the natural rate of population growth, it is in general possible to raise per capita output and hence welfare by lowering inflation (or increasing deflation) so as to induce greater real money holdings, even though the real rate of interest and net marginal product of capital are above the natural growth rate. It will generally not be optimal to increase the real money stock to the point where money holders are satiated, i.e. where the rate of deflation equals the net marginal product of capital. The welfare optimum will involve neither Phelps' Golden Rule capital stock nor Friedman's optimal quantity of money.

An alternative mechanism negating superneutrality in steady states is suggested by Brock (1974), who introduces a labor–leisure choice into Sidrauski's model. Since the additional first-order condition involves the marginal utilities of consumption and of leisure, it now becomes necessary for those two marginal utilities to be independent of money if the steady-state levels of capital, labor, and consumption are to be unaffected by changes in the rate of monetary growth. Brock shows that when money affects the marginal utility of leisure, money growth affects the labor supply curve and thus the steady-state stock of capital.[21]

A key feature of the Sidrauski model that allows it to exhibit superneutrality is the infinity of agents' horizons. Drazen (1981) shows that for a given individual who lives for two periods, both the substitution and the income effects on capital holdings of an increase in the return to money (lower inflation or higher deflation) are negative when consumption and money balances are normal goods. The negativity of the income effect can be explained as follows. An increase in the return to money arising from a reduction in inflation implies ceteris paribus higher income in the second period of life. Given the usual concavity conditions on utility, the agent will want to spread this increase over both periods. When consumption and real balances are "normal goods", this implies higher consumption and money balances in the first period. Since the usefulness of capital to the agent as an asset is only in transferring income from the first to the second period, a

---

[21]It is still possible to obtain invariance of the capital–labor ratio, provided that the production function exhibits constant returns to scale. Except in this limited sense, however, superneutrality is lost when the choice between labor and leisure is explicitly incorporated into the model.

redistribution of income in the opposite direction can be accomplished by lowering capital holdings. This negative income effect, combined with the unambiguously negative substitution effect, produces a negative total effect of an increase in the return to money.

Now, in view of the government budget identity, a reduction in monetary growth and inflation is associated with a reduction in transfer income, a lower deficit. The overall effect on the demand for capital of a reduction in the rate of monetary expansion is the sum of the effect (just described) of the increase in the return to money and the effect of the reduction of transfers. If transfers are distributed in proportion to first-period money holdings, then this overall effect is zero. (The transfers amount to nominal interest on money and exactly offset the effect of inflation on the real return to holding money.) If transfers are heavily weighted towards the old, it is possible that deflationary policy would increase demand for capital. This is because the reduction in the transfer income of the old would more than offset the effect described in the previous paragraph, inducing people to hold more capital in order to shift income and consumption to the second period of their lives.

Thus, the Tobin effect is observed if this does not occur (e.g. when transfers are sufficiently weighted towards the young).[22] Under this condition, Drazen shows that the result generally extends to the economy-wide capital–labor ratio.

Haliassos (1987) shows that superneutrality is not an inescapable feature of infinite-horizon setups, but is due to the commonly used but unrealistic assumption that portfolio adjustments are simultaneous across different agents. When portfolio holding periods are staggered, each portfolio is held over a period of time during which real rates of return change. Even when these changes are deterministic, staggering can generate a determinate optimal composition of portfolios: assets become imperfect substitutes under perfect foresight. Holding period returns are still tied to the rate of time preference as in the Sidrauski model. But the variability of rates of return and of return differentials within each holding period can be influenced through policy. Changes in the rate of growth of nominally denominated assets affect inflation and the real rate of return of money. Since relative asset supplies are unchanged, the optimal composition of private portfolios is also invariant to the policy change. But interest income on the optimal portfolio is affected. If the same level of consumption out of portfolio income is to be maintained, real rates on non-monetary assets have to adjust. It is also shown that real wealth and real taxes net of transfers are affected by the policy change.

---

[22]Tobin, and other contributors to this debate, were always assuming that transfers were independent of money holdings. If they were random or equal per capita, they would in Drazen's terms be weighted to the young.

Siegel (1983) shows that superneutrality will also fail in general when labor-augmenting (Harrod-neutral) technological change is incorporated into the model.[23] This creates an asymmetry between the production function and, therefore, the budget constraint, which are stationary in efficiency units, and the utility function, which is stationary in per capita values. The first-order equilibrium condition for the marginal product of capital involves the rate of growth of real per capita consumption and money holdings. In the absence of technical progress, these terms are zero. However, when technological change is present, these rates of growth are positive: real consumption and money holdings are constant only per efficiency unit of labor, i.e. the scale of each economic unit increases at the rate of technical progress. The coefficients on those rates of growth are functions of the marginal utility of consumption and of its derivatives with respect to per capita consumption and money holdings. Superneutrality now requires that these coefficients be unaffected by changes in monetary growth. This will be true for utility functions which are separable in consumption and money holdings; and for non-separable functions which are isoelastic in an index of real per capita consumption and real money holdings, $c^\gamma m^\beta$, where the sum of the constants satisfies $\gamma + \beta < 1$.

5.2. Superneutrality along the transition path

We now turn to the issue of whether changes in the rate of nominal money growth are superneutral when the economy is outside its steady state, but moving towards it.

Fischer (1979) considers a model similar to Sidrauski's with perfect foresight. He examines the class of utility functions displaying constant relative risk aversion, of which logarithmic utility is a special case. The result is that although in such a model the steady-state value of the capital stock is invariant to changes in the rate of monetary expansion, such superneutrality does not prevail on the transition path to the steady state, except in the case of logarithmic utility.[24] Fischer shows that higher rates of nominal monetary growth are associated with higher rates of capital accumulation on the transition path. Moreover, as the capital stock approaches its steady-state value from below, a larger rate of monetary expansion implies lower consumption. Fischer

---

[23] In similar vein, Tobin (1968) had shown that steady states with transactions requirements for money exist only if Harrod-neutral technological progress occurs at the same steady rate in both goods production and in transactions.

[24] Asako (1983) notes that for more general utility functions, a sufficient condition for super-neutrality on the transition path is that the function be separable in consumption and real money balances, i.e. $u_{cm} = 0$. Deriving necessary conditions for general utility functions is more difficult.

does not provide an estimate of the quantitative significance of these effects.

Cohen (1985) suggests a rationale for Fischer's results, using a model that emphasizes the distinction between consumers and producers. Nominal rates of interest vary along the transition path due to two conflicting factors: the increase in inflation pushes them upwards, while the decrease in real rates pushes them downwards. When the intertemporal elasticity of substitution is unity, the two effects cancel each other out and monetary policy cannot affect nominal interest rates. However, when the intertemporal elasticity of substitution is below (above) unity, the nominal rates on the transition path are above (below) their steady-state values. In those cases, monetary policy affects capital accumulation by influencing the rate of growth (or decline) of nominal rates towards their steady-state value.

This effect on accumulation comes about because the specification of the instantaneous utility function[25] allows consumption and real money holding to be treated as a composite commodity, the "price" of which is an increasing function of the nominal interest rate. Now when monetary policy raises all nominal rates, it also affects the equilibrium sequence of the relative price of the composite good from one period to another (which is a function of nominal interest rates). Cohen shows that the effect on interest rates has no consequence for the amount of consumption in his model. However, the effect on intertemporal relative prices of the composite good is such that an increased rate of monetary growth lowers the demand for the consumption good (unless elasticity is unity), while leaving the supply unaffected. The resulting decrease in consumption allows faster capital accumulation to take place all along the transition path.

Asako (1983) shows that it is possible for a utility function with constant relative risk aversion (CRRA) other than the logarithmic to violate super-neutrality on the transition path in a direction opposite from that suggested by Fischer. In particular, this is true of the CRRA utility functions with relative risk aversion exceeding unity when consumption and real money holdings are perfect complements, i.e. their desired ratio does not depend on economic conditions. In this case, the rate of capital accumulation is slower, the higher the rate of monetary expansion. Moreover, neither consumption nor the real money stock is affected by changes in money growth in the steady state. This superneutrality is even stronger than Sidrauski's, and it is due to the perfect complementarity of c and m.

---

[25] $U(c, m) = (1/(1 - s))(c^{\alpha} m^{1-\alpha})^{1-s}$, if $s \geq 0$ and $s \neq 1$,

$U(c, m) = \log c^{\alpha} m^{1-\alpha}$, if $s = 1$.

5.3. Empirical tests of superneutrality

Superneutrality asserts invariance of capital stock and consumption with respect to inflation rates and monetary growth. These are propositions about long-run paths. Invariance of capital implies, even derives from, invariance in the real interest rates to which marginal productivity of capital is equal in equilibrium. These invariances are all very difficult to test. Consequently, empirical research on superneutrality has focused primarily on tests for the existence and stability over time of the famous hypothesis about interest rates put forward by Fisher (1930) [and modified by Darby (1975)]. The Fisher hypothesis is that a change in inflation will be fully reflected in an equal change in nominal interest rates, without affecting the real rate of interest. Darby's modification restates the hypothesis in terms of after-tax real and nominal interest rates. One strand of the modern literature focuses on tests for the presence of a Fisher effect, sometimes allowing for taxation. The other strand focuses on the stability of the response of nominal rates to inflationary expectations over time. Here we illustrate both.

5.3.1. The presence of the Fisher effect

Tests of the Fisher hypothesis up to the early 1970s typically involved regressing the nominal interest rate on a distributed lag of past inflation rates as a proxy for expected inflation, a constant intended to represent the invariant real rate, and an error assumed to be distributed independently of past, present, and future price levels. The extraordinarily long lags typically implied by the estimates were taken as evidence against the Fisher hypothesis (even by Fisher himself).[26]

Sargent (1973) was the first to utilize rational expectations in testing the Fisher hypothesis. Sargent argues that even when Fisher's theory is correct, the estimated lag functions do not necessarily represent optimal forecasts of inflation. He combines rational expectations with the natural rate hypothesis (NRH) embodied in the Lucas aggregate supply curve to construct a model in which the real rate of interest is independent of the expected part of the money supply. His test of the Fisherian hypothesis is simply to test this model. He

---

[26]The first researcher to test the Fisher hypothesis was Fisher himself. In 1930 he concluded that "when prices are rising, the (nominal) rate of interest tends to be high, but not so high as it should be to compensate for the rise" (1930, p. 43). In addition, Fisher observed a relationship between interest rates and past inflation rates. He interpreted this as supporting a modified version that allows for less than perfect foresight and consequently effects that are smaller and slower than price changes.

does so indirectly by testing NRH, defined as the idea that unemployment is independent of the systematic part of the money supply.

Sargent proposes two tests of NRH. In the first, the unemployment rate is regressed on lagged unemployment rates and on other variables included in the information set in period $t - n - 1$, where n is the order of the autoregressive process followed by the unemployment disturbance. NRH implies that all those other variables are statistically insignificant, i.e. that the innovation in un-employment is not affected by past values of any variables, including policy variables. The alternative test proposed by Sargent involves estimating an equation for unemployment which incorporates not only lagged unemployment and the unexpected part of inflation, but also the expected part of inflation. The null (Fisherian) hypothesis is that the coefficient on expected inflation is zero, and it is tested against the alternative that it is not.

Although Sargent finds that the evidence on NRH (and hence on Fisher) is mixed, he points to the lack of an alternative model that would outperform NRH in tracking unemployment. Sargent feels that if an investigator has priors in favor of NRH, the evidence is not sufficient to reject them.

Fama (1975) suggests using a joint test of the hypotheses (i) that the expected real rate of return on Treasury bills is constant and (ii) that agents make optimal use of their information concerning inflation over the next month when setting the nominal interest rate today. The latter is a version of the efficient markets hypothesis (EMH).[27] If the hypotheses jointly hold, then it should not be possible to use any subset of information available as of $t - 1$ (e.g. the history of real rates) to come up with a better prediction of r than the constant $E(r)$. This in turn means that the autocorrelations for r are zero for all lags, and this can be tested by checking the sample autocorrelations for r.

A further set of tests can be obtained by generalizing the model of bill market equilibrium so that constancy of $E(r)$ becomes a special case. Specifical-ly, if estimating the regression

$$\pi_t = \alpha_0 + \alpha_1 R_t + \varepsilon_t \tag{5.1}$$

yields coefficient estimates that are inconsistent with the hypothesis that $\alpha_0 = -E(r)$ and $\alpha_1 = 1$, the model of a constant $E(r)$ is rejected. Market efficiency can then be tested by checking whether ε_t is autocorrelated. If EMH

---

[27] The nominal one-month rate of return on a one-month Treasury bill paying \$1 at time t is $R_t = (1 - v_{t-1})/v_{t-1}$, where v_{t-1} is the price of the bill determined in period $t - 1$. Fama postulates that the market sets v so that it perceives the expected real return on the bill to be the constant $E(r)$. This model of market equilibrium is combined with the assumption that the market makes optimal use of all available information concerning the stochastic rate of change of purchasing power π_t over the next month.

holds, R_t summarizes all available information about $E(\pi_t | I_{t-1})$, including past values of the disturbance. These past values should be of no use in predicting π_t, which implies that ε_t should be serially uncorrelated. This logic can be generalized to any piece of information in $t - 1$. An example is:

$$\pi_t = \alpha_0 + \alpha_1 R_t + \alpha_2 \pi_{t-1} + \varepsilon_t, \tag{5.2}$$

where EMH implies that α_2 is zero and ε_t is serially uncorrelated.

Although Fama's empirical results[28] did not reject his joint hypothesis, subsequent research has challenged their robustness. Nelson and Schwert (1977) argue that looking at the ex post real rate may generate an "errors in variables" problem, since it is possible for the autocorrelation function of the ex post real rate to be close to zero at all lags even if the ex ante real rate fluctuates considerably and is highly autocorrelated.[29] As for the test of whether $\alpha_2 = 0$ in (5.2), when the authors replace π_{t-1} with optimal predictors of inflation, which make use of more observations on past inflation and of the time series properties of the inflation rate, the coefficient on the optimal predictor is large and significant, putting EMH into question.

Garbade and Wachtel (1978) focus on equation (5.1), where the null hypothesis is that α_0 and α_1 are the same over three subperiods. They argue that the alternative specified by Fama, namely that the coefficients changed by a discrete amount from one subperiod to the next but remained constant within each subperiod, makes it quite unlikely that the null will be rejected in its favor. Instead they allow each coefficient to follow a random walk without drift. Fama's finding that α_1 is stable and equal to 1 cannot be rejected by their tests, either. The conclusion survives even when α_0 is assumed to depend linearly on time within each of six specified subintervals and the nature of this dependence is different for each one. However, when such piecewise-linear time-variation of α_0 is regarded as the alternative hypothesis, the null hypothesis of a constant real rate $-\alpha_0$ is rejected, irrespective of whether the constraint $\alpha_1 = 1$ is imposed or not.

The question whether nominal interest rates have adjusted sufficiently to compensate investors both for changes in (expected) inflation and for the

---

[28] Fama uses data on U.S. Treasury bills with one month to maturity over the period from January 1953 through July 1971, and for various subsamples. He also performs similar tests for bills of up to six months of maturity. In all cases, he assumes that the behavior of the Consumer Price Index is the relevant measure of inflation. The results of both autocorrelation and regression coefficient tests support EMH with respect to the history of inflation rates, and do not reject the model of constant expected real rates. Combining these two findings, Fama concludes that we cannot reject the hypothesis that all variation through time in R reflects variation in correctly-assessed expected rates of change in purchasing power.

[29] This happens when the variance of errors in inflationary expectations is large relative to the variance of the ex ante real rate.

effects of interest taxation is addressed by Tanzi (1980). Using data on six- and twelve-month Treasury bills, he ran the following regression over the 1952–75 period:

$$R_t = r_t + \beta E(\pi_t)/(1 - T_t),$$ (5.3)

where R is the lender's required rate, r is the after-tax rate he would have received if expected inflation were zero, $E(\pi_t)$ is expected inflation, and T is the tax rate on interest income. Tanzi rejects the hypothesis that $\beta = 1$. Since the estimate of β is below 1, he concludes that agents are not free of "fiscal illusion", and are not sufficiently compensated for the effects of changes in taxes on their nominal interest income.

While the Fisher hypothesis postulates constancy of the net marginal productivity of capital, most empirical papers use data on CPI-corrected returns on financial assets (i.e. nominally denominated interest-bearing claims such as Treasury bills). Carmichael and Stebbing (1983) point out that the poor results of existing tests may be partly due to a higher degree of substitutability at the margin between money and such financial assets than between financial assets and capital. One crucial fact about money is that its nominal rate of return is "regulated" (usually set equal to zero) and consequently changes in inflation change its real after-tax rate of return by the same amount. If nominally denominated assets are close substitutes for money, this one-to-one sensitivity to inflation should also be (approximately) true for their real after-tax rate, even if the marginal productivity of capital is fully governed by the rate of time preference and other parameters independent of inflation. This inverted Fisher hypothesis for financial assets is not rejected by data on three-month U.S. Treasury bills and by two Australian interest-rate series (short- and long-term).[30]

5.3.2. The Fisher effect over time

Tests of how the magnitude of the Fisher effect has behaved over time have mainly focused on two partitions of the available data sample. One is into the pre World War II and post World War II, while the other partitions the post World War II era into various subsamples. We briefly illustrate both.

Friedman and Schwartz (1976, 1982) and Summers (1983) have found essentially no evidence of the Fisher effect in the pre World War II period in either Britain or the United States. They have found much stronger correla-

---

[30]The U.S. sample is 1953 I–1978 IV; the Australian is early or mid-sixties to end of 1981. To test their hypothesis, Carmichael and Stebbing make use of portfolio arbitrage conditions on real after-tax rates of return among the three assets, and of the assumptions that expectations are unbiased and that individuals know their marginal tax rates.

tions between short-term nominal interest rates and either ex post inflation or other proxies for expected inflation rates in the post World War II period (especially post-1960). This led Friedman and Schwartz to suggest that perhaps financial markets "learned their Fisher" only gradually.

The findings concerning the United States were recently challenged by Barsky (1987). He argues that the observed difference in the magnitude of the Fisher effect is not due to a shift in any structural relationship but to differences in the stochastic process generating inflation. While inflation was essentially a white-noise process before World War I, it became a non-stationary ARIMA process in the post-1960 period. Barsky shows that an underlying Fisher effect is consistent with any observed correlation between current nominal interest rates and actual inflation rates in the current (or next) time period. The reason is that the latter simply reflect the persistence of inflation.

In addition, Barsky raises doubts as to whether regressions of nominal interest rates on inflation are reliable in assessing whether real rates are affected by changes in expected inflation. A case in point is that of the gold standard years prior to 1913, which look the least Fisherian in regressions involving nominal interest rates [e.g. Summers (1983)], but do not exhibit negative correlation between ex ante real rates and past inflation.[31]

Barsky attempts to reconcile this discrepancy by the fact that inflation in those years was virtually white noise. As a result, the variance of anticipated inflation was substantially lower than the variance of actual inflation, and OLS regression would lead to the incorrect conclusion that nominal interest rates failed to respond to inflation. Summers tries to allow for this by "band filtering" the data, i.e. considering only low-frequency components which can be thought of as easily forecastable. The hope is that then expected inflation can be proxied by actual inflation. McCallum (1984b) accepts the substantive conclusions of the Summers study, but points out that low-frequency estimation is affected by misspecification of the distinction between anticipated and unanticipated movements in the regressors.[32] Barsky shows that the covariance between anticipated and ex post inflation does not increase relative to the variance of inflation as the frequency is lowered. This suggests that band filtering in this case may not have resulted in a better proxy for expected inflation.[33]

Cargill and Meyer (1980) focus on the post World War II period and ask

---

[31]Another case is that of the postwar period, which looks Fisherian on the basis of nominal rate regressions, but exhibits a strong negative relationship between inflation and expected real returns on short-term instruments.

[32]See also their exchange in Summers (1986) and McCallum (1986).

[33]At any rate, given that expected inflation probably fluctuated very little in the pre-1913 period, that part of the sample is probably not very informative as to the validity of the Fisher hypothesis.

whether length of maturity is relevant for the existence and magnitude of the Fisher effect over time.[34] They run regressions of the form

$$R_t = \beta_0 + \beta_1 r_t + \beta_2 E(\pi_t) + u_t \tag{5.4}$$

over subperiods between 1954 and 1975. Coefficients on expected inflation, $E(\pi_t)$, are almost always positive and significant; they decline with increases in maturity. Many of the coefficients are close to or significantly above unity. However, estimates of β_2 vary significantly between subperiods. Estimates for some maturities decline quite substantially for the period 1970–75 relative to 1960–75.

6. Monetary policies

The previous section discussed substitutions of money for tax financing of a given path of government expenditures and the effects of the corresponding changes in the rate of nominal money growth. In this section we discuss shifts between alternative modes of non-tax financing of government expenditure. In most setups, fiscal policy is taken as given. In a few, taxes are also varied so as to eliminate effects of asset market exchanges on agents' opportunity sets.

Some of the models reviewed focus on the common type of open market operations, namely exchanges of money for nominal bonds. Others, however, discuss exchanges of money for real capital or for indexed bonds. Even when the term "capital" simply refers to stored amounts of the consumption good, money–capital exchanges should be distinguished from temporary increases in government expenditure G financed through money creation. The asset swaps considered are associated with a *given G*. We first investigate the relevance or irrelevance of various asset exchanges for the real allocation of resources. We then discuss shifts between bond and money financing which are necessary when certain financing policies are unsustainable over the longer run.

6.1. Asset exchanges

We start with models exhibiting neutrality of asset exchanges and then consider setups in which open market operations have been shown to be non-neutral.

---

[34]They consider a wide range of maturities of government and commercial financial instruments, and look at the "term structure" of inflationary expectations, so as to match each instrument with the (geometric) average of one-period expected inflation rates over its time to maturity.

6.1.1. Neutral asset exchanges

Wallace (1981) investigates whether there is a class of open-market exchanges between fiat money and "capital" (in the form of a stored consumption good) that would leave the equilibrium sequences for real consumption allocations and for the price level unaffected. He considers a two-period, pure-exchange, overlapping generations model with a single consumption good that is storable via a constant returns to scale, stochastic technology. Complete markets in contingent claims on second-period consumption are assumed. Open-market operations consist of purchases and costless storage by the government of the consumption good in exchange for fiat money.[35] Money is not dominated in return. The government sets the (possibly contingent) paths of government consumption, $G(t)$; of the endowment vector for each generation t, $w(t)$; of the path of government storage, $K^g(t)$; and of the nominal money supply path, $M(t)$. An equilibrium is described by a sequence of real consumption levels, prices of consumption claims, aggregate storage, prices of the good, and nominal money.

Wallace starts with an equilibrium for a policy $\{G(t), w(t), K^g(t) = 0\}$. He then identifies policies $\{G(t), \hat{w}(t), \hat{K}(t)\}$ which support the same equilibrium configuration (with the exception of the money sequence). The choice among them is irrelevant for the equilibrium outcome. While such policies leave the price path unaffected, they combine open market operations with changes in taxes net of transfers which "pay out" to agents any additional net interest income the government receives as a result of the change in its portfolio. This is necessary if private opportunity sets are to remain unaffected.[36] Wallace does point out that this analysis is probably most useful as a benchmark case for assessing the real effects of asset exchanges.

While Wallace's policies involve auxiliary fiscal changes, Chamley and Polemarchakis (1984) consider "pure" open market operations but alter the price process so as to pay out to private agents the altered returns on the government's portfolio. In addition, they do not assume the existence of a complete set of contingent markets. Suppose that the economy is in equilib-

---

[35] The supply of fiat money is costlessly manipulated by the government. In period t, consumers demand claims on consumption in period $t+1$, while firms (which are owned by members of generation t) supply those claims, storing the good and money in the process. In their roles as consumers, agents maximize their expected utility of consumption in the two periods of their life. As producers, they choose to undertake one or both of the two risky projects of storing money and of storing the good.

[36] Wallace shows that $\{\hat{K}^g(t)\}$ is any non-negative sequence bounded by $\{K(t)\}$, and $\{\hat{w}(t)\}$ is any endowment sequence that meets a particular set of restrictions. The point of the restrictions is to ensure (a) that the distribution of income among agents is unchanged, and (b) that the differences in net interest received by the government as a result of the change in its "portfolio" of the stored good and of money are offset by changes in taxes net of transfers. In this framework, the boundedness of $K^g(t)$ from above is necessary, because otherwise no feasible value of private storage exists that is consistent with unchanged total accumulation.

rium when the quantity of money is fixed for all time periods and government holdings of capital are zero (along with government expenditures and taxes for simplicity). Then suppose that the government announces a new contingent sequence for its capital holdings. The authors show that this policy change has no effect on the time paths of the allocation of goods and of the aggregate capital stock, as long as money maintains a non-zero value in terms of the capital good.[37] Individuals reduce their capital and increase their money holdings in a way that maintains both the value of each agent's portfolio and the real return on it. Thus, any intertemporal program that was feasible for a private agent before the policy change is also feasible after it. Moreover, the portfolio response of agents is consistent with equilibrium in the markets for capital and for money.[38]

The result extends to economies with many assets, in which case only the prices of the assets involved in the exchange are affected by it. It fails when short sales are bounded below or not feasible, and when open market exchanges involve money and assets denominated in nominal terms. The reason for the latter is the effect on the returns of a nominally denominated asset induced by the change in the path of the price of money. This effect is such that the conditions which the prices of money and of bonds have to satisfy for neutrality are not satisfied for a general distribution of total nominal returns on the nominal asset.

Peled (1985) focuses on neutrality of open market exchanges of fiat money for indexed government bonds in the context of a single-good, pure-exchange, overlapping generations model. Random endowments generate stochastic bond price and aggregate price levels and inflation. However, indexed bonds promise a given amount of the perishable consumption good. Peled considers a given path of taxation. He shows that if one starts with a financing scheme that results in money being willingly held, then one can change the path of bond issues almost arbitrarily and still be able to find offsetting changes in the path of money creation that would leave the paths of real consumption, taxes, and the price of bonds unaffected.[39] These exchanges do not affect the value of the

---

[37]A sufficient condition for a positive price of money in period t is that both the contemporaneous government capital holdings and the total return on capital be positive.

[38]Wallace's neutral policies can be seen as combinations of (1) an open market operation (given taxes net of transfers), which does affect the price of money, with (2) changes in the supply of money via taxes net of transfers that offset the first price effect without affecting the real quantity of money. Chamley and Polemarchakis show that monetary policies of this type do exist even in their more generalized framework. Sargent (1987, esp. p. 322) states a general neutrality theorem which encompasses those of Wallace, and Chamley and Polemarchakis as special cases.

[39]Note that not all financing policies which involve the same path of taxes and lead to the same government revenue leave the real allocation of resources unaffected. The added condition is that they also generate identical "deficit" paths for all periods $t > 1$ over which they are in effect. "Deficit" here refers to the change in the real value of government monetary plus non-monetary debt. When this is true, unchanged aggregate consumption is guaranteed to old agents and aggregate private saving is also unchanged.

government portfolio. The assumed existence of intragenerational markets for money and bonds is crucial for the result.[40]

Until recently it was though that irrelevance results could be obtained only in models where money is not dominated in return. Sargent and Smith (1987) show that such results can also be obtained in a class of models where money is dominated in real rate of return. In those models, money is dominated because some fraction of the population (the "poor") are assumed to be prevented by law from holding assets other than money. The "rich" can trade in all markets.[41] Specific assumptions about the distribution of income ensure that the poor cannot afford to hold any asset other than money. A byproduct of these assumptions is that the rich, who are not excluded from any market, will not hold money, but only stored goods and state-contingent claims to future consumption. In other respects, the overlapping generations setup is similar to that of Wallace (1981).

When open market exchanges of currency for "capital" (i.e. goods for storage) are undertaken, irrelevance with respect both to consumption and to the price system is ensured – as in Wallace – through lump-sum transfers or taxes which distribute the change in earnings on the government portfolio.[42] Sargent, Smith, and Wallace interpret the offsetting changes in taxes net of transfers, which are necessary for irrelevance in their models, as defining a "constant" fiscal policy. The difference here is that the rich are treated differently from the poor. Specifically, the poor must be induced to raise their saving to absorb the higher real stock of currency, while the rich must reduce their saving by the amount of capital purchased by the government. Irrelevance theorems when money is dominated due to legal restrictions seem to require that such restrictions be different across agents. For instance, if the original Wallace (1981) setup is augmented to include identical "reserve requirements" across all agents, money is dominated in return but irrelevance is not obtained.

Finally, Benninga and Protopapadakis (1984) adopt a specification for utility similar to that in Sidrauski (1967) in a two-period, Arrow–Debreu, state-preference economy with complete markets, heterogeneous consumers and firms, one good, and fixed labor supply. They ask whether shifts from one

---

[40]If such markets were absent prior to the government intervention, then the government could facilitate risk-sharing asset exchanges among diverse individuals through its open market operations. Then, government intervention would have real effects. On the other hand, neutrality is not contingent on the lump-sum nature of taxes.

[41]The empirical rationalization usually offered is that laws can exist (such as Peel's Bank Act of 1844) which impose a restriction on the minimum size of privately issued securities.

[42]The authors show that invariance can also be accomplished without variation in lump-sum taxes when the menu of assets is sufficiently enriched to allow the government to borrow from (and lend to) private agents. Again, the condition for irrelevance is that the open market operations in capital be accompanied by government exchanges in debt markets so as to leave private agents' budget sets unaltered.

financing mode to another, holding the revenue raised through the third mode constant, would be "neutral". They are considered "strongly neutral" when both consumption and money holdings are unaffected.

A shift between bonds and taxes will be strongly neutral if it leaves the present value of taxes (including "inflation taxes") for each consumer unchanged, and if the interest rate is unchanged. The first condition ensures that each agent's budget constraint remains unaltered by the policy shift; the second guarantees that real money holdings will also be unaffected. This result is a direct extension of those on debt neutrality to models incorporating money and uncertainty. In order for an open market purchase to be weakly neutral, a decline in the inflation rate must occur, lowering nominal interest rates, inducing agents to hold a larger real stock of money, while keeping the cost of holding money constant and allowing the government to receive more revenue from issuing money. This holds for a restricted class of utility functions: separability of utility in consumption and money is a sufficient condition for weak neutrality.[43] Finally, a shift in financing between money and taxes is weakly neutral only if the government undertakes an elaborate scheme of adjusting each individual's taxes in a way that offsets the changes in the cost to each individual of holding money.

Interestingly, Benninga and Protopapadakis show that in their model, no economy can be invariant under both policy shifts between money and taxes and policy shifts between money and debt. The reason is that if the present value of taxes is changed, then the cost of holding money and the revenue from money creation must also change for neutrality to hold. However, under debt–money neutrality government revenue from money creation is fixed.

6.1.2. Non-neutral asset exchanges

We now turn to models exhibiting non-neutrality of open market asset exchanges. Grossman and Weiss (1983) consider a pure exchange, Clower-constraint model with two types of infinitely-lived consumers, firms, and banks. Consumers of each type visit the bank once every two periods to withdraw money directly deposited into their accounts, in order to finance their perfectly foreseen consumption over the two periods.[44] Consumers are assumed to be the only ones who hold money.

When there is an open market purchase, the addition to the money stock flows into the banks and has to be absorbed wholly by a subset of the

---

[43]This is more restrictive than the conditions imposed by Sidrauski, due to the inclusion of uncertainty into the model.

[44]Deposits are not checkable. Firms deposit into consumers' accounts, since consumers own shares to firms' profits. In addition to shares, the asset menu includes both interest-bearing deposits and government bonds which are perfect substitutes for deposits.

population. This subset consists of the people who have exhausted previous money holdings and are there to make a withdrawal. Since money is only held for consumption purposes, agents are going to withdraw more only if they decide to consume more. Real and nominal interest rates have to drop in order to induce that group to decide to consume more. Moreover, price effects will only be gradual, since the members of this group will spend their increased holdings gradually until their next trip to the bank. Consumers of the other type cannot increase their nominal spending before their predetermined time comes to visit the bank. Thus, they respond to higher prices by reducing real consumption.[45]

A similar staggered-withdrawals setup is presented in Rotemberg (1984), except that his model incorporates capital, does not assume that output is constant, and postulates that money is withdrawn at the beginning of the period and is available for spending in the current and in the next period. The model is consistent with rate-of-return dominance of capital over money in the steady state. Rotemberg shows that there is no Tobin effect in his model, in the sense that the unique steady-state equilibrium size of the capital stock that involves positive consumption is independent of the rate of growth of the money stock. However, an increase in the rate of monetary growth, and hence in inflation, leads people to consume more right after they withdraw money; and less in the period in which they do not go to the bank and have to finance consumption with money withdrawn in the previous period. The extent of this distortion in the consumption path is partly determined by the assumption that the frequency of an agent's bank visits does not change with inflation.

Now consider an open market purchase of capital. If this had no effect on prices, consumption and hence withdrawals would also be unaffected: people at the bank would not want to hold the extra money made available to them. In fact, the price level has to rise. Rotemberg's numerical simulations of the unique non-explosive path show that the price increase results in a fall in consumption of those who do not visit the bank in that period, which raises capital, and hence output, in the following period, albeit by a small amount. How the magnitude of output response would be affected by allowing people to visit the bank more frequently in response to inflation is an open question.

Open market operations have also been shown to have real effects when

---

[45]In fact, it is possible to show that when utility is logarithmic (or when it is homothetic and demand for second-period consumption rises with inflation), the model generates damped oscillatory price behavior with overshooting after two periods and a fall in the current nominal and real rates. Two-period nominal interest rates also fluctuate, rising above their steady-state value on even dates and falling below it on odd dates, until the price path converges to its steady state. The oscillations are produced by the fact that in odd periods the types who exhaust their money holdings, and consequently have a propensity to spend out of them equal to one, are also the ones whose money holdings are larger than in the steady state. With output assumed fixed, such fluctuation in nominal spending generates fluctuations in the price level.

portfolio adjustments are staggered, even when we abstract from the transactions role of money. Haliassos (1987) presents such a setup in which even under infinite horizons and perfect foresight, an open market operation affects the level and variability of the real rates of return on non-monetary assets as well as the level of real wealth. The reason is that the open market operation affects the optimal composition of private portfolios. If a given level of consumption out of portfolio income is to be maintained, real rates of return have to adjust. Now rates of return on non-monetary assets absorb the brunt of adjustment, since the real rate on money is tied to the rate of growth of nominal government debt.

So far the models in this section postulate infinite horizons. Waldo (1985) constructs an overlapping generations, pure-exchange model in which the nominal and real interest rates fall and the price level rises less than proportionately to the money supply increase associated with an open market purchase. The measures of fiscal policy that are held constant are government spending and the total budget deficit, taking account of interest payments and inflation tax revenues. Thus, the effects on the total deficit of any variations in inflation and interest rates are offset through changes in lump-sum taxes.[46]

In Waldo's model the reason agents hold currency is to finance small transactions. Interest-bearing demand deposits, which are claims to government bonds, can only be transferred at a lump-sum cost, and are consequently used to effect large transactions. When an open market purchase takes place, the nominal interest rate falls to induce agents to substitute currency holdings for demand deposits. The excess demand for goods that results from the drop in nominal interest rates is then offset by an increase in the price level that reduces the real stock of wealth.

A different experiment, namely an increase in the rate of monetary growth (and of inflation), leads to a fall in currency demand and to an increase in goods demand. The price level rises, both to reduce the real currency supply and to lower goods demand. The effect on the nominal interest rate depends on the relative inflation elasticities of savings and currency. Even if the nominal interest rate rises, it does not do so by as much as inflation: the real interest rate definitely falls.[47]

---

[46]This allows inflation and the debt mix to be determined independently of each other and eliminates any income effects of inflation, so that results only depend on substitution effects. It is different from Sargent and Wallace (1981) where government spending and the narrowly defined deficit are held constant. In that model, open market purchases that lower interest rates imply lower inflation rates through the government budget identity.

[47]If one uses Waldo's setup but assumes that government spending and the primary budget deficit are held constant [i.e. the notion of constant policy in Sargent and Wallace (1981)], an open market purchase does put downward pressure on interest rates and (via the budget identity) on inflation rates,but the effects on savings and the price level are ambiguous. If inflation effects dominate, savings rise and the price level falls to clear the goods market. The opposite happens when interest rate effects dominate.

6.2. Consequences of persistent deficits

We turn now to the question of whether persistent budget deficits are inflationary. There are two sets of issues here. One is whether such deficits are financed by issuing bonds for a given money path, or vice versa. The other is whether it is the primary or the total budget deficit which is kept constant over time.

Smith (1982) considers a constant total budget deficit. He compares a "monetarist" policy of maintaining a target path for money while financing deficits through bonds to a "bondist" policy of maintaining a target path for the bond stock while issuing money to finance the deficit. He shows that in a dynamic IS/LM model, a zero-inflation steady state may not be stable under the monetarist strategy, whereas it is more likely to be stable under the bondist strategy. The rationale is that fixed tax rates and government spending (including debt service) make government saving procyclical. Under a bond target, the change in money supply dictated by the government budget identity is countercyclical. By contrast, under a monetary target, the government must sell bonds to the public when a drop in output causes an increase in the budget deficit. Although the dynamic behavior of the model is complicated, Smith suggests that crowding out effects play a crucial role in generating the instability associated with the monetarist policy.

Of course, such crowding out effects are absent in a Ricardian world. The issue of whether persistent bond-financed deficits are inflationary in such a setup was addressed by Barro (1976) and by McCallum (1984a). Barro suggests that they would be inflationary if the rate of growth of the bond stock exceeded the rate of growth of output, the simplest example being that of an economy without population growth. The reason is that in this case the present value of the government's future taxing capacity is bounded. McCallum agrees that persistent primary budget deficits are inflationary, but shows that the result does not carry over to total budget deficits. He points out that a positive growth rate of bonds can be permanently maintained in a stationary Ricardian economy, provided that this growth rate is smaller than the rate of time preference. This is because a household's disposable income also includes interest payments from the government. As a result, taxes can exceed household output and yet be smaller than disposable income. (Presumably the assumption of lump-sum taxation plays a crucial role here. Otherwise the distortionary consequences of such high taxes would be considerable.) It remains true that debt cannot grow forever faster than disposable income.[48]

One of the most controversial recent papers investigating the inflationary implications of persistent primary budget deficits is that by Sargent and Wallace

---

[48]These conclusions hold in per capita terms when the size of each household grows at a rate n and utility is a function of per capita consumption and money holdings.

(1981). They assume that persistent bond-financed deficits will eventually have to be monetized. The reason they invoke is an upper bound on the public's demand for bonds, but McCallum's analysis is also pertinent here. The strategy they consider is "monetarist" up to a point and from then on it becomes "bondist".

The fiscal authority is assumed to behave in its design of policy as a Stackelberg leader, whereas the monetary authority takes the role of a Stackelberg follower. All variations in the deficit considered are due to changes in G, since the size of after-tax per capita endowments is assumed constant and the economy is on its full-employment path with a real income growth equal to the constant rate of population growth, n. Monetary policy is determined by the choice of the rate of growth of the nominal stock of high-powered money, H. This rate of growth is assumed to be equal to θ up to time t^*, when the assumed arbitrary upper limit to private sector demand for bonds is attained. Thus, for $t < t^*$, the amount of bond financing is residually determined by the size of the primary deficit, the government budget constraint, and θ. From then on the amount of bond financing is determined by the requirement that the per capita bond stock be kept constant at that maximum level, while it is the rate of growth of H that is now residually determined.

The private sector in their model consists of the "rich" and the "poor", while the government consists of a fiscal and of a monetary authority. A transactions motive for holding money is not incorporated, nor is there any element of uncertainty. Bonds and claims to capital are assumed to be of sufficiently large denominations for the poor not to be able to afford them, and legal restrictions are assumed (somewhat artificially) to prevent the poor from pooling funds and the rich from acting as financial intermediaries for the poor. Thus, money is held only by the poor, while the rich hold their wealth in the form of bonds and of capital which bear the same real rate of return, R. It is assumed that R is fixed and that it exceeds the rate of population growth and the rate of return on money (equal to minus the inflation rate).

Buiter (1982) doubts whether this setup is appropriate for discussing issues of inflation and of government debt. First, in Sargent and Wallace's formulation, government spending, $G(t)$, is wasteful, since it does not enter in private utility functions and reduces the amount of resources available for consumption or investment. Second, the presence of the postulated constraints on the portfolio behavior of the poor imply that Pareto-optimal policies should involve a deflation rate of $-R$, thus making available to all agents intertemporal market terms of trade equal to the technological intertemporal terms of trade for the economy as a whole. Third, to the extent that the constraints imposed on the poor imply underaccumulation of capital, the government should act as a net lender to the private sector and/or give subsidies to the rich.

These objections notwithstanding, two interesting questions have been asked in the context of this model. First, what are the effects on the time path of inflation of adopting a more restrictive monetary policy today? Second, what are the effects on inflation of fiscal actions that result in larger real per capita total deficits? This second question includes cases of "fiscal irresponsibility", where fiscal authorities allow the deficit to exceed the maximum seignorage obtainable in steady state. We discuss both questions here.

6.2.1. Effects of monetary restriction

The effects of tighter money today are the focus of the Sargent–Wallace paper. On the basis of the setup described above, the authors derive two results. The first is that when money demand is independent of the inflation rate, a lower value of θ (and thus a lower rate of inflation) for $t < t^*$ always necessitates a higher rate of growth of money and higher inflation after t^*. This is because the lower θ for $t < t^*$ causes a higher level of the real per capita bond stock to be attained at $t = t^*$ and maintained thereafter. Since R is assumed to exceed n, this means that the size of the real per capita debt service (corrected for inflation and growth) for $t \geq t^*$ is larger. As a result, the rate of monetary growth (and consequently inflation) is also larger beyond t^* in order to finance the higher real per capita total (as opposed to primary) deficit.

The second result concerns the case where money demand decreases with expected inflation. Current inflation depends on the entire anticipated future path of the money supply. When a lower θ for $t < t^*$ implies higher rates of monetary growth after t^*, it becomes possible to construct examples in which these higher later rates dominate the lower earlier rates and produce higher inflation even before t^*. It should be noted, however, that this occurs only for specific parameter configurations.

Darby (1984) has noted that the Sargent–Wallace result in which monetary policy is fully dictated by the stance of fiscal policy requires that the real after-tax rate on bonds exceed the natural rate of growth of the economy. When the sign of this inequality is reversed, a given budget deficit can be dynamically consistent with a range of values for θ. As long as θ remains within this range, changes in monetary policy can take place today without having to be reversed over the longer run. Darby points to evidence showing that even long-term, before-tax yields on government bonds have not approached corresponding growth rates of real output in the United States. This is a fortiori true of after-tax yields.[49] Thus, there may be more flexibility in the choice of monetary policy than implied by the Sargent–Wallace analysis.

Buiter (1983b) suggests that even when the real rate on bonds exceeds the natural rate of growth and when money demand depends on expected inflation,

---

[49]This evidence is consistent with the analysis of Tobin (1986).

a lower value of θ for $t < t^*$ need not imply a higher rate of growth of the nominal money stock and higher inflation after t^*. While it is still true that the inflation rate for $t \geq t^*$ is higher the higher the real per capita bond stock, it is not clear that a lower value of θ for $t < t^*$ always implies a higher real per capita bond stock from t^* onwards. Specifically, a lower value of θ implies a higher real per capita bond stock for $t \geq t^*$ if it lowers the real discounted present value of the government's new money creation between $t = 0$ and $t = t^*$.

6.2.2. Effects of larger deficits

Buiter (1985) explores the consequences for the time path of inflation of fiscal policies that result in large real per capita total deficits, including the case where they exceed the "maximum seignorage" obtainable in a steady state. Real seignorage is defined as the amount of real resources that a government acquires in a period simply by virtue of the fact that private agents will hold the currency it prints. The per capita measure of this is equal in the steady state to the product of the real money stock times the sum of the inflation rate and the natural rate of growth of output. By raising inflation, the government also lowers real money demand. The two effects go against each other and there generally exists a maximum amount of real per capita seignorage that the government can extract.

Buiter examines the properties of the differential equation derived from the government budget constraint, assuming that the real per capita bond stock is kept constant at b and that nominal money demand per capita, m, depends inversely on the inflation rate, π:

$$\dot{m} = d + (R - n)b - (\pi + n)m , \qquad (6.1)$$

$$m = c_1 - c_2\pi , \quad c_1, c_2 > 0 , \qquad (6.2)$$

where d is the real primary deficit per capita, n is the natural rate of growth of output, and R is the real rate of return on bonds. The expression on the right-hand side of equation (6.1) is the per capita measure of the real, inflation- and growth-corrected budget deficit. Excessively high values of this measure are regarded as instances of "fiscal irresponsibility".

The point Buiter makes is that in the Sargent–Wallace model, the effect of fiscal irresponsibility can never be hyperinflation. In other words, fiscal policy in this model cannot generate unbounded increases in the inflation rate.

Specifically, in the case considered by Sargent and Wallace, where $d + (R - n)b$ is below the maximum amount of seignorage (or inflation tax) that could be attained in a steady state of the system, the above equation of motion has two equilibria (m, π), and there seems to be no economic criterion for choosing between them. If we consider the locally unstable equilibrium (as Sargent and Wallace do), an increase in the deficit will indeed raise the long-run rate of inflation, but by a finite amount. Alternatively, if the locally stable equilibrium is chosen, a finite reduction in the long-run inflation rate will result. This difference in signs mirrors the opposite effects on the amount of steady-state seignorage generated by a reduction in monetary growth.

However, it is also conceivable that the real total per capita deficit (adjusted for inflation and growth) will be set by the fiscal authority so irresponsibly as to exceed the maximum seignorage obtainable in the steady state. Buiter shows that in this case enough seignorage revenue could be generated so as to cover this difference through a process involving continuously increasing m, and continuously falling rates of inflation and monetary growth outside the steady state. This process is one of "hyperdisinflation", and it is unsustainable in the Sargent–Wallace model, since m in that model is bounded from above and cannot grow forever. The reason for this boundedness of m is that money is held by the poor to finance second-period consumption and both income and the supply of consumer goods are bounded. Indeed, some have argued (not entirely convincingly) that an unsustainable process would not even get started in a rational expectations world. The conclusion is that the case against fiscal irresponsibility provided by the Sargent–Wallace model emphasizing inflation, cannot rest on fears of hyperinflation, but only (at worst) on fears of finite increases in inflation rates.

7. Concluding remarks

There are two ways to evaluate a theoretical hypothesis. One is to ask how well it survives relaxations of assumptions, especially to see how dependent it is on patently unrealistic premises. An alternative criterion is the consistency of the theory's implications with empirical observations, the validity of its predictions. This test ignores the plausibility of assumptions. According to Milton Friedman's "methodology of positive economics", the crucial question is whether the economy behaves *as if* the theory were valid.

Our pragmatic view, following Tjalling Koopmans, is that all opportunities for testing should be seized, from the plausibility of primitive assumptions to the congruence of ultimate implications with observations. Empirical testing is too difficult, and too often ambiguous, to permit us to rely exclusively on the "as if" criterion in choosing among hypotheses.

Let us try to evaluate the three strong neutrality propositions reviewed in Sections 4, 5, and 6 by both kinds of criteria.

Debt neutrality fails the first criterion by a wide margin. In Section 4 we reviewed a series of papers showing how sensitive the Barro–Ricardo Equivalence theorem is to relaxing any one of numerous assumptions. Few economists can believe that all those assumptions hold in practice. But the profession, including even some of the harshest critics of debt neutrality, seems willing to overlook such unrealism and focus on the "as if" criterion instead.

We discussed the empirical literature but found the results inconclusive. More empirical research is needed and should be possible. Recent data on saving rates and deficits, especially in the United States, seem prima facie difficult to reconcile with debt neutrality. However, the inability of researchers to agree, even for identical sample periods and similar sets of variables, is not encouraging. We seem to need new tests as well as new data.

To reject debt neutrality is not to dismiss the sensible idea that expectations of future taxes, as of other future policies, affect current consumption and saving decisions, especially when there are credible signals of political and legislative intent.

We are reluctant to recommend more research on deficits, given the already huge volume of literature on the subject. However, there seems to be room for analysis of the effects of persistent budget deficits in a greater variety of circumstances. For example, what are the consequences of unsustainable policies not reversed before the situation gets "out of hand"? Both the profession and the lay public need a plausible "doomsday scenario" in debating the needs for and merits of fiscal austerity programs.

Superneutrality is the subject of a considerable literature examining critically its necessary assumptions. One necessary assumption for superneutrality, as well as for debt neutrality, is that consumer-savers' horizons are infinite. But this is not sufficient; a number of interesting papers identify departures from superneutrality even with infinite horizons. Although the literature provides a fairly good understanding of cases in which superneutrality fails, it is more difficult to dismiss this proposition as dependent on patently unrealistic assumptions than to dismiss debt neutrality. There is room for more research both on identifying conditions implying departures from superneutrality and on evaluating the realism of such conditions.

The most obvious gap, however, is in the empirical literature on superneutrality. The Fisher hypothesis has received much attention, but few papers test superneutrality directly. Perhaps more could be done following the methodology of Sargent's (1973) paper, specifying a model where superneutrality holds and carrying out joint tests of superneutrality and the underlying model. Sargent focused on the Fisher hypothesis, but the same methods could be used to test invariance of real per capita consumption or of the capital stock.

Testing superneutrality should not be the sole aim of research on the effects of inflation on capital accumulation. If there are such effects, it is important to identify their direction and importance, whether positive because of Mundell or Tobin effects or negative because of the real costs of economizing money balances.

Monetary policies, distinguished from fiscal policies, involve exchanges of assets between the government or its central bank and private agents. Models exhibiting irrelevance of asset exchanges show entire classes of policies that support the same equilibrium allocations. If this is correct, it does simplify the policy-maker's problem! Within this literature, there is still room for models exploring the precise conditions under which such policy classes exist. It is also interesting to examine whether the equilibrium in question is the only one supported by each policy in a given class. If there are multiple equilibria associated with each policy, irrelevance classes may be difficult to define.

Whether open market operations as typically implemented in practice are irrelevant, is a different question. A reader of this literature must keep in mind exactly what assets are being exchanged in each model. Some papers redefine the terms "open market operations" and "constant fiscal policy" and then try to justify their model-based redefinitions. It does not then follow that *all* feasible asset exchanges are irrelevant.

There is little empirical research related to this species of irrelevance literature. One reason may be that the asset swaps in the models do not resemble actually observed central bank operations. However, it should be possible to find historical approximations to at least some of the modeled asset exchanges and to test directly the hypothesis of neutrality. Indeed, if there are no such incidents, one may be tempted to ask whether it is the literature that is irrelevant, i.e. irrelevant to the monetary institutions and practices of real-world economies.

The foregoing remarks were stimulated by our surveys of neutrality literature in Sections 4–6. As they indicate, contemporary theory of fiscal and monetary policy is far removed from the practical concerns of policy-makers. In Section 3 we explained how current "microfoundations" methodology inevitably creates a wide gulf between theory and application. There was not always such a gulf. As our review in Section 2 of older traditions in macroeconomics indicates, fiscal theory and fiscal policy were once closely linked, each contributing to the other. The same was true of monetary theory and monetary policy. The major challenge to theorists today is to model enough of the heterogeneities, institutional idiosyncracies, and market imperfections of actual economies to make their theories useful to empirical researchers and interesting to policy practitioners.

References

Abel, A.B. and B.D. Bernheim (1986) 'Fiscal policy with impure intergenerational altruism', mimeo.
Abel, A.B., N.G. Mankiw, L.H. Summers and R.J. Zeckhauser (1986) 'Assessing dynamic efficiency: Theory and evidence', NBER Working Paper 2097.

Anderson, L.C. and K.M. Carlson (1970) 'A monetarist model of economic stabilization', *Federal Reserve Bank of St. Louis Review*, 54: 7–25.
Asako, K. (1983) 'The utility function and the superneutrality of money on the transition path', *Econometrica*, 51: 1593–1596.
Aschauer, D.A. (1985) 'Fiscal policy and aggregate demand', *American Economic Review*, 75: 117–127.
Barro, R.J. (1974) 'Are government bonds net wealth?', *Journal of Political Economy*, 82: 1095–1117.
Barro, R.J. (1976) 'Reply to Feldstein and Buchanan', *Journal of Political Economy*, 84: 343–350.
Barro, R.J. (1978) *The impact of social security on private saving: Evidence from the U.S. time series*. Washington: American Enterprise Institute.
Barro, R.J. (1979) 'On the determination of the public debt', *Journal of Political Economy*, 87: 940–971.
Barro, R.J. (1983) *Macroeconomics*. New York: Wiley.
Barsky, R.B. (1987) 'The Fisher hypothesis and the forecastability and persistence of inflation', *Journal of Monetary Economics*, 19: 3–24.
Barsky, R.B., N.G. Mankiw and S.P. Zeldes (1986) 'Ricardian consumers with Keynesian propensities', *American Economic Review*, 76: 676–691.
Barth, J.R., G. Iden and F.S. Russek (1986) 'Government debt, government spending, and private sector behavior', *American Economic Review*, 76: 1158–1167.
Benninga, S. and A. Protopapadakis (1984) 'The neutrality of the real equilibrium under alternative financing of government expenditures', *Journal of Monetary Economics*, 14: 183–208.
Bernheim D.B. (1987) 'Ricardian equivalence: An evaluation of theory and evidence', *NBER Macroeconomics Annual*, 2: 263–304.
Bernheim, D.B. and K. Bagwell (1988) 'Is everything neutral?', *Journal of Political Economy*, 96: 308–338.
Blanchard, O.J. (1985) 'Debt, deficits, and finite horizons', *Journal of Political Economy*, 93: 223–247.
Blinder, A.S. and R. Solow (1974): 'Analytical foundations of fiscal policy', in: *The economics of public finance*. Washington: Brookings Institution.
Boskin, M.J. (1978) 'Taxation, saving, and the rate of interest', *Journal of Political Economy*, 86: S3–S27.
Brock, W.A. (1974) 'Money and growth: The use of long run perfect foresight', *International Economic Review*, 15: 750–777.
Buchanan, J.M. (1964) 'Concerning future generations', in: J.M. Ferguson, ed., *Public debt and future generations*. Chapel Hill: The University of North Carolina Press.
Buiter, W.H. (1979) 'Government finance in an overlapping-generations model with gifts and bequests', in: G.M. von Furstenberg, ed., *Social security versus private saving*. Cambridge, Mass.: Ballinger.
Buiter, W.H. (1980) ' "Crowding out" of private capital formation by government borrowing in the presence of intergenerational gifts and bequests', *Greek Economic Review*, 2: 111–142.
Buiter, W.H. (1982) 'Comment on T.J. Sargent and N. Wallace "Some unpleasant monetarist arithmetic" ', NBER Working Paper 867.
Buiter, W.H. (1983a) 'The theory of optimum deficits and debt', NBER Working Paper 1232.
Buiter, W.H. (1983b) 'Deficits, crowding out, and inflation: The simple analytics', NBER Working Paper 1078.
Buiter, W.H. (1985) 'A fiscal theory of hyperdeflations? Some surprising monetarist arithmetic', NBER Technical Working Paper 52.
Buiter, W.H. and J. Carmichael (1984) 'Government debt: Comment', *American Economic Review*, 74: 762–765.
Buiter, W.H. and J. Tobin (1978) 'Debt neutrality: A brief review of doctrine and evidence', Cowles Foundation Paper 497.
Burbidge, J.B. (1983) 'Government debt in an overlapping-generations model with bequests and gifts', *American Economic Review*, 73: 222–227.
Burbidge, J.B. (1984) 'Government debt: Reply', *American Economic Review*, 74: 766–767.

Cargill, T.F. and R.A. Meyer (1980) 'The term structure of inflationary expectations and market efficiency', *Journal of Finance*, 35: 57–70.

Carmichael, J. (1982) 'On Barro's theorem of debt neutrality: The irrelevance of net wealth', *American Economic Review*, 72: 202–213.

Carmichael, J. and P.W. Stebbing (1983) 'Fisher's paradox and the theory of interest', *American Economic Review*, 73: 619–630.

Chamley, C. and H. Polemarchakis (1984) 'Assets, general equilibrium, and the neutrality of money', *Review of Economic Studies*, 51: 129–138.

Christ, C.F. (1968) 'A simple macroeconomic model with a government budget restraint', *Journal of Political Economy*, 76: 53–67.

Cohen, D. (1985) 'Inflation, wealth, and interest rates in an intertemporal optimizing model', *Journal of Monetary Economics*, 16: 73–85.

Currie, D. (1978) 'Macroeconomic policy and the government financing requirement: A survey of recent views', in: M. Artis and R. Nobay, eds., *Studies in contemporary economic analysis*, Vol. 1. London: Croom-Helm. (1978).

Darby, M.R. (1975) 'The financial and tax effects of monetary policy on interest rates', *Economic Inquiry*, 13: 266–276.

Darby, M.R. (1984) 'Some pleasant monetarist arithmetic,' *Federal Reserve Bank of Minneapolis Quarterly Review*, 1984: 32–37.

Diamond, P.A. (1965) 'National debt in a neoclassical growth model', *American Economic Review*, 55: 1126–1150.

Domar, E. (1944) 'The "burden of the debt" and the national income', *American Economic Review*, 34: 798–827; also in his *Essays in the theory of economic growth*. New York: Oxford University Press (1957).

Dornbusch, R. and J.A. Frenkel (1973) 'Inflation and growth: Alternative approaches', *Journal of Money, Credit and Banking*, 5: 141–156.

Drazen, A. (1978) 'Government debt, human capital, and bequests in a life-cycle model', *Journal of Political Economy*, 86: 505–516.

Drazen, A. (1981) 'Inflation and capital accumulation under a finite horizon', *Journal of Monetary Economics*, 8: 247–260.

Eisner, R. (1985) *How real is the deficit?* New York: Free Press.

Fama, E.F. (1975) 'Short-term interest rates as predictors of inflation', *American Economic Review*, 65: 269–282.

Feldstein, M. (1976) 'Perceived wealth in bonds and social security: A comment', *Journal of Political Economy*, 84: 331–336.

Feldstein, M. (1982) 'Government deficits and aggregate demand', *Journal of Monetary Economics*, 9: 1–20.

Feldstein, M. (1988) 'The effects of fiscal policies when incomes are uncertain: A contradiction to Ricardian equivalence', *American Economic Review*, 78: 14–23.

Feldstein, M. and D.W. Elmendorf (1987) 'Taxes, budget deficits, and consumer spending: Some new evidence', *American Economic Review*, forthcoming.

Feldstein, M. and S.C. Tsiang (1968) 'The interest rate taxation, and the personal savings incentive', *Quarterly Journal of Economics*, 82: 419–434.

Ferguson, J.M., ed. (1964) *Public debt and future generations*. Chapel Hill: The University of North Carolina Press.

Fischer, S. (1979) 'Capital accumulation on the transition path in a monetary optimizing model', *Econometrica*, 47: 1433–1439.

Fisher, I. (1930) *The theory of interest*. New York: Macmillan.

Fleming, J.M. (1962) 'Domestic financial policies under fixed and under floating exchange rates', *IMF Staff Papers*, 9: 363–379.

Friedman, B.M. (1977) 'Financial flow variables and the short-run determination of long-term interest rates', *Journal of Political Economy*, 85: 661–689.

Friedman, B.M. (1978) 'Crowding out or crowding in? Economic consequences of financing government deficits', *Brookings Papers on Economic Activity*, 9: 593–641.

Friedman, B.M. (1980) 'The determination of long-term interest rates: Implications for fiscal and monetary policies', *Journal of Money, Credit and Banking*, 12: 331–352.

Friedman, M. (1970) 'A theoretical framework for monetary analysis', *Journal of Political Economy*, 78: 193–238; Reprinted in R.J. Gordon, ed., *Milton Friedman's monetary framework*. Chicago: University of Chicago Press (1974), pp. 1–62.

Friedman, M. and A. Schwartz (1976) 'From Gibson to Fisher', *Explorations in Economic Research*, 3: 288–289.

Friedman, M. and A. Schwartz (1982) *Monetary trends in the United States and the United Kingdom*. Chicago: University of Chicago Press for the NBER.

Gale, D. (1983) *Money: In disequilibrium*. Cambridge: Cambridge University Press/Nisbet.

Garbade, K. and P. Wachtel (1978) 'Time variation in the relationship between inflation and interest rates', *Journal of Monetary Economics*, 4: 755–765.

Grossman, S. and L. Weiss (1983) 'A transactions-based model of the monetary transmission mechanism', *American Economic Review*, 73: 871–880.

Haliassos, M. (1987) 'Multi-asset economies with staggered portfolio adjustments', University of Maryland Working Paper 88-14.

Hansen, A.H. (1941) *Business cycles and national income*. New York: Norton.

Hansen, A.H. (1953) *A guide to Keynes*. New York: McGraw-Hill.

Hansson, I. and C. Stuart (1986) 'The Fisher hypothesis and international capital markets', *Journal of Political Economy*, 94: 1330–1337.

Hicks, J.R. (1937) 'Mr. Keynes and the "Classics"; A suggested interpretation', *Econometrica*, 5: 147–159.

Howrey, E.P. and S. Hymans (1978) 'The measurement and determination of loanable funds saving', *Brookings Papers on Economic Activity*, 3: 655–685.

Hubbard, R.G. and K.L. Judd (1986a) 'Finite lifetimes, borrowing constraints, and short-run fiscal policy', mimeo.

Hubbard, R.G. and K.L. Judd (1986b) 'Liquidity constraints, fiscal policy, and consumption', *Brookings Papers on Economic Activity*, 1986-1: 1–50.

Kahn, R.F. (1931) 'The relation of home investment to unemployment', *Economic Journal*, 41: 173–198.

Keynes, J.M. (1936) *The general theory of employment, interest, and money*. London: The Macmillan Press for The Royal Economic Society. (1973).

Kochin, L.A. (1974) 'Are future taxes anticipated by consumers?', *Journal of Money, Credit and Banking*, 6: 385–394.

Kormendi, R.C. (1983) 'Government debt, government spending, and private sector behavior', *American Economic Review*, 73: 994–1010.

Kotlikoff, L. and L.H. Summers (1981) 'The importance of intergenerational transfers in aggregate capital accumulation', *Journal of Political Economy*, 89: 706–732.

Laitner, J.P. (1979) 'Bequests, golden-age capital accumulation, and government debt', *Economica*, 46: 403–414.

Lerner, A.P. (1943) 'Functional finance and the federal debt', *Social Research*, 10: 38–51.

Lerner, A.P. (1944) *The economics of control*. New York: Macmillan.

Levhari, D. and D. Patinkin (1968) 'The role of money in a simple growth model', *American Economic Review*, 58: 713–753.

Lucas, R.E. (1976) 'Economic policy evaluation: A critique', in: K. Brunner and A. Meltzer, eds., *The Phillips curve and labor markets*, Carnegie-Rochester Conference Series on Public Policy, 1: 19–46.

McCallum, B.T. (1984a) 'Are bond-financed deficits inflationary? A Ricardian analysis', *Journal of Political Economy*, 92: 123–135.

McCallum, B.T. (1984b) 'On low-frequency estimates of long-run relationships in macroeconomics', *Journal of Monetary Economics*, 14: 3–14.

McCallum, B.T. (1986) 'Estimating the long-run relationship between interest rates and inflation: A reply', *Journal of Monetary Economics*, 18: 87–90.

Miller, M.H. and F. Modigliani (1961) 'Dividend policy, growth and the valuation of shares', *Journal of Business*, 34: 235–264.

Mirer, T.W. (1979) 'The wealth–age relation among the aged', *American Economic Review*, 69: 435–443.

Modigliani, F. (1964) 'Long-run implications of alternative fiscal policies and the burden of the national debt', in: J.M. Ferguson, ed., *Public debt and future generations*. Chapel Hill: The University of North Carolina Press.

Modigliani, F. and A. Ando (1976) 'Impacts of fiscal actions on aggregate income and the monetarist controversy: Theory and evidence', in: J.L. Stein, ed., *Monetarism*. Amsterdam: North-Holland, pp. 17–42.

Modigliani, F. and R. Brumberg (1954) 'Utility analysis and the consumption function: An interpretation of cross-section data', in: K.K. Kurihara, ed., *Post-Keynesian economics*. New Brunswick.

Modigliani, F. and A. Sterling (1986) 'Government debt, government spending, and private sector: Comment', *American Economic Review*, 76: 1168–1179.

Mundell, R.A. (1963a) 'Capital mobility and stabilization policies under fixed and floating exchange rates', *Canadian Journal of Economics and Political Science*, 29: 475–485.

Mundell, R.A. (1963b) 'Inflation and real interest', *Journal of Political Economy*, 71: 280–283.

Nelson, C.R. and G.W. Schwert (1977) 'Short-term interest rates as predictors of inflation: On testing the hypothesis that the real rate of interest is constant', *American Economic Review*, 67: 478–488.

O'Connell, S.A. and S.P. Zeldes (1987) 'Ponzi games and Ricardian equivalence', mimeo.

Patinkin, D. (1948) 'Price flexibility and full employment', *American Economic Review*, 38: 543–564.

Patinkin, D. (1956) *Money, interest, and prices*. Evanston: Row Peterson.

Peled, D. (1985) 'Stochastic inflation and government provision of indexed bonds', *Journal of Monetary Economics*, 15: 291–308.

Pigou, A.C. (1943) 'The classical stationary state', *Economic Journal*, 53: 343–351.

Pigou, A.C. (1947) 'Economic progress in a stable environment', *Economica*, 14: 180–190.

Plosser, C.I. (1982) 'Government financing decisions and asset returns', *Journal of Monetary Economics*, 9: 325–352.

Poole, W. (1970) 'Optimal choice of monetary policy instruments in a simple stochastic model', *Quarterly Journal of Economics*, 84: 197–216.

Porterba, J.M. and L.H. Summers (1986) 'Finite lifetimes and the effects of budget deficits on national savings', M.I.T. Working Paper 434.

Ricardo, D. (1817) *On the principles of political economy and taxation*, edited by Piero Sraffa with the collaboration of M.H. Dobb. Cambridge: Cambridge University Press for the Royal Economic Society (1951).

Rotemberg, J.J. (1984) 'A monetary equilibrium model with transactions costs', *Journal of Political Economy*, 92: 40–58.

Sargent, T.J. (1973) 'Rational expectations, the real rate of interest, and the natural rate of unemployment', *Brookings Papers on Economic Activity*, 1973-2: 429–472.

Sargent, T.J. (1987) *Dynamic macroeconomic theory*. Cambridge, Mass.: Harvard University Press.

Sargent, T.J. and B.D. Smith (1987) 'Irrelevance of open market operations in some economies with government currency being dominated in rate of return', *American Economic Review*, 77: 78–92.

Sargent, T.J. and N. Wallace (1981) 'Some unpleasant monetarist arithmetic', *Federal Reserve Bank of Minneapolis Quarterly Review*, 5: 1–17.

Seater, J.J. and R.S. Mariano (1985) 'New tests of the life cycle and tax discounting hypothesis', *Journal of Monetary Economics*, 15: 195–215.

Sidrauski, M. (1967) 'Rational choice and patterns of growth in a monetary economy', *American Economic Review*, 57: 534–544.

Siegel, J.J. (1983) 'Technological change and the superneutrality of money', *Journal of Money, Credit and Banking*, 15: 363–367.

Smith, G. (1982) 'Monetarism, bondism, and inflation', *Journal of Money, Credit and Banking*, 14: 278–286.

Summers, L.H. (1981) 'Capital taxation and accumulation in a life cycle growth model', *American Economic Review*, 71: 533–544.

Summers, L.H. (1982) 'Tax policy, the rate of return, and savings', NBER Working Paper 995.

Summers, L.H. (1983) 'The nonadjustment of nominal interest rates: A study of the Fisher effect', in: J. Tobin, ed., *Macroeconomic prices and quantities: Essays in memory of Arthur Okun*. Washington: Brookings Institution.

Summers, L.H. (1984) 'The after tax rate of return affects private savings', Harvard Institute of Economic Research Discussion Paper 1042.

Summers, L.H. (1986) 'Estimating the long-run relationship between interest rates and inflation: A response to McCallum'. *Journal of Monetary Economics*, 18: 77–86.

Tanner, E.J. (1979) 'An empirical investigation of tax discounting', *Journal of Money, Credit and Banking*, 11: 214–218.

Tanzi, V. (1980) 'Inflationary expectations, economic activity, taxes, and interest rates', *American Economic Review*, 70: 12–21.

Tobin, J. (1961) 'Money, capital, and other stores of value', *American Economic Review*, 51: 26–37.

Tobin, J. (1963) 'An essay on the principles of debt management', in: *Fiscal and debt management policies*, prepared for the Commission on Money and Credit. Englewood Cliffs: Prentice-Hall. Reprinted as *Cowles Foundation*, Paper No. 195, New Haven (1963).

Tobin, J. (1965a) 'Money and economic growth', *Econometrica*, 33: 671–684.

Tobin, J. (1965b) 'The burden of the public debt: A review article', *Journal of Finance*, 20: 679–682.

Tobin, J. (1968) 'Notes on optimal monetary growth', *Journal of Political Economy*, 76: 833–859.

Tobin, J. (1978) 'Comment from an academic scribbler' (on *Democracy in deficit*, by J.M. Buchanan and Richard E. Wagner), *Journal of Monetary Economics*, 4: 617–625.

Tobin, J. (1980) *Asset accumulation and economic activity*. Chicago: The University of Chicago Press.

Tobin, J. (1982) 'Money and finance in the macroeconomic process', *Journal of Money, Credit and Banking*, 14: 171–204.

Tobin, J. (1986a) 'The monetary–fiscal mix: Long-run implications', *American Economic Review*, 76: 213–218.

Tobin, J. (1986b) 'On the welfare macroeconomics of government financial policy', *Scandinavian Journal of Economics*, 88: 9–24.

Tobin, J. and W.H. Buiter (1976) 'Long run effects of fiscal and monetary policy on aggregate demand', in J.L. Stein, ed., *Monetarism*. Amsterdam: North Holland.

Tobin, J., W.C. Brainard, D. Backus and G. Smith (1980) 'A model of U.S. financial and nonfinancial economic behavior', *Journal of Money, Credit and Banking*, 12: 259–293.

Waldo, D.G. (1985) 'Open market operations in an overlapping generations model', *Journal of Political Economy*, 93: 1242–1257.

Wallace, N. (1981) 'A Modigliani–Miller theorem for open-market operations', *American Economic Review*, 71: 267–274.

Webb, D.C. (1981) 'The net wealth effect of government bonds when credit markets are imperfect', *Economic Journal*, 91: 405–414.

Weiss, A. and J.E. Stiglitz (1981) 'Credit rationing in markets with imperfect information', *American Economic Review*, 71: 393–410.

PART 7

MONEY, INFLATION, AND WELFARE

Chapter 18

INFLATION: THEORY AND EVIDENCE

BENNETT T. McCALLUM*

Carnegie-Mellon University and NBER

Contents

*The author is indebted to W.A. Brock, Zvi Eckstein, Stanley Fischer, Benjamin Friedman, Douglas Gale, Marvin Goodfriend, David Laidler, Ching-Sheng Mao, Avin Marty, Don Patinkin, and Michael Woodford for helpful comments and to the National Science Foundation for financial support (SES 84-08691).

Handbook of Monetary Economics, Volume II, Edited by B.M. Friedman and F.H. Hahn
© *Elsevier Science Publishers B.V., 1990*

1. Introduction

Inflation is a topic that is so broad as to be almost co-extensive with monetary economics. Consequently, there are many ways in which the present chapter overlaps with others in this Handbook. In particular, various topics that are considered in detail in other chapters are treated more briefly here.[1] It needs to be emphasized, accordingly, that the main purpose of the present discussion is not to attempt authoritative treatments of those specialized topics, but instead to provide a moderately general overview of the subject of inflation. To a significant extent, the aim is to offer a framework for coherent thought on that subject, both in terms of relevant theory and evidence regarding competing hypotheses.

During the years that have passed since the preparation of the ambitious survey article by Laidler and Parkin (1975), the nature of research in monetary economics has changed considerably. Rational expectations has become the mainstream hypothesis concerning expectational behavior, the "Ricardian Equivalence Theorem" has become a familiar notion in policy discussions, issues involving overlapping-generations models and cash-in-advance constraints have become common fare, "bubble" and "sunspot" phenomena have been extensively investigated, and problems associated with dynamic inconsistency of policy have been pondered. It is natural, then, that the outline of a survey today would be different from that of the Laidler–Parkin contribution, just as its outline differed from those of earlier surveys [e.g. Bronfenbrenner and Holzman (1963) and Johnson (1963)].

Nevertheless, one of the Laidler–Parkin organizational principles remains extremely useful. That principle is provided by the distinction between steady *ongoing* inflation, which will be anticipated by rational agents, and irregular *cyclical* outbursts of above- or below-normal inflation rates, which are likely to be unanticipated. While this distinction may be somewhat unclear in practice, it is an essential one in terms of theoretical analysis since the effects of anticipated and surprise inflation may be very different. Certain effects of the former, moreover, may be quantitatively important only if maintained over a long span of time. Accordingly, our discussion will make significant use of this distinction, with Sections 2 and 3 concerned with ongoing inflation and Section 4 pertaining to cyclical aspects of price level changes.

---

[1]The relationship between monetary and fiscal policy, necessitated by the government budget constraint, is treated much more extensively in Brunner and Meltzer, Chapter 9 in this Handbook, while bubbles and certain issues involving overlapping-generations models are explored in Brock, Chapter 7 in this Handbook. Also Woodford's Chapter 20 provides a more detailed consideration of the optimal inflation rate while Chapter 15 by Blanchard is concerned with aggregate supply or Phillips-curve issues.

Of the various new directions in monetary economics alluded to above, there are two that are evidently of fundamental importance. The first of these is the increased tendency of theoretical researchers to conduct their analysis in general equilibrium models in which private agents are depicted as solving dynamic optimization problems. The second is the increased interest in understanding *why* macroeconomic policy-makers – the monetary and fiscal authorities – behave as they do. The first of these two tendencies is clearly reflected in the present survey, with all of the analysis of Sections 2 and 3 being of a general equilibrium type. The second is also reflected to a substantial extent, though explicit recognition appears only toward the end of the chapter. There, in Section 5, we consider a line of analysis that is designed to explain the fact that inflation rates in industrial nations have been, over the past 40 years, positive to an overwhelming extent.

There is one contentious issue that it will be useful to address at the outset, before beginning the main analytical discussion. That issue is the extent to which validity should be assigned to Milton Friedman's famous dictum that "Inflation is always and everywhere a monetary phenomenon" (1963, p. 17). That particular statement has been strongly disputed by leading economists, including one of the editors of this Handbook [Hahn (1983)]. I would suggest, nevertheless, that there is in fact little professional disagreement with Friedman's position, when the latter is properly interpreted. In that regard it is essential to keep in mind that in the essay in question Friedman states that "inflation" will be taken to mean "a steady and sustained rise in prices" (1963, p. 1). Thus, his proposition does not constitute a denial of the fact that a shock which reduces an economy's productive capacity – a drought, a capital-destroying earthquake, or an increase in the real price that must be paid for imported goods – will in the absence of any monetary response lead to an increase in the general price level.[2] Nor does the Friedman position imply that an economy's ongoing inflation rate is determined solely by the rate of monetary growth; certainly the normal rate of output growth [Friedman (1963, p. 23)] and the pace of technical change in the payments industry are relevant.[3] But neither of

[2]An increase in monopoly power would, of course, do the same. But these are all examples of one-time effects on the price level, not the ongoing inflation rate. It is presumably agreed by both critics and supporters, incidentally, that Friedman's statement is a substantive proposition to the effect that inflation is brought about by money stock changes, not a tautological restatement of its definition as an ongoing decline in the value of money.

[3]The point is that these are the only two determinants of inflation (beside the money stock growth rate) in a steady state. This is so because all sensible monetary models imply relationships – be they ad hoc money-demand functions in Keynesian macroeconometric models or Euler equations in optimizing general equilibrium models – that link money balances willingly held to a real transaction measure (like output) and an opportunity-cost interest rate, the last of which must be constant over time in a steady state. In the model of Subsection 2.1 below, for example, the Euler equations (2.4), (2.5), and (2.6) together imply the relation $u_2(c_{t+1}, m_{t+1})/u_1(c_{t+1}, m_{t+1}) = \pi_t + f'(k_{t+1}) + \pi_t f'(k_{t+1})$. (Symbols are defined below.) The right-hand side of the latter will be equal to the nominal interest rate, R_t, so the steady-state relation is $u_2(c, m)/u_1(c, m) = R$. Technical change in the payments process would shift the u function, as explained in footnote 7.

those factors can plausibly contribute more than a few percentage points per year, and their contributions tend to work in opposite directions. Thus, their net effect can account for only (say) 0–2 percentage points per year on a sustained basis, a magnitude that is small in comparison to the contribution, during substantial inflations, of money growth.[4]

With respect to fiscal policy, matters cannot be summarized quite so briefly. But unless tax and spending patterns are such as to generate an unsustainable path – a possibility that will be described below in Subsection 2.3 – different fiscal rules will imply different ongoing inflation rates (as distinct from price levels) only if they result in different money stock growth rates. Basically, Friedman's dictum relies only on the presumption that money demand behavior is reasonably stable in real terms and that the volume of real transactions does not respond on a sustained basis to changes in the rate of money creation.

The one notable way in which substantial long-lasting inflation could in principle result without excessive money growth is via the route of speculative "bubble" effects on the general price level. It is not clear that many economists actually believe in the empirical relevance of this type of phenomenon, but there has been considerable interest in it as a matter of theory. The idea will, accordingly, be briefly considered (in Subsection 3.2).

Another topic that can usefully be mentioned here is that of money stock exogeneity. In this regard, the emphasis given by Friedman and Schwartz (1963) to various historical episodes involving autonomous shifts in monetary policy has led some critics to conclude that Friedman and other "monetarist" economists hold the view that monetary policy actions are exogenous. But while it is understandable how such a conclusion could be drawn, the conclusion is nevertheless seriously mistaken. For monetary policy actions to be exogenous, they would have to be entirely unresponsive to current and past macroeconomic conditions. Whether there is *any* researcher who holds such a belief is doubtful, and certainly monetarist economists do not. Friedman (1960) and Brunner and Meltzer (1983) may believe that money stock exogeneity

---

[4]This last statement might be disputed by pointing to the United States' experience of 1983–86, a period during which inflation rates averaged about 8 percent lower than money growth rates (measured by M1). A span of four years might arguably be considered as long enough to represent "sustained" in which case the evidence could appear to contradict Friedman's dictum. But it is important to recognize that the cost of holding money balances declined dramatically over this period, both because of interest rate reductions and regulatory changes that led to the introduction of checkable deposits (included in M1) on which interest is paid. Such a reduction would be expected to result in a sizeable increase in the quantity of real M1 balances held. If the money demand function were of the constant elasticity form and the elasticity with respect to the interest-cost variable were -0.20, for example, a reduction in the holding-cost measure from 0.12 to 0.02 would call for an increase in real balances of about 43 percent ($-0.2[\log 0.02 - \log 0.12] = \log 1.43$). The transitional effect is, in other words, large enough to keep inflation substantially below money growth rates for several years if the effects are spread over time.

would be desirable, but – as their writings abundantly demonstrate – they do not believe that such unresponsiveness has in fact prevailed.

A limitation of the discussion in this chapter is that it pertains to a closed economy. From a practical point of view that limitation is serious, as policy toward inflation in actual economies is significantly intertwined with terms-of-trade and exchange-rate considerations. But space constraints dictate the elimination of many relevant topics, and it is at least possible that theoretical clarity on essentials is actually enhanced by the absence of open-economy complications.[5]

Organizationally, the paper proceeds as follows. Section 2 begins with the development of a simplified but dynamic general equilibrium framework for the analysis of steady-state inflation. Some welfare considerations are included. Next, Section 3 discusses an alternative framework, the possibility of price level bubbles, and some relevant empirical evidence. In Section 4 attention is then shifted to the case of cyclical fluctuations, the main emphasis being given to alternative theories of the link between real and nominal variables – i.e. to Phillips-curve relationships. Again empirical evidence is briefly reviewed. Section 5 is, as mentioned above, concerned with analysis of policy behavior and, in particular, the explanation of a possible inflationary bias in the policy process. Finally, a few concluding comments are provided in Section 6.

2. Basic analysis of ongoing inflation

This section is devoted to a preliminary analysis of an economy with steady, ongoing inflation. But even though the analysis is concerned with alternative steady states, it begins with the specification of a general equilibrium model in which agents are depicted as solving dynamic optimization problems. Steady-state equilibria then emerge as special cases of more general dynamic equilibria. This procedure lessens the danger that agents' optimization problems are posed in a restrictive manner.

Two major simplifying devices will, on the other hand, be employed. First, all agents will be treated as alike in terms of preferences and production capabilities. Distributional matters are therefore neglected. Second, the model will be non-stochastic. Thus, the effects of uncertainty on agents' choices and utility levels are also neglected. The presumption is that these two omissions – which permit substantial simplification of the analysis – will not seriously affect the principal conclusions concerning steady states. Some consideration of the effects of uncertainty will be provided in Subsection 2.5.

---

[5]Empirical results are, of course, impaired by this neglect.

2.1. The Sidrauski model

The framework to be utilized is a discrete-time, perfect-foresight version of the well-known model of Sidrauski (1967), modified in ways to be described as we proceed. To avoid inessential clutter, we shall utilize a version with no depreciation or population growth. Thus, we consider an economy composed of a large number of similar households, each of which seeks at time t to maximize

$$u(c_t, m_t) + \beta u(c_{t+1}, m_{t+1}) + \beta^2 u(c_{t+2}, m_{t+2}) + \cdots. \tag{2.1}$$

Here c_t is consumption in period t while $m_t = M_t/P_t$, with M_t denoting the household's nominal money stock at the start of t and P_t the money price of the consumption good. The discount factor β equals $1/(1+\rho)$, where ρ is a positive time-preference parameter. Each household has access to a production function that is homogeneous of degree one in its two inputs, capital and labor. In the first version of the model labor is supplied inelastically, however, so the production function can be written as:

$$y_t = f(k_t), \tag{2.2}$$

where y_t is output and k_t is capital held at the start of t. The function f is taken to be well-behaved [Sidrauski (1967, p. 535)], so a unique positive value for k_{t+1} will be chosen in each period. Capital is output that is not consumed, so its price is the same as that of the consumption good. The real rate of return on capital held from t to $t+1$ is the marginal product $f'(k_{t+1})$.

An issue that arises immediately concerns the reason for the inclusion of m_t as an argument of the function u. The basic idea, described by many writers, is that holdings of the medium of exchange facilitate an agent's transactions. One way of expressing that idea is to assume that households derive utility only from consumption and leisure but the acquisition of consumption goods[6] requires "shopping" which reduces the time available for leisure or employment. In a monetary economy, however, the amount of shopping time required for a given amount of consumption depends negatively (up to some satiation level) upon the quantity of real money balances held by the household. If the shopping time is functionally related to c_t and m_t, substitution into the basic

---

[6]The model as written explicitly recognizes the existence of only one good. It is intended to serve, however, as a simplified representation of an economy in which each household sells a single product and makes purchases (at constant relative prices) of a large number of distinct consumption goods. That such an interpretation can be rigorously justified has been demonstrated by Lucas (1980a, p. 134), who remarks: "I imagine that this sort of elaboration is what we always have in mind when we work with aggregative models."

utility function yields an indirect utility function in which m_t appears.[7] This formalization does not justify every detail of Sidrauski's specification (2.1) as it brings in labor time as another argument and leads to somewhat different presumptions regarding the derivatives of u.[8] But it provides support for the general approach. For expositional reasons, our strategy will be to continue for the moment with Sidrauski's specification (2.1), in which u is assumed to be well-behaved, but to make modifications in what follows.

Regarding interactions with the government, it is assumed that in t each household receives transfers (net of taxes) in the real amount v_t. These are lump-sum in nature, i.e. the magnitude is regarded by each household as independent of its own assets and actions. A typical household's budget constraint for period t can then be written as:

$$f(k_t) + v_t = c_t + k_{t+1} - k_t + (1 + \pi_t)m_{t+1} - m_t, \qquad (2.3)$$

where $\pi_t = (P_{t+1} - P_t)/P_t$ is the inflation rate between t and $t + 1$. At time t, the household maximizes (2.1) subject to a sequence of constraints like (2.3), one for each period.[9] Under the assumption that u and f are both well-behaved, the first-order Euler conditions for the maximum problem can be written as equalities holding for each period. In the perfect-foresight case, these conditions become:

$$u_1(c_t, m_t) - \lambda_t = 0, \qquad (2.4)$$

$$\beta u_2(c_{t+1}, m_{t+1}) - \lambda_t(1 + \pi_t) + \beta\lambda_{t+1} = 0, \qquad (2.5)$$

$$-\lambda_t + \beta\lambda_{t+1}[f'(k_{t+1}) + 1] = 0. \qquad (2.6)$$

In addition, there are two transversality conditions:[10]

---

[7]Suppose that the basic within-period utility function is $\tilde{u}(c_t, l_t)$, where l_t is leisure in period t. Also suppose that shopping time in a period is $\psi(c_t, m_t)$, with $\psi_1 > 0$ and $\psi_2 < 0$. Then if the total time available per period is normalized at 1.0 and n_t is used to denote labor time, $l_t = 1 - n_t - \psi(c_t, m_t)$ and substitution yields $\tilde{u}(c_t, 1 - n_t - \psi(c_t, m_t)) \equiv u(c_t, m_t, n_t)$. Changes in payments technology will alter the function ψ and therefore u. It should be noted that the "cash-in-advance" constraint is simply a special case of the shopping-time model, one in which $\psi > 1$ when $m/c < 1$ and $\psi = 0$ for $m/c \geq 1$.

[8]See McCallum (1983a, p. 30). A more complete discussion of related matters is provided by Feenstra (1986).

[9]The general equilibrium nature of the model could be emphasized by permitting the household's supply of labor to differ from the amount used in production and likewise for capital, with discrepancies satisfied via competitive markets. But with all households alike, the equilibrium discrepancies would be zero. Consequently, the possibility is not recognized in (2.3) for the sake of notational simplicity.

[10]The role of the transversality conditions is to rule out paths that satisfy (2.3)–(2.6) but are undesirable to the household on a longer-term basis. They prevent the household, for example, from indefinitely accumulating assets at a rate so high that "future" consumption benefits are never obtained.

$$\lim_{t \to \infty} m_{t+1} \beta^{t-1} \lambda_t (1 + \pi_t) = 0 , \tag{2.7}$$

$$\lim_{t \to \infty} k_{t+1} \beta^{t-1} \lambda_t = 0 . \tag{2.8}$$

In the setting that has been specified, conditions (2.3)–(2.6) are necessary for a maximum while (2.3)–(2.8) are jointly sufficient.[11] Thus, if (2.7) and (2.8) are satisfied, the household's choices of c_t, m_{t+1}, k_{t+1}, and λ_t will be described (for given initial assets and paths of v_t and π_t) by the difference equations (2.3)–(2.6).

To complete the model we turn to the government. Abstracting temporarily from the possibility of borrowing, we write the government's budget constraint – in per-household terms – as follows:

$$M_{t+1} - M_t = P_t(g_t + v_t) .$$

Here g_t is real government purchases of output during t. Dividing by P_t and using the definitions of π_t and m_t, this constraint can be expressed in real terms as:

$$(1 + \pi_t)m_{t+1} - m_t = g_t + v_t . \tag{2.9}$$

It will be noted that, together the government and household budget constraints (2.9) and (2.3) imply the following overall resource constraint (or national income identity):

$$f(k_t) = c_t + k_{t+1} - k_t + g_t . \tag{2.10}$$

Because of this dependence, only two of these three constraints will be needed in the description of any equilibrium.

Consider now a situation in which time paths for M_t and g_t are chosen by the government.[12] Conditional upon those policy choices, competitive equilibrium paths for c_t, k_{t+1}, m_t, λ_t, π_t, P_t, and v_t are determined[13] by equations (2.3)–(2.6) and (2.9), plus the definitional identities:

$$m_t = M_t/P_t , \tag{2.11}$$

$$\pi_t = (P_{t+1} - P_t)/P_t . \tag{2.12}$$

---

[11]See Brock (1975). It should be mentioned that the contributions of Brock (1974, 1975) to the perfect-foresight analysis of the present type of model are so extensive that the class might justifiably be termed Sidrauski–Brock models.

[12]Other possibilities are that the government chooses paths for M_t and v_t or for g_t and v_t. The choice of a path for M_t is equivalent, it should be noted, to the choice of a path for the money-stock-growth rate, μ_t, defined as $\mu_t = (M_{t+1} - M_t)/M_t$.

[13]Provided that the transversality conditions are satisfied.

2.2. Steady-state analysis

Using the foregoing model, we now consider properties of steady states, i.e. dynamic equilibria in which every variable grows at some constant rate. Under present assumptions, with no technical progress or population growth, this condition requires that g_t, k_t, v_t, λ_t, c_t, and m_t must be constant over time, i.e. have growth rates of zero. To derive that implication, note that constant growth requires the ratio λ_{t+1}/λ_t to be constant, and that [by virtue of (2.6)] implies zero growth for k_t. Equation (2.10) then implies that $c_t + g_t$ must be constant, which can only be the case if both of those variables are constant.[14] An application of similar reasoning to (2.3) then implies zero growth for both m_t and v_t.

Given that these six variables must be constant over time, it is then possible to eliminate λ_t, M_t, and P_t and express the system as follows:

$$\beta u_2(c, m) = u_1(c, m)[1 + \pi - \beta],$$
$$1 = \beta[f'(k) + 1],$$
$$f(k) = c + g,$$
$$\pi m = g + v. \tag{2.13}$$

Here the first expression comes from (2.4) and (2.5); the second from (2.6); the third from (2.3) and (2.9); and the fourth from (2.9). With g and π given by policy,[15] these four relations determine the steady-state values of c, k, m, and v.

The implication that m_t is constant in a steady state means, of course, that the inflation rate will equal the (per capita) money growth rate (denoted μ). That equality would not be implied, however, if there were technical change that progressively shifted the production function or the shopping-time function. If, for example, (2.2) were replaced with

$$y_t = (1 + \alpha)^t f(k_t), \quad \alpha > 0, \tag{2.2'}$$

then g_t, k_t, and c_t would be required to grow at some positive rate. The same would be true for m_t, moreover, implying that inflation would be smaller than money growth. The difference between π and μ would, nevertheless, be fixed by technological considerations that are independent of μ itself.

---

[14]This follows from the useful fact that if (say) $z_t = x_t + y$, then z_t, x_t, and y_t can all grow at constant rates only if x_t and y_t each grow at the same rate. That is so because $\Delta z_t/z_t \equiv (x_t/z_t) \Delta x_t/x_t + (y_t/z_t) \Delta y_t/y_t$. Thus, the faster-growing of x_t and y_t would have an increasing influence on the growth rate of z_t.

[15]The sense in which π is given by government choice will be explained in the next sentence.

Of more interest in the present context is the question regarding "superneutrality": are the steady-state values of c, k, and y independent of π (and μ)? But in the present model it is a simple matter to determine by inspection of equations (2.13) that the answer is "yes". Specifically, the value of k is determined by the second of equations (2.13) alone. Then with g given by policy, the third equation determines c. Thus, we see that k, c, and $y = f(k)$ can be solved for without reference to the value of π. Alternative settings for the latter will have no effect on steady-state values of the main real variables.

Of course there is one real variable that is affected by π, namely m. Since $u_1 > 0$, different settings for π will, via the first of equations (2.13), require different levels of real money holdings. Indeed, the comparative steady-state derivative $dm/d\pi$ is equal to $u_1/(u_{22} - u_{12}u_2/u_1)\beta$, so with $u_{22} - u_{12}u_2/u_1 < 0$[16] real balances will be smaller the higher is the rate of inflation (i.e. the cost of holding money). A terminological question that arises is whether this non-invariance of m to the inflation rate means that the Sidrauski model does not have the property of superneutrality. In my opinion, that interpretation of the term would render it almost useless, since the set of interesting monetary models in which m is invariant to π is probably empty. Thus, the reasonable defining characteristic of superneutrality is the invariance[17] across steady states of all real variables excepting real money balances. This definition agrees with that of Patinkin (1987).

But while superneutrality thus defined is a property of the Sidrauski model as originally formulated, it does not survive even modest modifications. To demonstrate the non-robustness of the property, let us now drop the assumption – unreasonable in any event – that labor is supplied inelastically. Then the model's utility and production functions become:

$$u(c_t, m_t, n_t) + \beta u(c_{t+1}, m_{t+1}, n_{t+1}) + \cdots \tag{2.1$'$}$$

and

$$y_t = f(n_t, k_t), \tag{2.3$'$}$$

where n_t is the quantity of labor expended in production by a typical household during period t. It is of course assumed that $u_3 < 0$ with $u_{33} < 0$, that $f_2 > 0$ with $f_{22} < 0$, and that the functions continue to yield interior solutions. In the presence of these modifications, the following equation must be appended to the Euler equations (2.3)–(2.6) above:

$$u_3(c_t, m_t, n_t) + \lambda_t f_1(n_t, k_t) = 0. \tag{2.14}$$

---

[16]This condition is implied by Sidrauski's (1967, p. 535) assumption that neither c nor m is inferior.

[17]Invariance, that is, to alternative inflation rates.

Reinterpretation of expressions involving u and f is also required, of course. The resulting steady-state conditions that determine c, k, m, v, and n then become:

$$\beta u_2(c, m, n) = u_1(c, m, n)[1 + \pi - \beta] \,,$$
$$u_3(c, m, n) = -u_1(c, m, n)f_1(n, k) \,,$$
$$1 = \beta[f_2(n, k) + 1] \,, \tag{2.15}$$
$$f(n, k) = c + g \,,$$
$$\pi m = g + v \,.$$

The crucial difference is that the third of these relations no longer involves only one variable. Thus, it alone cannot determine k. Indeed, there is no subset of equations (2.15) that can be solved for real variables without the involvement of π. Thus, with this simple and appropriate modification, the Sidrauski model does not possess superneutrality – a point expressed clearly by Brock (1974).

Nevertheless, it warrants mention that if the ratio $u_3(c, m, n)/u_1(c, m, n)$ does not depend on m, then a subsystem of (2.15) *can* be solved for k, n, and c without involving m or π. Superneutrality will then prevail in this special case. Such a condition will obtain, moreover, if the function $u(c, m, n)$ is of the Cobb–Douglas form in terms of c, m, and $1 - n$. As such a form seems often to provide a good approximation to the data, it is perhaps reasonable to conclude that the modified Sidrauski model does not imply strict superneutrality, but does suggest that departures from superneutrality may be quantitatively unimportant.

2.3. Extensions

At this point it will be useful to add a third asset to the model. One obvious possibility would be private bonds, but with households all alike the equilibrium quantity held by each would have to be zero.[18] It is more interesting, therefore, to include government bonds. This inclusion, furthermore, has the benefit of modifying the government's budget constraint in a way that permits a clearer distinction to be drawn between monetary and fiscal policy actions.

To extend the model to include government bonds, let us specify that these

---

[18]That would not prevent determination of the rate of interest on such bonds, however. The additional Euler equation would give rise to a steady-state requirement that the nominal rate of interest be equal to $f'(k) + \pi + \pi f'(k)$.

are one-period securities that are sold in t at a money price of Q_t and redeemed in $t+1$ for one unit of money. Their nominal rate of return is then $R_t = (1 - Q_t)/Q_t$ and their real rate r_t is defined by $1 + r_t = (1 + R_t)/(1 + \pi_t)$. The number of such bonds purchased in t by a typical household is B_{t+1}. If we define $b_t = B_t/P_t$, the household budget constraint for t then becomes:

$$f(k_t) + v_t = c_t + k_{t+1} - k_t + (1 + \pi_t)m_{t+1} - m_t$$
$$+ (1 + r_t)^{-1}b_{t+1} - b_t , \tag{2.16}$$

instead of (2.3). This change has no effect on the Euler conditions (2.4)–(2.6) but adds to that set the following:

$$-\lambda_t(1 + r_t)^{-1} + \beta\lambda_{t+1} = 0 . \tag{2.17}$$

The latter condition is written as an equality to reflect an implicit assumption that households can choose positive or negative values for B_t – i.e. can lend to or borrow from the government. In addition, the household's problem now features a new transversality condition, which is:

$$\lim_{t\to\infty} b_{t+1}\beta^{t-1}\lambda_t(1 + r_t)^{-1} = 0 . \tag{2.18}$$

This has the effect of placing limits on the household's willingness to accumulate bonds and its ability to sell bonds.

With the inclusion of government bonds, the government's budget constraint becomes:

$$(1 + \pi_t)m_{t+1} - m_t + (1 + r_t)^{-1}b_{t+1} - b_t = g_t + v_t , \tag{2.19}$$

while this condition and (2.16) imply (2.10) just as (2.3) and (2.9) did before. With the additional asset recognized, government policy can specify time paths for three of the four variables M_t, g_t, v_t, and B_t, with the fourth determined by (2.19).

Within this extended model, let us now consider a competitive equilibrium under the assumption that the government is specifying time paths for M_t, g_t, and v_t. Then, provided that the three transversality conditions are satisfied, equations (2.4), (2.5), (2.6), (2.11), (2.12), (2.16), (2.17), and (2.19) determine time paths for c_t, k_t, m_t, λ_t, π_t, P_t, r_t, and b_t. A compressed steady-state version of the system, analogous to (2.13), can moreover be written as:

$$\beta u_2(c, m) = u_1(c, m)[1 + \pi - \beta],$$

$$1 = \beta[f'(k) + 1],$$

$$r = f'(k),\tag{2.20}$$

$$f(k) = c + g,$$

$$\pi m - br/(1 + r) = g + v.$$

These five equations determine steady-state values of c, m, k, r, and b.

A striking property of the system just summarized is that the values of variables other than b are unaffected by the government's choice of v. That can be shown by noting that the first four of equations (2.20) can be solved for c, k, r, and m (given the policy-set values of g and π). Any change in v then merely implies a change in b as dictated by the fifth equation, the government budget restraint.[19] Even the time path for P_t is invariant to v, since the path of M_t is exogenous and m is determined in the previously-discussed block.[20]

This result – the invariance of other variables to bond-financed changes in tax receipts – is typically referred to as the "Ricardian Equivalence Theorem", since the offsetting nature of taxes and bonds was clearly recognized, as a matter of theory, by Ricardo (1817). Today's considerable interest in models with this Ricardian property stems primarily from the work of Barro (1974, 1984).[21]

That the Ricardian equivalence result does not hold when tax/transfer magnitudes are geared to income or factor payments may be shown as follows. Suppose that v_t is replaced in the household and government's budget constraints by $\tau f(k_t)$, with τ being a tax rate on production. Then the first-order condition (2.6) will have $(1 - \tau)$ multiplying $f'(k_{t+1})$ so the second and third of equations (2.20) will have $(1 - \tau)f'(k)$ instead of $f'(k)$. Thus, the values of c, k, m, and r determined by the first four of equations (2.20) will depend on the value of τ. But that value will be linked to the value of b by the fifth of equations (2.20), so changes in b will lead to responses in c, k, m, and/or r.

Now consider again the case with lump-sum tax/transfer magnitudes. Since different paths of v and b imply different values for the government's budget position yet have no effect on other variables, the question arises of whether it

---

[19]We are still assuming that the system's transversality conditions are satisfied.

[20]A similar result holds, it should be added, outside the steady state. The set of equations (2.4), (2.5), (2.6), (2.10), and (2.17) and the identities for m_t and π_t make no reference to either v_t or b_t. Those seven equations therefore determine values of c_t, k_t, m_t, λ_t, π_t, P_t, and r_t without reference to v_t when the government sets paths for g_t, M_t, and either v_t or b_t.

[21]In particular, Barro (1974) shows that the result may hold with finite-lived individuals if they care about the utility of their offspring and leave non-zero bequests.

is possible to have an equilibrium with a permanent positive budget deficit. There is no problem if the deficit is financed by issuing money, but imagine an attempt to keep M_t constant and finance a positive deficit by the continuing sale of bonds. In this case, as it happens, the answer depends on the definition of "deficit" that is used. If the deficit is defined exclusive of interest payments, i.e. as the right-hand side of (2.19), then a positive value for $g_t + v_t$ and a constant M_t together imply that b_t must grow at a rate equal to the steady-state interest rate, which leads to the violation of the transversality condition (2.18). That fact is not itself conclusive, as transversality conditions are not in all cases necessary for optimality,[22] but it can be shown that in the case at hand the implied path for b_t is inconsistent with individual optimality [McCallum (1984a, p. 130)]. If, on the other hand, the "deficit" is defined more conventionally as inclusive of interest payments, as in

$$d_t = g_t + v_t + b_t R_{t-1}/(1 + R_{t-1}),\qquad\qquad(2.21)$$

then it is possible to have an equilibrium path with $d > 0$ in which all variables except v_t and b_t are constant. In this case b_t grows according to $b_{t+1} = b_t + d(1 + r)$ so its growth is more than overcome by the geometric shrinkage of β^{t-1}, leading to the satisfaction of (2.18). Thus, it is possible to have a zero-inflation equilibrium with $d > 0$ and an ever-growing stock of debt. But with d_t and g_t constant, (2.19) shows that taxes $(-v_t)$ will also be ever-growing. Indeed, the result at hand, taken from McCallum (1984a), does not violate the condition that the budget must be balanced in present-value terms when revenue from money creation is regarded as a tax.

Each of the results in this subsection remains valid, it should be added, if the model is generalized to permit (i) depreciation, (ii) population growth within each household, and (iii) variable labor supply as in (2.1′) and (2.3′).

2.4. Welfare

We now wish to consider effects of alternative steady inflation rates on the utility of a typical household. To keep the results from being excessively special, let us use the version of the model that treats labor supply as a variable – i.e. the non-superneutrality version with utility and production functions (2.1′) and (2.3′). In this case the steady-state values of c, k, m, n, and v are given (for policy-set values of g and π) by equations (2.15).

---

[22] In the case at hand, however, the production and utility functions possess enough concavity that Weitzman's (1973) conditions are satisfied and the transversality conditions are in fact necessary.

To evaluate the desirability of these equilibrium values, we now consider the "social planning" problem of choosing at $t = 1$, say, time paths of variables needed to maximize (2.1′) subject only to the economy's overall resource constraints. In per-household terms, these constraints are:

$$f(n_t, k_t) = c_t + k_{t+1} - k_t + g_t, \quad \text{for } t = 1, 2, \ldots. \tag{2.22}$$

The first-order conditions for this problem are (2.22) and those that follow, where $\phi_t \geq 0$ is the Lagrangian multiplier associated with (2.22):

$$u_1(c_t, m_t, n_t) - \phi_t = 0, \tag{2.23}$$

$$u_2(c_t, m_t, n_t) = 0, \tag{2.24}$$

$$u_3(c_t, m_t, n_t) + \phi_t f_1(n_t, k_t) = 0, \tag{2.25}$$

$$-\phi_t + \phi_{t+1}\beta[f_2(n_{t+1}, k_{t+1}) + 1] = 0, \tag{2.26}$$

$$-\phi_t \leq 0 \quad \text{with} \quad -\phi_t g_t = 0. \tag{2.27}$$

Now the last of these implies, since $\phi_t > 0$ by (2.23), that $g_t = 0$ – i.e. that government purchases of output must be zero. But this result obtains only because our setup has assigned no useful role to government purchases – by assumption these do not constitute capital or provide services valued by households. Consequently, since these assumptions are dubious at best, the $g_t = 0$ condition should not be taken literally as a conclusion regarding optimal fiscal policy. We set $g_t = 0$ in what follows *only* to assist in the investigation of the optimal inflation issue.

Proceeding then with $g = 0$, the steady-state version of the optimality conditions becomes:

$$u_2(c, m, n) = 0,$$
$$u_3(c, m, n) + u_1(c, m, n)f_1(n, k) = 0,$$
$$1 = \beta[f_2(n, k) + 1], \tag{2.28}$$
$$f(n, k) = c.$$

These determine optimal values of n, k, c, and m for $g = 0$ and the policy-set value of π. The question is: Are these values the same as those provided by the competitive equilibrium? Inspection of (2.15) indicates readily that the answer will be "yes" if and only if the right-hand side of the first of equations (2.15) equals zero, thereby satisfying the first of equations (2.28). And since u_1 is strictly positive, this equality will obtain only if $1 + \pi - \beta = 0$. Thus, social optimality requires an inflation rate of $\pi = \beta - 1$.

Interpretation of the latter is straightforward. In view of the steady-state condition $1 = \beta[f_2 + 1]$, the requisite inflation rate is given by $\pi = (P_{t+1}/P_t) - 1 = (1 + f_2)^{-1} - 1$, or $P_t/P_{t+1} = 1 + f_2$, or

$$\frac{(P_{t+1} - P_t)}{P_{t+1}} = -f_2(n, k) .$$ (2.29)

But this is, of course, immediately recognizable as the famous "Chicago Rule" developed most notably by Friedman (1969): deflate at a rate equal to the real rate of interest.[23] The logic of this requirement is simply that it is inefficient not to satiate agents with something – in this case, real money balances – that is socially costless to produce yet provides valuable services.

One matter that has received inadequate attention to this point is the behavior of the marginal-yield function, $u_2(c, m, n)$. In particular, satiation with real money balances requires that $u_2 = 0$ for some adequately large value for m. The shopping-time parable of footnote 7 clearly supports the existence of such a value: it is possible to hold more money than would be useful in a period under any circumstances. It is unclear, however, whether it is better to think of u_2 as becoming negative or as remaining equal to zero for m in excess of the satiation level.

The optimality result that we have obtained relies, it should be said, on the assumption that transfers (taxes) are administered in a lump-sum fashion. If instead government revenues – it is certainly appropriate to presume that some will be needed to finance positive government spending – are raised by income or factor-payment taxes, conditions (2.15) would be altered and would fail to match conditions (2.28), even with $\pi = \beta - 1$. It has been argued by Phelps (1973) that in this type of situation the optimal rate of inflation would be determined by the condition that all utilized revenue sources have the same marginal deadweight loss per unit of revenue. But this argument does not establish that a positive inflation rate would be optimal. First, it has been shown by Marty (1976) and Barro and Fischer (1976) that for the inflation tax this marginal "collection cost" is $-\eta/(1 + \eta)$, where η is the elasticity of money demand with respect to the interest rate.[24] A value of -0.25 for η would then imply a marginal collection cost of 33 percent, which seems quite high. From this type of consideration, Barro and Fischer (1976, p. 146) conclude that "while the Phelps proposition that inflationary finance should be chosen as part of the optimal public finance package is incontestable in principle, it may be

[23]While an early and incisive discussion of the Chicago Rule was provided by Marty (1961), the earliest statement that I have found is that of Friedman (1960, p. 70).

[24]Both Marty's analysis and that of Auernheimer (1974), on which Barro and Fischer draw, rely upon areas under money demand functions for their cost estimates. The agreement between our general-equilibrium result and that of Friedman (1969) leads me to guess that the money-demand approach is not misleading.

that, quantitatively, this argument would not lead to the choice of very much monetary expansion (and would likely lead to a negative rate of inflation)".[25]

Recently, a more definite and striking claim has been put forth by Kimbrough (1986), who argues that with money helping to facilitate transactions, the inflation tax is analogous to a tax on an intermediate good and therefore does not belong in an optimal tax package. Assuming that money's transaction effects appear as described above in footnote 7, Kimbrough shows this to be the case in a setting in which there is a consumption tax and a fixed capital stock.[26] A similar result was previously obtained by Lucas and Stokey (1983) using a variant of the cash-in-advance constraint. The Kimbrough and Lucas–Stokey arguments attempt to restore the optimality of the Chicago Rule under the restriction that government revenue must be raised without lump-sum taxation; their generality is questioned in Chapter 20 by Woodford in this Handbook.

The foregoing discussion has been concerned only with the "shoe-leather" cost of inflation, the failure to satiate agents with a service-yielding asset that is costless to produce. As many writers have emphasized, this cost is quite small in magnitude for inflation rates of (say) 20 percent per annum or below. Since rates well below that figure seem to give rise to considerable distress in actual economies, an important question is "why?". This topic has been extensively examined by Fischer in a series of papers that are summarized in Fischer (1984). Further summarization of the points is difficult, but in general the significant non-shoe-leather costs identified by Fischer are either due to the non-adaptation of institutional features designed for a non-inflationary world (e.g. non-indexation of government debt and tax schedules) or to relative price variability that is not actually associated with inflation in any tight logical way. Thus, anyone who believes that "inflation is associated with the decline of public morality, the rise and fall of nations, and more weighty matters than money triangles and the efficiency of the price system" [Fischer (1984, pp. 45–46)] will be somewhat disappointed by the outcome of Fischer's review. But, as he says, "with no long-run tradeoff between inflation and unemployment, there is nothing to be said for moderate rates of inflation except that they are costly to reduce" (1984, p. 46). Furthermore, the non-adaptations mentioned above may be of great practical importance. If, for example, the non-indexation of tax schedules is taken as given, then the cost of inflation

---

[25]In general, the Barro–Fischer (1976) paper provides an excellent brief summary of matters discussed in the present section. That paper asks, however: "why would the private sector hold any real capital at all when the opportunity cost of holding money is driven all the way down to zero?" (1976, p. 144). The answer is that any reduction in the stock of capital would raise its yield above that on money and lead asset holders to move back into capital.

[26]Actually, Kimbrough's shopping-time specification is somewhat less general than that of footnote 7 and differs in assuming that end-of-period, rather than start-of-period, real balances facilitate transactions.

might be regarded as including the resource misallocation – possibly quite substantial – induced by the interaction of inflation and inflation-sensitive taxes.

2.5. Stochastic shocks

One significant limitation of the analysis of the previous four subsections is its neglect of uncertainty. It is my impression that propositions of the comparative steady-state type, with which this section is concerned, are not very sensitive to the presence or absence of uncertainty. A bit of interesting theoretical evidence relating to one of the topics – i.e. superneutrality – has recently been provided by Danthine, Donaldson and Smith (1987). These authors investigate the effects of stochastic shocks to the production function in a model otherwise similar to that of Subsection 2.1 above. They find that the existence of this type of technological uncertainty leads to the negation of the strict superneutrality result implied by equations (2.13) above.[27] The magnitude of this effect is, however, tiny. For a "representative" set of parameter values, stochastic simulations indicate that the mean value of the steady-state distribution of the capital stock changes only from 0.18485 to 0.18629 when the money growth rate is changed from zero to 500 percent per period.[28]

A consideration of the robustness of Ricardian equivalence results to the recognition of uncertainty has been undertaken by Chan (1983). His basic result is that debt–tax equivalence continues to hold in the presence of uncertainty if each household's *share* of an uncertain future tax burden is fixed and if there exist private securities that can be combined to act as a perfect substitute for the government's bonds. In cases in which these conditions do not obtain, a bond-financed tax change will typically have some effect on current aggregate demand, but the direction of the effect is – as conjectured by Barro (1974, p. 1115) – dependent upon the precise specification of the utility function and other aspects of the environment. Mention should also be made of the theoretical approach suggested by Blanchard (1985), which involves agents with uncertain lifetimes. If these agents do not have bequest motives, then some departure from Ricardian properties is implied.

In addition, it would be of considerable interest to know whether the "Chicago Rule" for optimal inflation would remain valid – as a prescription for

---

[27]This result can be obtained by noting that the relevant version of (2.6) becomes $E\lambda = \beta E[\lambda f'(k) + \lambda]$. Since λ_{t+1} and k_{t+1} are not independent, it is not possible to cancel out $E\lambda$. Consequently, the system does not decompose in the way that (2.13) does.

[28]More precisely, the comparison is for $\mu = 0$ and $\mu = 5$; see Danthine, Donaldson and Smith (1987, p. 491). The case under discussion features a Cobb–Douglas production function and non-separable preferences with constant relative risk aversion.

the *average* inflation rate – in the presence of stochastic shocks to the system. Intuition suggests that the situation would be similar to that pertaining to superneutrality, i.e. that the conclusions based on deterministic models would be approximately valid. In terms of formal analysis, I have not found investigations in terms of the Sidrauski model itself, but Lucas and Stokey (1983) have considered the matter using a model of the cash-in-advance type. Since they specify that the cash-in-advance constraint pertains to only a subset of the consumption goods – formally, to one of the model's two composite goods – with credit purchases possible for the other, their model is quite similar to a one-good Sidrauski setup; see Lucas and Stokey (1983, p. 80). In this setting, with randomly fluctuating government expenditures, Lucas and Stokey indicate that efficiency "requires... a nominal interest rate identically zero, brought about by a deflation induced by continuous withdrawals of money from circulation" (1983, p. 82).[29] It must be said that the model in question includes no capital goods, but introduction of these would not seem to seem to affect the *necessity* of monetary satiation, which would be induced by an inflation path that kept the private cost of holding money close to zero.

3. Issues regarding ongoing inflation

Having presented a basic outline of one contemporary model for analyzing ongoing inflation, we now turn to important areas of disagreement and relevant evidence. First, in Subsection 3.1 we consider the extent to which our previous conclusions are affected by adoption of an analytical framework in which agents have finite lifetimes, in contrast to the Sidrauski assumption of everlasting households. Second, in Subsection 3.2 the much-discussed possibility of "hyperinflationary" speculative bubbles is briefly reviewed. Then in Subsection 3.3 some consideration of existing empirical evidence – and difficulties in bringing evidence to bear on the outstanding issues – is provided.

3.1. Overlapping-generations models

The last decade has witnessed a significant volume of monetary analysis conducted in the context of models in which a new generation of individual agents, each with a finite life span of two (or more) periods, is born each period. These agents' perspectives on consumption versus saving naturally change as they age, so at any point in time the economy includes agents with different desires regarding the accumulation of wealth, even if agents are all

---

[29]A similar result has been obtained by Krugman, Persson and Svensson (1985).

born with the same lifetime utility function and production possibilities. This feature makes the overlapping-generations (OG) framework an attractive vehicle for the analysis of theoretical issues regarding saving and the accumulation of wealth.

Of the monetary analysis that has been conducted in OG models, a substantial fraction has incorporated the point of view according to which "it is not legitimate to take fiat money to be an argument of anyone's utility function or of any engineering production function" [Wallace (1980, p. 49)]. Adherents to that point of view have also avoided relationships such as the shopping-time function of footnote 7 above or the cash-in-advance constraint favored by Lucas (1980a) and others. The resulting models have generated predictions regarding inflation and other monetary phenomena that are very different from those of the Sidrauski-type framework.[30]

It has been argued, however, that most of the unusual features of these models stem from their neglect of the medium-of-exchange function of money. McCallum (1983a) shows, for example, that three of the most striking implications of the Wallace (1980) model vanish if it is modified, by the addition of shopping-time considerations, to reflect this function.[31] Incisive arguments of a similar nature have been put forth by Tobin (1980b) and Patinkin (1983).

The basic point of this line of argument is that it is the transaction-facilitating property of money that makes it a distinctive asset, so any model that totally neglects that property is apt to yield misleading conclusions regarding actual monetary phenomena. It is unfortunate, perhaps, that the representation of such phenomena cannot be incorporated in a more satisfying manner than by making money an argument of a production or utility function, but to "capture" this property in that inadequate way is better than to miss it entirely.[32]

Adopting this latter point of view, a number of writers have used OG models with cash-in-advance or money-in-the-utility-function features to analyze questions regarding inflation or other monetary phenomena.[33] The issue to be addressed here is whether these monetary OG models, with finite-lived agents, yield different conclusions than those obtained in Section 2 above.

With respect to superneutrality, it is well known to be the case that the OG model does not generally have that property; this is implied by the analyses of Stein (1971), Drazen (1981), and others. In fact, Drazen shows that under a

---

[30]See, for example, Wallace (1980) or Bryant and Wallace (1979).

[31]Wallace's three implications are that money will not be demanded if its growth rate exceeds that of output; that steady states with valued money will be Pareto-optimal if and only if money growth is non-positive; and that open-market operations have no effect on the price level.

[32]This position is developed most extensively by McCallum (1983a).

[33]Examples include Stein (1971), Drazen (1981), Helpman and Sadka (1979), Weiss (1980), McCallum (1987), Lucas (1980a), and Woodford (1987).

fairly wide set of conditions the capital–labor will be positively related to the inflation rate. It is possible to argue, however, that such effects are unlikely to be quantitatively important.[34] In any event, since the Sidrauski model implies exact superneutrality only with an unrealistic assumption, there is no major disagreement in this regard.

Next, there is the Ricardian property of the Sidrauski model, i.e. the invariance of other variables to debt-financed alterations in the magnitude of lump-sum tax collections. In this case, the OG model does yield a different prediction.[35] In particular, as Diamond's (1965) pioneering analysis demonstrated in a non-monetary setting, the steady-state values of important macroeconomic variables will depend (for given time paths of the money stock and government purchases) upon the magnitude of a tax-transfer variable analogous to v of Section 2.

The third main conclusion of Section 2 was that, with lump-sum tax-transfer magnitudes, social optimality requires adherence to the Chicago Rule prescription: a rate of deflation equal to the marginal product of capital. For the OG model with money, McCallum (1987) shows that this condition is again necessary for optimality in the following sense: if the economy does not have an overabundance of capital,[36] then unless the Chicago Rule condition obtains it would be possible to enhance one generations's utility without reducing the utility of any other generation. Since the analyses of Scheinkman (1980b), Tirole (1985), and McCallum (1987) indicate that capital overaccumulation will not occur in a competitive equilibrium in any economy that possesses a positive quantity of a non-augmentable and productive asset such as land, the conclusion regarding Pareto optimality is much the same as in Section 2.

It should be said that the foregoing conclusion pertains to a Pareto-type comparison recognizing different generations and an arbitrary initial stock of capital. If, instead, the analysis seeks to determine the inflation rate that will yield the highest steady-state utility – the same for all generations – then there will be a relevant tradeoff, with increased real money balances being associated with reduced levels of the capital stock. In this case, different specifications of utility and production functions will result in different optimal inflation rates, but these will typically be greater than the Chicago Rule rate – see Fischer (1986). But Abel (1987) has demonstrated the following: if there is also a fiscal

[34] If the ratio of the marginal utility of consumption (MUC) when old to the MUC when young is independent of money holdings, then departures from superneutrality will occur only to the extent that money is a significant form of wealth. But in the United States, the value of outside money is only about 1 percent of the value of tangible real assets.

[35] Here the term "OG model" is being used in a sense that does not include setups, like those of Barro (1974), that feature operative intergenerational altruism.

[36] That is, does not have so much capital that the net marginal product is less than the rate of aggregate output growth. The possibility of such a situation has been stressed by Diamond (1965), Phelps (1966), Cass and Yaari (1967), and many others.

instrument available – i.e. lump-sum intergenerational transfers – then the optimal steady-state policy will involve Golden Rule capital accumulation and monetary satiation. The latter is attained by equalization of the pecuniary rates of return on money and capital, just as called for by the Chicago Rule.

Before moving on, let us briefly return our attention to the class of OG models that does not give any transaction-facilitating role to the asset termed money. In such models it is possible, despite this omission, to devise assumptions that will permit the coexistence of valued money and other assets. That can be accomplished, for example, by assuming that money and other assets have different risk characteristics [Wallace (1981)] or by assuming that certain groups are prevented by law from holding particular assets [Sargent and Wallace (1982)]. In such settings it will frequently be the case that open-market swaps of money for other assets, undertaken by the monetary policy authority, will have no effect on aggregate output or the price level – a result that Wallace (1981) attributes to a "Modigliani–Miller Theorem". The important thing to recognize about these results is merely that money does not, in the relevant models, serve as a medium of exchange. If it did, then its rate of return would be lower (in the absence of satiation-inducing policy) than on other assets with similar risk characteristics, and open-market swaps for similar-risk assets would have the traditionally-posited type of effect on aggregate demand. One way of explaining this is to note that while a tax-financed increase in, for example, government bond holdings would have no effect on aggregate demand in a Ricardian model because of tax capitalization, a tax-financed increase in the money stock would have a positive effect (as there is no implied change in future taxes necessitated by the changed money stock). But an appropriate combination of the two operations is analytically equivalent to an open-market operation, so it follows that an open-market purchase of bonds has a positive net effect on nominal wealth. The same type of effect obtains, moreover, in a non-Ricardian model, although its workings are weaker and the analysis less transparent. The upshot of these considerations is that nominal "Modigliani–Miller" results for open-market operations do not obtain in models in which money has a transaction-facilitating role. Such results hold in the Wallace and Sargent–Wallace examples only because they pertain to assets swaps in which the two assets serve as media of exchange to precisely the same extent. These swaps are not open-market operations in the usual sense of the term.

A distantly related but quite distinct piece by Sargent and Wallace (1981), entitled "Some Unpleasant Monetarist Arithmetic", has been one of the most widely discussed publications of recent years on the subject of inflation. The main reason for this attention is the apparent suggestion that an economy's monetary authority cannot, by its own base-money creation choices, prevent inflation if an irresponsible fiscal authority embarks upon a course of action that implies continuing deficits (defined net of interest). Formally, the paper's argument is only that paths of base money and fiscal variables are unavoidably related by the government budget constraint in a way that makes non-inflationary base-money creation inconsistent with continuing real deficits. Whether the monetary authority has control over inflation thus depends on "which authority moves first, the monetary authority or the fiscal authority? In other words, who imposes discipline on whom?" (1981, p. 7). But the paper's analysis assumes that the fiscal authority "moves first", in the sense that a real deficit sequence is taken as given. In this way the paper seems to suggest that in fact a monetary authority, which can adjust the monetary base by open-market operations, may be technically dominated by a fiscal authority. But consideration indicates that this suggestion is misleading. To see this, suppose that the monetary authority seeks to avoid inflation (by creating base money slowly) while the fiscal authority attempts to follow a purchase/taxation plan that implies a continuing real deficit. In a case of this type, the monetary authority will be technically able to force the fiscal authority to submit to its discipline, in contrast with the Sargent–Wallace assumption. The reason is that the monetary authority has direct control over the monetary base while the fiscal authority does not have direct control over the deficit; it has direct control only over taxes and its bond offerings. In the case under consideration, then, the fiscal authority will be unable to carry out its plan because it will simply not have the requisite purchasing power. It can achieve its planned purchases, but only by increasing taxes and departing from its planned deficit path. Thus, a truly determined monetary authority will always have its way. It is of course true that actual fiscal authorities often use *political* means to induce monetary authorities to cooperate in irresponsible undertakings, but the Sargent–Wallace (1981) analysis is not designed to investigate such political forces. The analysis provides, consequently, no reason for believing that a monetary authority cannot prevent inflation, if it wishes to do so.

In sum, the messages regarding inflation generated by OG models are not significantly different from those stemming from Sidrauski-type models, provided that the transaction-facilitating services of money are treated the same in each case.

3.2. Bubble inflation

A great deal of professional attention has been given, during the last dozen or so years, to the possible existence of rational asset-price *bubbles* – i.e. to equilibria in which a component of the price process exists only because it is arbitrarily expected to exist, yet does so in a manner that does not violate expectational rationality.[37] In its simplest form, this sort of phenomenon can be

---

[37]I know of no general-purpose survey of the topic. Specific aspects have been usefully discussed by Taylor (1986), Brock (Chapter 7 in this Handbook), and Woodford (1984).

represented as follows. Suppose that market clearing in period t requires that

$$\psi(P_t, P^e_{t+1}) = 0 \,, \tag{3.1}$$

where ψ is an excess demand function, P_t is the current price in question, and P^e_{t+1} is the period-t expectation of P_{t+1}.[38] In a perfect-foresight context P^e_{t+1} will equal P_{t+1}, but (3.1) will remain a condition designed to explain P_t on the basis of the given expectational magnitude, P_{t+1}. In particular, (3.1) is *not* an ordinary difference equation relating P_{t+1} to a given value of P_t. This has been stressed by Whiteman (1984).

One approach to solving the model (3.1) is to find a function that expresses P_t in terms of the system's relevant state variables. Since no other non-expectational variables appear in (3.1), a natural conjecture in this case is that P_t is constant over time.[39] The conjectured solution is $P_t = P$, with P to be determined. Since under this conjecture it will also be true that $P^e_{t+1} = P$, the relation $\psi(P, P) = 0$ can be solved for P.[40]

But suppose that instead the analyst conjectures that $P_t = \pi(P_{t-1})$, i.e. that P_t is functionally dependent on its most recent value. Then it must also be true that $P_{t+1} = \pi(P_t)$. Substitution into (3.1) in this case gives $\psi[P_t, \pi(P_t)] = 0$, which serves to determine the function π.[41] But adoption of this latter solution, $P_t = \pi(P_{t-1})$, instead of $P_t = P$ is tantamount to assuming that agents base their expectations on "extraneous" state variables, for the implied dependence of P^e_{t+1} on P_t is not dictated by the model (3.1). In that sense, $P_t = \pi(P_{t-1})$ defines a family of bubble or bootstrap solutions, one for each conceivable initial value for P_{t-1}.[42] Unless that value happens by chance to equal P, the time path will then differ from $P_t = P$. And the discrepancy, $P_t - P$, will in this case constitute the bubble or bootstrap component of the solution.

The sort of phenomenon illustrated in the foregoing arises much more generally in models in which the price at which some market clears is dependent upon current expectations of future values of that price. An issue that has been extensively investigated is whether the assumption of competitive equilibrium with optimizing, forward-looking agents is sufficient to rule out

[38]An example is provided by the Cagan (1956) model of the price level with rational expectations and a constant money stock.

[39]More generally, the conjecture would be that P_t depends only on the variables that explicitly appear in the model at hand. The procedure under discussion is developed more fully for linear models in McCallum (1983c).

[40]Here I am assuming that this solution for P exists and is unique. The non-uniqueness that results from bubbles is of a different type, one that will be described momentarily.

[41]There may be more than one solution for π, only one of which will normally give the same stationary value for P_t as the P defined above.

[42]This multiplicity arises because the model (3.1) itself does not refer to any lagged price; it suggests that historical initial conditions are irrelevant.

bubble equilibria of the type described. The answer seems to be that while some types of bubble phenomena are precluded – e.g. paths with exploding *relative* prices – others are not. In particular, it seems that in an economy with fiat money, optimizing behavior does not rule out bubbles in which real money balances fall continually, asymptotically approaching zero.[43] This implies the possibility of an ever-increasing price level in an economy with a constant money stock – a situation which may be termed an inflationary bubble. The existence of this logical possibility has been taken by Hahn (1983, pp. 11–13, 71) as grounds for objecting to the monetarist notion that, in his words, "a necessary and sufficient condition for inflation is an increasing stock of money".

That competitive theory fails to exclude inflationary bubbles does not mean, however, that they occur in actual economies. Accordingly, this becomes an appropriate point to begin our review of empirical evidence relating to the issues of Sections 2 and 3.

3.3. Empirical evidence

Interesting attempts to determine whether bubble behavior prevailed during the famous German hyperinflation of 1920–23 have been conducted by Flood and Garber (1980) and Burmeister and Wall (1982). These test attempts are not entirely convincing, however, because of the restrictiveness of the utilized assumptions regarding behavior of the monetary authorities – in particular, the maintained assumption that the money supply is generated exogenously. In addition, they suffer from a technical problem, created by the existence of an exploding regressor, regarding the asymptotic distribution theory needed for formal tests. This problem is briefly mentioned by Flood and Garber (1980) in their footnote 18 (p. 754).[44]

One extremely simple test procedure, proposed by Diba and Grossman (1984), has been implemented for the German hyperinflation by Hamilton and Whiteman (1985). The basic idea is that the existence of an inflationary bubble implies that the bubble component of the price level process is explosive. In a model with a log-linear demand function, this implies that stationarity of the time series for log P_t will not be obtained by differencing that series the same number of times as is just adequate to induce stationarity of log M_t. Thus, the graphs presented by Hamilton and Whiteman (1985, p. 369), which show that

---

[43]Important contributions in this line of analysis have been made by Gale (1973), Brock (1975), Calvo (1979), and Obstfeld and Rogoff (1983).

[44]Recently, a test strategy that avoids this problem has been implemented in a preliminary manner by Casella (1989). The strategy was previously developed in a different context by West (1987).

second differencing is just adequate to eliminate a growing mean for both log M_t and log P_t, constitute evidence against the hypothesis that the German hyperinflation represented an inflationary bubble. Unfortunately, the logic of this simple test seems to rely on the assumption of a log-linear money demand function. Researchers who consider that assumption dubious may then find the conclusion unpersuasive.

In any event, it cannot be claimed that any type of formal test for the presence of bubbles has been conducted for a wide variety of inflationary episodes. Thus, there currently exists no compelling body of evidence adequate to firmly rule out bubble inflation. There is no formal evidence tending to support its existence, however. This writer would hazard a guess that continued study of the issue will not lend support to the notion that inflationary bubble phenomena are of empirical significance.

Let us now turn to issues raised in Section 2. In attempting to bring evidence to bear on propositions concerning steady-state properties of an economy, one is faced with the necessity of using data that do not conform neatly to comparative steady-state experiments. Instead, actual data sets reflect the experiences of economies undergoing fluctuations due to various types of shocks and administered by monetary authorities that rarely (if ever) make clear-cut policy regime changes of the type envisioned by comparative steady-state analysis. Now, in principle this fact need not deter the researcher, who can proceed by estimating a fully-specified dynamic model – one that tracks the economy's period-by-period fluctuations – and then determining its steady-state properties by analytical means. In practice, however, the approach is unappealing because of the necessity of specifying and estimating a model that satisfactorily reflects the economy's dynamic behavior. To do so, one must not only model portfolio balance and savings vs. consumption behavior, as in the examples of Section 2, but also the aggregate-supply or Phillips-curve relationship that we have yet to discuss. And, as Section 4 will indicate, there is little agreement concerning this critical component of any dynamic macroeconomic model.

Consequently, attempts have been made to reach conclusions regarding steady-state properties – in particular, superneutrality – by means of strategies that do not rely upon specification of the system's period-to-period dynamics. Most notably, Lucas (1980b) and Geweke (1986) have devised procedures for investigating *low-frequency* relationships among variables in analytical settings that are (except for the list of relevant variables) model-free. The general idea of the approach seems to be that "low frequency" corresponds to "long run", with the latter concept in turn presumably related to steady-state properties, including superneutrality. Before discussing a weakness with the approach, let us note that both Lucas and Geweke report findings that are ostensibly supportive of the hypothesis of neutrality. In particular, Lucas (1980b) shows that inflation rates are related to money growth rates with a coefficient near to unity when a low-pass filter is used to remove high-frequency components of the two series.[45] Similarly, Geweke (1986) finds that output and ex post real interest rates are not significantly influenced by past money growth rates when only the lowest-frequency component of his measure of influence is considered.[46] His finding, that real money balances *are* influenced by money growth is, as indicated in Subsection 2.2, consistent with an appropriate definition of superneutrality.

A difficulty with this type of test has been described in McCallum (1984b), which shows that the presumption that low-frequency measures will reflect comparative steady-state properties is not generally warranted. The problem is that the relevant steady-state relationships pertain to anticipated movements, while low-frequency statistics will usually[47] reflect a mixture of anticipated and unanticipated effects. The weak link in the test strategy is essentially the same as that discussed definitively by Sargent (1971): in any system in which responses are different to anticipated and unanticipated variations, sums of distributed-lag coefficients will not correspond to comparative steady-state effects [see also Lucas (1972b)]. McCallum's (1984b) demonstration merely emphasizes that this principle remains true if the data series are subjected to Fourier transforms prior to analysis.

Cross-section evidence, pertaining to time-averaged experiences of different economies, is not subject to the above-mentioned difficulty. Thus, it is arguable that such evidence provides a more reliable guide to comparative steady-state properties than single-economy studies. In this regard the cross-country data sets compiled by Harberger (1978) and Barro (1984) exhibit a tendency to support the hypothesis that inflation rates vary approximately point-for-point with money growth rates. This type of examination has its own flaws, of course. For example, it relies on an implicit assumption that within a given economy the same money growth rate is achieved in each period included in the sample. Consequently, such evidence is certainly not adequate to sustain any conclusions regarding the rather delicate issue of superneutrality.

The other positive issue raised in Section 2 is the extent to which actual economies exhibit Ricardian properties. Empirical studies conducted prior to 1986 have recently been reviewed by Seater (1985), Bernheim (1987), and Leiderman and Blejer (1988). Seater concludes that "the [Ricardian] hypoth-

---

[45]Lucas's sample consists of M1 and CPI rates of change for the United States over the period 1955–75. One observation, for the second quarter, was used for each year.

[46]Geweke's concept, termed "feedback", is essentially a measure of the extent to which Granger causality occurs, one designed so as to permit a decomposition by frequency. Geweke's (1986) data is also for the United States, but his tests involve quarterly postwar time series as well as annual observations for 1870–1978, with tests pertaining to subperiods designed to reflect different policy regimes.

[47]Reference here is to results based on model-free procedures of the type under discussion.

esis is supported by virtually all the direct tests of it" (1985, p. 124) but recognizes that most of this "evidence consists of failures to reject the hypothesis and therefore may be of questionable power" (p. 125). In addition, he recognizes that contradictory indirect evidence has been provided by various studies of the consumption function which reject variants of the permanent-income hypothesis. (The latter topic, currently the subject of intensive investigation by a number of scholars, cannot adequately be reviewed here.) Bernheim (1987) expresses doubt "that it is possible to identify in a convincing way the relevant structural relationships through macro time series". But, partly on the basis of "indirect" and cross-country evidence, he finds the data to be strongly anti-Ricardian. By contrast, the conclusions of Leiderman and Blejer cannot be categorized so easily. They mention studies that seem to give both types of answers, and leave the reader with the impression that it is not yet settled whether the Ricardian proposition provides a reasonably good empirical approximation.

4. Inflation and output fluctuations

In this section we shift our attention from steady states to cyclical fluctuations. This shift leads to a variety of issues pertaining to Phillips-curve phenomena – i.e. to the relationship between inflation (or money growth) and employment (or output) levels measured relative to their normal or "natural-rate" values. Since it is by way of this relationship that monetary policy actions have their main effects on employment and output,[48] the precise nature of the relationship is of critical importance in the context of macroeconomic stabilization policy. Consequently, the area is one of the most extensively studied in all of economics. Nevertheless, there remains much disagreement concerning the Phillips (or aggregate supply) relationship. A cynic might guess that this lack of consensus stems from the desire on the part of researchers for intellectual product differentiation, but such a guess would in my opinion be unjustified. Instead, the main reason for a lack of consensus is the combined importance and difficulty of the subject. Specifically, it is inherently difficult to devise a theory to explain the nature of a relationship between real and nominal variables while respecting the axiom, fundamental to neoclassical economic theory, that rational agents are concerned only with real variables.

Relevant aspects of the story begin with Phillips's (1958) hypothesis that changes in money wage rates are induced primarily by recent values of the unemployment rate, the latter being a measure of the excess supply of labor. This hypothesis attracted much support because of its policy relevance, the

---

[48]This claim will be discussed in Subsection 4.3.

interesting U.K. evidence reported by Phillips, and the fact that this sort of wage-change relation was just what was needed to convert the static Keynesian model – as interpreted by Modigliani (1944) and others, with its inexplicably given level of the money wage – into a usable dynamic framework. But, as is well known, Friedman (1966, 1968) and Phelps (1967) argued convincingly that the relationship should be expressed in terms of *real*, not nominal, wage changes. The modified relation would still be usable with the Keynesian model of aggregate demand, but would avoid an implausible implication of Phillips's original formulation, i.e. that unemployment could be kept permanently low (or output permanently high) by acceptance of a constant but "high" rate of inflation. The Friedman and Phelps versions involved expected changes in real wage rates and used the rather mechanical adaptive expectations formula to account for expectational behavior. Lucas then developed the case for rational expectations and explored its implications in papers (1972a, 1973) that set the stage for contemporary debates.

In the following subsections we review the leading alternative Phillips curve hypotheses (as of 1986) as well as selected bits of evidence that are useful in discriminating among them. Because of the impossibility of covering the enormous literature in any detail in the space permitted, these reviews will be extremely brief and will mention only a small fraction of the worthwhile work that has been done in the area.

4.1. Alternative theories

Currently there are four basic types of Phillips-curve or aggregate-supply theories that attract substantial support from knowledgeable economists. These may be categorized as follows.

  (i) flexible-price, monetary misperception models;
 (ii) sticky-price expectational models;
(iii) NAIRU models; and
 (iv) real business cycle models.

The characteristics of the four classes will be described in turn.

Models of type (i), developed primarily by Lucas (1972a, 1973),[49] posit the existence of suppliers who base their production-rate decisions on the relative prices of their own products. The two cited papers rely upon different relative price variables. In particular, Lucas's (1972a) general-equilibrium model emphasizes the current own-product price in relation to the expected value of a future general price level, a comparison that reflects the expected rate of return from current savings.[50] By contrast, his (1973) model compares the current

---

[49]Significant elaborations were provided by Barro (1976) and Cukierman (1979).

[50]In the (1972a) model, non-interest-bearing money is the only store of value.

own-product price with the current general price level.[51] The two models are alike, however, in assuming that individual suppliers are ignorant of the current general price level and the current aggregate money stock. Their optimizing choices must accordingly be based on uncertain *perceptions* regarding these nominal aggregative magnitudes. Thus, when a seller finds that his own product price – the "local" price, in one terminology – is unusually high, that may be because the aggregate money stock is unusually large or because relative demand conditions are unusually favorable to his product. The rational supply response, then, is a weighted average of the responses that would be appropriate to the two possibilities if known to prevail, with weights depending on the (known) extent to which local price variability is on average a consequence of the two possibilities.

In each of the Lucas models aggregate output responds to inflation only if it is unanticipated; high or even increasing rates of inflation will induce no output response if they are predictable on the basis of suppliers' knowledge of the economy's workings. For some plausible ways of completing the model, consequently, the Lucas supply theories both give rise to *policy ineffectiveness propositions*. Both result in models, that is, possessing the property that the stochastic behavior of output is entirely unaffected by the monetary authority's choice of parameters characterizing systematic aspects of policy behavior.[52]

This striking property induced, not surprisingly, a large volume of research designed to explore the robustness of the ineffectiveness proposition under the assumption of rational expectations.[53] One of the more notable contributions was Fischer's (1977) development of a model that is representative of our class (ii),[54] i.e. models with rational expectations but prices that are not free to adjust to market-clearing values within each period. In Fischer's specification, nominal wages for periods t and $t+1$ are set for half of the workforce at the start of each period t. The values pertaining to periods t and $t+1$ may be different and each of them is set, in light of existing price-level expectations, so

---

[51]The idea behind this particular comparison, together with the informational discrepancy mentioned below, has been described by Sargent (1979, p. 381) as reflecting the notion that "the labor supplier works in one market but shops in many other markets", so that he cares about the price of his own services in relation to the current price of "an economy-wide bundle of goods". There seems, however, to be a logical flaw with this interpretation: how can the purchaser of these various goods fail to discover their current prices? Also, Lucas's (1973) model posits market clearing only in the aggregate, not in each market separately. In general, the logic of the (1973) model is different from, and less satisfactory than, that of the (1972a) model.

[52]This property was brought to the profession's attention most notably by Sargent and Wallace (1975). The proposition presumes that systematic components of policy can be related to past, but not current, values of variables.

[53]Reviews of that literature are provided by Barro (1981), McCallum (1980), and Taylor (1985).

[54]Others include Phelps and Taylor (1977), Gray (1976), and – subject to caveats mentioned below – Taylor (1979, 1980).

as to make the expected real wage for each period equal to its (expected) market-clearing value. Shocks occur, however, which typically result in price levels different from those anticipated, so real wages will usually be unequal to the market-clearing values. Employment and output are then determined so as to equate the marginal product of labor to the current real wage.[55]

With preset nominal wages, surprise inflation will result in a lower-than-expected real wage (for both groups of workers) and therefore, with Fischer's employment-determination assumption, a greater-than-normal level of aggregate output. But this model does not have the policy-ineffectiveness property: if demand shocks are serially correlated, then monetary policy rules can be designed to affect the variance of the output process – essentially because policy can in this case be made to respond to shocks that occur after some currently-prevailing wages were set. The unconditional *mean* of the output process cannot be affected by the choice of policy-rule parameters, however, if effects of the type discussed in Subsection 2.2 are ruled out.[56] In this sense, then, the Fischer model satisfies the *natural rate hypothesis* as defined by Lucas (1972b): there is *no* monetary policy that will keep output permanently high in relation to its natural-rate path. The same will be true, moreover, for other models of class (ii) in which prices are preset at expected market-clearing levels.

A third category of aggregate supply models is one which builds on the concept of a "non-accelerating-inflation rate of unemployment" (NAIRU). Each such model posits a stable Phillips-type relation between unemployment (or output relative to its reference path) and the acceleration magnitude, i.e. the period-to-period change in the inflation rate. Distributed-lag specifications may be employed, as in Tobin's (1980a, p. 68) formulation, which explains each quarter's inflation rate by the previous quarter's unemployment rate and an average of the previous eight quarters' inflation rates. In NAIRU models it is not always clear whether past inflation values enter as proxies for inflationary expectations or to reflect "catch-up or "inertia" effects that have no justification in terms of neoclassical theory. In any event, NAIRU models do not satisfy the natural-rate property: if there exists a stable negative relationship between unemployment and the change in inflation, then the unemployment

---

[55] Barro (1977b) has emphasized that this assumption regarding employment determination is as critical for the model's properties as the wage-setting feature. He has pointed out that other employment determination rules could be combined with the staggered wage process and that some would yield higher levels of utility, ex post, for workers and employers.

[56] It is entirely appropriate to rule out such effects in the context of the issue at hand. The point is not that such effects are non-existent, but rather that they should be thought of as affecting the "normal" or "natural rate" level of output, not the deviation of output from that reference value. The issue at hand is the effectiveness of stabilization policy, which is concerned with these deviations.

rate can be permanently lowered by permanent acceptance of an increased value of the acceleration magnitude.[57]

The last category in our four-way classification scheme pertains to so-called "real business cycle" models. In these models the specification of the Phillips-curve relationship is a simple one; it is assumed that there is no such relation. There is, more precisely, no wage–price mechanism that would transmit monetary disturbances into output or unemployment effects.[58] Any observed correlations between output and (say) money growth are, according to this viewpoint, the consequence of "reverse causation", i.e. responses of the money stock to output fluctuations brought about by real shocks to technology or perhaps preferences. This line of research, initiated by Kydland and Prescott (1982), Long and Plosser (1983), and King and Plosser (1984), has been quite prominent in recent years (i.e. 1984–86). In part this popularity is no doubt due to the theoretical attractiveness of the basic notion that there is no Phillips relation; as mentioned before, it is difficult to account for such a relation on the basis of strict neoclassical reasoning.

There is one important formulation whose position in terms of the foregoing categorization is unclear, namely the staggered-wage models of Taylor (1979, 1980). In these models nominal wages (or prices) are set each period for a fraction of the sellers, as in the Fischer (1977) setup, and maintained for two or more periods. And again the preset values are selected on the basis of rational and forward-looking expectations. But the principle governing the level at which they are set is not to equate expected supply and demand quantities, but rather to keep in step with wages (or prices) pertaining to the other portion of the workforce, with an adjustment reflecting expected excess demand. In the two-group, two-period case this approach gives rise to a relation of the form:

$$x_t = 0.5\mathrm{E}_{t-1}[(x_{t+1} + x_{t-1})] + 0.5\gamma\mathrm{E}_{t-1}[(y_t - \bar{y}_t) + (y_{t+1} - \bar{y}_{t+1})], \quad \gamma > 0,$$

$$(4.1)$$

where x_t is the log of the wage set (for half the workforce) at the start of t and $y_t - \bar{y}_t$ is a logarithmetic measure of output relative to normal. Now clearly this equation can be rearranged to yield:

$$0 = (\mathrm{E}_{t-1}x_{t+1} - x_t) - (x_t - x_{t-1}) + \gamma\mathrm{E}_{t-1}[(y_t - \bar{y}_t) + (y_{t+1} - \bar{y}_{t+1})].$$

$$(4.2)$$

---

[57]It might be objected that in actual practice accelerations are never permanent. But that does not constitute a denial that the NAIRU models possess a distinctive feature. And *if* that feature is judged plausible (implausible), then it constitutes a mark in favor of (against) the class of models even if the hypothetical experiment used in defining the feature never occurs.

[58]Thus, we are again abstracting from effects of the type discussed in Subsection 2.2.

And with rational expectations it must be true that realized values of x_t and $y_t - \bar{y}_t$ will differ only randomly from expected values. Consequently, the last equation can be seen to imply that different acceleration magnitudes will be permanently associated with different levels of excess demand. Thus, Taylor's formulation, like NAIRU models, does not satisfy the natural rate hypothesis. The nature of the implied association is unlike that of the NAIRU models, however; higher values of $\Delta x_{t+1} - \Delta x_t$ give rise to *lower* values of $y_t - \bar{y}_t$. Thus, Taylor's approach does not fall cleanly into either category (ii) or (iii).

4.2. Evaluation of alternative theories

A very large number of empirical studies have been conducted with the object of determining which type of Phillips-curve theory conforms most closely to the facts, but conclusions are not clear-cut. A major reason for this inconclusiveness is one that plagues attempts to test economic propositions of many types, namely that any formal statistical test must rely upon maintained hypotheses that are about as dubious as the proposition under explicit scrutiny. In evaluating the evidence, consequently, it is necessary to utilize a subjective blend of statistical and theoretical findings.[59]

The empirical studies conducted by Barro (1977a, 1978) provided a substantial boost toward acceptance of the monetary misperception models of Lucas, since the results suggested that unanticipated changes in U.S. money growth rates have strong effects on employment and output with anticipated changes having insignificant effects. Barro's results relied, however, on some debatable assumptions concerning the basic specification of the monetary policy rule and the presence of lagged money surprise terms in the unemployment (or output) equation.[60] Both features can be defended, but the defense leaves room for skepticism. Later studies by Gordon (1982) and Mishkin (1982) yielded conclusions that conflict with Barro's by attributing significant explanatory power to anticipated money growth rates, a finding that is inconsistent with Lucas's models.

A line of argument that may be more convincing to some readers relies on the observation that information regarding aggregate money stock magnitudes (and price indices) is available to the public both promptly and cheaply. And since knowledge of current money stock magnitudes would eliminate the effect

---

[59]For a thoughtful alternative evaluation, see King and Dotsey (1987).

[60]Lagged surprise terms need to be rationalized by some argument that has them entering to reflect adjustment-cost effects, which might be more directly expressed in terms of a lagged value of the employment or output variable. Sargent (1976) showed that if lagged money surprises are permitted, identification of unanticipated money changes must rely upon exclusion restrictions that presume considerable knowledge of monetary policy behavior.

of monetary surprises on output in the Lucas models,[61] this observation tends to turn the misperceptions theory into one of the real business cycle class (iv).[62]

With regard to the latter, one reason for its recent popularity is the demonstration by Kydland and Prescott (1982) that simulations with a model, in which a stochastic technology shock provides the *sole* source of fluctuations, provides a fairly good match to actual U.S. data in several respects.[63] A second likely reason is Sims' (1980) demonstration that monthly money stock innovations explain very little of the variance of industrial production when a nominal interest rate is included in a small VAR system. It has been argued,[64] however, that this fact is easily reconciled with a belief in the potency of monetary policy surprises. Basically, the argument is that there is no reason to interpret *money stock* residuals in a VAR system with surprise actions of the *monetary authority*, especially when the latter typically focuses his attention on monthly interest rate movements.

A third boost for real business cycle models has come from recent recognition that arguments of Nelson and Plosser (1982) concerning alternative data detrending procedures – i.e. differencing versus linear trend removal – are conceptually interesting and quantitatively important. The Nelson–Plosser suggestion that it is possible to separate trend from cyclical components of observed time series, and that the cyclical component contributes comparatively little variability to GNP and employment series, is open to objection [McCallum (1986)]. But is is possible to reject this specific suggestion and still view other considerations raised by Nelson and Plosser to be of considerable importance. Eichenbaum and Singleton (1986) have shown, for example, that analysis with differenced series indicates much weaker Granger causality from

---

[61] It has been suggested that this difficulty might not prevail if the "true" monetary aggregate were unobservable and thus measured with error. It was shown by King (1981), however, that if observations are available on a proxy variable that differs only randomly from the true aggregate, then output (or employment) should be unrelated to movements in measured monetary aggregates. This suggestion seems unsatisfactory, therefore, for one who accepts the facts to be as indicated by the Barro (1977a, 1978), Gordon (1982), or Mishkin (1982) studies.

[62] It should be kept in mind that this objection to Lucas's theory would not be applicable to prewar periods, when aggregate data was much more difficult to obtain. The greater availability of such data may, in accordance with the Lucas models, be one reason for the reduced severity of business cycle fluctuations in the postwar period.

[63] In particular, real GNP autocorrelations, correlations of GNP with other variables, and variances of other variables are reasonably well matched provided that the variance of GNP is itself consistent with actual data. The latter condition is obtained in the Kydland–Prescott (1982) study by choice of the variance of the (unobserved) technology shock. There are various respects in which the Kydland–Prescott model does not provide a good match with actual data. On this subject, see Summers (1987) and McCallum (1989).

[64] See, for example, McCallum (1983b). The point, that a neglect of monetary policy operating procedures may seriously distort econometric results, is applicable in a variety of issues.

monetary to real variables than does analysis with series detrended by removal of linear trend terms. There is currently much activity in this area of research; some time will probably be needed before reliable conclusions can be drawn.

With regard to the NAIRU class of models, the main point would seem to be that their key implication – i.e. that output can be permanently raised (relative to normal) by monetary means – is implausible enough to warrant rejection on purely theoretical grounds. Empirically, furthermore, experiences with accelerating inflation seem not to have been accompanied by unusually high output levels.

The remaining class of theories is type (ii), sticky-price models that do not imply irrationality on the part of individual agents. In this case the class is wide enough that it is difficult to conceive of evidence that would reflect badly on all its members. For example, to whatever extent the failure of real wages to move countercyclically tends to discredit the Fischer (1977) mechanism,[65] this failure is not at all inconsistent with specifications in which nominal wages are set à la Fischer but employment is demand-determined at preset *product* prices with current real wages irrelevant for employment decisions.[66] The main objection to the broad class of theories, consequently, has stemmed from the analytical difficulty of explaining why price stickiness relevant for quantity determination would pertain to nominal as opposed to real prices. In other words, if prices are to be preset (for whatever reason) why are they not preset in real terms by means of indexation (or linkage) arrangements? One possibility, suggested in McCallum (1986), is that for many specific product prices the benefits to individuals of the insurance provided by such arrangements would be extremely small. If this is so, then the transaction costs necessitated by such arrangements might be adequate to inhibit their use, even though these costs are themselves very small. And the aggregate consequences could be substantial, as the argument of Akerlof and Yellen (1985) illustrates.

On the basis of the foregoing considerations, empirical and theoretical, it would appear that there is at present no evidence or reason that clearly compels one to reject theories of either the sticky-price or real-business cycle type. Such evidence should in principle be obtainable, however, as the theories have implications that differ more markedly than is the case with sticky-price and monetary misperception models.

---

[65] This failure cannot entirely discredit the Fischer model, as technology shocks will lead to procyclical real wages even under its assumptions. If these predominate over demand shocks, then the gross correlations could be as observed.

[66] This sort of scheme has been described by McCallum (1982). Reasons why current wages may be unimportant in employment determination have been explored at length by Hall (1980), whose analysis complements that of Barro (1977b).

4.3. Other sources of non-neutrality

At this point we need briefly to consider cyclical output–inflation correlations that are brought about not via the Phillips-curve mechanisms discussed above, but by monetary "non-neutralities" that work by altering the natural-rate path of output. That such non-neutralities may exist should be apparent from the discussion in Sections 2 and 3, where it was concluded that precise steady-state superneutrality is not implied by OG models or by models of the Sidrauski type except under stringent restrictions. Clearly, the same behavior patterns that cause (per capita) values of capital, employment, and consumption to depend upon inflation rates, when comparisons are made across steady states, will give rise to related effects of anticipated inflation on a period-by-period basis. If, for example, the steady-state capital stock is increased by anticipated inflation, as in the model of Drazen (1981), then output may also be related to inflation at business-cycle frequencies.

There are two reasons, however, for devoting much less attention to these sources of non-neutrality than to those discussed in Subsection 4.1. The first of these concerns the fundamentally different nature of the implied cyclical variations. In particular, variations resulting from effects of anticipated inflation on the capital stock (or on the capital–labor ratio) are appropriately thought of as variations in the natural rate of output, rather than departures from the latter, for these variations would occur even with perfectly flexible prices and complete information on the part of individual agents.[67] They do not involve inefficiencies in the utilization of existing resources, as is the case with output variations of the Phillips-curve type.

Secondly, there are various reasons for believing that monetary effects on natural-rate values of output are not empirically of great importance. Of these reasons, three will be mentioned. First, the magnitude of the full effect of anticipated inflation on output is unlikely to be large. Even though precise superneutrality is not predicted by the models of Sections 2 and 3, it is apt to provide a good approximation to actuality. Second, such effects as do occur would tend to affect output slowly, for the existing capital stock is large in relation to plausible variations in annual investment flows. Finally, the direction of effect predicted by theoretical analysis is unclear. While higher inflation unambiguously increases output in Drazen's (1981) overlapping-generations setup, it does the opposite in other models such as those of Stockman (1981) and Kimbrough (1986).

In sum, it would appear that monetary effects on output at business cycle

---

[67]Typically, "natural rate" values would be defined relative to such reference conditions. No general definition is here attempted, however, for the appropriate definition will differ from model to model.

frequencies are probably due primarily to fluctuations in output in relation to its natural or normal values, rather than fluctuations in normal values themselves.

5. Positive analysis of monetary policy

In this section we turn our attention to a topic of a different type, namely: Why is it that substantial (positive) inflation has been a predominant feature of the postwar era?[68] Of course the models of Sections 2 and 3 suggest that sustained inflation will not occur in the absence of excessive money growth,[69] but acceptance of that view just alters the form of the question, which then becomes: Why do current-day monetary authorities permit money growth rates that result on average in positive inflation? In response, it is tempting to point to the demise of commodity-money standards. But suppose that it was agreed that adherence to such a standard would prevent sustained inflation. This agreement would still leave unanswered the question of why the monetary authority, in an economy with a fiat money system, would not choose a zero or negative average rate of inflation.[70]

The most prominent attempt to address this issue appears in a line of work initiated by Barro (1983) and Barro and Gordon (1983a), who built upon insights developed by Calvo (1978) and especially Kydland and Prescott (1977). In this section we discuss the basic model used in this line of work, briefly consider extensions involving reputational considerations, and touch upon a few more general matters regarding the positive analysis of monetary policy.

5.1. Effects of discretionary policy implementation

In the prototype model developed by Kydland and Prescott (1977) and spelled out by Barro and Gordon (1983a), the monetary authority's objectives are

---

[68]For the United States, for example, the price level in mid-1986 (as measured by the CPI) stood at 5.6 times its 1946 value. By way of comparison, it is interesting to note that the 1940 price level, as measured by the WPI, was only 1.3 times its value as of 1776. (This calculation splices the official WPI to the Warren and Pearson values in 1890.)

[69]What rate is excessive depends, as mentioned in Section 1, on output growth and the rate of technical progress in transaction technology. But these factors are both small and tend to oppose each other so a non-inflationary money growth rate will be within 1 or 2 (annual) percentage points of zero.

[70]That this choice lies within the monetary authority's power seems indisputable, for large economies or ones with floating exchange rates, since the time span under discussion is a matter of decades.

represented by a loss function in which the arguments are the squared deviations of unemployment and inflation from values determined by considerations of allocational efficiency.[71,72] It will simplify matters without distortion of the argument, however, if we simply take the loss function to be decreasing in the current money growth surprise (unanticipated money growth reduces unemployment) and increasing in the square of money growth itself.[73] There are also discounted values of similar terms included for all future periods, but for the moment these can be ignored. If, with such an objective function, the monetary authority were to adopt a *policy rule* by choosing among constant money growth rates, it would recognize that surprise values will average to zero whatever its choice so that the chosen money growth rate would be zero. Similarly, an *average* growth rate of zero would be implied by the optimal choice of a rule when a broader class of rules is considered.

But suppose that, instead, the authority implements its objectives in a so-called discretionary manner,[74] i.e. by selecting current money growth rates on a period-by-period basis. In each period, that is, the prevailing *expected* money growth rate is taken as a given piece of data – an initial condition. The current surprise is then apparently under the authority's control, so the loss-minimizing choice of the current money growth rate is that which just equates the marginal benefit of surprise money growth to the marginal cost of money growth per se. With the objective function as specified, this optimal value will be strictly positive. But rational private agents understand this policy process well enough that their expectations regarding money growth are correct on average. Thus, the surprise magnitude is zero on average, over any large number of periods, even though the magnitude within each period is

---

[71]The unemployment term is of the form $(Un_t - k\bar{U}n_t)^2$, with $\bar{U}n_t$ the natural-rate value of Un_t and $k < 1$. The latter condition reflects the assumption that the monetary authority's "target" value of unemployment is below the natural-rate value. Barro and Gordon (1983a) interpret this as reflecting some externality that makes the socially optimal value of Un_t less than $\bar{U}n_t$, and are consequently able to claim that there is no discrepancy between the policy-maker's objectives and private agents' preferences. The analysis would remain the same, of course, if the $k < 1$ condition were interpreted as merely reflecting a desire by the policy-maker for an excessively low rate of unemployment.

[72]The analysis relies upon the plausible assumption that deviations of inflation from the efficient rate are increasingly costly at the margin. Use of the squared deviation is designed to reflect that condition in a tractable manner.

[73]In this setup there is no need to distinguish between money growth and inflation rates. Accordingly, we shall here use the terms interchangeably. The allocationally efficient rate of growth is taken to be zero only for convenience; in principle it would be whatever rate leads to the optimal steady inflation rate.

[74]This terminology is due to Kydland and Prescott (1977). It does not agree with that used in earlier versions of the "rules vs. discretion" debate, which were (in today's terms) actually concerned with non-activist vs. activist policy. That a *rule* can be activist – i.e. be responsive to recent conditions – should need no explanation here.

under the control of the monetary authority. Consequently, there is on average no benefit – no extra employment – materializing from surprises. On average, then, the discretionary regime features more money growth (i.e. inflation) but the same amount of surprise money growth (i.e. unemployment) as with an optimal rule.

As a matter of positive analysis, this model suggests that excessive money growth (i.e. positive inflation) is attributable to the fact that actual monetary authorities are not bound by rules, either self-imposed rules or ones stipulated externally. Instead, they conduct policy in a way that involves repeatedly taking account of the fact that for *given* expectations a lower money growth rate would result temporarily in more unemployment, while repeatedly ignoring the effect of these growth rates on the expectations that are subsequently given.

These points can be succinctly illustrated by means of a specific algebraic example, utilized by Barro and Gordon (1983b). In this example, the monetary authority seeks at time t to minimize the loss function:

$$z_t + \beta z_{t+1} + \beta^2 z_{t+2} + \cdots , \tag{5.1}$$

where β is a discount factor $(0 < \beta < 1)$. The per-period losses are given by:

$$z_t = (a/2)\pi_t^2 - b(\pi_t - \pi_t^e) , \quad a, b > 0 , \tag{5.2}$$

where π_t represents inflation or money growth in t with π_t^e the previously-formed expectation of π_t. Rule-like optimization involves a once-and-for all choice of π_t values under the condition that $\pi_t - \pi_t^e$ will, for whatever choice, equal zero on average. In these circumstances, the optimal choice will be $\pi_t = 0$ for all t. But if π_t^e is taken as given in period t, and π_{t+j}^e values are viewed as independent of π_t for $j = 1, 2, \ldots$, then the value of π_t that will minimize (5.1) is the discretionary value $\pi_t = b/a > 0$. This will, under discretion, be chosen at each t.

There are alternative interpretations that can be given to the foregoing model. In particular, the beneficial aspect of actual money growth can be thought of as reflecting government revenues from money creation. And although the details of an appropriate specification would then be different, the conclusion regarding the inflationary tendency of a discretionary regime would again be obtained [Barro (1983)]. An interpretive issue is whether the policymaker's objective function should be viewed as accurately reflecting preferences of the public. The affirmative position taken by Barro and Gordon (1983a, pp. 593–594) has been challenged by Cukierman (1986, p. 9). But whatever the outcome of that dispute, it is germane primarily to the normative uses of the model. From the perspective of understanding why inflation is observed, all that matters is whether the specification of the policy-maker's objectives is sufficiently accurate, empirically.[75]

An interesting elaboration of the foregoing model has been provided by Cukierman and Meltzer (1986), who begin with a framework like that of Barro and Gordon (1983a) but extend it so as to accommodate imperfect control of, and noisy announcements about, money growth rates. In addition, Cukierman and Meltzer postulate stochastically changing objectives of the monetary authority and assume that these fluctuations in objectives are not directly observable by the public. Two examples of the additional results that are obtained from this extended framework are, first, that the monetary authority will choose to have relatively looser control procedures if his rate of time preference is relatively high and, second, that looser control leads to a higher average rate of money growth.

There are a number of objections to the basic Barro–Gordon framework that could be raised. One, mentioned by Grossman and Van Huyck (1986), is that the excessive money-growth result is not obtained if the objective function is respecified to reflect a dislike for expected (rather than actual) inflation. This seems to be a criticism directed more at the model's normative merits, however, than at its merits as a positive theory of inflation, for actual policy-makers seem to be concerned with costs of *realized* inflation, rather than the ones emphasized by economic theorists. From this positive perspective, however, another objection might be that actual policy-makers have not based their period-by-period optimality calculations on models in which private agents' expectations are rational. While rationality may in fact have prevailed, so the argument goes, the Fed and other central banks have not recognized that to be the case and have modelled (perhaps implicitly) agents' expectations by means of fixed forecasting formulae.

To consider the force of this last objection, let us examine an example in which the monetary authority has the specific loss function (5.1) and (5.2), but believes, in contrast to the previous example, that agents form expectations according to the fixed formula:

$$\pi_t^e = 0.5(\pi_{t-1} + \pi_{t-2}).$$ (5.3)

Now in this case the monetary authority believes that his choice of π_t will affect future expectations, i.e. π_{t+1}^e and π_{t+2}^e. His optimal choice at t of inflation or money growth is then as follows:

$$\tilde{\pi}_{t+j} = (b/a)[1 - 0.5(\beta + \beta^2)], \quad j = 0, 1, 2, \ldots.$$ (5.4)

---

[75]With regard to actual Federal Reserve objectives, interesting support for the view that the principal aims are avoidance of inflation and unemployment is provided by Pierce (1974).

Thus, instead of the value b/a chosen under the Barro–Gordon expectational assumption, the π_t value will depart from zero only to the extent that the authority's preferences exhibit impatience (i.e. $\beta < 1$). But it would seem extremely likely that the objectives of actual monetary authorities do have that property, so the point of view suggested by this objection continues to predict a positive inflation rate. That rate remains undesirable, moreover, in the sense that the experienced inflation induces no extra employment. It should be added that while this example does not feature the rules vs. discretion distinction, it does not contradict the *normative* force of the Kydland–Prescott demonstration as pertaining to an economy in which expectations are rational and the policy authority recognizes that rationality.

5.2. *Reputational considerations*

The objection to the basic model that has been most prominent in the literature is neither of the ones mentioned above, but one that is based on its neglect of reputational effects. In particular, recent papers by Barro and Gordon (1983b), Barro (1986), Backus and Driffill (1985), Grossman and Van Huyck (1986), and others have proceeded in repeated-game formulations that explore the possibility that reputational forces can lead to outcomes closer to those obtained under rules than discretion in the basic Kydland–Prescott setup.

In the model of Barro and Gordon (1983b), it is assumed that the monetary authority announces the intention to create money or inflate at a specified rate, say π^*, that is smaller than the discretionary value $\hat{\pi}$. Private agents expect this value to be chosen in each period so long as the authority's actual choices do not depart from $\pi_t = \pi^*$. If, however, at some date t^0 there occurs a discrepancy, $\pi_t^0 \neq \pi^*$, then agents expect that the discretionary value $\hat{\pi}$ will prevail in $t^0 + 1$ and possibly for some additional periods, after which expectations revert to $\pi_t^e = \pi^*$. Under these assumptions, the equilibrium outcomes tend to concentrate on the value π^*, and that value is shown to lie between 0 and $\hat{\pi}$, i.e. between the values pertaining to the pure cases discussed previously. Thus, reputational considerations are helpful, according to the analysis, but do not provide a complete substitute for the presence of a well-designed rule. Two problems with this particular model have, however, been pointed out by Barro (1986) and Rogoff (1987). First, it requires the monetary authority to have an infinite planning horizon: if the horizon is finite the purely discretionary outcome will prevail in each period. Second, the number of periods, for which the expected inflation rate is $\hat{\pi}$ (rather than π^*) after the occurrence of a $\pi_t \neq \pi^*$ discrepancy, is arbitrary and the equilibrium value of π^* itself depends on that number. These problems are, as Barro and Rogoff recognize, quite serious in the context of the issues at hand.

Partly for that reason, Barro (1986) has considered an alternative approach that involves uncertainty on the part of agents about the "type" of policy-maker that is in office as the monetary authority. Different types, in this context, correspond to different degrees of commitment to low inflation, with these differences apparently reflecting preferences – or some sort of political affiliation – since the same commitment technology would presumably be available to all potential policy-makers. The model's attractiveness is considerably enhanced, in view of this interpretation, by Rogoff's (1987) extension to a case with a continuum of policy-maker types – an extension that has the virtue of eliminating the need to assume a randomized strategy on the part of the policy-maker. Each new incumbent begins his term, according to the model, with zero money growth for a number (possibly zero) of periods. Afterwards, an uncommitted policy-maker, who has been masquerading as a committed type in order to develop exploitable expectations of low inflation, switches to the discretionary value. During the initial interval, agents' expectations involve the subjective probability (which is revised as experience accumulates) of the incumbent policy-maker being of the uncommitted type. Because the policy-maker who is uncommitted succeeds in generating a positive monetary surprise at the end of his term, the model implies that, conditional upon the public's prior subjective probability regarding types, the expected value of the loss function is lower for the uncommitted type. Expected losses for either type are, however, smaller the greater is the subjective probability that the policy-maker will be of the committed type. Institutions that more frequently place committed inflation-avoiders in the policy-making office therefore produce better outcomes on average (over a large number of terms), according to the assumed loss function, as well as lower average inflation rates.

While this alternative framework avoids the two particular problems noted above, it has weaknesses of its own. As Barro (1986, p. 20) notes, it "would seem preferable to generate predictions for inflation that depended less on individual traits of policymakers and more on basic institutional factors". To that might be added the related objection that the analysis is incomplete, so long as it includes no description of the process determining the "type" of policy-maker that is selected each term. In a setting in which types matter, the type that attains office should be treated as an endogenous variable.

5.3. Private objectives of the monetary authority

The models described above are open to the criticism that they unrealistically presume altruistic behavior on the part of the monetary authority. Actual policy decisions are made by purposeful individuals or groups of individuals whose actions are strongly influenced by matters affecting their own income, prestige, and working conditions – none of which is represented in the Barro–Gordon objective function. In this vein, insightful discussions of Federal Reserve behavior have been provided by Hetzel (1986), Lombra and Moran (1980), Kane (1982), and others.

It seems clear that the point of view represented by these authors has much merit; full understanding of policy behavior requires some attention to the actual motives of policy-makers. But it also seems clear that a truly satisfactory analysis of this type will be extremely difficult. For policy-makers' objectives are partly concerned with attainment and retention of policy positions, the filling of which is part of a nation's political process. Adequate treatment of this aspect of behavior then requires an adequate model of the political system – including voter behavior, if the nation in question is one in which the democratic process plays a significant role. And despite many worthwhile efforts,[76] the profession is currently a long way from having a widely-accepted model of that type.[77]

There is one way, nevertheless, in which reasoning about the private interest of policy-makers seems highly relevant to the concerns of this chapter. In particular, Friedman (1985, pp. 60–61) has suggested that the prestige of the top monetary policy-maker – e.g. the Chairman of the Board of Governors of the Federal Reserve System – depends strongly on the amount of attention accorded his actions by the news media. And this amount is certainly strongly increased by the perception that the Board of Governors has discretionary power: a legislated rule for monetary policy would sharply reduce the media's attention to the Fed's Chairman. Now, it seems clear that this observation should be interpreted in a manner that is not so highly personalized, but refers to many more individuals. Thus, it would appear to be the case that the prestige – and perhaps in some cases the pecuniary income in subsequent career positions – of Board Members and various professional employees of the Fed (including researchers) is enhanced by the public's perception that the Fed has important discretionary power. To the extent that this viewpoint is accepted, it might then seem unlikely that the Fed would willingly adopt behavioral rules that would eliminate the discretionary aspects – and, according to the analysis of Subsection 5.1, the inflationary bias – of U.S. monetary policy behavior. A more hopeful alternative scenario would have the Fed choosing to behave in a rule-like manner, by abstaining from attempts to

---

[76]A recent example is provided by Alesina (1987).

[77]Cukierman and Meltzer (1986) interpret the stochastic objectives of the policy-maker in their model as reflecting desires to remain in office, with the chances of doing so believed by the policy-maker to depend on inflation and employment. Furthermore, the relative importance of these two determinants of popularity "shifts in unpredictable ways as individuals within the decision-making body of government change their positions, alliances, and views" (1986, p. 1103). Treatment of political influences as stochastic and exogenous illustrates the absence of a well-developed theory of such influences.

exploit the temporary fixity of expectations, while retaining the image and prestige of a crucial policy-making organization.

6. Concluding remarks

It may have been noted that the discussion in this chapter had devoted little explicit attention to the topic of hyperinflation, on which there is a substantial literature initiated by the famous study of Cagan (1956) and given a large boost by the innovative analysis of Sargent and Wallace (1973).[78] The reason for our lack of emphasis is that most of the relevant theoretical points are subsumed in our general discussion. Furthermore, much of the recent work on hyperinflation has been principally concerned with the development and application of econometric techniques appropriate under the hypothesis of rational expectations. Unless bubble phenomena were operative during the relevant episodes, which seems unlikely, the main substantive question that needs to be understood is why the monetary authorities permitted the outlandish money stock growth rates that occurred. Despite interesting historical investigations by Sargent (1982), Capie (1986), and others, this question remains unanswered.

Also slighted in our discussion has been the recent outburst of writings on commodity-money arrangements and, more generally, on monetary standards; a prominent example is provided by papers in the July 1983 issue of the *Journal of Monetary Economics*. Much of the work on monetary standards has been stimulating and continuing efforts may ultimately aid in the design of institutions that would avoid the inflationary tendency discussed above in Subsection 5.1. At present, however, it remains unclear how to achieve the adoption of such a standard or to prevent the violation of one that is nominally in force.

It is a difficult matter to summarize what is already a fairly compressed summarization. It may nevertheless be useful to conclude this chapter with an attempt briefly to identify the main themes that are implied by the discussion of Sections 1–5. The first of these is that, with regard to ongoing inflation, the principal conclusions of theoretical analyses are not very sensitive to details of model specification, so long as the latter posits rational agents devoid of money

---

[78]As is well known, Cagan's study attempted to lend support to the hypothesis that money demand functions do not shift about erratically by showing that such functions remained in place through the exceptionally stressful periods of seven twentieth-century European hyperinflations (Austria 1921–22; Germany 1922–23; Greece 1943–44; Hungary 1923–24; Hungary 1945–46; Poland 1923–24; and Russia 1921–24). Cagan's work was remarkable for its time, but his principal conclusion was somewhat undetermined by econometric procedures that would today be judged as flawed; the basic regression specification included an endogenous variable as a regressor and took no account of severely autocorrelated residuals. Also, as B. Friedman (1978) has noted, Cagan's dynamic stability analysis incorrectly applied a stability condition appropriate for a continuous-time formulation to an empirical model estimated with discrete-time data.

illusion. Whether one assumes finite-lived or infinite-lived agents, such models suggest (i) that steady-state inflation rates will conform fairly closely to money growth rates, (ii) that superneutrality is not strictly implied but departures should be minor, and (iii) that socially optimal inflation rates are probably zero or negative. Bubble inflation provides a possible exception to point (i) as a matter of theory, but there is little reason to believe that such a phenomenon is of significance empirically. With regard to irregular inflation, and the cyclical interaction of nominal and real variables, there is considerably less professional agreement. Four classes of aggregate-supply or Phillips-curve theories are currently in use by researchers and at least two of these have been able thus far to withstand attempts at refutation. Perhaps the most important issue regarding inflation is why policy authorities have behaved, over the last 40 years, in a manner that permitted a many-fold increase in the price level in most industrial nations. A full answer to that question will require a much better theory of the political process than is currently available. An important hypothesis regarding inflationary bias has been suggested, nevertheless, by models that focus on the effects of period-by-period (i.e. "discretionary") decision-making by a monetary authority that seeks, in a fiat-money regime, to avoid unemployment as well as inflation.

References

Abel, A.B. (1987) 'Optimal monetary growth', *Journal of Monetary Economics*, 19: 437–450.

Akerlof, G.A. and J. Yellen (1985) 'Can small deviations from rationality make significant differences to economic equilibria?', *American Economic Review*, 75: 708–720.

Alesina, A. (1987) 'Macroeconomic policy in a two-party system as a repeated game', *Quarterly Journal of Economics*, 102: 651–678.

Auernheimer, L. (1974) 'The honest government's guide to inflationary finance', *Journal of Political Economy*, 82: 598–606.

Backus, D. and J. Driffill (1985) 'Inflation and reputation', *American Economic Review*, 75: 530–538.

Barro, R.J. (1974) 'Are government bonds net wealth?', *Journal of Political Economy*, 82: 1095–1117.

Barro, R.J. (1976) 'Rational expectations and the role of monetary policy', *Journal of Monetary Economics*, 2: 1–32.

Barro, R.J. (1977a) 'Unanticipated money growth and unemployment in the United States', *American Economic Review*, 67: 101–115.

Barro, R.J. (1977b) 'Long term contracting, sticky prices, and monetary policy', *Journal of Monetary Economics*, 3: 305–316.

Barro, R.J. (1978) 'Unanticipated money, output, and the price level in the United States', *Journal of Political Economy*, 86: 549–580.

Barro, R.J. (1981) 'The equilibrium approach to business cycles', in: J. Barro, ed., *Money, expectations, and business cycles*. New York: Academic Press.

Barro, R.J. (1983) 'Inflationary finance under discretion and rules', *Canadian Journal of Economics*, 16: 1–16.

Barro, R.J. (1984) *Macroeconomics*. New York: Wiley.

Barro, R.J. (1986) 'Reputation in a model of monetary policy with incomplete information', *Journal of Monetary Economics*, 17: 3–20.

Barro, R.J. and D.B. Gordon (1983a) 'A positive theory of monetary policy in a natural rate model', *Journal of Political Economy*, 91: 589–610.

Barro, R.J. and D.B. Gordon (1983b) 'Rules, discretion, and reputation in a model of monetary policy', *Journal of Monetary Economics*, 12: 101–121.

Barro, R.J. and S. Fischer (1976) 'Recent developments in monetary theory', *Journal of Monetary Economics*, 2: 133–167.

Bernheim, B.D. (1987) 'Ricardian equivalence: an evaluation of theory and evidence', *NBER macroeconomics annual 1987*: 263–304.

Blanchard, O.J. (1985) 'Debt, deficits, and finite horizons', *Journal of Political Economy*, 93: 223–247.

Brock, W.A. (1974) 'Money and growth: The case of long-run perfect foresight', *International Economic Review*, 15: 750–777.

Brock, W.A. (1975) 'A simple perfect foresight monetary model', *Journal of Monetary Economics*, 1: 133–150.

Bronfenbrenner, M. and F.D. Holtzman (1963) 'A survey of inflation theory', *American Economic Review*, 53: 593–661.

Brunner, K. and A.H. Meltzer (1983) 'Strategies and tactics for monetary control', *Carnegie-Rochester Conference Series on Public Policy*, 18: 59–104.

Bryant, J. and N. Wallace (1979) 'The inefficiency of interest-bearing national debt', *Journal of Political Economy*, 87: 365–381.

Burmeister, E. and K. Wall (1982) 'Kalman filtering estimation of unobserved rational expectations with an application to the German hyperinflation', *Journal of Econometrics*, 20: 255–284.

Cagan, P. (1956) 'The monetary dynamics of hyperinflation', in: M. Friedman, ed., *Studies in the quantity theory of money*. Chicago: University of Chicago Press.

Calvo, G. (1978) 'Optimal seigniorage from money creation', *Journal of Monetary Economics*, 4: 503–517.

Calvo, G. (1979) 'On models of money and perfect foresight', *International Economic Review*, 20: 83–103.

Capie, F. (1986) 'Conditions in which very rapid inflation has appeared', *Carnegie-Rochester Conference Series on Public Policy*, 24: 115–168.

Casella, A. (1989) 'Testing for price level bubbles: The German hyperinflation once more', *Journal of Monetary Economics*, 24: 109–122.

Cass, D. and M.E. Yaari (1967) 'Individual saving, aggregate capital accumulation, and efficient growth', in: K. Shell, ed., *Essays in the theory of optimal economic growth*. Cambridge, Mass.: M.I.T. press.

Chan, L.K.C. (1983) 'Uncertainty and the neutrality of government financing policy', *Journal of Monetary Economics*, 11: 351–372.

Cukierman, A. (1979) 'Rational expectations and the role of monetary policy: A generalization', *Journal of Monetary Economics*, 5: 213–230.

Cukierman, A. (1986) 'Central bank behavior and credibility – some recent developments', *Federal Reserve Bank of St. Louis Review*, 68: 5–17.

Cukierman, A. and A.H. Meltzer (1986) 'A theory of ambiguity, credibility, and inflation under discretion and asymmetric information', *Econometrica*, 54: 1099–1128.

Danthine, J.P., J.B. Donaldson and L. Smith (1987) 'On the supeneutrality of money in a stochastic dynamic macroeconomic model', *Journal of Monetary Economics*, 20: 475–499.

Diamond, P.A. (1965) 'National debt in a neoclassical growth model', *American Economic Review*, 55: 1126–1150.

Diba, B.T. and H.I. Grossman (1984) 'Rational bubbles in the price of gold', National Bureau of Economic Research, Working Paper 1300.

Drazen, A. (1981) 'Inflation and capital accumulation under a finite horizon', *Journal of Monetary Economics*, 8: 247–260.

Eichenbaum, M. and K.J. Singleton (1986) 'Do equilibrium real business cycle theories explain postwar U.S. business cycles?', *NBER Macroeconomics Annual*, 1: 91–135.

Feenstra, R.C. (1986) 'Functional equivalence between liquidity costs and the utility of money', *Journal of Monetary Economics*, 17: 27–291.

Fischer, S. (1977) 'Long-term contracts, rational expectations, and the optimal money supply rule', *Journal of Political Economy*, 85: 191–206.

Fischer, S. (1984) 'The benefits of price stability', in: *Price stability and public policy*. Kansas City: Federal Reserve Bank of Kansas City.

Fischer, S. (1986) 'Monetary rules and commodity money schemes under uncertainty', *Journal of Monetary Economics*, 17: 21–35.

Flood, R.P. and P.M. Garber (1980) 'Market fundamentals vs. price level bubbles: The first tests', *Journal of Political Economy*, 88: 745–770.

Friedman, B.M. (1978) 'Stability and rationality in models of hyperinflation', *International Economic review*, 19: 45–64.

Friedman, M. (1960) *A program for monetary stability*. New York: Fordham University Press.

Friedman, M. (1963) *Inflation: Causes and consequences*. New York: Asia Publishing House.

Friedman, M. (1966) 'Comments', in: G.P. Shultz and R.Z. Aliber, eds., *Guidelines, informal controls, and the market place*. Chicago: University of Chicago Press.

Friedman, M. (1968) 'The role of monetary policy', *American Economic Review*, 58: 1–17.

Friedman, M. (1969) *The optimum quantity of money and other essays*. Chicago: Aldine.

Friedman, M. (1985) 'How to give monetarism a bad name', in: *Monetarism, inflation, and the federal reserve*. Joint Economic Committee, Congress of the United States. Washington: U.S. Government Printing Office.

Friedman, M. and A.J. Schwartz (1963) *A monetary history of the United States, 1867–1960*. Princeton: Princeton University Press.

Gale, D. (1973) 'Pure exchange equilibrium of dynamic economic models', *Journal of Economic Theory*, 6: 12–36.

Geweke, J. (1986) 'The superneutrality of money in the United States: An interpretation of the evidence', *Econometrica*, 54: 1–22.

Gordon, R.J. (1982) 'Price inertia and policy ineffectiveness in the United States, 1890–1980', *Journal of Political Economy*, 90: 1087–1117.

Gray, J.A. (1976) 'Wage indexation: A macroeconomic approach', *Journal of Monetary Economics*, 2: 221–236.

Grossman, H.I. and J.B. Van Huyck (1986) 'Seigniorage, inflation, and reputation', *Journal of Monetary Economics*, 18: 21–31.

Hahn, F. (1983) *Money and inflation*. Cambridge, Mass.: M.I.T. Press.

Hall, R.E. (1980) 'Employment fluctuations and wage rigidity', *Brookings Papers on Economic Activity*, 1980-1: 91–123.

Hamilton, J.D. and C.H. Whiteman (1985) 'The observable implications of self-fulfilling expectations', *Journal of Monetary Economics*, 16: 353–374.

Harberger, A.C. (1978) 'A primer on inflation', *Journal of Money, Credit and Banking*, 10: 505–521.

Helpman, E. and E. Sadka (1979) 'Optimal financing of the government's budget: Taxes, bonds, or money?', *American Economic Review*, 69: 152–160.

Hetzel, R.L. (1986) 'A Congressional mandate for monetary policy', *Cato Journal*, 5: 797–820.

Johnson, H.G. (1963) 'A survey of theories of inflation', *Indian Economic Review*, 6: 29–69.

Kane, E.J. (1982) 'External pressure and the operations of the Fed', in: R.E. Lombra and W.E. Witte, eds., *Political economy of international and domestic monetary relations*. Ames: Iowa State University Press.

Kimbrough, K.P. (1986) 'Inflation, employment, and welfare in the presence of transaction costs', *Journal of Money, Credit, and Banking*, 18: 127–140.

King, R.G. (1981) 'Monetary information and monetary neutrality', *Journal of Monetary Economics*, 7: 195–206.

King, R.G. and M. Dotsey (1987) 'Rational expectations and the business cycle', in: *The new Palgrave: A dictionary of economic theory and doctrine*. London: Macmillan.

King, R.G. and C.I. Plosser (1984) 'Money, credit, and prices in a real business cycle', *American Economic Review*, 74: 363–380.

Krugman, P.R., T. Persson and L.E.O. Svensson (1985) 'Inflation, interest rates, and welfare', *Quarterly Journal of Economics*, 100: 677–695.

Kydland, F.E. and E.S. Prescott (1977) 'Rules rather than discretion: The inconsistency of optimal plans', *Journal of Political Economy*, 85: 473–491.

Kydland, F.E. and E.S. Prescott (1982) 'Time to build and aggregate fluctuations', *Econometrica*, 50: 1345–1370.

Laidler, D. and M. Parkin (1975) 'Inflation: A survey', *Economic Journal*, 85: 741–809.

Leiderman, L. and M.I. Blejer (1988) 'Modelling and testing Ricardian equivalence: A survey', *International Monetary Fund Staff Papers*, 35: 1–35.

Lombra, R. and M. Moran (1980) 'Policy advice and policymaking at the federal reserve', *Carnegie-Rochester Conference Series on Public Policy*, 13: 9–68.

Long, J.B., Jr. and C.I. Plosser (1983) 'Real business cycles', *Journal of Political Economy*, 91: 39–69.

Lucas, R.E., Jr. (1972a) 'Expectations and the neutrality of money', *Journal of Economic Theory*, 4: 103–124.

Lucas, R.E., Jr. (1972b) 'Econometric testing of the natural rate hypothesis,' in: O. Eckstein, ed., *The econometrics of price determination*. Washington: Board of Governors of the Federal Reserve System.

Lucas, R.E., Jr. (1973) 'Some international evidence on output–inflation tradeoffs', *American Economic Review*, 63: 326–334.

Lucas, R.E., Jr. (1980a) 'Equilibrium in a pure currency economy', in: J.H. Kareken and N. Wallace, eds., *Models of monetary economies*. Minneapolis: Federal Reserve Bank of Minneapolis.

Lucas, R.E., Jr. (1980b) 'Two illustrations of the quantity theory of money', *American Economic Review*, 70: 1005–1014.

Lucas, R.E., Jr. (1985) 'Models of business cycles', Yrjo Jahnsson Lectures, Helsinki.

Lucas, R.E., Jr. and N. Stokey (1983) 'Optimal fiscal and monetary policy in an economy without capital', *Journal of Monetary Economics*, 12: 55–93.

Marty, A.L. (1961) 'Gurley and Shaw on money in a theory of finance', *Journal of Political Economy*, 69: 56–62.

Marty, A.L. (1976) 'A note on the welfare cost of money creation', *Journal of Monetary Economics*, 2: 121–124.

McCallum, B.T. (1980) 'Rational expectations and macroeconomic stabilization policy: An overview', *Journal of Money, Credit and Banking*, 12: 716–746.

McCallum, B.T. (1982) 'Macroeconomics after a decade of rational expectations: Some critical issues', *Federal Reserve Bank of Richmond Economic Review*, 68: 3–12.

McCallum, B.T. (1983a) 'The role of overlapping-generations models in monetary economics', *Carnegie-Rochester Conference Series in Public Policy*, 18: 9–44.

McCallum, B.T. (1983b) 'A reconsideration of Sims's evidence concerning monetarism', *Economics Letters*, 13: 167–171.

McCallum, B.T. (1983c) 'On non-uniqueness in rational expectations models: An attempt at perspective', *Journal of Monetary Economics*, 11: 139–168.

McCallum, B.T. (1984a) 'Are bond-financed deficits inflationary? A Ricardian analysis', *Journal of Political Economy*, 92: 123–135.

McCallum, B.T. (1984b) 'On low-frequency estimates of long-run relationships in macroeconomics', *Journal of Monetary Economics*, 14: 3–14.

McCallum, B.T. (1986) 'On "real" and "sticky-price" theories of the business cycle', *Journal of Money, Credit and Banking*, 18: 397–414.

McCallum, B.T. (1987) 'The optimal inflation rate in an overlapping-generations economy with land', in: W.A. Barnett and K.J. Singleton, eds., *New approaches in monetary economics*. Cambridge: Cambridge University Press.

McCallum, B.T. (1989) 'Real business cycle models', in: R.J. Barro, ed., *Modern business cycle theory*. Cambridge, Mass.: Harvard University Press.

Mishkin, F.S. (1982) 'Does anticipated monetary policy matter? An econometric investigation', *Journal of Political Economy*, 90: 22–51.

Modigliani, F. (1944) 'Liquidity preference and the theory of interest and money', *Econometrica*, 12: 45–88.

Nelson, C.R. and C.I. Plosser (1982) 'Trends and random walks in macroeconomic time series: Some evidence and implications', *Journal of Monetary Economics*, 10: 139–162.

Obstfeld, M. and K. Rogoff (1983) 'Speculative hyperinflations in maximizing models: Can we rule them out?', *Journal of Political Economy*, 91: 675–687.

Patinkin, D. (1983) 'Monetary economics', in: E.C. Brown and R.M. Solow, eds., *Paul Samuelson and modern economic theory*. New York: McGraw-Hill.

Patinkin, D. (1987) 'Neutrality', in: *The new Palgrave: A dictionary of economic theory and doctrine*. London: Macmillan.

Phelps, E.S. (1966) *Golden rules of economic growth*. New York: W.W. Norton and Co.

Phelps, E.S. (1967) 'Phillips curves, expectations of inflation, and optimal unemployment over time', *Economica*, 34: 254–281.

Phelps, E.S. (1973) 'Inflation in a theory of public finance', *Swedish Journal of Economics*, 75: 67–82.

Phelps, E.S. and J.B. Taylor (1977) 'Stabilizing powers of monetary policy under rational expectations', *Journal of Political Economy*, 85; 163–190.

Phillips, A.W. (1958) 'The relation between unemployment and the rate of change of money wage rates in the United Kingdom, 1861–1957', *Economica*, 25: 283–300.

Pierce, J.L. (1974) 'Quantitative analysis for decisions at the Federal Reserve', *Annals of Economic and Social Measurement*, 3: 11–19.

Ricardo, D. (1817) *Principles of political economy and taxation*. London: Murray.

Rogoff, K. (1987) 'Reputational constraints on monetary policy', *Carnegie-Rochester Conference Series on Public Policy*, 26: 141–182.

Sargent, T.J. (1971) 'A note on the accelerationist controversy', *Journal of Money, Credit and Banking*, 3: 50–60.

Sargent, T.J. (1976) 'The observational equivalence of natural and unnatural rate theories of macroeconomics', *Journal of Political Economy*, 84: 631–640.

Sargent, T.J. (1979) *Macroeconomic theory*. New York: Academic Press.

Sargent, T.J. (1982) 'The ends of four big inflations', in: R.E. Hall, ed., *Inflation*. Chicago: University of Chicago Press for NBER.

Sargent, T.J. and N. Wallace (1973) 'Rational expectations and the dynamics of hyperinflation', *International Economic Review*, 14: 328–350.

Sargent, T.J. and N. Wallace (1975) ' "Rational" expectations, the optimal monetary instrument, and the optimal money supply rule', *Journal of Political Economy*, 83: 241–254.

Sargent, T.J. and N. Wallace (1981) 'Some unpleasant monetarist arithmetic', *Federal Reserve Bank of Minneapolis Quarterly Review* 5: 1–17.

Sargent, T.J. and N. Wallace (1982) 'The real bills doctrine vs. the quantity theory: A reconsideration', *Journal of Political Economy*, 90: 1212–1236.

Scheinkman, J.A. (1980a) 'Discussion', in: J.H. Kareken and N. Wallace, eds., *Models of monetary economies*. Minneapolis: Federal Reserve Bank of Minneapolis.

Scheinkman, J.A. (1980b) 'Notes on asset trading in an overlapping generations model', Working Paper, University of Chicago.

Seater, J. (1985) 'Does government debt matter? A review', *Journal of Monetary Economics*, 16: 121–131.

Sidrauski, M. (1967) 'Rational choice and patterns of growth in a monetary economy', *American Economic Review Papers and Proceedings*, 57: 534–544.

Sims, C.A. (1980) 'A comparison of interwar and postwar business cycles: Monetarism reconsidered', *American Economic Review Papers and Proceedings*, 70: 250–257.

Stein, J.L. (1971) *Money and capacity growth*. New York: Columbia University Press.

Stockman, A.C. (1981) 'Anticipated inflation and the capital stock in a cash-in-advance economy', *Journal of Monetary Economics*, 8: 387–393.

Summers, L.H. (1987) 'Some skeptical observations on real business cycle theories', *Federal Reserve Bank of Minneapolis Quarterly Review*, 10: 23–27.

Taylor, J.B. (1979) 'Staggered wage setting in a macro model', *American Economic Review Papers and Proceedings*, 69: 108–113.

Taylor, J.B. (1980) 'Aggregate dynamics and staggered contracts', *Journal of Political Economy*, 88: 1–23.

Taylor, J.B. (1985) 'Rational expectations models in macroeconomics', in: K.J. Arrow and S. Honkapohja, eds., *Frontiers of economics*. Oxford: Basil Blackwell.

Taylor, J.B. (1986) 'New econometric techniques for macroeconomic policy evaluation', in: Z. Griliches and M.D. Intriligator, eds., *Handbook of econometrics*, Vol. 3. Amsterdam: North-Holland.

Tirole, J. (1985) 'Asset bubbles and overlapping generations', *Econometrica*, 53: 1071–1100.

Tobin, J. (1980a) 'Stabilization policy ten years after', *Brookings Papers on Economic Activity*, 1980-1: 19–71.

Tobin, J. (1980b) 'Discussion', in: J.H. Kareken and N. Wallace, eds., *Models of monetary economies*. Minneapolis: Federal Reserve Bank of Minneapolis.

Wallace, N. (1980) 'The overlapping generations model of fiat money', in: J.H. Kareken and N. Wallace, eds., *Models of monetary economies*. Minneapolis: Federal Reserve Bank of Minneapolis.

Wallace, N. (1981) 'A Modigliani–Miller theorem for open-market operations', *American Economic Review*, 71: 267–274.

Wallace, N. (1983) 'A legal restrictions theory of the demand for "money" and the role of monetary policy', *Federal Reserve Bank of Minneapolis Quarterly Review*, 7: 1–7.

Weiss, L. (1980) 'The effects of money supply on economic welfare in the steady state', *Econometrica*, 48: 565–576.

Weitzman, M.L. (1973) 'Duality theory for infinite horizon convex models', *Management Science*, 19: 783–789.

West, K.D. (1987) 'A specification test for speculative bubbles', *Quarterly Journal of Economics*, 102: 553–580.

Whiteman, C.H. (1984) *Linear rational expectations models: A user's guide*. Minneapolis: University of Minnesota Press.

Woodford, M. (1984) 'Indeterminacy of equilibrium in the overlapping-generations model: A survey', Working Paper, Columbia University.

Woodford, M. (1987) 'Credit policy and the price level in a cash-in-advance economy', in: W.A. Barrett and K.J. Singleton, eds., *New approaches in monetary economics*. Cambridge: Cambridge University Press.

Chapter 19

COSTS OF INFLATION

JOHN DRIFFILL, GRAYHAM E. MIZON and ALISTAIR ULPH

University of Southampton

Contents

Handbook of Monetary Economics, Volume II, Edited by B.M. Friedman and F.H. Hahn
© *Elsevier Science Publishers B.V., 1990*

1. Introduction

Economic policy in most Western countries over the past ten years has given prominence to reducing the rate of inflation, with consequences in some countries like the United Kingdom of high rates of unemployment. Attempts to justify this policy stance often consist of listing some of the alleged undesirable consequences of inflation, but with little attempt to assess the orders of magnitude of the economic losses associated with these consequences. In this chapter we review the attempts that have been made by economists to evaluate the costs imposed on an economy by inflation. We begin, in Section 2, with the simplest case of perfectly anticipated inflation where there are no other distortions to the economy. In this case inflation is viewed as a tax on real money balances, and the evaluation of the costs of inflation is a standard application of the welfare effects of a single distortion. The consequences of this inflation tax are that people will seek to make less use of money, and this has implications for the holding of other assets. The analysis is then extended to allow for the possibility of other distortions in the economy, of which we consider two related to the tax system: the non-existence of lump-sum taxes (so that some tax on real money balances may be desirable), and the failure of tax systems in practice to be fully indexed.

Perfectly anticipated inflation with complete indexation is not often what people have in mind when they talk of the need to reduce inflation; rather it is the fear that higher rates of inflation will be related to either greater uncertainty about inflation or greater variability in relative prices, the latter underlying the notion that high rates of inflation may undermine the operation of the price system in achieving an efficient allocation of resources. In Section 3 we outline a number of models that might lead us to think that such relationships could exist and their implications for the evaluation of the costs of inflation. The two main sets of models are those that assume that agents are unable to monitor accurately changes in the aggregate price level, and those that analyse why it may be rational for agents not to adjust nominal prices in line with inflation (either because there are costs of adjusting prices, or because of asymmetric information).

The ultimate objective in analysing the costs of inflation is to obtain some empirical estimates of the welfare effects of policies to control the rate of inflation, and in Section 4 we turn to an appraisal of the econometric evidence that has been used to assess the costs of inflation. We pay particular attention to the work that seeks to establish links between the rate of inflation and either the unpredictability of inflation or the extent of variability in relative prices.

Finally, in Section 5 we draw some conclusions about what the theoretical and empirical work surveyed in the previous sections suggests about policies towards inflation.

2. The welfare costs of anticipated inflation

In this section we summarise the analysis of the welfare costs of perfectly anticipated inflation. To structure the discussion we shall use a variant of the framework employed by Fischer (1981b). Consider then a single agent (all the literature summarised in this section ignores distributional issues), who lives for two periods, and consumes a single good in both periods. He chooses C_1, M, B to maximise

$$\phi(C_1) + \beta\psi(C_2)$$

subject to

$$P_1C_1 + M + B = W - P_1T\left(C_1, \frac{M}{P_1}, \frac{B}{P_1}\right),\tag{2.1}$$

$$P_2C_2 = M + B(1 + R),\tag{2.2}$$

where C_1 and C_2 are consumption of the single good in periods 1 and 2, M is nominal money holdings, B nominal bond holdings, R is the nominal interest rate, and T specifies the real transactions costs associated with real purchases. This is introduced to provide a rationale for holding money when bonds pay a positive nominal interest rate; it could be specified to include C_2 as an argument, but C_2 is effectively pinned down by (2.2). To ensure that money is held in equilibrium we require that $T_2 < T_3$, and it will later prove useful to consider the simplification $T_2 = 0$.

Letting $m = M/P_1$, $b = B/P_1$, $w = W/P_1$, and $1 + r = z \cdot (1 + R)$ denote real money balances, real bond holdings, real wealth, and real gross returns on bonds (where $z = P_1/P_2 = 1 - \pi$, with π the rate of inflation), respectively, (2.1) and (2.2) can be rewritten in real terms as:

$$C_1 + m + b = w - T(C_1, m, b),\tag{2.3}$$

$$C_2 = z \cdot m + b(1 + r).\tag{2.4}$$

[Note that the definition of π means that inflation is defined as $(P_2 - P_1)/P_2$ rather than the more usual $(P_2 - P_1)/P_1$.]

The first-order conditions are:

$$\phi' = \lambda(1 + T_1),$$
$$\beta\psi' \cdot z = \lambda(1 + T_2), \tag{2.5}$$
$$\beta\psi' \cdot (1 + r) = \lambda(1 + T_3),$$

from which one derives demand functions $C_1(w, z, r)$, $m(w, z, r)$, $b(w, z, r)$ and indirect utility function $V(w, z, r)$. It is readily checked in the usual way that $\partial V/\partial w = \lambda$, and letting ζ denote a general parameter, a little manipulation yields:

$$\frac{\partial V}{\partial \zeta} = \frac{\partial V}{\partial w} \cdot \frac{\partial w}{\partial \zeta} + \beta\psi'\left[m \cdot \frac{\partial z}{\partial \zeta} + b \cdot \frac{\partial(1 + r)}{\partial \zeta}\right]. \tag{2.6}$$

If ζ increases from ζ_0 to ζ_1, one then calculates the compensating variation, C, associated with this change as:

$$V(w + C, \zeta_1, \ldots) = V(w, \zeta_0, \ldots)$$

or

$$C = \int_{\zeta_1}^{\zeta_0} \left(\frac{\partial V}{\partial \zeta} \bigg/ \frac{\partial V}{\partial w}\right) d\zeta. \tag{2.7}$$

From (2.6) one obtains various expressions for the welfare loss from inflation depending on what is assumed about other adjustments in the economy, and in the rest of this section we consider three cases of increasing generality.

2.1. Real interest constant, lump-sum taxes

In (2.6) let ζ be the inflation rate π, and assume that inflation leaves real wealth, w, and real interest rates, r, unaffected. Then, assuming $\partial V/\partial w$ is constant, so that compensated and Marshallian demand curves are equivalent, the expression for the welfare cost of inflation is:

$$C = \int_{\pi_1}^{\pi_0} m(\pi) \, d\pi. \tag{2.8}$$

This measure yields the welfare triangle measure of the cost of inflation familiar from the seminal work of Bailey (1956). The position is illustrated in Figure 19.1. Supposing that inflation enters the money demand function only

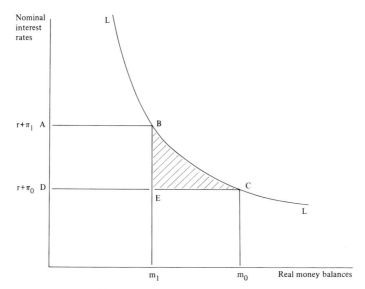

Figure 19.1. Welfare costs of inflation.

through its impact on nominal interest rates, then the loss of consumer surplus given by (2.8) is the area $ABCD$. The nominal money stock is increased by printing money, and real money balances are constant. The increase in inflation yields additional revenue to the government equal to the area $ABED$ [the extra "inflation tax" $(\pi_1 - \pi_0)$ times the stock of real balance m_1] and if it is assumed that this is used to reduce lump-sum taxes on consumers, then the net cost to the consumer is the deadweight loss BEC. Using data on a number of hyperinflations drawn from Cagan (1956), Bailey calculated the welfare losses associated with inflation, and showed that as inflation approaches infinity the loss to the economy (effectively from elimination of money) could be between 30 and 50 percent of national income. [For related discussion and elaboration see Marty (1976), Tatom (1976, 1979), and Tower (1971).]

Behind this measure of the cost of inflation is the notion that as inflation rises the velocity of circulation also rises as people seek to carry out a given set of transactions with a smaller stock of real money balances, and Bailey gave an informal account of how people will economise in their use of money. They will concentrate their shopping closer to the receipt of income and since shopkeepers will also be trying to reduce their stocks of goods this will lead to more queuing or searching to find stores still open (the "shoe leather effect"); this substitution of search time for real money balance is presumably at the expense of leisure, since real income (and wealth) is assumed unaffected. People may substitute other media of exchange, such as foreign currencies, or resort to barter arrangements, and again these may require increases in search time to find partners willing to use such substitutes.

A more formal analysis of the way in which inflation affects the process of conducting transactions can be found in the work of Barro (1970, 1972). The analysis is based on a simple inventory model of money demand by firms and households. Firms received a continuous flow of income which rises at a rate equal to the rate of inflation. They have to pay their employees wage payments which are fixed in real terms, and with their revenue stream depreciating over time firms would clearly like to pay out their revenue continuously as wages. But making wage payments incurs a fixed real cost, α, which acts to reduce the frequency of payments. For any given payment period, t, employers will have a real money demand function, m^e, and a cost per unit of time, γ^e, given (approximately) by:

$$\gamma^e = \tfrac{1}{2} y\pi t + \frac{\alpha}{t} \tag{2.9}$$

and

$$m^e = \tfrac{1}{2} y \cdot t , \tag{2.10}$$

where y is real income and π the rate of inflation.

Recipients of these disbursements by firms (for simplicity they will be thought of as workers) face a real rate of interest, r, assumed the same for all workers. For a payment persion, t, workers lose both the interest forgone on their money holding and depreciation of the money paid out at the beginning of the period, and this leads to the corresponding expression for workers for money demand, m^w, and costs per unit of time for any given payment period t, γ^w, given by:

$$\gamma^w = \tfrac{1}{2} y \cdot t(\pi + 2r) , \tag{2.11}$$

$$m^w = \tfrac{1}{2} y \cdot t . \tag{2.12}$$

Choosing the optimal payment period t^* to minimise $\gamma^e + \gamma^w$ yields the familiar square root formulae:

$$t^* = \sqrt{\alpha/y(r + \pi)} , \tag{2.13}$$

with money demand $m = m^w + m^e$ given by:

$$m = y \cdot t^* = \sqrt{\alpha y/(r + \pi)} . \tag{2.14}$$

Both money demand and payment period are decreasing functions of inflation with elasticities $-\frac{1}{2}$.

Suppose, in addition to reducing the payment period, agents switch to alternative exchange media. Barro captured this by assuming that some proportion $\phi(\pi)$ of transactions is not monetised. Then (2.14) is modified to yield a demand function for real money balances:

$$m = \frac{[1 - \phi(\pi)]\sqrt{\alpha y}}{\sqrt{(r + \pi)}} . \tag{2.14'}$$

Using the same data as Bailey (i.e. Cagan's data on hyperinflations) Barro (1972) computed measures of welfare cost. He showed that for positive inflation rates the marginal welfare cost of inflation exceeds 50 percent of the additional government revenue raised by an increase in inflation.

2.2. Inflation affects real wealth and real interest rates

In the original work on the cost of inflation summarised in the previous subsection it was assumed that inflation would not affect real wealth or the real rate of interest. It can thus be taken to apply only to short-run costs of inflation. [See Cathcart (1974) and Chappell (1981) for attempts at long-run analysis, but which do not address the issues raised below.] In the long run, inflation may affect both real wealth and real interest rates. In that case the expression for $\partial V / \partial \pi$ in (2.6) becomes:

$$\frac{\partial V}{\partial \pi} = \frac{\partial V}{\partial w} \cdot \frac{\partial w}{\partial \pi} + \beta \psi' \left[b \cdot \frac{\partial (1 + r)}{\partial \pi} - m \right]. \tag{2.15}$$

There are three reasons why inflation might be expected to have long-run effects on the real interest rate and real income or wealth. First, as Tobin (1955, 1965) noted, the effect of higher inflation in reducing the demand for real money balances is effectively a switch in the portfolio of assets held in the economy; in particular, lower real money balances may be associated with increased holdings of physical capital, and this would raise output per head and reduce the real interest rate. This is the "Tobin" effect. Second, as Feldstein (1976) noted, in addition to these portfolio effects there may be *savings* effects if the savings rate depends on the real rate of interest as would be suggested by life-cycle models of savings. Finally, depending on assumptions about the structure of taxation, higher inflation rates will have implications for the government budget constraint and these offsetting fiscal policies may have further effects. In this subsection we shall maintain the assumption that the government uses either lump-sum taxes or inflation to finance its budget, and so focus only on the first two factors.

To analyse these effects the literature has taken the one-sector neoclassical growth model familiar from Solow (1956) and added a monetary asset. To give the flavour of such models and illustrate the portfolio and savings effects, we outline a variant of the Feldstein (1976) model in which all taxes are lump sum.

There is a single good which can be used for both consumption and investment plus money; the labour force (equals population) grows at an exogenously fixed rate, n. The production side of the economy is summarised by an aggregate constant returns to scale production function written in per capita terms as:

$$y = f(k),\tag{2.16}$$

where $f' > 0$ and $f'' < 0$. Capital lasts for ever so firms invest until the marginal product of capital equals the real interest rate:

$$f'(k) = r.\tag{2.17}$$

Households hold two assets, real outside money, which in per capita terms is m, and the real value of corporate bonds, which, since bond financing is assumed to be the only source of funding for firms, is equivalent to the real value of the capital stock. The portfolio behaviour of households is captured by having the desired ratio of real money to capital held by households as a decreasing function of the nominal interest rate:

$$\frac{m}{k} = L(r + \pi), \quad L' < 0,\tag{2.18}$$

where π is again the rate of inflation. In steady state m/k will be constant. Since the capital stock will be growing at rate n in steady state, this requires that the rate of growth of the money supply, μ, be given by:

$$\mu = \pi + n.\tag{2.19}$$

Disposable household income is equal to national income less lump-sum taxes and the fall in the real value of money balances, or, in per capita terms

$$h = y - t - \pi.m,$$

where t is lump-sum taxes per head and h is disposable income per head. Lump-sum taxes will be equal to the difference between government expenditure per head, which is assumed to be a constant fraction γ of output per head, and the increase in the money supply, so $t = \gamma \cdot y - \mu \cdot m$, and using (2.19) this yields the expression for per capita disposable household income:

$$h = y(1 - \gamma) + m \cdot n . \tag{2.20}$$

Finally, households are assumed to save a proportion of their disposable income, $\sigma(r)$, which depends on the real rate of interest. In the steady state per capita savings are used to finance capital accumulation and additional real money balances, so:

$$\sigma(r)h = nk + nm . \tag{2.21}$$

It appears from (2.20) that per capita disposable household income is unaffected by the inflation rate, for given values of output per head, y, and real money balances, m, since changes in the inflation tax are offset by changes in the lump-sum tax per head. However, this does *not* induce a superneutrality result because of the assumed portfolio behaviour of households, (2.18). Individual households take the inflation rate, the lump-sum tax, the real interest rate, and other economy-wide variables as being independent of their behaviour, and consequently perceive the nominal interest rate as being the marginal cost of holding money rather than capital. They ignore the fact that, when all households behave the same way, holding lower money balances will be associated with a higher lump-sum tax.

Equations (2.16)–(2.21) summarise the steady-state growth behaviour of this simple economy, and tie down the six endogenous variables, y, k, r, π, m, and h, as functions of the exogenous government policy variable, μ. Eliminating y, r, m, and h, we get:

$$\sigma[f'(k)] \cdot (1 - \gamma) \cdot \frac{f(k)}{k} = n\{1 + [1 - \sigma(f'(k))] \cdot L[f'(k) - \pi]\} . \tag{2.22}$$

Totally differentiating (2.22) with respect to π yields:

$$\frac{dk}{d\pi} = \frac{n(1 - \sigma) \cdot L'}{\psi} , \tag{2.23}$$

where

$$\psi = \sigma'f''\left[(1 - \gamma)\frac{f(k)}{k} + nL\right] + \frac{\sigma(1 - \gamma)}{k}\left[f'(k) - \frac{f(k)}{k}\right] - n(1 - \sigma)L'f'' . \tag{2.24}$$

By concavity of f, ψ is negative if $\sigma' \geq 0$. Since the numerator of (2.23) is clearly negative, we have $dk/d\pi \geq 0$. If $\sigma' = 0$, so there is no savings effect, then we are left solely with the Tobin effect, that as inflation increases the steady-state capital–labour ratio rises, thereby increasing output per head, and reducing the real interest rate. This arises solely from liquidity preference behaviour, with households switching away from real money balances to real capital. If $\sigma' > 0$, then the qualitative conclusions remain unaltered, but the absolute size of the effect of inflation on the capital–output ratio will be reduced, as one might expect, since the switch out of real money is now partly into increased consumption to avoid the effects of inflation.

Returning to equation (2.15) we can see that to the extent that higher inflation reduces the real rate of interest this will tend to exacerbate the welfare costs of inflation (at least for those households that are net lenders), while the increase in real per capita income will reduce the welfare cost. In quantitative terms it is usually argued that these additional terms are likely to be small relative to the traditional measure of the welfare costs, for the simple reason that the real money stock is typically small relative to the real capital stock [of the order of one-fortieth – see Green and Sheshinski (1977)] so that the extent to which a switch out of real money into capital will affect real interest rates is likely to be small.

2.3. Lump-sum taxes not available

In the analysis so far it has been assumed that fiscal policy is operated by means of lump-sum taxes, so that revenue from inflation is redistributed by either reducing lump-sum taxes or providing lump-sum subsidies. Provided this is so, positive rates of inflation are undesirable, and in the context of the Bailey model the optimal rate of inflation is minus the real rate of interest [see also Friedman (1969)].

Lump-sum taxes are unlikely to be available (at least to the extent required to fully finance government expenditure) and this modifies the above argument in an important way. For now the revenue from inflation can be used to reduce distorting taxation, yielding a welfare gain that is larger than just the size of the tax revenue (area *ABDE* in Figure 19.1). For an arbitrary set of taxes, it is clearly possible that there could be welfare gains from inflation if this allows the reduction of the most distorting taxes.

In this subsection we survey the two broad strands that have emerged in the literature in relation to taxes. First, a number of authors have constructed models which purport to capture in a simple way the operation of the tax systems observed in a number of Western economies, and used these to reappraise the evaluation of the costs of inflation. One feature of the operation of tax systems that is particularly important in relation to inflation is the extent to which the tax structure is fully indexed, and obvious examples of failures to index are the operation of progressive income taxes with tax brackets that are not adjusted in line with inflation, or the taxation of the inflationary component of nominal interest. This can have interesting consequences – for example, higher inflation may lead to the need for *higher* taxes because the tax system may actually be subsidising firms (see below).

The second area of work addresses the following question. While for some arbitrary set of taxes one could clearly make a case for higher inflation if the revenue from inflation was used to reduce the most distorting taxes, a more stringent question is to ask what can be said about the optimal level of inflation when it is assumed that other taxes in the economy are optimally set. In other words, the optimal rate of inflation is seen as arising as part of the solution of a standard optimal tax problem, in which real money balances are one of the commodities on which taxes can be levied.

2.3.1. Analysis of existing tax structures

The taxes which are likely to be of particular interest in terms of the extent to which the tax structure is indexed are taxes on income from capital or earnings, and because of the way in which costs of inflation have been related to changes in interest rates taxes on capital have received considerable attention. To illustrate the way in which such taxes can affect the conclusions reached when there are only lump-sum taxes, we return to the model used by Feldstein (1976) introduced in the previous subsection, and consider the impact of introducing taxes on corporate profits and personal income tax on interest receipts. All other taxes, including those on labour income, are assumed to be lump-sum taxes, and these are adjusted to ensure that the government budget constraint is met.

The pertinent features of the corporation tax structure in terms of the distortion it creates between the marginal product of capital and the real interest rate are its treatment of depreciation and interest deductability [see King (1975) for a simple account]. We continue to assume no depreciation [but see Feldstein, Green and Sheshinski (1978) for an examination of the impact of the tax treatment of depreciation]. Let τ_1 denote the tax rate at which the real component of interest payments can be deducted from profits and τ_2 the rate at which the inflation component can be deducted. Then the net of tax cost of capital to producers is $(1 - \tau_1)r - \tau_2\pi$ and firms will invest up to the point where this is equal to the net of tax marginal product of capital, $(1 - \tau_1)f'(k)$. Then the condition for investment is no longer (2.17) but is now:

$$f'(k) = r - \left(\frac{\tau_2}{1 - \tau_1}\right)\pi .$$ (2.17′)

As this makes clear, a fully indexed corporate tax system would occur if $\tau_2 = 0$, and this would leave investment decisions undistorted. In practice, tax systems tend to ignore the distinction between real and nominal interest, i.e. $\tau_1 = \tau_2 = \tau$, say.

On the household side we suppose analogously that real interest receipts are taxed at a rate θ_1 and nominal interest receipts at a rate θ_2. Then the net of tax *nominal* interest rate, which is what affects the liquidity preference decision, is $(1 - \theta_1)r + (1 - \theta_2)\pi$, while the net of tax real interest rate, which is what affects the savings decision, is $(1 - \theta_1)r - \theta_2 \pi$. Thus, the liquidity preference and savings decisions, (2.18) and (2.21), are now modified by the existence of the personal income tax system as reflected in (2.18') and (2.21'):

$$\frac{m}{k} = L[(1 - \theta_1)r + (1 - \theta_2)\pi] , \qquad (2.18')$$

$$\sigma[(1 - \theta_1)r - \theta_2 \pi] \cdot h = nk + nm . \qquad (2.21')$$

Full indexation of the personal income tax system corresponds to $\theta_2 = 0$, and again actual tax systems frequently ignore the distinction between real and nominal interest receipts, so that $\theta_1 = \theta_2 = \theta$.

To assess the implications of the introduction of this tax system, we first consider the impact of an increase in inflation on the capital–output ratio. The analogue of (2.23) and (2.24) is now:

$$dk/d\pi = \zeta/\hat{\psi} , \qquad (2.23')$$

where

$$\hat{\psi} = (1 - \theta_1)f'' \left[\frac{h}{k} - n(1 - \sigma)L' \right] + \frac{\sigma(1 - \gamma)}{k} \left[f'(k -) - \frac{f(k)}{k} \right], \qquad (2.24')$$

$$\zeta = [\beta + (1 - \theta_2)]n(1 - \sigma)L' - (\beta - \theta_2)\sigma' \frac{h}{k} , \qquad (2.25)$$

$$\beta = (1 - \theta_1)\tau_2/(1 - \tau_1) . \qquad (2.26)$$

By the same argument as we had before, if $\sigma' \geq 0$, $\hat{\psi}$ is negative, and, provided $\theta_1 \leq 1$, $\tau_1 \leq 1$, the first term in ζ is negative. However, the second term in ζ depends on the sign of $\beta - \theta_2$, which depends purely on the parameters of the tax system, and so could take any sign.

Consider two special cases. Suppose first that the tax system is fully indexed. Then $\beta = \theta_2 = \tau_2 = 0$, $dk/d\pi$ is positive, and the only difference from the lump-sum tax analysis is that the first term in $\hat{\psi}$ is smaller than the corresponding term in ψ. So the introduction of a fully indexed corporate and personal income tax system will increase $dk/d\pi$. Now consider the more usual case where $\tau_1 = \tau_2 = \tau$ and $\theta_1 = \theta_2 = \theta$. If $\tau = \theta$, then again $\beta + (1 - \theta_2) = 1$ and $\beta - \theta_2 = 0$, and the results for the fully indexed case apply. If $\tau > \theta$, the second term in ζ will be negative, so $dk/d\pi$ will still be non-negative, but larger in magnitude than if this second effect had not been present. The rationale can be seen if we consider the net real return to households, which is:

$$r^n = (1 - \theta)f'(k) + \frac{(\tau - \theta)}{1 - \tau}\pi . \tag{2.27}$$

Given k, an increase in inflation will *raise* the real return to savings, since firms are being subsidised on the inflation component of interest at a greater rate than households are being taxed. Thus, the savings effect will now work in the same direction as the portfolio effect, and encourage an increase in the desired holdings of real capital. Clearly, the implications are reversed if $\tau < \theta$.

There are two further implications of (2.27) which are of relevance for evaluation of welfare effects. First, because the operation of the tax system involves subsidising firms for the inflation component of interest rates, and taxing households, it turns out [Feldstein (1976), Green and Sheshinski (1977)] that as π rises the need for tax revenue *rises* if $\tau > \theta$. So the assumption that inflation is a *substitute* for tax revenue need not hold if the tax system is not indexed. Second, for $\tau > \theta$, small rates of inflation will tend to reduce the wedge between the consumer's net of tax real rate of return and the marginal product of capital that would otherwise be induced by the operation of the tax system. These two factors will have opposite impacts on welfare.

Even within the framework of the model proposed by Feldstein, assessing the welfare implications of different inflation tax rates, turns out to be impossible at any level of generality. Alternative specifications of the economy or the operation of the tax system introduces a further source of complications [see Green and Sheshinski (1977), Feldstein, Green and Sheshinski (1978), Feldstein and Summers (1979), and Marty (1978), for alternative models, and for an analysis of the implications for international capital mobility, Hartman (1979)]. The one result which does seem to be robust is that for plausible ranges of parameter values, the Tobin effect survives and higher inflation rates lead to higher capital output ratios in steady state.

2.3.2. Optimal taxes

It is perhaps not too surprising that it is going to be difficult to say much in general about the welfare effects of inflation for a fairly arbitrarily specified tax system. It would be hoped that by restricting attention to a (second-best)optimal structure of taxes one might be able to derive more general propositions about the desirability of using inflation as a means of funding government expenditure.

Following the seminal paper by Phelps (1973), the early literature using this optimal tax approach [see also Burmeister and Phelps (1971), Siegel (1978), Marty (1978), and Feldstein (1979)] reversed the conclusion of the Bailey (1956) and Friedman (1969) analyses that the optimal rate of inflation was the negative of the real interest rate. In the presence of optimally set distorting taxation it was shown that a positive inflation rate was optimal, on the grounds that quantities of all taxable goods including real money balances should be reduced to provide resources for public expenditure.

Using a more general intertemporal framework, Drazen (1979) shows that this conclusion may be wrong, and that there are assumptions under which the Bailey/Friedman results would hold even if there are no lump-sum taxes. The framework employed is an extension of the steady-state growth models considered so far to allow for many consumer goods (suppose there are j such goods) and variable labour supply. Population (equals labour force) grows at the exogenously given rate n; $y_1 \cdots y_j$ denotes output per head of the j consumer goods; $c_1 \cdots c_j$ denotes consumption per head; and $g_1 \cdots g_j$ denotes a fixed vector of government purchases of the j consumption goods. k denotes the per capita stock of a single non-depreciating capital good, y_k the production of this good, again in per capita terms. Letting ℓ denote per capita labour supply, the production function is written as:

$$F(y_1 \cdots y_j, y_k) = f(k, \ell) \,, \tag{2.28}$$

where F and f are homogeneous of degree 1.

Nominal producer prices P_i for goods are deflated by an index $P = P(P_i \cdots P_j)$, where P is an arbitrarily chosen linearly homogeneous function of goods prices. Deflated producer prices ("real prices"), $p_i \equiv P_i/P(P_i \cdots P_j)$, are thus independent of the absolute price level, and in steady state at whatever inflation rate, are constant over time. Other real variables (the money stock, consumer prices, and tax rates) are defined analogously as the appropriate nominal variable deflated by the index $P(\cdot)$. Real producer prices are denoted p_i, consumer prices q_i, with $q_i = p_i + t_i$, where t_i is the tax rate, $i = 1 \cdots j, k, \ell$.

It is assumed that the real resource consumed by transactions is the time of agents. Holding money balances reduces this time. This device causes real money balances to appear as an argument of agents' utility function, and allows the claim in this model that this is equivalent to the presence of real transaction costs. At the same time it leaves budget constraints (importantly the government's budget constraint and the economy's resource constraints) unaffected. Real money balances, m, are held by consumers to facilitate transactions, and this is equivalent to assuming that consumers have a per period utility function

$U(c_1, \ldots, c_j, \ell, m)$; households live for ever and maximise the present value of life-time utility, using a utility discount rate δ. The only assets available to households for effecting intertemporal allocation are money and the capital good. Letting μ denote the rate of growth of the money supply, a government choice variable, inflation, in the steady state is again $\pi = \mu - n$.

Consumer optimisation yields a steady-state indirect utility function, $V(q_1 \ldots q_j, q_k, q_\ell, \mu)$, with respect to all consumer prices and the rate of growth of the money supply. The analogues of Roy's Identity are:

$$\frac{\partial V}{\partial q_i} = \alpha\left(-c_i + \delta \frac{\partial m}{\partial q_i} + \delta q_k \cdot \frac{\partial k}{\partial q_i}\right), \quad i = 1 \cdots j, \ell, \tag{2.29}$$

$$\frac{\partial V}{\partial q_k} = \alpha\left(-nk + \delta \frac{\partial m}{\partial q_k} + \delta q_k \cdot \frac{\partial k}{\partial q_k}\right), \tag{2.30}$$

$$\frac{\partial V}{\partial \mu} = \alpha\left(-m + \delta \frac{\partial m}{\partial \mu} + \delta q_k \cdot \frac{\partial k}{\partial \mu}\right). \tag{2.31}$$

In the static world we would have $\partial V / \partial q_i = -\alpha c_i$, but with intertemporal resource allocation, a change in a consumer price will affect not just current consumption but also lifetime wealth through the holding of money and capital, and these considerations are reflected in the second and third terms of (2.29)–(2.31).

The government now chooses its taxes and the inflation rate to maximise $\int_0^\infty V(\ ) e^{-\delta t} \, dt$ subject to its budget constraint, or equivalently, as is familiar from the optimal tax literature [Diamond and Mirrlees (1971)], the production constraint. Drazen then shows that the optimal rate of growth of the money supply, μ^*, is given by:

$$\mu^* = -\frac{1}{m} \frac{\lambda}{\alpha} \sum_{i=1}^{j} p_i c_i \varepsilon_{i\mu} + \delta \varepsilon_{\mu\mu} + \frac{1}{m} \delta q_k \varepsilon_{k\mu}$$

$$-\frac{1}{m} \frac{\lambda}{\alpha} \left[k\varepsilon_{k\mu}\left(p_k\left(n - \frac{f_k}{p_k}\right)\right) - \ell f_\ell \varepsilon_{\ell\mu}\right], \tag{2.32}$$

where $\varepsilon_{i\mu} = (\partial c_i / \partial \mu) \cdot (\mu / c_i)$ denote cross elasticities. The first term measures the value of the resources that would be released from the private sector for production of government goods. What matters then is the extent to which the use of inflation reduces the consumption of goods that are relatively expensive to produce. The term is multiplied by λ / α, which is the marginal cost of raising revenue by distorting taxation; with lump-sum taxes this equals one, but in general exceeds 1. The second and third terms correspond to the more traditional measures of welfare cost. The second term is related to the familiar

Bailey measure of the distorting effect of inflation, reflecting the change in steady-state holdings of money balances caused by inflation; the third term is effectively the Tobin effect, reflecting changes in the per capita steady-state holding of capital. The final term reflects the impact of inflation on factor supplies. Since money economises on resources for transactions, a reduction in real money balances might be expected to reduce labour supply. While the second term will be negative, and the third would be positive for reasons given earlier, the first and last terms will be more difficult to sign. To the extent that inflation does release resources for taxation over all consumer goods, the first term will also be positive (this is explicitly the Phelps argument for a positive rate of increase in the money supply).

One particular case where the Bailey/Friedman conclusion would emerge would be where the utility function of consumers was Cobb–Douglas, implying negative unit own price elasticity ($\varepsilon_{\mu\mu} = -1$), and zero across price elasticities ($\varepsilon_{i\mu} = \varepsilon_{k\mu} = \varepsilon_{\ell\mu} = 0$). Then (2.32) reduces to $\mu^* = -\delta$, and $\pi = -(f_k/p_k)/(1 + \tau_k)$, so inflation is the negative of the rate of return on capital received by households.

When cross elasticities are non-zero, the other terms in (2.32) are pertinent, and in principle these could have any sign, leaving the optimal rate of change of the money supply unsigned.

2.4. Summary

The previous subsections have outlined the developments that have taken place in the past thirty years in the evaluation of the cost of perfectly anticipated inflation. The starting point was the simple Bailey/Friedman analysis in which inflation affects only the demand for money balances and this cost can be represented by the usual measure of distortion in a single market. This was extended to allow for the fact that decreased holding of real money balances would have repercussions for the real interest rate and real incomes through effects on holdings of real capital or other assets. As long as lump-sum taxes are available, it will still be optimal not to use inflation as a means of raising finance; the final part of this section has considered the implications when the government has to use distorting taxes, especially taxes that may not be fully indexed. While this provides some reasons for having a positive rate of growth of the money supply, it remains an empirical matter how the various factors now balance out.

The conclusion of Fischer (1981b) was that the arguments for using inflation as a means of raising revenue relative to distorting taxes is not very strong, since the marginal cost of raising revenue in this way is larger than for other taxes, such as income tax. He concluded that the simple Bailey measure would lead to a cost of about 0.3 percent of GNP for a 10 percent inflation rate.

Including the effects of distortions caused by non-indexed tax systems might cause this to rise to 0.7 percent of GNP, and, allowing for the roughness of the calculations involved, figures as high as 2 or 3 percent would not be implausible. In his discussion of Fischer's paper, Lucas (1981) came up with similar order of magnitude figures. While these costs are significant, they scarcely provide support for the view that inflation must necessarily always be reduced.

However, much of the popular concern about inflation stems from fears that high rates of inflation will lead to the breakdown of the operation of the price mechanism, either because higher rates of inflation are associated with increased uncertainty about inflation, or because it is associated with increased variability of relative prices. The rest of this chapter will assess the theoretical and empirical basis of such claims.

3. Uncertainty about inflation rates and relative prices

In this section we discuss models in which inflation is stochastic and is associated with variations in relative prices across industries and over time, for one reason or another. We take four types of model which appear to be representative of recent analyses bearing on the costs of inflation. In the main, it appears that there has been little formal calculation of these costs. Authors have worked out the effects of inflation – or the effects of the exogenous processes causing it – on prices and quantities, but have not often pursued the subject as far as working out the welfare effects. In addition, tractable models deal with particular aspects of economic decisions, so the results are illustrative of costs of inflation which may arise through one set of decisions or another, and individual pieces of analysis tend not to give a very complete picture.

The models which are described in what follows are formalised and specialised. Two draw on Cukierman's work on relative price variations, which he describes as "relative/aggregate" and "permanent/transitory" confusion, and are based on arguably ad hoc assumptions about information. They rely on suppliers of goods making quantity decisions on the basis or imperfect knowledge of the relevant prices. The third is a simple partial equilibrium example of allocative inefficiencies caused when agents make a price decision (rather than a quantity decision) with imperfect information. The fourth class of model is based on the assumption that price adjustment is costly, either because of "menu costs" or quadratic adjustment costs.

3.1. Models in which agents confuse aggregate and relative price changes

Cukierman (1984) takes Lucas's (1973) model with many markets and imperfectly informed agents, and explores the effects of supply shocks and

demand (money supply) shocks on equilibrium outcomes, and he looks at some
of the ways in which welfare is affected. The basic set-up of the model is well
known. Prices and quantities are normally expressed in logs in what follows.
The economy consists of many markets, indexed by v. In each market, supply
contains both a deterministic, steadily growing component, and a "cyclical
component", thus:

$$y_t^s(v) = y_{nt} + y_{ct}(v) , \tag{3.1}$$

where y_{nt} is the deterministic component which grows through time,

$$y_{nt} = \alpha + \beta t , \tag{3.2}$$

and $y_{ct}(v)$ is the "cyclical" component which depends positively on the
perceived relative price in the market:

$$y_{ct}(v) = \gamma[p_t(v) - E(Q_t | I_t(v))] , \quad \gamma > 0 . \tag{3.3}$$

Here $E(Q_t | I_t(v))]$ is the expected value of the average economy-wide price
level, Q_t, in market v given information $I_t(v)$ available there. Q_t is a weighted
geometric mean of individual market prices, with weights $u(v)$ which sum to
one. Namely,

$$Q_t \equiv \sum_v u(v)p_t(v) . \tag{3.4}$$

Demand in each market depends on the (log of the) nominal money stock, x_t,
which is stochastic, a random demand shift variable, $w_t(v)$, and the price level
in the market:

$$y_t^d(v) = x_t + w_t(v) - p_t(v) . \tag{3.5}$$

It is assumed that changes in the log of the money stock are normally
distributed with mean δ and variance σ_x^2, and individual market demand shocks
are independently distributed, normally with zero mean and variance σ_w^2. Thus
we have $\Delta x_t \sim N(\delta, \sigma_x^2)$ and $w_t(v) \sim N(0, \sigma_w^2)$. The innovation in the money
stock is denoted ε_t, so that we can write $x_t = x_{t-1} + \delta + \varepsilon_t$.

The motivation for this structure is drawn from Lucas (1973), who in turn
refers to Lucas and Rapping (1969). It may be assumed that behind the supply
curve lies a labour market which is cleared by a perfectly flexible nominal
wage, and that the form of (3.3) reflects the behaviour of both suppliers and
demanders of labour in market v. The firms in v which demand labour up to

the point where the marginal product equals the real product wage know both the price of their output, $p_t(v)$, and the money wage they face, whereas the workers in v know only the nominal wage and the price of locally produced goods, $p_t(v)$, but not the price of their consumption bundle Q_t which contains goods from all markets. This information structure induces the supply curve (3.3). In support of a supply curve like (3.3), Lucas (1973) invokes the model of Lucas and Rapping (1969) which is derived from a model of utility-maximising worker/consumers, and the model of Lucas (1972).

The demand side of the model is justified by Lucas (1973) as a convenient simplification by means of which ". . . the entire burden of accounting for the breakdown of nominal income into real output and price is placed on the aggregate supply side". It may be justified as the result of a transactions technology which limits nominal demand each period to the product of the money stock and a randomly fluctuating velocity of circulation, i.e. by assuming a vertical but randomly shifting LM curve.

When all agents know the price level Q_t with certainty in the current period, then $E[Q_t | I_t(v)] = Q_t$, and under such circumstances there is no confusion between relative and aggregate prices. The solution for the market equilibrium price in each market is then:

$$p_t(v) = \frac{1}{1+\gamma} \left[-(\alpha + \beta t) + x_t + \gamma Q_t + w_t(v) \right], \tag{3.6}$$

and the economy-wide average price is:

$$Q_t = -\alpha - \beta t + x_t , \tag{3.7}$$

so the relative price in each market is given by:

$$p_t(v) - Q_t = w_t(v)/(1+\gamma) . \tag{3.8}$$

With full information on prices in all markets, then, no confusion between aggregate and relative price changes occurs. Prices in the economy as a whole, Q_t, are proportional to the money stock, and relative prices (and therefore outputs) depend only on relative demand shifts, and not at all on the money supply.

Consider now an economy in which agents do not know Q_t in period t but only learn it with a one-period lag, and know only prices in the market in which they trade. Suppose that agents have the following beliefs. Prices $p_t(v)$ are distributed around the economy-wide average price Q_t with a deviation $z_t(v)$ which is normally distributed with mean zero and variance τ^2. The average price, Q_t, is unknown, and itself has mean $\bar{Q}_t$ and variable σ^2. Thus, beliefs are that

$$P_t(v) = Q_t + z_t(v),$$ (3.9)

where $Q_t \sim N(\bar{Q}_t, \sigma^2)$ and $z_t(v) \sim N(0, \tau^2)$. Given these, and their informa-tion set $I_t(v)$, the agents in market v predict the value of Q_t to be

$$E[Q_t | I_t(v)] = (1 - \theta)p_t(v) + \theta \bar{Q}_t,$$ (3.10)

where $\theta = \tau^2/(\tau^2 + \sigma^2)$.

If agents form beliefs in this way, then the equilibrium price in market v will be obtained by substituting (3.10) into the supply equation (3.1), and equating with demand (3.5), giving a price:

$$p_t(v) = \frac{1}{1 + \gamma\theta} [x_t - \alpha - \beta t + \gamma\theta \bar{Q}_t + w_t(v)].$$ (3.11)

Aggregating across markets yields:

$$Q_t = \frac{1}{1 + \gamma\theta} [x_{t-1} + \delta - \alpha - \beta t + \gamma\theta \bar{Q}_t + \varepsilon_t] + \frac{\sum_v u(v)w_t(v)}{1 + \gamma\theta}.$$ (3.12)

It is assumed that there is a large number of markets and thus $\sum_v u(v)w_t(v)/(1 + \gamma\theta)$ converges in probability to zero [Cukierman and Wachtel (1979)]. $\bar{Q}_t$ is the agents' prior belief about Q_t based on information available before period t, i.e. knowing the realisations in period $t - 1$, but before having observed the period t price in their own market. Cukierman denotes this information set I_t. Hence, taking expectations in (3.11) over ε_t, we get an expression for $\bar{Q}_t$ which is:

$$\bar{Q}_t = x_{t-1} + \delta - \alpha - \beta t.$$ (3.13)

Substituting (3.13) back into (3.12), the latter can be written as:

$$Q_t = \bar{Q}_t + \varepsilon_t/(1 + \gamma\theta),$$ (3.14)

and (3.11) then can be rewritten in the form:

$$p_t(v) - Q_t = w_t(v)/(1 + \gamma\theta) \equiv z_t(v).$$ (3.15)

It is clear from expressions (3.14) and (3.15) that agents' beliefs about prices, expressed in (3.9) and (3.10), above are rational if $\tau^2 = \sigma_w^2/(1 + \gamma\theta)^2$ and if $\sigma^2 = \sigma_x^2/(1 + \gamma\theta)^2$. This implies that $\theta = \sigma_w^2/(\sigma_w^2 + \sigma_x^2)$.

The effect of imperfect information on output decisions can be calculated by going back to the supply equation (3.1). The "cyclical" component of supply in market ν is

$$y_{ct}(\nu) = \gamma[p_t(\nu) - E(Q_t \mid I_t(\nu))] = \gamma\theta[p_t(\nu) - \bar{Q}_t]$$

$$= \frac{\gamma\theta}{1 + \gamma\theta}[\varepsilon_t + w_t(\nu)], \tag{3.16}$$

and the weighted average of this across all markets is

$$y_{ct} \equiv \sum_\nu u(\nu)y_{ct}(\nu) = \frac{\gamma\theta}{1 + \gamma\theta}\varepsilon_t. \tag{3.17}$$

Cukierman argues therefore that the presence of imperfect information causes output in individual markets to depend on aggregate money shocks, rather than simply on relative demand shocks, as is the case when information is perfect. There is an average response of supply across all markets which is proportional to the money demand shock, and the factor of proportionality, $\gamma\theta/(1 + \gamma\theta)$, is a decreasing function of the variance of the rate of money growth, σ_x^2.

Thus, one way in which costs are imposed on the economy is through inappropriate output responses to real and monetary shocks. Under perfect information, cyclical output in each market is, from (3.3) and (3.8):

$$y_{ct} = \frac{\gamma}{1 + \gamma} w_t(\nu), \tag{3.18}$$

as compared with (3.16) under imperfect information. Confusion causes too small a response to real shocks and too large a response to monetary shocks.

The analysis described above provides a framework within which inflation, price variation across markets, and output fluctuations are generated endogenously, and which could be used to evaluate welfare levels associated with alternative monetary policies and patterns of real demand disturbances. This last step is not performed explicitly by Cukierman, and it does not appear to have been undertaken elsewhere in the literature as yet.

A point made clear by setting up an internally consistent model in this way is that there is (at least in this particular model) no necessary connection between the average level of inflation and its variability, or its unpredictability. The relation between these quantities depends on the money supply process and the other exogenous driving variables of the model. Any costs of inflation drawn from a further analysis of models of this kind are clearly not costs of inflation per se but of the monetary policies which underly it.

The above model derives effects of misperceptions on output levels and prices, but does not discuss intertemporal allocations of resources explicitly. Cukierman extends the analysis to embrace this aspect of an economy by grafting on to it a bond market, and exploring the model's implications for expected inflation rates and activity in bond markets. To this we now turn.

Imperfect information naturally induces a variety of expectations of inflation across markets. If all agents face the same nominal interest rate on bonds, they typically will have different subjective real rates, and so bond market equilibruim will not lead to an efficient allocation of resources over time. Some borrowers will borrow too much, and others too little. Cukierman offers the following analysis, based on the above model.

The average economy-wide price level at time $t + 1$, Q_{t+1}, is given by (3.13) and (3.14) above, and is:

$$Q_{t+1} = x_t + \delta - \alpha - \beta(t + 1) + \frac{\varepsilon_{t+1}}{1 + \gamma\theta}$$

$$= \bar{Q}_t + \delta - \beta + \varepsilon_t + \frac{\varepsilon_{t+1}}{1 + \gamma\theta}.$$

In market v at time t agents know $\bar{Q}_t$ but not x_t nor ε_t, and certainly not ε_{t+1}, so their best estimate of $\bar{Q}_{t+1}$ is:

$$E[Q_{t+1} | I_t(v)] = \bar{Q}_t + \delta - \beta + (1 - \theta)(\varepsilon_t + w_t(v)),$$

since $(1 - \theta)(\varepsilon_t + w_t(v))$ is their best estimate of ε_t [as can be deduced from (3.10), (3.14), and (3.15)]. Hence, estimates of future prices vary across markets.

The current economy-wide price level, Q_t, is given by (3.14) above, but agents do not know it. Their best estimate of it, given (3.14) and (3.15), is:

$$E[Q_t | I_t(v)] = \bar{Q}_t + (1 - \theta)(\varepsilon_t + w_t(v))/(1 + \gamma\theta). \tag{3.19}$$

If expected inflation is defined by

$$\pi_t^*(v) \equiv E[Q_{t+1} | I_t(v)] - E[Q_t | I_t(v)]$$

$$= \delta - \beta + \frac{\gamma\theta(1 - \theta)}{1 + \gamma\theta} (\varepsilon_t + w_t(v)), \tag{3.20}$$

then the variance of inflation expectations across markets is:

$$V(\pi^*(\nu)) = \left\{ \frac{\gamma\theta(1-\theta)}{1+\gamma\theta} \right\}^2 \sigma_w^2 . \tag{3.21}$$

This turns out only to be increasing in the variance of the money growth rate, σ_x^2, under certain conditions.

Turning now to the actual rate of inflation defined by $Q_{t+1} - Q_t$, the difference in actual average price levels at $t+1$ and at t, we have, from (3.13), (3.14), and the identity $x_t = x_{t-1} + \delta + \varepsilon_t$, that

$$\pi_{t+1} = \delta - \beta + (\varepsilon_{t+1} + \gamma\theta\varepsilon_t)/(1+\gamma\theta) . \tag{3.22}$$

For an individual in market ν, the difference between the actual and expected inflation rate, $\pi_t^*(\nu) - \pi_{t+1}$, will depend on both real and monetary shocks. In fact we have, from (3.20) and (3.22) above, the result that

$$\pi_{t+1} - \pi_t^*(\nu) = \frac{\varepsilon_{t+1}}{1+\gamma\theta} + \frac{\theta^2\gamma}{1+\gamma\theta}\varepsilon_t - \frac{\gamma\theta(1-\theta)}{1+\gamma\theta} w_t(\nu) , \tag{3.23}$$

and consequently the expected squared inflation error for the individual in market ν is:

$$V(FE) = [\{1 + (\theta^2\gamma)^2\}\sigma_x^2 + (\gamma\theta)^2(1-\theta)^2\sigma_w^2]/[1+\gamma\theta]^2 . \tag{3.24}$$

The last part of the expression (in σ_w^2) reflects the variation of inflation expectations across markets, and the first part (in σ_x^2) reflects average economy-wide inflation errors.

Cukierman (1984), drawing on an earlier paper of his [Cukierman (1978)], analyses the effects of the variation of inflation expectations on the allocative efficiency of the bond market as follows. He supposes that there are many borrowers and lenders in the market, and the supplies and demands of bonds of borrower, B, and lender, L, are:

$$I_B = \{a_B - [n - \pi^*(B)]\}/b_B , \tag{3.25}$$

and

$$I_L = \{a_L - [n - \pi^*(L)]\}/b_L , \tag{3.26}$$

where n is the nominal interest rate and $\pi^*(\cdot)$ is the appropriate expected inflation rate. Summing over borrowers and lenders and equating aggregate supplies and demands yields an equilibrium nominal interest rate:

$$n = \sum_s v_s a_s + \sum_s v_s \pi^*(s) \tag{3.27}$$

where s is used to index both lenders and borrowers, so the sum is taken over all participants in the market, and $v_s \equiv (1/b_s)/(\sum_s (1/b_s))$. The real rate of interest faced by trader i is then:

$$r_i = n - \pi^*(i) . \tag{3.28}$$

If an average inflation expectation is defined by $\bar{\pi}^* = \sum_s v_s \pi^*(s)$, and an average real interest rate by $R = n - \bar{\pi}^*$, then the individual's real interest rate can be written as the average R less the excess of his expected inflation rate over the average, namely

$$r_i = R + \bar{\pi}^* - \pi^*(i) . \tag{3.29}$$

When all traders have the same inflation expectations, their common real rate of interest is of course R. In any case, R is the weighted average of the r_i, since $R = \sum_i v_i r_i$.

Cukierman computes the losses suffered by traders in bond markets as a result of forecasting the real interest rate incorrectly by the welfare triangle. Agent i makes a forecasting error, $r_i - r$ (where r is the ex post real rate), which equals his inflation forecast error, $\pi_{t+1} - \pi_t^*(i)$, his supply of bonds exceeds the optimum by $(1/b_i)(\pi_{t+1} - \pi_t^*(i))$, and his welfare loss is $[\pi_{t+1} - \pi_t^*(i)]^2/2b_i$. The expected value of the loss computed over all markets and time periods is then (assuming all b_i equal) proportional to the mean squared inflation error in equation (3.23) above. This depends on both the variance of inflation across markets, and on the variance of average economy-wide inflation forecasting errors.

There are two further ways in which unanticipated inflation and variation in expected inflation rates across markets may induce social costs. One is by inducing more trading in bonds, and causing real resources to be used up in that activity. The other is by causing unanticipated redistributions of wealth among agents. Cukierman (1984) touches on both of these aspects briefly, using the model outlined above. He computes $\text{var}(I_i)$, the variance of an individual trader's position in bonds, to measure the effect on the amount of trading, and concludes that it depends positively on the overall variance of inflationary expectations and, for given overall variance, negatively on the correlation of expectations of different traders. The expected value of unanticipated losses for the typical trader before positions are known are shown to increase with the overall variance of inflationary expectations [Cukierman (1984, pp. 78–80)].

3.2. Models in which agents cannot forecast future prices perfectly

Cukierman (1982, 1984) and others have made much of the distinction between permanent and transitory shocks to the money supply and relative demands as a reason why monetary policies may have real effects, and why a transitory shock to the money supply may have persistent effects, on output. Cukierman (1984) offers the following model in order to examine the implications for monetary policy and the allocative efficiency of the price system.

The economy is assumed to consist of many markets for goods, as before, which are competitive and clear instantaneously. Production takes a period and producers have to decide in $t-1$ how much to bring to market in t, and do so on the basis of the expected price in the market (ν) in question relative to the expected economy-wide average price. Supply in market ν at time t is:

$$y_t^s(\nu) = \beta_\nu t + \gamma_\nu [E_{t-1} p_t(\nu) - E_{t-1} Q_t], \tag{3.30}$$

where $\beta_\nu t$ is a deterministic growing component of supply and $\gamma_\nu > 0$ is the elasticity of supply with respect to the expected relative price difference. Demand for the good depends on nominal demand, $n_t(\nu)$, relative to price, $p_t(\nu)$, with elasticity $-\psi(<0)$, namely

$$y_t^d(\nu) = \psi_\nu [n_t(\nu) - p_t(\nu)], \tag{3.31}$$

and nominal demand in market ν depends on a relative demand shock, $x_t(\nu)$, which contains both permanent and transitory parts, and money stock, $\delta_t + m_t + \varepsilon_t(\nu)$. Thus,

$$n_t(\nu) = x_t(\nu) + \delta t + m_t + \varepsilon_t(\nu), \tag{3.32}$$

and $x_t(\nu) = x_t^p(\nu) + x_t^q(\nu)$, $\Delta x_t^p \sim N(0, \sigma_{xp}^2)$, $x_t^q \sim N(0, \sigma_{xq}^2)$, $\varepsilon_t(\nu) \sim N(0, \sigma_\varepsilon^2)$, and $\Delta m_t \sim N(0, \sigma_m^2)$. The economy-wide average, Q_t, is a weighted average of the $p_t(\nu)$ as in (2.4) above.

Equating supply and demand, (3.30) and (3.31), gives the equilibrium price in each market ν as:

$$p_t(\nu) = (\delta - \beta_\nu/\psi_y)t + x_t(\nu) + m_t + \varepsilon_t(\nu)$$

$$- \frac{\gamma_\nu}{\psi_\nu} [E_{t-1} p_t(\nu) - E_{t-1} Q_t]. \tag{3.33}$$

To focus on agents' imperfect forecasting ability as the source of the problem, it is assumed that agents in all markets know all current prices, $p_t(\nu)$. Taking expectations of (3.33) at $t-1$ enables derivation of an expression for $E_{t-1}p_t(\nu)$, which is:

$$E_{t-1}p_t(\nu) = (1 - d_\nu)[\delta t + E_{t-1}x_t(\nu) + E_{t-1}m_t]$$
$$- \frac{\beta_\nu t}{\psi_\nu + \gamma_\nu} + d_\nu E_{t-1}Q_t , \tag{3.34}$$

where $d_\nu \equiv \gamma_\nu / (\psi_\nu + \gamma_\nu)$. Aggregating over all markets gives an expression for $E_{t-1}Q_t$, namely

$$E_{t-1}Q_t = \delta t + E_{t-1}m_t + \sum_\nu w(\nu)\psi_\nu E_{t-1}x_t(\nu) - \sum_\nu w(\nu)\beta_\nu t , \tag{3.35}$$

where

$$\bar{d} \equiv \sum_v u(\nu)d_\nu \quad \text{and} \quad w(\nu) \equiv \frac{1}{1 - \bar{d}} \cdot \frac{u(\nu)}{\psi_\nu + \gamma_\nu} ,$$

and thus $\sum_\nu w(\nu)\psi_\nu = 1$. Forecasts of the money stock, m_t, and the relative demand shock, $x_t(\nu)$, are based on past data and knowledge of the underlying stochastic processes. For the money stock, agents have observations on past values, m_{t-1}, m_{t-2}, etc. For x_t, agents observe only the sum of x_t and ε_t [as can be inferred from (3.33)]. Given the stochastic processes involved, optimal forecasts are distributed lags with geometrically declining weights on past data, with the rate of decay being a function of the variances of the permanent and transitory components of the relevant variables.

The output in each market [equation (3.30)] depends on the expected relative price, which from (3.34) and (3.35) is:

$$E_{t-1}p_t(s) - E_{t-1}Q_t = (1 - d_s)\left[E_{t-1}x_t(s) - \sum_\nu w(\nu)\psi_\nu E_{t-1}x_t(\nu) \right]$$
$$- \frac{1}{\psi_s + \gamma_s}\left[\beta_s - \psi_s \sum_\nu w(\nu)\beta_\nu \right]t . \tag{3.36}$$

Equation (3.36) shows that the expected relative price depends on the expected relative demand for the good s (the first term on the RHS), and on the relative productivity of the s industry (the second term on the RHS). Expected money supplies have no effect in this set-up because agents are assumed to know all current prices, and money affects all equiproportionally. Moreover, money has no effect on the forecasting of future values of $x_t(\nu)$. So here only real factors affect relative price and output decisions in individual markets. Cukierman does, however, include in these factors the "differential monetary noise", $\varepsilon_t(\nu)$, which was included in the demand function (3.32) and which he attributes to monetary policy.

The effect on output of agents not knowing the permanent value of $x_t(\nu)$, i.e. not having "full current information" about the state of the economy, is computed by examining the difference,

$$D_c(s) = y_t(s) - y_t^*(s)$$
$$= \gamma_s \{ E_{t-1} p_t(s) - E_{t-1} Q_t - [p_{t-1}^p(s) - Q_{t-1}^p] \} , \qquad (3.37)$$

between the output actually produced and what would be produced if agents knew the actual state of the economy at $t-1$, and knew the values of the permanent components of prices and of the underlying driving variables in the economy, $x_t(s)$. Cukierman shows that $D_c(s)$ can be expressed in terms of differences between the best forecast of $x_t(\nu)$ and its permanent value, namely $E_{t-1} x_t(\nu) - x_{t-1}^p(\nu)$. The expected value of $D_c(s)$ is zero, and its variance is shown to be an increasing function of either the variance of transitory relative demand shocks, or the variance of permanent relative demand shocks, whether caused by real or monetary factors [the $\varepsilon_t(\nu)$].

The essence of the model described here appears to be that agents cannot forecast future values of relevant variables perfectly, and have to make output decisions one period ahead of the date on which their output is sold on the market. The allocation of shocks to categories of permanent and transitory does not have a great deal of content, since many ARMA(1, 1) processes can be represented as being the sum of a permanent and a transitory component, and forecasting errors of the type analysed here would emerge regardless of the processes driving the exogenous variables. It may also be worth noting here that the connection between any costs of inflation and monetary policy appear to be tenuous in this model. Since it is assumed that agents in each market know all current prices, money is neutral, except for the "differential money demand shock", $\varepsilon_t(\nu)$, which appears to be observationally equivalent to a relative demand shock, $x_t(\nu)$. "Costs" of inflation arise entirely out of relative demand shocks. Thus, although the model described above has been used quite frequently in the context of the persistent effects of transitory shocks, and models of stagflation, and it may indeed be a realistic model of relative price variation, it may be argued that it does not provide a suitable vehicle for articulating the costs of inflation.

3.3. Production inefficiency with unpredictable inflation

In Cukierman's (1984) analysis of permanent/transitory confusion, agents have to plan goods supply one period ahead, and their imperfect forecasting ability gives rise to an inefficient allocation of resources relative to that which would occur if they could forecast better. However, the wage and employment decisions underlying the supply curve were not explored. A simple piece of analysis by Katz and Rosenberg (1983) (KR) does this, and shows that an inefficient allocation can be induced by unpredictable inflation when nominal wages are fixed in advance of knowing the product price. Whereas in Cukierman (1984) suppliers had to make supply decisions on the basis of expected prices, it is here assumed that suppliers of labour have to make a nominal wage decision before knowing the prices of consumption goods, and supply whatever quantity of labour is demanded when those prices become known.

It is assumed that the economy has a strictly concave production function:

$$X = F(N) , \tag{3.38}$$

with $F' > 0$ and $F'' < 0$. When the real wage is W, employment N is such that the marginal product of labour equals the real wage:

$$F'(N) = W , \tag{3.39}$$

and so employment is a function of the real wage:

$$N = G(W) , \tag{3.40}$$

where $G_W = 1/F'' < 0$, and $G_{WW} = -F'''/F''^3$.

It is assumed that the nominal wage is set before the price level is known, and in such a way as to generate a fixed expected real wage rate. The actual real wage rate will be a random variable if prices fluctuate randomly due to money supply unpredictability or due to other unpredictable events. The expected level of employment will be:

$$\bar{N} = E\{G(W)\} \tag{3.41}$$

and

$$\bar{X} = E\{F(G(W))\} , \tag{3.42}$$

Drawing on results of Rothschild and Stiglitz (1970, 1971), KR show that a mean-preserving increase in the variability of W will raise $\bar{N}$ if $G(\cdot)$ is (strictly) convex in W and lower it if $G(\cdot)$ is (strictly) concave in W. Mean employment is raised or lowered by real wage variability according as

$$G_{WW} = -F'''/F''^3 \gtreqless 0 . \tag{3.43}$$

Similarly, mean output is raised or lowered according as

$$[F\{G(W)\}]_{WW} = F''G_W^2 + F'G_{WW} = \frac{1}{F''} - \frac{F'F'''}{F''^3} \gtreqless 0 . \tag{3.44}$$

KR go on to show that the effect of an increase in the variance of W (σ^2) on $\bar{N}$ and $\bar{X}$ is:

$$d\bar{N}/d\sigma^2 = G_{WW}/2 \tag{3.45}$$

and

$$d\bar{X}/d\sigma^2 = (F''G_W^2 + F'G_{WW})/2 . \tag{3.46}$$

In these expressions the partial derivatives are evaluated at the mean of the distribution of real wages. The ratio of the effect on mean output to the effect on mean employment is:

$$\frac{d\bar{X}}{d\sigma^2} \Big/ \frac{d\bar{N}}{d\sigma^2} = F' - \frac{F''^2}{F'''} . \tag{3.47}$$

Thus, if $F''' > 0$, mean employment rises with σ^2, but the increase in mean output is less than the marginal product of labour at the mean real wage. If $F''' < 0$, then mean employment declines, and the decline in output relative to the decline in employment is greater than the marginal product of labour at the mean real wage. In either case, then, it appears that increasing the variability of real wages reduces the efficiency of production.

3.4. Menu costs of price adjustment and the costs of inflation

A large body of literature has grown up in which it is postulated that firms face a fixed "menu" cost every time they change their price. The purpose of this approach seems largely to have been to rationalise the observation that firms in fact change prices infrequently by large amounts, and to investigate the effects of this kind of behaviour for the economy. It seems to have been particularly useful in formulating hypotheses about the relationship between the overall inflation rate and the variability of prices. Whether it can offer any useful insights into the cost of inflation is less clear, since to some degree it involves simply assuming at the outset that inflation is costly.

Prominent contributors to this line of inquiry have been Sheshinski and Weiss (1977, 1983), Caplin and Spulber (1985, 1987), Rotemberg (1982, 1983a,

1983b), Mussa (1981), Danziger (1983, 1984, 1987), and Kuran (1983, 1986a, 1986b).

Sheshinski and Weiss (1977) (SW) showed that when a monopolistically competitive firm faces a constant known inflation rate and has a fixed cost of making price changes, its optimal policy is to change the (nominal) price upwards whenever the real price falls to some critical low value, s, so that immediately after the price change the real price achieves a certain higher value, S – an (s, S) price policy. When the rate of inflation increases, s falls and S rises, so the range of variation of real prices between nominal adjustments increases. The interval of time between price changes may or may not increase depending on the shape of the firm's profit function. Higher adjustment costs naturally increase the intervals between price changes, but the effects of the real interest rate are not unambiguous.

Sheshinski and Weiss's basic (1977) model has the following structure. The firm charges a nominal price, p_t; the rate of inflation is a constant g and so the general price level at time t is $\bar{p}_t = e^{gt}$; $z_t \equiv p_t / \bar{p}_t$ is the firm's real price. Demand at time t is denoted $q_t = f(z_t)$, a function of the firm's real price. Real unit production costs are denoted by $c(q_t)$. Hence, the firm's real profits at t are $F(z_t) \equiv [z_t - c(f(z_t))] f(z_t)$. The real cost of a nominal price adjustment is denoted β, the real interest rate is r, and V_0 denotes the present discounted value of real profits at time 0.

SW consider the real profits of the firm when it contemplates price changes at times $t = 0, t_1, t_2, t_3$, etc. and the nominal price in the interval $[t_\tau, t_\tau + 1)$ is p_τ, so the real price is $p_\tau e^{-gt}$. Total real profits in the interval, including the cost of changing the price at $t_\tau + 1$, are:

$$\int_{t_\tau}^{t_{\tau+1}} F(p_\tau e^{-gt}) e^{-rt} \, dt - \beta e^{-rt_{\tau+1}} .$$

Summing this over price changes τ gives the expression:

$$V_0 = \sum_{\tau=0}^{\infty} \left[\int_{t_\tau}^{t_{\tau+1}} F(p_\tau e^{-gt}) e^{-rt} \, dt - \beta e^{-rt_{\tau+1}} \right]. \tag{3.48}$$

The firm chooses $\{t_\tau\}$ and $\{p_\tau\}$, for $\tau = 1, 2, 3, \ldots$, so as to maximise V_0. Assuming that an interior maximum for V_0 exists, the first-order conditions are:

$$\partial V_0 / \partial t_\tau = [-F(p_\tau e^{-gt_\tau}) + F(p_{\tau-1} e^{-gt_\tau}) + \beta r] e^{-rt_\tau} = 0 \tag{3.49}$$

and

$$\partial V_0 / \partial p_\tau = \int_{t_\tau}^{t_{\tau+1}} F'(p_\tau e^{-gt}) e^{-(r+g)t} \, dt = 0 , \quad \tau = 1, 2, \ldots . \tag{3.50}$$

Equation (3.49) is the condition that a marginal delay in a price change should have zero value, given the prices charged before and after. (3.50) is the condition that, given the dates on which prices are changed, a marginal change in the nominal price charged between any two such dates has no value. SW are able to show that, because the real optimal policy at any date τ after the first price change is independent of any initial conditions, the optimal policy involves a fixed interval ε between price changes, so that $t_{\tau+1} = t_\tau + \varepsilon$, and the real price varies between two fixed values, s and S, with $S = s\, e^{g\varepsilon}$:

SW note in conclusion that a natural way of measuring the effects of inflation on social welfare, in the context of their partial equilibrium analysis, would be to compute the present discounted value of consumers' surplus. The net consumers' surplus associated with a real price z is:

$$G(z) = F(z) + \int_z^\infty f(z)\, \mathrm{d}z \, ,$$

and the present discounted value of $G(z)$ less the costs of price adjustment could be computed and used to measure the costs of inflation. (This suggestion by SW does not appear to have been taken up by subsequent authors in this area.)

It should be noted that the pricing behaviour and the pattern of production over time produced by this model assume that firms meet all demand out of current production. There are no possibilities of holding inventories for smoothing production (since goods are assumed to be non-storable). Nor do firms consider letting some demand go unmet at the price they are currently charging. The introduction of inventory holding would presumably reduce costs associated with variations in the rate of production and introduce costs of inventory holding.

In the later paper [Sheshinski and Weiss (1983)] the deterministic model is replaced by one in which inflation is stochastic, and the optimum pricing policy remains (s, S) as before. The stochastic process for inflation is that the economy has two states, between which it moves randomly. In state zero, inflation is zero, and in state one, it is a constant rate $g > 0$. The sojourn times in each state are i.i.d. random variables, with exponential distributions. The (s, S) result depends on the form of the stochastic process driving prices. As SW note: ". . . the assumptions that the process is monotone with only one state of positive growth and one state of zero growth are required for two bounds only to describe the optimal policy".

Danziger (1984) considers the optimal (s, S) pricing rule using a slightly different stochastic process for the price level, though it shares with SW the feature that prices can either stay the same or go up, but not go down. Danziger (1983), following Bordo (1980), considers price adjustment with stochastic inflation, and assumes that firms, when they change price, also fix the length of time for which the new price is to endure. While he is able to investigate the effects of inflation uncertainty and variability under this assumption, it is not clear that this price behaviour of firms is optimal, though it may contain a degree of descriptive realism. Naish (1986) investigates the implications of SW-type price adjustment costs for the trade-off between firms' average output level and the permanent fully anticipated inflation rate.

While Sheshinski and Weiss (1983) put their analysis in a partial equilibrium framework, Caplin and Spulber (CS) draw on the model to generate a general equilibrium model of inflation and relative price variability, in which price variability is a result of optimal responses by firms to general inflation. They consider an economy with a continuum of small monopolistically competitive firms, each pursuing an (s, S) relative price policy, and forming expectations of inflation rationally. Inflation is driven by a money supply process which parallels the inflation process assumed by SW (1983): money supply is constant (in state 1) or grows at a constant rate g (in state 2), and sojourn times in each state are i.i.d. random variables with exponential distributions. CS are able to show that there is an equilibrium in which relative prices of firms are uniformly distributed over the interval $(s, S]$. This work draws on Caplin (1985) which investigates the implications for aggregate demand of firms pursuing (S, s) inventory policies.

CS use a discrete time version of SW (1983), in which the log of the firm's real price, $r(t) \equiv p(t) - P(t)$, varies between s and S, while aggregate inflation, $\Pi(t) \equiv P(t) - P(t-1)$, follows a two-state stochastic process. The firm's nominal price change is defined as $\Delta(t) \equiv p(t) - p(t-1)$, and thus the relative price change is $r(t) - r(t-1) = \Delta(t) - \Pi(t)$. The stochastic process for $\Pi(t)$ has zero inflation in state 1, and continuous inflation at a rate g in state 2.

CS show that the individual firm's inflation rate is a mean-preserving spread of the aggregate inflation rate, namely they can write:

$$\Delta(t) = \Pi(t) + \varepsilon(t) , \tag{3.51}$$

where $\mathrm{E}(\varepsilon(t) \,|\, \Pi(t)) = 0$ and $V(\Delta(t)) = V(\Pi(t)) + V(\varepsilon(t)) > V(\Pi(t))$. In the general equilibrium, the aggregate inflation rate is a divisia index of individual firm inflation rates. The distribution of individual firms' prices over $(s, S]$ is uniform at each date. The index of relative price variability across firms, defined as

$$VI(t) \equiv \frac{1}{D} \int_0^D (\Delta_i(t) - \Pi(t))^2 \, \mathrm{d}i ,$$

where $D \equiv S - s$, is shown to be simply related to the variance of individual prices. In fact, the expected value of relative price variability, $EVI(t)$, is equal to the difference between the variance of individual price inflation, $V(\Delta_i(t))$, and the variance of aggregate inflation, $V(\Pi(t))$. That is,

$$EVI(t) = V(\Delta_i(t)) - V(\Pi(t)) .$$

This means that the variance of individual price inflation is the sum of aggregate inflation variation and relative inflation variation in this set-up.

Turning to comparative dynamic exercises, CS show that increases in the level and variability of inflation tend to increase the variability of relative prices, allowing for the dependence of (s, S) on the aggregate inflation process. The precise results depend on how the money supply process is changed.

The effects of costs of adjustment of price changes have been discussed extensively also by Rotemberg (1982, 1983a, 1983b) and Mussa (1981), using a different framework from SW, namely one in which adjustment costs are convex – typically quadratic in the price change – in a discrete time model. Firms then tend to change prices every period, and have an incentive to smooth price changes over time rather than to bunch them as they do when the costs are fixed. Rotemberg develops the implications for the business cycle. However, he does not implicitly develop the implications of his analysis for the costs of inflation. The real effects of inflation in the kind of world he describes are pursued also by Kuran (1983, 1986a, 1986b) who examines the effects of inflation on the average output level of firms, and on employment. His argument is that as a firm's relative price varies during the period when its nominal price is fixed, demand for its product will vary and, on average, its output may be higher or lower than if relative price remained at its average level. Similar arguments apply to the firm's employment level. These factors are used to illustrate the absence of superneutrality of money in the presence of price adjustment costs. The employment and output effects of inflation presumably have welfare effects, but assessing the magnitude of any such effects has not been undertaken as yet.

3.5. Summary and conclusions

Section 3 of the chapter has examined models in which either imperfect information or costs of adjustment lead, in some cases, to an association between inflation and price variability. The literature reviewed mainly focuses on articulating the real effects of inflation, and only tangentially deals with its welfare costs, though it provides frameworks which could be developed so as to give measures of welfare costs. A general point which is reinforced by this literature is that aggregate inflation, its variability over time, its unpredictability, and the variability in prices across an economy, are all endogenous variables within some general equilibrium model. The associations which emerge between them depend on the nature of the exogenous driving forces of the model. There is no general or necessary connection between, say, the average aggregate inflation rate and the variability of prices across firms.

The costs of inflation are frequently assumed to be associated with the variability in relative prices across firms, and with both the variability and unpredictability of the aggregate inflation rate. Okun (1975) gives a broad discussion of these costs. His arguments draw on his concept of "customer markets" in which the high costs of acquiring information lead to enduring relationships between workers and employers, and between customers and suppliers. In an economy containing both these customer markets and also "auction markets", inflation causes relative price variation, since prices in customer markets respond more slowly than those in auction markets. This, in Okun's view, has enormous welfare costs, and he remarks:

> Prolonged and intense inflation upsets many habits of economic life, confronting consumers with price increases and price dispersions that send them shopping; making them doubt their ability to maintain their living standards, and downgrade the value of their career jobs and long-term savings; and forcing them to compile more information and try to predict the future – costly and risky activities and that they are poorly qualified to execute and bound to view with anxiety [Okun (1975, p. 383)].

Okun's summary remarks, and his more detailed discussion in the paper, express a view of the costs of inflation which is widely held. His arguments are, however, somewhat loose and it is not clear that all would withstand close scrutiny. The models outlined above formalise a number of mechanisms which may give rise to an association between inflation and price variability, and move in the direction of formalising some of the arguments he makes, but, while precise, they are considerably more narrow in their scope than his view. It appears to remain the case that the man-in-the-street notions of the costs of inflation have not been formalized in rigorous theoretical models.

4. Costs of inflation: Empirical evidence

4.1. Introduction

For any theory to be taken seriously, and in particular used as a basis for policy analysis and prescription (no matter what its pedigree or its elegance), it is essential for its empirical relevance and veracity to be established. Hence, it is not surprising that there is a large literature concerned with the empirical underpinnings of the major tenets of the theories which purport to identify the costs of inflation. In this section we describe briefly the main hypotheses which have been analysed empirically and the results obtained. In reviewing the results available in the literature we critically appraise the econometric methodology which typically has been employed. In particular, we argue that the confirmationist methodology which is commonly adopted provides extremely fragile support for the theories adumbrating the costs of inflation. The quality and usefulness of econometric models is not established simply by noting that their statistical properties confirm the associated economic theory hypotheses. Model evaluation requires much more than economic theory consistency and goodness of fit. Only by checking a model's congruence with all the available sources of information, including the rival explanations provided by alternative theories, can we hope to establish a model's credentials. For more details of this view of econometric modelling see Hendry and Mizon (1985) and for discussion of methods of implementation see Hendry and Richard (1982). Pagan (1987) discusses this and other approaches to econometric modelling, but points often are made most tellingly by demonstration, and this is the approach we take in this section. In the particular context of the relationship between relative price variability and the aggregate rate of inflation we present empirical results, using data for the United Kingdom, which illustrate the dangers of confirmationism by showing the fragility of simple models that might be used for assessing whether there is a highly significant positive relationship between these variables.

4.2. Review of the empirical literature

"It is well known that the costs of inflation depend on the source of the inflation, on whether and when the inflation was anticipated, and on the institutional structure of the economy" [Fischer (1981a)]. If the institutional structure of the economy is construed to include the behavioural structure of the economy, we might expect the empirical literature on the costs of inflation to be concerned with the analysis of:

   (i) the causes of inflation;
   (ii) relevant behavioural relationships;
   (iii) distinguishing the effects of anticipated and unanticipated inflation; and
   (iv) the relative importance of inflation variability and uncertainty about the (expected) rate of inflation.

Although the importance of determining the causes of inflation is widely acknowledged [see, for example, the papers and references in Hall (1982)], the empirical literature of this topic rarely is associated directly with the costs of inflation. Since inflation is not a policy instrument, nor is it an autonomous variable [see Aldrich (1988) for a discussion of the nature of autonomous variables and their relationship to exogenous variables], but is regarded as an important barometer of the success of government economic policies, an understanding of the determinants of aggregate prices and their rates of inflation is essential if it is desired to "control" inflation and so avoid, or lessen, its attendant costs. Sargan (1980) is an excellent example of the econometric analysis of price determination, and McCallum, Chapter 18 in this Handbook, reviews the literature on the causes of inflation.

The empirical literature associated with the costs of inflation is much more concerned with issues (ii)–(iv) above. Indeed, it is the linkages between inflation, inflation variability, and/or inflation uncertainty and the rest of the economy (real and monetary) that has been a focus of attention. The assessment of the effects of anticipated inflation, which Pagan, Hall and Trivedi (1983) argue is usefully interpreted in the framework of the Fisher effect relating nominal and real interest rates via inflation, has spawned a large literature [see, for example, Levi and Makin (1978, 1979)] and was discussed in Section 2. Similarly, the literature on the real effects of unanticipated inflation, particularly that concerned with the Phillips curve, is extensive and discussed in detail elsewhere, e.g. Ashenfelter and Layard (1986). Hence, in this section we concentrate on discussion of the empirical literature which analyses the relationship between inflation variability, inflation uncertainty, and the level of inflation. Since a number of surveys of this area already exist [e.g. Fischer (1981a), Taylor (1981), and Marquez and Vining (1984)] we provide only a brief review in this section, but then critically evaluate the extant econometric evidence.

Prior to summarising the main results obtained in this literature it is important that we remind ourselves of the distinction between simple and partial correlations. As is well known, two variables can have a highly significant *simple* correlation as a result of having a common driving variable or common trend, but once the influence of the common variable has been partialled out or removed there may be no correlation between them, i.e. the *partial* correlation between the two variables is not significantly different from zero. Hence, before we use the correlation structure of data to make inferences, we should be clear in our minds whether it is simple or partial correlations, or both, that are relevant for our analysis. It is rare for economists or econometricians to be interested in closed models, and so the typical model has some exogenous variables, and the parameters of interest are functions of the parameters of the distribution of the endogenous variables *conditional* on the exogenous variables. Consequently, particularly when it is a correlation between two endogenous variables that we are interested in, it is a *partial* correlation not a *simple* correlation that is relevant – the linear influence of the exogenous variables needs to be partialled out. It is therefore surprising that much of the early literature on relative price variability and inflation looked only at simple correlations between these variables.

An equally elementary, but nonetheless fundamental, point concerns the partition of variables into endogenous and exogenous variables. Despite the fact that in Western economies (other than very small open economies) the rate of inflation is not an autonomous variable, a major concern of empirical studies has been to assess the impact of inflation on relative price variability, on its variance, and on inflation uncertainty, with the level of inflation treated as an *exogenous* variable. In addition to potential econometric problems, this causes logical problems, for as Fischer (1981a) puts it: "since the inflation rate is not an exogenous variable to the economy, there is some logical difficulty in discussing the costs of inflation per se rather than the costs and benefits of alternative policy choices". However, just as partial and general equilibrium analyses have valid but distinct roles, so it is possible to analyse models which treat inflation as an exogenous variable, and this will be relevant *provided* that the parameters of interest (e.g. partial responses, elasticities, and propensities) are those of the conditional distribution which has inflation among the valid conditioning variables. A corollary of this is that an inferential minefield faces the investigator who attempts to compare models, and results from models, which are based on distributions that condition on different variables [Mizon (1984), Mizon and Richard (1986) and Lu and Mizon (1988) contain further discussion of this point].

We now summarise the empirical literature on the relationship between the level and variability of inflation and relative price variability.

4.2.1. Inflation variability

The basic issue of interest is whether aggregate inflation is more variable when its average level is higher, this having been conjectured to be the case by Okun (1971) and Friedman (1977). In fact, Okun (1971) supported his view by reporting that there was a positive association between the standard deviation of the annual increase in the GNP deflator and its average value, using data for 17 OECD countries during the period 1951–68. Logue and Willett (1976) reported similar results for a more comprehensive data set, but they did note that this "strong relationship breaks down, however, when the sample is disaggregated". When a simple correlation between the standard deviation and the average of the inflation rates for 41 countries across the period 1948–70 is being calculated, it is not surprising that the absence of spatial and temporal homogeneity causes the correlation to differ for disaggregated data. However, the converse, i.e. that aggregation, or more accurately inappropriately assumed homogeneity, may be the reason for there being a strong positive correlation between inflation and its variability, is equally important, although attention is drawn to it less often. Foster (1978) provides similar results to those of Logue and Willett, but he uses average absolute changes in the inflation rate rather than the standard deviation as a measure of variability.

In discussing the variability of inflation it is important to distinguish cross-sectional from time-series variability. Although the theories about the relationship between the variability and the level of inflation are no doubt concerned with the relationship between the time-series variance of inflation and its mean, the majority of the evidence that has been published is concerned with the relationship between the cross-sectional mean and variance of inflation and how it varies over time. In addition, we note that it is the relationship between the *unconditional* mean and variance of the cross-section (which is assumed to be constant cross-sectionally, though not necessarily through time), which is analysed in the studies mentioned above. Hence, the available evidence based on cross-section data seems to be of limited relevance.

4.2.2. Relative price variability and inflation

As described in Section 3, there are many theories which predict that relative price variability and aggregate inflation will be positively related. Authors of such theories include Lucas (1973), Cukierman (1979), Amihud and Mendelson (1982) and Hercowitz (1981). The possibility of there being such a relationship was considered in empirical work long before these theories were developed – see, for example, Mills (1972) and Graham (1930). Glejser (1965) used cross-section data for 15 European countries to calculate the correlation between the inflation rate and the standard deviation of relative prices, and duly found it to be positive. One of the first studies (in recent times) to use time-series data to analyse the relationship between relative price variability and inflation was that of Vining and Elwertowski (1976). They used graphs as the basis for their comments on the relationship between the standard deviation of the changes in relative prices and the inflation rate, using wholesale price data and retail price data for the United States over the period 1948–74. In fact, using the data provided in tables 1 and 2 of Vining and Elwertowski (1976), the simple correlation coefficients between these standard deviations and the inflation rates are 0.4435 and 0.2225 for the wholesale prices and retail prices, respectively. Note that the *t*-statistics for testing the null hypothesis that the correlation coefficient is zero are 2.47 and 1.41, respectively, so that there is little evidence for concluding that "there is a strong positive association between inflation and relative price variability", which many authors subsequently have asserted as an appropriate interpretation of the Vining and Elwertowski results. We also note that further analysis of these correlations using OLS regression on PC GIVE [see Hendry (1987)] reveals that the *t*-values using White (1980) heteroskedastic consistent standard errors are 0.94 and 0.61 for the wholesale prices and retail prices, respectively. In addition to the regressions of the standard deviations of relative price changes on the average inflation rates yielding highly heteroskedastic residuals for both price series, the residuals for the retail price data are serially correlated and the regression has a significant Reset [see Ramsey (1969)] test statistic. More telling than each of these unfavourable diagnostic test statistics, and probably the reason for them, is the fact that the estimated correlation coefficients are extremely sensitive to changes in the sample period used. For example, if the final observation, that for 1974, is omitted, the estimated correlations are 0.152 and −0.066, respectively, with corresponding *t*-statistics (based on heteroskedastic consistent standard errors) of 0.41 and −0.21!

Hence, the information contained in tables 1 and 2 and the associated graphs of Vining and Elwertowski (1976) do not provide convincing evidence of a strong positive relationship between relative price variability and inflation in the United States. Indeed, after outlining six theories linking inflation and relative price variability, Fischer (1981b) analyses more recent data for the United States and concludes that "it is evident from the contrasts between the regression results for different periods that there is no simple stable relation between relative price variability and inflation". Fischer then demonstrates that the relationship between these variables in the United States post-1956 is dominated by food and energy and shocks, and that the evidence for West Germany and Japan yields similar conclusions. In an attempt to avoid the loss of information that results from using a single statistic to measure relative price variability, Taylor (1981) uses a diagram to present information on the relationship between relative price variability and inflation non-parametrically. On the basis of this he concludes, amongst other things, that: (i) inflation and relative price variability are both higher in the 1970s than in the 1960s and (ii) energy price movements dominate both variables in 1973 and 1979; conclusions which are consonant with those of Fischer. Taylor then provides a summary of the contract model, previously developed in Taylor (1980a, 1980b), which provides an alternative rationalisation for a positive association between relative price variability and inflation to that provided by the "information based" models of Cukierman and Hercowitz.

Despite the nature of the evidence using U.S. data, it has commonly been summarised as providing confirmation for the hypothesis that there is a strong positive association between inflation and relative price variability, e.g. Marquez and Vining (1984) – though they do comment that the relationship need not be stable through time! In contrast, studies using data for the United Kingdom, e.g. Hesselman (1983), Leser (1983), Mizon, Safford and Thomas (1983), and Mizon and Thomas (1988), have found there to be no evidence of a strong positive relationship between inflation and relative price variability.

Indeed, Mizon, Safford and Thomas (1983) found that major determinants of relative price variability are the tax rate and associated changes made in the Chancellor of the Exchequer's Budget statements, in addition to the energy price changes of the 1970s. In so far as the tax system is non-lump-sum, it is often, by design but also by default, distortionary. Similarly, aggregate inflation as a tax on money has the potential to be distortionary, but the evidence, for the United Kingdom at least, is that aggregate inflation has less impact on relative price variability than changes in other tax rates and major shifts in the prices of key commodities like oil. In the light of these findings, and those of Blinder (1982) and Fischer (1981a, 1981b), it seems that once the effects of events like the oil price "shocks" have been allowed for there is little or no empirical evidence for higher aggregate inflation causing greater relative price variability.

4.2.3. Relative price variability and "shocks"

Anticipated inflation and anticipated changes in monetary aggregates should, by definition, have less immediate impact on relative price variability than unanticipated changes or "shocks". The importance of food and energy price shocks referred to above suggests that the partition of variables into anticipated and unanticipated components could well be valuable in further analysis of the determinants of relative price variability. Indeed, a number of the theoretical models reviewed in Section 3 involve expectations of prices, and surprises or shocks. Therefore, there are theoretical models (e.g. those involving rational expectations), as well as there being pragmatic empirical grounds, for exploring the explanatory value of shocks. Parks (1978) was one of the first to experiment with such an approach. Using a random walk with drift to model aggregate inflation, he found the square of the unanticipated inflation rate to be the most statistically significant explanatory variable for relative price variability. In particular, this squared inflation shock was much more important than the inflation rate in explaining relative price variability. The measure of relative price variability used was that denoted by VP_t in the literature, and defined as:

$$VP_t = \sum_{i=1}^{n} w_{it}^* (DP_{it} - DP_t)^2 ,$$

when the aggregate rate of inflation DP_t is defined as:

$$DP_t = \sum_{i=1}^{n} w_{it}^* DB_{it} ,$$

and when n is the number of commodities, w_{it}^* is the average expenditure share on the ith commodity in years t and $t-1$, P_{it} is the log of the price of the ith commodity at time t (i.e. $P_{it} = \log p_{it}$), P_t is an aggregate price index (e.g. a geometric mean of the p_{it}'s), and D is the first difference operator. Note that aside from any other considerations, the dimension of VP_t would suggest that DP_t^2 rather than DP_t, and $(DP_t - DP_t^*)^2$ rather than $(DP_t - DP_t^*)$, are the relevant explanatory variables, when DP_t^* is the anticipated inflation rate, which Parks generated using the random walk with drift model as $DP_t^* = DP_{t-1} + \hat{\mu}$. Similar dimensional considerations no doubt lead other investigators, e.g. Vining and Elwertowski (1976), to use the standard deviation of relative price variability $\sqrt{VP_t}$, rather than VP_t, when checking for a positive association between it and the inflation rate DP_t.

Hercowitz (1982), using an equation derived in Hercowitz (1981), examined the hypothesis that VP is related to aggregate monetary and real shocks. Using annual wholesale price indices for the United States to compute VP, and the unanticipated money growth series estimated by Barro (1978), Hercowitz found no support for the hypothesis that money shocks affect VP. These results were at variance with the general tenor of the earlier work of Vining and Elwertowski (1976) and Parks (1978). It is also relevant to point out that Hercowitz in his studies noted that his estimated models had serially correlated residuals and non-constant parameters. Hence, Hercowitz's results had cast doubt on the strength of the empirical support for a strong relationship between relative price variability, inflation (anticipated and unanticipated), and monetary shocks, as well as indicating the potential fragility of the empirical results on this topic, including his own. That regressions relating VP to functions of DP and real and monetary shocks would be expected to have heteroskedastic and serially correlated residuals within the framework of Lucas (1973) type models, was mentioned in the important paper by Pagan, Hall and Trivedi (1983). This serves to emphasise the point made earlier, that it is important to test a model's congruence with all the available information, for in the absence of such congruence valid inferences are extremely difficult to achieve.

In a more recent study Silver (1988) explores a VP–DP type relationship using highly disaggregated U.K. data. This study relates the variability of price across retail outlets (as measured by the coefficient of variation) for *each* of 57 food products, to the anticipated and unanticipated price of that product for the period 1968–84. The anticipated price was generated by an AR(1) model for each product. A number of different functional forms were employed for the relationship for each of the 57 products, with the results indicating that there is no significant relationship for approximately half of the products, and that for the vast majority of the products which had a significant relationship it was negative.

4.2.4. Inflation uncertainty

It has been argued that it is the unpredictability of inflation that is a major source of the welfare loss associated with inflation. For example, Friedman (1977) conjectured that higher inflation rates are typically associated with higher inflation variability and often more forecast uncertainty as well, so that for risk-averse economic agents there is a loss. Of course the fact that inflation is variable does not mean that it is unpredicatable: variability and uncertainty are distinct properties. If we ignore deterministic variability as being less relevant and uninteresting, we can still distinguish two types of stochastic variability – those associated with conditional and unconditional variance. The inflation variability that was the concern of Subsection 4.2.1 was the unconditional variance of inflation. However, variability can be decomposed into predictable and unpredictable components. For example, a regression model which explains the aggregate inflation rate, $\Delta \log P_t$, as a linear function of variables from an information set, I_t, yields residuals the variance of which is a measure of the unpredictability of inflation. This residual variance is of course nothing other than an obvious sample estimate of the conditional variance of inflation, when the conditioning is with respect to the variables in I_t. In this subsection we look at some of the literature which has assessed the influence of inflation on the conditional variance of aggregate inflation and the conditional variance of relative price variability.

Pagan, Hall and Trivedi (1983) note that if it is presumed that there will always be an increase in the unanticipated rate of inflation if there is a rise in the actual inflation rate, it is necessary to distinguish between absolute and proportional variability. In particular, they define inflation to be absolutely more variable if the elasticity of the conditional variance of inflation with respect to the level of inflation is positive, and it is proportionally more variable if the elasticity is greater than unity. Pagan et al. then use Australian data to test for absolute and proportional inflation variability. Letting $\psi_t = (DP_t - D\hat{P}_t)$ and defining $E(\varphi_t^2 \mid I_t) = \sigma_t^2$ they then generated $D\hat{P}_t$ in two different ways. First, they used for $D\hat{P}_t$ the median of the price expectation of consumers included in a survey conducted over the period 1973 quarter 1 to 1981 quarter 2. Secondly, $D\hat{P}_t$ was generated via an autoregressive process with an initial lag of 4 corresponding to the assumption that expectations are formed about inflation over the next four quarters. For both sets of inflation expectations they could not reject the hypothesis that $\beta = 1$ when it was assumed that $\sigma_t^2 = \gamma DP_{t-1}^{\beta}$, and allowance was made in the analysis for both serial correlation and heteroskedasticity. Hence, for their particular parametric model, and for their data, Pagan, Hall and Trivedi (1983) did no reject the hypothesis of proportional variability in inflation.

Engle (1983) used U.S. data to test for ARCH effects [see Engle (1982)] and for the influence of the rate of inflation on the conditional variance of aggregate inflation. For this analysis the information set I_t included lagged inflation, the rate of change of wages, the rate of change of money supply, and the rate of change of the import deflator. Engle (1983) concludes that the conditional or unanticipated variance of inflation:

> in the seventies was not slightly greater than in the sixties and both were well below the variances in the late forties and early fifties. Although the level of inflation in the seventies was high, it was predictable based on available information and, hence, the variance did not increase.

Hence, the broadly similar approaches of Pagan, Hall and Trivedi (1983) and Engle (1983), both of which used sophisticated econometric techniques, taken jointly yield inconclusive evidence on the hypothesis that inflation uncertainty increases with the level of inflation. On the one hand, Pagan et al. using Australian data do not reject the hypothesis in its strictest form of proportional variability, but on the other Engle was able to reject the hypothesis using U.S. data.

The relative price variability measure VP_t provides an example of a cross-sectional variance, namely the variance of inflation rates across n commodities. The models discussed in Subsection 4.2.3 were essentially concerned with the problem of finding an appropriate specification for the conditional mean of VP_t, with functions of the aggregate inflation rate DP_t included in the set of potential conditioning variables. In this sense the literature on the relationship between VP_t and DP_t is analogous to that concerned with inflation uncertainty. Furthermore, one of the assertions in Friedman (1977) was that increases in the conditional (time-series) variance of inflation will lead to increases in relative price variability measures like VP_t. It has been argued above that to date the empirical evidence for either, or both, of these variances increasing with the aggregate rate of inflation is weak.

Cukierman and Wachtel (1979) analysed the relationship between the variance of inflation expectations and the variance of inflation, and the variance of the rate of change of nominal income. In their empirical work the first variance was proxied by the variance of inflation expectations from the Livingston and Michigan Survey Research Center surveys. The latter two variances were proxied by moving variances of the corresponding observed rates of change. The regressions which they report show the variance of the inflation expectations from both surveys to be positively related to the moving variances. Hence, it is claimed that the results support the proposition that there is a positive relationship between the variability of inflation and the spread of expected inflation over different markets. However, no test statistics for serial correlation and heteroskedasticity in the equation residuals are given, and so we do not know whether the usual OLS standard errors, which the authors have used, are appropriate.

4.2.5. The distribution of inflation

Although it is of less direct relevance to the costs of inflation we now briefly refer to the literature which has been concerned with the shape of the distribution of prices. One of the key assumptions in the theories of Lucas (1973) and Cukierman (1979, 1982) is that the logarithms of prices P_{it} are normally distributed. This assumption has been shown to be inappropriate by a number of authors using different data sets. Examples are: Vining and Elwertowski (1976), Blejer (1983), Buck and Gahlen (1983), and Mizon, Safford and Thomas (1986), who all show that the hypothesis that ΔP_{it} is normally distributed is overwhelmingly rejected. Hence, one of the foundations on which many of the theories of the costs of inflation are built is inconsistent with the empirical evidence.

4.2.6. Causality

The finding that there is a positive association between two variables of interest does not convey any information about their causal ordering. Hence, if it is desired to use the observed positive association in the design of policy prescriptions it is likely to be of interest to ask which variable causes which. It is not possible to provide an answer to this question simply using correlations. Furthermore, it is usual for the variables whose correlation is of interest to be endogenous variables within the class of models typically used, and in that context exogenous variables are more natural "causes". However, many authors have employed the Granger causality concept, which is essentially one of temporal precedence or feedback, to explore the nature of the relationship between variables like VP_t and DP_t. Marquez and Vining (1984) summarise much of this literature by noting that the conclusion is invariably that neither VP_t nor DP_t appears to unidirectionally Granger-cause the other, and that they are best described by a joint process with feedback. This leads authors such as Fischer to the conjecture that there are other variables which are "driving" both relative price variability and aggregate inflation. Noting the important influence that oil and food price shocks apparently have had on VP_t in the United States at least, this is an unsurprising conjecture.

4.3. Pitfalls of confirmationism

In this subsection we illustrate the dangers inherent in confirmationism by analysing the relationship between VP_t and DP_t using the retail price data for the United Kingdom used in Mizon, Safford and Thomas (1986) and Mizon and Thomas (1988).

4.3.1. Relative price variability and inflation

In confronting the hypothesis that there is more variability in relative prices when the aggregate rate of inflation is higher with empirical evidence, it is first necessary to decide on appropriate definitions for these variables. Although much of the literature uses VP_t (or $\sqrt{VP_t}$) as the measure of relative price variability and DP_t as the inflation rate, it is not clear that these are the most appropriate measures. First, note from the definition of VP_t given in Subsection 4.2.3 above that this is a weighted sample variance of the individual commodity inflation rates, i.e. a weighted sample variance of $\Delta \log p_{it} = DP_{it}$, or equivalently of $\Delta \log(p_{it}/P_t) = DP_{it} - DP_t$. Hence, it is the dispersion of *rates of change* of the log relative prices which is being used, rather than the dispersion of the log relative prices themselves. Whilst it could be argued that the log prices may be integrated of order one or more [see Engle and Granger (1987)] so that the time-series variance of such variables is unbounded, it is relevant to note that it is the cross-sectional variance that is being measured, and in any case it is less likely that the log *relative* prices will be non-stationary. Secondly, although Taylor (1981) suggests that the variance of rates of change rather than the level of log relative prices might have been used in order to remove the signal (which is unlikely to induce costs), and so enable the analysis to concentrate on the noise (which does induce costs), identifying "true signal" with a stochastic trend is very restrictive, as in fact Taylor points out. Pagan and Ullah (1986) contains more discussion of this issue in the particular context of variables like VP_t being used as measures of risk, which it is in the costs of inflation literature.

We now draw on the results in Mizon and Thomas (1988) which use VP_t and DP_t as the basic measures of relative price variability and inflation to illustrate what might go wrong in looking at the simple correlations between these variables. Figures 19.2 and 19.3 provide the graphs of VP_t and DP_t, respectively, for monthly seasonally unadjusted U.K. data covering the period 1964(1) to 1983(12), with 37 categories of goods (i.e. $n = 37$). The simple correlation between these variables over this period is 0.595, with a t-value, using regular OLS standard errors, of 11.41 – impressive evidence indeed of a strong positive relationship between VP_t and DP_t!

If for the moment we assume that the simple correlation coefficients between VP_t and DP_t is an appropriate parameter of interest, we must check how robust this estimate of it is. In particular, we would wish to avoid basing policy recommendations on a fragile parameter estimate. Table 19.1, equation (1), provides diagnostic test statistics for the regression of VP_t on DP_t over the period 1964(1) to 1983(12), from which it is clear that the usual inferences

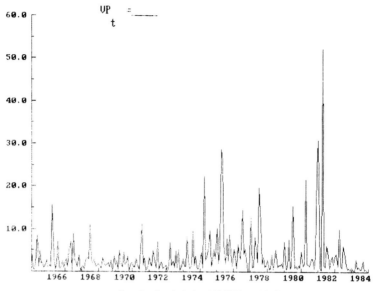

Sample Period is 1964(1) -- 1983(12)

Figure 19.2

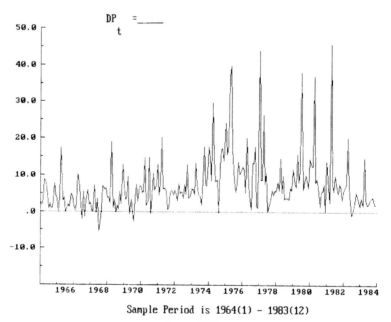

Sample Period is 1964(1) - 1983(12)

Figure 19.3

Table 19.1
Eq. (1): modelling *VP* by OLS. Sample is 1964(1) to 1983(12)

Variable	Coefficient	Std · error	HCSE	*t*-value	*t*(HCSE)
constant	0.47542	0.40442	0.72592	1.176	0.65
DP	0.44311	0.03882	0.11395	11.415	3.89

$R^2 = 0.3538$ $\sigma = 4.5295$ $F(1,238) = 130.31$ $DW = 1.645$
Residual autoregression of order   12

LAG	1	2	3	4	5	6	7	8
Coeff.	0.1794	−0.0604	0.1691	0.1378	−0.0868	−0.0667	−0.1168	0.0241
S.E.'s	0.0669	0.0678	0.0680	0.0690	0.0696	0.0691	0.0691	0.0691

LAG	9	10	11	12
Coeff.	−0.0163	0.0177	−0.0388	0.2069
S.E.'s	0.0684	0.0675	0.0675	0.0665

Testing for serial correlation from lags 1 to 1
$Chi^2[1] = 7.538$ and $F\text{-Form}[1,237] = 7.68$

$Arch[1,236] = 6.88$ $Hetero[2,235] = 32.87$ $Reset[2,236] = 44.95$
$Skewness = 3.451$ $Excess\ kurtosis = 16.371$ $Norm[2] = 3130.24$

Eq. (2) modelling *VP* by OLS. Sample is 1964(1) to 1974(12) less 24 forecasts

Variable	Coefficient	Std · error	HCSE	*t*-value	Partial R_2
constant	1.94545	0.33270	0.49614	5.84753	0.2439
DP	0.13607	0.05401	0.10192	2.51933	0.0565

$R^2 = 0.0564948$ $\sigma = 2.43322887$ $F(1,106) = 6.35$ $DW = 2.086$
Tests of Parameter CONSTANCY over: 1973(1) − 1974(12)

Forecast $Chi^2(24)/24 = 3.26$
Chow test (24,106)   = 3.08

Testing for serial correlation from lags 1 to 1
$Chi^2[1] = 7.538$ and $F\text{-Form}[1,237] = 7.68$

$Arch[1,104] = 0.44$ $Hetero[2,103] = 10.24$ $Reset[2,104] = 21.46$
$Skewness = 2.535$ $Excess\ kurtosis = 7.199$ $Norm[2] = 342.43$

	1964(1)–1983(12)		1964(1)–1972(12)		1973(1)–1983(12)	
	Mean	SD	Mean	SD	Mean	SD
VP	3.67	5.62	2.54	2.49	4.59	7.12
DP	7.20	7.55	4.38	4.36	9.51	8.75
r		0.595		0.234		0.629
t		11.41		2.52		9.23
t(HCSE)		3.89		1.33		3.67

Note: These results were generated using *PC GIVE* (version 5.1). Hendry (1987) describes the program and gives definitions of the test statistics which have been used in compiling this table.

based on this estimated correlation coefficient are likely to be very misleading. For example, the residuals from this regression have significant serial correlation, ARCH effects, heteroskedasticity, and non-normal skewness and kurtosis. In addition, the Reset test statistic indicates that it is inappropriate to relate VP_t to DP_t linearly. The fragility of the simple correlation coefficient between VP_t and DP_t is further evidenced by the predictive failure of the regression when its parameters are estimated using data for the period 1964(1) to 1972(12) and it is used to forecast VP_t over the period 1973(1) to 1983(12) – see the forecast χ^2 and the Chow test statistics for equation (2) of Table 19.1. In fact, many similar simple regressions suffer predictive failure if the sample periods used for estimation terminate around the time of the first oil price shock in 1972. Indeed, inspection of the descriptive statistics at the foot of Table 19.1 shows that the means of both VP_t and DP_t roughly doubled after the oil price shock, and that the standard deviation of VP_t almost trebled whilst that of DP_t doubled. The estimated correlation coefficient between these variables of 0.595 over the whole sample period is also seen to be dominated by the co-movements of VP_t and DP_t after 1972(12) – the estimated correlation coefficient between them over the period 1964(1) to 1972(12) being smaller and not significantly different from zero using t-statistic based on the HCSE. Note that Figures 19.2 and 19.3 suggest that the high correlation after 1972 may be the result of a few "shocks" which had large impacts on both VP_t and DP_t, namely the two oil price hikes, the large change in VAT rates in 1979, and major Budget tax rate changes. This is therefore analogous to Fischer's finding, mentioned above, that in the United States the relationship between relative price variability and inflation is dominated by the changes in food and oil prices. An important difference though is the fact that in the United Kingdom many of the "shocks" which are driving inflation and relative price variability are government-induced changes, fiscal and monetary, associated with the institution of an annual Budget. This serves to highlight the point that inflation per se does not cause welfare losses, but is itself the result of government economic policy (no matter what instruments are being used to implement the policy) and external "shocks".

An alternative reaction to the finding of significant heteroskedasticity in the residuals and the Reset test statistic indicating the use of an inappropriate functional form for the relationship between VP_t and DP_t, is to consider other functions for the relationship. In particular, remembering that VP_t and DP_t are essentially sample variances and means of $\Delta \log p_{it}$, the results of Rao (1952) suggest that a linear relationship between the logarithm of VP_t and DP_t be tried. Furthermore, a logarithmic transformation is often a variance stabilising transformation, and so it is possible that $\log VP_t$ may not have a marked change in variance pre- and post-1973. In fact, $\log VP_t$ has a standard deviation of 0.874 for the period 1964(1) to 1972(12), and of 1.175 for the period 1973(1) to 1983(12), so that there is a much smaller increase in dispersion following the first oil price increase. However, although the regression of $\log VP_t$ on DP_t for the full sample period yields an estimated correlation coefficient of 0.508 with a regular t-value of 9.09 and an HCSE-based t-value of 9.99, and the residuals exhibit less non-normal skewness and kurtosis, the residuals are serially correlated and heteroskedastic. Moreover, if the regression is run for the period pre-1973 the estimated correlation coefficient is 0.274 with an HCSE-based t-value of 2.60, so that there is much less evidence of a strong positive association between inflation and relative price variability.

If, in addition to noting the manifest fragility of the estimated simple correlation coefficient between VP_t and DP_t, we recognise that it is more likely that a partial rather than a simple correlation coefficient is of interest, we are led to consider other variables to include in the analysis. Potential variables would be functions of money supply, interest rates, wage rates, and exchange rates. To bring such variables into consideration as additional regressors now would represent a model rescue operation without a guide. In particular, such as approach would be constantly changing the relevant information set and so implicitly changing the parameters of interest. A preferable strategy, which avoids the limitations inherent in such simple-to-general modelling, is to formulate a general model (i.e. one embracing all potentially relevant variables) which has had its congruence with the available information established, and then to seek parsimonious models (i.e. simpler models nested within the general model) which are also congruent. Mizon and Thomas (1988) adopted such a strategy using the economic theory framework of Lucas (1973) as further developed in Pagan, Hall and Trivedi (1983), but without considering models involving $\log VP_t$. Their results indicate that significantly more of the variation in VP_t is explained when a larger set of explanatory variables is used, especially when auxiliary regressions are employed to generate anticipated and unanticipated components for them. In particular, Budget and seasonal dummy variables have an important role, and "surprises" in bilateral exchange rates contribute to the explanation of VP_t. However, there still appears to be a role for aggregate inflation (the inflation rate in the Retail Price Index in this case) in explaining VP_t. Their work though, despite developing a model which was congruent with most of the available information, did not lead to a model which was congruent with *all* the available information in that there was evidence of heteroskedasticity in the residuals. The model that they report though does have the important property of encompassing rival models which have been proposed for the explanation of relative price variability; see Mizon (1984) for further discussion of the importance of this property in modelling. Hence, the finding that there was a significant positive association between relative price variability and aggregate inflation must still be treated circumspectly.

5. Conclusions

The view that there are many costs associated with inflation, and especially with high and variable rates of inflation, is widely held. Indeed, the governments in many Western economies have in recent years had the lowering of the rate of inflation as a major objective of economic policy. In order to justify these policies it is necessary not only to identify and estimate the *net* costs of inflation per se, but also to assess the costs of the policies adopted to reduce inflation. In this chapter we have reviewed the economic theory and empirical evidence which has been concerned with the costs of inflation. Although there is now a large literature on the economic theory for there being links between inflation and inflation variability and uncertainty, both of which are thought to be costly links, there still remains a gap between the costs of the formal theory and those of intuition. In addition, there is as yet little theory available to enable us to directly estimate the welfare costs of inflation. Finally, we have argued that the empirical relevance of the hypothesised links between inflation and risk, as captured by increased inflation variability and inflation uncertainty, has not yet been satisfactorily established. The costs of inflation is an important topic, and one which is likely to benefit from new research.

References

Aldrich, J. (1988) 'Autonomy', *Oxford Economic Papers*, 41: 15–34.

Amihud, Y. and H. Mendelson (1982) 'Relative price dispersion and economic shocks: An inventory-adjustment approach', *Journal of Money, Credit and Banking*, 14: 390–398.

Ashenfelter, O. and P.R.G. Layard, eds. (1986) *The handbook of labor economics*. Amsterdam: North-Holland.

Bailey, M. (1956) 'The welfare cost of inflationary finance', *Journal of Political Economy*, 64: 93: 93–110.

Barro, R.J. (1970) 'Inflation, the payment period and the demand for money', *Journal of Political Economy*, 78: 1228–1263.

Barro, R.J. (1972) 'Inflationary finance and the welfare cost of inflation', *Journal of Political Economy*, 80: 978–1001.

Barro, R.J. (1978) 'Unanticipated money, output and the price level in the U.S.', *Journal of Political Economy*, 86: 549–580.

Blejer, M.I. (1983) 'On the anatomy of inflation – the variability of relative commodity prices in Argentina', *Journal of Money, Credit and Banking*, 15: 469–482.

Blejer, M.I. and L. Leiderman (1980) 'On the real effects of inflation and price variability: Some empirical evidence', *Review of Economics and Statistics*, 62: 539–544.

Blejer, M.I. and L. Leiderman (1982) 'Inflation and relative price variability in the open economy', *European Economic Review*, 18: 387–402.

Blinder, A.S. (1982) 'The anatomy of double-digit inflation in the 1970's', in R.E. Hall, ed., *Inflation: Causes and effect*, NBER Project Report. Chicago: University of Chicago Press.

Bordo, M.D. (1980) 'The effect of monetary change on commodity prices and the role of long-term contracts', *Journal of Political Economy*, 88: 1088–1109.

Buck, A. and B. Gahlen (1983) 'On the normality of relative price changes', *Economics Letters*, 11: 231–236.

Burmeister, E. and E.S. Phelps (1971) 'Money, public debt, inflation and real interest', *Journal of Money, Credit and Banking*, 3: 153–182.

Cagan, P. (1956), 'The monetary dynamics of hyperinflation', in: M. Friedman, ed., *Studies in the quantity theory of money*. Chicago: University of Chicago Press.

Caplin, A. (1985) 'The variability of aggregate demand with (S, s) inventory policies', *Econometrica*, 53: 1395–1409.

Caplin, A. and D.F. Spulber (1985) 'Inflation, menu costs and price variability', Discussion Paper 1181, Harvard Institute for Economic Research.

Caplin, A. and D.F. Spulber (1987) 'Menu costs and the neutrality of money', *Quarterly Journal of Economics*, 102: 703–726.

Cathcart, C.D. (1974) 'Monetary dynamics, growth and the efficiency of inflation finance', *Journal of Money, Credit and Banking*, 6: 169–190.

Chappell, D. (1981) 'On the revenue maximising rate of inflation', *Journal of Money, Credit and Banking*, 13: 391–392.

Cukierman, A. (1978) 'Heterogeneous inflationary expectations, Fisher's theory of interest, and the allocative efficiency of the bond market', *Economic Letters*, 1: 151–156.

Cukierman, A. (1979) 'The relationship between relative prices and the general price level: A suggested interpretation', *American Economic Review*, 69: 444–447.

Cukierman, A. (1982) 'Relative price variability, inflation, and the allocative efficiency of the price mechanism', *Journal of Monetary Economics*, 9: 131–162.

Cukierman, A. (1984) *Inflation, stagflation, relative prices, and imperfect information*. Cambridge: Cambridge University Press.

Cukierman, A. and P. Wachtel (1979) 'Differential inflationary expectations and the variability of the rate of inflation: Theory and evidence', *American Economic Review*, 72: 508–512.

Danziger, L. (1983) 'Price adjustments with stochastic inflation', *International Economic Review*, 24: 699–707.

Danziger, L. (1984) 'Stochastic inflation and the optimal policy of price adjustment', *Economic Enquiry*, 22: 98–108.

Danziger, L. (1987) 'Inflation, fixed cost of price adjustment, and measurement of relative-price variability: Theory and evidence', *American Economic Review*, 77: 704–713.

Diamond, P. and J. Mirrlees (1971) 'Optimum taxation and public production', *American Economic Review*, 61: 8–27, 261–278.

Drazen, A. (1979) 'The optimal rate of inflation revisited', *Journal of Monetary Economics*, 5: 231–248.

Engle, R.F. (1982) 'Autoregressive conditional heteroskedasticity with estimates of the variance of UK inflation', *Econometrica*, 38: 410–421.

Engle, R.F. (1983) 'Estimates of the variance of US inflation based on the ARCH model', *Journal of Money, Credit and Banking*, 15: 286–301.

Engle, R.F. and C.W.J. Granger (1987) 'Cointegration and error correction: Representation, estimation and testing', *Econometrica*, 55: 251–276.

Feldstein, M.S. (1976) 'Inflation, income taxes, and the rate of interest – a theoretical analysis', *American Economic Review*, 66: 809–820.

Feldstein, M.S. (1979) 'The welfare cost of permanent inflation and optimal short run economic policy', *Journal of Political Economy*, 87: 749–768.

Feldstein, M.S., J. Green and F. Sheshinski (1978) 'Inflation and taxes in a growing economy with debt and equity finance', *Journal of Political Economy*, 86: 553–570.

Feldstein, M. and L. Summers (1979) 'Inflation and the taxaton of capital income in the corporate sector', *National Tax Journal*, 32: 445–470.

Fischer, S. (1981a) 'Relative shocks, relative price variability, and inflation', *Brookings Papers on Economic Activity*, 2: 381–431.

Fischer, S. (1981b) 'Towards an understanding of the costs of inflation, II', in: K. Brunner and A. Meltzer, eds., *The costs and consequences of inflation*, Vol. 15, Carnegie-Rochester Conference Series on Public Policy. Amsterdam: North-Holland, pp. 5–41.

Fischer, S. and F. Modigliani (1975) 'Towards an understanding of the real effects and costs of inflation', *Weltwirtschaftliches Archiv*, 114: 810–833.

Foster, E. (1978) 'The variability of inflation', *Review of Economics and Statistics*, 60: 346–350.

Friedman, M. (1969) 'The optimum supply of money', in: M. Friedman, ed., *The optimum supply of money and other essays*. Chicago: University of Chicago Press.

Friedman, M. (1977) 'Nobel lecture: Inflation and unemployment', *Journal of Political Economy*, 85: 451–472.

Froyen, R.T. and Ward, R.N. (1984) 'The changing relationship between aggregate price and output – the British experience', *Economica*, 51: 53–67.

Glejser, J. (1965) 'Inflation, productivity and relative prices – a statistical study', *The Review of Economics and Statistics*, 47: 76–80.

Graham, F.D. (1930) *Exchange, prices and production in hyperinflations: Germany 1920–1923*. Princeton: Princeton University Press.

Green, J. and E. Sheshinski (1977) 'Budget displacement effects of inflationary finance', *American Economic Review*: 67: 671–682.

Hall, R.E., ed. (1982) *Inflation: Causes and effects*, NBER Project Report, Chicago: University of Chicago Press.

Hartman, D.G. (1979) 'Taxation and the effects of inflation in the real capital stock in an open economy', *International Economic Review*, 20: 417–425.

Hendry, D.F. (1987) *Users manual for PC GIVE*, vesion 5.0. Oxford: Oxford Institute of Economics and Statistics.

Hendry, D.F. and G.E. Mizon (1985) 'Procrustean econometrics: Or stretching and squeezing data', Discussion Paper 69, Centre for Economic Policy Research, London.

Hendry, D.F. and J-F. Richard (1982) 'On the formulation of empirical models in dynamic econometrics', *Journal of Econometrics*, 20: 3–33.

Hercowitz, Z. (1981) 'Money and the price dispersion of relative prices', *Journal of Political Economy*, 89: 328–356.

Hercowitz, Z. (1982) 'Money and price dispersion in the United States', *Journal of Monetary Economics*, 10: 25–37.

Hesselman, L. (1983) 'The macroeconomic role of relative price variability in the USA and the UK'. *Applied Economics*, 15: 225–233.

Katz, E. and J. Rosenberg (1983) 'Inflation variability, real wage variability, and production inefficiency', *Economica*, 50: 469–475.

King, M. (1975) 'Taxation, corporate financial policy, and the cost of capital – a comment', *Journal of Public Economics*, 4: 271–279.

Kuran, T. (1983) 'Asymmetric price rigidity and inflationary bias', *American Economic Review*, 73: 373–382.

Kuran, T. (1986a) 'Price adjustment, anticipated inflation, and output', *Quarterly Journal of Economics*, 101: 407–418.

Kuran, T. (1996b) 'Anticipated inflation and aggregate employment: The case of costly price adjustment', *Economic Enquiry*, 24: 293–311.

Leser, C.V. (1983) 'Short run and long run relative price changes', *Journal of the Royal Statistical Society*, 146: 172–181.

Levi, M.D. and J.H. Makin (1978) 'Anticipated inflation and interest rates: Further interpretations of findings on the Fisher equation', *American Economic Review*, 68: 801–812.

Levi, M.D. and J.H. Makin (1979) 'Phillips, Friedman and the measured impact of inflation on interest', *Journal of Finance*, 34: 35–52.

Logue, D. and T. Willett (1976) 'A note on the relationship between the rate and variability of inflation', *Economica*, 43: 151–158.

Lu, M. and G.E. Mizon (1988) 'Model comparison via sectoral encompassing', paper presented to the ESRC Macroeconomic Research Bureau Conference, University of Warwick, July 1988.

Lucas, R.E. (1972) 'Expectations and the neutrality of money', *Journal of Economic Theory*, 4: 103–124.

Lucas, R.E. (1973) 'Some international evidence on output–inflation tradeoffs', *American Economic Review*, 63: 526–534.

Lucas, R.E. (1981) 'Discussion of Stanley Fischer, "Towards an understanding of the costs of inflation: II" ', in: K. Brunner and A. Meltzer, eds., *The costs and consequences of inflation*, Carnegie-Rochester Conference Series on Public Policy, Vol. 15. Amsterdam: North-Holland, pp. 43–52.

Lucas, R.E. and L.A. Rapping (1969) 'Real wages, employment, and inflation', *Journal of Political Economy*, 77: 721–754.

Marquez, J. and D. Vining (1984) 'Inflation and relative price behavior: A survey of the literature', in: M. Ballobon, ed., *Economic perspectives: An annual survey of economics*, Vol. 3. New York: Harwood Academic Publishers, pp. 1–52.

Marty, A.L. (1976) 'A note on the welfare cost of money creation', *Journal of Monetary Economics*, 2: 121–124.

Marty, A.L. (1978) 'Inflation, taxes and the public debt', *Journal of Money, Credit and Banking*, 10: 437–452.

Mills, F.C. (1927) *The behavior of prices*. New York: National Bureau of Economic Research.

Mizon, G.E. (1984) 'The encompassing approach in econometrics', in: D.F. Hendry and K.F. Wallis, eds., *Econometrics and quantitative economics*. Oxford: Basil Blackwell, pp. 135–172.

Mizon, G.E. and J-F. Richard (1986) 'The encompassing principle and its application to nonnested hypotheses', *Econometrica*, 54: 657–678.

Mizon, G.E. and S.H. Thomas (1988) 'Relative price variability and inflation in an open economy: A monthly model for the UK 1972–1983', in: G.W. McKenzie, ed., *International competitiveness in the UK Economy*. London: Macmillan.

Mizon, G.E., J.C. Safford and S.H. Thomas (1983) 'Relative price variability and inflation: Empirical evidence for the U.K.', Economics Department, University of Southampton, mimeo.

Mizon, G.E., J.C. Safford and S.H. Thomas (1986) 'The distribution of consumer price changes in the UK', Discussion Paper in Economics and Econometrics 8626, University of Southampton.

Moore, J.H. (1984) 'The costs of inflation: Some theoretical issues', Discussion Paper 19, Centre for Economic Policy Research, London.

Mussa, M. (1981) 'Sticky prices and disequilibrium adjustment in a rational model of the inflationary process', *American Economic Review*, 71: 1020–1027.

Naish, H.F. (1986) 'Price adjustment costs and the output–inflation trade-off', *Economica*, 53: 219–230.

Okun, A. (1971) 'The mirage of steady inflation', *Brookings Papers on Economic Analysis*, 2: 435–498.

Okun, A.M. (1975) 'Inflation: Its mechanics and welfare costs', *Brooking Papers*, 2: 351–390.

Pagan, A.R. (1987) 'Three econometric methodologies: A critical appraisal', *Journal of Economic Surveys*, 1: 3–24.

Pagan, A.R., A.D. Hall and P.K. Trivedi (1983) 'Assessing the variability of inflation', *Review of Economic Studies*, 50: 585–596.

Pagan, A.R. and A. Ullah (1986) 'The econometric analysis of models with risk terms', Discussion Paper 127, Centre for Economic Policy Research, London.

Parks, R.W. (1978) 'Inflation and relative price variability', *Journal of Political Economy*, 86: 79–85.

Phelps, E.S. (1973) 'Inflation in a theory of public finance', *Swedish Journal of Economics*, 75: 67–82.

Ramsey, J.B. (1969) 'Tests for specification errors in classical linear least squares regression analysis', *Journal of the Royal Statistical Society*, B31: 350–371.

Rao, C.R. (1952) *Advanced statistical methods in biometric research*. London: Wiley, p. 124.

Rotemberg, J.J. (1982) 'Monopolistic price adjustment and aggregate output', *Review of Economic Studies*, 49: 517–531.

Rotemberg, J.J. (1983a) 'Aggregate consequences of fixed costs of price adjustment', *American Economic Review*, 73: 433–436.

Rotemberg, J.J. (1983b) 'Supply shocks, sticky prices, and monetary policy', *Journal of Money, Credit and Banking*, 15: 489–498.

Rothschild, M. and J.E. Stiglitz (1971) 'Increasing risk I: A definition', *Journal of Economic Theory*, 2: 225–243.

Rothschild, M. and J.E. Stiglitz (1971) 'Increasing risk II: A definition', *Journal of Economic Theory*, 3: 66–84.

Sargan, J.D. (1980) 'A model of wage–price inflation', *Review of Economic Studies*, 67: 97–112.

Sheshinski, E. and Y. Weiss (1977) 'Inflation and the costs of price adjustment', *Review of Economic Studies*, 44: 287–303.

Sheshinski, E. and Y. Weiss (1983) 'Optimum pricing policy under stochastic inflation', *Review of Economic Studies*. 50: 513–529.

Siegel, J. (1978) 'Notes on optimal taxation and the optimal rate of inflation', *Journal of Monetary Economics*, 4: 297–305.

Silver, M.S. (1988) 'Average price, unanticipated prices and price variability in the UK for individual products', *Applied Economics*, 20: 569–594.

Solow, R. (1956) 'A contribution to the theory of economic growth', *Quarterly Journal of Economics*, 70: 65–94.

Tatom, J.A. (1976) 'The welfare costs of inflation', *Federal Reserve Bank of St. Louis Review*, 53: 9–22.

Tatom, J.A. (1979) 'The marginal welfare cost of the revenue from money creation and the "optimal" rate of inflation', *The Manchester School*, 47: 359–368.

Taylor, J.B. (1980a) 'Aggregate dynamics and staggered contracts', *Journal of Political Economy*, 88: 1–23.

Taylor, J.B. (1980b) 'Output and price stability: An international comparison', *Journal of Economic Dynamics and Control*, 2: 109–132.

Taylor, J.B. (1981) 'On the relation between the variability of inflation and the average inflation rate', *Carnegie-Rochester Conference Series on Public Policy*, 15: 57–86.

Tobin, J. (1955) 'A dynamic aggregative model', *Journal of Political Economy*, 23: 103–115.

Tobin, J. (1965) 'Money and economic growth', *Econometrica*, 33: 671–684.

Tobin, J. (1986) 'On the welfare macroeconomics of government financial policy', *Scandinavian Journal of Economics*, 88: 9–24.

Tower, E. (1971) 'More on the welfare cost of inflationary finance', *Journal of Money, Credit and Banking*, 3: 850–860.

Vining, D.R. and T.C. Elwertowski (1976) 'The relationship between relative prices and the general price level', *American Economic Review*, 66: 699–708.

White, H. (1980) 'A heteroskedasticity-consistent convariance matrix estimator and direct test for heteroskedasticity', *Econometrica*. 48: 817–838.

Chapter 20

THE OPTIMUM QUANTITY OF MONEY

MICHAEL WOODFORD*

University of Chicago

Contents

*I would like to thank Tim Kehoe and David Levine for extremely helpful discussions of the issues treated here, and Buz Brock, Robert Lucas, Bennett McCallum, Julio Rotemberg, and the editors for helpful comments on an earlier draft. I would also like to thank the Institute for Economic Analysis, Universitat Autònoma de Barcelona, and the Department of Economics, European University Institute, Florence, for their hospitality during the writing of the first draft, and the National Science Foundation and the Graduate School of Business, University of Chicago, for research support.

Handbook of Monetary Economics, Volume II, Edited by B.M. Friedman and F.H. Hahn
© *Elsevier Science Publishers B.V., 1990*

0. Introduction

Milton's Friedman's (1969) doctrine regarding the "optimum quantity of money" – according to which an optimal monetary policy would involve a steady contraction of the money supply at a rate sufficient to bring the nominal interest rate down to zero – is undoubtedly one of the most celebrated propositions in modern monetary theory, probably *the* most celebrated proposition in what one might call "pure" monetary theory, by which I mean the branch of the subject which abstracts from business cycle phenomena. It has spawned an extensive literature criticizing and extending Friedman's analysis, and no small amount of controversy.

The reasons for the degree of interest in Friedman's argument are not difficult to discern. On the one hand, Friedman deploys some simple but deep ideas from the modern theory of competitive equilibrium, having to do with the characterization of a Pareto optimal allocation of resources and the interpretation of certain necessary conditions for efficiency in terms of equilibrium prices and rates of return, and puts them to use in an argument whose simplicity and elegance suggest that the conclusions reached might be of reasonably general validity. And on the other hand, the conclusions that Friedman reaches are of apparent relevance to some of the most hotly debated issues of practical economic policymaking, and his proposed policy rule is of such striking simplicity that its implications for practical policy are quite clear.

The discussion to follow will show that the matter is considerably more complicated than Friedman's simple argument would suggest. One consequence of this is that Friedman's promise of a straightforward link between theoretical argument and practical policy analysis will not in fact be borne out. The quantitative importance of the various effects discussed above that work opposite to the one stressed by Friedman is hard to judge on the basis of the kinds of simple examples presented below. Further work based upon numerical simulations is probably necessary in order to get much sense of this; for the kinds of simplifying assumptions that have to be made in order to allow analytical solutions to be derived for the examples discussed below often severely limit one's ability to directly apply the results to actual economies. It is probably time that work in this area turned more toward computational issues. In any event, the general equilibrium literature has shown that the question of optimal monetary policy cannot be be settled – in the sense of producing explicit quantitative advice for policymakers – without needing to specify in relative detail a model of how money is used in the economy.

It is reasonably certain, of course, that the optimal rate of money growth, even taking into account the sort of factors discussed here, will not be too large. Surely high rates of money growth are mainly destructive, and so at least in broad outline Friedman's conclusions remain important. As far as the choice between moderate deflation and moderate inflation is concerned, there are many considerations beyond Friedman's to be taken into account. But even Friedman would not attach too much significance to the choice between different relatively low steady rates of money growth. (The numerical estimates of Kehoe et al. (1989) find extremely small welfare gains from an optimal rate of inflation even in cases where the optimum does involve a positive rate of money growth.) Doubtless other issues such as whether or not cyclical variation in money growth is superior to steady money growth are of greater practical importance than the choice between alternative low steady rates of inflation, with which the literature on the "optimum quantity of money" has largely been concerned.

As a result, conclusions from this literature for practical policy analysis have been few thus far. Nonetheless, the sort of theoretical elaboration to which the literature has led is a necessary first step in the development of a monetary theory that could be relied upon to provide insight into more important questions. A sound understanding of the behavior of monetary economies in an idealized state of stationary equilibrium is surely necessary before one can begin to think clearly about the adjustment to shocks and stabilization policies, and we will see that even this preliminary problem is full of unsuspected complexities. It is shown, for example, that treating the demand for real money balances as a function simply of the cost of holding such balances, instead of explicitly modeling the interdependence of money demand with other supply and demand decisions, can lead to conclusions of doubtful empirical relevance; that taking explicit account of the fact that the usefulness of money requires that money balances be changing hands in response to changes in conditions, rather than modeling the entire money supply as being always held by the same representative consumer, can make a great difference for one's conclusions about the effects of monetary policy upon the real allocation of resources; that taking explicit account of the distinct interests of successive generations, rather than modeling the economy as a collection of infinite lived consumers, can have important effects for the welfare evaluation of alternative policies, even when the policies in question are not explicitly concerned with life-cycle or intergenerational issues; that the optimal monetary policy is crucially dependent upon what set of fiscal policies are available for use in conjunction with it (i.e. what sort of taxes are reduced or transfers are made possible by the government's revenue from seignorage); that rational expectations equilibrium is often indeterminate in monetary economies and that the choice of policy can affect whether this is so or not; that monetary policies formulated in terms of a target sequence of interest rates are not equivalent to policies formulated in terms of a target sequence for the money supply, so that it does not suffice to consider only alternative policies of the latter sort; and that monetary policies formulated in terms of a target sequence of interest rates are not necessarily "underdetermined" or specially prone to result in price-level indeterminacy. All of these findings are likely to be of importance as we seek to understand more subtle issues of monetary policy with the help of even more complex models.

I will not here attempt to survey all of the contributions to the debate opened by Friedman's paper; a useful résumé of the early literature is provided by Bewley (1980). My concern will instead be to set out what I consider to be the current state of knowledge regarding the problem. One issue regarding the history of thought, however, is perhaps worth brief attention. I will throughout this chapter associate the doctrine being discussed with the name of Friedman. In fact, as Bewley points out, many authors had previously discussed at least some aspects of this doctrine prior to the appearance of Friedman's essay; particular mention should be made of Samuelson (1968), which presents a formal model. Nonetheless, it seems proper to identify the doctrine with Friedman. Not only does Friedman take the analysis further than Samuelson, particularly with reference to the policy prescription that I have called the Friedman Rule – Samuelson (1968) notes that competitive equilibrium would be inefficient in the case of a positive nominal interest rate, but does not suggest a remedy, although Samuelson (1969) indicates an awareness of the possibility of bringing down nominal interest rates through contraction of the money supply – but Friedman is largely responsible for the degree of attention that the proposition came to receive, due to his bold assertion of its implications for practical policy.

1. The argument for the Friedman Rule

In order better to consider the degree of general validity of Friedman's argument, it is useful to distinguish two (distinct though not unrelated) theses, both of which seem to be implied by what Friedman says.

Friedman Proposition (*Weak Form*)

In order for competitive equilibrium in a monetary economy to result in an efficient allocation of resources, it is necessary that the nominal rate of interest be zero, or at any rate (in the case of stochastic returns on some assets) that there be no asset whose nominal yield is always non-negative and sometimes positive, so that the returns to this asset strictly dominate the return to holding money.

Friedman Proposition (Strong Form)

The best monetary policy, from the point of view of maximizing the welfare of consumers (the welfare of some representative consumer or, presumably, some measure of average welfare in the case of heterogeneous consumers), would be to maintain a rate of growth of the money supply that is so low (quite likely involving steady contraction of the money supply) as to make the nominal interest rate (on assets with a riskless nominal return, such as Treasury securities) as low as possible (typically, zero).

The strong form of the Friedman proposition is often stated in a form that specifies a particular rate of contraction of the money supply in terms of "real" features of the economy, such as the rate of time preference of consumers or the real rate of return on physical capital. Friedman, indeed, states his proposal in these terms, for he takes the view that the equilibrium real rate of interest (at least in a long-run stationary equilibrium) is independent of the rate of money growth (and determined by "real" factors of the kind just mentioned). It then follows from the elementary quantity-theoretic proposition that the rate of inflation should be equal to the rate of money supply growth (minus some rate of growth of the demand for real balances, if one likes, that should also in a stationary equilibrium be independent of the rate of growth of the money supply) that in order to reduce the nominal interest rate to zero it is necessary to contract the money supply at a rate equal to the equilibrium real rate of interest (minus the rate of growth of the demand for real balances). I have not stated even the "strong form" of the Friedman proposition in so strong a form as this, because the problems with the strong form that I wish to discuss below have nothing to do with the by now well-known fact that "superneutrality" propositions of the kind assumed by the Friedman (i.e. the notion that there is an equilibrium real rate of interest that can be defined independently of the rate of money supply growth or other aspects of monetary policy) are valid only under quite special circumstances.[1] Instead, I wish to consider whether it is really the case that the highest level of welfare is associated with so low a rate of money growth as is necessary to reduce the nominal rate of interest to zero, whatever that rate of money growth may be.

It should also be noted that the strong form proposition that I have stated refers to maximizing some measure of average consumer welfare. Some authors [e.g. Bewley (1980, 1983)] have interpreted Friedman's view to be (and have themselves discussed a proposition that would assert) that a suffici-

---

[1]This is, for example, the main criticism of the Friedman proposition in Stein (1970). For a summary of reasons why superneutrality need not obtain, see Orphanides and Solow, Chapter 6 in this Handbook.

ently low rate of money supply growth can bring about a Pareto optimal equilibrium. Such a claim would be both stronger and weaker than the claim I have stated, in certain respects. I have chosen the formulation given here because, on the one hand, it is too easy to provide counter-examples to the other sort of proposition. One need only assume the existence of some kind of market imperfection that gives rise to inefficiency of some kind that cannot be cured through monetary policy, and the proposed claim would be refuted; but this would tell one nothing about whether a steady contraction of the money supply might still not be welfare improving. And on the other hand, as I will argue below, even in those cases in which a sufficient rate of contraction of the money supply suffices to make possible a Pareto optimal equilibrium, it is not clear that such an equilibrium should be preferable to an inefficient equilibrium attainable through some high rate of money supply growth; for as examples in Subsection 2.3 demonstrate, this might require that weight placed on the utilities of some consumers relative to those of others be arbitrarily large.

To be brief, I will argue that the weak form of the Friedman proposition is valid for a wide range of types of monetary economies, but that the conditions under which the strong form is valid are considerably more special. Hence, the Friedman Rule for the rate of growth of the money supply can only be argued to characterize optimal policy under special circumstances. In particular, a number of reasons will be given for which it can be desirable to allow money growth and inflation greater than is specified by the Friedman Rule, temporarily or even permanently.

In arguing that passage from the weak to the strong form of the proposition requires quite special assumptions, I will be elaborating upon a line of criticism that was first suggested in early responses to Friedman's paper by Clower (1970) and especially Hahn (1971, 1973). These early critics of Friedman's view, while identifying a number of respects in which the cases in which the result could easily be shown to be valid were extremely special, and cogently arguing that a desirable monetary theory ought to incorporate a number of other features, did not succeed in explicitly demonstrating that a more adequate monetary theory could be developed and that it would lead to conclusions different from Friedman's. I will restrict my attention here to describing the various explicit models yielding conclusions different from Friedman's that have been presented in the literature to date, without, of course, meaning to deny that important features of the role of money in actual economies might fail to be captured by any of the models yet developed. I will also attempt, to the extent possible, to relate the various known Friedman and anti-Friedman cases to one another and where possible to give some sense of the considerations that should lead one to consider one sort of model or another to be a useful description of actual monetary economies and actual monetary policy choices.

Subsection 1.1 argues for the general validity of the weak form of the Friedman proposition. Subsection 1.2 then discusses some special cases in which the strong form can also be shown to be valid. Cases in which the strong form of the Friedman proposition is invalid are then treated in Section 2. In all of the cases treated in that section, the problem is formulated as one of choosing between alternative possible steady rates of money growth on the basis of a comparison of the stationary equilibria associated with them, and in all of these cases lower rates of money growth are indeed associated with a lower stationary equilibrium value for the nominal interest rate; but it is shown that a nominal interest rate as low as that called for by Friedman may not be desirable. Section 3, on the contrary, takes up the issue of whether the goal of a low nominal interest rate is always best served by a policy of low money growth, and whether the problem of an optimal monetary policy need be formulated as one of choosing an optimal rate of growth of the money supply, instead of, for example, choosing an interest rate target.

1.1. Efficiency and the rate of return on money

In order to see why a lower rate of return on money than on other assets (i.e. a positive nominal interest rate on other assets, supposing that the nominal yield on monetary assets is fixed at zero, as for example is true of currency) will quite generally indicate a failure of the allocation of resources in the economy to be efficient (Pareto optimal), it is necessary to consider how it could be possible for such a rate of return differential to exist in equilibrium. One simple reason would be a supposition that money balances yield something of value to the possessor in addition to the value of the goods for which they can be exchanged at some future date. This idea is reflected in one of the most often-used formal models of a monetary economy, the Sidrauski–Brock model (presented in the following subsection), by writing the level of real money balances held by a given consumer as an argument of his utility function along with his levels of consumption and leisure, and supposing that at least in the case of a sufficiently low level of real balances, utility is increasing in the level of real balances. In the case of such a model, a positive nominal interest rate on some non-monetary asset (that does not similarly yield utility to its possessor in addition to serving as a store of value) will exist in equilibrium only if the consumers who hold money have a positive marginal utility of additional real money balances in at least some possible future state. But a positive marginal utility of money is inconsistent with Pareto optimality, insofar as real money balances are not a scarce resource; the quantity in existence is in principle unlimited, as one simply needs for goods to be assigned sufficiently low money prices. Hence, the weak form of the Friedman proposition would

apply to such an economy. This is, indeed, more or less the argument that
Friedman gives.

It is not necessary, in interpreting a model of this kind, to suppose that the
rate of return differential results from a pure *preference* for money balances
over other forms of wealth. Instead, the usual interpretation would be that
holding real money balances reduces the degree to which carrying out transactions (e.g. purchasing the goods that one consumes) requires one to expend
either physical resources (the frequently mentioned "shoe-leather costs") or
time [as in the "shopping time" model of Kimbrough (1986a, 1986b)] that
would otherwise have alternative uses. Explicit representation of the nature of
these real costs of carrying out transactions does not in any way affect the
above conclusion: given that real money balances are not scarce, a Pareto
optimal allocation of resources must involve the use of real money balances to
economize on these other resources to the fullest extent possible, which in turn
will imply that this cannot be a reason for money to be dominated in rate of
return.

A closely related model of equilibrium money demand, which is sometimes
regarded as providing a more explicit account of how money balances can be of
value, involves the assumption that certain goods can be purchased only in
exchange for money, which money must have been held at the beginning of the
period in which the purchase is to be made. [The first formal model incorporating such a "cash-in-advance" constraint was proposed by Clower (1967); a
recent application of the idea to issues of the kind with which we are concerned
here is provided by Lucas and Stokey (1983).] This idea too allows for the
possibility of an equilibrium with a positive nominal interest rate, but it will
also generally be the case that a positive nominal interest rate implies
inefficiency. Suppose that the cash-in-advance constraint applies to purchases
of some goods (the "cash goods" of Lucas and Stokey) but not to others (their
"credit goods"). Let λ_t^i denote the marginal utility to consumer i of an
additional unit of money at the beginning of period t. If u_{1t}^i denotes the
marginal utility to consumer i of an additional unit of consumption of some
cash good in period t, u_{2t}^i denotes the corresponding marginal utility of some
credit good, and p_{1t} and p_{2t} denote the money prices of the two goods in period
t, then among the first-order conditions for optimal consumption behavior by
consumer i will be the relations:

$$u_{1t}^i = \lambda_t^i p_{1t} , \tag{1.1a}$$

$$u_{2t}^i = E_t[\lambda_{t+1}^i] p_{2t} , \tag{1.1b}$$

$$\lambda_t^i \geq E_t[\lambda_{t+1}^i] . \tag{1.1c}$$

(Here I am assuming that consumer *i* consumes a positive quantity of both goods 1 and 2 in period *t*, or at any rate that there is no binding non-negativity constraint on his choices of how much of either good to consume.) The different time subscripts in conditions (1.1a) and (1.1b) reflect the fact that an increase in consumption of good 1 and would require a diversion of beginning-of-period money balances from other uses, while an increase in consumption of good 2 will only mean a reduction of end-of-period money balances, since cash in advance is not required for the latter purchase. The expectation occurs in condition (1.1b) to allow for the fact that the marginal utility of money balances at the beginning of the following period may depend upon the realization of random variables that are not yet known when period *t* purchases are made. Condition (1.1c) holds because one possible use of beginning-of-period money balances is to simply hold them over into the following period. If (1.1c) holds with strict inequality, the cash-in-advance constraint is binding.

One obvious way of defining a nominal interest rate for such an economy would be to suppose that there is a competitive market for one-period money loans, such that money loaned in period *t* can be used by the borrower to purchase cash goods in period *t*, and that the money repaid can be used by the creditor to purchase cash goods in period *t* + 1. (Lucas and Stokey discuss in some detail the market organization and timing of transactions that may be assumed to make sense of this.) If the nominal interest rate i_t on such loans is fixed at the time of the loan, then in equilibrium this rate will have to satisfy:

$$1 + i_t = \lambda_t^i / E_t[\lambda_{t+1}^i] . \tag{1.2}$$

Thus, the nominal interest rate is positive if and only if the cash-in-advance constraint binds.

Now suppose that there exists a well-defined technological marginal rate of transformation between goods 1 and 2; then in a competitive equilibrium, a profit-maximizing choice of the mix of goods produced will imply that this marginal rate of transformation will equal the price ratio p_{1t}/p_{2t}. But a necessary condition for a Pareto optimal allocation of resources is that for each consumer *i*, the marginal rate of transformation equal the consumer's marginal rate of substitution, u_{1t}^i/u_{2t}^i. Hence, a necessary condition for a competitive equilibium to be Pareto optimal is $u_{1t}^i/u_{2t}^i = p_{1t}/p_{2t}$, which from (1.1a) and (1.1b) implies $E_t[\lambda_{t+1}^i] = \lambda_t^i$. From (1.2), this then implies a nominal interest rate equal to zero. A positive nominal interest rate implies inefficiency insofar as it will mean that cash goods will be more expensive for consumers relative to credit goods, than is true of their relative resource costs, so that consumers will substitute away from cash goods to a greater extent than is consistent with efficiency.

It should be obvious from this sketch that counter-examples are possible. For example, if there are no "credit goods", as in the economy described in chapter 5 of Sargent (1987), then no distortion of the choice between cash and credit goods occurs, and equilibria with positive nominal interest rates can be Pareto optimal. Sargent's example is thus a counter-example to even the weak form of the Friedman proposition. Counter-examples could also be given in which there are both cash and credit goods, but no technological possibility of transformation between the two. Consider, for example, an economy in which both types of goods are in fixed supply, given by the endowments of consumers, and in which consumers must sell all of their endowments of the cash goods, purchasing any of these goods that they themselves wish to consume on the cash market. Then again there is no distortion, since all consumers face the same relative prices for all goods, and there are no producer prices that these need to be equal to. However, these counter-examples are plainly extremely special. The non-existence of credit goods, as in the Sargent example, requires that one assume that the supply of output is fixed exogenously by an endowment; for if one were to assume instead an endogenous supply of labor which could be used to produce the various kinds of consumption goods, then leisure would be a "credit good", and the existence of an endogenous labor supply would suffice to make any equilibrium with a positive nominal interest rate inefficient. Similarly, even in the case of the pure endowment economy, it is essential for the counter-example that no consumer be allowed to consume any of his own endowment of any cash good without paying cash for it; otherwise [as in the model of Grandmont and Younes (1973)], an equilibrium with a positive nominal interest rate would generally be inefficient, since a consumer who was a net purchaser of some cash good and another consumer who was a net seller of that same good would face different relative prices. This kind of counter-example also depends upon an assumption that the division between cash goods and credit goods be the same for all consumers, whereas, as Lucas and Stokey point out, this need not be the case.

Similar conclusions are reached in the case of models of the demand for fiat money that do not so directly postulate a special role for money as opposed to other assets, but that allow money to earn a different rate of return in equilibrium because of different costs of transactions involving money as opposed to those involving other assets. One simple example of such an alternative model is the "legal restrictions" model used by Sargent and Wallace (1982) and Bryant and Wallace (1984), and discussed in Subsections 2.3, 3.1, and 3.2 below. In this model the coexistence of money with other assets earning a higher return (bonds) is explained by the existence of a legal restriction upon the minimum denomination in which bonds can be issued (and in which the liabilities of any intermediaries that purchase bonds can be issued), so that small savers are forced to hold money while large savers can hold the higher-yielding bonds. But in such a model a higher return on bonds implies a different marginal rate of substitution between present and future consumption for consumers who issue bonds or hold bonds, on the one hand, and consumers who hold money on the other; hence Pareto efficiency would require that the returns on money and bonds be equalized, i.e. a zero nominal interest rate on bonds.

Another type of legal restriction that might account for the coexistence of money with assets earning a higher return is the existence of reserve requirements for certain kinds of financial intermediaries, that require these intermediaries to hold a certain fraction of their assets in the form of money. [This sort of theory of money demand is developed by Fama (1980), and is used in addressing issues relating to optimal monetary policy by Freeman (1987) and Smith (1988). An example of such a model is discussed further in Sections A.4 and A.5 in the appendix] One must, of course, assume that for certain purposes financing by means of the regulated intermediaries is indispensable, so that the reserve requirement simply does not mean that these institutions cannot afford to operate. If, for example, one supposes that accumulation of physical capital can be financed only by the regulated intermediaries (e.g. because an indivisibility prevents small savers from being able to own capital directly, and a legal restriction prevents other kinds of intermediaries from serving this function), then small savers who hold the liabilities of competitive regulated intermediaries are effectively able to accumulate physical capital only if they are willing to hold real money balances along with it in a certain fixed proportion. [Smith (1988), in fact, treats the reserve requirement as applying directly to savers' accumulation of capital, dispensing with intermediaries altogether.] In such a model, a Pareto optimal equilibrium will in general require that consumers' marginal rate of substitution between consumption in one period and in the following period be equal to the technological marginal rate of transformation between those two goods, which is to say, to the real return on physical capital. But consumers' marginal rate of substitution will be equated with the real return on the asset that they are able to accumulate, namely the liabilities of the regulated intermediaries, and this return will be a weighted average of the returns on money and on physical capital. Hence, the allocation of resources must be efficient unless money earns the same return as physical capital, so that the nominal return on physical capital (and on the loans made by the intermediary) is zero.

Another example of such a model would be one in which some consumers are not able to trade the higher-yielding assets in certain periods, while money can always be exchanged for goods. For example, in the sort of model considered by Rotemberg (1984) and Grossman and Weiss (1983), it is assumed that a higher-yielding asset coexists with money, but that some consumers can only purchase or sell the asset in odd periods, while the others can only purchase or sell it in even periods. (The idea is that non-convex transactions costs make unprofitable more frequent asset market transactions, but the formal model simply imposes these restrictions upon the timing of access to the asset market.) Then a consumer who has access to the asset market only in odd periods may divide his wealth in such a period between money and the higher-yielding asset, the money balances being intended to allow him to consume in excess of his endowment in the following period, when he is unable to sell any of his holdings of the higher-yielding asset. This possibility also obviously requires that consumers be unable to borrow in the periods in which they do not have access to the asset market, which one may represent by assuming a non-negativity constraint on money balances. In such a model, the existence of a higher return on the other asset again implies that equilibrium will under very general conditions be inefficient. Efficiency will (except in the case of a corner solution) require that the marginal rates of substitution (MRS) between consumption in different periods be the same for all consumer types. But then the MRS between any two consecutive periods must equal the real return on money for all consumers, since this is true for those that hold money from the one period to the next. It follows that the MRS for a given consumer between two periods in which he has access to the asset market must equal the real return on money over that time interval; but it must also equal the real return over the same time interval on the alternative asset.

Finally, it is worth mentioning a possible extension of the weak form of the Friedman proposition to certain economies in which money is the only asset. Bewley (1980, 1983) presents a formal treatment of Friedman's ideas for the case of an economy in which money (the only asset) is held in order to allow consumers to alter their time pattern of consumption relative to their pattern of endowment income. Since there is no nominal interest rate in an economy in which money is the only asset,[2] Bewley makes not reference to what I have called the weak form of the Friedman proposition; instead he is simply concerned directly with the issue of the welfare consequences of a rate of contraction of the money supply equal to consumers' rate of time preference. This work might not seem to fit easily the analytical framework I have chosen to use here, both because of my emphasis on the importance of distinguishing between the weak and strong forms of Friedman's doctrine, and because even my "strong form" of the Friedman proposition refers to a nominal interest rate. But it is possible to state both "weak form" and "strong form" propositions analogous to those given above for this kind of economy as well, and again it turns out that the weak form has considerably more general validity.

---

[2] In fact, Bewley refers to a nominal interest rate of another sort than that referred to in my statement of the Friedman proposition – a nominal rate of interest that the monetary authority pays on money balances. The relationship of this sort of nominal interest rate to the Friedman condition for efficiency is taken up below, especially in Subsection 3.3.

Statement of such propositions for Bewley's type of model (discussed further in Subsection 2.2 below) will accordingly increase the degree of continuity between our treatment of the various types of models of the role of money.

In Bewley's model, as with the models discussed above, optimizing consumer behavior will generally mean that for any consumer i who holds money at the end of period t, there must hold a first-order condition of the form

$$1 = E_t[R_m(t, t+1)\text{MRS}^i(t, t+1)^{-1}], \qquad (1.3)$$

where I here am allowing both the return to holding money and the marginal rate of substitution to be possibly stochastic, i.e. dependent upon the realization of some period $t + 1$ state variable. (This condition assumes that consumption is non-zero, or at any rate that no non-negativity constraint on consumption is binding, either in period t or in any possible state in period $t + 1$. This assumption will in fact not hold for all of the examples of Bewley economies discussed below, and hence the first-order conditions for an optimal consumption program given below do not always have this form. Nonetheless, it should be obvious that the case assumed here is not very restrictive; it is rather the examples presented below that represent quite special cases.) On the other hand, in the case of a consumer who holds no money at the end of period t, the right-hand side of (1.3) may be larger than 1, because of the existence of a constraint requiring that each consumer's money balances be non-negative at the end of each period; this means that consumers are unable to borrow against future endowment income. If for some consumer j, the right-hand side of (1.3) is larger than 1, we can say that *his borrowing constraint is binding in period t*. As usual, a Pareto optimal allocation of resources will require that $\text{MRS}^i(t, t + 1)$ be the same for all i, in all periods t and $t + 1$, and for all possible realizations of the random state variables. Hence, an equilibrium can in general involve a Pareto optimal allocation of resources only if no consumer's borrowing constraint ever binds, under any possible realization of the state variables.[3]

Now it is possible, in the case of a given equilibrium, to speak of the value of assets that are not in fact traded, by asking at what price the various consumers would be willing to buy to sell such an asset if they were able to. Hence, we can define a nominal interest rate for a Bewley economy by considering the price at which consumers would be willing to buy or sell bonds promising to pay a fixed quantity of money in the following period, regardless of the state realized then. Consumers who hold money at the end of period t would be willing to buy such bonds even if they paid a zero nominal interest rate,

---

[3]This is only true, of course, if the Pareto optimal allocation cannot involve a corner solution, i.e. an allocation in which some consumer type is at his lowest feasible level of consumption in some period. An exception is the Levine example discussed in Subsection 2.2 below.

whereas consumers whose borrowing constraint binds in period t would be willing to sell such bonds at some positive nominal interest rate. If we define "the" nominal interest rate in period t (call it i_t) to be the supremum of the set of interest rates at which some consumer would be willing to sell such a bond if he were able to, then

$$1 + i_t = \sup_i \mathrm{E}_t[R_m(t, t+1)\mathrm{MRS}^i(t, t+1)^{-1}]. \tag{1.4}$$

The advantage of this definition is that we have then established the general validity of the following analog of the weak form of the Friedman proposition for Bewley economies: *An equilibrium is Pareto optimal only if the nominal interest rate defined in (1.4) is always zero.* We can also then reformulate Bewley's inquiry as an attempt to determine whether or not one can formally demonstrate a strong form Friedman proposition, according to which it should be possible to bring about a Pareto optimal equilibrium by choosing a sufficiently low rate of money growth. The idea behind such a claim would be that a high enough real return on money balances might allow the existence of an equilibrium in which consumers always hold large enough real balances for their borrowing constraints never to bind. As is discussed further in Subsection 2.2, there are special cases in which this strong form proposition can be shown to be correct, but also others in which it is not.

1.2. A case in which the Friedman Rule is optimal

The strong form of the Friedman proposition hardly follows trivially from the weak form discussed in the previous subsection. In certain special cases, however, Friedman's argument can be shown to be valid. One of the simplest (and best known) examples is due to Brock (1975). [For further development of this type of model, see Benhabib and Bull (1983).]

Brock considers the type of explicit general equilibrium model of a monetary economy first used by Sidrauski (1967). In such an economy there exist a large number of identical infinitely-lived consumers, each of whom seeks to maximize

$$\sum_{t=0}^{\infty} \beta^t U(c_t, n_t, M_t/P_t), \tag{1.5}$$

where c_t represents consumption in period t, n_t represents labor supply, M_t represents (nominal outside) money balances held at the beginning of period t, and P_t represents the price of the consumption good in terms of money in period t. Let us suppose that U is strictly increasing in consumption, strictly decreasing in labor supply, and strictly increasing in real money balances as long as $M_t/P_t < m^*(c_t, n_t)$, but non-increasing for $M_t/P_t \geq m^*(c_t, n_t)$, where $m^*(c_t, n_t)$ represents the finite level of real money balances with which consumers will be "satiated with liquidity" (Friedman's "optimum quantity of money"). Also, let us assume that U is strictly concave and twice continuously differentiable in all three arguments. Finally, let the discount factor β lie between zero and one.

The representative consumer faces an infinite sequence of budget constraints of the form:

$$P_t c_t + M_{t+1} + B_{t+1} \leq W_t n_t + M_t + (1 + i_t) B_t + T_t , \qquad (1.6)$$

where W_t represents the nominal wage, B_t represents the quantity of one-period bonds held at the beginning of period t (valued at their purchase price in terms of money in the previous period), i_t represents the nominal interest rate paid on bonds maturing in period t, and T_t represents the nominal value of lump-sum transfers paid to the representative consumer in period t (negative in the case of lump-sum taxation). If we assume a simple technology according to which one unit of labor can be converted into one unit of the perishable consumption good, then goods market clearing in period t requires that

$$c_t + g_t = n_t , \qquad (1.7a)$$

where g_t represents the level of government purchases in period t. This technology also implies that in competitive equilibrium:

$$W_t = P_t . \qquad (1.7b)$$

Finally, if we assume that the government neither issues nor purchases bonds, clearing of the bond market will require $B_t = 0$ each period, since the representative consumer will be neither able to borrow nor lend. (The bond market is included in our formalism in order to be able to define a nominal interest rate in terms of which to discuss the Friedman propositions stated above.)

Let us consider the set of possible stationary equilibria of such an economy, i.e. equilibria in which consumption, labor supply, government purchases, real money balances (M_t/P_t), the nominal interest rate, the real quantity of lump-sum transfers or taxes (T_t/P_t), the real wage (W_t/P_t), and the rate of inflation (P_{t+1}/P_t) are all constant over time. Let these constant values be denoted c, n, g, m, i, t, w, and $1 + \pi$. In a stationary equilibrium these quantities must satisfy:

$$\frac{U_n}{U_c} (c, n, m) = w , \qquad (1.8a)$$

$$\frac{U_m}{U_c}(c, n, m) = i \,, \tag{1.8b}$$

$$1 + i = \beta^{-1}(1 + \pi) \,, \tag{1.8c}$$

$$c + m\pi = wn + t \,, \tag{1.8d}$$

$$c + g = n \,, \tag{1.8e}$$

$$i \geq 0 \,, \tag{1.8f}$$

$$w = 1 \,. \tag{1.8g}$$

Conditions (1.8a)–(1.8c) follow from the first-order conditions for optimal choice of labor supply, money balances, and borrowing or lending, under the assumption of stationarity. Condition (1.8d) follows from the consumer budget constraint (1.6) under the assumption of stationarity (given that the loan market clears with $B_t = 0$ each period), and condition (1.8e) from the market-clearing condition (1.7a). Condition (1.8f) does not actually follow from our assumptions above (a negative nominal interest rate could exist if consumers held real money balances in excess of m^*), but it seems reasonable to ignore the possibility of equilibria of that kind, since it would only be necessary to assume the existence of *one* consumer with zero cost of holding additional money balances in order for a negative nominal interest rate to be inconsistent with the absence of pure arbitrage profits for that consumer (who could borrow an unbounded amount at the negative interest rate in order to finance holdings of money balances earning a zero nominal interest rate). Condition (1.8g) follows from (1.7b). It is included as a separate equation here because when distorting taxes are considered in Subsection 2.1, (1.8g) must be modified while (1.8a) continues to hold. Finally, we should add to these conditions the stipulation that if real money balances are indeed constant over time, π must be the constant rate of growth of the money supply as well as the constant rate of inflation.

Conversely, any set of constant values (where c, n, and m are positive) satisfying (1.8a)–(1.8g) will represent a possible stationary equilibrium. The different such solutions represent the different possible stationary equilibria among which the government may choose by choosing an appropriate rate of money growth, supposing that the level of government purchases has been independently determined upon other grounds. Note that by choosing the rate of money growth, the government can directly choose the stationary value of π; (1.8a)–(1.8e) and (1.8g) then determine the stationary values of c, n, m, i, w, and t, and (1.8f) will be satisfied assuming that the rate of money growth satisfies $1 + \pi \geq \beta$. The government has only one variable to choose here (given g), since the choice of a desired rate of growth of the money supply commits it to bringing about lump-sum transfers or taxes of exactly the size necessary to bring that about. (Rather than bothering to present conditions under which the solution for the other variables must be unique for each choice of π, I will simply assume that the government can in any event bring about any of the possible stationary equilibria that it likes.) Note also that a consequence of (1.8c) is that the stationary real rate of return on bonds is unaffected by the rate of money growth; hence there is a unique rate of money growth that results in a stationary equilibrium with a nominal interest rate equal to zero, and, as Friedman argues, it is a contraction of the money supply at a rate equal to the rate of time preference of the representative consumer, i.e. $\pi = \beta - 1$. This is the rate of contraction prescribed by the Friedman Rule.

We can formulate Friedman's problem as the determination of which among the possible choices of π results in values of c, n, and m that lead to the highest level of utility for the representative consumer, i.e. to the highest value of $U(c, n, m)$. The problem is easily solved, for one observes that the highest technologically feasible level of utility can in fact be obtained through a stationary equilibrium belonging to this class. The only technological constraint upon feasible allocations $\{c_t, n_t, m_t\}$ is that $c_t + g \leq n_t$ every period. Because of the additive separability of the utility function (1.5) and the lack of any intertemporal linkages in the feasibility constraint, the choice of optimal feasible allocations reduces to the independent choice of (c_t, n_t, m_t) in each period t to maximize $U(c_t, n_t, m_t)$ subject to the constraint $c_t + g \leq n_t$. The optimal allocation is thus obviously a stationary one. Because of the concavity of U, under standard boundary conditions on U this problem will have an interior solution characterized by:

$$U_m(c, n, m) = 0 , \tag{1.9a}$$

$$U_c(c, n, m) + U_n(c, n, m) = 0 . \tag{1.9b}$$

Conditions (1.9) will furthermore have a unique solution, for strict concavity implies that there cannot be more than one point on the hyperplane $c + g = n$ that is tangent to an indifference curve of U. Comparison with conditions (1.8) indicates that this stationary allocation is in fact the unique stationary equilibrium allocation associated with the rate of money growth $\pi = \beta - 1$, the rate of contraction of the money supply called for by Friedman. Thus, for this sort of economy (at least if one ignores the possible existence of equilibria other than the stationary one – an issue taken up in Subsection 2.4 below) the Friedman Rule would indeed be the optimal monetary policy in a quite unambiguous sense.

A closely related model, albeit one that provides a more explicit representation of the way in which holding real money balances allows consumers to increase their level of utility, is the cash-in-advance model of Wilson (1979) and Lucas and Stokey (1983). The nature of the cash-in-advance constraint has been described in the previous subsection. In addition to the specifications already mentioned, Lucas and Stokey assume the existence of a large number of identical infinitely-lived consumers, each of whom seeks to maximize

$$\sum_{t=0}^{\infty} \beta^{t} V(c_{1t}, c_{2t}, n_{t}) \, ,$$

where c_{1t} represents consumption of a "cash good", c_{2t} represents consumption of a "credit good", n_{t} represents labor supply, and V is a strictly concave function that is monotonically increasing in both kinds of consumption and monotonically decreasing in labor supply. Note that there is no direct effect upon utility from holding real balances; their advantages are entirely owing to the cash-in-advance constraint. Lucas and Stokey also assume that both the cash good and the credit good are perishable goods produced using labor at constant returns to scale, one unit of labor for each unit of consumption goods produced; as a result, in competitive equilibrium, the same price p_{t} will be the money price of both consumption goods and the nominal wage in period t.

In any equilibrium of this model, the utility received by the representative consumer during any period t can be written as a function of his beginning-of-period real money balances m_{t}, his aggregate consumption purchases $c_{t} = c_{1t} + c_{2t}$, and his labor supply n_{t}, i.e.

$$U(c_{t}, n_{t}, m_{t}) = \max V(c_{1t}, c_{2t}, n_{t})$$

$$\text{s.t. } c_{1t} + c_{2t} \leq c_{t}, \ c_{1t} \leq m_{t} \, . \tag{1.10}$$

With this reinterpretation of our previous notation, all of the equations (1.5)–(1.8) now apply to the Lucas–Stokey model. In this case, condition (1.8f) is plainly necessary, since (1.10) implies $U_{m} \geq 0$.

Thus, the set of possible stationary equilibrium allocations continues to be described by the same set of equations, and the welfare evaluation of these allocations also remains the same. As a result we again may conclude that the unique stationary equilibrium consistent with the rate of contraction of the money supply called for by Friedman achieves the allocation of resources that maximizes the utility of the representative consumer subject to the constraint of technological feasibility. In this case it is possible to be completely explicit about the way in which the welfare of the representative consumer is increased by such a policy since the utility function does not specify any direct utility from real balances.

Grandmont and Younes (1973) obtain a similar result in the case of another type of cash-in-advance economy, consisting of a finite number of types of infinitely-lived consumers with differing endowments of the several types of cash goods that exist each period. In this economy there are no credit goods but, as explained above, consumers do not need cash in order to consume their own endowment of any good. Each type of consumer is assumed to have additively separable preferences and all are assumed to have a common discount factor, so that there is an unambiguous Friedman Rule for the economy, $\pi = \beta - 1$. Grandmont and Younes show that under very general assumptions, any stationary equilibrium is inefficient in the case of a constant money supply, while any stationary equilibrium is Pareto efficient in the case of a steady contraction of the money supply in accordance with the Friedman Rule.

2. Is a higher return on money balances necessarily better?

In this section I discuss reasons why the strong form of the Friedman proposition may be invalid, despite the general validity of the weak form. The essential criticism is that the best policy, from among those available, need not always be one that results in an allocation of resources that is Pareto optimal in the full ("first-best") sense. Of course, in the presence of a sufficiently large set of policy instruments (in particular, a sufficiently large number of distinct ways in which lump-sum taxes or transfers can be distributed), so that a second welfare theorem obtains, i.e. the entire Pareto frontier (derived with reference only to the constraints imposed by the production technology) can be reached by appropriate choice of policy, it is obvious that a desirable policy choice will be one that reaches a point on that frontier. And if all points on the Pareto frontier are characterized by money earning as high a return as other assets, then a desirable policy choice will surely bring that about, among other things.

But one may not have available so large a set of policy instruments. Indeed, it is arguable that the question of optimal monetary policy arises only when one does not; for if a sufficiently large set of types of lump-sum taxes or transfers are possible, an optimal pattern of resource allocation will be possible without anyone ever holding money. [This argument assumes that there are not in fact any valuable "liquidity services" that are uniquely provided by money balances, but rather that money is held in order to allow a pattern of exchanges of real goods and services that would not otherwise be possible in equilibrium, as in the models of money presented by Samuelson (1958), Wallace (1980), Townsend (1980), or Bewley (1980, 1983), among others.] One can contrive examples in which the complete Pareto frontier cannot be reached with available policy tools other than monetary policy, and in which it nonetheless can entirely be reached using monetary policy, for example the cash-in-advance economy of the previous section; but this is plainly a rather special result. Hahn (1971, 1973) in particular has often argued that realistic models of the role of money in actual economies will involve market imperfections so severe that no monetary policy will result in a fully Pareto optimal equilibrium. In any event, the case of a limited set of policy instruments is of considerable interest, and even in quite simple examples one often finds that the set of allocations that can be attained includes only part of, or perhaps none of, the Pareto frontier.

We have seen in the previous section that money earning as high a return as other assets is typically a *necessary* condition for Pareto optimality. But it may not be *sufficient*, and so the mere fact that certain monetary policies reduce the nominal interest rate to zero does not mean that they result in an efficient allocation of resources. In the presence of additional distortions, no available policy may achieve a "first-best" allocation, and among the allocations that are attainable, the best one need not be any of the ones that happen to reduce the nominal interest rate to zero. This idea is familiar from the "theory of the second best" in public finance. Examples of other distortions that might remain even when the Friedman Rule is implemented, and whose effects might be sufficiently reduced by a higher rate of money growth to make that higher rate of money growth more desirable on balance, include the distortion of incentives by excise taxes used to bring about the steady contraction of the money supply or to finance government purchases that might otherwise be financed through money creation (Subsection 2.1 below), and inefficiencies in the allocation of consumption across individuals due to the non-existence of markets for insurance against individual income fluctuations (Subsection 2.2).

But even if some monetary policies (which, among other things, make the return on money equal to that on other assets) can be shown to result in a Pareto optimal equilibrium, it does not follow that the best policy must be one of those. If only part of the Pareto frontier belongs to the set of attainable allocations, then the best attainable allocation need not lie on the Pareto frontier. Of course, in such a case, there exists *some* social welfare function for which the optimal policy would be on the Pareto frontier (and so would have to satisfy the Friedman Rule); but it is important to note that the kind of social welfare function required may be very inegalitarian. For example, it is shown in Section 2.3 below that an increase in the rate of money growth may increase average welfare across generations (in the case of an economy made up of overlapping generations of finite-lived consumers) by lowering the real rate of return so as to bring about a more desirable life-cycle profile of control over resources, even when the lower rate of money growth would actually be Pareto optimal (but would maximize a social welfare function only if it weights more heavily the utilities of early generations than later ones).

Finally, even if there exists a monetary policy that allows as an equilibrium the allocation of resources which is most desirable, i.e. which maximizes one's social welfare function subject only to the constraints imposed by technical feasibility, this may not suffice to make that policy desirable. For models of monetary economies often have the property that perfect foresight (or rational expectations) equilibrium is not unique for a given policy regime; accordingly, a policy other than that which would allow the optimal equilibrium might nonetheless be preferred, simply in order to rule out certain undesirable equilibria that would also be possible under that rule. It is argued in Subsection 2.4 below that large multiplicities of equilibria, including the possibility of "sunspot" equilibria and endogenous equilibrium cycles, are more often possible in the case of low rates of money growth (or actual contraction of the money supply) than in the case of higher rates of money growth; this provides another possible reason for not reducing the rate of growth of the money supply to the extent called for by the Friedman Rule.

2.1. The possible desirability of an "inflation tax" when only distorting taxes are available

One important reason why the rate of money growth that reduces the nominal interest rate to zero may not maximize welfare was first pointed out by Phelps (1972, 1973). [The argument is further developed by Marty (1976), Siegel (1978), Drazen (1979), and Chamley (1985).] Phelps points out that if lump-sum taxation is not possible (contrary to what was assumed in the examples presented in Subsection 1.2), then the government will not be able to satisfy all of the conditions for a Pareto optimal equilibrium. Even if the Friedman Rule is implemented (resulting in a nominal interest rate of zero), there will be distortions introduced by the indirect taxes on various goods that must be levied in order to allow the government to bring about a steady contraction of the money supply; and if the government wishes to finance some positive level of purchases (but seeks to maximize the welfare of the private sector subject to this constraint) these indirect taxes will be still higher. A higher rate of money growth than is called for by the Friedman Rule could allow reduction of the distorting indirect taxes, and for this reason might increase welfare even though it introduces another distortion. In fact, Phelps argues (by analogy with a familiar result in the theory of optimal taxation introduced by Ramsey) that optimal taxation will often require *some* use of each of the available distorting taxes in order to reduce the extent to which any of the others must be used, among which taxes should be counted the "inflation tax" (i.e. the possibility of reducing the amount of revenue that must be raised through other taxes by increasing the money supply at a rate faster than that called for by Friedman, at the expense of driving a wedge between the marginal cost of producing real money balances and their marginal value to the private sector). Thus, Phelps argues, the optimal rate of money growth will surely be at least somewhat higher than that called for by Friedman in such a case.

This argument has been widely cited, and as a result some, who have observed that a positive nominal interest rate is not always (second-best) optimal in the case of other ways of modeling the demand for real money balances, have supposed that the result depends upon whether real balances are modeled as a direct source of utility (in which case Phelps' analogy with the standard Ramsey tax problem is presumed to be correct) or instead as simply facilitating certain kinds of transactions. But the problem is not so much that the analogy with taxation of a consumption good is less valid in these other models. Instead, it is important to remember that even in the Ramsey problem the optimal tax package need not involve a positive tax rate on all goods; this can only be shown under certain assumptions about the response of demands to prices. The standard formula for Ramsey taxes is:

$$\sum_i t_i \frac{\partial x_i}{\partial q_k} = \mu x_k \, , \tag{2.1}$$

where t_i is the excise tax on good i, x_i is the quantity purchased of that good, and q_i is the after-tax price of that good. In the case that the representative consumer purchases a positive quantity of each of the goods being summed over, this formula will imply that each of the taxes t_i must be positive, *if* the matrix of derivatives of the demand functions has an inverse all of whose elements are negative. (For in this case the vector t would have to be either entirely positive or entirely negative, and since in the optimal equilibrium the government must succeed in financing some positive quantity of expenditures, it must be entirely positive.) As usual a sufficient condition for the matrix of derivatives to have an inverse with this property is that all of the goods be *gross substitutes*, i.e. that the demand for each good be a decreasing function of its own price and an increasing function of the prices of all other goods. [See, for example, Takayama (1985, theorem 4.D.3).] While this is a familiar assumption it is well known to be rather restrictive. Even more restrictive, of course, are the conditions under which it is valid to ignore the cross-price effects, so that one finds that the sign and magnitude of the tax on a given good should depend only upon the elasticity of demand for that good with respect to its own price. This is in fact the basis for Phelps' conclusion that the tax rate on "liquidity" should be positive, as well as for his conclusion that "if, as is so often maintained, the demand for money is highly interest-inelastic, then liquidity is an attractive candidate for heavy taxation – at least from the standpoint of monetary and fiscal efficiency" (1973, p. 82). The result just referred to regarding gross substitutes provides some clarification of Phelps' claim that the cross-price effects would have to be "of a special sort" in order for it not to be optimal to tax all goods.

The situation is in fact exactly the same in the case of the optimal rate of inflation in a dynamic model of the kind considered here: a "gross substitutes" condition on the various demand functions (including the demand for real money balances) suffices to insure that the optimal tax package include a positive tax on all goods, including inflation at a rate greater than that called for by the Friedman Rule. The anti-Phelps case is also possible,[4] however, because the "gross substitutes" condition does not hold for all well-behaved utility functions. Thus, in order to understand why the Friedman proposition can continue to be valid even in the case of only distorting taxes, it is necessary to undertake a proper general equilibrium analysis, rather than relying upon the sort of partial equilibrium analysis of money demand typically used by Friedman himself.

In the appendix it is shown that the following analog of (2.1) characterizes the (second-best) optimal constant rate of money growth in the Sidrauski–Brock model presented earlier, if the only available tax is a proportional tax on consumption:

$$\begin{bmatrix} c_p m_p \\ c_\rho m_\rho \end{bmatrix} \left[\left(\frac{1 + \pi - \beta}{\beta} \right) p + \mu(1 + \pi) \left(\frac{1 - \beta}{\beta} \right) p \right] = \mu \begin{bmatrix} c \\ m \end{bmatrix}. \qquad (2.2)$$

Here p denotes the after-tax price of consumption when labor is the numeraire (i.e. $p = 1/w$, and $p - 1$ is the tax rate on consumption), and $\rho = p\pi$ (i.e. ρ is the government's seignorage revenue in units of the labor numeraire, per unit of real money balances held by the representative consumer). The "demand functions", $c(p, \rho)$ and $m(p, \rho)$, represent solutions to the modified versions of equations (1.8a)–(1.8d) for given values of p and ρ, i.e. the stationary levels of consumption and real balances associated with the stationary equilibrium corresponding to a given choice of a constant tax rate and of a constant rate of money growth. The vector on the left-hand side of (2.2) plays the role of the vector of tax rates in (2.1), and again, a "gross substitutes" condition on the demand derivatives (i.e. c_p, $m_p < 0$, c_ρ, $m_\rho > 0$) implies that this vector must be strictly positive in the case that $g > 0$, which in turn implies that $1 + \pi - \beta > 0$, so that the optimum will be characterized by inflation in excess of that called for by the Friedman Rule, and by a positive nominal interest rate.

This result indicates a reasonably direct parallelism between the Phelps

---

[4]This is shown using approaches different from the one developed below in Drazen (1979) and Woodford (1989).

problem and the standard Ramsey tax result. It is worth pointing out, however, that the conditions on the matrix of "demand " derivatives required for the result may be even less innocuous in the case of the demand for real balances (and the inflation "tax" on real balances) than in the case of other goods. One might, for example, think it reasonable that the stationary level of consumption c should be decreasing, rather than increasing, in ρ, for fixed p; if real balances and consumption purchases are roughly complementary, because money is needed to carry out the purchases, then a lower return to holding money balances may well result in substitution toward leisure and away from consumption. Similarly, the stationary demand for real balances m might well be decreasing, rather than increasing, in p (i.e. might be increasing in the real wage) for fixed ρ, insofar as a higher real wage that results in both higher labor supply and higher consumption might require a higher level of real balances with which to carry out the consumption expenditures. Hence the "gross substitutes" assumption is far from compelling in this case, and might even seem a case of doubtful interest. The case assumed by Phelps himself, i.e. zero off-diagonal elements in the matrix in (2.4), would similarly appear not to be of great practical interest.

This is the basis of the criticism of Lucas and Stokey (1983, p. 82), who suggest that their cash-in-advance model of a monetary economy would lead to conclusions quite different from Phelps':

> [Our model] leads ... to a substantial difference with Phelps's argument that "liquidity" should be viewed as an *additional* good, with a presumption that an efficient tax program involves a positive inflation tax. In our framework, "liquidity" (currency balances) is not a good, but rather the *means* to the acquisition of a subset of ordinary consumption goods. If one wishes to tax this subset at a higher rate than goods generally, the inflation tax is a means for doing so, but a positive interest-elasticity of money demand is clearly not sufficient to make this case.

It is not true, of course, that there is any *formal* difference between the sort of results that are obtained for a Sidrauski–Brock type of model, as considered above, and those that can be obtained for the Lucas–Stokey model. As noted earlier, the Lucas–Stokey model is formally identical to a Sidrauski–Brock model with a particular sort of utility function $U(c, n, m)$; and, not surprisingly, both Phelps and anti-Phelps results occur for some utility functions, as in the case of the Sidrauski–Brock model. But Lucas and Stokey are correct to state that their interpretation has some effect upon the validity of "the presumption" that the Phelps result should obtain. For if such a presumption is suggested in the case of the Sidrauski–Brock model on the basis of a supposition that the assumption of "gross substitutes" makes sense, then no similar presumption will be valid in the case of the Lucas–Stokey model. There the corresponding "presumption" would surely be that cash and credit goods should be gross substitutes, rather than aggregate consumption and real money balances. But *this* gross substitutes assumption is not sufficient to imply that $1 + \pi - \beta > 0$. Similarly, if one regards as valid the assumption that cross-price effects should be small, the cross-price effects that should be assumed to be zero would be between cash goods and credit goods, rather than between consumption and real balances; but this case does not lead to Phelps' conclusion that a low interest elasticity of money demand suffices to indicate that the optimal "inflation tax" should be large. The appropriate lesson, however, is not that more explicit microfoundations make so much of a difference – supposing that the Sidrauski–Brock model is interpreted with care – but rather that the case of the Sidrauski–Brock model itself for which Phelps' analysis is correct is a more special case than at first thought it might have appeared.

The Phelps argument has also been criticized by Kimbrough (1986a, 1986b). Kimbrough argues that while the argument may be correct for a model in which money is modeled as directly affecting consumers' utility, the Friedman Rule will nonetheless be optimal if money balances are valued instead because they affect the technology through which transactions are carried out, freeing real resources that would otherwise be used up by the transactions technology. He argues that it is so because in the latter case real money balances are an "intermediate good", and it is known from the standard literature on optimal taxation [e.g. Diamond and Mirrlees (1971)] that the optimal tax rate on an intermediate good is zero (production efficiency continues to be desirable) even when the government must finance a positive level of purchases through distorting taxes (so that full Pareto optimality will be unattainable).

Kimbrough (1986a) demonstrates the optimality of the Friedman Rule, even in the second-best case, for the case of a "shopping time" transactions technology according to which the representative consumer must spend a quantity of time equal to $g(M_{t+1}/P_t c_t)c_t$ in order to purchase consumption goods in the quantity c_t, where the representative consumer has preferences simply over his level of consumption in each period and the time remaining to him for leisure. Here M_{t+1} represents money balances held *at the end* of the period in which the consumption purchases are made (and hence money balances held at the beginning of the following period), P_t is again the money price of consumption goods inclusive of tax, and g is a convex function reaching a minimum at a finite positive ratio of real balances to consumption. Kimbrough argues (1986b, p. 137) that the Friedman Rule should also be valid for "any economy in which, in equilibrium, scarce resources are used up in the transactions process and agents can economize on these transactions costs by holding money", because money is an "intermediate good" in all such cases.

Since this claim has been cited approvingly by a number of authors, it is worth pointing out that the analogy with the treatment of "intermediate goods" in the standard optimal taxation problem is not generally valid and that Kimbrough's result does not in fact have the generality claimed for it. Details are given in Woodford (1989), where it is shown that Kimbrough's result depends upon the form assumed for the transactions technology function – both his assumption of constant returns to scale in the transaction technology[5] and his assumption that it is end-of-period balances, rather than beginning-of-period balances, that affects the time required to carry out transactions.[6] The general result in the case of the shopping time technology model is the same as for the general class of Sidrauski models, i.e. either the Phelps result or the anti-Phelps result is possible, depending upon details of the specification. Kimbrough's example may, however, shed further light upon the plausibility of specifications of the general Sidrauski framework (to which the shopping time model belongs as a special case) for which the Phelps result is invalid.

2.2. Expansionary monetary policy as a substitute for private insurance

Both the Sidrauski–Brock type of model (including the "shopping time" interpretation of this model) and the closely related Lucas–Stokey cash-in-advance model, discussed above, oversimplify the role of money in actual economies in very many respects. In particular, the use of a representative consumer model implies that the distribution of money balances across agents in the economy never changes; some motive is introduced in order to induce the representative consumer to hold at all times a certain positive quantity of money, but the advantages of holding money must be of some sort that do not require money balances to ever be used up by anyone. In the case of the Sidrauski–Brock or "shopping time" model, this requires one to postulate advantages to holding real money balances whose nature is not explicitly modeled. In the case of the Lucas–Stokey model, the use of money in exchange is modeled explicitly, and an explicit representation is given of the way in which the exchange of real goods and services is changed by the presence of real money balances, but the pattern of exchanges that is assumed in order to make the use of money in purchases consistent with the existence of a representative consumer is extremely artificial. (The representative consumer does use up his money balances, in order to make purchases of "cash goods",

---

[5]The importance of this assumption for Kimbrough's result has also been discussed by Faig (1988) and Guidotti and Vegh (1988).

[6]The beginning-of-period specification, which is more common in the literature on Sidrauski–Brock models, is more easily reconciled with an explicit account of the way that transactions are organized that creates a role for money balances in facilitating transactions, such as the model of Lucas and Stokey (1983) discussed earlier. With that specification, the Phelps result is possible even in the case of a constant returns to scale transactions technology.

with the result that for a certain part of each "period" no one holds the economy's money supply; the money is all tied up in the payments mechanism, no longer being available to be spent by the consumers who have just used it to purchase "cash goods", but also not yet available for spending by the consumers who sold those goods. The existence of a time lag between when the buyer of "cash goods" parts with his claim to the money and when the seller can exercise his claim to it is crucial to the existence of an equilibrium demand for a positive quantity of real balances in this model.)

A more satisfactory model of the role of money in facilitating transactions would involve accumulation and decumulation of money balances by a given consumer at different points in time, depending upon the particular transactions into which he enters, with one consumer's reduction in his money balances implying another's increased holdings of money; in such a model, the advantage of holding money would consist exactly in the possibility of running down one's money balances at some future date or under certain contingencies. Such a model is necessarily not a representative agent model. As a result, alternative monetary policies will affect welfare, not only by changing the real return on money balances, but also by redistributing purchasing power between consumers who are differently situated. It will be shown that the redistribution associated with a policy of steady monetary expansion may well increase average utility, while that associated with the policy of contraction of the money supply called for by Friedman may decrease it; these effects would then tend to counteract the effects upon the incentive to hold money balances that Friedman considers. Consequently, the maximum level of some weighted sum of utilities may be associated with a higher rate of money growth and inflation than is called for by the Friedman Rule.

It is also often argued that money balances may be held at least in part because of the possibility of using stocks of liquid assets to "self-insure" against the consequences of otherwise uninsurable variations in desire to consume or in income. This sort of "precautionary demand" for money can also not be represented within a representative agent framework. The very idea of an inefficiency in the use of resources due to the absence of insurance markets (or, more generally, of complete markets for contingent claims of the kind assumed in the Arrow–Debreu model) makes sense only when consumers are not all identical, for only then would there be any desire to arrange state-contingent exchanges. But in a model with heterogeneous consumers it is possible to represent a role for money balances as at least a partial substitute for such insurance contracts (which one may suppose cannot be written because of imperfect information problems of one sort or another). And such a view of the role of money is not without consequence for one's view of the welfare consequences of alternative rates of money growth and inflation, for depending upon how the new money is injected into the economy, a policy of monetary expansion may help to supply some of the insurance against contingencies of "liquidity constraint" that consumers are unable to arrange through private contracts. This sort of effect is again a consequence of the particular sort of redistribution of purchasing power between consumers in different situations that results from an expansionary policy. Such results provide a further illustration of why the strong form of the Friedman proposition need not be valid, which is quite distinct from the considerations introduced in the previous subsection; that is, deflation at the rate called for by the Friedman Rule may not be desirable, even if lump-sum taxation is possible.

2.2.1. Welfare costs of inflation in the Bewley–Levine model

A rigorous model of the role of money along the lines just sketched has been presented by Bewley (1980, 1983), and further developed by Levine (1986a, 1986b, 1987, 1988). In the Bewley model, there is a finite number (greater than one) of distinct types of infinitely-lived consumers, each of whom seeks to maximize the expected value of an infinite sum of discounted single-period utilities of consumption; the rates of time preference of the different consumer types need not be identical. As in the Lucas–Stokey model, consumers' preferences do not include any direct preference for holding money; money is held only as a means to achieving a more desirable consumption allocation. Unlike in the Lucas–Stokey model, there is no assumption that goods cannot be directly exchanged for goods or that one cannot consume one's own current endowment or that there is any time lag before money accepted in exchange for goods can be spent again. Money balances are useful only insofar as they can be used in certain periods to allow consumption of a value greater than the value of a consumer's endowment in that period. Money is necessary for this purpose because of an assumption that consumers are unable to borrow against future endowment income; any consumption in excess of one's current endowment must be financed out of one's cash balances. [The non-existence of private credit might be explained by spatial decentralization of exchange as in the "turnpike" models of Townsend (1980), or by imperfect information problems of the sort discussed by Bryant (1980).] It is also tacitly assumed in most models of this sort that fiat money is the only available store of value that can serve the purpose of allowing consumption allocations to differ from endowment patterns; in this respect the Bewley model is similar to (and unsatisfactory for many of the same reasons as) the simple overlapping generations model of the demand for fiat money discussed by Wallace (1980). One might, however, extend this class of models to allow for the coexistence of money and other assets (possibly earning a higher rate of return) by introducing transactions costs associated with the use of other assets to finance consumption purchases. Levine (1986a) gives conditions for the existence of an equilibrium with valued fiat money in the presence of a large set of different assets which are subject to various constraints regarding the states in which markets for the various assets are open, but it is obvious that one might equally well represent differential degrees of "liquidity" by differing costs of transacting in different markets that are however always open.

In models of this sort it is evident that there need not be any demand for intrinsically valueless money balances at all; but Bewley (1983) and Levine (1986a, 1987) give sufficient conditions for the existence of an equilibrium in which a positive quantity of real money balances is held (in aggregate) at all times. The conditions have to do both with a sufficient degree of inefficiency of the autarchic consumption allocation (which in turn depends upon endowments being sufficiently variable either over time or across different random states, and the marginal utility of consumption increasing sufficiently rapidly in response to consumption declines, or upon sufficiently large variations in the marginal utility of consumption due to variations over time or across states in the taste for consumption), and with a sufficiently high rate of return on money balances (i.e. with a sufficiently low rate of inflation as a result of a sufficiently low rate of money growth) relative to the consumers' rates of time preference (which accordingly must not be too large), so that holding money is not too costly a way of arranging a more desirable consumption allocation.

Bewley's analysis of the welfare properties of monetary equilibria in models of this kind supports Friedman's general argument in one important respect. He shows that under quite general conditions, equilibrium cannot be Pareto optimal if the money supply is not contracted steadily, or, in fact, if the rate of steady contraction of the money supply is less than all consumers' rates of time preference. As in Friedman's argument, the reason is that in that case insufficient real balances will be held, in the sense that they are too small, at least at certain times, to allow for complete self-insurance against variations in income and/or tastes for consumption. Since Bewley's model is more general in certain respects than the class of deterministic models described in Section 1, it is appropriate to state his result here with some precision.

Bewley considers an economy consisting of a finite number of infinitely-lived consumers. (As usual, we really mean a large number of each of a finite number of types of consumers, so that competitive equilibrium makes sense.) Consumer i seeks to maximize the expected value of a sum of discounted utilities:

$$\sum_{t=0}^{\infty} \delta_i^t u_i(c_t^i, s_t),$$

where the discount factor satisfies $0 < \delta_i < 1$, where the L-vector c_t^i is the consumption by consumer i in period t, and where s_t represents an aggregate state variable which may affect consumers' tastes. The single-period utility function $u_i(c, s)$ is twice differentiable with respect to c, strictly increasing in each of the L consumption goods, and strictly concave in c, for each of the possible values of s. The aggregate state variable $\{s_t\}$ follows a finite state Markov process with stationary transition probabilities, ergodic and with no transient states. In each period, consumer i has a non-negative L-vector ω_t^i of endowments of the consumption goods. This endowment depends only upon the aggregate state s_t, but may be different in different states; thus, consumers may wish to obtain a consumption pattern that differs from their endowment pattern either because endowments fluctuate while their preferences do not, or because preferences fluctuate while their endowment does not. It is assumed that each consumer has a non-zero endowment in at least one of the possible aggregate states s, and that in each aggregate state s, the aggregate endowment vector $\sum_i \omega_t^i$ is positive in all L goods.

   The L consumption goods in each period are all assumed to be perishable; an intrinsically valueless government-issued fiat money is the only asset that can be held from one period to the next. Bewley considers only monetary policies in which the money supply grows at a constant rate π, which may be negative (steady contraction of the money supply), and in which the increase or decrease in the money supply each period comes about through lump-sum transfers or taxes which are distributed across consumers according to a fixed set of proportions $\tau_i > 0$ (with $\sum_i \tau_i = 1$) that do not vary with the aggregate state of the economy.[7] Consumer i's money balances evolve over time according to the relation:

$$M_t^i = (1 + \pi)^{-1} M_{t-1}^i + p_t'[\omega_t^i - c_t^i] + \tau_i(\pi/1 + \pi) , \qquad (2.3)$$

where M_t^i represents the fraction of the total money supply in period t that is held by consumer i at the end of period t and p_t represents the L-vector of consumption goods prices in period t, deflated by the period t money supply. (Note that if consumption goods prices in terms of money rise steadily at the rate of money growth π, the prices p will remain constant.) A program of consumption (contingent, of course, upon the history of realizations of the aggregate state) for consumer i is *feasible*, given his initial money balances M_{-1}^i and a price process [i.e. a specification of p_t as a function of the history of aggregate states $(s_0, s_1, \ldots, s_t)$, for each $t \geq 0$], if and only if (2.3) implies that, given that consumption program, $M_t^i \geq 0$ for all t, for all possible histories of realizations of the aggregate state. This inequality reflects the impossibility of borrowing against future endowment income, discussed above. Bewley

---

[7]Bewley actually assumes a constant money supply and interest payments on money balances, which may be negative, financed out of lump-sum taxes (transfers in the case of negative interest). This is equivalent, however, to the formalism presented here; Bewley's interest rate r corresponds to $-\pi/1 + \pi$ in our notation. See Subsection 3.3 below for further discussion.

defines a *monetary equilibrium* (for given initial money balances and a given rate of money growth π) as a price process and a consumption allocation [i.e. a specification of c_t^i for each i as a function of the history of aggregate states $(s_0, s_1, \ldots, s_t)$, for each $t \geq 0$] such that for each i, the specified consumption program c_t^i maximizes the expected utility of consumer i, among the class of feasible consumption programs for i, given the specified price process and consumer i's initial money balances; total consumption demand $\sum_i c_t^i$ adds up to the total endowment $\sum_i \omega_t^i$ in all periods and for all histories of the aggregate states; and all components of the price vector p_t are bounded uniformly away from zero and from infinity, for all t and for all histories of the aggregate states. The last clause of this definition is worthy of special comment. The fact that prices deflated by the money supply remain forever bounded away from both zero and infinity means that real balances in the economy fluctuate around some constant positive level, rather than either declining asymptotically to zero [in a self-fulfilling hyperinflation of the sort known to be possible in many equilibrium models of fiat money – see, for example, Scheinkman (1980) or Woodford (1988)] or growing asymptotically without bound [in a self-fulfilling deflation of the sort that is shown to be possible under certain circumstances by Brock (1975) and Woodford (1988)]. The fact that monetary equilibrium is *defined* by Bewley to have this property restricts somewhat the generality of the results to be described below since self-fulfilling inflations are often possible in equilibrium (assuming that one drops the last clause from Bewley's definition). In models of this type, the self-fulfilling deflations are often possible in the case that the money supply is steadily contracted, as is illustrated in the appendix.

Bewley's result (1980, theorem 2) is the following: *if $1 + \pi > \delta_i$ for all i, then any monetary equilibrium in which every consumer consumes a positive quantity of at least one consumption good in every period and for every possible history of the aggregate states involves an allocation of consumption that is not Pareto optimal.* As just noted, this result in fact only guarantees that with too high a rate of money growth there cannot exist a Pareto optimal equilibrium in which the quantity of real balances remains bounded forever. One can easily reject as well the possibility that an equilibrium in which real balances approach zero asymptotically (if such equilibria exist) could ever be Pareto optimal; this follows directly from the fact that equilibria in which fiat money has no value are not Pareto optimal, under very general conditions [see Levine (1987)]. An equilibrium in which real balances grow without bound, however, might be Pareto optimal even when the rate of money growth exceeds that called for by the Friedman Rule, as shown by an example in the appendix.

This example provides a qualification to Bewley's result, but not one that really lessens the support that Bewley's result provides for the Friedman proposition. For the example does not contradict the proposition (quite generally valid for the Bewley model) that Pareto optimality requires that the borrowing constraints never bind. (This is the version of the weak form of the Friedman proposition that applies to the present model, since if a borrowing constraint were ever to bind it would imply the existence of a consumer who would be willing to issue securities that would yield a positive nominal interest rate were he able to do so.) Nor does it contradict the general thesis that contraction of the money supply is necessary for a Pareto optimal equilibrium to be possible, for equilibria in which real balances grow without bound of the kind illustrated in the appendix are possible only in the case $\pi < 0$. This can be shown using a proof of the sort given by Levine (1987) for the case of a constant money supply; the essence of the argument is that an equilibrium with real balances growing without bound would have to imply oversaving (violation of a transversality condition) by at least one consumer, in the case that consumers do not hold any money in order to be able to pay future taxes.

The example in Section A.2 in the appendix even provides support for the strong form of the Friedman proposition, if (as with our consideration of the Sidrauski–Brock model in Section 1 and in the previous subsection) one limits oneself to comparing the welfare properties of different possible stationary equilibria (by which I here mean equilibria with a constant level of real balances). Instead of the equilibrium represented by equations (A.4), one might consider the stationary equilibrium in which $p_t = p$ for all t; $M_t^1 = 1$ for all odd t, 0 for all even t; $M_t^2 = 0$ for all odd t, 1 for all even t; $c_t^1 = d$ for all odd t, $a + b - d$ for all even t; and $c_t^2 = a + b - d$ for all odd t, d for all even t; where the quantities p and d satisfy:

$$u'(d) = \delta(1 + \pi)^{-1}u'(a + b - d) ,\tag{2.4a}$$

$$(a + b)/2 \le d < a ,\tag{2.4b}$$

$$p = (2 + \pi)/((2 + 2\pi)(a - d)) .\tag{2.4c}$$

Now a solution d to (2.4a) clearly cannot exist that satisfies the first inequality in (2.4b) unless $\pi \ge \delta - 1$, so that this is a necessary condition for the existence of a stationary equilibrium of the form (2.4). On the other hand, it is also easily seen that a unique solution for p and d satisfying conditions (2.4) exists in the case of any rate of money growth in the range

$$\delta \le 1 + \pi < \delta u'(b)/u'(a) ,\tag{2.5}$$

which interval is non-empty given that $a > b$.

How do the welfare properties of the different stationary equilibria compare as one varies π over the range (2.5)? Since there are two types of consumers in this model, the appropriate measure of welfare is not so unambiguous as in the case of the representative agent models considered previously, but given the symmetry of the model, the average of the lifetime utilities to the two types is surely not an unreasonable choice. This welfare measure is proportional to $u(d) + u(a + b - d)$, and so is a decreasing function of d, for d in the range (2.4b). Furthermore, it is clear from (2.4a) that d is an increasing function of π. Hence, over the range (2.5), average welfare is a monotonically decreasing function of the rate of growth of the money supply. Furthermore, the choice $\pi = \delta - 1$, in accordance with the Friedman Rule, not only makes possible the stationary equilibrium with the highest level of average utility, but makes possible a stationary equilibrium that is Pareto optimal, since in that case $d = (a + b)/2$, and as noted above this is the consumption allocation that maximizes average utility among all feasible allocations. (None of the stationary equilibria for $\pi > \delta - 1$ is Pareto optimal, since in these equilibria the borrowing constraint binds for one type of consumer or the other in every period, keeping the marginal rates of substitution between successive periods' consumption always unequal between the two types.) Hence, if one restricts one's attention to the stationary equilibria associated with different rates of money growth, the rate of contraction called for by the Friedman Rule is clearly preferable to all higher rates of money growth.

This example has been much discussed. [See, for example, Sargent (1987, ch. 6); Townsend (1980) also restricts his attention to a stationary equilibrium that is formally analogous to this one.] It is therefore important to stress that the conclusions just summarized are not at all robust. One problem, already referred to, has to do with the neglect of other equilibria that may also be associated with a given rate of money growth; there can be optimal equilibria associated with higher rates of money growth than that called for by the Friedman Rule, and suboptimal equilibria (e.g. equilibria involving real balances going asymptotically to zero) associated with low rates of money growth, including that called for by the Friedman Rule. But more important is the fact that even the conclusions just sketched regarding the comparative welfare properties of stationary equilibria do not generalize to the case of *stochastic* endowment processes, as opposed to the rigid deterministic alternation between even and odd periods assumed above. Since the case of a deterministic alternation is surely extremely special (given that fluctuations of a certain magnitude in the endowments are necessary in order for equilibria with valued fiat money to be possible at all), and since it is only the case of stochastic endowment variation (or equivalently, preference variation) that can represent the idea of a precautionary demand for money, this greatly reduces the interest of the conclusion that can be drawn from the deterministic example.

2.2.2. Consequences of stochastic endowments or tastes

One important difference in the case of a stochastic endowment process, demonstrated by Bewley (1983), is that there may not exist any monetary equilibria in which real balances remain bounded away from zero if the money supply is contracted at or even near the rate called for by the Friedman Rule. Hence, the mere fact that higher rates of money growth prevent an equilibrium from being Pareto optimal may not justify an attempt to implement the Friedman Rule. For the whole point of Friedman's advice is to achieve conditions that would make possible an equilibrium in which consumers hold an adequate level of money balances to insure a high degree of "liquidity"; but contraction of the money supply may prevent the existence of an equilibrium in which money balances exist in sufficient quantity to provide consumers with any "liquidity" at all.

This possibility can be illustrated by the following simple example. Suppose that the probability of transition from any aggregate state to any other is positive, and suppose also (contrary to one of the assumptions stated above) that for each consumer i there is at least one aggregate state in which he has no endowment. (Suppose also that consumption must be non-negative all periods.) Then consider the possibility of an equilibrium with $\pi < 0$. In any period, and for any positive integer N (no matter how large), consumer i knows that there is a positive probability that he will have zero endowment in each of the following N periods. Since a feasible consumption program for i must be such that i's money balances will remain non-negative under all possible histories of realizations of the aggregate state, consumer i must choose to hold money balances sufficient to allow him to pay his tax liability (which is positive each period since $\pi < 0$) even if his endowment turns out to be zero for an arbitrarily large number of periods in succession. This means that he must choose $M_t^i \geq \tau_i$ in every period. But summing over all consumers implies that in equilibrium one would have to have $M_t^i = \tau_i$ for all i and for all t. From (2.3) this implies that $c_t^i = \omega_t^i$ for all i and for all t. Thus, there can be no equilibrium in which any consumers are able to achieve a consumption allocation that is more desirable than their endowment patterns by accumulating and decumulating money balances; there can be no monetary equilibrium in which welfare is any higher than it is in the case that money does not exist or is not valued. This means that a policy with $\pi < 0$ can be worse than a policy of choosing a zero or low positive rate of money growth, insofar as in the latter case equilibria would exist in which money balances are held in excess of those needed to insure feasibility, and so in which consumers are able to use their money balances to achieve consumption allocations preferable to their endowment patterns. [I specify a *low* positive rate of money growth, for too large a rate of money growth can render impossible any equilibrium with valued fiat money, as is discussed in some detail by Levine (1987). In the case of the deterministic example presented above, a rate of money growth equal to or greater than the upper bound in (2.8) will prevent the existence not only of a stationary equilibrium, but of any equilibrium with valued fiat money.]

Bewley (1983) discusses this problem in terms of possible non-existence of monetary equilibrium if the rate of money growth is too low, which he shows can occur even for rates of contraction of the money supply that are less than all consumers' rate of time preference and even if consumer endowments are always bounded away from zero. But one must recall again that for Bewley "monetary equilibrium" means an equilibrium in which the price level is bounded forever. There may still exist equilibria in which money has a positive value, but in which real balances asymptotically approach zero (because price deflation is not as rapid as the contraction of the money supply), for reasons similar to those demonstrated in Woodford (1988). But in any event, in such cases the choice of too low a rate of money growth *forces demonetization* of the economy – exactly the opposite of Friedman's objective.

The problem that arises, in the case of stochastic endowment (and or preference) processes, has to do with the distributional consequences of money growth or contraction, and with the extent to which the sort of redistribution brought about tends to ameliorate or to worsen the problems caused by the inability of consumers to contract to insure one another against the risk of endowment or preference variations. For note that the reason why, in the above example, a steady contraction of the money supply results in insufficient real balances to provide consumers with any "liquidity" at all, is that the taxes levied in order to contract the money supply make worse the needs for liquidity faced by consumers in the state in which they have zero endowment. If the allocation of the lump-sum taxes across consumers were not required to be constant, and instead the tax rate were reduced on consumers who had especially low income in the current state, the problem would not arise to the same extent; it would be easier to arrange equilibria in which a low rate of money growth coincided with real balances forever bounded away from zero. But this would be exactly the case in which it would be possible to use fiscal policy to effectively provide the kind of insurance that private contracts would supply in the case of idealized Arrow–Debreu markets. When the allocation of the tax burden is fixed, contraction of the money supply actually makes the need for such state-contingent transfers worse, whereas a policy of mild expansion of the money supply would tend to substitute partially for the missing insurance markets, insofar as the problem of consumers running out of purchasing power in the event of a long sequence of periods in which their endowments remained low would be mitigated by the existence of the lump-sum transfers which would increase such consumers' share of the total money supply.

The tendency of the transfers associated with a policy of constant growth of the money supply, in the case that the allocation of taxes and transfers is not state-contingent, to substitute for the existence of private insurance markets is demonstrated most strikingly by an example due to Levine (1986b, 1988), in which it is possible through an appropriate choice of the money growth rate to obtain an equilibrium which is Pareto optimal, *but a positive rate of money growth is required for Pareto optimality*. The example is quite special, but it serves to identify in an ideal case an effect of money growth that operates in the opposite direction to the sort of incentive effect stressed by Friedman, which countervailing effect is also operative (alongside the Friedman effect) in more general models of the Bewley type.

Levine's example is as follows. There are two types of consumer, in equal numbers. There are two aggregate states, in one of which $u^1(c) = ac$ and $u^2(c) = bc$, where $a > b$, and in the other of which $u^1(c) = bc$ and $u^2(c) = ac$. (That is, utility is always linear, but marginal utilities are subject to stochastic variation.) In each period there is a probability $\varepsilon > 0$ that the aggregate state will remain the same in the following period, and a probability $1 - \varepsilon > 0$ that the marginal utilities of the two consumer types will be reversed. Both consumer types have the same discount factor $\delta < 1$, and both have an endowment of one unit of the single consumption good each period. In this economy the equilibrium without valued fiat money is inefficient, because both types consume one unit of the good in each period, while the expected utility of both could be made higher by allocating a larger share of consumption to each type in the periods in which he has a high marginal utility. (In fact, it is easy to see that the only Pareto optimal allocation that does not involve one consumer type consuming everything in all periods is the one in which in every period the consumer type whose marginal utility is higher consumes everything.)

Levine looks at equilibria with valued fiat money that take a special form; this particular class of equilibria is a sort of generalization to the case of stochastic preference variations of the kind of stationary equilibrium that would be possible in the case of deterministic alternation of preferences. The equilibria that Levine considers are *two-state Markov equilibria*, in which, while the deflated price level is not constant, it follows a two-state Markov process. The deflated price level depends only upon whether the aggregate state is currently the same as in the previous period (a "boom" period) or has changed since the previous period (a "recession" period). In these equilibria the entire money supply is held at the end of each period by those consumers who had low marginal utility during that period. This means that at the beginning of every "boom" period the distribution of money balances is the same (all are held by the consumers who currently have a high marginal utility, prior to the lump-sum transfers), and similarly at the beginning of every "recession" period (all are held by consumers who currently have a low marginal utility); hence it is not surprising that in such an equilibrium the price level should be the same in all "boom" periods and likewise in all "recession" periods.

Levine shows that for many values of the preference parameters of the model there will exist an interval of rates of money growth consistent with the existence of a two-state Markov equilibrium, and that in such cases there is a unique two-state Markov equilibrium in that interval. This makes it possible to compare the welfare properties of similar equilibria associated with different rates of money growth, as in the example above where we considered the stationary equilibria associated with different rates of money growth. As in the previous example, one must keep in mind that there may exist many other equilibria as well for these same rates of money growth, which achieve different levels of welfare. Nonetheless, the exercise is of interest, not least for the contrast it provides to the previous example. Levine shows that for some parameter values and rates of money growth, a Pareto optimal equilibrium is attained (with the consumption allocation described above); for others, one obtains an inefficient equilibrium in which the consumers with high marginal utility consume all of the good in "boom" periods, but only part of it in "recession" periods.[8] In the appendix I derive the conditions under which a Pareto optimal equilibrium occurs. It is shown that these conditions can only be satisfied in the case of a positive rate of money growth, and also that for some parameter values there does exist a range of positive rates of money growth for which the conditions are satisfied.

One might wish to compare the two-state Markov equilibria associated with different rates of money growth according to a welfare criterion like that used above in comparing alternative stationary equilibria. The obvious analogous measure in the present case would be the average level of ex ante expected utility over all consumers, with the different possible initial states of the economy weighted according to the frequency with which they occur over the long run (i.e. an initial "boom" state with probability $1 - \varepsilon$, an initial "recession" state with probability ε). Under this measure, the highest level of welfare

---

[8]This accounts for the names given to the two types of periods; in "recession" periods less trade occurs than would be efficient, due to maldistribution of liquidity in the economy – the consumers with the high marginal utility happen to have low money balances. If one were to extend the model by allowing for endogenous labor supply instead of an exogenously given endowment, one could obtain examples of "business cycles" in which equilibrium output would be lower in the "recession" periods. Levine's example is, in this regard, essentially a simplified discrete-time version of the continuous-time model with endogenous labor supply considered by Scheinkman and Weiss (1986). Scheinkman and Weiss also demonstrate that a redistribution of money balances of the sort that would be associated with a one-time increase in the money supply through a uniform lump-sum transfer would result in a Pareto improvement, although they do not consider the consequences of continuing (and hence anticipated) money growth.

achievable by any feasible allocation is achieved by the efficient equilibrium (if one is possible); so that if there exists a range of values for π that satisfy conditions (A.6) in the appendix, this range of rates of money growth will maximize the welfare criterion. Even when there exist no values of π that satisfy all of these conditions, however, there may exist a range of values of π for which inefficient two-state Markov equilibria exist, and again one can ask which rate of money growth maximizes the welfare criterion. Levine (1986b) shows that this will not be the rate of money growth called for by the Friedman Rule, nor will it be the lowest rate of money growth consistent with the existence of an equilibrium of this type. Instead, the optimal rate of money growth (within the range consistent with such an equilibrium) is always either greater than zero, or is the highest rate of money growth consistent with the existence of a two-state Markov equilibrium in the case that no positive rates of money growth are in that range. Again, the reason is that a certain rate of steady growth of the money supply helps to provide consumers with some insurance against the situation of finding themselves repeatedly with a high marginal utility of consumption and being unable to purchase much because of their depleted cash balances.

The Levine example, in which full Pareto optimality is possible in the case of a positive rate of money growth, is obviously extremely special. The exact linearity of the utility functions is not essential, but it is crucial that the consumers' optimization problem has a *corner solution*: whenever any consumer chooses to hold money, he chooses zero consumption, i.e. to hold as large money balances as possible. As a result, small changes in the expected rate of return on money balances would not affect the size of the money balances that any consumers choose to hold under any circumstances. Hence, Friedman's reason for rates of money growth higher than $\delta - 1$ to result in inefficiency is inoperative in this case. In general, one should not expect a corner solution to obtain under all possible states, and so the Friedman sort of inefficiency should exist in the case of positive rates of money growth, albeit alongside the sort of role for money growth as a substitute for insurance markets revealed in a pure form by the Levine example. One can still, in the case of more general preferences, consider the range of rates of money growth consistent with the existence of a two-state Markov equilibrium, and compare the levels of welfare (using the sort of measure just described) associated with the two-state Markov equilibria corresponding to different rates of money growth. Kehoe, Levine and Woodford (1989) do this for the case of a logarithmic utility function (in which case consumption is never chosen to be zero). They show that the change in welfare resulting from a small increase in the rate of money growth can be written as the sum of two terms, one positive (representing the redistribution effect at work in the Levine example) and one negative (representing the effect upon the incentive to hold real balances stressed by Friedman). Because of the existence of the positive term, the optimal rate of money growth is often not the lowest rate of money growth consistent with the existence of such an equilibrium; Kehoe et al. show that for some parameter values the optimal rate of money growth is greater than zero.

An obvious question about all of these results, in which the distributional effects of money growth or contraction are important because of their exacerbation or amelioration of problems due to the incompleteness of financial markets, is how contrived the specifications made above are in terms both of the particular market structure that is assumed to exist and of the particular class of alternative government policies that are considered. In particular, one might wonder if these results do not depend crucially upon consideration of an unnecessarily restricted class of monetary policies, or upon assuming away the existence of other types of government policy instruments (e.g. fiscal policy choices or social insurance programs) that if used optimally would result in the absence of these redistributive effects that we have seen can counterbalance the Friedman-type effects of money growth. Levine (1988) has addressed this issue by considering the entire class of possible consumption allocations that could be implemented by some incentive-compatible mechanism, given a particular specification of what information is public and what is private, and indicating a sense in which an optimal government policy from among this class must involve the existence of an asset like the fiat money considered above that is redistributed across consumers in the way that results from monetary expansion in the above examples. The informational assumptions under which this result is obtained must then themselves be justified as far as realism is concerned; but Levine argues, convincingly I think, that private information of some sort similar to the kind he assumes must exist if the use of money is to play any role at all in a desirable institutional structure, and if the sorts of market imperfections that explain the use of money in actual economies are to be reconciled with individual rationality. [The argument here is in many respects similar to Hahn's (1973) concern to found monetary theory upon assumptions that make money "essential".]

2.3. The return on money and the life-cycle allocation of resources

In this subsection I wish to consider the effects upon the intertemporal allocation of resources of alternative rates of money growth, in models which take account of the fact that consumers in fact have finite lifetimes and that the economy is made up of overlapping generations of such consumers. Even when the role of money in the economy is similar in such models to models with a representative consumer or a finite number of consumer types, the choice of demographic structure is far from innocuous where the welfare evaluation of alternative possible monetary equilibria is concerned. In particular, consideration of the distinct interests of successive generations of consumers in a given economy is especially important as a way of seeing the flaw in a view that would argue that the achievement of a Pareto optimal equilibrium is an end in itself. For it will be seen that in some cases the only Pareto optimal equilibrium that can be achieved using a given set of monetary policy instruments is one that corresponds to maximization of a weighted sum of utilities only if the weights on certain generations' utilities are extremely large relative to the weights placed on other generations' utilities.

2.3.1. The overlapping generations model of fiat money

To begin it will be useful to recall the standard analysis of the welfare effects of alternative rates of money growth in the familiar overlapping generations model of fiat money, as developed by Wallace (1980) and Brock and Scheinkman (1980). These authors consider an economy made up of overlapping generations of identical consumers, each of whom lives for two consecutive periods, with an equal number in each generation. Each consumer seeks to maximize $u(c_1, c_2)$, where c_1 represents his level of consumption during the first period of life and c_2 his level of consumption during his second period of life, and where u is increasing in both arguments and strictly concave. (As in most of the literature on overlapping generations models in monetary economics, I assume the existence of a single perishable consumption good each period, although this is not crucial for the results to follow. Nor is the assumption of only two periods of life per consumer essential.) Each consumer is assumed to be endowed with a quantity e_1 of the consumption good in his first period of life and a quantity e_2 in his second. The only asset is assumed to be fiat money, which is assumed to be growing (or contracting) in quantity at some constant rate; this growth or contraction of the money supply is brought about through lump-sum taxes or transfers. The total lump-sum taxes or transfers made in a given period are assumed to be divided in the proportions t_1/t_2 between consumers currently in the first period of life and consumers currently in the second period of life (where $t_1 + t_2 = 1$; t_1, $t_2 \geq 0$); these proportions are assumed to be the same in all periods and not subject to choice by the monetary authority. The only policy choice with which we are concerned is accordingly the rate of growth π of the money supply.

A consumer faces the lifetime budget constraints:

$$c_1 + m = e_1 + t_1 h , \tag{2.6a}$$

$$c_2 = e_2 + t_2 h + m R_m , \tag{2.6b}$$

where h is the total quantity of lump-sum transfers per period per new consumer born that period (the same each period in the case of a stationary equilibrium), m is the quantity of real money balances per consumer held at the end of the first period of life, and R_m is the gross real return on money held from the first period of life to the second (p_t/p_{t+1}, if p_t is the money price of the consumption good in period t). His optimizing choice of c_1, c_2 and m is characterized by

$$\frac{u_1}{u_2}(c_1, c_2) = R_m , \tag{2.6c}$$

together with conditions (2.6a) and (2.6b). (I will ignore the possibility of a corner solution, which can easily be ruled out by assuming appropriate boundary conditions for the utility function.) In a stationary equilibrium, in which the allocation of consumption between young and old agents, and likewise the level of real balances, is the same each period, goods market clearing requires that in each period

$$c_1 + c_2 = e_1 + e_2 . \tag{2.7a}$$

In order for real balances to be constant over time, the rate of inflation must be constant and equal to the rate of money growth π, so that in a stationary equilibrium one must have

$$R_m = (1 + \pi)^{-1} \tag{2.7b}$$

every period. [Note that these conditions imply the further relationship $h = m(\pi/1 + \pi)$.] Any set of values for c_1, c_2, m, h, and R_m satisfying all five of conditions (2.6) and (2.7), and such that c_1, c_2, m, $R_m > 0$, will describe a stationary money equilibrium.

There are two distinct ways in which one might wish to compare the welfare properties of alternative stationary equilibria. One way (followed by much of the literature on this model) would be to ask which stationary equilibria are Pareto optimal. It can be shown that a stationary consumption allocation (c_1, c_2) satisfying (2.12a) is Pareto optimal if and only if

$$\frac{u_1}{u_2}(c_1, c_2) \geq 1 . \tag{2.8}$$

[For a very general treatment of Pareto optimality in overlapping generations exchange economies, see Balasko and Shell (1980).] When this condition is not

satisfied, the consumption allocation is inefficient, not because there exist any
two consumers with different marginal rates of substitution between the same
two goods (this is impossible given our assumption of only two-period lives and
only one consumer type per generation), but because of the existence of
dynamic inefficiency of the kind first studied by Malinvaud. The construction of
a Pareto superior feasible allocation is possible, but it requires changing the
consumption allocations of every member of an infinite sequence of consumers
extending into the indefinite future.

Comparing (2.8) with (2.6c) and (2.7b) indicates that the stationary equilibrium associated with a given constant rate of money growth will be Pareto
optimal *if and only if* $\pi \leq 0$. This result, which Wallace stresses, might appear
to vindicate the Friedman proposition, since it indicates that efficiency requires
(and is also guaranteed by) a sufficiently low rate of money growth. [Brock and
Scheinkman explicitly argue that results of this kind show that the sort of
results by Brock (1975) for the case of a Sidrauski-type model are not
dependent upon that way of modeling the role of money.] But despite the
similar conclusion, the reason behind it is quite different from Friedman's. A
non-positive rate of money growth is not required for efficiency because it is
necessary to keep the nominal interest rate at zero; in this model, the nominal
interest rate is zero in *any* monetary equilibrium (including the stationary
equilibria with $\pi > 0$), because money would not be held if any other asset
yielded a higher return. (A nominal interest rate can be defined for the
economy just described by introducing a market for one-period loans, which
market will clear with zero borrowing and lending and a real return on loans
equal to the real return on money.) Instead, a positive rate of money growth
creates an inefficiency because the real rate of return available on savings is
reduced (something that Friedman assumes will *not* be affected by the rate of
money growth) and made lower than the economy's growth rate (here assumed
to be zero), resulting in dynamic inefficiency.

An alternative criterion for comparing alternative stationary equilibria would
be to compare the stationary levels of utility $u(c_1, c_2)$ associated with different
possible equilibria. Maximization of $u(c_1, c_2)$ subject to the constraint (2.12a)
requires the first-order condition:

$$\frac{u_1}{u_2}(c_1, c_2) = 1 ,$$

from which one sees immediately that the maximum stationary level of utility is
achieved when $\pi = 0$. (Stationary equilibria with $\pi < 0$ are Pareto optimal
despite the fact that the stationary level of utility is lower, because they allow
the initial old generation, who hold the money supply at the beginning of the
first period and consume only in that period, to obtain a higher level of

consumption than they receive in the stationary equilibrium with $\pi = 0$. These consumers, unlike all subsequent generations, are better off the higher the equilibrium level of real balances m, because this determines the value of the money that they initially hold.) Hence $\pi = 0$ is the uniquely optimal rate of money growth under such a criterion.

Of course, every Pareto optimal consumption allocation maximizes *some* social welfare function that is increasing in (and dependent only upon) the levels of utility achieved by the various consumers. The choice of any among the set of Pareto optimal equilibria could be justified by appropriate weighting of the utilities of different generations in one's social welfare function. However, a stationary equilibrium with $\pi < 0$ corresponds to a sequence of welfare weights that decreases geometrically over time at the rate $1 + \pi$. (Assuming that the social welfare function is a weighted average of utilities, the weights associated with a given Pareto optimal equilibrium can be uniquely identified, given that we have assumed the same utility function for all generations.) That is, the welfare of early generations is weighted most heavily, with the weight on later generations eventually becoming arbitrarily small compared to the weight on the early generations. A social welfare function with such extreme differences in the weights on different generations is unattractive. The stationary equilibrium with $\pi = 0$ achieves the uniquely optimal allocation in the case of a social welfare function with equal weights on all generations' utilities. Furthermore, if one considers any welfare index of the form:

$$W = \lim_{N \to \infty} \left[\sum_{s=1}^{N} \lambda_s u_s \right] \Big/ \left[\sum_{s=1}^{N} \lambda_s \right],$$

where u_s represents the level of utility received by members of generation s and where $\{\lambda_s\}$ is a sequence of positive weights that are both bounded above and bounded away from zero (so that there is an upper bound on the ratio between the weights assigned any two generations), then the stationary equilibrium that achieves the highest stationary level of utility will also achieve a higher level of the index W than any other stationary equilibrium. In this sense use of the criterion of maximum stationary utility simply requires that one not be willing to assign utility weights to different generations that make the weight on some generations' utility larger than that on certain other generations' utility by an arbitrarily large amount.

The conclusions reached using the criterion of Pareto optimality on the one hand and that of maximum stationary utility on the other are not contradictory in the present case, since the policy that leads to the maximum level of stationary utility is *one* of those that results in a Pareto optimal equilibrium. But this is somewhat coincidental, and in the case of more complicated models the rate of money growth required for Pareto optimality may be lower than the one that would maximize stationary utility. Indeed, this is often the case for overlapping generations models in which market imperfections exist that allow the equilibrium rate of return on money to be lower than that on other assets – exactly the case with which Friedman's argument is concerned.

2.3.2. An example with legal restrictions upon financial intermediation

The following provides a simple example.[9] Consider the "legal restrictions model" of how money can be dominated in rate of return, used by Sargent and Wallace (1982) and Bryant and Wallace (1984). In the simplest version of this model, there are overlapping generations of two-period-lived consumers, as above, but each generation consists of three distinct consumer types. Type 1 consumers ("small savers") have life-cycle consumption preferences and a life-cycle endowment pattern such that, over the range of rates of return on savings and possible tax-transfer policies with which we are concerned, they wish always to save a positive quantity in the first period of life, but a quantity too small to allow them to buy bonds (given the legal restriction on the minimum denomination in which bonds can be issued), so that their savings will always be held entirely in the form of money. Type 2 consumers ("large savers") have preferences and endowments such that over this range of rates of return and tax-transfer policies they wish always to save a quantity large enough to allow them to invest in bonds. Type 3 consumers ("borrowers") wish to consume in excess of their endowment during the first period of life, for all rates of return and tax-transfer policies in the range referred to, and so issue bonds. Fiat money, the quantity of which grows at a rate determined by the monetary authority, and the bonds issued by type 3 consumers are the only assets; as before there is a single perishable consumption good per period.

As before, we wish to compare alternative steady rates of growth or contraction of the money supply, for a fixed distribution of whatever lump-sum taxes or transfers occur across the six types of consumers present in each period (young small savers, old small savers, young large savers, etc.), which distribution is assumed not to be subject to choice by the monetary authority. A case which is especially simple to analyze is that in which all taxes or transfers are to type 1 consumers. In this case, variations in the rate of money growth (and hence in the size of the lump-sum taxes or transfers that must be made) have no effect upon the budget constraints of either type 2 or type 3 consumers, and hence no effect upon their borrowing or saving decisions. Let $S_2(R)$ be the aggregate net savings of young type 2 consumers, as a function of

---

[9]The basic idea is drawn from the example presented by Wallace (1987). I have complicated Wallace's example in order to introduce a second asset so that it is clear that the rate of contraction of the money supply required for Pareto optimality is in fact the rate called for by the Friedman Rule.

the gross real return R on bonds, and $S_3(R)$ the corresponding function for young type 3 consumers. (For the rates of return with which we are concerned, $S_2(R) > 0$ while $S_3(R) < 0$.) Then the rate of return that clears the bond market must satisfy:

$$S_2(R) + S_3(R) = 0 , \tag{2.9}$$

as well as $R \geq R_m$. (If the latter condition were not satisfied, then large savers would hold money rather than bonds.) The solution to (2.9) is evidently independent of the rate of money growth; let us suppose that there exists a solution R^* within the range of rates of return for which the assumptions made above about consumer behavior hold. The stationary equilibrium level of real balances m and level of lump-sum transfers h, for any given constant rate of money growth π, will be given by the solution to equations (2.6) and (2.7), where the utility function and endowments referred to in these equations are those of a type 1 consumer.

Let us suppose that the preferences and endowments of type 1 consumers are such that equations (2.6) and (2.7) have a solution with $m > 0$ for the case $\pi = 0$, and that the solution to (2.9) satisfies $R^* > 1$. Then in the case of a constant money supply, there will exist a stationary equilibrium of the kind described (i.e. in which all money is held by small savers, all bonds by large savers), with $R_m = 1$, $R = R^*$, and hence a positive nominal interest rate on bonds. This equilibrium will be Pareto inefficient, as discussed in Subsection 1.1, because the marginal rates of substitution between consumption in the first and second periods of life will be different for type 1 consumers (MRS $= R_m$) than for type 2 and 3 consumers (MRS $= R$). Furthermore, as argued by Friedman, a steady contraction of the money supply at an appropriate rate can lower the nominal interest rate to zero and bring about a Pareto optimal equilibrium. For if one chooses $\pi < 0$, equations (2.6) and (2.7) continue to have a solution with $m > 0$, describing the behavior of type 1 consumers in a stationary equilibrium; the equilibrium rate of return on money will be $R_m = (1 + \pi)^{-1}$. The solution to (2.9) will continue to be R^*. As long as $(1 + \pi)^{-1} \leq R^*$, these equations will continue to describe a stationary equilib-rium. As π is lowered, the equilibrium real rate of return on money increases, while the equilibrium real rate of return on bonds remains unchanged; thus the nominal return on bonds falls. If one chooses π such that $(1 + \pi)^{-1} = R^*$, the rate of return on money becomes as large as that on bonds, so that the nominal rate of interest falls to zero. This is the rate of deflation called for by the Friedman Rule. One can easily verify that the resulting stationary equilibrium is Pareto optimal, since not only do all consumers have the same marginal rate of substitution between any two goods, but the equilibrium real rate of return exceeds the economy's growth rate, so that no dynamic inefficiency exists.

However, implementation of the Friedman Rule does not move the economy to a more desirable stationary equilibrium according to the criterion of maximum stationary utility. In the new stationary equilibrium, the rate of return on bonds is unchanged; hence the budget constraints facing type 2 and 3 consumers are unchanged, and the stationary consumption allocations received by consumers of these types are unchanged. The stationary level of utility received by type 1 consumers depends upon the rate of money growth in the same way as did that of the single consumer type in the simple overlapping generations model considered above: it is maximized when $\pi = 0$, and so is reduced by a contraction of the money supply at the rate necessary to bring the nominal interest rate down to zero. If one's welfare criterion is any weighted average of the stationary levels of utility achieved by the different consumer types, the best stationary equilibrium is achieved by a policy of zero money growth, even though this means a positive nominal interest rate and, consequently, inefficiency.

The point is that the only Pareto optimal equilibrium that can be achieved through policies of this kind (alternative choices of π) is one that maximizes one's social welfare function only if one is willing to place a much higher weight on the welfare of early generations of type 1 consumers than upon later generations of type 1 consumers. The measures that are needed in order to cure the inefficiency associated with a positive nominal interest rate (i.e. raising the rate of return on money balances) have an adverse side-effect: they raise the rate of return available to small savers in a way that distorts the life-cycle consumption pattern of these consumers so as to make their stationary level of utility lower. This happens insofar as reducing the nominal interest rate to zero requires the real return on money balances to be made higher than the economy's rate of growth, which is the rate of return that leads to optimal life-cycle consumption choices (for reasons similar to those behind Phelps' "golden rule").

The result is in no way dependent upon special features of the "legal restrictions" model of how money can be dominated in rate of return by other assets. Similar results may be derived for a wide variety of types of overlapping generations models in which some kind of market imperfection allows an equilibrium to exist in which not all assets earn the same rate of return. For example, Weiss (1980) finds that maximization of the stationary level of utility requires a rate of money growth higher than that which would reduce the nominal interest rate to zero in a model with a single consumer type per generation whose utility function depends upon the level of real balances held at the beginning of the second period of life; and in Woodford (1985) I find a similar result in a model with a single consumer type per generation that is subject to a cash-in-advance constraint.

It is important to note the role in such results of the assumption that the class of alternative policies do not include a fully general menu of possible lump-sum tax and transfer policies, so that the choice of a rate of money growth implies a particular level of redistributive taxes or transfers with a particular pattern. The kind of result just obained is not crucially dependent upon the assumption that the lump-sum taxes or transfers go entirely to type 1 consumers; had we compared alternative rate of money growth for some other fixed distribution of the taxes or transfers, a similar result would be obtained. (If some of the lump-sum taxes are levied upon type 2 or 3 consumers, then a reduction of π slightly below zero would increase the stationary level of utility of type 1 consumers, since they would not pay all of the taxes but would be the only consumers to benefit from the increased rate of return on money balances. But the stationary level of utility of type 2 or 3 consumers would be reduced by any reduction of π below zero for the same reason, and with an appropriate weighting of the stationary utilities of the three types of consumers in one's welfare criterion, it could still be judged undesirable to contract the money supply at all, despite the fact that this would be needed to bring the nominal interest rate down to zero.) But the result obtained does depend upon an assumption that, for example, tax-transfer policies are not possible in which some consumer types (at certain points in the life cycle) receive transfers while others are taxed. With a fully general set of lump-sum taxes and transfers available, it would be possible to choose a policy regime that would make possible an equilibrium with a consumption allocation that maximized any desired weighted average of the stationary levels of utility of the three types of consumers, subject only to the constraint of the aggregate endowment available to distribute; and such a first-best allocation would necessarily be Pareto optimal, so that with a large enough set of policy instruments there is no conflict between the two welfare objectives. It follows immediately from the first-order conditions for the maximization of

$$W = \sum_{s=1}^{3} \lambda_s u_s \tag{2.10}$$

subject to a constraint that aggregate consumption not exceed the aggregate endowment each period, that in any such first-best allocation the marginal rate of substitution between first- and second-period consumption is 1 for each consumer type. Hence, in any such first-best equilibrium, one would have $R = R_m = 1$; the rates of return on both assets would be equalized (as called for by the Friedman Rule), but this would not involve raising the rate of return on money above the economy's growth rate (as was argued above to be undesirable).

The following is a simple example of such a first-best equilibrium. Suppose that $S_2(1) + S_3(1) < 0$, because aggregate net saving by the type 2 and 3 consumers is an increasing function of R, and $R^* > 1$. Consider a policy regime with $\pi = 0$, so that aggregate net transfers each period will be zero. However, let young type 2 consumers receive a lump-sum transfer equal in aggregate to $-[S_2(1) + S_3(1)]$, while old type 2 consumers are required to pay a lump-sum tax of equal size. This will not change the lifetime budget constraints of type 2 consumers if they face a real return on bonds of $R = 1$, but will increase their desired saving in that event by exactly the amount of the transfer, so that the aggregate saving of type 2 consumers in this case will equal $-S_3(1)$. As a result, the bond market will clear at $R = 1$. As before, $R_m = 1$ follows from the fact that $\pi = 0$. This is a Pareto optimal equilibrium, because the marginal rates of substitution of all consumers are equalized and the real rate of return faced by all consumers is no less than the economy's rate of growth (i.e. zero). It also achieves the consumption allocation that maximizes (2.10) subject to the constraint associated with the aggregate endowment, if one chooses the weights $\{\lambda_s\}$ inversely proportional to each consumer type's marginal utility of consumption in this allocation.

The conclusion, that availability of a sufficiently broad set of possible lump-sum taxes and transfers will make the Friedman Rule necessarily a part of the policy that maximizes any welfare criterion based upon the stationary levels of utility received by the various consumer types in a stationary overlapping generations model, is quite general. This explains, for example, the result to this effect of Abel's (1987) in the case of an overlapping generations model in which consumers receive utility from holding real money balances, and of Woodford (1985) in the case of an overlapping generations model with a cash-in-advance constraint. The general idea is that, even in the case of many different kinds of market imperfections of the kind that make possible equilibria with money dominated in rate of return, it is possible to prove a Second Welfare Theorem: with a sufficiently broad set of lump-sum taxes and transfers available, the complete set of Pareto optimal allocations can be supported as equilibria. In such a case the policy that maximizes any social welfare function is necessarily one of these, and as explained in Subsection 1.1, it is very generally true that a Pareto optimal equilibrium will have to have a zero nominal interest rate.

Does this mean that results of the kind illustrated above [or by the results of Weiss (1980), Wallace (1987), and so on] should not be regarded as indicating a realistic reason for choosing a rate of money growth greater than that called for by the Friedman Rule, insofar as the results depend upon a possibly artificial restriction upon the set of available policy instruments? This is essentially the same objection that was raised in the previous subsection, which was also concerned with possible welfare effects of the rate of money growth that were critically dependent upon the redistributional aspect of such policy choices. There are again various ways in which one might seek to answer this objection. One is to explicitly describe informational constraints that would limit the set of tax-transfer policies available to government policymakers and argue for their realism. Wallace (1987) proceeds along these lines, insofar as he argues that the same kind of presumed problems of imperfect information that would make it possible for equilibrium to be inefficient with a constant money supply (so that a sufficient rate of contraction of the money supply is necessary to achieve Pareto optimality) should also limit the set of feasible tax policies available to the government to the particular class he considers. Rather than further developing explicit examples of this kind, however, I shall content myself with arguing that any model of a monetary economy that allows a role for money of the sort that is conventionally assumed (in both theoretical and empirical work on money demand) must be based upon an assumption that alternative rates of growth of the money supply necessarily imply certain patterns of redistribution, rather than that the redistributive aspect of money supply growth and contraction is completely arbitrary.

Let us consider, for example, the proposition that there is a relatively stable demand for nominal money balances as a function of the level of money prices, some measure of real activity in the economy, and perhaps certain interest rates, which relation is not too much affected by monetary policy changes (as long as those are not really extreme), so that changes in the money supply necessarily bring with them changes in the level of money prices, the level of real activity, interest rates, or some combination of the three. In particular, open market operations between money and bonds (that earn a higher rate of interest than does money), the main way through which changes in the money supply are brought about in economies such as the United States, are argued to have effects of this sort, and of a predictable sort. But the sort of effects that are usually argued to occur need not be associated with open market operations at all, in rigorous general equilibrium models of money demand of the kind we have been discussing here, *if the redistributive aspect of the open market operation is allowed to be completely arbitrary.* For example, Sargent and Smith (1986) argue, in the case of a "legal restrictions" model of the kind considered above, that if a particular pattern of lump-sum taxes and transfers is associated with open market operations between money and bonds, such open market operations will be completely *neutral*, not only in the sense of having no effects on real activity or upon interest rates, but also of having no effect upon the equilibrium price level either. (The idea is that if the open market operation is accompanied by a pattern of lump-sum taxes and transfers that are appropriately differentiated among different consumer types and between young and old consumers of those types, the aggregate demands for real money balances and for bonds, at the previously prevailing equilibrium prices, are changed by the open market operation by exactly the same amount as are the available supplies of these assets, so that all markets continue to clear at the same prices as before. The lifetime budget constraints of all consumers also remain unchanged, and so the real uses of resources by the private sector are in no way changed by the open market operation. All of these results would continue to hold, it should be noted, if, instead of the model with perfect price flexibility assumed by Sargent and Smith, one introduced price stickiness or a "Lucas supply curve".) Sargent and Smith argue that the sort of open market operation that has exactly this distributional impact should be considered a "pure" open market operation, while a combination of the sale or purchase of government bonds by the monetary authority with any other pattern of lump-sum taxes and transfers should be considered a combination of an open market operation with a certain redistributive fiscal intervention. This particular way of distinguishing between "monetary policy" choices and "fiscal policy" choices is quite non-standard and has a number of disadvantages. But their neutrality result does clearly make the point that if the open market operations actually engaged in by the Federal Reserve do have certain characteristic effects (e.g. if a permanent increase in the money supply through this means eventually results in a roughly proportional increase in the price level, rather than having no effect or even decreasing the price level) it must be because the redistributive aspect of the way in which such interventions actually occur is of one particular sort rather than happening to coincide upon different occasions with very different patterns of taxes and transfers; at least the range of variation in the redistributive aspect of actual open market operations must be considerably more restrictive than the range of possible combinations of monetary and fiscal interventions considered by Sargent and Smith.[10] The most plausible explanation of this would be that the range of feasible fiscal interventions under the circumstances actually faced by policymakers is considerably smaller than that considered by Sargent and Smith. But in this case one cannot argue that the entire set of Pareto optimal allocations can be supported as equilibria by appropriate choices of monetary and fiscal policies, and so there is no reason to suppose that in general the second-best policy from the point of view of maximizing stationary utility will be one that reduces the nominal interest rate to zero.

2.3.3. Money growth and welfare in models with capital accumulation

Related considerations also help to clarify a point made by a number of early critics of Friedman's argument, in particular Hahn (1971). Hahn argues that a

---

[10] The possibility of a "neutrality" result of this kind for open market operations is not dependent upon special features of the type of "legal restrictions" model of the respective demands for money and bonds used by Sargent and Smith. Indeed, the basic argument behind their result was first made by Kaldor (1970) in a criticism of the theoretical foundations of Friedman's notion of a stable demand for real balances.

higher rate of return on money balances would discourage capital accumulation, insofar as more savings would be held in the form of money rather than direct or indirect claims to physical capital, and that the effects on income of the lower capital stock might have a more important effect on welfare than the increased "liquidity" associated with the higher level of real balances. This argument is clearly not correct for all possible economies. It is not necessarily true that a higher real return on money balances must result in a lower equilibrium capital stock. If, for example, one introduces a standard constant-returns, one-sector production technology into the Sidrauski–Brock model described in Subsection 1.2, the level of capital stock associated with a stationary equilibrium will always be such that the marginal product of capital is equal to the rate of time preference of the representative consumer; if one assumes an inelastic labor supply, the level of capital stock for which this is true is independent of the rate of inflation. In such a model the level of capital stock associated with a stationary equilibrium is unchanged as the rate of return on money is made closer to the rate of return on physical capital through deflation. Nor is it necessarily true that an increase in the equilibrium capital stock, when this is the effect of a higher rate of money growth, must mean a higher level of consumer welfare. If one introduces a one-sector production technology into the simple overlapping generations model with no market imperfections described above [e.g. in the manner of Diamond (1965)], then one finds that in a stationary equilibrium the level of capital stock is such that the marginal product of capital equals the rate of return on money, which is determined solely by the rate of money growth. If one assumes an inelastic labor supply (as Diamond does), this would establish an inverse relationship between the stationary equilibrium capital stock and the rate of money growth. But in this case, choice of any rate of money growth greater than that consistent with Pareto optimality (i.e. $\pi > 0$) will result in a capital stock higher than the "golden rule" capital stock, and hence *lower* aggregate consumption.

A rate of money growth higher than that which would result in a rate of return on money as high as that on physical capital *is* often optimal (in the sense of maximizing stationary utility) in overlapping generations economies where market imperfections allow money to be dominated in rate of return, so that the real return to physical capital can exceed the economy's growth rate even while the real return on money (due to steady money growth) is less than it. A number of such examples have been presented in the literature, including those of Fischer (1986), Romer (1986), and Woodford (1983). Nonetheless, the nature of the interaction between money growth, capital accumulation, and the life-cycle allocation of resources in these examples is somewhat complex, and not really of the kind suggested by Hahn's argument. That is, the reason that an increase in the rate of money growth can increase welfare is not really that a lower return on money makes capital accumulation more attractive. In these examples the "inflation tax" effectively brings about a fiscal transfer from later to earlier periods of life, which increases welfare if the real rate of return on saving exceeds the population growth rate. The effect can be reversed if money growth occurs through transfers to consumers at the end of their lives (while effectively "taxing" them over their entire lifetimes), even though in that case increased money growth reduces the return on money to exactly the same extent.

Furthermore, the increase in stationary welfare due to the higher rate of money growth may occur even if it does not result in any substitution from money to capital. Suppose that in the "legal restrictions" model we eliminate the type 3 consumers (borrowers), and instead let the type 2 consumers (large savers) hold physical capital earning a return $R > 1$, while, as before, type 1 consumers (small savers) must hold money. Just as above, the stationary level of utility of the type 1 consumers is maximized by choosing $R_m = 1$, while the stationary utility of the type 2 consumers is unaffected. But neither consumer type substitutes between capital and money balances as the rate of return on money is lowered.

Indeed, a result of this kind is possible even when physical capital and real balances are *complements*, so that a lower rate of return on money results in *less* capital accumulation. An example is described in the appendix, in which legal restrictions exist that require real money balances to be held in an amount that is at least as large as a certain multiple of the value of one's wealth held in the form of physical capital. (One may interpret this as an economy in which because of indivisibilities capital cannot be directly owned by individual savers, so that accumulation of physical capital must be financed by intermediaries who provide small-denomination liabilities – deposits – to the ultimate savers. If these intermediaries are perfectly competitive but are subject to a "reserve requirement" that requires them to hold a fraction $k/1 + k$ of the funds deposited with them in the form of money, then the deposits held by the savers will effectively be claims to a bundle of physical capital and real money balances in the ratio 1 to k.) In this sort of economy, as noted by Gale (1983) and Orphanides and Solow (1988), there will typically be a reverse "Tobin effect", i.e. a reduction in the real return on money balances due to higher inflation will decrease rather than increase the equilibrium capital stock. But the overlapping generations example presented in the appendix shows that a higher rate of money growth than that called for by the Friedman Rule may be optimal (in the sense of maximizing the stationary level of utility), *despite* the fact that a lower rate of money growth would increase the steady state capital stock as well as lowering the rate-of-return differential between money and capital.

Finally, it should be noted that many of the results exhibited for economies with capital accumulation do not actually depend upon the existence of productive capital; preferences could be found for which exactly the same relationship between money growth and welfare would exist in the case of a pure exchange economy, by replacing the possibility of physically transforming goods in one period into goods in another period by the possibility of altering some consumer's consumption of the goods in the two periods without changing his utility. This also indicates that the effect of inflation upon capital accumulation cannot be what is essential in those examples.

The results of this subsection should make it clear that the use of models with a finite number of infinitely lived consumers, rather than overlapping generations of infinitely-lived consumers, is far from an inconsequential choice when the issue to be analyzed concerns welfare comparisons across alternative policy regimes. It is sometimes argued that overlapping generations models would be useful for monetary theory only insofar as one were interested in having a model of the demand for money that does not involve any market imperfections that could allow money to be held despite being dominated in rate of return. But this is clearly not the case; in the models just described, money is not held simply as a store of value like any other asset, yet results are obtained regarding the welfare consequences of money growth that are different from those that would be obtained in the case of a similar model of money demand but with a finite number of infinitely-lived consumer types. In particular, in the latter case a rate of money growth that resulted in a Pareto optimal allocation would not be so unreasonable a candidate for a desirable policy, insofar as the set of utility weights for which the equilibrium allocation would be optimal would generally not be extremely unequal.

2.4. Consequences of the rate of money growth for determinacy of the equilibrium value of money

To this point I have assumed the perspective of most of the literature on the "optimum quantity of money", which is to say that I have simply compared the welfare properties of the stationary equilibria (or at any rate stationary Markovian equilibria involving fluctuations only of the simplest kind consistent with the existence of stochastic fundamentals) corresponding to different possible rates of money growth. But many equilibrium models of monetary economies have the property that the equilibrium corresponding to a given monetary policy need not be unique, and indeed multiple equilibria could have been exhibited in the case of most of the models considered above had we considered a broader class of possible equilibria. These other equilibria may well be relevant for our consideration of the optimal rate of growth of the money supply. For one rate of money growth need not be considered preferable to another, even if the stationary equilibrium corresponding to the first is clearly preferable to that corresponding the second, if the first policy also makes possible other equilibria that are worse than any of the equilibria consistent with the second policy.

Such considerations can weigh against adoption of the sort of contractionary policy called for by Friedman, even if one supposes that none of the problems discussed in the previous three subsections is empirically significant, insofar as a steady contraction of the money supply can result in indeterminacy of equilibrium under circumstances in which it would be unique (and stationary) in the case of a higher rate of money growth. Furthermore, some of the other (non-stationary) equilibria in the case of the lower rate of money growth may involve a lower level of welfare than would be associated with the stationary equilibrium obtained with the higher rate of money growth, insofar as fluctuations in either the allocation of resources (in the absence of any change in fundamentals) or in the price level may reduce consumer welfare. [The possible welfare loss due to fluctuations in the allocation of resources results from consumer risk aversion, and can be explicitly derived in equilibrium models of the kind considered here; fluctuations in the price level are not harmful in the sort of models considered here insofar as they are not accompanied by quantity fluctuations, but they could be harmful in a more complicated model which preserved essentially the same account of the demand for money balances but incorporated imperfect information problems of the kind modeled by Lucas (1972). For an argument that price level indeterminacy is itself an indication that a particular policy regime is an undesirable one, see Sargent (1988).]

In Woodford (1988) I analyze the complete set of rational expectations equilibria (including "sunspot equilibria" involving sunspot variables with arbitrary stochastic properties), for different constant rates of money supply growth, in the case of the representative consumer cash-in-advance model of Lucas and Stokey (1983), discussed in Section 1. It will be recalled that if we simply compare the stationary equilibria consistent with alternative rates of money growth, the highest level of utility for the representative consumer is associated with the rate of contraction of the money supply called for by Friedman, i.e. $\pi = \beta - 1$. Owing to the continuity of the various functions characterizing stationary equilibrium, levels of utility nearly this high (and higher than those associated with higher rates of money growth) will also be associated with rates of contraction of the money supply close to (but not quite as large as) that called for by Friedman. However, there may also be other equilibria besides the stationary equilibria previously considered. In fact, indeterminacy of perfect foresight (deterministic) equilibrium and the existence of sunspot equilibria can much more easily occur in the case of lower rates of money growth than in the case of higher. "Self-fulfilling deflations" (equilibria in which the level of real balances asymptotically becomes arbitrarily large, as in the example given in Section A.2 of the appendix) are necessarily possible when $0 > \pi \geq \beta - 1$ – exactly the cases in which the steady-state equilibrium has desirable properties – and when such equilibria exist, there is necessarily a continuum of perfect foresight equilibria and a very large set of sunspot equilibria. The set of sunspot equilibria includes equilibria in which, even asymptotically, the level of real balances is not always high; reversions to low levels of real balances (due to rapid inflation) occur in certain sunspot states, resulting in a binding cash-in-advance constraint in those states. As a result, the sunspot state affects the real allocation of resources. On the other hand, if $\pi \geq 0$, self-fulfilling deflations are impossible (the level of real balances is bounded in all equilibria), and equilibrium may be unique. In this case, the unique equilibrium involves no response to sunspot states.

For some preference specifications, there can exist large sets of equilibria in which real balances remain forever bounded both above and away from zero, although they are not constant at the steady-state level ("bounded equilibrium fluctuations"). When indeterminacy of this kind exists, again there necessarily exist sunspot equilibria of this kind, and in sunspot equilibria of this kind the sunspot states necessarily affect the allocation of resources. This kind of indeterminacy can occur even for positive rates of money growth, but again it is generally associated with relatively low rates of money growth. At least in the case of additively separable preferences (along with some additional regularity conditions that are relatively unrestrictive), it can be shown that there necessarily exists some critical rate of money growth such that bounded equilibrium fluctuations are impossible for any rate of money growth at least that high, and the critical rate is not so high as to result in non-existence of a monetary steady state. Thus, there exist preference specifications for which a high enough rate of money growth results in uniqueness of monetary equilibrium (and the impossibility of sunspot equilibria), but the rate of money growth required may be well above zero. Thus, insofar as price level determinacy (or the prevention of surprise movements in the price level) is an aim of policy, it might provide a reason for not reducing the rate of money growth too far.

While no comparably thorough analysis of the complete set of possible rational expectations equilibria has been carried out for any other model, similar results appear to hold for a number of types of equilibrium models of money. Brock (1975) discusses the possibility of multiple perfect foresight equilibria in the Sidrauski model, and shows in particular that a continuum of self-fulfilling deflations are possible when π is near the rate called for by Friedman. Sunspot equilibria are also easily shown to exist in that case. Because the Lucas–Stokey model is formally isomorphic to a particular case of the Sidrauski–Brock model, the conclusions reported above regarding bounded equilibrium fluctuations will also apply to that model for at least some kinds of preferences. Grandmont (1986) considers the existence of deterministic equilibrium cycles and stationary Markovian sunspot equilibria in the overlapping generations model of Wallace (1980), for the case of utility additively separable between periods of life, and shows that neither is possible in the case of a high enough rate of money growth. His results can be shown to extend to the entire class of bounded equilibrium fluctuations, and since self-fulfilling deflations are impossible in that class of models, a high enough rate of money growth again suffices to rule out indeterminacy of either sort. The problem has not been much studied in the case of Bewley–Levine models, but it will be recalled that the example of a continuum of self-fulfilling deflations discussed in Subsection 2.2.1 depended upon $\pi < 0$.

Further discussion of the consequences of alternative monetary policy regimes for price level determinacy and the existence of sunspot equilibria can be found in Subsections 3.2 and 3.3 below.

3. Is control of money supply growth the only way to insure an efficient return on money?

In the previous section I have accepted the conventional formulation of the problem of the optimum quantity of money as a comparison of the consequences of alternative steady rates of growth or contraction of the money supply. In this section I wish to take up another sort of question about Friedman's analysis. Even supposing that it is possible to achieve a Pareto optimal equilibrium through an appropriate choice of monetary policy and even supposing that efficiency in this sense is a desirable goal of monetary policy, must one think of the range of choices as simply one or another steady rate of money supply growth? In particular, given that Friedman's argument is first that a zero nominal rate of interest is necessary for efficiency, and then secondly that a low rate of money growth is necessary in order to achieve it, an obvious question is whether Friedman's is in fact the only way to think about policies that would keep nominal interest rates low. On the one hand, one might wonder whether a low rate of growth of the money supply is an inevitable feature of a policy aimed at keeping nominal interest rates low, given that discussions of monetary policy options in the short run often associate a lower rate of money growth with an increase in nominal interest rates. And on the other, one might wonder whether, even granted that maintenance of low nominal interest rates will involve a steady low rate of money growth, it is necessarily the case that the best way to formulate a policy aimed at keeping the economy in such an equilibrium is by fixing an exogenous growth path for the money supply, to which the monetary authority is committed regardless of what the equilibrium level of interest rates might turn out to be. Two simple proposals are (1) for the monetary authority to commit itself directly to a desired target path for nominal interest rates regardless of what rate of money supply growth this might turn out to involve, or (2) for the rates of return on money and other assets to be equalized through interest payments on money balances. These two issues are taken up in sequence. Because most of the literature has been concerned with the effects of alternative choices of an exogenously specified money growth rate, these issues have not yet been very thoroughly studied. As a result I will not be able to give the same sort of synthetic exposition here as above. Instead I will have to be content to present a few simple examples that are intended more to be provocative than to suggest general answers to the questions just raised.

3.1. Low nominal interest rates may require temporary money growth and inflation

Even in the case of economies for which there is a one-to-one correspondence between possible equilibrium paths for the nominal interest rate and possible paths for the money supply, so that choice of a target path for one necessarily implies choice of a target path for the other, the way to permanently reduce the nominal interest rate to zero (in order to achieve the sort of efficiency gains with which Friedman is concerned) may not be to immediately commit oneself to a steady low rate of growth of the money supply. In particular, it may not be appropriate to immediately adopt that rate of money growth that is known to be required for a stationary equilibrium with a zero nominal interest rate. For if the economy does not start from initial conditions (i.e. an initial distribution of asset holdings) consistent with the zero-interest stationary equilibrium, adoption of that steady rate of money growth may result not only in failure to reach a zero nominal interest rate immediately, but in failure to ever reach it; while alternative monetary policies might be possible that would bring the nominal interest rate to zero immediately.

Consider again the "legal restrictions" model of Subsection 2.3, but suppose now that no lump-sum taxes on transfers are possible. Instead, let us suppose that the government can borrow from the private sector (on the same terms as type 3 consumers, i.e. its bonds are also subject to the minimum denomination requirement) and that similarly the central bank can acquire private debt (so that the government is a net lender to the private sector). Variations in the money supply will then have to come about through *open market operations* between money and bonds. (Again, an assumption of limitations upon the set of fiscal instruments available is crucial for establishing a determinate rate of money growth necessary in order to have a stationary equilibrium with a particular level of nominal interest rates.) Let $S_1(R_m)$ denote the aggregate real net savings of type 1 consumers as a function of the rate of return on money, and $S_j(R)$, for $j = 2, 3$, denote as before the aggregate real net savings of type j consumers fas a function of the real return on bonds. (A similar saving function for type 1 consumers is now well defined because we now assume no taxes or transfers.) The conditions for money market and bond market equilibrium in period t are then:

$$S_1(P_t/P_{t+1}) = M_t/P_t , \tag{3.1}$$

$$S_2(R_t) + S_3(R_t) = B_t/P_t , \tag{3.2}$$

where P_t represents the money price of the consumption good in period t, R_t represents the real return expected to be earned on bonds held from period t to period $t + 1$, M_t represents the money supply held at the end of period t, and B_t represents the money value of the net holdings of government debt by the private sector at the end of period t. (B_t is negative in a period in which the government is a net lender to the private sector.) The government chooses the evolution over time of the outstanding quantities of money and government bonds subject to the budget constraint:

$$M_t + B_t = M_{t-1} + (R_{t-1}P_t/P_{t-1})B_{t-1} . \tag{3.3}$$

Here $R_{t-1}P_t/P_{t-1}$, the nominal interest rate on bonds issued in period $t - 1$, will be fixed in period $t - 1$; hence, the entire right-hand side of (3.3) is predetermined at the beginning of period t. The government's only choice is how the total outstanding nominal value of its liabilities, $M_t + B_t$, is to be divided between money and bonds.

Let a stationary equilibrium be one in which real money balances $m = M_t/P_t$, net real government debt $b = B_t/P_t$, and the real rates of return on both money and bonds are all constant. Equation (3.3) implies that in a stationary equilibrium one must have:

$$(1 - R_m)m = (R - 1)b .$$

This, together with (3.1) and (3.2), implies:

$$(1 - R_m)S_1(R_m) = (R - 1)[S_2(R) + S_3(R)] . \tag{3.4}$$

This indicates the relationship that must exist between the return on bonds R and the return on money R_m (and hence the rate of money growth and inflation) in a stationary equilibrium. Conversely, any pair (R, R_m) that satisfy (3.4), with $R \geq R_m$ and both R and R_m drawn from the range of rates of return for which the behavioral assumptions made earlier hold (type 1 consumers save but not enough to be able to purchase bonds, etc.), will describe a stationary equilibrium.

Now let us make some additional assumptions about the form of the savings functions: that all net savings functions are increasing in the rate of return on savings (a "gross substitutes" assumption), and furthermore that $S_2(1) + S_3(1) < 0$, while $S_1(1) + S_2(1) + S_3(1) > 0$. In this case we observe the following about the set of solutions to (3.4). First, there are two distinct stationary equilibria with a constant money supply (and hence $R_m = 1$): one with $R = 1$, and one with $R = R^* > 1$, where R^* is the unique solution to (2.9). In the first stationary equilibrium, $m > 0$ and $b < 0$ (the government is a net lender), although total government liabilities $m + b$ remain positive; in the second (the equilibrium with a constant money supply discussed in Subsection 2.3), $m > 0$ and $b = 0$. Second, there are two distinct stationary equilibria with a zero nominal interest rate (i.e. with $R = R_m$): one with $R = 1$ (the same equilibrium just discussed), and one with $R = R^{**} < 1$, where R^{**} is the unique solution to

$$S_1(R) + S_2(R) + S_3(R) = 0 .$$

Now under the assumptions made above the equilibrium with $R = R_m = 1$ is the unique Pareto optimal equilibrium that can be attained solely through the use of open market operations (i.e. involving no lump-sum taxes or transfers), for Pareto optimality requires both $R = R_m$ (so that all consumers have identical marginal rates of substitution) and $R \geq 1$ (so that there is no dynamic inefficiency). Furthermore, it is also the unique stationary equilibrium of this type that achieves an allocation on the stationary utility frontier, i.e. for which there exists a set of utility weights, all of which are bounded above and away from zero, such that this equilibrium achieves the maximum feasible level of average utility. Hence, either from the point of view of achieving efficiency or of maximizing at least one non-extreme weighted average of utilities, the stationary equilibrium with $R = R_m = 1$ is the most desirable one.

Now this equilibrium does not require money growth if one starts from initial conditions consistent with the stationary equilibrium, i.e. if one starts out with a money supply in excess of total government liabilities by a ratio of $S_1(1)/[S_1(1) + S_2(1) + S_3(1)]$. Suppose instead that in the past the government has followed a laissez-faire policy, i.e. a constant money supply but also no government borrowing or lending, and that as a result the initial asset holdings of the private sector are those associated with the stationary equilibrium with $R_m = 1$, $R = R^*$. In this case, initially the nominal value of total government liabilities (the predetermined value for $M_1 + B_1$) is exactly equal to the money supply (M_0). If a policy of zero money growth is followed ($M_t = M_0$ for all t), then it follows that $B_t = 0$ forever, so that $R_t = R^*$ forever. One possible equilibrium path for the price level is for it to remain constant forever (i.e. the stationary equilibrium with $R_m = 1$, $R = R^*$). If there are other equilibria they involve self-fulfilling inflations in which the value of money goes asymptotically to zero in which the real return on money is always negative. Hence, in all possible equilibria under this policy, nominal interest rates are positive forever, and always equal at least to $R^* - 1$. The allocation of resources will not be Pareto optimal and the average levels of utility of the different consumer types will necessarily be inside the frontier of feasible values.

Yet under these initial conditions the optimal stationary equilibrium can be achieved. In order to reach it, an open market operation is needed to obtain the ratio B_1/M_1 associated with that equilibrium; once the correct composition of government liabilities is obtained, the money supply can be held constant forever. Since the optimal stationary equilibrium requires $M_1/M_1 + B_1 = k = S_1(1)/[S_1(1) + S_2(1) + S_3(1)] > 1$, and since the initial conditions require that $M_1 + B_1 = M_0$, the optimal stationary equilibrium will require $M_1/M_0 = k > 1$, i.e. money growth in the first period, although no further money growth is required. Since in the optimal stationary equilibrium the level of real money balances is the same $[S_1(1)]$ as in the previous stationary equilibrium, the transition to the optimal stationary equilibrium will also require $P_1/P_0 = k > 1$, i.e. inflation in the first period, although no further inflation is required. Note that this inflation does not create any inefficiency since it does not result in high nominal interest rates. This does not mean, of course, that no one is hurt by it; the initial holders of money (the initial old consumers of type 1) are worse off the higher is P_1. A social welfare function giving sufficient importance to the welfare of this group might well lead a government to prefer a policy of more gradual transition to the optimal stationary equilibrium in order to have lower inflation in the first period, at the expense of Pareto optimality.

This result does not depend upon special features of the "legal restrictions" model. Similar results are obtained in Woodford (1985, 1987) for the case of an overlapping generations model in which all consumers are identical and live for three consecutive periods, and all consumption purchases are subject to a cash-in-advance constraint. In that model, the initial conditions that may or may not be consistent with the optimal stationary equilibrium have to do with the distribution of money holdings at the beginning of the first period between consumers in the second and consumers in the third period of their lives. Again there are two stationary equilibria with zero money growth, one with $R = R_m = 1$ (the unique Pareto optimal stationary equilibrium, which achieves the maximum feasible stationary level of utility), which requires the government to be a net lender, and one with $R_m = 1$, $R > 1$ (and hence a positive nominal interest rate), consistent with laissez-faire. The first involves a larger fraction of the money supply being, at the start of each period, in the hands of consumers starting their second period of life rather than their third. If laissez-faire has prevailed in the past, the initial distribution of money balances is such that, if the money supply continues to be held constant forever, the inefficient stationary equilibrium will continue forever.

On the other hand, it is possible to achieve a Pareto optimal equilibrium by choosing in each period the quantity of open market operations by the central bank necessary to bring about a zero nominal interest rate. In the first period this will require an expansion of the money supply and an increase in the price level. (The expansion of the money supply is needed because the interest rate can be lowered only if the central bank supplies additional credit. The increase in the price level is necessary in order to reduce the value of the money balances initially held by consumers in the second and third periods of life, thus inducing them to consume less, allowing the goods market to clear despite the increased demand on the part of consumers in the first period of life due to the lower cost of borrowed funds.) However, consistent pursuit of this policy results in asymptotic convergence to the optimal stationary equilibrium. This example is of interest because it demonstrates the possible need for temporary money growth and inflation during the transition to a non-inflationary stationary equilibrium in an example where the transition to the more desirable stationary equilibrium cannot be achieved in the first period alone (i.e. by a single open market operation). The case for moving, at least eventually, to what I have called the optimal stationary equilibrium is also stronger in this case because of the existence of a single consumer type per generation. In this case, any welfare criterion based upon a weighted average of the utility levels of all generations with weights that are uniformly bounded above and away from zero will make any policy that results in eventual convergence to that stationary equilibrium preferable to the policy of never allowing any growth in the money supply.

A similar result is also obtained in Woodford (1987) for the Lucas–Stokey model, and for other models in Wallace (1988). Finally, it should be noted that the need for high money growth in order to keep nominal interest rates low need not disappear, even asymptotically; if there are continuing shocks that affect asset demands, maintenance of low nominal interest rates may involve recurrent episodes of high money growth. This is illustrated in the case of a "legal restrictions" model with time-varying endowments by Sargent and Wallace (1982), but the proposition is also easily seen to be true of a wide class of monetary models.

It is worth emphasizing that in all of these examples the possible desirability of temporary money growth and inflation depends upon the assumed absence of fiscal policy instruments. If lump-sum taxation were possible in the "legal restrictions" economy, then it would be possible to bring about the composition of government liabilities B_1/M_1 associated with the optimal stationary equilibrium without having to make M_1 any larger than M_0 (and so also without inflation), since tax collections could be used to make $M_1 + B_1$ smaller than M_0. It would similarly make possible intervention in the loan market to bring down nominal interest rates in the cash-in-advance example without a coincident increase in the total money supply. On the other hand, if one supposes (not implausibly) that the only available taxes are all distorting taxes, it would remain the case, in either of these examples, that the unique policy leading to a

Pareto optimal equilibrium was the one involving temporary money growth and inflation, for Pareto optimality would require that the distorting taxes not be used.

3.2. Can a central bank peg the nominal interest rate?

Doubtless much of the controversy surrounding the results of Sargent and Wallace (1982) just referred to arises from the fact that they choose to describe their optimal policy as one of pegging nominal interest rates through a "discount window", rather than (as I have described it above) talking about cyclical variations in the outstanding quantity of money that might be brought about by open market operations. This raises an interesting issue: if the object of optimal monetary policy (in accordance with Friedman's argument) is to bring about a zero nominal interest rate, why does monetary policy need to be formulated in terms of a target rate of money supply growth at all (constant or otherwise)? Why not simply target the nominal interest rate directly? This becomes a particularly pressing issue if one supposes that, for reasons of the kind discussed in the previous subsection, the time path for the money supply needed in order to maintain a zero nominal interest rate forever does not involve constant growth. Then an argument against trying to keep nominal interest rates always exactly zero might be that detailed knowledge of the true structure of the economy would be necessary to know how exactly the rate of money growth should be varied. But if it is possible simply to instruct the Federal Reserve to conduct open market operations when and in the amounts necessary to keep nominal interest rates on target, and if (as Friedman argues) the desired level of nominal interest rates is not time varying and can be known from an economic argument of very general validity that does not require one to commit oneself to any detailed model of the economy, this would not seem to be an obstacle.

But it is often argued that a monetary policy conducted along those lines would prove disastrous. One type of argument, which may be traced back to Wicksell and Robertson and finds a well-known modern expression in Friedman (1968), asserts that a policy of pegging nominal interest rates would be desirable only if exactly the right interest rate target were chosen (an unlikely outcome, particularly since the "natural rate of interest" might vary over time); attempting to maintain nominal interest rates at a level below their "natural rate" would require perpetual and indeed accelerating money growth and inflation, that would probably make the policy unsustainable after some finite period of time, while attempting to maintain them above their "natural rate" would require a corresponding acceleration of deflation. Such an argument depends upon a belief that there is a unique equilibrium real rate of interest determined completely independently of monetary policy, and that monetary expansion can bring about a temporary reduction in the real rate of interest only by bringing about a situation of disequilibrium in which lenders are mistaken about the real return that they receive because inflation is higher than they expect it to be; such a disequilibrium can then be maintained, if at all, only by an ever-accelerating inflation in order to keep inflation ahead of lenders' expectations. But this is plainly not true of many coherent equilibrium models; there may be many different real rates of interest that can exist in equilibrium, even in stationary equilibrium, depending upon the monetary policy regime.[11] In the case of the "legal restrictions" example of the previous subsection, there exist solutions to (3.4) for a large number of different possible stationary real interest rates R, and, as noted above, there are even two distinct stationary real rates of interest that are consistent with zero money growth and a constant price level. The same is true of my [Woodford (1985, 1987)] cash-in-advance model, and indeed of very many overlapping generations models. As a result, there is no general reason to suppose that attempting to permanently lower the nominal interest rate, even if this requires monetary expansion and inflation at first, must result in perpetual acceleration of inflation or in eventual infeasibility of the policy.

A second argument against interest-rate pegging asserts that such a policy regime makes the price level indeterminate, resulting in the possibility not only of inflation or deflation without bound at the time that such a policy regime is initiated, but of continuing unexpected fluctuations of the price level in response to "sunspot" events (as discussed in Subsection 2.4). This argument has been made, for example, by Sargent and Wallace (1975) and by Sargent (1979, pp. 92–95).[12] The argument is as follows. The level of money prices is determined by the requirement that the real value of the nominal money supplied by the central bank be equal to the private sector's demand for real balances, which will depend upon the nominal interest rate as well as upon factors such as the level of real economic activity. If the money supply rule is simply to supply as large a nominal quantity as is demanded given a certain nominal interest rate, then this relation leaves the money price level indeterminate insofar as a higher price level would still equate money supply and demand if a proportionately higher quantity of money were supplied, as it would be under the policy regime described. Nor do any other equilibrium conditions resolve this indeterminacy (at least in the IS–LM model considered

---

[11] The possible non-uniqueness of the "natural rate of interest" was mentioned by many early critics of Wicksell's doctrine, such as Cassel and von Mises, as a reason why the "cumulative process" of accelerating inflation need not continue forever in the face of continued low nominal interest rates. See Kohn (1989).

[12] The idea that pegging the nominal interest rate would lead to an indeterminate price level in an aggregative Keynesian model was pointed out by authors such as Modigliani (1944) and Patinkin (1965, p. 309); for further discussion, see Kohn (1989). Sargent and Wallace (1975) develop the idea in the context of an explicitly dynamic model with rational expectations. Sargent and Wallace themselves repudiate the doctrine in their (1982) paper.

by Sargent and Wallace), for the current price level enters them only insofar as some of them involve the expected rate of inflation (in particular, the relation between the level of nominal interest rates and the saving and investment determinants of the equilibrium real rate), and so an arbitrary change in the current price level would still be consistent with equilibrium as long as the expected future price level were increased proportionately. This in turn is consistent with rational expectations equilibrium given that the future price level is similarly indeterminate, if the nominal interest rate peg is to be maintained forever. Indeterminacy of this kind would be undesirable, as discussed in Subsection 2.4, especially if unexpected inflation distorts the allocation of resources due to the existence of a "Lucas supply curve", for in this case "sunspot" fluctuations in the price level would result in unnecessary deviations of equilibrium supply from the full-information level.

But indeterminacy of the kind discussed by Sargent and Wallace, due to an exact homogeneity of the equilibrium conditions in the sequence of price levels given a policy of pegging the nominal interest rate,[13] will in fact almost never exist in a complete general equilibrium model, as opposed to the sort of Keynesian aggregative model that they consider. For there are many reasons for the equilibrium conditions to not be perfectly homogeneous even in the case of an interest rate peg. First of all, even in the case that variations in the money supply are to be brought about entirely through lump-sum taxes or transfers, it will usually be reasonable to assume a fixed distribution of lump-sum taxes or transfers across consumers that will in general not coincide with the distribution of previous money balances across consumers that happens to exist, as in the models presented in Subsections 2.2 and 2.3. As a result the increase or decrease in the aggregate money supply that would be necessary to accommodate a given change in the current price level would change the distribution of money balances across consumers, and so would in general have a real effect on the economy. Secondly, in the case that the variations in the money supply are to be brought about through open market operations (with the schedule of tax collections being unaffected) rather than through taxes or transfers (with the outstanding government debt being unaffected), the homogeneity result will not be true even for a representative consumer model. For the increase or decrease in the money supply that would be necessary to accommodate a given change in the current price level carries with it a change in the net indebtedness of the government to the private sector, which will affect the budget constraints of consumers and so have a real effect on the economy. (Both of these kinds of effects are ignored in the IS–LM model used by Sargent and Wallace. There are of course no possible

---

[13]McCallum (1986) distinguishes between "indeterminacy" of the sort that results from interest rate pegging in the Sargent–Wallace (1975) model and mere "non-uniqueness" of equilibrium of the sort exhibited by the examples of Subsection 2.4.

distributional effects in an aggregative model of that kind; and there are also no consequences of changes in net government indebtedness because the consumption/saving decision in that model does not depend upon consumers' intertemporal budget constraint.)

Of course, the mere fact that exact homogeneity will almost never hold does not prove that there might not nonetheless be a severe indeterminacy of rational expectations equilibrium as a result of an interest rate peg. However, this would not necessarily prove that a policy formulated in terms of an exogenous rate of money growth is to be preferred to one that specifies an exogenous nominal interest rate path, for it has been shown in Subsection 2.4 that equilibrium can be indeterminate even in the case of an exogenously specified rate of money growth. Indeed, at least in some cases to be described below, *equilibrium is unique in the case of an interest rate target even though it would be indeterminate if the central bank tried to bring about the same equilibrium through a policy that specified a target path for the money supply.*

An example is provided by the "legal restrictions" model of the previous subsection. Suppose that the central bank seeks to bring about the Pareto optimal equilibrium described above through a program of open market operations, and that the policy regime adopted is one in which the central bank stands ready to exchange money for bonds at a price that fixes the nominal interest rate on bonds at zero [as in the "discount window" regime of Sargent and Wallace (1982)]. Then a perfect foresight equilibrium will be a set of sequences $\{M_t, P_t, B_t\}$ that satisfy (3.1)–(3.3) for all periods $t \geq 1$, with a given value for the right-hand side of (3.3) in period 1 (an initial condition), and with the expression P_t/P_{t+1} substituted for R_t in all of the equations. Since (3.3) implies in this case that $M_t + B_t$ will be constant over time, and since its initial value is given as an initial condition, we can let this constant value be written $M + B$, understood to be a constant whose value is exogenously given. Then (3.1) and (3.2) imply that in any perfect foresight equilibrium the price level sequence $\{P_t\}$ must satisfy

$$S_1(P_t/P_{t+1}) + S_2(P_t/P_{t+1}) + S_3(P_t/P_{t+1}) = (M + B)/P_t \qquad (3.5)$$

for all periods. In addition to this requirement, neither (3.1) nor (3.2) actually need hold with equality, but only

$$S_1(P_t/P_{t+1}) \leq M_t/P_t , \qquad (3.6)$$

since in the case of a zero nominal rate type 2 consumers are indifferent between holding money and bonds. To every price level sequence satisfying (3.5), there corresponds a perfect foresight equilibrium, for a sequence $\{M_t\}$ can then necessarily be found that satisfies (3.6). Now let us again suppose that all of the net saving functions S_j are monotonically increasing, and also that

$$\lim_{R \to 0} S_1(R) + S_2(R) + S_3(R) = \underline{S} > 0 , \tag{3.7a}$$

$$\lim_{R \to \infty} S_1(R) + S_2(R) + S_3(R) = \bar{S} < \infty . \tag{3.7b}$$

(The latter condition can be interpreted as reflecting the fact that the aggregate endowment of young agents out of which saving can occur is finite.) In this case, (3.5) has a unique solution $P_t = \phi(P_{t+1})$ for all $P_{t+1} > 0$, and ϕ is a monotonically increasing function, whose value always lies between $M + B/\bar{S}$ and $M + B/\underline{S}$. Furthermore, $\phi(P)/P$ will be a monotonically decreasing function of P. Hence, there will be a unique price level P^* for which $\phi(P^*) = P^*$, and one will have $\phi(P) > P$ for all $P < P^*$, $\phi(P) < P$ for all $P > P^*$. It follows that price sequences that satisfy (3.5) must be of one of three types: either $P_t = P^*$ for all t; or $P_t < P^*$ for all t, and the price level is monotonically decreasing; or $P_t > P^*$ for all t, and the price level is monotonically increasing. In the second case one obtains a contradiction by noting that the sequence cannot converge to any positive price level since the stationary equilibrium is unique, but that it cannot ever fall below the lower bound $M + B/\bar{S}$ either. In the third case one obtains a contradiction as well, since the sequence cannot converge but also cannot ever exceed the upper bound $M + B/\underline{S}$. Hence, only the sequence in which $P_t = P^*$ for all t satisfies (3.5), and perfect foresight equilibrium is unique. (The sequences $\{M_t, B_t\}$ associated with the equilibrium are not unique, but the equilibrium allocation of resources and real rates of return are uniquely defined.)

Hence, it is possible for a policy that pegs the nominal interest rate to result in a determinate price level.[14] Furthermore, in an economy of this kind a policy

---

[14]It is important to notice that the specification that there are to be no taxes or transfers is also an important part of the policy. McCallum (1986) argues that the price level would be indeterminate in the model of Sargent and Wallace (1982) – essentially the model just considered – in the case of a "pure interest rate peg", because the initial quantity of money in the hands of the public should be treated as something chosen by the monetary authority, through an initial tax or transfer, rather than as an exogenously given datum. Since the desire to peg the nominal interest rate at zero does not determine a unique value for this initial transfer, he argues, there exists a continuum of equilibria corresponding to different sizes of transfers. This would be true here, and equally true of the determinacy result in Woodford (1985, 1987, 1988). However, this does not seem to me to show that the sort of indeterminacy result exhibited for IS–LM models such as that of Sargent and Wallace (1975) is equally valid in the case of these latter models; in the case of the IS–LM model, it does not matter if one specifies that the money supply grows only through open market operations and that there are to be no taxes or transfers, because consumers' budget constraints do not affect the behavior postulated in that model. As far as the practical issue is concerned of whether or not an interest rate target alone suffices to specify a well-defined monetary policy, one must seek to determine whether the determination of the overall level of taxes and transfers is properly taken as exogenous by the central bank, or whether this is something that should be determined as an aspect of monetary policy. The question is not one of logic but rather of fact regarding the way in which monetary and fiscal policy decisions are coordinated within an actual institutional framework.

that specifies an exogenous path for the money supply can result in indeterminacy. Consider, for example, the policy of maintaining a constant money supply M (starting from an initial condition of no outstanding government debt or credit). Under this policy regime the real rate of return on bonds is always equal to R^*, the solution to (2.9), while any price level sequence $\{P_t\}$ that satisfies (3.1) with $M_t = M$ for all t is consistent with perfect foresight equilibrium. In the case that there exists an $\underline{R} > 0$ such that $S_1(\underline{R}) = 0$, then there will exist an uncountably infinite number of such equilibria, in which the price level increases asymptotically without bound (self-fulfilling inflations of the kind discussed in Subsection 2.4), in addition to the stationary equilibrium with a constant price level discussed in Subsection 2.3 and Section 3. (Note that the assumption that such an $\underline{R} > 0$ exists is consistent with (3.7a); it is possible for $S_1(R)$ and $S_3(R)$ to both be negative for small R, as long as $S_2(R)$ is still positive.)

Interest rate pegging also results in a unique monetary equilibrium, no matter what sequence of interest rate targets is chosen, in the cash-in-advance overlapping generations economy treated in Woodford (1985, 1987). In that model, monetary equilibrium is also unique in the case of any sequence of money supply targets, so that the two ways of formulating the central bank's conduct of open market operations are equivalent. (This analysis, like that above, assumes the absence of taxes or transfers. If taxes and transfers of arbitrary size are allowed as an additional dimension of monetary policy, then the sequence of interest rate targets and of money supply targets can be chosen largely independently.)

Conditions (which are not very restrictive) are given in Woodford (1988) under which interest rate pegging results in a unique monetary equilibrium, in the case of a constant positive interest rate that may be arbitrarily small, in the Lucas–Stokey model. The unique equilibrium involves a constant allocation of resources over time, and by choosing an interest rate that is close enough to zero, this constant allocation can be made arbitrarily close to the stationary allocation that maximizes the welfare of the representative consumer. It also involves a constant rate of inflation that is lower the lower the interest rate chosen. If one were to attempt to bring about the same desirable stationary allocation of resources and low rate of inflation through exogenous specification of a constant rate of money growth, then equilibrium is typically indeterminate (as discussed in Subsection 2.4). Not only will there often exist the possibility of "self-fulfilling inflations", as in the legal restrictions example just presented, but in the case of negative rates of money growth (as would be necessary to achieve an especially low nominal interest rate) there will necessarily exist the possibility of "self-fulfilling deflations", just as in the example of a Bewley–Levine economy discussed in Subsection 2.2, and in some cases there exist large sets of equilibria in which the price level fluctuates forever while remaining bounded above and away from zero.

These examples indicate that it is far from obvious that interest rate pegging is more likely to result in price level indeterminacy than a policy that fixes a money supply growth path. On the other hand, contrary examples can also be devised. In Woodford (1986a) I consider a cash-in-advance economy with two kinds of infinitely-lived consumers and a segmentation of financial markets similar to that of the "legal restrictions" model considered above, i.e. small savers ("workers") hold only money while large savers ("capitalists") hold only interest-earning assets (claims to capital) and borrow the money necessary for their purchases each period from the central bank. This model has a Wicksellian structure in that the consequence of an elastic supply of loans (inside money) at a fixed nominal interest rate will be expansion of the money supply and inflation when investment demand increases and contraction of the money supply and deflation when investment demand declines. In this model I show that an elastic supply of inside money by the central bank results in the existence of sunspot equilibria in which fluctuations in the profit expectations of capitalists are self-fulfilling, whereas a policy of maintaining a fixed quantity of money (and instead letting the interest rate fluctuate) rules out fluctuations of this kind and makes the stationary equilibrium the unique rational expectations equilibrium. This latter sort of model may have more of the structure that critics of an elastic money supply have had in mind. An understanding of whether or not such policies have desirable consequences under empirically realistic conditions will depend upon analysis of this issue for a broader range of theoretical models.

3.3. Interest on money balances as a way of equalizing returns

Another approach to the elimination of the inefficiency pointed to by Friedman, that again acts directly to equalize the returns on money and other assets rather than counting upon contraction of the money supply to have this effect, is for the government to pay a positive nominal interest rate on money balances equal to the nominal return available on other assets. This method is discussed by Friedman (1960) as an alternative to a steady contraction of the money supply, and many commentators upon Friedman's proposal have favored this method on the ground that it would avoid the need for steadily declining prices, something that many have felt it would be difficult to bring about in reality due to supposed "downward inflexibility" of money wages or other prices. The most frequently discussed aspect of the proposal (because most obviously feasible) is the payment of interest upon the reserves that commercial banks hold on deposit at the Federal Reserve. If these reserves represented the only demand for the monetary base, then (assuming also the absence of any legal limit on the interest that could be paid to depositors by commercial banks, and perfect competition among banks for deposits) such a measure would suffice to eliminate Friedman's inefficiency. But in reality the public holds currency as well as deposits with financial intermediaries, and so the inefficiency would not be eliminated unless the rate of return on currency could also be made equal to that on other assets offering a riskless nominal return. Interest payments on currency held by the public would obviously be much harder to arrange, providing one important reason to prefer the deflationary scheme.

But for analytical purposes let us abstract from such problems and suppose that direct interest payments on money balances are possible. What would the consequences be? A simple but important result, valid for equilibrium models of money of all types, is the following: *Two monetary policies that differ in the rate of nominal interest payments on money balances, but involve the same size of (and distribution of) real lump-sum tax collections and transfer payments, as well as the same quantity of real government purchases and the same quantity of real outstanding government debt or credit at all times, so that the additional interest payments in one case must be financed through an increase in the money supply, will be consistent with exactly the same set of equilibria, in the sense that both the real allocation of resources and the quantity of (and distribution of) real money balances in equilibrium will be the same.* The reason is that the nominal interest payments on money balances simply increase the nominal value of each consumer's money balances but not their distribution, so that their effect can be entirely undone by a proportional increase in the level of money prices. An equilibrium with a rate of nominal interest payments r on money and a rate of growth of the money supply π will be identical (as far as the real allocation of resources, real rates of return, the distribution of real money balances, and so on are concerned) to an equilibrium that would be possible with zero interest on money and a rate of money growth of π', where $1 + \pi' = (1 + \pi)/(1 + r)$, with the same pattern of real taxes and transfers. [This is shown explicitly by Grandmont and Younes (1973) for the case of their cash-in-advance economy.] As a result there has been no loss of generality in our restricting our attention to the case of zero interest on money up to this point; and there is equally no loss of generality in Bewley's (1980, 1983) restriction of attention to the case of a constant money supply but variable interest payments.

There is also obviously no advantage to be gained from a policy of interest payments on money as opposed to contraction of the money supply, as far as the consequences for perfect foresight or rational expectations equilibria with symmetric information and perfectly flexible prices are concerned. If, however, one supposes that there is some kind of cost associated with changes in the price level (especially stochastic changes in the price level of the sort involved in the equilibria of the Bewley model discussed above, due to an inability to costlessly diffuse throughout the economy the information needed to allow perfectly coordinated prices changes), this could be a reason to prefer a particular combination of money supply growth or contraction and interest rate payments that would allow the general level of money prices to remain fixed. Similarly, if one supposes that information about individual consumers' money balances is not costlessly available to the government, this could be a reason for using the rate of money supply growth as a policy instrument rather than the rate of interest paid on money (above all in the case that one desires to tax money balances, as in the Levine example of Subsection 2.2).

It should also be noted that a policy of paying interest on money is equivalent to a policy of steady contraction of the money supply only if the rate of nominal interest payments on money is fixed exogenously (just as the rate of contraction of the money supply is fixed exogenously in the cases studied in Subsection 1.2 and Section 2), rather than being allowed to depend on endogenous variables. In fact, discussions of the interest-on-money proposal frequently assume that the rate of interest to be paid on money should be determined by reference to the market-determined nominal interest yields of other assets, *not* by some such formula as "pay interest at a rate equal to the representative consumer's rate of time preference". Indeed, Friedman's own discussion of this proposal indicates that he imagines that the rate of interest paid on money should be varied over time in response to observed variations in market yields on short-term government debt.[15] This makes the proposal to pay interest on money importantly different from the proposal to contract the money supply at a constant rate.

One difference is obviously that the response to shocks (to the real return to physical capital, to rates of time preference, etc.) will be different in the two cases. But even in the case of a stationary economy, the two policies will not in general be equivalent. Even though a given stationary equilibrium for a particular stationary economy might be equally consistent with a policy rule that specifies an exogenous rate of money growth and one that specifies the rate of interest payments on money as a function of market interest rates on other assets, the entire *set* of equilibria consistent with the two policy rules need not be the same. In particular, the response of the rate of interest on

---

[15]Friedman's reason is presumably a recognition that shocks to the supply and/or demand for credit should result in fluctuations in the real rate of interest even in a Pareto optimal equilibrium, as in the model of Sargent and Wallace (1982). But this should also imply that, if interest is not paid on money, the rate of contraction of the money supply necessary for efficiency would not be constant, as Sargent and Wallace argue. Friedman's avoidance of this conclusion in the case of his discussion of the optimal rate of contraction of the money supply may be attributable to a belief that the price level fluctuations that would result from a Sargent–Wallace type of policy would cause misallocations of resources independent of those due to a positive nominal interest rate. If this point of view is accepted, this would be an important reason to prefer interest payments on money to the deflationary scheme.

money to changes in other nominal interest rates might make the equilibrium level of nominal interest rates indeterminate when it would not be in the case of an exogenous rate of money growth (or an exogenous rate of interest on money). As a simple example, consider any of the economies discussed above for which there existed an equilibrium (with zero interest on money) in which the nominal interest rate is always zero. Now suppose that the policy rule is modified as follows: the real lump-sum taxes or transfers remain as before, but now there is to be paid interest on money equal to whatever the nominal interest rate on the alternative asset (say, bonds) may be, financed by printing new money. It should be evident (from the general proposition stated above) that in this case the nominal interest rate will be completely indeterminate; the same equilibrium allocation of resources and distribution of real money balances is consistent with absolutely any nominal interest rate. This indeterminacy might seem to be of no consequence, since the allocation of resources is unaffected. But the rate of inflation is also indeterminate, and so if one modifies the model to allow for real effects of unanticipated price level changes, one might easily find this kind of policy regime would lead to an indeterminacy of the equilibrium allocation of resources as well.

The type of indeterminacy just described is also cured by specifying taxes to respond to the level of nominal interest payments, e.g. a rule such as "total tax collections each period are to be equal in value to total interest payments on money, whatever those may be". But even when taxes do vary with the level of interest payments in this way, feedback from market interest rates to the rate of interest paid on money (and hence the level of taxes) can make the equilibrium nominal interest rate indeterminate, even when it would not be with an exogenously fixed rate of interest on money. An example due to Smith (1988) illustrates this.[16] The economy he considers is a special case of the "reserve requirements" example discussed in Section A.4 in the appendix, modified to allow for the payment of interest on money holdings. The gross real return on savings (i.e. on deposits with the regulated intermediary) is equal to

$$R_{dt+1} = \phi R + (1 - \phi)(1 + r_{t+1})(P_t/P_{t+1}),$$

---

[16]Sargent and Wallace (1985) demonstrate the possibility of indeterminacy resulting from a scheme that pays interest on money equal to the return on an alternative asset due to the fact that, in the model they consider, there is nothing to tie down the equilibrium return on the alternative asset. The alternative asset for them is privately issued debt; because all of the consumers in a position to borrow from one another have identical preferences and endowments, the bond market must clear at whatever rate of return makes consumers willing neither to issue nor acquire bonds, which in turn will be whatever rate of return is available on money. The circularity results in indeterminacy even of stationary equilibrium in their model. Smith avoids an indeterminacy of this sort by assuming the existence of physical capital with a technologically determined real return, as explained below.

where R is the constant gross real return on physical capital, P_t is the period t price level, r_{t+1} is the nominal rate of interest paid in period $t+1$ on money (the intermediary's reserves) held from period t to period $t+1$, and ϕ is the fraction of the intermediary's assets that can be held in the form of physical capital. Smith considers two policy regimes, one with $r_{t+1} = 0$ (the type of economy considered earlier), and one [which he interprets as representing Friedman's (1960) proposal] in which $1 + r_{t+1} = RP_{t+1}/P_t$, so that the returns on physical capital and money are equalized ex post. He gives conditions on consumer preferences under which equilibrium is determinate and sunspot equilibria do not exist (at least with the class of possible sunspot equilibria that he considers) in the case of the policy with no interest payments on money, but equilibrium is indeterminate and sunspot equilibria do exist in the case of the rate of return equalizing policy. The sunspot equilibria in the latter case will result in unnecessary randomization of the allocation of resources in the economy, quite apart from any undesirable effects (not modelled here) associated with fluctuations in prices, and Smith argues that this is an indesirable consequence of Friedman's proposal.

In the appendix I extend the class of policy regimes considered to include two general categories. In the first, $r_{t+1} = r$ is an exogenous constant. (The case of $r = 0$ considered by Smith is a special case of this type.) In the second, r_{t+1} varies so as to maintain a constant spread between the ex post nominal interest paid on money and the ex post nominal yield on physical capital, i.e. $(1 + r_{t+1})(P_t/P_{t+1})$ is held constant. [A special case of this is the interest on money rule assumed by Smith, according to which the spread is kept always equal to zero, i.e. $(1 + r_{t+1})(P_t/P_{t+1}) = R$.] Consideration of the broader class of policies shows that it is not so much the average level of interest payments on money (or the average return differential between money and capital) that matters for the existence or not of sunspot equilibria of the kind exhibited by Smith, as the question of whether a given average level of interest payments is implemented through a policy of the first category or of the second. Under conditions discussed in the appendix, the indeterminacy and sunspot equilibria are not present in the case of constant-r policies, even when r is quite high; and on the other hand, indeterminacy and sunspot equilibria are possible in the case of constant ex post spread policies even when the average rate of nominal interest payments on money is zero.

As in the previous subsection, we find that two monetary policies that might appear to be equivalent insofar as both are consistent with the same stationary equilibrium can differ in their consequences for the determinacy of equilibrium. Smith's result also provides another illustration of the point made above in Subsection 2.4, namely that a policy that equates the rate of return on money to that on other assets so as to eliminate the Friedman inefficiency may result in indeterminacy.

Appendix

A.1. Derivation of (2.2)

The derivation of an analog to the standard Ramsey tax formula proceeds as follows. We first must modify our notation in equations (1.8) to let labor be the numeraire (which without loss of generality we can assume is not taxed). Let p be the after-tax price of the consumption good (i.e. $p = 1/w$, and $p - 1$ is the tax on the consumption good), and let $\rho = p\pi$ (i.e. ρ is the government's seignorage revenue in units of the labor numeraire, per unit of real money balances held by the representative consumer). Then (1.8d) becomes:

$$pc + \rho m = n ,\tag{A.1}$$

and the other equations in (1.8) are similarly modified. It is useful to define an "indirect utility function":

$$V(p, \rho) = U(c(p, \rho), n(p, \rho), m(p, \rho)) ,$$

where the c, n, and m "demand functions" represent solutions to the modified versions of equations (1.8a)–(1.8d) for given values of p and ρ. [These are not quite demand functions in the usual sense, and V is not quite an indirect utility function, because these functions do not represent the solution to a problem of maximizing $U(c, n, m)$ subject to a budget constraint that depends only upon the given values for p and ρ; instead we are, in effect, solving the representative consumer's optimization problem for given price sequences represented by p and ρ *and for a given level of initial real money balances*, and then varying the assumed level of initial real money balances until one is found such that the solution sequences for consumption, labor supply, and real money balances take on constant values. For our purposes it suffices that such functions be well-defined near the optimal stationary equilibrium.] Then the government's problem[17] can be equivalently formulated as the choice of values for p and ρ to maximize $V(p, \rho)$ subject to the constraint:

$$c(p, \rho) + g \le n(p, \rho) .$$

---

[17] A criticism of this conception of the government's problem that I will not take up here concerns the appropriateness of simply comparing the levels of utility associated with alternative possible stationary equilibria. A better formulation of the problem would be to compare the different possible paths for the economy, corresponding to different policy choices, starting from given initial conditions (in particular, initial asset stocks), and ask what sequence of policy choices (not necessarily stationary) would represent optimizing behavior by the government. This sort of problem is treated by Turnovsky and Brock (1980), Lucas and Stokey (1983), and Chamley (1985).

The optimal stationary equilibrium will then obviously be characterized by first-order conditions of the form:

$$V_p = U_c c_p + U_n n_p + U_m m_p = \lambda [c_p - n_p] ,$$ (A.2a)

$$V_\rho = U_c c_\rho + U_n n_\rho + U_m m_\rho = \lambda [c_\rho - n_\rho] ,$$ (A.2b)

where λ is a (positive) Lagrange multiplier. Furthermore, differentiation of condition (A.1) yields:

$$n_p = c + pc_p + \rho m_p ,$$ (A.3a)

$$n_\rho = m + pc_\rho + \rho m_\rho .$$ (A.3b)

Using these relations one can eliminate n_p and n_ρ from equations (A.2), and using (1.8a)–(1.8c) one can eliminate U_m and U_n. One is left with the two equations in (2.2), where $\mu = (U_c/p - \lambda)/\lambda$. This is a system of equations analogous to the usual Ramsey tax formulas, with the qualifications given above regarding the extent to which the functions c and m can be interpreted as "demand functions".

Now suppose that, by analogy with the argument referred to above for the Ramsey case, we assume that the matrix of derivatives of the "demand functions" above has the sign pattern associated with "gross substitutes", i.e. that c_p, m_ρ, n_p, $n_\rho < 0$, c_ρ, $m_p > 0$. Then if c, $m > 0$, equations (A.3) imply that there exists a positive vector (i.e. $[p, \rho]$) which, when multiplied by the matrix in (2.2), yields a negative vector; this together with the sign pattern of the matrix allows us to apply theorem 4.D.3 of Takayama (1985). It follows that the inverse of the matrix must be entirely negative. Then since m and c have the same sign (positive), the two elements of the vector on the left-hand side above (the analog of the vector of tax rates in the Ramsey formula) must also have the same sign. Can that common sign be negative? The second element of the vector of "tax rates" can also be written $\rho + (U_c/\lambda)$ $(1 + \pi)(1 - \beta)/\beta$, and both U_c and λ must be positive, so that if the entire expression were negative, ρ would have to be negative. But (A.1) together with (1.8e) implies that:

$$(p - 1)c + \rho m = g .$$

If the level of government purchases g is positive, it is impossible that both $p - 1$ and ρ be negative. Hence, the vector of "tax rates" must be entirely positive, rather than entirely negative. This in turn means that μ is negative, from which it follows that the positive "tax rate" on money requires $1 + \pi - \beta > 0$. Thus, the optimum will be characterized by inflation in excess of that called for by the Friedman Rule, and by a positive nominal interest rate.

A.2. Example of self-fulfilling deflations in the Bewley model (Subsection 2.2.1)

Suppose that there are two infinitely-lived consumer types that exist in equal numbers. Type 1 consumers have an endowment of a units of the single consumption good in odd periods and b units in even periods, while type 2 consumers have b in odd periods and a in even. Let us suppose that $a > b$. Each type seeks to maximize

$$\sum_{t=0}^{\infty} \delta^t u(c_t^i),$$

i.e. their discount factors and utility functions are identical, and the utility functions do not vary from period to period. This is a special case of Bewley's model, in which there are two aggregate states and the alternation between them is purely deterministic. Note that the economy is one in which an efficient allocation of resources cannot be achieved in equilibrium if fiat money does not exist or is not valued in equilibrium. For without fiat money the only equilibrium would be one in which each consumer consumes exactly his endowment in each period. Then the marginal rate of substitution between period t consumption and period $t + 1$ consumption would never be the same for type 1 and type 2 consumers (assuming that u is strictly concave), and so the consumption allocation would not be efficient.

Now consider the case of a steady contraction of the money supply, but at a rate less than that called for by the Friedman Rule, i.e. suppose that $\delta - 1 < \pi < 0$. Suppose also that $\tau_1 = \tau_2 = \frac{1}{2}$. Then the following is an equilibrium:

$$M_t^1 = \tfrac{1}{2} - p_0\left(\frac{\delta}{1+\delta}\right)\left(\frac{a+b}{2}\right)\left(-\frac{\delta}{1+\pi}\right)^t, \tag{A.4a}$$

$$M_t^2 = \tfrac{1}{2} + p_0\left(\frac{\delta}{1+\delta}\right)\left(\frac{a+b}{2}\right)\left(-\frac{\delta}{1+\pi}\right)^t, \tag{A.4b}$$

$$c_t^1 = c_t^2 = \frac{a+b}{2}, \tag{A.4c}$$

$$p_t = p_0\left(\frac{\delta}{1+\pi}\right)^t, \tag{A.4d}$$

for all t, where p_0 can be chosen to take any value in the interval:

$$0 < p_0 \leq \frac{1+\delta}{1+\pi}\frac{1}{a+b}. \tag{A.4e}$$

[Recall that M_t^i in (2.3) denotes the *fraction* of the total money supply held by

i, not the nominal quantity held; hence (A.4a) plus (A.4b) sum to one at all times.] These specifications are consistent with (2.3) for all t, and given (A.4e) they imply non-negative money balances for all consumers in all periods. Because consumption is constant for all consumers and the real rate of return on holding money is always equal to δ^{-1}, the first-order conditions for optimal consumption are all satisfied for all consumers. It is also easily verified that the transversality condition,

$$\lim_{t \to \infty} \delta^t u'(c_t^i) M_t^i / p_t = 0 ,$$

holds for $i = 1$, 2, so that the consumption programs (A.4c) are optimal given the price process (A.4d) and the initial money balances. (Note that this last result would *not* obtain in the case $\pi \geq 0$.) Hence the specification (A.4) satisfies all of the conditions required for a monetary equilibrium, *except* Bewley's requirement that the deflated price level remain bounded away from zero; (A.4d) implies that the deflated price level approaches zero asymptotically, so that real money balances become unboundedly large in this equilibrium. It is also easily seen that such an equilibrium is Pareto optimal; the consumption allocation (A.4c) represents the unique allocation that maximizes the average utility of the two types of consumers.

A.3. Levine's example (Subsection 2.2.2)

The structure of the economy has been described in the text; here I derive the conditions under which there exists a two-state Markov equilibrium (as described in the text) in which the allocation of resources is Pareto optimal. Given that in a Pareto optimal equilibrium the consumers with low marginal utility must sell all of their endowment to the consumers with high marginal utility, and given that the entire money supply must end up in the hands of the consumers with low marginal utility at the end of each period, it is evident that the deflated price level process must be:

$$p^b = (2 + \pi)/(2 + 2\pi) ,$$

$$p^r = \pi/(2 + 2\pi) ,$$

where p^b is the deflated price level in "boom" periods and p^r in "recessions". [In a "recession" period, consumers with high marginal utility also had high marginal utility in the previous period, and so held no money at the end of that period. They accordingly hold a fraction $\pi/(2 + 2\pi)$ of the money supply in the current period, after the lump-sum transfer. Since they hold no money at the end of the current period, this is the amount they spend; and if the equilibrium allocation is optimal, they must receive one unit of consumption good for it, so that $p^r = \pi/(2 + 2\pi)$. One calculates p^b in a similar fashion.] This is already enough to indicate that such an equilibrium is not possible except in the case of a positive rate of money growth, for the price level must be positive in "recession" periods. The problem with negative money growth is as follows. If there is to be a two-state Markov equilibrium, in a "recession" period high marginal utility consumers (who were also high marginal utility in the previous period) must have no money balances at the beginning of the period, and if $\pi < 0$, they must also pay a lump-sum tax. In order to pay the tax they will have to sell some of their endowment to low marginal utility consumers, and a fortiori they will be unable to purchase the endowment of the low marginal utility consumers. [While this demonstration pertains only to the case of a two-state Markov equilibrium, Levine (1988) shows that for essentially the same reason there cannot be a Pareto optimal equilibrium of *any* kind in the case of any monetary policy in which the money supply never increases, including any constant rates of money growth $\pi \leq 0$.]

It remains to be shown that a Pareto optimal equilibrium can occur for some positive rates of money growth. The efficient consumption allocation will be chosen by optimizing consumers who face the above price process only if the following first-order conditions are satisfied:

$$(a/p^b) \geq (\delta/1 + \pi)[\varepsilon(a/p^r) + (1 - \varepsilon)(\mu^b/p^b)] \,, \tag{A.5a}$$

$$(\mu^b/p^b) = (\delta/1 + \pi)[\varepsilon(\mu^r/p^r) + (1 - \varepsilon)(a/p^b)] \,, \tag{A.5b}$$

$$(a/p^r) \geq (\delta/1 + \pi)[\varepsilon(a/p^r) + (1 - \varepsilon)(\mu^b/p^b)] \,, \tag{A.5c}$$

$$(\mu^r/p^r) = (\delta/1 + \pi)[\varepsilon(\mu^r/p^r) + (1 - \varepsilon)(a/p^b)] \,, \tag{A.5d}$$

$$\mu^b \geq b \,, \tag{A.5e}$$

$$\mu^r \geq b \,. \tag{A.5f}$$

Here conditions (A.5a)–(A.5d) relate respectively to the saving decisions of high-marginal-utility consumers in a "boom" period, low-marginal-utility consumers in a "boom", high-marginal-utility consumers in a "recession", and low-marginal-utility consumers in a "recession". Each condition states that the marginal utility of money balances in the current period must be at least as great as the marginal utility associated with money balances in the current period that are to be held over into the following period, which in turn depends upon the marginal utility of money balances in each of the two possible states that might occur in the following period. The conditions hold with equality in the case of low-marginal-utility consumers because they choose to hold money over into the following period. The symbols μ^b and μ^r denote the marginal utility of real money balances for a low-marginal-utility consumer in "boom" and "recession" periods, respectively; conditions (A.5e) and (A.5f) indicate that these must be at least as large as the marginal utility of consumption in the current period. I have written a for the marginal utility of real money balances for a high-marginal-utility consumer in equations (A.5a)–(A.5d), because these consumers always choose to consume in the current period.

Conditions (A.5b) and (A.5d) can be solved for μ^b and μ^r, and the values obtained can be substituted into the remaining four inequalities. Also substituting for the equilibrium price levels as a function of the rate of money growth, one obtains the following four inequalities in terms of the parameters and the rate of money growth:

$$\frac{\delta(1-\varepsilon)}{1+\pi-\delta\varepsilon} \geq \frac{b}{a} \,, \tag{A.6a}$$

$$\frac{\pi}{2+\pi} \frac{\delta(1-\varepsilon)}{1+\pi-\delta\varepsilon} \geq \frac{b}{a} \,, \tag{A.6b}$$

$$\frac{\pi}{2+\pi} \left[\frac{\delta(1-\varepsilon)}{1+\pi-\delta\varepsilon}\right]^2 \leq 1 \,, \tag{A.6c}$$

$$\frac{\pi}{2+\pi} \left[1 - \frac{\delta^2(1-\varepsilon)^2}{(1+\pi)(1+\pi-\delta\varepsilon)}\right] \geq \frac{\delta\varepsilon}{1+\pi} \,. \tag{A.6d}$$

These inequalities indicate the range of values for π that are consistent with the existence of a Pareto optimal two-state Markov equilibrium, for given values of the other parameters. It is evident that in order for the left-hand sides of both (A.6a) and (A.6b) to be positive, π must be positive, so that, again, such an equilibrium is inconsistent with a policy of steady contraction of the money supply. Given $\pi > 0$, however, (A.6c) necessarily holds, and (A.6a) follows from (A.6b). Hence the range of possible rates of money growth consistent with efficiency is determined by (A.6b) and (A.6d). It is easy to see that both inequalities are satisfied by some positive rates of money growth, for some values of the other parameters. For example, given any $\pi > 0$, (A.6b) necessarily holds for b/a small enough, and (A.6d) necessarily holds for ε small enough. On the other hand, for given positive values of b/a and ε, neither inequality is satisfied by π too close to zero. Hence, when a Pareto optimal equilibrium is possible, there will be a positive rate of money growth that is the minimum rate consistent with the efficient equilibrium. For rates of money growth lower than this (including negative rates), it is not necessarily the case that a two-state Markov equilibrium becomes impossible; Levine (1986b) shows that often a two-state Markov equilibrium will continue to exist, but that it will necessarily be inefficient in the way described above.

A.4. A reserve requirement example (Subsection 2.3.3)

Consider an economy made up of overlapping generations of identical two-period-lived consumers, and suppose again that the single good can be either consumed or stored (as physical capital), in which case each unit of it yields $R > 1$ units in the following period. But suppose now that consumers are required to hold k units of real money balances for each unit of physical capital accumulated; this is the only reason for money to be held, assuming that $R_m \le R$. In this case, the gross real return on savings will be $R_d = \phi R + (1 - \phi) R_m$, where $\phi = 1/1 + k$. (As discussed in the text, this can be interpreted as the return on deposits with a regulated financial intermediary; all saving will be held in this form given that $R_m \le R_d$.) As a result, the life-cycle saving decision of a typical consumer will satisfy the first-order condition:

$$\frac{u_1}{u_2}(c_1, c_2) = R_d . \tag{A.7}$$

Furthermore, the consumer budget constraint,

$$c_2 - e_2 = [e_1 - c_1] R_d + \tau$$

(where τ represents the lump-sum transfer to a consumer during the second period of life) together with the government budget constraint,

$$\tau = (1 - R_m)m = (1 - R_m)(1 - \phi)[e_1 - c_1]$$

(where m represents the quantity of real money balances held at the end of the first period of life, and the existence of a stationary equilibrium is assumed), imply that in any stationary equilibrium the stationary consumption allocation (c_1, c_2) will have to satisfy:

$$c_2 - e_2 = [e_1 - c_1](\phi R + (1 - \phi)) \tag{A.8}$$

Conditions (A.7) and (A.8) determine the stationary consumption allocation given R_m, which in turn is determined as usual by the rate of money growth. If the marginal rate of substitution u_1/u_2 is an increasing function of c_2 and a decreasing function of c_1 (as will be the case, for example, if preferences are additively separable), then (A.7) and (A.8) imply that a lower value for R_m will result in both lower real balances and a lower steady-state capital stock.

Nonetheless, the optimal rate of money growth, from the point of view of maximizing stationary utility, is higher than the rate that would reduce the nominal interest rate to zero. For the line determined by (A.8) is unaffected by changes in R_m, and the point of highest utility on this line is the point tangent to an indifference curve, i.e. the point at which

$$\frac{u_1}{u_2}(c_1, c_2) = \phi R + (1 - \phi).$$

Comparison with (A.7) indicates that this point is obtained as the stationary consumption allocation if and only if $R_m = 1$. On the other hand, the Friedman Rule would call for a rate of return $R_m = R$, since only in that case is the marginal rate of substitution of consumers between their first and second periods of life [R_d, from (A.7)] equated to the true marginal rate of transformation between those two goods in production (R).

A.5. Smith's example (Subsection 3.3)

Consider again the "reserve requirement" example just presented, for the special case of an additively separable utility function $u(c_1, c_2) = U(c_1) + V(c_2)$, where both U and V are increasing concave functions, and a zero endowment in the second period of life. (We can then simply denote the first period endowment by e.) Let us also now suppose that interest is paid on money, while the money supply remains constant. The analog of (A.7) for a non-stationary equilibrium is then:

$$U'(c_{1t}) = R_{dt+1}V'(c_{2t+1}). \tag{A.9}$$

Here the overall return on savings is:

$$R_{dt+1} = \phi R + (1 - \phi)(1 + r_{t+1})(P_t/P_{t+1}), \tag{A.10}$$

as noted in the text, where r_{t+1} is the nominal rate of interest paid on money balances in period $t + 1$. The consumer's budget constraint implies:

$$\begin{aligned}
c_{2t+1} &= R_{dt+1}[e - c_{1t}] + \tau_{t+1} \\
&= [e - c_{1t}](R_{dt+1} - r_{t+1}(1 - \phi)(P_t/P_{t+1})) \\
&= [e - c_{1t}](\phi R + (1 - \phi)(P_t/P_{t+1})),
\end{aligned} \tag{A.11}$$

where the second line follows from the specification that a lump-sum tax will be levied in exactly the amount needed to pay the interest on money balances, and the third line follows from (A.10). [Note that this generalizes (A.8).] Since real money balances in period t are equal to $(1 - \phi)[e - c_{1t}]$, it follows that

$$P_t/P_{t+1} = [e - c_{1t+1}]/[e - c_{1t}].$$

Substituting this into (A.10) and (A.11) yields an equilibrium condition of the form $F(c_{1t}, c_{1t+1}, r_{t+1}) = 0$.

Now I wish to compare the consequences of two different sorts of specifications of r_{t+1}. In the first, $r_{t+1} = r$ is an exogenous constant. In the second, r_{t+1} varies so as to maintain a constant spread between the ex post nominal interest paid on money and the ex post nominal yield on physical capital; i.e. $(1 + r_{t+1})(P_t/P_{t+1})$ is held constant. [A special case of this rule is considered by Smith, according to which the spread is kept always equal to zero, i.e. $(1 + r_{t+1})(P_t/P_{t+1} = R.$] In both cases the equilibrium condition reduces to an equation of the form $F(c_{1t}, c_{1t+1}) = 0$. The different possible stationary equilibria (solutions with c_{1t} constant) corresponding to different rates of interest on money are also the same in both cases. But the *complete* set of equilibria may be different in the case of two specifications that each result in the same stationary equilibrium. In particular, it is of interest to ask whether there can be a continuum of distinct perfect foresight equilibria that all converge asymptotically to the same stationary equilibrium. In each case the answer to this question depends upon whether or not $|F_2/F_1| > 1$, where the derivatives of the function F are evaluated at the stationary equilibrium values for (c_{1t}, c_{1t+1}). [See Woodford (1984, 1986a, 1986b).] If this inequality holds, perfect foresight equilibrium is indeterminate near the stationary equilibrium, and the different possible equilibrium sequences for $\{c_{1t}\}$ correspond to different possible equilibrium sequences for the nominal interest yields on capital and money.

The specification chosen affects only the form of (A.10). In the case of a constant interest rate on money, R_{dt+1} is an increasing function of c_{1t} and a decreasing function of c_{1t+1}, whereas in the case of the constant spread, R_{dt+1} is a constant. The effect of the variations in R_{dt+1} in the former case is clearly to add a positive term to F_1 and a negative term to F_2 [if F represents the right-hand side minus the left-hand side of (A.9)], evaluated at any given stationary equilibrium; it is also evident that $F_1 + F_2$ is unaffected. When R_{dt+1} is a constant, it is evident that F_1 and F_2 are both positive. Hence, in any event $F_1 > 0$ and $F_1 + F_2 > 0$, so that perfect foresight equilibrium is indeterminate near the stationary equilibrium if and only if $F_2 > F_1$. And the effect of the variations in R_{dt+1} will plainly make this harder; one observes that *if perfect foresight equilibrium is indeterminate near a given stationary equilibrium in the case of a constant interest rate on money, then it will necessarily also be indeterminate near that same stationary equilibrium in the case of a constant ex post interest rate spread, but the converse is not true.* Furthermore, one can show that a sufficient condition to rule out indeterminacy in the case of a constant interest rate on money is that the utility function V have a low enough coefficient of relative risk aversion, specifically, that $-cV''(c)/V'(c) \leq R^{-1}$ for all c. But even when this condition holds it is possible to have indeterminacy in the case of a constant spread, as Smith shows for the case of a policy that equates the ex post returns on money and capital.

Finally, just as in the case discussed in Subsection 2.4, the indeterminacy of perfect foresight equilibrium near the stationary equilibrium in this sense is a sufficient condition for the existence of *stationary sunspot equilibria* in which stochastic fluctuations in the nominal interest rate (and in the rate of inflation) continue to occur forever in response to self-fulfilling revisions of expectations on the part of consumers. This in turn will result in unnecessary randomization of the allocation of resources in the economy, quite apart from any undesirable effects (not modelled here) associated with fluctuations in prices.

As in the previous subsection, we find that two monetary policies that might appear to be equivalent insofar as both are consistent with the same stationary equilibrium can differ in their consequences for the determinacy of equilibrium. Smith's result also provides another illustration of the point made above in Subsection 2.4, namely that a policy that equates the rate of return on money to that on other assets so as to eliminate the Friedman inefficiency may result in indeterminacy. It is worth noting, however, that in Smith's example it is not simply the attempt to increase the rate of return on money that creates the problem. His result might make it seem so, insofar as he only compares two policy regimes – one in which there are no interest payments on money ($r = 0$) and one in which the ex post returns on money and capital are equated ($R_d = R$) – and shows that is possible for stationary sunspot equilibria to exist in the latter case under conditions on preferences that would preclude such equilibria in the former case. But we have seen that the result actually has to do with the difference between a constant-r policy and a constant-R_d policy, and not at all with the difference in the average rates of return on money in the two cases that he considers.

Nonetheless, the problematic aspect of the policy regime considered by Smith, the fact that ex post returns on money are made always equal to those on capital, *is* a natural consequence of an effort to adjust asset returns so as to insure Pareto optimality. Specifically, one of the necessary conditions for an equilibrium to be Pareto optimal in an economy of the kind considered by Smith is that

$$U'(c_{1t}) = R\, E_t[V'(c_{2t+1})] . \tag{A.12}$$

(This is the condition that is necessary in order for there to exist a set of contingent claims prices that would at one and the same time make the consumption allocation chosen by each consumer the minimum-cost way of achieving the level of expected utility and make the production technology earn exactly zero profits.) On the other hand, any equilibrium of the kind discussed above must be such that

$$U'(c_{1t}) = E_t[R_{dt+1}V'(c_{2t+1})] .$$

(A.13)

[This generalizes (A.9) to the case of possibly stochastic returns.] In order to insure that (A.12) holds necessarily in whatever equilibrium is realized, without reference to any other equations of the model (that might allow one to determine exactly what sorts of fluctuations in the price level if any are possible in equilibrium), it is evidently necessary to make R_{dt+1} always equal to R; any other way of having r_{t+1} depend upon the realization of P_{t+1} would not guarantee that (A.13) would imply (A.12) for all possible distributions of realizations for P_{t+1}. Smith's policy regime, that can create indeterminacy, would thus appear to be in the spirit of Friedman's proposal.

References

Abel, A.B. (1987) 'Optimal monetary growth', *Journal of Monetary Economics*, 19: 437–450.

Balasko, Y. and K. Shell (1980) 'The overlapping generations model. I. The case of pure exchange without money', *Journal of Economic Theory*, 23: 281–306.

Benhabib, J. and C. Bull (1983) 'The optimal quantity of money: A formal treatment', *International Economic Review*, 24: 101–111.

Bewley, T. (1980) 'The optimum quantity of money', in: J.H. Kareken and N. Wallace, eds., *Models of monetary economies*. Minneapolis: Federal Reserve Bank of Minneapolis.

Bewley, T. (1983) 'A difficulty with the optimum quantity of money', *Econometrica*, 51: 1485–1504.

Brock, W.A. (1975) 'A simple perfect foresight monetary model', *Journal of Monetary Economics*, 1: 133–150.

Brock, W.A. and J.A. Scheinkman (1980) 'Some remarks on monetary policy in an overlapping generations model', in: J.H. Kareken and N. Wallace, eds., *Models of monetary economies*. Minneapolis: Federal Reserve Bank of Minneapolis.

Bryant, J. (1980) 'Transaction demand for money and moral hazard', in: J.H. Kareken and N. Wallace, eds., *Models of monetary economies*. Minneapolis: Federal Reserve Bank of Minneapolis.

Bryant, J. and N. Wallace (1984) 'A price discrimination analysis of monetary policy', *Review of Economic Studies*, 51: 279–288.

Cagan, P. (1956) 'The monetary dynamics of hyperinflation', in: M. Friedman, ed., *Studies in the quantity theory of money*. Chicago: University of Chicago Press.

Chamley, C. (1985) 'On a simple rule for the optimal inflation rate in second best taxation', *Journal of Public Economics*, 26: 35–50.

Clower, R.W. (1967) 'A reconsideration of the micro-foundations of monetary theory', *Western Economic journal*, 6: 1–9.

Clower, R.W. (1970) 'Is there an optimal money supply?', *Journal of Finance*, 25: 425–433.

Diamond, P.A. (1965) 'National debt in a neoclassical growth model', *American Economic Review*, 55: 1126–1150.

Diamond, P.A. and J.A. Mirrlees (1971) 'Optimal taxation and public production, I: Production efficiency', *American Economic Review*, 61: 8–27.

Drazen, A. (1979) 'The optimal rate of inflation revisited', *Journal of Monetary Economics*, 5: 231–248.

Faig, M. (1988) 'Characterization of the optimal tax on money when it functions as a medium of exchange', *Journal of Monetary Economics*, 22: 137–148.

Fama, E.F. (1980) 'Banking in the theory of finance', *Journal of Monetary Economics*, 6: 39–57.

Fischer, S. (1986) 'Monetary rules and commodity money schemes under uncertainty', *Journal of Monetary Economics* 17: 21–35.

Friedman, M. (1960) *A program for monetary stability*. New York: Fordham University Press.

Friedman, M. (1968) 'The role of monetary policy', *American Economic Review*, 58: 1–17.

Friedman, M. (1969) 'The optimum quantity of money', in: *The optimum quantity of money and other essays*. Chicago: Aldine.

Gale, D. (1983) *Money: In disequilibrium*. Cambridge: Cambridge University Press.

Grandmont, J.-M. (1986) 'Stabilizing competitive business cycles', *Journal of Economic Theory*, 40: 57–76.

Grandmont, J.-M. and Y. Younes (1973) 'On the efficiency of a monetary equilibrium', *Review of Economic Studies*, 40: 149–165.

Grossman, S. and L. Weiss (1983) 'A transactions-based model of the monetary transmission mechanism', *American Economic Review*, 73: 871–880.

Guidotti, P.E. and C.A. Vegh (1988) 'The optimal inflation tax when money reduces transactions costs: A reconsideration', International Monetary Fund, unpublished.

Hahn, F.H. (1971) 'Professor Friedman's views on money', *Economica*, 38: 61–80.

Hahn, F.H. (1973) 'On the foundations of monetary theory', in: M. Parkin and A.R. Nobay, eds., *Essays in monetary economics*. New York: Harper & Row.

Kaldor, N. (1970) 'The "new" monetarism', *Lloyd's Bank Review*, July.

Kehoe, T.J., D.K. Levine and M. Woodford (1989) 'The optimum quantity of money revisited', Federal Reserve Bank of Minneapolis, Working Paper 404.

Kimbrough, K.P. (1986a) 'The optimum quantity of money rule in the theory of public finance', *Journal of Monetary Economics*, 18: 277–284.

Kimbrough, K.P. (1986b) 'Inflation, employment, and welfare in the presence of transaction costs', *Journal of Money, Credit and Banking*, 18: 127–140.

Kohn, M. (1989) 'The finance constraint theory of money: A progress report', Dartmouth College, unpublished.

Levine, D.K. (1986a) 'Liquidity with random market closure', U.C.L.A., unpublished.

Levine, D.K. (1986b) 'Borrowing constraints and expansionary policy', U.C.L.A., unpublished.

Levine, D.K. (1987) 'Efficiency and the value of money', U.C.L.A., unpublished.

Levine, D.K. (1988) 'Asset trading mechanisms and expansionary policy', Federal Reserve Bank of Minneapolis, Working Paper 385.

Lucas, R.E., Jr. (1972) 'Expectations and the neutrality of money', *Journal of Economic Theory*, 4: 103–124.

Lucas, R.E., Jr. and N.L. Stokey (1973) 'Optimal fiscal and monetary policy in an economy without capital', *Journal of Monetary Economics*, 12: 55–93.

Marty, A.L. (1976) 'A note on the welfare cost of money creation', *Journal of Monetary Economics*, 2: 121–124.

McCallum, B.T. (1986) 'Some issues concerning interest rate pegging, price level determinacy, and the real bills doctrine', *Journal of Monetary Economics*, 17: 135–160.

Modigliani, F. (1944) 'Liquidity preference and the theory of interest and money', *Econometrica*, 12: 45–88.

Patinkin, D. (1965) *Money, interest and prices*, 2nd edn. New York: Harper & Row.

Phelps, E.S. (1972) *Inflation policy and unemployment theory*. New York: Norton.

Phelps, E.S. (1973) 'Inflation in the theory of public finance', *Swedish Journal of Economics*, 75: 67–82.

Romer, D. (1986) 'A simple general equilibrium version of the Baumol–Tobin model', *Quarterly Journal of Economics*, 101: 663–685.

Rotemberg, J.J. (1984) 'A monetary equilibrium model with transactions costs', *Journal of Political Economy*, 92: 40–58.

Samuelson, P.A. (1958) 'An exact consumption-loan model of interest with or without the social contrivance of money', *Journal of Political Economy*, 66: 467–482.

Samuelson, P.A. (1968) 'What classical and neoclassical monetary theory really was', *Canadian Journal of Economics*, 1: 1–15.

Samuelson, P.A. (1969) 'Nonoptimality of money holding under *laissez-faire*', *Canadian Journal of Economics*, 2: 303–308.

Sargent, T.J. (1979) *Macroeconomic theory*. New York: Academic Press.

Sargent, T.J. (1987) *Dynamic macroeconomic theory*. Cambridge, Mass.: Harvard University Press.

Sargent, T.J. (1988) 'Elements of monetary reform', Hoover Institution, unpublished.

Sargent, T. J. and B.D. Smith (1986) 'Irrelevance of open market operations in some economies with government currency being dominated in rate of return', Hoover Institution, unpublished.

Sargent, T.J. and N. Wallace (1975) ' "Rational" expectations, the optimal monetary instrument, and the optimal money supply rule', *Journal of Political Economy*, 83: 241–254.

Sargent, T.J. and N. Wallace (1982) 'The real bills doctrine versus the quantity theory: A reconsideration', *Journal of Political Economy*, 90: 1212–1236.

Sargent, T.J. and N. Wallace (1985) 'Interest on reserves', *Journal of Monetary Economics*, 15: 279–290.

Scheinkman, J.A. (1980) 'Discussion', in: J.H. Kareken and N. Wallace, eds., *Models of monetary economies*. Minneapolis: Federal Reserve Bank of Minneapolis.

Scheinkman, J.A. and L. Weiss (1986) 'Borrowing constraints and aggregate economic activity', *Econometrica*, 54: 23–45.

Sidrauski, M. (1967) 'Rational choice and patterns of growth in a monetary economy', *American Economic Review, Papers and Proceedings*, 57: 534–544.

Siegel, J. (1978) 'Notes on optimal taxation and the optimal rate of inflation', *Journal of Monetary Economics*, 4: 297–305.

Smith, B.D. (1986) 'Interest on reserves and sunspot equilibria: Friedman's proposal reconsidered', Univ. of Western Ontario, unpublished.

Stein, J.L. (1970) 'The optimum quantity of money', *Journal of Money, Credit and Banking*, 2: 397–419.

Takayama, A. (1985) *Mathematical economics*, 2nd edn. New York: Cambridge University Press.

Townsend, R.M. (1980) 'Models of money with spatially separated agents', in: J.H. Kareken and N. Wallace, eds., *Models of monetary economies*. Minneapolis: Federal Reserve Bank of Minneapolis.

Townsend, R.M. (1987) 'Optimal activist currency rules', University of Chicago, unpublished.

Turnovsky, S.J. and W.A. Brock (1980) 'Time consistency and optimal government policies in perfect foresight equilibrium', *Journal of Public Economics*, 13: 183–212.

Wallace, N. (1980) 'The overlapping generations model of fiat money', in: J.H. Kareken and N. Wallace, eds., *Models of monetary economies*. Minneapolis: Federal Reserve Bank of Minneapolis.

Wallace, N. (1987) 'Some unsolved problems in monetary theory', in: W.A. Barnett and K.J. Singleton, eds., *New approaches in monetary economics*. New York: Cambridge University Press.

Wallace, N. (1989) 'Some alternative monetary models and their implications for the role of open-market policy', in: R.J. Barro, ed., *Modern business cycle theory*. Cambridge, Mass.: Harvard University Press.

Weiss, L. (1980) 'The effects of money supply on economic welfare in the steady state', *Econometrica*, 48: 565–576.

Wilson, C.A. (1979) 'An infinite horizon model with money', in: J.R. Green and J.A. Scheinkman, eds., *General equilibrium, growth and trade: Essays in honor of Lionel McKenzie*. New York: Academic Press.

Woodford, M. (1983) 'Transaction costs, liquidity, and optimal inflation', in: *Essays in intertemporal economics*, Ph.D. dissertation, M.I.T.

Woodford, M. (1984) 'Indeterminacy of equilibrium in the overlapping generations model: A survey', Columbia University, unpublished.

Woodford, M. (1985) 'Interest and prices in a cash-in-advance economy', Discussion Paper 281 Columbia University.

Woodford, M. (1986a) 'Stationary sunspot equilibria in a finance constrained economy', *Journal of Economic Theory*, 40: 128–137.

Woodford, M. (1986b) 'Stationary sunspot equilibria: The case of small fluctuations around a deterministic steady state', University of Chicago, unpublished.

Woodford, M. (1987) 'Credit policy and the price level in a cash-in-advance economy', in: W.A. Barnett and K.J. Singleton, eds., *New approaches in monetary economics*. New York: Cambridge University Press.

Woodford, M. (1988) 'Monetary policy and price level determinacy in a cash-in-advance economy', University of Chicago, unpublished.

Woodford, M. (1989) 'Liquidity services as an intermediate good in the theory of public finance', University of Chicago, unpublished.

PART 8

MONETARY POLICY

Chapter 21

RULES VERSUS DISCRETION IN MONETARY POLICY

STANLEY FISCHER*

World Bank and Massachusetts Institute of Technology

Contents

*I am grateful to Olivier Blanchard, Ben Friedman and Milton Friedman for helpful comments, and the National Science Foundation for research support.

Handbook of Monetary Economics, Volume II, Edited by B.M. Friedman and F.H. Hahn
© *Elsevier Science Publishers B.V., 1990*

1. Introduction

Discretionary monetary policy has long been an anomaly to liberal economists. Henry Simons addressed the issue[1] in his classic paper "Rules versus Authorities in Monetary Policy" (1948, original in 1936):

> The monetary problem stands out today as the great intellectual challenge to the liberal faith.... The liberal creed demands the organization of our economic life largely through individual participation in a game *with definite rules*.... [D]efinite, stable, legislative rules of the game as to money are of paramount importance to the survival of a system based on freedom of enterprise (pp. 160–162, emphasis in original).

Simons posed the issue as one of rules versus authority, or rules versus discretion. That dichotomy should rather be seen as a continuum, in which the extent of discretion left to the monetary authority is determined by the specificity of the objectives it is given, and the immediacy of the link between its actions and the attainment of those objectives. At one extreme of discretion, a monetary authority could have the full powers of the Fed (to buy and sell securities, set the discount rate, reserve requirements, and other regulations) and be given the objective of promoting economic well-being. Both the objective, economic well-being, and the link between the monetary authority's actions and the attainment of the objective are vague. At the other extreme, the central bank could be directed to expand its holdings of government securities weekly, at an annual rate of 4 percent per year.

Intermediate arrangements exist in several countries, in which the central bank is given general objectives but required to report regularly and justify its plan of action for a reasonable period ahead. Its plans may be summarized by money and interest rate targets. It may also be required to report on the execution and outcome of past policies. The reports may be made to the legislature, to the Treasury, or to the public. In the last case, public criticism and the inherent threat that the legislature will intervene constitute the limits on the powers of the institution.

Simons considered alternative monetary rules, including constancy of the quantity of money but, noting "the danger of sharp changes on the velocity

---

[1]It had been discussed a century earlier in the context of the dispute between the currency and banking schools [Viner (1955, ch. V)]. Fetter (1965, p. 174) quotes the Chancellor of the Exchequer saying in 1839: "I deny the applicability of the general principle of the freedom of trade to the question of making money."

side" (p. 164), concluded that the optimal rule, at least for an interim period, was for the central bank to stabilize the price level. Mints (1950) likewise supported a price level rule for the United States. Milton Friedman (1948), after echoing Simons' point of principle, developed a framework in which fiscal and monetary policy would operate automatically. It included 100 percent reserve money, essentially constant government spending and tax rates, and, through full monetary financing of deficits, countercyclical monetary growth.

Friedman (1948) raised the question of whether long and variable lags in the operation of policy might cause the active (though automatic) countercyclical policy of the framework to be destabilizing. In *A Program for Monetary Stability* (1959), he argued, on the basis of research later published in Friedman and Schwartz (1963), that the Fed has frequently been a source of economic instability. Given the record and the theoretical implications of long and variable lags, Friedman advocated the rule that the growth rate of money be held constant.[2] On the general issue of rules versus discretion, he suggested that discretion had permitted destabilizing shifts in monetary policy as the central bank had been swayed by public opinion and political pressures; and that, because the criteria for judging the performance of the monetary authority are so imprecise, the Fed's discretionary powers had enabled it to escape serious public scrutiny.

A new set of arguments in the rules versus discretion debate developed from the dynamic inconsistency literature brought to macroeconomics by Kydland and Prescott (1977). At the formal level, Friedman's analysis suffered from the logical weakness that discretion seemed to dominate rules: if a particular rule would stabilize the economy, then discretionary policy-makers could always behave that way – and retain the flexibility to change the rule as needed.[3] The dynamic inconsistency literature showed that precommitment by monetary authorities could improve the behavior of the economy.

In this chapter I first discuss the gold standard as a quasi-automatic monetary policy regime, then in Section 3 turn to the issues raised by the Chicago school. Alternative monetary rules are examined in Section 4. The modern literature, centered around the concept of dynamic inconsistency, and its relevance to the rules versus discretion debate is the focus of Sections 5 through 7.

[2]Friedman (1959) explains the switch from his earlier framework as resulting from the empirical evidence. Cogent criticism of the 100 percent money proposal and the linking of monetary and fiscal policy by Clark Warburton (1966, ch. 16, original in 1952) may also have played a role. Warburton (1966, ch. 17, original in 1952) came close to advocating a constant money growth rule, suggesting an annual growth rate averaging 4–5 percent, with variations of not much more than 1–2 percent per annum to allow for changes in velocity. Selden (1962) reviews the development of support for the constant growth rate rule, giving substantial credit to Warburton.

[3]However, Friedman did confront the issue of why a formal rule might be preferable to a discretionary policy, making an analogy to the Bill of Rights (1962, pp. 239–241).

2. The gold standard

A pure gold standard is a fully automatic monetary system. The specie-flow mechanism in which the money stock adjusts through the balance of payments reveals the equilibrating tendencies inherent in the system. With all goods traded and their prices equalized worldwide, adjustment comes purely through wealth effects as the outflow of gold (specie) from a country with a current account deficit reduces the flow of spending in that country. With non-traded goods in each country, adjustments in the relative price of home goods that shift domestic spending between home and traded goods provide an additional stabilizing mechanism, as in Hume's analysis.[4]

Although far from fully automatic, in its heyday the gold standard was as close to a monetary system operated by rule as there has been. I therefore briefly review both the operation of the system and nineteenth-century analyses of it, primarily in the United Kingdom where the theory and practice of central banking developed. The context was one in which commercial banking was developing rapidly and the question of the effects of changes in the quantity of bank deposits on the economy was being discussed.

The debate between the currency and banking schools preceding Peel's Bank Act in 1844 that determined the formal structure of the Bank of England explicitly addressed the rules versus discretion issue. The currency school argued that the quantity of currency should vary precisely as it would if all money were gold, meaning that the balance of payments should determine changes in the quantity of currency; they did not view bank deposits as money; and they favored the use of monetary rules rather than discretion. The banking school disagreed on these issues. Both schools believed that the currency should be kept convertible into gold.[5]

The temper of the times, soon to produce the Corn Laws, favored the use of markets and not discretionary authority. The Bank Act, reflecting currency school views,[6] put a strict limit on the Bank's issue of fiduciary money and required all other Bank of England notes to be backed 100 percent by gold.[7] The Bank of England had claimed since 1832 to be determining the quantity of currency by following currency school principles,[8] but the currency school was

---

[4]Viner (1955, ch. VI) presents a full analysis of gold standard mechanisms.

[5]Good descriptions of the views of the two schools are contained in Mints (1945, ch. VI), and Fetter (1965, ch. VI).

[6]Included in this school were Lord Overstone, G.W. Norman (grandfather of Montagu Norman), and Robert Torrens. Peel himself recognized that in a crisis, discretionary authority might have to be exercised [Kindleberger (1978, p. 173)].

[7]Silver was permitted to constitute up to one-fifth of reserves, but the Bank did not deal in silver after 1850.

[8]This was the so-called Palmer rule, described in 1832 by J. Horsley Palmer, governor of the Bank of England, as guiding the Bank's operations [Fetter (1965, pp. 132–133)].

nonetheless severely critical of the Bank's misuse of its discretionary powers.[9]

Banking school opponents of the Bill argued both that it was a mistake to treat only currency as money, and that the gold standard rule for determining the stock of money was, in any case unwise, since the appropriate behavior of the money stock depended on whether movements in the Bank of England's reserve were caused by domestic or foreign disturbances, and on whether the disturbances were permanent or temporary [Viner (1955, p. 261)].[10] Although the banking school's real bills doctrine appeared to suggest a rule for Bank of England operations, the school did not propose an alternative legislative rule. Viner's (1955, p. 281) summary of their position describes the general view of proponents of discretion: "Reliance must be had on the good sense and the competence of those who had charge of the credit operations of the banking system."

Despite the 1844 Bank Act, British monetary policy during the period from the Bank Act until 1914 was actively managed. The need for management arose, as the banking school had anticipated, from the presence of fractional reserve banking. Claims on the Bank of England were throughout the period as good as gold. Virtually the entire gold reserve of the country was held by the Bank of England.[11] In several crises, the Bank in lending freely to meet largely internal drains of currency exceeded the legal limit on its uncovered liabilities. It was typically later indemnified by Act of Parliament.

The central role to be played by bank rate in the operation of the gold standard was not anticipated in 1844.[12] International capital flows, responding to interest rate differentials, moved gold far more rapidly than the classical specie-flow mechanism. During the heyday of the international gold standard, from 1880 to World War I, an informal set of "rules of the game"[13] is said to have developed to describe the discretionary actions that monetary authorities were to take in support of the system. A country suffering a current account deficit was supposed to tighten domestic credit, thereby protecting the gold

---

[9]Viner (1955, p. 254) strongly supports their criticisms: ". . . during the period from about 1800 to about 1860 the Bank of England almost continuously displayed an inexcusable degree of incompetence or unwillingness to fulfill the requirements which could reasonably be demanded of a central bank".

[10]Fetter (1965, ch. VI) describes the views of the critics of the Bank Act, including Tooke, Fullarton, and John Stuart Mill.

[11]This was the situation decried by Bagehot (1906, original in 1873), who argued that it would have been better for the commercial banks to hold their own gold reserves. But he saw no way of moving from the current situation to the preferred alternative, instead vigorously developing the view that in a crisis the Bank should lend freely against "all good banking securities".

[12]On the operation of the gold standard, see Bordo and Schwartz (1984), particularly the introductory essay by Bordo, and Eichengreen (1985). The Eichengreen volume contains several classic sources; among others, W.M. Scammell's "The Working of the Gold Standard" repays reading.

[13]Moggridge [in Bordo and Schwartz (1984, p. 195)] says that the phrase was coined and came into use only in 1930.

reserve and gold convertibility by reducing both capital outflows and domestic demand.[14]

The rules of the game were not formally agreed to, not well defined, and may not have been implemented. The Macmillan Committee (1931, paragraphs 46–47), unable to define operating rules of the gold standard, set out principles to which central banks in a gold standard system would subscribe, including the stability of price levels and exchange rates as goals of policy, and the avoidance of non-cooperative behavior. Goodhart (1972) defined the main rule to be protection of the gold reserve through bank rate, and found that the Bank followed the rule. Bloomfield (1959), examining data for eleven countries over the period 1880–1914, showed that central banks predominantly violated the rule that domestic policy actions should reinforce the specie-flow mechanism.[15] This is suggestive of sterilization, which was certainly common in the gold-exchange standard after World War I,[16] notably in the failure of the United States and France to expand their money supplies in response to gold inflows.

There is no question that the gold standard monetary system did not operate by rule. In the first instance, countries sometimes left and sometimes returned to the gold standard, by discretion. And even when they were on the gold standard, the central bank (in the United States, sometimes the Treasury) took an active, if not always successful, role in managing the system to maintain convertibility. The Bank of England manipulated bank rate actively, by discretion, mainly to protect the gold reserve.[17] The "rules of the game" were far from being well defined.

[14]The Cunliffe Commission's First Interim Report on the return of the United Kingdom to gold at the end of World War I contained a clear statement of the common understanding:

Whenever before the war the Bank's reserves were being depleted, the rate of discount was raised. This . . . by reacting upon the rates for money generally, acted as a check which operated in two ways. On the one hand, raised money rates tended directly to attract gold to this country or to keep here gold that might have left. On the other hand, by lessening the demands for loans for business purposes, they tended to check expenditure and so to lower prices in this country, with the result that imports were discouraged and exports encouraged and the exchanges thereby turned in our favour. Unless this two-fold check is kept in working order the whole currency system will be imperilled (paragraph 18).

[15]Econometric results presented by Dutton (1984) confirm the view that the Bank was not obeying the rules of the game, though he broadens the rules to preclude the Bank reacting countercyclically to domestic contraction. See also papers on Germany, Sweden, and Italy by, respectively, McGouldrick, Jonung, and Fratianni and Spinelli, in Bordo and Schwartz (1984), suggesting the rules were not followed.

[16]Bloomfield's examination of the pre-World War I data follows the format of Nurkse's (1944) research on inter-War monetary policy.

[17]Sayers (1958, ch. 2) provides a concise account of the period after 1873, noting that the Bank's concern to protect its own income interfered with the development of its central banking activities. Hawtrey (1962) covers a longer period and puts more emphasis on the mechanism by which bank rate affected real activity: he saw the link as being mainly through inventory demand, and for that reason emphasized that *changes* in the rate, which led to inventory accumulation or decumulation, were more significant than the level of the rate.

Nonetheless, the gold standard came closer to a regime of rules than the current system. The key difference is that monetary policy had a clearly defined objective that was, for most of the period, within the power of the monetary authority to achieve: to maintain convertibility of the currency into gold at a fixed price. Whether or not the rule enhanced economic stability relative to alternative feasible policies is another matter.

3. The Chicago school and rules versus discretion

The Federal Reserve System was originally expected to operate within a gold-standard setting, although in specifying that the money stock was to be elastic, the Federal Reserve Act provided a contradictory guide to monetary policy. Because it started operating during World War I when many of the belligerents were effectively not on the gold standard, the System "began operations with no effective legislative criterion for determining the total stock of money. The discretionary judgment of a group of men was inevitably substituted for the quasi-automatic discipline of the gold standard" [Friedman and Schwartz (1963, p. 193)].

The discretionary operation of monetary policy created little controversy so long as it was successful during the 1920s. Proposals for monetary reform in the United States proliferated after the debacle of monetary policy in the Great Depression. Impressed by bank failures, a group of Chicago economists in 1933 advocated a system in which banks would hold 100 percent reserves against checkable deposits.[18] With 100 percent reserves, bank runs could not reduce the money stock, as they had in the Great Depression. Proponents included Irving Fisher (1945, original in 1935)[19] whose simplest plan required the money stock to be held constant after a currency commision had bought sufficient government securities to bring reserves up to 100 percent. Among the alternatives proposed by Fisher were constancy of the per capita nominal money stock and a price stabilization rule. Fisher also implied that interest might be paid on reserves.

Although the Chicago arguments for rules were originally developed in the context of the 100 percent reserve plan, they are not inherently related. Simons and Fisher could easily have advocated stabilizing the price level in a fractional reserve system. Friedman could later advocate the constant growth rate rule without requiring the economy first to move to 100 percent money.

A change to 100 percent reserves would have removed one potential weakness in an automatic system – the danger that a loss of confidence would

[18]Hart (1952, 1935 in original) provides an account and critique of the "Chicago Plan", which he says was independently developed by Lauchlin Currie at Harvard.

[19]In the preface, Fisher thanks members of the Chicago group and acknowledges their memorandum on the 100 percent plan as the original source of many of the ideas in the book.

lead to runs on banks. But it should have been anticipated then, and is clear now from the fate of regulation in the seventies, that it would have been impossible to maintain the restriction against the use of all other financial intermediary liabilities as means of payment.[20] The system would have required frequent legislative or discretionary rule changes to keep up with private sector attempts to circumvent the artificial barrier, and would have increased monetary uncertainty. Rather than prevent sharp changes in velocity, the 100 percent reserve proposal, by mandating the use of inefficient methods of banking, would have ensured continuing shifts in velocity.[21] Monetary rules are discussed in the remainder of this chapter without reference to 100 percent reserves.

It is useful to distinguish two levels of argument in the rules versus discretion debate. The first is general, examining the case in principle for rules rather than discretion, without necessarily specifying the rule or details of the discretionary system. The second is specific, discussing whether the money supply should vary one way or the other, or whether nominal interest rates should be fixed, and may be relevant to both discretionary and rules systems.

Friedman's general arguments for rules rather than discretion are that a rule enables the monetary authority to withstand political pressures, provides criteria for judging its performance, and ensures certainty about economic policy for private agents. His specific argument for a constant growth rate rule was entirely pragmatic, i.e. that this would reduce economic instability. I briefly discuss Friedman's general case for rules and then, in the next section, examine alternative operating rules.

Insulating the central bank from political pressures is, I believe, a worthy purpose, though it accords ill with a general preference for democratic decision-making.[22] The other two arguments are unpersuasive. What good is it to evaluate the performance of the central bank if it is engaged in an exercise that is irrelevant to the behavior of the macroeconomic variables that matter? Far better to require the central bank each year, or quarter, to explain its actions, and to subject the explanation to the uncertain evaluations of an

---

[20]Simons (1948, p. 172) was aware of the difficulties. He thought that a way of handling them could be found "when we conceive the problem broadly as that of achieving a financial structure in which the volume of short-term borrowing would be minimized, and in which only the government would be able to create (and destroy) either effective circulating media or obligations generally acceptable as hoards media".

[21]The payment of interest on reserves would reduce the incentive to invent non-bank depository institutions, though it is unlikely even so that attempts to differentiate sharply between banks and other intermediaries in order to control the quantity of "money" would be successful.

[22]Friedman (1962) remarks on the inherently undemocratic nature of central banking, referring to the implicit view of Emile Moreau, a governor of the Bank of France between the Wars, that he, Norman, Schacht, and Strong could run the economies of the world if only they were left alone to do so. The more recent view is that central banks follow the prevailing political winds. Society of course makes arrangements to shield other types of decision-making – for instance, legal – from immediate political pressures.

imprecise science – as we do at present. Certainty about economic policy is not a compelling argument for rules either. Economic agents want certainty about prices and about output; banks aside, they have no inherent interest in the behavior of the stock of money. If a discretionary policy that produced an unpredictable path for money ensured price stability and full employment, the uncertainty about monetary policy would be of no account.

Leaving aside the dynamic inconsistency argument that will be discussed later, it is difficult to evaluate the argument of principle made by Simons and most proponents of rules. A successful discretionary monetary policy that maintains reasonable price stability and employment will likely do more to maintain the general use of free markets and personal freedoms than an unsuccessful rule that causes discontent over the basic organization of the economy. I will therefore analyze alternative policies with differing degrees of discretion in terms of the likely economic outcomes, leaving the reader to factor in his or her preference for rules as a matter of principle.

4. Alternative rules

In this section I consider alternative monetary policies: the Friedman constant money growth rule; the possibility of feedback monetary rules, including the frequent modern proposals for a nominal GNP rule; the Fisher–Simons rule of a price level target; and the Fisher "compensated dollar" proposal. I do not consider exchange rate based rules.

4.1. The constant growth rate rule

Friedman's argument for the constant growth rate rule[23] rather than an active feedback rule is that there are long and variable lags in the effects of monetary policy. Thus, any active policy that responds to current events may have its effects only at an inappropriate time. Let Y_t be the level of a target variable, say nominal GNP, and m_t be the level of the money stock. The aim of policy is to minimize the variance of Y_t, conditional on information available up to period $(t-1)$. Suppose that

$$Y_t = \sum_1^n \alpha_{i,t} Y_{t-1} + \sum_0^k \beta_{j,t} m_{t-j} + \varepsilon_t , \tag{1}$$

---

[23]After some discussion, Friedman (1960) proposes there be no seasonal variation in the growth rate of money. This would restore the seasonal to interest rates.

where $\alpha_{i,t}$ and $\beta_{j,t}$ are stochastic coefficients, and ε_t is a disturbance term, which can be taken to be white noise.

Consider now the role of lags. First, in the absence of lags, active policy may be unnecessary: if the α_i in (1) were identically zero, and given that ε is white noise, active monetary policy could not reduce the variance of nominal GNP. Long lags in the system, reflected in the α_i, make policy potentially more useful. The mechanisms that produce such lags are likely also to cause monetary policy to work with long lags. Long lags in the effects of policy by themselves are not necessarily an impediment to the successful use of active countercyclical policy [Fischer and Cooper (1973)]. If the coefficients in (1) were not stochastic, then optimal monetary policy could exactly offset the lagged effects of earlier disturbances and monetary policy by setting

$$ m_t = -[\beta_0]^{-1} \left[\sum_1^n \alpha_i Y_{t-i} + \sum_1^k \beta_j m_{t-j} \right]. \tag{2} $$

One difficulty with the policy in (2) is that it could produce instrument instability, requiring ever larger changes in the money stock to offset its lagged effects [Holbrook (1972)]. It would be more likely to do so the more slowly the effects of money on output build up; if β_0 were small, the rule (2) would call for large fluctuations in the money stock. In that sense long lags of policy could make the active policy in (2) undesirable, but allowing for costs of instrument instability in the objective function, optimal policy would still in this model be active.

Uncertainty about the lag coefficients, the $\beta_{j,t}$, means that active use of monetary policy adds variability to income. Active policy can still be used, cautiously, to reduce the variance of output, but the gain may be small.[24] The presence of variable lags, then, makes optimal policy less active, and in that sense is an argument in favor of the constant growth rate rule. Totally inactive policy could be optimal if the mere use of active policy adds uncertainty to the system independent of the particular active policy followed.[25]

Friedman's evidence for long and variable lags in the effects of money is based on a comparison of turning points in the growth rate of money and cyclical peaks in activity in NBER reference cycles.[26] Reduced-form evidence, for example of the St. Louis Fed model [or Barro (1978), or Mishkin (1983)], typically finds a reasonably close connection between money growth and the subsequent behavior of nominal GNP.[27] In the St. Louis model active monetary

[24] This is the effect of multiplier uncertainty, discussed by Brainard (1967).

[25] This could be the case if economic agents viewed the Fed as either being totally inactive, or else potentially a source of instability – as implicit in Friedman's development of the case for a constant growth rate rule.

[26] Friedman (1969, original in 1961) discusses his evidence and criticisms of it.

[27] The variability of lags found by Friedman could result from the omission of other factors that move the cycle, such as fiscal policy.

policy can be stabilizing even when lags are treated as stochastic [Cooper and Fischer (1974)].

In the above example, a zero (logarithm of the) money stock minimizes the noise added to the system by active monetary policy. The question arises of what is the corresponding monetary policy in practice [Diamond (1985)]. Friedman regards a policy of maintaining a constant growth rate of money as inactive, though even in this case the monetary rule has to specify whether past misses in attaining the given growth rate are to be ignored or corrected. Also to be considered are the questions of which monetary variable to target, and whether an alternative policy such as attempting to fix the nominal interest rate might produce a lower variance of the target variable.[28]

Except if the argument for a rule is based on the principle of minimizing the Fed's discretion, these questions cannot be answered without using an analytic and, ultimately, an empirical model. The Fed's discretion is minimized by giving it a task that it can accomplish exactly, the simplest of which is to require it to increase its portfolio each week at a given annual rate, say 4 or 0 percent.[29] Statistical inference would place the minimum uncertainty about the outcome of policy at the historical average level of the monetary variable in the regression relating the behavior of the target variable (real output, or nominal GNP) to the instrument variable.

The strongest argument against a constant growth rate rule for money is that the velocity of all money stocks has varied substantially and with some short-run predictability. It can be argued that these variations are themselves induced by unstable monetary policy, but it is hard to believe that shocks to the demand for money that cause interest rate movements and technical progress in the payments system will not cause continuing future changes in velocity. Because the behavior of the stock of money per se is not the ultimate goal of policy, there is no reason other than the fear that any active policy will degenerate for not taking such changes into account in setting monetary targets.

4.2. Interest rate versus money targets

In a famous article, Poole (1970) analyzed in the context of a fixed price IS–LM model the question of whether output would be more stable if monetary policy held the interest rate or the quantity of money fixed in the

---

[28]So long as a base level of a nominal variable such as the money stock is specified, an interest rate pegging rule need not produce indeterminacy of the money stock. See Blanchard and Fischer (1988, ch. 10) and McCallum (1981).

[29]It is because he believes the Fed's authority should be minimized that Friedman has recently moved from his former proposal that the money growth rule target M1 or M2 to the view that the monetary base should be held constant.

face of shocks to the IS curve (shocks from investment, consumption, or government demand for goods) and the LM curve (money demand shocks). The well-known answer is that interest rate pegging stabilizes output if shocks are primarily from money demand, and that money stock fixing is preferable if shocks are primarily from the IS curve.

If the price level is allowed to vary, and with rational expectations, monetary policy cannot affect the behavior of output unless the monetary authority has an informational advantage, or equivalently if some prices are fixed before monetary policy decisions are made.[30] Assume, as seems realistic, that the monetary authority can react after wages are set. In a model with IS and LM curves, plus an aggregate supply curve in which output is an increasing function of the price level relative to the expected price level, results similar to Poole's are obtained with respect to IS and LM shocks. The relative impact of a supply shock under money and interest rate rules depends on the parameters in the model: when the level of output is relatively little affected by price level movements, money stock targeting stabilizes output relative to interest rate targeting.[31]

4.3. Nominal GNP targeting

Among monetary rules that allow for changing velocity, a nominal GNP rule has received considerable attention.[32] The rule would specify a target path for nominal GNP, for instance one that grows at x percent. If the target path for nominal GNP is pre-specified for all time, policy accepts a linear and one-for-one tradeoff between changes in the price level and output. This implies, for instance, acceptance of the need for a recession of 5 percent of real GNP in the face of a supply shock that raises the price level 5 percent. It is unlikely that such a tradeoff would be accepted if the choice were put explicitly.

Nonetheless, suppose that a target path for nominal GNP has been specified. Monetary policy would then be chosen each period to bring GNP as close as possible to the specified path. Given lags in the operation of money, and if current money growth has small effects on current nominal GNP, such a policy is likely to produce instrument instability and ever-increasing fluctuations in the money stock.[33] The nominal GNP rule would then have to be calculated

---

[30]I abstract here from Mundell–Tobin and other effects through which changes in the growth rate of money affect real variables even when all markets clear.

[31]These results are developed in detail in Blanchard and Fischer (1988, ch. 10).

[32]For instance, Bean (1983) and Taylor (1985).

[33]Instrument instability would not be a problem if we had full confidence in our models, but we can be sure that the models will not continue to describe reality if the money supply fluctuates more than it ever has historically.

imposing some costs on variations in money growth. Taylor (1985) examines economic performance with nominal GNP targeting, emphasizing the difficulties caused by the lagged responses of output and prices to previous policy.

Once the impacts of past shocks, including the lagged effects of monetary policy, are recognized, an alternative mode of GNP targeting may be employed in which the monetary authority announces policies that are expected gradually to bring the economy back to a target path. Or the aim might be to produce a given growth rate of GNP each year, with past deviations from target forgiven. The simplest method of calculating the required growth rate of money is to use a forecasting equation for velocity to derive the growth rate of money implied by the intermediate target levels of GNP. This was the policy followed by the Bundesbank from 1974 to 1980, with target money growth set annually [Fischer (1988)].

A related interpretation is that under nominal GNP targeting, the monetary authority announces each period a nominal GNP target rather than a target growth rate of money. With the nominal GNP target justified in public, this is a policy that gives the monetary authority the discretion to adjust money growth in response to changes in velocity within the period. From the control theory viewpoint this change makes it possible in principle to come closer to achieving targets. Whether that would actually happen would depend on the monetary authority's success at predicting velocity and the extent to which the greater discretion would enable it to pursue other objectives.

On this interpretation, in the context of a simple three-equation macro-economic model – consisting of IS and LM curves plus the Lucas supply function – a policy that fixes nominal GNP within a period completely offsets the effects of demand shocks (shocks entering the IS and LM curves) on output and prices. Thus, if the ultimate goals of policy are to keep output and the price level at some target level, monetary policy that successfully targets nominal GNP is appropriate when the economy is affected by demand shocks. However, obviously, an adverse supply shock would raise the price level above its target level and reduce output below its target level [Blanchard and Fischer (1988, ch. 10)].

4.4. Price level rules

As in the case of nominal GNP targeting, a price level rule can be viewed either as the specification of the objective of monetary policy or the basis for an operating rule. The Fisher–Simons price level rule is in Simons merely the specification of a target for monetary policy. Fisher (1945, p. 25) makes the specific proposal that the Fed expand the money stock when the price level falls below target and contract when the price level rises above target. The dynamic properties of such a policy cannot be evaluated without an explicit model; lags in the operation of monetary policy raise the possibility that the policy would actually be destabilizing, particularly because monetary policy seems to operate more slowly on prices than on real GNP. This suggests that a Fisher–Simons rule could cause significant fluctuations in real GNP in trying to stabilize the price level.

Fisher's "compensated dollar" proposal [Fisher (1920)], recently revived by Hall (1983), proposes that the dollar be exchangeable into gold, but that the value of gold that is exchanged for a dollar be fixed in real terms, defined say by the CPI. The notion is that the gold standard check on excess issue of currency would still be available, the simple gold standard criterion of maintaining convertibility would still be there, but the secular effects of changes in the relative price of gold on the aggregate price level would disappear.[34] The proposal gives the Fed a simple rule to follow – maintain convertibility – and appears to promise price level stability. The difficulty with the scheme is that its dynamics are not understood, particularly whether there would be destabilizing speculation against the standard. For instance, if the price of gold were adjusted monthly in accordance with the change in the CPI, anticipated changes in the CPI would allow individuals to speculate by buying or selling gold in advance of the change in parity. Probably the imposition of sufficiently large transactions costs would reduce the extent of such speculation, but the desirability and consequences of such costs have not been explored. Furthermore, it is entirely unclear how the scheme induces the wage flexibility that must be needed if the aggregate price level is to be stable.

4.5. The methodological problem

None of these alternative policy proposals commands wide assent within the profession. Since Lucas's policy evaluation critique (1976), there has been no accepted way of evaluating detailed policy proposals.[35] There has been a tendency to evaluate proposals either in very simple econometric models, which are set up as much for tractability as for realism, or in very simple theoretical models, also marked mainly by tractability. One such model that provides considerable insight is the three-equation macro model consisting of IS and LM curves plus an aggregate supply curve. However, few appear to be convinced by such exercises – and they are right, for how a policy would

[34]In the introduction to the U.S. edition of Morgan-Webb (1934), James H. Rand Jr. claims this is precisely the policy followed in Britain after its 1931 departure from the gold standard.
[35]This includes the constant growth rate rule which represents a significant change from previous practice and therefore may induce changes in economic structure in unexpected ways.

operate in practice depends to a considerable extent on the lags with which policy affects the relevant target variables.

Yet policy evaluation and Fed policy-making continue. Economists with experience confidently pronounce on the errors of the Fed's ways. The Fed continues to make discretionary policy, recently with considerable success in terms of its objectives. Each is using implicit and sometimes explicit models, of considerable sophistication.

The natural vehicles for studying alternative policy rules are the large-scale econometric models, some of which have met the market test of commercial success. Given an econometric model, an objective function, and computing ability, optimal feedback rules for monetary policy can be calculated. However, given the variety and inadequacies of existing models, it would be difficult to justify enshrining any of these rules in legislation. Until and if ever a new generation of models that meets the demanding standards of the profession is developed, there will be no generally accepted professional basis for discussing alternative policy rules.

What monetary policies should be adopted in the meantime? At a minimum, it is clear that monetary policy should adjust for predictable changes in velocity. It might be possible to find simple feedback rules that perform well in a variety of models,[36] and to recommend them as a basis for monetary policy. They could serve in the first instance as an indicator of what monetary policy should be. Prudence would suggest years of public and professional discussion before an attempt was made to put such rules into legislation.[37] It also suggests that the rule include procedures for its own amendment.

5. Dynamic inconsistency: The basic example

Until 1977 it appeared that discretion dominated rules, since any good rule could be adopted by discretion.[38] The concept of dynamic inconsistency, brought to macroeconomics in the rules versus discretion context [Kydland and Prescott (1977)] completely changed the debate.[39]

Dynamic inconsistency occurs when a future policy decision that forms part of an optimal plan formulated at an initial date is no longer optimal from the

[36]Cooper and Fischer (1972) found feedback rules that reacted to the behavior of inflation and unemployment which stabilized output in both the St. Louis and MPS models.

[37]Friedman in 1948 offered his monetary and fiscal framework very much as a tentative proposal for professional discussion.

[38]Friedman (1972) had argued that a policy adopted by rule would stabilize private sector expectations relative to the same policy carried out by discretion, but the basis for that argument was not clear.

[39]In this section I draw freely on my 1986 survey article [Fischer (1986)]; see also Cukierman (1985).

viewpoint of a later date, even though no new information has appeared in the meantime. An example of dynamic inconsistency due to Prescott (1977), developed in Fischer (1980), is that of optimal taxation in a system with capital. Under rational expectations the solution gives tax rates that are optimal conditional on their being expected by private agents. But once capital is in place, its supply is inelastic and a government acting to maximize the welfare of the representative individual would tax capital more heavily. The problem is that if the public expected the government to violate its announcement, economic welfare would be lower than if the government could commit itself to following through on its promised tax rate.[40]

The application to the rules versus discretion debate comes from the claim that policy will be dynamically consistent if determined by rules. By contrast, a government or central bank with discretion may, under rational expectations, be expected to make the short-run optimal decision every time it can, therefore gains nothing from its opportunism, and on average produces a worse outcome than would a government able to tie its hands.

In this section I present a simple Phillips-curve example of dynamic inconsistency, and discuss the relevance to the rules versus discretion debate of the example. In the next section I present extensions that take reputation into account.[41]

5.1. Basic example

Suppose that the policy-maker has a single period loss function quadratic in the rate of inflation (π) and in the deviation of real output (y) from a target level:

$$L(\cdot) = a\pi^2 + (y - ky^*)^2, \quad a > 0, k > 1. \tag{3}$$

Here y^* can be interpreted as full employment output. The target level of output exceeds the natural rate.

The assumption $k > 1$ is crucial. The most plausible justification is that tax distortions cause the natural rate of employment to be too low. That justification allows the loss function $L(\cdot)$ to be consistent with the single period utility function of private agents. An alternative view is that the government has

---

[40]Precisely the same problem occurs with the optimal inflation tax and money holding [Calvo (1978)]; the monetary authority can always impose a lump-sum tax by discretely increasing the money supply and, once the private sector has formed expectations, is tempted to do so.

[41]This structure was introduced by Kydland and Prescott (1977) and developed by Barro and Gordon (1983a, 1983b), Backus and Driffill (1985a, 1985b), Canzoneri (1985), Rogoff (1985), and others.

different tastes than the private sector.[42] In any event, dynamic inconsistency may occur whether or not the private sector and the government have the same tastes.

The intertemporal loss function, a discounted sum of the form

$$M_t(\cdot) = \sum_0^\infty (1 + \delta)^{-i} L_{t+i}(\cdot),$$
(4)

may more plausibly differ between the private sector and the government in a system with periodic elections that can end the life of the government. In this case the government may have a shorter horizon than the private sector.

An expectational Phillips curve describes the relationship between output and inflation each period:

$$y = y^* + b(\pi - \pi^e),$$
(5)

where π^e is the expected rate of inflation.

Consider first a one-period game. The policy-maker sets the inflation rate. Under discretion the expected inflation rate is taken as given, implying:

$$\pi = (a + b^2)^{-1} b[(k - 1)y^* + b\pi^e].$$
(6)

If expectations are correct, the inflation rate will be positive at the level

$$\pi_d = a^{-1} b(k - 1)y^*,$$
(7)

where subscript d represents "discretion". Note that the inflation rate is higher the larger is b, and thus the greater the output gain from unanticipated inflation, the larger is the distortion $(k - 1)y^*$, and the smaller is a (the less costly is inflation).

The implied value of the loss function under discretion is:

$$L_d = (k - 1)^2 y^{*2}(1 + a^{-1} b^2).$$
(8)

This equilibrium is evidently worse for the government (and if it has the same utility function, the private sector) than a zero inflation equilibrium. The zero inflation equilibrium, the precommitment solution, gives a value of the loss

---

[42]More sophisticated theories that recognize heterogeneity in private sector tastes and that seek to ground the government's objective function in the electoral process could produce a utility function for some governments that would seek to raise output above the natural rate. Cukierman (1985) contains an extended discussion of this point.

function equal to:

$$L_p = (k-1)^2 y^{*2}. \tag{9}$$

Why, in this game, does the policy-maker not choose an inflation rate of zero, thereby attaining L_p rather than L_d? Under the rules of the game, in which the private sector commits itself first to a given π^e, $\pi = \pi^e = 0$ is not a Nash equilibrium. Once the private sector has committed itself to $\pi^e = 0$, the policy-maker will choose the positive rate of inflation implied by (6). The inflation rate π_d in (7) is a Nash equilibrium that, if expected by the private sector, will be implemented by the government.[43] If the policy-maker could somehow commit herself to choosing $\pi = 0$, she could obtain the distorted second-best outcome L_p.

For discussing reputational equilibrium we want also to calculate the inflation rate and value of the utility function in the fooling solution in which individuals expect the policy-maker to create zero inflation but she instead acts opportunistically. With $\pi^e = 0$, the optimal discretionary rate of inflation is from (6):

$$\pi_f = (a + b^2)^{-1}[b(k-1)y^*]. \tag{10}$$

The corresponding value of the loss function is:

$$L_f = (1 + a^{-1}b^2)^{-1}(k-1)^2 y^{*2}. \tag{11}$$

Thus:

$$L_f = (1 + a^{-1}b^2)^{-1}L_p \equiv (1 + \theta)^{-1}L_p,$$
$$L_d = (1 + a^{-1}b^2)L_p = (1 + \theta)L_p. \tag{12}$$

Note that $\theta = b^2/a$ is, loosely, a measure of the utility gain from unexpected inflation: b gives the increase in output and a the utility loss from higher inflation.

We thus have the fundamental set of inequalities that demonstrates the benefits of precommitment:

$$L_f < L_p < L_d. \tag{13}$$

---

[43]It is also the only Nash equilibrium. It is tempting when talking of the private sector "moving first" to think of it setting its expectation strategically. If π^e were a private sector strategic variable, it could be set at the value that would from (6) induce $\pi = 0$. According to the algebra that would result in $y = ky^*$ and produce a first-best solution. But that would not be an equilibrium because π and π^e would be different. In other words, it is inconsistent to argue that the public "sets" π^e at a negative number in order to achieve $\pi = 0$.

The discretionary solution produces the largest loss, resulting as it does in a positive rate of inflation with no output gain. Therefore, one suspects the policy-maker would want to choose a zero inflation rate to attain L_p. But because the loss function is lower when the government succeeds in fooling the private sector than when it acts consistently $(L_f < L_p)$, the government is tempted to violate expectations if the private sector should be lulled into expecting zero inflation. In striving to obtain output gains by fooling the public, the government succeeds only in raising the inflation rate and producing the worst of the three outcomes in (13).

Accordingly, Kydland and Prescott argued, policy-makers should be constrained by rule. That would enable them to attain the precommitted solution, admittedly not the best possible, but better than the discretionary alternative.

5.2. Preliminary discussion

How persuasive is this? Should we expect discretionary policy-makers always to choose the short-run optimal solution, or might they take into account the consequences for future expectations of any current decisions to pursue short-run gains? Before presenting models with reputation, we briefly discuss the general problem of dynamic inconsistency.

Societies deal routinely and continuously with situations in which dynamic inconsistency could occur. So do individuals.[44] Wealth in general, and the national debt in particular, are standing invitations to surprise taxation, which is rarely explicitly imposed. Implicit social security obligations are honored and protected. Property rights are protected by law and understood to be essential to economic efficiency in a market environment. Central banks with discretionary powers successfully run low-inflation policies in several countries, including Germany, Japan, and Switzerland.[45]

The law, constitutional or less fundamental, is obviously one solution to the dynamic inconsistency problem. But not all potential dynamic inconsistency situations are dealt with by the law. This raises the questions of which issues are and should be handled through the law and which by discretionary

---

[44]Elster (1979) and Schelling (1984) are stimulating references, dealing in part with individual inconsistencies and problems of self-control.

[45]The dynamic inconsistency literature in macroeconomics has been almost exclusively concerned with the alleged inflationary bias of macroeconomic policy. Even aside from Switzerland and Germany, it is clear from history that inflationary bias is only a sometime thing. At the ends of the Napoleonic and Civil Wars, and World War I, Britain and the United States deflated to get back to fixed gold parities. These episodes too deserve attention in the dynamic inconsistency literature. A challenge for the theory of dynamic inconsistency is to explain why countries were able to institute mechanisms to suppress their inflationary bias until the end of the World War II, and to explain why the bias is worse in some countries than others.

policy-making. The ability to describe future contingencies fully must be an important element in this choice.

A potentially fruitful way of thinking about the constitutional law–law–rule–discretion continuum is to view policies as involving a tradeoff between the benefits of flexibility and the costs of dynamic inconsistency.[46] Depending on the policy, the legal system makes an ex ante choice of the costs that should be attached to attempts to change it. Discretionary policies, such as monetary policy, can be changed at low cost; rules fixed by law such as much of fiscal policy are changeable at greater cost; rules fixed by constitutional law such as the rights of private property or interstate commerce are in principle also changeable but at yet greater cost.

5.3. Non-rules solutions

One way of reducing the inflationary bias of the basic example, developed by Rogoff (1985), is to appoint conservative policy-makers. Suppose society's loss function is (3). Let a_b (b for banker) be the policy-maker's weight on inflation in his personal loss function. Giving such an individual full discretion results in a loss for society of

$$L_b = [1 + b^2/a_b]L_p . \tag{14}$$

The more conservative the policy-maker, the closer the society comes to achieving the precommitted equilibrium.

The notion of appointing conservative central bankers is certainly suggestive. Further reasons to appoint them relate to the benefits of reputation, to be examined below.

Another non-rules solution is to put in place incentives for successor governments to behave consistently. This is the approach that has been followed in a model involving government debt, but not capital, by Lucas and Stokey (1983), and in a model including, in addition, monetary policy, by Persson, Persson and Svensson (1985). The general principle, explained by Persson and Svensson (1984), is to place the successor decision-makers in a situation where the penalty for deviating from the precommitted consistent plan balances at the margin the benefit of doing so. In principle such arrangements can be made in any situations where the full set of states of nature can be specified ex ante.

---

[46]Rogoff (1985) suggests this tradeoff, which is examined further in Section 7 below. Cukierman and Meltzer (1986) include similar considerations in their analysis of a government's choice between discretion and rules.

The Lucas–Stokey and Persson–Svensson solutions raise delicate issues. Dynamic inconsistency does not disappear. Rather, the solution assumes that the government will not violate certain explicit obligations, such as repaying the debt, even though there is an incentive to do so. Without a theory of reputation such solutions have to be regarded as incomplete. We turn now to models with reputation.

6. Dynamic inconsistency and reputational equilibrium

The basic Phillips-curve example invites the question of whether the decision-maker cannot, by behaving consistently, reach a better result than the one-period discretionary outcome. Perhaps by showing forbearance, investing in reputation, a central bank can induce the private sector to believe that it will not produce unexpected inflation.

There indeed exist reputational equilibria in which the monetary authority is expected and induced to behave consistently so long as it does so. The key to analyzing such equilibria is the specification of private sector expectations.

Suppose that the horizon is infinite and that policy-makers have the loss function $M_t(\cdot)$ in (4). Denote the inflation rate (7) associated with discretionary policy in the one period problem by π_d. The inflation rate associated with the precommitted monetary policy is $\pi_p = 0$.

We start with expectations based on the private sector's viewing the policy-maker as either reliable or opportunistic. If the inflation rate has ever been anything other than the precommitted rate of zero, the expected inflation rate from then on will be π_d from (7). If the government has hitherto produced the precommitted inflation rate, $\pi_p = 0$, it is expected to continue doing so.

Why these particular expectations? They will turn out to be justified, or rational. But, as in many cases, they are not the only rational expectations, or in game-theory terminology, perfect, equilibria. The problem of multiple rational expectations solutions to intertemporal games is well known. Below we give another example of a consistent set of expectations.

Given these expectations, consider a government that has always behaved consistently, now considering whether to continue producing zero inflation or whether rather to fool the public. If it cheats, it gains in that period:

$$\text{temptation} = L_p - L_f = \theta L_p / (1 + \theta) . \tag{15}$$

It then has to pay for its cheating by being expected to produce the discretionary solution forever. If that is what is expected, that is the best thing for the government to do. The loss from discretionary policy in one period relative to the precommitted equilibrium is:

$$\text{loss} = L_d - L_p = \theta L_p . \tag{16}$$

Note that both the temptation and the loss are increasing in θ.

The gain from acting opportunistically is then equal to the temptation minus the present discounted value of the loss that starts a period later:

$$\text{gain from opportunism} = \text{temptation} - \text{loss}/\delta$$
$$= \theta L_p[\delta - (1 + \theta)][\delta(1 + \theta)]^{-1} . \tag{17}$$

The government will act opportunistically if it has a very high discount rate, and it will then be expected to, and will, behave that way in every succeeding period. It will keep the inflation rate at zero if the discount rate is low or if θ is high. The role of θ in determining whether the government keeps inflation at zero appears paradoxical in that when θ is high, the short-run gain from unanticipated inflation is high. But since both the gain and the loss are increasing in θ, the net effect is a priori indeterminate, and depends on the curvature of the loss function.

Note that in this certainty setting a reputational equilibrium is possible only if the horizon is infinite. Otherwise the government would be sure in the last period to produce the discretionary outcome whatever the private sector's expectation, and working backwards would be expected to do the same in the first period.

6.1. The Barro–Gordon example

Barro and Gordon (1983b) produce another example of a reputational equilibrium in this type of model. Their expectations assumption is that if the government fails to produce the expected inflation rate this period, the private sector expects the discretionary inflation rate next period; if they produce the expected inflation rate this period, they are expected to do so again next period.

The first question is whether a zero inflation rate can be sustained as an equilibrium. The loss from opportunism lasts only one period, before the government regains credibility and is faced with the same decision it has in the initial period. Thus, the gain from opportunism in this case is, using (15) and (16):

$$\text{gain} = \text{temptation} - \text{loss}/(1 + \delta)$$
$$= \theta L_p[(\delta - \theta)/(1 + \delta)(1 + \theta)] . \tag{18}$$

With a high discount rate the government will produce higher than expected inflation in period 1. In period 2 it produces the discretionary rate π_a. It regains trust by doing what was expected, but then promptly violates it in period 3. Thus, the initial set of expectations was not rational.

With a low discount rate and high θ the government will produce zero inflation.[47] If, by accident, it were to violate that rule, the public would expect π_d to be followed by zero inflation, and the government would indeed act that way. Thus, with low δ the assumed expectations are rational.

For the high δ case, Barro and Gordon are able to show that there is an equilibrium if $\delta\theta < 1$, that is only if the government is not too impatient. If $\delta\theta > 1$, it will go to the discretionary solution. If it is not too impatient, the equilibrium inflation rate in this reputational equilibrium lies between the zero inflation that would be attainable under precommitment and π_d that occurs if the government is entirely short-sighted.

The nature of the rules equilibrium is that the government will carry out the rule because there is no advantage to not doing so. If it should by miscalculation deviate, then it will next period implement π_d given that it is expected to do so. It regains credibility and thereafter is happy to implement the rule again. The equilibrium is perfect – though it is far from unique, as Barro–Gordon recognize and discuss.

6.2. Multiple equilibria

Perhaps there are many possible equilibria in the real world, and it is pure accident that a particular situation exists. Nonetheless, it would be preferable if theory could narrow down the range of possibilities.

The description of the private sector's response to the government's deviation as a punishment raises the hope that the design of an optimal punishment strategy will reduce the multiplicity of equilibria. But unless the private sector is thought of as a single union, it is difficult to conceive how it can select an optimal punishment as opposed to optimally calculating expectations.

The more promising route probably lies in enriching the description of the environment in which the policy-makers and the private sector operate.

6.3. A randomizing government

Tabellini (1983, 1985), Backus and Driffill (1985a, 1985b), and Barro (1985) apply the Kreps–Wilson (1982) reputation model to the inflation problem.

---

[47]In the Barro–Gordon model zero inflation is not an equilibrium because of differing assumptions on the utility function.

Tabellini, and Backus and Driffill consider a monopoly union setting wages in a game with a monetary authority. The alternative assumption, made by Barro, is that private agents are homogeneous and not engaged in strategic considerations vis-à-vis the policy-maker. The union versus central bank game may be appropriate for Europe, but in the United States context the notion that private agents cannot combine against the monetary authority is more attractive than the alternative.

The horizon is finite. The public believes there are two possible types of policy-maker, the strong and the weak. The strong never inflates. The weak has the same utility function as the public, is always tempted to produce unanticipated inflation, but by pretending to be strong can build up a reputation for strength. The weak policy-maker potentially engages in a mixed (randomizing) strategy, picking a probability of acting tough (or alternatively, producing inflation) in each period, and letting the dice decide the policy choice. If in any period the dice makes him act weak, the public understands he is weak, and in each subsequent period he obtains only the discretionary outcome.

The general form of the solution is as follows.[48] For a long-horizon problem the policy-maker will start out not randomizing at all and not producing inflation (this will keep his reputation unchanged). Because private agents are uncertain of the policy-maker's type, inflation is below its expected level all this time, causing a small recession. Eventually the end beckons, and the policy-maker begins to randomize. During this period his reputation is improving and the probability of playing strong is falling. Then, towards the end, maybe only in the last period, he inflates for sure.

One result that emerges from this framework is that as the horizon goes to infinity, and provided the discount rate is reasonable, the reputational equilibrium with zero inflation is attained. The reasoning is similar to that above: the penalty for revealing your weakness is a very long period of inferior performance.

Neither the elegance nor the suggestiveness of the Kreps–Wilson construct can be denied. But the analysis, by focusing entirely on the weak policy-maker who has made it through without inflating, draws attention away from the implausibility of the underlying view of the policy-maker's actions. It is difficult to believe a model of reputation in which a central bank creates inflation because the dice fell one way rather than another.[49]

---

[48]A two-period example is worked out in full detail in Fischer (1986).
[49]While Fed policy that conditions on the stock market or the exchange rate is stochastic in outcome, the Fed is not in those cases purely randomizing.

7. Flexibility and rules

The models of the preceding two sections appear to prove the clear dominance of rules over discretion; reputational models show that policy-makers under discretion may, but will not necessarily, produce the optimal outcome that rules ensure.

However, the issue is not closed. A basic argument for activist policy is that the policy-makers can handle certain disturbances more flexibly and more cheaply than can a myriad of private agents. For instance, there is no good reason why a shift in the demand for money should be transmitted to prices, causing all economic agents to adjust prices and wages when the money-creating authorities can respond instead. One of the most important arguments for discretionary policy is that it leaves the policy-maker the flexibility to respond rapidly to contingencies not foreseen or not describable in the potential rule.

Suppose that a disturbance ε is observed by the policy-maker each period, after private sector expectations have been determined, and that the nature of the disturbance cannot be described in the monetary rule.[50] We generalize the supply function (5) to:

$$y = y^* + b(\pi - \pi^e) + \varepsilon . \tag{19}$$

Here ε is a disturbance with expectation zero that is not serially correlated and that is not known to private agents when they make their wage decisions. (We do not show time subscripts.) Denote the variance of ε by σ^2. The social loss function is now the expectation of $L(\cdot)$ in equation (3).

The monetary authority is in a position to respond to realizations of ε, but π^e, representing wage-setting, is determined before ε is known. There is no pre-commitment, and no consideration of reputation, so that the discretionary solution is chosen each period. The inflation rate is:

$$\pi = (a + b^2)^{-1} b[(k - 1)y^* + b\pi^e - \varepsilon] , \tag{20}$$

implying π^e is the same as under certainty, namely

$$\pi^e = (b/a)(k - 1)y^*$$

and

$$\pi = (b/a)(k - 1)y^* - (a + b^2)^{-1} b\varepsilon . \tag{20'}$$

---

[50]This example is closely related to the analysis by Rogoff (1985).

In this solution the monetary authority responds to supply shocks, allowing them to affect both output and inflation: an adverse supply shock both raises the inflation rate and reduces output below the natural rate.[51]

The expected value of the loss function under these conditions is calculated as:

$$\mathrm{E}(L) = (1 + \theta)(k - 1)^2 y^{*2} + (1 + \theta)^{-1}\sigma^2 , \qquad \theta \equiv b^2/a . \tag{21}$$

Suppose, alternatively, that the monetary authority had no discretion and that the money supply was held rigidly constant. Assume also that the quantity theory holds, with

$$m = y^* = p + y , \tag{22}$$

where p is the (logarithm of the) price level, and the money stock is set at the level which is expected to produce $p = 0$. Suppose that last period the (logarithm of the) price level was zero. The expected price level and inflation rate this period are also zero.

The expected value of the loss function under a constant money rule can then be shown to be:

$$\mathrm{E}(L_m) = (k - 1)^2 y^{*2} + (1 + a)(1 + b)^{-2}\sigma^2 . \tag{23}$$

The first term is larger under discretion, reflecting the basic dynamic inconsistency result. The second term is larger under the constant money rule, reflecting the benefits to society of flexible monetary policy.

There is thus a basic tradeoff between the gains from dynamic consistency and the loss of flexibility in imposing a monetary rule. To the extent that the central bank has a longer horizon than one period – and this may be one reason that the law attempts to isolate central bank management from political pressures – it may be able to establish a reputation that serves the same purpose as a monetary rule.

8. Concluding comments

The rules versus discretion debate in monetary policy is at least 150 years old. There has, in that time, been no monetary system that operated without the exercise of substantial discretionary authority – to be sure more so at some

---

[51] I am assuming that the target level of output does not change with the supply shock. That assumption does not affect the basic point being made here.

times, such as after the collapse of the gold standard, and in some countries, than others.

The pre-1977 arguments of principle for rules lacked any convincing demonstration that rules might systematically be better than discretion. That demonstration came with the dynamic inconsistency literature. However, given the possible benefits of the flexibility of monetary policy under discretion, and the role of reputation, the dynamic inconsistency literature does not establish the superiority of rules.

In thinking about monetary policy and rules, it is useful to discuss who the monetary policy-makers will be.[52] For concreteness, consider the example of the United States. At one extreme the decision on monetary policy could be made on the basis of current knowledge and enshrined in the constitution. That is unlikely to happen, given the difficulties of amending the constitution. Nor, given the uncertainties over monetary policy, should serious economists argue for such an amendment. It surely ill behooves a profession that completely failed to anticipate the variability of real exchange rates under a floating exchange rate system to believe that it is capable of specifying a monetary policy that should be changed only through the tortuous process of constitutional amendment. The choice in the United States is thus not between a monetary policy determined by rule for all time, and discretion, but between a monetary policy specified by the Congress and one chosen by the Fed. Current U.S. fiscal policy does not suggest that the Congress would do a better job of choosing monetary policy than the Fed, though that is not to say that the Fed cannot do better.

The Chicago school's emphasis on rules versus discretion was misleading as was its emphasis on the desirability of rules as such. There is a continuum of monetary policies, some giving more discretion to the central bank than others. It is difficult to attach much virtue to a rule merely because it is a rule if it produces poor economic performance. Accordingly, more valuable than the rules versus discretion debate is the substantive discussion of alternative monetary policies that accompanied it. That discussion has sputtered since being derailed by the econometric evaluation critique, but is too important to be suppressed much longer.

---

[52] In commenting on an earlier draft of this chapter, Milton Friedman stated:

The major comment is the omission of what I have increasingly come to regard as Hamlet on this issue [rules versus discretion], namely the public choice perspective. To illustrate, . . . you talk about a loss function for "the policymaker" that includes solely inflation and the deviation of real output from a target level. If we bring this down to earth, these are likely to be only very indirectly related to the real objectives of the actual policymakers. From revealed preference, I suspect that by far and away the two most important variables in their loss function are avoiding accountability on the one hand and achieving public prestige on the other. A loss function that contains those two elements as its main argument will I believe come far closer to rationalizing the behavior of the Federal Reserve over the past 73 years than one such as you have used.

References

Andersen, L.C. and K.M. Carlson (1970) 'A monetarist model for economic stabilization', *FRB of St. Louis Review*, April: 7–25.

Backus, D. and J. Driffill (1985a) 'Rational expectations and policy credibility following a change in regime', *Review of Economic Studies*, 52: 211–222.

Backus, D. and J. Driffill (1985b) 'Inflation and reputation', *American Economic Review*, 75: 530–538.

Bagehot, W. (1906) *Lombard Street*. London: Kegan, Paul, Trench, Trubner.

Barro, R.J. (1978) 'Unanticipated money, output, and the price level in the United States', *Journal of Political Economy*, 86: 549–580.

Barro, R.J. (1985) 'Reputation in a model of monetary policy with incomplete information', University of Rochester, manuscript.

Barro, R.J. and D. Gordon (1983a) 'A positive theory of monetary policy in a natural rate model', *Journal of Political Economy*, 91: 589–610.

Barro, R.J. and D. Gordon (1983b) 'Rules, discretion and reputation in a model of monetary policy', *Journal of Monetary Economics*, 12: 101–122.

Bean, C.R. (1983) 'Targeting nominal income: An appraisal', *Economic Journal*, 93: 806–819.

Blanchard, O.J. and S. Fisher (1988) *Lectures in macroeconomics*. Cambridge, Mass.: MIT Press.

Bloomfield, A.I. (1959) *Monetary policy under the international gold standard: 1880–1914*. New York: Federal Reserve Bank.

Bordo, M.D. and A.J. Schwartz, eds. (1984) *A retrospective on the classical gold standard, 1821–1931*. Chicago: University of Chicago Press.

Brainard, W. (1967) 'Uncertainty and the effectiveness of policy', *American Economic Review, Papers and Proceedings*, 57: 411–425.

Calvo, G. (1978) 'On the time consistency of optimal policy in a monetary economy', *Econometrica*, 46: 1411–1428.

Canzoneri, M.B. (1985) 'Monetary policy games and the role of private information', *American Economic Review*, 75: 1056–1070.

Cooper, J.P. and S. Fischer (1972) 'Stochastic simulation of monetary rules in two macroeconometric models', *Journal of the American Statistical Association*, 67: 750–760.

Cooper, J.P. and S. Fischer (1974) 'Monetary and fiscal policy in the fully stochastic St. Louis model', *Journal of Money, Credit and Banking*, 6: 1–22.

Cukierman, A. (1985) 'Central bank behavior and credibility – some recent developments', Tel Aviv University, manuscript.

Cukierman, A. and A.H. Meltzer (1986) 'A positive theory of discretionary policy, the cost of democratic government and the benefits of a constitution', *Economic Inquiry*, 24: 363–365.

Diamond, P.A. (1985) 'Ignorance and monetary policy', M.I.T., mimeo.

Dutton, J. (1984) 'The Bank of England and the rules of the game under the International Gold Standard', in: D. Bordo and A.J. Schwartz, eds., *A retrospective on the classical gold standard, 1821–1931*. Chicago: University of Chicago Press.

Eichengreen, B., ed. (1985) *The gold standard in theory and history*. New York: Methuen.

Elster, J. (1979) *Ulysses and the sirens*. Cambridge: Cambridge University Press.

Fetter, F.W. (1965) *The development of British monetary orthodoxy*. Cambridge, Mass.: Harvard University Press.

Fischer, S. (1980) 'Dynamic inconsistency, cooperation and the benevolent dissembling government', *Journal of Economic Dynamics and Control*, 2: 93–107.

Fischer, S. (1986) 'Time Consistent Monetary and Fiscal Policies: A Survey', M.I.T., mimeo.

Fischer, S. (1988) 'Monetary policy and performance in the U.S., Japan and Europe, 1973–1986', in: Y. Suzuki and M. Olcabe, eds., *Toward a world of economic stability: Optimal monetary framework and policy*. Tokyo: University of Tokyo Press.

Fischer, S. and J.P. Cooper (1973) 'Stabilization policy and lags', *Journal of Political Economy*, 81: 847–877.

Fisher, I. (1920). *Stabilizing the dollar*. New York: Macmillan.

Fisher, I. (1945) *100% money*. New Haven: City Printing Company.

Friedman, M. (1948) 'A monetary and fiscal framework for economic stability', reprinted in: M. Friedman, *Essays in positive economics*. Chicago: Chicago University Press (1953).

Friedman, M. (1959) *A program for monetary stability*. New York: Fordham University Press.

Friedman, M. (1962) 'Should there be an independent monetary authority? 'in L.B. Yeager, ed., *In search of a monetary constitution*. Cambridge, Mass.: Harvard University Press.

Friedman, M. (1969) 'The lag in effect of monetary policy', in: M. Friedman, *The optimum quantity of money*. Chicago: Aldine.

Friedman, M. (1972) 'The case for a monetary rule', *Newsweek*, 7 February: 67.

Friedman, M. and A.J. Schwartz (1963) *A monetary history of the United States, 1867–1960*. Princeton: Princeton University Press.

Goodhart, C.A.E. (1972) *The business of banking*. London: Weidenfeld and Nicholson.

Hall, R.E. (1983) 'Monetary strategy with an elastic price standard', in: *Price stability and public policy*. Kansas City: Federal Reserve Bank, pp. 137–159.

Hart, A.G. (1952) 'The "Chicago plan" of monetary reform', in: F.A. Lutz and L.W. Mints, eds., *Readings in monetary theory*. London: George Allen and Unwin.

Hawtrey, R.G. (1962) *A century of bank rate*. New York: Augustus M. Kelley reprint series.

Holbrook, R.S. (1972) 'Optimal economic policy and the problem of instrument instability', *American Economic Review*, 62: 57–65.

Kindleberger, C.P. (1978) *Manias, panics, and crashes*. New York: Basic Books.

Kreps, D. and R. Wilson (1982) 'Reputation and imperfect competition', *Journal of Economic Theory*, 27: 253–279.

Kydland, F.E. and E.C. Prescott (1977) 'Rules rather than discretion: The inconsistency of optimal plans', *Journal of Political Economy*, 85: 473–492.

Lucas, R.E. (1976) 'Econometric policy evaluation: A critique', in: Carnegie-Rochester Conference Series on Public Policy, Vol. 1, *The Phillips curve and labor markets*, pp. 19–46.

Lucas, R.E. and N.L. Stokey (1983) 'Optimal fiscal and monetary policy in an economy without capital', *Journal of Monetary Economics*, 12: 55–94.

McCallum, B.T. (1981) 'Price level determinacy with an interest rate rule and rational expectations', *Journal of Monetary Economics*, 8: 319–329.

Mints, L.W. (1945) *A history of banking theory*. Chicago: University of Chicago Press.

Mints, L.W. (1950) *Monetary policy for a competitive society*. New York: McGraw-Hill.

Mishkin, F.S. (1983) *A rational expectations approach to macroeconomics*. Chicago: University of Chicago Press.

Morgan-Webb, (1934). *The rise and fall of the gold standard*. New York: Macmillan.

Nurkse, R. (1944) *International currency experience*. League of Nations (Arno Press, 1978).

Persson, T. and L.E.O. Svensson (1984) 'Time-consistent fiscal policy and government cash-flow', *Journal of Monetary Economics*, 14: 365–374.

Persson, M., T. Persson and L.E.O. Svensson (1985) 'Time consistency of fiscal and monetary policy', Seminar Paper 331, Institute for International Economic Studies, Stockholm.

Poole, W. (1970) 'Optimal choice of monetary policy instruments in a simple stochastic macro model', *Quarterly Journal of Economics*, 84: 197–216.

Prescott, E.C. (1977) 'Should control theory be used for economic stabilization?', in: Carnegie-Rochester Conference Series on Public Policy, Vol. 7, *Optimal policies, control theory and technology exports*.

Rogoff, K. (1985) 'The optimal degree of commitment to an intermediate monetary target', *Quarterly Journal of Economics*, 100: 1169–1190.

Sayers, R.S. (1958) *Central banking after Bagehot*. Oxford: Clarendon Press.

Schelling, T.C. (1984) *Choice and consequence*. Cambridge, Mass.: Harvard University Press.

Selden, R.T. (1962) 'Stable monetary growth', in: L.B. Yeager, ed., *In search of a monetary constitution*. Cambridge, Mass.: Harvard University Press.

Simons, H.C. (1948) *Economic policy for a free society*. Chicago: University of Chicago Press.

Tabellini, G. (1983) 'Accommodative monetary policy and central bank reputation', University of California, Los Angeles, manuscript.

Tabellini, G. (1985) 'Centralized wage setting and monetary policy in a reputational equilibrium', University of California, Los Angeles, manuscript.

Taylor, J.B. (1985) 'What would nominal GNP targetting do to the business cycle?', in: Carnegie-Rochester Conference Series on Public Policy, Vol. 22, *Understanding monetary regimes*, pp. 61–84.

Viner, J. (1955) *Studies in the theory of international trade*. London: George, Allen, and Unwin.

Warburton, C. (1966) *Depression, inflation, and monetary policy*. Baltimore: Johns Hopkins Press.

British parliamentary reports on international finance, The Cunliffe Committee and the Macmillan Committee Reports (Arno Press, 1978).

Chapter 22

TARGETS AND INSTRUMENTS OF MONETARY POLICY

BENJAMIN M. FRIEDMAN*

Harvard University

Contents

*I am grateful to Alan Viard for research assistance; to Bennett McCallum, Allan Meltzer and William Poole for helpful comments; and to the National Science Foundation and the Harvard Program for Financial Research for research support.

Handbook of Monetary Economics, Volume II, Edited by B.M. Friedman and F.H. Hahn
© *Elsevier Science Publishers B.V., 1990*

1. Introduction

The desire to provide normative guidance to public policy is a fundamental theme that has motivated much of monetary economics, almost since the inception of the subject as a recognizable field of economic inquiry. The connection is readily understandable. Because "money" in any modern economy is a commodity either provided by government or, at the least, provided by the private sector under authority and conditions set by government, the link connecting monetary influences on economic activity to specific actions by identifiable public institutions is immediate and direct. Investigating how those public institutions' actions affect the principal dimensions of macro-economic activity has traditionally constituted the heart of what monetary economics is all about. As long as some macroeconomic outcomes are clearly preferable to others – stable prices rather than inflation, for example, or prosperity rather than widespread unemployment – the question of which government actions are more likely to lead to more desirable outcomes is not just natural but inevitable.

The literature of targets and instruments of monetary policy has evolved in response to the desire to bring monetary economics even closer to the actual operations of central banks. Following the vocabulary made familiar in a broader policy context by Tinbergen (1952) and others at the outset of the post World War II period, research on the subject has proceeded from the distinction between prices or quantities that a central bank can uniquely determine, directly through its own operations (the "instruments" of monetary policy), and those aspects of economic activity that it intends for its operations, along with other elements of public policy as well as independent forces, to affect (the "targets"). In addition, because of the role often advocated in the specific context of monetary policy for economic variables that neither fall under the central bank's direct control nor possess social significance on their own – the leading example, of course, is the stock of money or its rate of growth – the literature has also emphasized yet a third category of prices or quantities now commonly understood as "intermediate targets".

The apparent practical importance of this line of research has increased significantly during the course of the post-war period, as central banks around the world have demonstrated their willingness not merely to change the conceptual framework underlying their monetary policy operations but, in-deed, to do so in response both to abstract analysis and to the associated empirical research which it has spawned. This process gained momentum in the 1970s, as many central banks adopted different forms of monetary aggregate targets, and it has continued in the 1980s as the growing disenchantment with such targets has created a conceptual vacuum at the core of the monetary policy process in many countries. At the same time, specific new questions raised by the application of these ideas to actual policy operations have continued throughout this period to provide fresh ground for new research, so that the interaction between policy practice and policy research has been a two-way influence.

Notwithstanding this quite practical orientation, the literature of targets and instruments of monetary policy also bears fundamental connections to a variety of broader economic and political questions. Most obvious among these are the issues of rules versus discretion, and of an active versus a passive orientation, in economic policy more generally.[1] For example, having a specific in-stitutionalized target regularizes monetary policy responses to entire categories of independent influences and events. Whether a target implies some kind of rule even more broadly, however, and if so whether the rule is necessarily simple and nonresponsive, remain open and serious questions. In addition, as is frequently the case in debates of rules versus discretion ("government by laws versus government by men"), a motivation often advanced for some kinds of monetary policy targets is to provide a mechanism for holding economic policymakers politically accountable.

This chapter surveys the major conceptual developments in the literature of targets and instruments of money policy, with particular emphasis on the broader, "strategic" issues defining the overall framework within which policy operates. The chapter therefore devotes less attention to empirical findings and to more detailed questions about institutional arrangements, both of which have tended, on the whole, to be a good deal more specific to the case of individual countries.[2] Another limitation worth noting at the outset is that this chapter focuses primarily on the analysis of monetary policy in closed economies.[3]

Section 2 examines "the instrument problem" – that is, the selection of the specific price or quantity which the central bank directly and immediately controls – beginning with the standard analysis introduced by Poole (1970) comparing the relative merits in this context of interest rates and monetary aggregates. A central issue that goes beyond Poole's demand-side-only analysis arises, however, as soon as behavior governing the supply of goods and services also matters in a nontrivial way. It is then necessary first to resolve such prior questions as whether systematic monetary policy affects just nominal magnitudes or also affects real economic activity, and, in turn, to determine

---

[1] See the treatment of rules versus discretion in Chapter 21 by Stanley Fischer in this Handbook.

[2] See, for example, the useful surveys by Cagan (1982) and McCallum (1985), and the more recent references cited in Friedman and Kuttner (1988).

[3] See the treatment of monetary policy in open economies in Chapter 23 by Rudiger Dornbusch and Alberto Giovannini in this Handbook.

the appropriate objective to be pursued by monetary policy. Extension of the Poole analysis to models including a role for aggregate supply behavior hinges crucially on such matters.

Section 3 considers the implications of the fact that what most people mean by "money" in discussions of monetary policy is not a plausible policy instrument at all because it is endogenous in the kind of fractional reserve banking system common to most modern market economies. Hence, money is at best an "intermediate target" of monetary policy. Under what circumstances is it useful to have a monetary policy based on money – or, for that matter, any analogous endogenous variable – as an intermediate target? If an economy's reality does not meet these conditions, is there any other role for such endogenous variables in the monetary policy process?

Section 4 turns to the subsidiary issue, which has been of great practical importance at various times and in various countries, of how the central bank can best control a monetary aggregate should it choose to do so. In part the issues here are analogous to those that arise in the Poole analysis and extensntions to it, but the literature of this subject has also prominently featured questions about the structure of the fractional reserve banking system which renders money endogenous in the first place. Such practical issues as what constitutes the best short-run forecasting process, and what degree of monetary control generates undesirable side-effects like interest rate volatility or even potential dynamic instability, have also been important here.

Section 5 reviews more briefly several specific issues that have also arisen within the literature of targets and instruments of monetary policy. These include the implications of alternative monetary policy frameworks for the information available to the economy's private sector, the positive empirical question of when and whether any given central bank has actually based its operations on one kind of targeting strategy or another, and the empirical basis for making normative selections of monetary policy targets and instruments.

Section 6 briefly draws connections to some broader issues, including rules versus discretion and activism versus nonresponsiveness, as well as to the long-standing issue, "why money?".

2. The instrument problem

A central bank operating in a modern fractional reserve banking system typically has several different tools at its disposal for affecting private economic and financial behavior. In most economies these include the ability to de-termine (usually within legislatively specified limits) what reserves banks and other depository institutions must hold in relation to their deposits, to vary the supply of such reserves by buying and selling securities (usually government securities) for the central bank's own account, to lend reserves directly to banks, to set minimum conditions for particular kinds of credit transactions (for example, stock market margin requirements), and to regulate a variety of aspects of ordinary banking and other financial activities.[4] Among these several devices, the buying and selling of securities – usually called "open market operations" – is typically the primary focus of the monetary policy function.[5]

The "instrument problem" of monetary policy arises because of the need to specify how the central bank will conduct its open market operations. In particular, the instrument problem is the choice of a variable to be set directly by the central bank via buying and selling securities, and hence the value of which is to serve as the principal guide in carrying out that buying and selling function. Because open market operations are in essence a trading activity, the instrument variable used may be either a quantity or a price. The central bank may buy or sell a specified amount of securities, thereby inelastically providing or withdrawing that amount of bank reserves. Alternatively, it may buy or sell whatever amount of securities other traders in the market want to transact at a specified price, thereby elastically letting "the market" determine the quantity of reserves to be held at that price. Beyond this more fundamental choice, of course, it is also necessary for the central bank to decide exactly which quantity variable it is setting (for example, total reserves, nonborrowed reserves, the monetary base, reserves or the monetary base adjusted for changes in reserve requirements, and so on), or, alternatively, just which price variable (for example, the interest rate on overnight interbank reserve borrowings, the Treasury bill rate, and so forth).

Whether to key open market operations to a quantity or a price is an issue of first-order importance in normative monetary economics, and has been so for a long time.[6] The modern literature of the subject dates from the formalization by Poole (1970) of the insight that the optimal choice between quantity and price in this context depends both on familiar parameters describing economic behavior and on the relative magnitudes of the different sources of uncertainty affecting the economy.[7] In the context of the instrument problem – in contrast

---

[4]Throughout the remainder of this chapter, "banks" will be taken to include all financial intermediaries making loans and taking deposits subject to reserve requirements set by the central bank or a parallel regulatory body.

[5]In some countries, direct lending of reserves – the "discount window" – is also of substantial importance. More typically, however, variations in discount policy are considered significant largely to the extent that they are signals of intended future open market operations. See Lombra and Torto (1977) and Poole (1985) for evidence pertinent to the U.S. case.

[6]See, for example, Cagan's (1978) review of the bullionist controversy in England in the nineteenth century, and Friedman and Schwartz's (1963) account of the debate over gold (or bimetallic) standards in the United States.

[7]This idea was familiar in a less formal way earlier on, however. For example, the debate between Friedman and Meiselman (1963, 1965) and Ando and Modigliani (1965a, 1965b), over the relative stability of the money-income and investment-multiplier relations, was clearly in part about the usefulness of money as a target of monetary policy, although neither side expressed the issues in Poole's terms of IS and LM curve variances. See also Brunner and Meltzer (1964, 1967, 1969) and the papers in Federal Reserve Bank of Boston (1969) for key pre-1970 contributions.

to the intermediate target problem, which is the subject of Section 3 below – Poole's analysis related the choice between exogenously setting a monetary quantity and exogenously setting an interest rate to the relative magnitudes of the unpredictable elements of the nonbank public's behavior in the market for goods and services and the market for financial assets, respectively.

2.1. Models based only on aggregate demand

Poole's analysis relied on a simplified one-period Hicks–Keynes framework including an aggregate spending (IS) relation and an aggregate money market equilibrium (LM) relation:

$$y = -\alpha_1 r + u , \tag{1}$$

$$m = \beta_1 y - \beta_2 r + v , \tag{2}$$

where y is income; m is "money", supplied by central bank securities sales and withdrawn by securities purchases; r is the interest rate (the price of the securities bought and sold); u and v are zero-mean disturbances to aggregate spending and money demand, respectively, with variances σ_u^2 and σ_v^2 and covariance σ_{uv}; coefficients α_1, β_1 and β_2 are all non-negative; and all variables are in natural logarithms, so that (with constant terms omitted) they bear the interpretation of deviations from deterministic base values.[8] Here disturbances u and v reflect not only the stochastic character of private spending and money demand behavior but also any other uncertainties due to influences on such behavior from fiscal or other policy actions, changes in asset values, events abroad, or any other factors assumed to be independent of monetary policy actions.

The model consisting of (1) and (2) is prototypical of the vehicles used for formal analysis of this kind, in that the number of solvable restrictions exceeds by one the number of potentially endogenous variables, so that there is one degree of freedom left to represent the choice of a policymaker. On the assumption that the central bank's objective is to stabilize income around its deterministic normal value, and that the values of all coefficients are known, this model has the solution

$$E(y^2)|_r = \sigma_u^2 \tag{3}$$

---

[8]These conventions of notation – all constants set to zero, lower-case variables in logarithmic form and interpreted as deviations from equilibrium values, all coefficients non-negative – will be maintained throughout this chapter.

when the interest rate is the chosen instrument, and

$$E(y^2)|_m = \frac{\beta_2^2 \sigma_u^2 + \alpha_1^2 \sigma_v^2 - 2\alpha_1 \beta_2 \sigma_{uv}}{(\alpha_1 \beta_1 + \beta_2)^2} \tag{4}$$

when the money stock is the instrument.

Comparison of (3) and (4) clearly indicates the nature of the trade-off involved in choosing the instrument of monetary policy. Fixing the interest rate – that is, supplying money perfectly elastically – shields income from any disturbances affecting portfolio behavior but provides no protection against disturbances to spending behavior. By contrast, inelastically fixing the money stock forces the interest rate to rise or fall so as partially to damp the impact of disturbances to spending, with the extent of damping given by $0 \leq \beta_2^2/(\alpha_1 \beta_1 + \beta_2)^2 \leq 1$, but only at the cost of exposing income to disturbances to portfolio behavior. Given values of the three "slope" coefficients (and the correlation between the two disturbances), a larger variance of disturbances to portfolio behavior therefore makes the money stock more likely to be the preferable instrument, and vice versa.[9] In the end, however, the choice is inherently empirical. Which instrument is preferable, in the sense of delivering a smaller variance for income, depends on the values of the two respective variances (and the covariance) as well as on the values of the model's three behavioral parameters.

The choice of either instrument amounts to a rule requiring, at least for the single time period under consideration, specified responses of open market operations to the two classes of disturbances under study. From the standpoint of the price of securities, money as the instrument means varying the price in response to either form of disturbance, while the interest rate as the instrument means varying the price in response to neither. From the perspective of the quantity of securities, the interest rate as the instrument means buying or selling in response to either form of disturbance, while money as the instrument means – subject to the qualification below – buying or selling in response to neither.

Poole also demonstrated that, if the central bank is able to implement a more richly structured response system, in general there exists a policy rule that dominates either the simple interest rate instrument or the simple money stock instrument. In particular, supplying money neither perfectly elastically nor perfectly inelastically but rather according to a more general relation of the form (again omitting the constant term):

$$m = \gamma_1 r, \tag{5}$$

[9]If $\sigma_u^2 = \sigma_v^2 = 0$, the problem is trivial and either instrument implies $E(y^2) = 0$.

for the optimal choice of γ_1, delivers a value of $E(y^2)$ at least as small as the smaller of $E(y^2)|_r$ and $E(y^2)|_m$. The solution for the optimal elasticity of money supply is

$$\gamma_1 = \frac{-\beta_1\beta_2\sigma_u^2 + \alpha_1\sigma_v^2 + (\alpha_1\beta_1 - \beta_2)\sigma_{uv}}{\beta_1\sigma_u^2 + \sigma_{uv}}, \tag{6}$$

for which the value of the objective is

$$E(y)^2\big|_{\gamma_1} = \frac{\sigma_u^2\sigma_v^2\left[1 - \left(\dfrac{\sigma_{uv}}{\sigma_u\sigma_v}\right)^2\right]}{\beta_1^2\sigma_u^2 + \sigma_v^2 + 2\beta_1\sigma_{uv}}. \tag{7}$$

The greater generality of the finite-elasticity response policy is readily apparent in that use of the interest rate as a straight instrument ($\gamma_1 = \infty$) follows for $\sigma_u^2 = 0$ (and, of course, then $\sigma_{uv} = 0$), while use of money as a straight instrument follows for combinations of values of σ_u^2 and σ_v^2 (and σ_{uv}) for which $\gamma_1 = 0$.

Apart from these two special cases, the central bank's optimal policy amounts to closing Poole's three-variable–two-restriction model by addding a third nontrivial restriction, rather than by taking a unique variable as exogenous. Moreover, inspection of (6) shows that, even apart from effects due to the covariance of the two disturbances, it is impossible to say a priori whether this optimal response policy is to supply money with positive or negative interest elasticity. The choice is again empirical. In intuitive terms, the optimal money supply response amounts to whatever is necessary to offset the slope and variation in money demand behavior, so as to give the model's solved-out money market equilibrium schedule the optimum degree of interest elasticity, given the relative variance of the two disturbance terms.[10]

The Poole analysis in this general form has proved highly useful in a variety of different settings, including not just monetary policy issues but such questions as fixed versus flexible exchange rates and nominal versus indexed wages.[11] The common features of this kind of analysis include the relation of a policy choice to the relative variances of different sources of uncertainty affecting the relevant aspects of economic behavior, the dependence of optimal actions also on key behavioral parameters, and the dominance in general of optimally structured constraints over simply fixing one variable or another. A key part of its contribution has been to establish the inescapably empirical nature of policy questions like those under study here.

[10]See Tobin (1983) for a useful intuitive discussion along these lines.

[11]For examples of applications to these specific contexts see Aizenmann and Frenkel (1985), Gray (1976), and Fischer (1977b).

2.2. Supply–demand models with neutral monetary policy

At least since the mid-1970s, when the effects of price increases imposed by the international petroleum cartel greatly increased macroeconomists' interest in many aspects of aggregate supply behavior, a major thrust of the literature of targets and instruments of monetary policy has been to move beyond a demand-only framework to models incorporating nontrivial representations of aggregate supply. Extending Poole's analysis to a complete supply–demand context is not straightforward, however. One reason is that doing so immediately raises the issue of whether systematic monetary policy is or is not neutral, in the sense of affecting only nominal magnitudes while leaving real economic activity unchanged. Moreover, in models in which monetary policy does affect both nominal and real magnitudes, there is no ready analog to the obvious policy objective of stabilizing "income" in Poole's model.

For models in which monetary policy is neutral, Sargent and Wallace (1975) demonstrated that the classic choice between money and the interest rate as the exogenous policy variable is really no choice at all in that, with rational expectations, prices in the goods and services market are indeterminate under an interest rate instrument. A simplified version of Sargent and Wallace's model expands Poole's IS–LM framework both by adding the representation of aggregate supply behavior due to Lucas (1972, 1973) and by distinguishing between real and nominal magnitudes for both quantity variables and interest rates. The resulting three-equation–four-variable model is then

$$x_t = -\alpha_1[r_t - (E_{t-1}(p_{t+1}) - p_t)] + u_t , \tag{8}$$

$$m_t - p_t = \beta_1 x_t - \beta_2 r_t + v_t , \tag{9}$$

$$x_t = \gamma_1(p_t - E_{t-1}(p_t)) + \gamma_2 x_{t-1} + z_t , \tag{10}$$

where x now denotes *real* output and spending; p is the price level; r is specifically the *nominal* interest rate; z is a zero-mean disturbance to aggregate supply, with variance σ_z^2; E_{t-1} denotes the expectation operator conditional on information as of time $t - 1$; and all variables are again in logarithms, and all constants are omitted.

Because of the structure of (10), with its imposition of a "natural rate" of output except for price misperceptions and the random disturbance z, any predetermined nonstochastic value of m_t that economic agents are assumed to incorporate into expectations $E_{t-1}(\cdot)$ effects neither the expected value nor any other aspect of the distribution describing x_t. Monetary policy is neutral.[12]

---

[12] Sargent and Wallace (1975) also demonstrated that under rational expectations the real interest rate $[r_t - (E_{t-1}(p_{t+1}) - p_t)]$ is invariant with respect to such choice of m_t.

Money is a plausible instrument variable; but it affects prices only, not real output.

By contrast, the model simply breaks down if the exogenous policy instrument is not money but the interest rate. In that case, the model's real variables are overdetermined, while there exists an extra degree of freedom in the solution for all nominal magnitudes. Both the price level and the nominal money stock are indeterminate. Unless prices are of no concern to policymakers at all, therefore, the Sargent–Wallace analysis indicates that the interest rate instrument is not just inferior but implausible on an a priori basis. Unlike in Poole's analysis, the instrument problem is not an empirical issue.

McCallum (1981) subsequently demonstrated, however, that this indeterminancy of prices under an interest rate instrument would follow only in the case in which the central bank's ultimate objective placed no weight at all on prices – what McCallum termed a "pure interest rate peg". By contrast, as long as the central bank places at least some weight on prices in formulating monetary policy, the model does yield a determinate solution for all variables.

McCallum actually showed this result for the case in which the central bank's objectives include money, rather than prices, so that the interest rate is exogenously set as a linear combination of an arbitrary value (r_{t-1} in McCallum's example based on a preference for interest rate smoothing over time) and the value consistent with any arbitrarily selected value for the money stock, and hence the policy rule is

$$r_t = \phi r_t^* + (1 - \phi)r_{t-1} , \tag{11}$$

where r_t^* is r_t such that $E_{t-1}(m_t | r_t) = m_t^*$ for m_t^* arbitrary. It is clear, however, that McCallum's result carries over to the case in which the central bank's objective includes not just money but any nominal variable. For example, a joint preference for smooth interest rates and stable prices, which would again imply (11) where r_t^* is instead r_t such that $E_{t-1}(p_t | r_t) = p_{t-1}$, would work just as well. At an intuitive level, the Sargent–Wallace indeterminacy result simply amounts to the point that there must be some nominal anchor to determine the absolute price level in any economy. Exogenously fixing the nominal money stock is one way to provide such an anchor, but there are also many others.

2.3. Supply–demand models with non-neutral monetary policy

Even in models based on rational expectations and aggregate supply behavior that exhibits the natural rate property, systematic monetary policy may affect real economic activity for a variety of reasons. Following the early contributions of Fischer (1977a) and Phelps and Taylor (1977), the literature has primarily emphasized failures of neutrality due to less than perfectly flexible wages and/or prices. At its most basic level, the point has long been familiar. An economy needs a nominal anchor to determine its absolute price level, but it does not need two of them. Money can be neutral only if it is the only exogenously set nominal variable.[13]

The immediate effect of introducing some inflexibility to either wages or prices in this context is to alter the aggregate supply function. For example, Fischer's equivalent to a reduced form for (8)–(10), based on two-period nominal wage contracts and assuming $\gamma_1 = 1$ for simplicity, is

$$x_t = \tfrac{1}{3}m_t + \tfrac{1}{2}(e_{1t} + e_{2t}) + \tfrac{1}{6}E_{t-1}(e_{1t} - e_{2t}) + \tfrac{1}{3}E_{t-2}(e_{1t} - e_{2t}), \tag{12}$$

where e_1 is the disturbance to aggregate supply expressed as a function of the real wage, and e_2 is the disturbance to aggregate demand expressed as a function of real balances [that is, a solved-out form of (8) and (9)] with elasticity also assumed equal to one. Phelps and Taylor's equivalent, based on a model with prices fixed one period in advance, is

$$x_t = \theta_1(E_{t-1}(p_t) - p_{t-1}) + \theta_2(m_t - p_{t-1}) + e_t, \tag{13}$$

where θ_1 and θ_2 are combinations of the coefficients in their model's underlying behavioral equations, and e is a combination of the disturbances in these equations. Still another variant that has figured prominently in the literature of targets and instruments of monetary policy is Bean's (1983):

$$x_t = \gamma_1[(p_t - E_{t-1}(p_t)) + \gamma_2 E_{t-1}(z_t)] + \gamma_3 z_t, \tag{14}$$

where z is now the technological disturbance to an underlying Cobb–Douglas production function, and the three coefficients bear the structural interpretations

$$\gamma_1 = \frac{1 - \phi}{\phi}, \qquad \gamma_2 = \frac{\theta}{\phi + \theta}, \qquad \gamma_3 = \frac{1}{\phi}, \tag{15}$$

where $-1/\phi$ is the wage elasticity of labor demand [in other words, where $(1 - \phi)$ is the labor coefficient in the production function], and $1/\theta$ is the wage elasticity of labor supply. Yet another variant prominently used in the analysis

---

[13]Standard references on this subject include Modigliani (1963) and Patinkin (1965). Although the more recent literature has focused on explicit (and analytically tractable) rigidities like contracts specifying fixed nominal wages, it is more plausible to regard wage and price rigidities of a more implicit nature as pervasive throughout the economy; see, for example, Fischer (1980).

of monetary policy is Turnovsky's (1987):

$$x_t = \gamma_1(p_t - E_{t-1}(p_t)) + \gamma_2 E_{t-1}(z_t) + \gamma_3 E_t(z_t) + z_t,$$ (16)

where the coefficients bear the structural interpretation

$$\gamma_1 = \gamma_3(1 - \tau), \qquad \gamma_2 = \gamma_3\left(\frac{\theta}{\theta + \phi}\right), \qquad \gamma_3 = \frac{1 - \phi}{\phi},$$ (17)

where $-1/\phi$ and $1/\theta$ are again the wage elasticities of labor demand and labor supply, respectively; τ is the extent to which wages are indexed to prices, $0 \le \tau \le 1$; and $E_t(z_t)$ indicates the contemporaneous perception of z_t, which may or may not equal z_t.

Any of these supply functions renders monetary policy non-neutral, even under rational expectations, so that further analysis of the instrument problem requires a particular policy objective specifying the weight placed on real versus nominal targets. Perhaps for that reason – and also perhaps because of the widespread dissatisfaction with the results of using interest rates in this role earlier on – there has been little analysis in the literature examining the choice of monetary policy instrument at this level. Such an analysis is easily possible, however, as an example based on the model used by Aizenmann and Frenkel (1986) – though carrying out an exercise they did not undertake – readily illustrates.

In order to establish a plausible objective for monetary policy in the presence of potential disturbances to aggregate supply, Aizenmann and Frenkel based their analysis on maintaining equilibrium in the labor market characterized by labor demand,

$$l^d = \phi(p - w + z),$$ (18)

and labor supply,

$$l^s = \theta(w - p),$$ (19)

where w is the (logarithm of the) nominal wage, and z is a zero-mean percentage disturbance to production for given capital and labor. If (18) represents the first-order condition derived from a Cobb–Douglas production function with labor coefficient δ, then $\phi = 1/(1 - \delta)$ and the quantity of output is

$$x = \phi[\delta(p - w) + z].$$ (20)

The corresponding market-clearing equilibrium is invariant to the specification of aggregate demand or to any disturbances affecting aggregate demand, of course, but it does vary with z. In particular, $l^d = l^s$ implies

$$(w - p)^e = \frac{\phi}{\phi + \theta} z ,$$

$$l^e = \theta \left(\frac{\phi}{\phi + \theta} \right) z , \qquad x^e = (1 + \theta) \left(\frac{\phi}{\phi + \theta} \right) z , \tag{21}$$

where the e superscript indicates equilibrium values.[14] In the absence of some specific impediment, the ordinary working of the labor market would establish a new equilibrium at these values following the emergence of any nonzero realization of the production disturbance z. At the same time, nothing in the equilibration process represented by (21) anchors the value of any nominal magnitude (wages w, prices p, or nominal income $x + p$).

Following Gray (1976), Fisher (1977a), and Phelps and Taylor (1977), it is useful to suppose that the impediment which prevents the automatic establishment of the new equilibrium given in (21) is less than perfect flexibility of nominal wages. In the limit, if nominal wages are rigid ($w = 0$), then reaching the equilibrium in (21) requires $p = -[\phi/(\phi + \theta)]z$. If the model's demand side is as in (8) and (9), and the zero-mean property of z implies zero expected price inflation in this one-period context, then the monetary policy that exactly delivers the price movement required to achieve the market-clearing real wage despite the rigidity of nominal wages can be expressed equivalently as[15]

$$m^e = v - \left(\frac{\beta_2}{\alpha_1} \right) u + \left(\frac{\phi}{\phi + \theta} \right) \left[(1 + \theta) \left(\beta_1 - \frac{\beta_2}{\alpha_1} \right) - 1 \right] z \tag{22}$$

or

$$r^e = \frac{1}{\alpha_1} u - \left(\frac{1 + \theta}{\alpha_1} \right) \left(\frac{\phi}{\phi + \theta} \right) z . \tag{23}$$

Here the equilibrium movement in the money stock accommodates any disturbance to money demand on a one-for-one basis, fully offsets any disturbance to real aggregate demand (with allowance for the relevant elasticities α_1 and β_2), and responds to the supply disturbance in just the fashion necessary to

[14] To recall, all constants are suppressed, so that (21) gives equilibrium values stated as percentage deviations around the corresponding deterministic values that would obtain with $z = 0$.

[15] Alternatively, if the zero-mean property of z were taken to imply $E_{t-1}(p_{t+1}) = 0$, then (22) would be unaltered but (23) would be

$$r^e = \frac{1}{\alpha_1} u - \frac{1 + \alpha_1 + \theta}{\alpha_1} \left(\frac{\phi}{\phi + \theta} \right) z .$$

deliver $p = -[\phi/(\phi + \theta)]z$.[16] The equilibrium movement in the interest rate does not depend at all on the money demand disturbance, but it again fully offsets any real aggregate demand disturbance (with allowance for α_1) and it again responds to the supply disturbance so as to deliver $p = -[\phi/(\phi + \theta)]z$.

Clearly, implementing the monetary policy described by m^e or r^e requires knowledge of the realizations of the model's three disturbance terms (only u and z in the case of r^e). In the absence of such knowledge, the choice that corresponds to the classic form of the monetary policy instrument problem would be to fix either $m = 0$ or $r = 0$, consistent with a zero prior expectation for each disturbance. Either $m = 0$ or $r = 0$, however, delivers values of output, prices, labor input, and real wages that will then differ from the corresponding market-clearing equilibrium. In order to evaluate the relative merits of these two policy alternatives in so rich an environment, it is therefore necessary to have a well-specified policy objective. For example, if the sole criterion of monetary policy is the variance of output around the equilibrium given in (21), then the solution to the instrument problem hinges on a comparison between

$$E(x - x^e)^2\big|_m = \frac{\beta_2^2(\phi - 1)^2}{\lambda^2}\sigma_u^2 + \frac{\alpha_1^2(\phi - 1)^2}{\lambda^2}\sigma_v^2$$

$$+ \left[\frac{\alpha_1^2(\beta_2 + 1)^2}{\lambda^2} - \frac{2\alpha_1(\beta_2 + 1)(\theta + 1)}{\lambda(\phi + \theta)} + \frac{(\theta + 1)^2}{(\phi + \theta)^2}\right]\phi^2\sigma_z^2 \tag{24}$$

and

$$E(x - x^e)^2\big|_r = \frac{(\phi - 1)^2}{(\phi - 1 + \alpha_1)^2}\sigma_u^2 + \left[\frac{\alpha_1^2}{(\phi - 1 + \alpha_1)^2} - \frac{2\alpha_1(\theta + 1)}{(\phi - 1 + \alpha_1)(\phi + \theta)}\right.$$

$$\left. + \frac{(\theta + 1)^2}{(\phi + \theta)^2}\right]\phi^2\sigma_z^2, \tag{25}$$

where $\lambda = \alpha_1\beta_1\delta\phi + \beta_2(\alpha_1 + \delta\phi) + \alpha_1$, and for simplicity both expressions omit all relevant covariance terms.[17] Alternatively, if the sole objective of monetary policy is to stabilize output around the deterministic ($x = 0$) value, rather than around the new market-clearing equilibrium value – in other words, to avoid fluctuations in output, even in response to real production shocks – the choice

---

[16]Fischer (1985) used a similar model assuming $\beta_1 = 1$ and $\theta = 0$ to argue that the optimal money supply policy is unresponsive to supply disturbances, but that result is clearly a special case. For more general values of β_1 and θ, dm^e/dz may be positive or negative.

[17]In other words, the solution shown here rests on the assumption that the three disturbances are independent.

between $m = 0$ and $r = 0$ hinges on the comparison of

$$E(x^2)\big|_m = \frac{\beta_2^2(\phi - 1)^2}{\lambda^2} \sigma_u^2 + \frac{\alpha_1^2(\phi - 1)^2}{\lambda^2} \sigma_v^2 + \frac{\alpha_1^2(\beta_2 + 1)^2\phi^2}{\lambda^2} \sigma_z^2 \quad (26)$$

and

$$E(x^2)\big|_r = \frac{(\phi - 1)^2}{(\phi - 1 + \alpha_1)^2} \sigma_u^2 + \frac{\alpha_1^2\phi^2}{(\phi - 1 + \alpha_1)^2} \sigma_z^2, \quad (27)$$

where again both expressions omit all covariance terms. Both of these comparisons are clearly empirical matters.[18]

While there is no reason to presume that the stabilization of output per se, around either the ex ante or the ex post equilibrium, is necessarily the only criterion governing monetary policy, at least some other suggested objectives amount to the same thing. For example, the policy objective suggested by Aizenmann and Frenkel for their own model is equivalent to minimizing the expected area of a triangle representing the welfare loss due to disequilibrium in the labor market in terms of consumers' and producers' surplus. On the assumption that firms are always on their labor demand curves, so that $l = l^d$ regardless of whether $l^d \gtrless l^s$, that measure for this model is:

$$\Delta = \tfrac{1}{2}(l - l^e)[(w - p)^s - (w - p)], \quad (28)$$

where $(w - p)^s$ is the supply price of labor, equal to $(1/\theta)l$ from (19).[19] For this policy objective, however, the solution to the instrument problem simply hinges on the comparison of

$$E(\Delta)\big|_m = \kappa \cdot E(x - x^e)^2\big|_m \quad (29)$$

and

$$E(\Delta)\big|_r = \kappa \cdot E(x - x^e)^2\big|_r, \quad (30)$$

where $\kappa = \phi(\phi + \theta)/2\theta(\phi - 1)^2$.

In sum, the basic insight of the Poole analysis – relating the choice of instrument of monetary policy to the relative variances of different categories of disturbances affecting the economy, as well as to the values of specifically

---

[18]As is familiar, in both cases $r = 0$ shields x from any disturbance to money demand, while $m = 0$ exposes x to the money demand disturbance but damps the spending disturbance.

[19]Alternatively, the assumption $l = \min\{l^s, l^d\}$ would lead to a criterion that switched according to $l^d \gtrless l^s$.

identifiable parameters of economic behavior – carries over to models incorporating nontrivial aggregate supply behavior, as long as there is some contradiction of perfectly classical assumptions that prevents the economy from automatically equilibrating on its own in the first palace (and, at the same time, renders monetary policy non-neutral).[20]

3. The intermediate target problem

A potentially important problem inherent in the entire mode of analysis reviewed in Section 2 is that what most people mean by "money" in discussions of monetary policy is not a quantity set directly by the central bank. Under the kind of fractional reserve banking system in use in almost all modern economies in the Western world, most of the money used by the public, either as a means of payment or as a liquid store of value, represents the liabilities of private depository institutions. Although the central bank can influence the money-creating activities of these institutions, that influence is not the same as its being able to set the money stock exogenously, as if money were a genuine policy instrument. Instead, the quantity variable which the central bank can set directly, if it chooses, is at best some measure of its own liabilities – for example, bank reserves or the monetary base (reserves plus currency).

One solution to this problem, of course, is simply to define "money" so that it is potentially exogenous – that is, to define money as some measure of the central bank's direct liabilities – regardless of common usage. In that case "money demand" functions like (2) or (9) represent the derived demand for central bank liabilities, based on the underlying fractional reserve system (and, if the measure used is the monetary base, on the public's demand for currency), and the analysis can proceed just as before. Nevertheless, this confounding of the respective portfolio behavior of the banking system and the nonbank public runs counter to the rich and long-standing tradition of distinct analysis of money demand behavior (meaning that of the nonbank public) and money supply behavior (meaning that of the banking system). In addition, keeping the two analytically separate in this context as well is more consistent with the principle of distinguishing among the respective implications of disturbances to the economy arising from different sources.[21]

---

[20] The role of rigid nominal wages in providing this impediment to equilibrium (and hence a source of policy non-neutrality) makes clear the intimate connection between the problem of choosing a monetary policy instrument with the degree of wage indexation (here zero) taken as given, and the problem of choosing a wage indexation system with the conduct of monetary policy taken as given. This equivalence is explicit in, for example, Karni (1983), Aizenmann and Frenkel (1986), and Turnovsky (1987).

[21] For example, Brunner and Meltzer (1964, 1972, 1976 and elsewhere) have consistently taken this approach.

Merely extending the analysis of the instrument problem in Section 2 to allow for the endogeneity of "money" is fairly straightforward. Following Modigliani, Rasche and Cooper (1970), and others, a standard representation of bank portfolio behavior that can be construed as either the supply of money or the demand for reserves is

$$m = \delta_1 h + \delta_2 r + q , \tag{31}$$

where h is the quantity of nonborrowed reserves (or any other potentially exogenous measure of central bank liabilities), and q is a zero-mean disturbance with variance σ_q^2.[22] The classic instrument problem is then the choice between reserves and the interest rate, rather than between money and the interest rate, as the variable to be set exogenously by monetary policy.

Combining (31) with (1) and (2) gives an expanded version of the demand-only model analyzed in Section 2, for which the solution is again as in (3) for the interest rate instrument and

$$E(y^2)|_h = \frac{1}{(\alpha_1 \beta_1 + \beta_2 + \delta_2)^2} [(\beta_2 + \delta_2)^2 \sigma_u^2 + \alpha_1^2 \sigma_v^2 + \alpha_1^2 \sigma_q^2$$
$$- 2\alpha_1(\beta_2 + \delta_2)\sigma_{uv} + 2\alpha_1(\beta_2 + \delta_2)\sigma_{uq} - 2\alpha_1^2 \sigma_{vq}] \tag{32}$$

for the reserves instrument, where σ_{uq} and σ_{vq} are the covariances of q with u and v, respectively. As in the comparison betwen (3) and (4), the advantage of supplying reserves perfectly inelastically is to damp the effect on income due to disturbances to aggregate demand, with damping factor:

$$0 \leq \frac{(\beta_2 + \delta_2)^2}{(\alpha_1 \beta_1 + \beta_2 + \delta_2)^2} \leq 1 .$$

The associated disadvantage is that doing so exposes income to effects due to disturbances to both money demand behavior and money supply (reserves demand) behavior, both of which a policy of supplying reserves perfectly

---

[22]To be strictly accurate, what economists usually construe as nonborrowed reserves (or the nonborrowed monetary base) is not a quantity directly set by the central bank either. In the United States, for example, such technical factors as float, Treasury deposits at Federal Reserve Banks, Federal Reserve holdings of foreign currencies, gold flows, and accounts of foreign central banks all stand between the economist's concept and the quantity directly altered by the Federal Reserve's securities transactions. Moreover, economists almost always refer to nonborrowed reserves on a seasonally adjusted basis, and on a basis adjusted to reflect changes in reserve requirements. Omitting such matters from attention in a survey like this reflects the usual presumption that, over whatever is the minimum time horizon that matters for macroeconomic purposes, the central bank can successfully offset such factors to within a tolerance sufficient to allow analysts outside the central bank to neglect them altogether.

elastically would eliminate. Similarly, combining (31) with a supply–demand model like that consisting of (8), (9), and (18)–(20) would have analogously straightforward effects on comparisons like (24) versus (25), or (26) versus (27).

By contrast, the issue that is not straightforward when money is endogenous is what role money itself can or should play in the monetary policy process. The intermediate target problem is the choice of just such a variable, usually a readily observable financial quantity (or price), that the central bank will treat, for purposes of some interim-run time horizon, as if it were the target of monetary policy – even though everyone recognizes that the quantity (or price) in question actually bears no ultimate significance at all. What it means to base monetary policy on an intermediate target, and under what conditions doing so is sensible, has been the focus of a substantial literature.

3.1. General statement of the problem

It is easiest to understand the use of any given intermediate target variable for monetary policy as a two-stage procedure. In the first stage, the central bank determines the value of the intermediate target which would be consistent with the desired ultimate policy objective under a variety of ex ante assumptions – for example, zero values for all relevant disturbances. At the second stage, the central bank proceeds, in some ex post fashion, to treat achieving this value of the intermediate target (set ex ante) as if doing so were the objective governing policy. In practice many central banks have implemented intermediate target strategies at least approximately according to this two-stage manner.

The distinction between the "ex ante" assumptions employed in the first stage of this process and whatever makes the second stage "ex post" is clearly crucial. Since the passage of time per se is not a significant issue here, the literature analyzing the intermediate target problem has largely focused on the availability of new information as time passes. The key role of the intermediate target variable, then, is to provide a rule for processing and acting on this new information.

Friedman (1977) suggested several plausible circumstances under which money (or, for that matter, any other endogenous variable) may provide such useful information. All arise in a dynamic setting in which a relevant value of the intermediate target variable is observable before some policy decision, or some adjustment to an earlier policy decision, is made, while the corresponding value(s) of the variable(s) constituting the ultimate policy objective are not. This realization of the intermediate target is then part of the information set underlying the choice of a final value for the policy instrument.

The most obvious context in which this kind of segmented information flow arises is an inherently dynamic system in which the relevant economic behavior exhibits leads and lags distributed through time. For example, if people demand money for transactions purposes, and tend on average to accumulate money in advance of actual spending, then in general the observed value of the money stock at any time conveys information about the future strength of aggregate demand. Similarly, in models in which some individuals' or businesses' ability to spend depends in part on their ability to borrow, and loan transactions tend to precede actual spending, the observed volume of credit conveys information about the future state of aggregate demand. In either case, such information is at least potentially useful whenever monetary policy actions affect economic behavior with a lag.

An endogenous variable like the money stock can also provide such useful information, even in the absence of behavioral economic lags, if there are lags in the availability of relevant data. For example, in a context in which disturbances to economic behavior are serially correlated, observations of the recent values of key endogenous variables convey information that is potentially useful for anticipating future outcomes. If observations of endogenous financial variables like money (or credit, or interest rates) are available on a more timely basis than observations of variables like income and prices – as is the case in most economies – then the information given by those financial variables in general has a role to play in setting the optimal value of the policy instrument. Equivalently, if observations of financial variables are available continuously throughout the "period" of analysis but observations of variables like income and prices are not, and if it is possible for the central bank to adjust the value of its policy instrument as time passes within the period, then again these available observations in general have a role to play in the policymaking process.

Even so, finding that some variable like money conveys potentially useful information is not the same as establishing that the central bank should specifically use that variable as an intermediate target. Much of the literature of the intermediate target problem has focused on analyzing just this distinction.

3.2. Intermediate targets in models based only on aggregate demand

Friedman (1975, 1977) analyzed the intermediate target problem in the context of a demand-only model consisting of (1), (2), and (31), with serially correlated disturbances. For zero expectations of disturbances u, v, and q, whether the policy that delivers the smaller variance of income in such a model is $r = 0$ or $h = 0$ depends upon the comparison of (3) and (32).[23] In either case, the

---

[23]As in the Poole analysis reviewed in Section 2, in general the policy that minimizes the variance of income is to supply reserves with some nonzero yet finite elasticity.

potential role in this context for money, an endogenous variable in both cases, is to provide information indicating a likely nonzero realization of some relevant disturbance, and therefore – if this information is in hand in time to react to it – warranting a different value of the policy instrument.

If each of the three disturbances u, v, and q follows a first-order autoregressive process with autocorrelations ρ_u, ρ_v, and ρ_q, respectively, knowing the values of each of the model's three endogenous variables at time $t-1$ facilitates using (1), (2), and (31) to discover the values of u_{t-1}, v_{t-1}, and q_{t-1} and then calculating "informed" expectations of the three disturbances for period t as $\rho_u u_{t-1}$, $\rho_v v_{t-1}$, and $\rho_q q_{t-1}$. The optimal value of the policy instrument for period t, given this information, is then

$$r_t = \frac{\rho_u}{\alpha_1} u_{t-1} \tag{33}$$

under the interest rate instrument, or

$$h_t = -\frac{1}{\alpha_1 \delta_1} [(\beta_2 + \delta_2)\rho_u u_{t-1} - \alpha_1 \rho_v v_{t-1} + \alpha_1 \rho_q q_{t-1}] \tag{34}$$

under the reserves instrument. By contrast, if observations of m_{t-1} and whichever of r_{t-1} or h_{t-1} was endogenous are available, but y_{t-1} remains unknown, it is not possible to solve (1), (2), and (31) for u_{t-1}, v_{t-1}, and q_{t-1}, and hence not possible to implement directly either (33) or (34).

Using money as an intermediate target variable in this context amounts to setting r or h instead so as to achieve $E_{t-1}(m_t) = 0$.[24] This policy is either

$$r_t = \frac{1}{\alpha_1 \beta_1 + \beta_2} \left[\frac{\beta_1^2 \rho_u \sigma_u^2 + \rho_v \sigma_v^2 + \beta_1 (\rho_u + \rho_v)\sigma_{uv}}{\beta_1^2 \sigma_u^2 + \sigma_v^2 + 2\beta_1 \sigma_{uv}} \right] m_{t-1} , \tag{35}$$

with an interest rate instrument, or

$$h_t = \frac{(\alpha_1 \beta_1 + \beta_2 + \delta_2)}{\delta_1 (\alpha_1 \beta_1 + \beta_2)} \cdot \frac{\omega_1}{\omega_2} \cdot m_{t-1} , \tag{36}$$

where ω_1 and ω_2 are appropriately weighted combinations of all three variances (σ_u^2, σ_v^2, and σ_q^2) and all three corresponding covariances, with a reserves instrument. Hence, under either instrument the model breaks down in such a way that targeting the money stock in this context requires responding only to the information contained in m_{t-1} but not whichever of h_{t-1} or r_{t-1} is endogenous.

---

[24] With zero expectations for all three disturbances, the policy consistent with $E(m) = 0$ would be just $r = 0$ or $h = 0$.

The criticism of this policy argued in Friedman (1975) is that in general neither (35) nor (36) is the policy that actually minimizes the variance of income, given the available information contained in the observations m_{t-1} and either r_{t-1} or h_{t-1}. The policy that minimizes $E_{t-1}(y_t^2)$ is instead either

$$r_t = \frac{1}{\alpha_1} \left[\frac{\beta_1 \rho_u \sigma_u^2 + \rho_u \sigma_{uv}}{\beta_1^2 \sigma_u^2 + \sigma_v^2 + 2\beta_1 \sigma_{uv}} \right] m_{t-1} \tag{37}$$

or

$$h_t = -\frac{\alpha_1 \beta_1 + \beta_2 + \delta_2}{\alpha_1 \delta_1} \cdot \frac{\omega_3}{\omega_4} \cdot m_{t-1}, \tag{38}$$

where ω_3 and ω_4 are analogous (though not identical) to ω_1 and ω_2. Comparison of (35) to (37) [or of (36) to (38)] shows that treating money as an intermediate target of monetary policy does not in general deliver the instrument value consistent with minimizing the variance of income, given the information contained in lagged values of the endogenous financial variables. Under special conditions, of course, the two may be identical. For example, Friedman pointed out that if $\beta_2 = \sigma_v^2 = 0$ – that is, if money demand is both interest inelastic and nonstochastic – then both (35) and (37) trivially reduce to $r_t = -(\rho_u/\alpha_1\beta_1)m_{t-1}$. In general, however, the policy based on money as an intermediate target variable is not even the best way for monetary policy to take advantage of the information contained in observations of money itself, much less an optimum way of processing all available information in general.[25]

3.3. Intermediate targets in supply–demand models

For the same reason that they make the analysis of the instrument problem so straightforward, demand-only models like the one used above offer only limited possibilities for investigation of various intermediate targets of monetary policy. Because "income" is typically such a model's only endogenous nonfinancial variable, and hence the obvious ultimate policy target, there is no remaining nonfinancial variable to suggest as an intermediate target. The choice of an intermediate target must therefore be from among the model's set of endogenous financial variables.

Models incorporating both aggregate supply and aggregate demand behavior also admit analysis of policies based on the use of some financial variable as an intermediate target variable, although the literature has not pursued this aspect

[25]Specifically, the variance $E_{t-1}(y_t^2)$ that follows from (35) or (36) is in general greater than the corresponding variance given in (37) or (38), respectively.

of the subject in any depth.[26] For example, making the money stock endogenous in a model like that of Aizenmann and Frenkel (1986) would merely require adding a money supply function like (31) to the system consisting of (8), (9), and (18)–(20). The policy of exogenously setting $m = 0$, analyzed in Section 2, would not then be feasible, but treating money as an intermediate target variable – that is, setting either reserves or the interest rate such that either $E_{t-1}(m_t | r_t) = 0$ or $E_{t-1}(m_t | h_t) = 0$ for any given information set – would be. Computing the resulting variances corresponding to $E(x - x^e)^2$ in (24) and (25), $E(x^2)$ in (26) and (27), or $E(\Delta)$ in (29) and (30), would then be relatively straightforward. The general inferiority of any such policy, compared to the policy of setting either r or h at the value derived by directly minimizing the ultimate policy objective, would emerge in a way that is analogous to the result shown above for the demand-only model.

Analysis of intermediate monetary policy targets within supply–demand models has instead primarily focused on the potential use of nonfinancial variables like prices or nominal income. In this context, too, it is crucial to distinguish between analysis based on supply–demand models in which systematic monetary policy is neutral and the contrasting analysis of non-neutral policy. When policy does not affect the distribution of real magnitudes, the price level (or, equivalently, nominal income) becomes the only plausible *ultimate* macroeconomic policy target. Hence the analysis of price or nominal income targets in such models typically has little if anything to do with the intermediate target problem. By contrast, when policy does affect real magnitudes, a price target for monetary policy is clearly an *intermediate* target (unless real variables receive no weight at all in policymakers' preferences), and a nominal income target is also an *intermediate* target unless the ultimate policy objective also exhibits the one-for-one weighting system implicit in the $y = x + p$ definition.[27]

Aizenmann and Frenkel (1986), for example, analyzed both a price target and a nominal income target as if these variables were potential policy instruments – that is, on the assumption that either $p = 0$ or $x + p = 0$ in the model used above could be set exogenously. They showed that, in their model with nominal wages rigid, fixing nominal income is equivalent to holding employment constant, while fixing prices is trivially equivalent to fixing the real wage. Which of these alternatives is preferable therefore depends on the

---

[26]A plausible reason is that the analytical shortcomings of using money as an intermediate target variable were already known before the use of supply–demand models for the analysis of monetary policy issues became widespread.

[27]Hall's (1984) work, discussed below, makes this concept explicit; some proponents of nominal income targeting appear to have based their advocacy of the idea on just this notion. Others, like Tobin (1983) and McCallum (1984), have relied more on the stochastic structure of aggregate supply behavior. See the discussion below.

relative wage elasticities of labor demand (ϕ) and labor supply (θ) – and, of course, on the objective governing policy. For the welfare-analytic objective given in (28), for example, the choice between $p = 0$ and $x + p = 0$ depends on the comparison between

$$E(\Delta)|_p = \frac{1}{2} \left[\frac{\phi}{\theta(\phi + \theta)} \right] \phi^2 \sigma_z^2 \tag{39}$$

and

$$E(\Delta)|_{x+p} = \frac{1}{2} \left[\frac{\phi}{\theta(\phi + \theta)} \right] \theta^2 \sigma_z^2 , \tag{40}$$

so that the price target is more likely to be prefereable if labor *demand* is the less elastic, while the nominal income target is more likely to be preferable if labor *supply* is the less elastic.

In fact, no central bank operating in a market economy can simply set either prices or nominal income exogenously. The feasible analogs to the policies considered in (39) and (40) would therefore consist of evaluating $E(\Delta)$ – or, for that matter, any other specific objective – not for $p = 0$ and $x + p = 0$ but for the respective values of reserves or the interest rate consistent with $E_{t-1}(p_t) = 0$ and $E_{t-1}(x_t + p_t) = 0$ for a given information set in general indicating nonzero expectations for the model's disturbance terms.[28]

The principal contribution in the literature to date that has investigated either price or nominal income targeting along these lines is Bean's (1983) analysis of nominal income targets, based on the aggregate supply function given in (14) together with the solved-out aggregate demand relation

$$x_t = \psi(m_t - p_t) + e_t , \tag{41}$$

where for simplicity "money" is taken as the exogenous policy instrument.[29] As in the analysis above of the demand-only model, the potential role for an intermediate target variable here arises from the assumption of serially corre-lated disturbances. Specifically, Bean assumed that each of z in (14) and e in

---

[28] If the expectations of all disturbances are zero, then $r = 0$ or $h = 0$ implies $E(p) = E(x + p) = 0$, and targeting prices or nominal income is indistinguishable from any other kind of policy.
[29] The usual interpretation of an aggregate demand function like (41) is as a solved-out IS–LM system. If the underlying spending and money demand relations are as in (8) and (9), then (apart from price expectations) $\psi = \alpha_1/(\alpha_1\beta_1 + \beta_2)$ and $e = [1/(\alpha_1\beta_1 + \beta_2)](\beta_2 u - \alpha_1 v)$. Alternatively, allowing for the endogeneity of money as in the analysis above based on the demand-only model would require writing (41) as $x = \psi(\delta_1 h - p) + e$, which can similarly be interpreted as a solved-out version of (8), (9) and (31) where now $\psi = \alpha_1/(\alpha_1\beta_1 + \beta_2 + \delta_2)$ and $e = [(\beta_2 + \delta_2)u - \alpha_1(v - q)]/(\alpha_1\beta_1 + \beta_2 + \delta_2)$. Use of either version, of course, presumes that the central bank does not choose r as the policy instrument.

(41) consists of the sum of a random walk component and a white noise component. Bean also posited as the objective governing monetary policy minimizing the variance of real output around the corresponding equilibrium value in the presence of supply shock z, which for (14) is just

$$x_t - x_t^e = \gamma_1[(p_t - E_{t-1}(p_t)) + \gamma_2(z_t - E_{t-1}(z_t))] . \tag{42}$$

Given observations on the model's endogenous variables in period $t-1$, the policy that minimizes $E_{t-1}(x_t - x_t^e)^2$ in the presence of rigid nominal wages is a feedback rule relating m_t to the random walk components of z and e in period $t-1$, but not to the corresponding white noise components. Either fixing the money stock at $m_t = 0$ without reacting to this information or using nominal income as an intermediate target variable – that is, setting m_t so as to render $E_{t-1}(x_t + p_t | m_t) = 0$ – is in general inferior to this optimal feedback policy. The resulting variances are, respectively,

$$E_{t-1}(x_t - x_t^e)^2|_m = \Sigma^2 + \left(\frac{\gamma_1}{\gamma_1 + \psi}\right)^2 [\sigma_{ep}^2 + (\gamma_2(\gamma_1 + \psi) - \gamma_3)^2 \sigma_{zp}^2] \tag{43}$$

and

$$E_{t-1}(x_t - x_t^e)^2|_{E_{t-1}(x+p)} = \Sigma^2 + \left(\frac{\gamma_1}{\gamma_1 + \psi}\right)^2 [\gamma_2(\gamma_1 + \psi) - \gamma_3 - \psi + 1]^2 \sigma_{zp}^2 , \tag{44}$$

where Σ^2 is the minimum feasible value of $E_{t-1}(x_t - x_t^e)^2$ achieved by the optimal feedback policy, and σ_{ep}^2 and σ_{zp}^2 are the one-period variances of the *random walk* components of the disturbances to aggregate demand and aggregate supply, respectively.[30]

The $m = 0$ policy is inferior to the optimal feedback rule, therefore, in that it always fails to take proper account of what is known about the demand disturbance, and except when $\psi = 1$ it fails to take proper account of the supply disturbance. Similarly, although the policy of setting $E_{t-1}(x_t + p_t) = 0$ does eliminate the effect of the predictable component of the demand disturbance, it too is inferior to the optimal feedback policy in that it fails to take proper account of the supply disturbance [except trivially when $\gamma_2 = 1$, which from (15) implies an inelastic labor supply, so that supply disturbances do not affect the equilibrium output level in the first place]. Hence the choice between these two suboptimal policies rests on the comparison between (43) and (44). Because a sufficient condition for the variance in (44) to be less than that in

---

[30]The minimum value Σ^2 is in general nonzero because of the white noise components of z and e, and the one-period innovations to the random walk components of z and e.

(43) is $\psi < 1$, and indeed the available empirical evidence suggest a less-than-unity elasticity of real aggregate demand with respect to real balances, Bean concluded that monetary policy based on nominal income as an intermediate target is likely to be preferable to a policy based on exogenously fixing "money".[31]

West (1986), however, showed that this apparently straightforward conclusion hinges crucially on the choice of minimizing $E_{t-1}(x_t - x_t^e)^2$ as the objective governing monetary policy. As an example, West showed that when minimizing $E_{t-1}(x_t^2)$ is the policy objective, the conclusion in a highly similar model is just the opposite. In that case a nominal income target is preferable to a fixed money stock if and only if the elasticity of aggregate demand with respect to real balances is *greater* than unity.[32] The main point here, therefore, is not just the inherently empirical nature of the key choices involved in designing monetary policy but also, in a model encompassing both supply and demand, the importance of the choice of policy objective.

A further generalization of the idea of using either a price or a nominal income target for monetary policy is Hall's (1984) analysis of an "elastic" price target, whereby the central bank sets its policy instrument so as to achieve

$$E_{t-1}(p_t) = \xi U_t , \tag{45}$$

where U is the difference between the actual unemployment rate and the corresponding "full employment" benchmark, and the base from which the percentage price deviation p is measured (here normalized to zero, as usual) is specifically intended to be constant over time. When the targeting rule's elasticity ξ equals the reciprocal of the elasticity relating unemployment to real income – that is the "Okun's Law" coefficient (usually estimated empirically to be around one-third for the United States) – this elastic price standard is equivalent to nominal income targeting. A larger value of ξ places relatively greater implicit weight on unemployment (real output), while a smaller value places relatively greater implicit weight on the price level. Instead of making explicit the objective implied by (45) and working out analytically the relevant variances that follow from implementing it under some specific model, Hall performed simulations based on empirical estimates of the time series of the respective disturbances to aggregate demand and aggregate supply for the

---

[31] Bean did not consider the further problem associated with the endogeneity of most plausible definitions of "money". See again footnote 29.

[32] West's result is both necessary and sufficient, while Bean's is merely sufficient, because of the simpler structure of West's model. Instead of (14), West used the aggregate supply function in (10), with adaptive price expectations as the device rendering monetary policy non-neutral. (West showed that it is the difference in objective, not the difference in supply behavior, which accounts for the difference between his result and Bean's.)

United States, and on an assumed value (one-half) for the elasticity of the supply curve relating price setting to the level of unemployment.

In a similar vein, Taylor (1985) used simulations of a bivariate autoregressive process generating prices and real income, estimated using U.S. time-series data, to evaluate several different versions of a nominal income targeting procedure. Taylor also explicitly considered, but did not simulate, a generalization of this procedure analogous to Hall's elastic price standard. In their reliance on empirical simulations rather than analytical solutions, both Taylor's and Hall's analyses are in the spirit of the earlier empirical work evaluating alternative monetary policy rules on the basis of simulations of large macroeconometric models.[33] Nevertheless, generalization of the use of prices or nominal income as an intermediate target variable to a rule like (45), with its readily intuitive constant-elasticity form, is easily compatible with the more explicitly analytical line of development of this literature in recent years.

3.4. The information variable approach

The repeated analytical demonstration of the inferiority of using some endogenous variable as an intermediate target of monetary policy, compared to a more general feedback rule optimally relating the value of the policy instrument to the observed value of that variable, has shaped the subsequent monetary policy literature in recognizable ways. It was readily apparent in work like that of Friedman (1975) and Bean (1983) that the optimal feedback rule which dominates the intermediate target strategy is a vehicle for exploiting the information contained in observations of the endogenous variable in question. Under such a rule, the endogenous variable is not an intermediate target but an "information variable" in the sense earlier made explicit in a monetary policy setting by Kareken et al. (1973), and suggested still earlier (with the label "indicator") by Brunner and Meltzer (1967).

The basic idea at work in the information variable approach is again dynamic, arising in just the context discussed above, of either behavioral lags or economic lags as the motivation for the intermediate target strategy. Observations of a variable like the money stock are potentially useful for anticipating future stochastic movements of variables like income and prices that enter the central bank's objective, or for estimating contemporaneous stochastic movements of these variables before the relevant direct data became available. In either case, feedback rules like those derived by Friedman and Bean constitute the optimal way of exploiting that information, given the assumed behavioral model and policy objective.[34]

---

[33]See for, example, Cooper and Fischer (1972a, 1972b).

[34]LeRoy and Waud (1977) made the dynamic nature of this approach still more explicit by drawing the analogy between the use of an information variable and Kalman filtering.

One implication of this "information variable" approach is that issues of behavioral causation, which had dominated much of the earlier discussion, become secondary.[35] Whether the money stock does or does not "cause" future movement of income or prices is not the issue here. All that matters is whether observed values of the money stock provide information that helps predict future movements of these variables. Hence statistical analysis along the lines of Granger (1969) and Sims (1972) are apt, despite questions about whether such tests are capable of saying anything about economic causation.[36] In addition, Friedman (1984b) showed that tests of whether or not money provides such information can also be performed within a structural model context.

Another implication of the conceptual shift from an intermediate target approach to an information variable context is that there is no longer any compelling reason to limit the focus of the central banks's policy-setting rule to only one such endogenous variable. In principle, of course, it is always possible to employ some appropriately weighted combination of two or more endogenous variables as an intermediate target. In practice, however, the intermediate targets proposed in the literature have almost always been univariate or, like nominal income, an unweighted combination usually regarded as a single variable anyway.[37] By contrast, under an information variable approach there is no reason to restrict monetary policy to respond only to one endogenous variable, unless there is evidence suggesting that observations of that one variable contain all (or nearly all) of the available information relevant to achieving the central bank's objectives. Instead, it is in general optimal to follow the approach, intuitively outlined earlier on by Guttentag (1966), of exploiting all relevant sources of information.

Friedman (1982a, 1983) explored along these lines the implications of basing monetary policy on both a money stock variable and a credit variable, on the basis of empirical evidence for the United States showing not only that credit (defined as the outstanding indebtedness of all U.S. obligors other than financial intermediaries) contains approximately as much information about subsequent movements of income and prices as does any conventional measure of money, but also that the interaction between the effects of credit and the narrow (M1) money stock is such that both variables together provide significantly more information in this context than does either taken alone. At an intuitive level, the principal argument here is that using a credit variable in this

---

[35]Tobin (1970) is the classic statement of the objection to money as an intermediate target based on questions of causation.

[36]What remains, of course, is the question of whether the results of Granger–Sims tests, based on data from a sample in which the central bank conducted monetary policy under one set of principles, continue to be pertinent after a change in those principles. See Lucas (1976) and Sims (1982) for opposing viewpoints on this issue.

[37]Hall's (1984) "elastic price standard" is an exception.

way diversifies the information base underlying monetary policy responses to observations of ongoing events, in that credit describes the liability side of the nonbank public's balance sheet while measures of money describe the asset side. Subsequent contributions by other researchers investigated further the potential role of a credit variable in guiding monetary policy, relying either on empirical evidence on the relationship of credit to macroeconomic variables or on theoretical arguments along the lines of Blinder and Stiglitz (1983) or Bernanke and Gertler (1989). In addition, Modigliani and Papademos (1983) developed a theoretical argument relating the relative usefulness of money and credit variables in this context to issues of financial market structure.

Like the optimal feedback rules derived in the various models considered above, the information variable approach to monetary policy – whether based on one information variable, or two, or many – makes explicit the need for a clearly articulated objective to govern policy, as well as a model stating the relationship between the variable(s) comprising that objective and the central bank's policy instrument. Given these basic tools, the question of what further role additional endogenous variables can play in the policy process is largely an empirical issue of what (if any) readily observable financial prices or quantities contain potentially useful information to guide the setting of the policy instrument in order best to achieve the objective.[38] At the same time, the optimal choice of policy instrument is not independent of the potential use of information variables in this way. Which instrument delivers the smallest variance for a given objective in a given model depends in general on the appropriately conditioned variances of the principal stochastic disturbances affecting economic behavior, and variances conditional on different information sets are not the same.

4. Implementing monetary targets: The instrument problem once again

Notwithstanding the analytical shortcomings of monetary (or other) intermediate targets as a basis for monetary policy, beginning in the 1970s central banks in an increasing number of countries adopted – or at least professed to adopt – monetary aggregate targets. Given the endogeneity of the quantities that most of these central banks meant by "money", the issue of how best to achieve these targets became a logical next step in the development of the targets and instruments literature, indeed a step that antedated either the

---

[38]A further question in this context is why restrict the information variables to financial ones. Unlike the intermediate target strategy, the information variable strategy can in general be centered on nonfinancial variables. Although this point is familiar enough [see, for example, Friedman (1984a)], the literature to date has not explored in a formal way the possibility of feedback rules based explicitly on nonfinancial sources of information.

attention to supply shocks or the formal analysis of the intermediate target strategy emphasized in Section 3.

The separate literature of controlling monetary aggregates made clear the fundamentally two-stage character of the monetary policy process based on an intermediate target variable. Here the existence of a specified target value for the money stock, presumably determined via some prior analysis involving macroeconomic variables of genuine policy consequence, is simply a given. The remaining question is how the central bank is to set its exogenous policy instrument so as to render the actual value of the money stock as close as possible to this target value, in the context of different stochastic disturbances affecting money supply and money demand. The fact that the realizations of these disturbances will in general affect the value of the money stock that is consistent with achieving the underlying macroeconomic objectives of this policy – which is, in the end, the basic analytical flaw in the intermediate target strategy itself – went unconsidered here.

4.1. Analysis under fixed institutional arrangements

Pierce and Thomson (1972) first explicitly framed the money stock control problem in a conceptual framework analogous to Poole's (1970), also using a demand-only model like Poole's. More specifically, they examined whether nonborrowed reserves or a short-term interest rate is the superior policy instrument for minimizing the variance of the money stock around some given target value when money is determined by the interaction of the money demand and supply functions (2) and (31), with income taken as predetermined but not known with certainty in advance. The alternative solutions to this problem are

$$E(m^2)|_r = \sigma_v^2 + \beta_1^2 \sigma_y^2 + 2\beta_1 \sigma_{vy} , \tag{46}$$

$$\begin{aligned} E(m^2)\Big|_h &= \frac{1}{(\beta_2 + \delta_2)^2} [\delta_2^2 \sigma_v^2 + \beta_2^2 \sigma_q^2 + (\beta_1 \delta_2)^2 \sigma_y^2 \\ &\quad - 2\delta_2 \beta_2 \sigma_{vq} + 2\beta_1 \delta_2^2 \sigma_{vy} - 2\beta_1 \beta_2 \delta_2 \sigma_{qy}] , \end{aligned} \tag{47}$$

where σ_y^2 is the variance of the forecasting error associated with y (and covariances σ_{vy} and σ_{qy} are defined analogously).

The result here is parallel to those derived above. Which policy instrument minimizes $E(m^2)$ depends on the relative magnitudes of the three relevant variances (and the covariances), and on the respective elasticities describing the nonbank public's money demand behavior and the banking system's money supply behavior. The interest rate instrument exposes the money stock to money demand disturbances and to effects on money demand due to un-expected movements in income, both on a one-for-one basis, but entirely shields the money stock from money supply disturbances. The reserves instru-ment damps money demand disturbances and the effects of unexpected income variation, both with damping factor $0 \leq \delta_2^2/(\beta_2^2 + \delta_2^2) \leq 1$, but exposes the money stock to money supply disturbances. Which instrument is superior under these assumptions is an empirical matter.[39]

McCallum and Hoehn (1983) carried out an analogous investigation in the context of the supply–demand model consisting of (8)–(10) and (31).[40] Here the alternative solutions are (apart from covariance terms)

$$
E(m_t^2)|_r = \sigma_v^2 + \left(\frac{1 + \beta_1\gamma_1}{\alpha_1 + \gamma_1}\right)^2 \sigma_u^2 + \left(\frac{\alpha_1\beta_1 - 1}{\alpha_1 + \gamma_1}\right)^2 \sigma_z^2 \tag{48}
$$

and

$$
E(m_t^2)|_h = \frac{1}{(1 + \psi)^2}\left[\sigma_v^2 + \left(\frac{1 + \beta_1\gamma_1}{a_1 + \gamma_1}\right)^2 \sigma_u^2 + \left(\frac{\alpha_1\beta_1 - 1}{\alpha_1 + \gamma_1}\right)^2 \sigma_z^2 + \psi^2\sigma_q^2\right],
$$
$$\tag{49}$$

where

$$
\psi = \frac{1}{\delta_2}\left[\alpha_1\left(\frac{1 + \beta_1\gamma_1}{\alpha_1 + \beta_1}\right) + \beta_2\right].
$$

As usual, the interest rate instrument exposes the money stock to disturbances to money demand behavior on a one-for-one basis, and to disturbances to real spending and to aggregate supply weighted by the relevant elasticities. The reserves policy damps the effect on money due to all three of these distur-bances, with damping factor $0 \leq 1/(1 + \psi)^2 \leq 1$, but exposes the money stock to disturbances to money supply behavior. Which instrument is superior is again an empirical question.

4.2. Analysis of alternative institutional arrangements

Although it is possible to think of numerous changes in the institutional structure of a country's financial markets that might affect its central bank's

---

[39] It is also straightforward to calculate the optimal elasticity of reserves supply, analogous to Poole's optimal elasticity of money supply in (6), that will in general dominate either $r = 0$ or $h = 0$.

[40] Because systematic monetary policy does not affect real variables in their model, the only basis for choosing a target value for the money stock is presumably to influence prices. The basic flaw in the intermediate target strategy still obtains, however.

ability to achieve the objectives motivating monetary policy, the monetary economics literature has not taken up such suggestions in any systematic way.[41] By contrast, suggestions for changing institutional arrangements so as to improve the efficacy of the central bank's control over the money stock have attracted substantial attention.

Given the fractional reserve system underlying the money supply process in nearly all market economies, the chief focus of this attention has been the structure of reserve requirements. Davis (1971) early on catalogued many of the familiar slippages in the control of monetary aggregates via open market operations, and Poole and Lieberman (1972) subsequently elaborated the potential importance in the U.S. context of more uniform reserve requirements, both across different forms of monetary liabilities and across different categories of money-issuing institutions. Especially in the context of the large realized month-to-month (and even quarter-to-quarter) variations in U.S. money growth during the 1979–82 period, during which the Federal Reserve System publicly maintained that controlling money growth was its chief operating priority, the specific aspect of this subject that attracted the most attention was the presence of a time lag in the requirement that banks hold reserves based on their deposits.

McCallum and Hoehn (1983) analyzed the implications of lagged reserve requirements in the context of the supply–demand model consisting of (8)–(10), as immediately above, and instead of (31) a reserves demand relationship given by

$$m_{t-1} = \delta_1 h_t + \delta_2 r_t + q_t . \tag{50}$$

Because the money-supply/reserves-demand equation does not affect the determination of the money stock anyway when the exogenous monetary policy instrument is the interest rate, the substitution of (50) for (31) leaves $E(m_t^2)|_r$ in (48) unchanged. By contrast, under lagged reserve requirements the corresponding variance when the stock of reserves is the policy instrument is

$$E(m_t^2)|_h = \sigma_v^2 + \left(\frac{1 + \beta_1 \gamma_1}{\alpha_1 + \gamma_1}\right)^2 \sigma_u^2 + \left(\frac{\alpha_1 \beta_1 - 1}{\alpha_1 + \gamma_1}\right)^2 \sigma_z^2 + \psi^2 \sigma_q^2 . \tag{51}$$

Because the exogenous reserves policy in this context is equivalent to the exogenous interest rate policy except for the addition of some slippage (σ_q^2) in setting the interest rate, it is clearly inferior in that it provides no damping of the three disturbance terms in (48), but merely adds a fourth.

[41]A possible exception here is the large literature on institutional arrangements facilitating (more typically, impeding) the coordination of monetary and fiscal policies. That subject lies beyond the scope of this survey, however.

Under a system of lagged reserve requirements, therefore, the interest rate unambiguously dominates the stock of reserves as the policy instrument for controlling the money stock.[42] Despite the unusual (for this literature) emergence of a result that is not inherently empirical, the subsequent literature on this issue has nonetheless largely focused on empirical questions like how large the increase in variance from (49) to (51) really is, especially in more fully specified and disaggregated models of money supply and demand, and to what extent the use of the reserve demand relation (50) together with macroeconomic relations like (8)–(10) is consistent with the typically very short time delay involved in most actual lagged reserve systems.[43]

Apart from the timing, coverage, and uniformity of reserve requirements, the principal issues of institutional arrangements discussed in the literature of controlling money as an intermediate policy target have been the central bank's discount window procedure for lending reserves to banks, responses to technical factors like variations in float and currency in circulation, problems of timeliness and accuracy of data, and the ever-present problem of seasonal adjustment. Poole and Lieberman's (1972) early review of the subject encompassed most of these issues, and more recently Levin and Meek (1981), Santomero (1983), Goodfriend (1983), and others have focused in particular on the role of discount window borrowing.

4.3. Problems of volatility and instability

Another set of issues that arises when the central bank uses some measure of money as an intermediate target, especially in the context of reserves as the exogenous policy instrument, is the prospect of excessive volatility of interest rates. In simple models like those analyzed above, there is no apparent reason why interest rate volatility should be a policy concern. In fact, however, most central banks have historically sought to minimize interest rate volatility, and it is not difficult to posit richer models of income determination in which interest rate volatility can matter.[44]

In a one-period context, interest rate volatility simply means the variance of

---

[42] In most models the same conclusion would hold for the choice of a policy instrument to affect prices or (with a source of non-neutrality) income.

[43] For example, the U.S. case which motivated McCallum and Hoehn's analysis involved a two-week lag. By contrast, the shortest time period introduced in macroeconomic discussions along the lines of (8)–(10) is usually one calendar quarter, and it is often much longer. Subsequently, the Federal Reserve System shortened the lag to two days, but this change did not put an end to analysis of its operations as a lagged reserve requirement; see, for example, Goodfriend (1984).

[44] Even so, given the traditional importance of the subject in both academic and practical discussions of monetary policy it is surprising how little literature has arisen examining such potential effects. Three exceptions are Poole (1976), Johnson (1981) and Friedman (1982b).

the interest rate – or, more generally, of the entire constellation of interest rates – around the corresponding expected value(s). Here the connection to the choice of policy instrument is clear enough. Under an interest rate instrument, whatever interest rate the central bank sets exogenously has zero variance in this sense. Under a reserves instrument, the variance is nonzero. In the model consisting of (8)–(10) and (31), for example, the one-period variance of r when h is exogenous in general incorporates the respective variances (and covariances) for each of u, v, z, and q. Under most familiar theories of asset pricing, this larger one-period variance for a specified short-term interest rate implies larger one-period variances for other interest rates as well.

In a dynamic context, the question is both richer and more subtle. Here the issue is not just the within-period variance of any interest rate around its expected value but the movement of interest rates from one time period to the next, including whatever deterministic component renders each period's expected value not the same as the prior period's realization. Although the literature has typically been vague at best in distinguishing these two senses of interest rate volatility, central banks have typically exhibited concern for both. Within the research literature, the empirical work of Tinsley et al. (1982a, 1982b) has been an exception in focusing explicitly on interest rate volatility in both senses. Whether interest rate volatility in this second, dynamic sense is likely to be greater under an interest rate instrument or some other policy strategy is not clear a priori. Using a reserves instrument, or using money as an intermediate target, exposes each period's interest rate to a variety of shocks as in the models analyzed above. By contrast, if use of an interest rate instrument leads to increased variation in price inflation, and if realized inflation affects the central bank's subsequent setting of the interest rate – as is the case, for example, if the inflation rate exhibits inertia, and the interest rate that matters for economic activity is the real interest rate – then the period-to-period variance of (nominal) interest rates may be greater under an interest rate instrument. More generally, any monetary policy system that results in a volatile inflation rate is likely to increase the period-to-period volatility of nominal interest rates.

Finally, in a dynamic context the extent of period-to-period interest rate volatility also depends on the objective specifying how rapildy the central bank seeks to restore income (or prices, or money) to the corresponding targeted path, once a departure from that path has occurred. The point at issue here is a straightforward appliction of Holbrook's (1972) analysis of the problem of instrument instability, which can arise whenever the effects of policy instruments on policy targets are distributed through time. Ciccolo (1974), Enzler and Johnson (1981), Freedman (1983), and others have analyzed the potential instability that can result from excessively close control of a money target, given the extensive evidence indicating that money demand behavior exhibits a lagged response to interest rates.[45] The point is presumably applicable in a broader context as well, given the even more substantial evidence documenting lags in the response of nonfinancial behavior to movements in financial prices and quantities.

5. Other issues

In addition to the central analytical issues reviewed in Sections 2, 3, and 4, the literature of targets and instruments of monetary policy has also encompassed a variety of specific related questions. The most prominent among these include the implications of the central bank's operating procedures for the behavior of the private sector, positive questions about whether central banks did or did not in fact use a particular operating procedure during a particular time period (a question often taken up in the context of a central bank's own public assertion that it did so), and the voluminous empirical literature examining which financial quantities best display the properties appropriate for a monetary policy target.

5.1. Monetary policy and private information

A central theme running throughout the targets and instruments literature, and especially in the analysis of the intermediate target problem as laid out in Section 3, is the central bank's exploitation of available information. At the same time, however, it should be clear that the structure of the policy process – what potential instrument variable is exogenous, what (if any) intermediate target variable provides the basis for automatic responses of the instrument, and so on – also affects the information available to the economy's private sector. To the extent that that is so, holding private-sector behavior fixed for purposes of analysis like that above is potentially misleading.[46]

Dotsey and King (1986), building on King's (1982, 1983) earlier work, reconsidered Poole's (1970) original evaluation of interest rate versus money stock instruments in the context of a model in which private-sector decision-makers learn from observing market prices, including nominal interest rates, and in which inadequacies of information are by assumption the only impedi-

---

[45]See also Higgins (1982), Radecki (1984), Lane (1984), and McCallum (1985).

[46]The basic point here is related to Lucas's (1976) criticism of economic policymaking based on econometric models, but here it is more general in form in that what changes is private agents' information sets. A more direct application of Lucas's point is Walsh's (1984) analysis of the consequences of the choice of instrument variable for money demand behavior.

ment to achieving the equilibrium level of output.[47] Their analysis shows that an interest rate target rule, by which the central bank uses a feedback rule to set $E_{t-1}(r_t)$ on the basis of observed economic outcomes in period $t - 1$, but then allows disturbances to the economy to affect the corresponding actual realization r_t, is equivalent to a feedback rule similarly relating the value of the money stock to observed economic outcomes. Dotsey and King also showed that in their model either of these feedback rules in general dominates either a fixed interest rate policy or a fixed money stock policy, so that the analogy to Poole's original result is even more complete.

Siegel (1985) used a much simpler model, again incorporating flexible prices, to consider what properties make a monetary aggregate a useful "indicator" of unobservable variables like income and prices. As in Dotsey and King's work, but in contrast to the line of analysis in Sections 2–4, the presumption is that with full information the private economy on its own will operate at equilibrium, so that the purpose of variables that provide information is to facilitate this private-sector process rather than to enable the central bank to assist the private sector in reaching equilibrium. Siegel showed that monetary assets with demands that are *not* income elastic in general provide the most information about both prices and real income, while monetary assets with demands that are highly income elastic provide the most information about nominal income. Siegel also emphasized the more familiar point that monetary assets that are extremely closely related to the reserve base provide little information about any endogenous variables when the central bank uses reserves as its exogenous policy instrument. Both of these conclusions are especially relevant in the context of the empirical literature discussed below. Moreover, Siegel's conclusions are also favorable to simultaneously using more than one aggregate as information variables, along the lines discussed in Section 3.

5.2. What the central bank did or did not do

The adoption of at least some form of monetary target for monetary policy became widespread during the 1970s – at least according to what central banks said about their own policies. By contrast, economists and other observers of monetary policy (both official and private) have often expressed doubts that some central banks' adoption of such targets was more than rhetorical. Most often, skepticism of this kind has ensued when an announced policy based on a monetary aggregate target did not deliver the results previously claimed on

---

[47] In other words, no nominal rigidity provides a source of non-neutrality like that considered in Sections 2 and 3.

behalf of such a policy by its advocates. A logical question in that case is whether the policy was unsuccessful or, alternatively, was simply never tried. This issue became especially lively in the United States in the wake of the emphasis on monetary aggregate targets which the Federal Reserve System officially said it adopted in 1979 and abandoned in 1982.[48]

An early contribution along these lines was DeRosa and Stern's (1977) effort to establish whether the Federal Reserve System had adopted (at least in part) a monetary aggregate target in 1970. Their analysis, which largely set the pattern for future efforts along these lines, involved empirically estimating a central bank reaction function of the form

$$\Delta r_t = f(\Delta M_{t-1} - \Delta M^*_{t-1}, X_{t-1}),$$ (52)

where Δr is the change in the interest rate used as the exogenous policy instrument, ΔM is the growth rate of whatever monetary aggregate is in question as the supposed intermediate policy target, ΔM^* is the corresponding announced target value, and X is a vector of other variables (like price inflation or unemployment) to which monetary policy may plausibly respond.[49] Addressing the question of the adoption of a monetary target as of a specific date then amounts to testing for a change in the reaction function coefficients, in particular the coefficient on the $(\Delta M - \Delta M^*)$ term, at that point in the data sample. DeRosa and Stern reported statistically significant evidence of such a change for the United States in 1970.

The subsequent literature has evolved along roughly the same lines. Prominent examples for the U.S. case are tests by Feige and McGee (1979) and by Lombra and Moran (1980) for Federal Reserve behavior following the 1975 adoption of a Congressional resolution calling for monetary aggregate targets, and by Hoehn (1983) and Spindt and Tarhan (1987) for Federal Reserve behavior during the controversial 1979–82 period. In each case, the evidence again indicated a statistically significant change at the time posited.

As Lombra and Moran emphasized, however, statistical significance and economic significance are not always the same. In their results, for example, the post-1975 response of the federal funds rate to observed deviations of money growth from the corresponding target value was statistically significant, but so small (compared to the benchmark provided by empirical estimates of the interest elasticity of money demand) as to cast doubt on how large a role the monetary target actually played in the Federal Reserve System's decisions

---

[48]See, for example, the discussion among B. Friedman (1984b), M. Friedman (1984), and McCallum (1984).
[49]Conceptual antecedents of this procedure are Reuber (1964) and Friedlaender (1973). The switch to upper-case notation here reflects the fact that variables are not necessarily in logarithms, and do not necessarily bear the interpretation of deviations from deterministic base values.

setting interest rates. This point has featured prominently in the subsequent literature, especially since empirical estimates almost always indicate a very small (in absolute value) interest elasticity of money demand in the short run, so that a correspondingly large response of interest rates to observed movements in the money stock would be necessary to correct such movements within any short time frame.

5.3. Evidence comparing alternative target variables

One of the most troublesome contrasts between the world described by simple models like those surveyed throughout this chapter and the world in which actual central banks make monetary policy is the multiplicity (in the latter) of different deposit instruments, and hence the multiplicity of different monetary aggregates. Before it can take advantage of the insights of a typical model including a single variable labeled "*M*" and called "money", therefore, a central bank operating in any well-developed financial system must decide just which variable "*M*" is. Moreover, the experience of many countries has now cast strong doubt on the proposition, sometimes offered as a way of minimizing the importance of this choice, that all of the potential "*M*'s" typically move together anyway. That may be so in the context of a hyperinflation, but in countries experiencing ordinary business fluctuations under moderate inflation different "*M*'s" often display widely disparate growth rates, even for periods of several years at a time. Hence even saying whether monetary policy is tight or easy, or has tightened or eased, often depends crucially on which deposit aggregate is construed as "money".

The approach that the literature has taken to this question is primarily empirical, and the resulting body of available empirical research is both large and extensive, covering different time periods and different countries and employing a variety of statistical methodologies. Although it is not the purpose of this chapter to survey this empirical literature in any detail, it is useful nonetheless to indicate how its main strands relate to the analytical issues discussed in Sections 2–4.[50]

By far the greatest part of this empirical research, and the part with the longest history, has investigated the connection between alternative financial aggregates and macroeconomic variables plausibly construed as defining the ultimate objectives of monetary policy. The earlier efforts along these lines primarily employed the statistical methodology that grew out of the work of Friedman and Meiselman (1963) and Andersen and Jordan (1968). The

---

[50]For references to many of the specific contributions over the years, see again Cagan (1982), McCallum (1985), and Friedman and Kuttner (1988).

question usually asked in this line of research is which aggregate delivers the best "fit" when employed as M in equations of the form

$$\Delta Y_t = f\left(\sum_{i=1}^{n} \omega_i \Delta M_{t-i}, X_{t-1} \right), \tag{53}$$

where ΔY is the growth rate of nominal income, ΔM is the growth rate of the aggregate, X is a vector of other variables affecting ΔY (frequently used elements of X include a fiscal policy measure and a dummy variable indicating major labor union strikes), and the ω_i are a set of distributed lag weights to be estimated. Following the work of Granger (1969) and Sims (1972), however, the question more typically asked has become not just whether some M can predict the future variation of Y but, more specifically, whether M can predict that part of the variation in Y not already predictable from the observed movement of Y itself. This subsequent line of research has therefore relied on equations of the form

$$\Delta Y_t = f\left(\sum_{i=1}^{n} \omega_i \Delta M_{t-i}, \sum_{i=1}^{n} \phi_i \Delta Y_{t-i} \right), \tag{54}$$

where the ϕ_i are distributed lag coefficients analogous to the ω_i.

Empirical research along the lines of either (53) or (54) bears a fairly direct relation to the analytical issues under discussion in Sections 2–4. In either case, the object is to find the aggregate that, if employed by the central bank as its intermediate target variable in the case of deposit or loan aggregates that are necessarily endogenous, or if employed as the exogenous policy instrument in the case of aggregates like nonborrowed reserves or the monetary base, would deliver a smaller variance of income about its expected value. Furthermore, the recognition that nominal income may be less relevant than real income and prices separately in defining the ultimate objective of monetary policy has often led to trivariate (and sometimes higher-order) generalizations of (54), with separate equations for real income and prices, respectively.

An even more traditional line of empirical work that some researchers have also brought to bear on the selection of an aggregate for monetary policy purposes is the estimation of money demand functions. Here the connection to the analytical issues considered in Section 2–4 is even more straightforward. While equations like (53) or (54) at best represent reduced-form solutions to the models that typically underlie the analytical side of this literature, empirical money demand functions are, in principle, direct implementations of equations like (9) which are clearly central to the analysis. Consequently, empirical estimation of money demand functions can provide values of such crucial behavioral parameters as elasticities β_1 and β_2 and variance σ_v^2 in (9). Especially in the wake of the trend toward deregulation and private innovation in the financial markets of many countries, the literature of empirically estimated money demand functions has grown enormously in recent years.[51]

There has also been a substantial amount of empirical research focusing on the relationship between alternative monetary aggregates and variables that comprise potential exogenous instruments of monetary policy. Here what is at issue is the monetary control problem, as outlined in Section 4, and the connection to the underlying analytical issues is typically both direct and explicit. Much of the work along these lines has exploited empirical models of money demand and money supply to estimate the variance that would be associated with the use of a specific instrument variable (for example, non-borrowed reserves or the federal funds rate) to affect a given endogenous monetary aggregate used as an intermediate target variable.[52] An alternative approach, employed by Johannes and Rasche (1979), is to use time-series methods to estimate what amounts to a reduced-form equivalent of such models.

Two specific aspects common to all three of these lines of empirical research bear explicit comment as they relate to the literature of targets and instruments of monetary policy. First, whether or not "money" exhibits properties that bear implications for choosing a particular monetary policy framework is increasingly not an independently testable question, at least on the basis of historical data, because central banks can and do use the results of statistical studies like those described above as a basis for deciding how to define "money" in the first place.[53] Second, a striking feature of this entire field of empirical investigation is the remarkable extent to which researchers who otherwise profess strong sympathy with Lucas's (1976) criticism of the use of econometric models for policy purposes, on the ground that a change in policy procedures will in general induce a change in economic behavior and will therefore invalidate the model, have simply ignored this criticism as it applies to these kinds of exercises as a basis for selecting the best "*M*".

6. Some broader issues

In conclusion it is also useful to consider briefly the relationship between the main line of analytical issues developed in the targets and instruments litera-ture and some other broad issues involved in the conduct of monetary policy.

---

[51]See, for example, the papers cited by Judd and Scadding (1982) and Roley (1985).

[52]See, for example, Pindyck and Roberts (1976), Sivesind and Hurley (1980), and Lindsey et al. (1984).

[53]See, for example, the empirical evidence presented by Simpson et al. (1979) in support of the Federal Reserve System's 1980 redefinition of the U.S. monetary aggregates.

The most obviously relevant among these are the traditional issues of rules versus discretion, and of activism versus nonresponsiveness, in the making of economic policy more generally.[54]

In a single-period context, the entire subject of targets and instruments of monetary policy falls squarely into the general discussion of rules for guiding policy. In this sense the choice of an exogenous policy instrument, and in some cases also of an intermediate policy target, amounts to picking a rule for determining how the economic system – here including the actions of the central bank – will translate the various disturbances to which the economy is subject into effects on its overall performance. Some of these implied rules are simple. Others, including feedback rules of the kind derived in Section 3, are more complicated. In the end, however, within the context of a single period each is a rule nonetheless.

Following the work of Kydland and Prescott (1977) and Barro and Gordon (1983), however, the modern literature of rules versus discretion is mostly about what happens in a dynamic context, and here the connection to the targets and instruments literature is less straightforward. Is the central bank presumed to make the same choice of instrument variable (and intermediate target variable, if any) in each period? What aspects of the economy's condition inherited from the previous period does it take into account in defining the objective which motivates its actions in each period? What kind of feedback rules does it employ in relating the value of its instrument (and its intermediate target, if any) to those conditions? In what way does its objective take account of the implications of its current actions for future time periods? The relationship between the issues reviewed in Sections 2–4 and the rules versus discretion debate hinges importantly on the answers to questions like these.

One line of thinking that implicitly addresses many of these questions, clearly articulated by Tobin (1983), for example, is that in the world of actual policymaking "rules" necessarily mean simple rules. In that case the analytical issues reviewed in this chapter do bear quite directly on the rules versus discretion debate, since the typical outcome of the line of analysis surveyed here is to demonstrate the inferiority in general of simple rules – fix the reserve base, fix an interest rate, fix the expected value of the money stock, and so on – compared to rules specifying responses that take account of at least some of the available information about the disturbances affecting economic behavior. If rules must be simple ones, therefore, the targets and instruments literature not only demonstrates the qualitative inferiority of rules but provides guidelines for quantifying that inferiority. Nevertheless, the issue remains

---

[54]Again see the review of these issues in Stanley Fischer's contribution (Chapter 21) to this Handbook.

open, not only because of questions about the empirical magnitudes involved but also because others who have thought about these issues – for example, McCallum (1985) – reject the view that rules must be simple in order to be relevant in practice.

The literature of targets and instruments of monetary policy is also closely related to the issue of activism versus nonresponsiveness. Nonresponsiveness essentially means a simple rule – fix this, or fix that – while activism means responding to initial conditions, or to evidence of disturbances, according to one feedback rule or another. Even so, because the nonresponsive rules that have attracted the most attention over the years have typically referred to some endogenous variable like money, rather than to some variable that the central bank can set directly (like nonborrowed reserves), in the end the real question is not whether or not to respond to anything at all but rather which classes of phenomena merit a response and which do not. This kind of question is clearly at the analytical heart of the targets and instruments literature surveyed in Sections 2–4.

Framing the issue in this way also makes clear the limited applicability of Friedman's (1953) classic criticism of activist policy on the ground that varying policy from the no-response, or base, position in general introduces uncertainty, and with sufficient ignorance may introduce sufficient uncertainty to increase the variance of the policy objective rather than reduce it. The targets and instruments literature brings to center attention the problem of defining the base position in the first place in a stochastic environment. Does it refer to an interest rate, to the reserve base, or to money? Does it refer to levels or to changes of whatever variable is at issue?

Analysis along the lines of the targets and instruments literature indicates how to answer such questions on the basis of any given model, and typically any given model will imply that in general at least some degree of responsiveness dominates a purely nonresponsive policy, even after allowing for uncertainty surrounding the model's coefficients, as illustrated by Brainard (1967). Although many economists have argued as if an even deeper level of uncertainty – in particular, ignorance about what is the right model – somehow implies that fixing some measure of *money* constitutes the appropriate definition of the base position for purposes of this issue, there is no obvious reason to accept this presumption. In the absence of at least some articulated model indicating the likely implications of the central bank's policy actions for its policy objectives, no conclusions of this kind are possible at all. There is no more reason for presuming that qualitative propositions about "money" uniquely survive the absence of a model than for the presumption that empirical evidence involving "money" uniquely survives Lucas's (1976) point about public policy and private behavior.

Finally, although it is easy enough as a matter of abstract analysis to discuss all of these aspects of monetary policy as if "policy" and "politics" did not have the same root, political considerations are hardly irrelevant to the issues involved in the targets and instruments literature. A frequently expressed motivation underlying the intermediate target strategy – articulated by Poole (1980), for example – is to provide a mechanism enabling higher governmental authorities as well as the general public to hold the central bank politically accountable for its conduct of monetary policy. Whether this argument is compelling must in the end depend both upon the quantitative degree of inferiority of the intermediate target strategy compared to a given alternative, determined along the lines analyzed here, and on the risks and consequences associated with what the relevant central bank decision-makers may do in the absence of such an accountability mechanism. That these risks and consequences are difficult to specify does not necessarily make them less real. At least thus far, however, this difficulty has largely prevented the development of any substantial body of monetary policy research incorporating them.

References

Aizenmann, J. and J.A. Frenkel (1985) 'Optimal wage indexation, foreign exchange intervention, and monetary policy', *American Economic Review*, 75: 402–423.

Aizenmann, J. and J.A. Frenkel (1986) 'Supply shocks, wage indexation, and monetary accommodation', *Journal of Money, Credit and Banking*, 18: 304–322.

Andersen, L.C. and J.L. Jordan (1968) 'Monetary and fiscal actions: A test of their relative importance in economic stabilization', Federal Reserve Bank of St. Louis, *Review*, 50: 11–24.

Ando, A. and F. Modigliani (1965a) 'The relative stability of monetary velocity and the investment multiplier', *American Economic Review*, 55: 693–728.

Ando, A. and F. Modigliani (1965b) 'Rejoinder', *American Econommic Review*, 55: 786–790.

Barro, R.J. and D.B. Gordon (1983) 'Rules, discretion, and reputation in a model of monetary policy', *Journal of Monetary Economics*, 12: 101–121.

Bean, C.R. (1983) 'Targeting nominal income: An appraisal', *Economic Journal*, 93: 806–819.

Bernanke, B.S. and M. Gertler (1986) 'Agency costs, collateral, and business fluctuations', *American Economic Review*, 79: 14–31.

Blinder, A.S. and J.E. Stiglitz (1983) 'Money, credit constraints, and economic activity', *American Economic Review*, 73: 297–302.

Brainard, W. (1967) 'Uncertainty and the effectiveness of policy', *American Economic Review*, 57: 411–425.

Brunner, K. and A.H. Meltzer (1964) 'The Federal Reserve's attachment to the free reserve concept', U.S. Congress, House Committee on Banking and Currency, Subcommittee on Dosmestic Finance. 88th Congress, 2nd Session. Washington: U.S. Government Printing Office.

Brunner, K. and A.H. Meltzer (1967) 'The meaning of monetary indicators', in: Horwich, ed., *Monetary process and policy: Symposium*. Homewood: Richard D. Irwin.

Brunner, K. and A.H. Meltzer (1969) 'The nature of the policy problem', in: K. Brunner, ed., *Targets and indicators of monetary policy*. San Francisco: Chandler Publishing Company.

Brunner, K. and A.H. Meltzer (1972) 'Money, debt, and economic activity', *Journal of Political Economy*, 80: 951–977.

Brunner, K. and A.H. Meltzer (1976) 'An aggregative theory for a closed economy,' in: Stein, ed., *Monetarism*. Amsterdam: North-Holland.

Cagan, P. (1978) 'Monetarism in historical perspective', in: Mayer et al., eds., *The structure of monetarism*. New York: W.W. Norton & Company.

Cagan, P. (1982) 'The choice among monetary aggregates as targets and guides for monetary policy', *Journal of Money, Credit, and Banking*, 14: 661–686.

Ciccolo, J.H. (1974) 'Is short-run monetary control feasible?', in: Federal Reserve Bank of New York, *Monetary aggregates and monetary policy*. New York.

Cooper, J.P. and S. Fischer (1972a) 'Simulations of monetary rules in the FRB–MIT–Penn model', *Journal of Money, Credit and Banking*, 4: 384–396.

Cooper, J.P. and S. Fischer (1972b) 'Stochastic simulation of monetary rules in two macroeconometric models', *Journal of the American Statistical Association*, 67: 750–760.

Davis, R.G. (1971) 'Short-run targets for open market operations', in: Board of Governors of the Federal Reserve System, *Open market policies and operating procedures – staff studies*. Washington.

DeRosa, P. and G.H. Stern (1977) 'Monetary control and the federal funds rate', *Journal of Monetary Economics*, 3: 217–230.

Dotsey, M. and R.G. King (1986) 'Informational implications of interest rate rules', *American Economic Review*, 76: 33–42.

Enzler, J. and L. Johnson (1981) 'Cycles resulting from money stock targeting', in: Board of Governors of the Federal Reserve System, *New monetary control procedures*, Vol. I. Washington.

Federal Reserve Bank of Boston (1969) *Controlling monetary aggregates*. Boston.

Feige, E.L. and R. McGee (1979) 'Has the federal reserve shifted from a policy of interest rate targets to a policy of monetary aggregate targets?', *Journal of Money, Credit and Banking*, 11: 381–404.

Fischer, S. (1977a) 'Long-term contracts, rational expectations, and the optimal money supply rule', *Journal of Political Economy*, 85: 191–205.

Fischer, S. (1977b) 'Long-term contracting, sticky prices, and monetary policy: A comment,' *Journal of Monetary Economics*, 3: 317–323.

Fischer, S. (1980) 'On activist monetary policy with rational expectations', in: S. Fischer, ed., *Rational expectations and economic policy*. Chicago: University of Chicago Press.

Fischer, S. (1985) 'Supply shocks, wage stickiness, and accommodation', *Journal of Money, Credit and Banking*, 17: 1–15.

Freedman, C. (1983) 'Some theoretical aspects of base control', in: Purvis, ed., *The Canadian balance of payments: Perspectives and policy issues*. Montreal: Institute for Research on Public Policy.

Friedlander, A.F. (1973) 'Macro policy goals and revealed preference', *Quarterly Journal of Economics*, 87: 25–43.

Friedman, B.M. (1975) 'Targets, instruments, and indicators of monetary policy', *Journal of Monetary Economics*, 1: 443–473.

Friedman, B.M. (1977) 'The inefficiency of short-run monetary targets for monetary policy', *Brookings Papers on Economic Activity*, 1977-2: 293–335.

Friedman, B.M. (1982a) 'Time to reexamine the monetary targets framework', Federal Reserve Bank of Boston, *New England Economic Review* March/April: 15–23.

Friedman, B.M. (1982b) 'Federal reserve policy, interest rate volatility, and the U.S. capital raising mechanism', *Journal of Money, Credit and Banking*, 14: 721–745.

Friedman, B.M. (1983) 'The roles of money and credit in macroeconomic analysis', in: J. Tobin, ed., *Macroeconomics, prices and quantities: Essays in memory of Arthur M. Okun*. Washington: The Brookings Institution.

Friedman, B.M. (1984a) 'Lessons from the 1979–82 monetary policy experiment', *American Economic Review*, 74: 382–387.

Friedman, B.M. (1984b) 'The value of intermediate targets in implementing monetary policy', in: Federal Reserve Bank of Kansas City, *Price stability and public policy*. Kansas City.

Friedman, B.M. and K.H. Kuttner (1988) 'Money, income and prices after the 1980s', National Bureau of Economic Research, mimeo.

Friedman, M. (1953) 'The effects of a full-employment policy on economic stability: A formal analysis', in: M. Friedman, *Essays in positive economics*. Chicago: University of Chicago Press.

Friedman, M. (1984) 'Lessons from the 1979–82 monetary policy experiment', *American Economic Review*, 74: 397–400.

Friedman, M. and D. Meiselman (1963) 'The relative stability of monetary velocity and the investment multiplier in the United States, 1897–1958', in: Commision on Money and Credit, *Stabilization policies*. Englewood Cliffs: Prentice-Hall.

Friedman, M. and D. Meiselman (1965) 'Reply to Ando and Modigliani and to DePrano and Mayer', *American Economic Review*, 55: 753–785.

Friedman, M. and A.J. Schwartz (1963) *A monetary history of the United States, 1867–1960*. Princeton University Press.

Goodfriend, M. (1983) 'Discount window borrowing, monetary policy, and the post-October 6, 1979 Federal Reserve operating procedure', *Journal of Monetary Economics*, 12: 343–356.

Goodfriend, M. (1984) 'The promises and pitfalls of contemporaneous reserve requirements for the implementation of monetary policy', Federal Reserve Bank of Richmond, *Economic Review*, 70: 3–12.

Granger, C.W.J. (1969) 'Investigating causal relations by econometric models and cross spectral methods', *Econometrica*, 37: 424–438.

Gray, J.A. (1976) 'Wage indexation: A macroeconomic approach', *Journal of Monetary Economics*, 2: 221–235.

Guttentag, J.F. (1966) 'The strategy of open market operations', *Quarterly Journal of Economics*, 80: 1–30.

Hall, R.E. (1984) 'Monetary policy with an elastic price standard', in: Federal Reserve Bank of Kansas City, *Price stability and public policy*. Kansas City.

Higgins, B. (1982) 'Should the federal reserve fine tune monetary growth?', Federal Reserve Bank of Kansas City, *Economic Review*, 67: 3–16.

Hoehn, J. G. (1983) 'Recent monetary control procedures and the response of interest rates to fluctuations in money growth', Federal Reserve Bank of Dallas, *Economic Review*, September: 1–10.

Holbrook, R.S. (1972) 'Optimal economic policy and the problem of instrument instability', *American Economic Review*, 62: 57–65.

Johannes, J.M. and R.H. Rasche (1979) 'Predicting the money multiplier', *Journal of Monetary Economics*, 5: 301–325.

Johnson, D. et al. (1981) 'Interest rate variability under the new operating procedures and the initial response in financial markets', in: Board of Governors of the Federal Reserve System, *New monetary control procedures*, Vol. I. Washington.

Judd, J.P. and J.L. Scadding (1982) 'The search for a stable money demand function: A survey of the post-1973 literature', *Journal of Economic Literature*, 20: 993–1023.

Kareken, J.H., T. Muench and N. Wallace (1973) 'Optimal open market strategy: The use of information variables', *American Economic Review*, 63: 156–172.

Karni, E. (1983) 'On optimal wage indexation', *Journal of Political Economy*, 91: 282–292.

King, R.G. (1982) 'Monetary policy and the information content of prices', *Journal of Political Economy*, 90: 247–279.

King, R.G. (1983) 'On the economics of private money', *Journal of Monetary Economics*, 12: 127–185.

Kydland, F.E. and E.C. Prescott (1977) 'Rules rather than discretion: The inconsistency of optimal plans', *Journal of Political Economy*, 85: 473–491.

Lane, T.D. (1984) 'Instrument instability and short-term monetary control', *Journal of Monetary Economics*, 14: 209–224.

LeRoy, S.F. and R.N. Waud (1977) 'Applications of the Kalman filter in short-run monetary control', *International Economic Review*, 18: 195–207.

Levin, F. and P. Meek (1981) 'Implementing the new procedures: The view from the trading desk', in: Board of Governors of the Federal Reserve System, *New monetary control procedures*, Vol. I. Washington.

Lindsey, D.E., H.T. Farr, G.P. Gillum, K.J. Kopechy and R.D. Porter (1984) 'Short-run monetary control: Evidence under a non-borrowed reserve operating procedure', *Journal of Monetary Economics*, 13: 87–111.

Lombra, R. and M. Moran (1980) 'Policy advice and policymaking at the Federal Reserve', in: K. Brunner and A.H. Meltzer, eds., *Monetary institutions and the policy process*. Amsterdam: North-Holland.

Lombra, R.E. and R.G. Torto (1977) 'Discount rate changes and announcement effects', *Quarterly Journal of Economics*, 91: 171–176.

Lucas, R.E., Jr. (1972) 'Expectations and the neutrality of money', *Journal of Economic Theory*, 4: 103–124.

Lucas, R.E., Jr. (1973) 'Some international evidence on output–inflation tradeoffs', *American Economic Review*, 63: 326–334.

Lucas, R.E., Jr. (1976) 'Econometric policy evaluation: A critique', in: K. Brunner and A.H. Meltzer, eds., *The Phillips curve and labor markets*. Amsterdam: North-Holland.

McCallum, B.T. (1981) 'Price level determinacy with an interest rate policy rule and rational expectations', *Journal of Monetary Economics*, 8: 319–329.

McCallum, B.T. (1984) 'Monetarist rules in the light of recent experience', *American Economic Review*, 74: 388–391.

McCallum, B.T. (1985) 'On consequences and criticisms of monetary targeting', *Journal of Money, Credit and Banking*, 17: 570–597.

McCallum, B.T. and J.G. Hoehn (1983) 'Instrument choice for money stock control with contemporaneous and lagged reserve requirements', *Journal of Money, Credit and Banking*, 15: 96–101.

Modigliani, F. (1963) 'The monetary mechanism and its interaction with real phenomena', *Review of Economics and Statistics*, 45: 79–107.

Modigliani, F. and L.D. Papademos (1983) 'The structure of financial markets and the monetary mechanism', in: Federal Reserve Bank of Boston, *Controlling monetary aggregates* III. Boston.

Modigliani, F., R. Rasche and J.P. Cooper (1970) 'Central bank policy, the money supply, and the short-term rate of interest', *Journal of Money, Credit and Banking*, 2: 166–218.

Patinkin, D. (1965) *Money, interest, and prices: An integration of monetary and value theory*. New York: Harper and Row.

Phelps, E.S. and J.B. Taylor (1977) 'Stabilizing powers of monetary policy under rational expectations', *Journal of Political Economy*, 85: 163–190.

Pierce, J.L. and T.D. Thomson (1972) 'Some issues in controlling the stock of money', in: Federal Reserve Bank of Boston, *Controlling monetary aggregates* II: *The implementation*. Boston.

Pindyck, R.S. and S.M. Roberts (1976) 'Instruments, intermediate targets, and monetary controllability', *International Economic Review*, 17: 627–650.

Poole, W. (1970) 'Optimal choice of monetary policy instrument in a simple stochastic macro model', *Quarterly Journal of Economics*, 84: 197–216.

Poole, W. (1976) 'Interest rate stability as a policy goal', Federal Reserve Bank of Boston, *New England Economic Review*, May/June: 30–37.

Poole, W. (1980) 'Comments of James Tobin, "Stabilization policy ten years after"', *Brookings Papers on Economic Activity*, 1980-1: 79–85.

Poole, W. (1985) 'The discount window', in: Joint Economic Committee, *Monetarism, inflation, and the Federal Reserve*. 99th Congress, 1st Session. Washington: U.S. Government Printing Office.

Poole, W. and C. Lieberman (1972) 'Improving monetary control', *Brookings Papers on Economic Activity*, 1972-2: 293–335.

Radecki, L.J. (1984) 'Targeting in a dynamic model', Federal Reserve Bank of New York, *Quarterly Review*, Summer: 9–15.

Reuber, G.L. (1964) 'The objectives of Canadian monetary policy, 1949–61: Empirical "Trade-offs" and the reaction function of the authorities', *Journal of Political Economy*, 72: 109–132.

Roley, V. (1985) 'Money demand predictability', *Journal of Money, Credit and Banking*, 17: 611–641.

Santomero, A.M. (1983) 'Controlling monetary aggregates: The discount window', *The Journal of Finance*, 38: 827–844.

Sargent, T.J. and N. Wallace (1975) ' "Rational" expectations, the optimal monetary instrument, and the optimal money supply rule', *Journal of Political Economy*, 83: 241–254.

Siegel, J.J. (1985) 'Monetary aggregates as indicators of economic activity: A theoretical analysis', University of Pennsylvania, mimeo.

Simpson, T.D., et al. (1979) 'A proposal for redefining the monetary aggregates', *Federal Reserve Bulletin*, 65: 13–42.

Sims, C.A. (1972) 'Money, income, and causality', *American Economic Review*, 62: 540–552.

Sims, C.A. (1982) 'Policy analysis with econometric models', *Brookings Papers on Economic Activity*, 1982-1: 107–152.

Sivesind, C. and K. Hurley (1980) 'Choosing an operating target for monetary policy', *Quarterly Journal of Economics*, 94, 199–203.

Spindt, P.A. and V. Tarhan (1987) 'The Federal Reserve's new operating procedures: A post mortem', *Journal of Monetary Economics*, 19: 107–123.

Taylor, J.B. (1985) 'What would nominal income targetting do to the business cycle?', in: K. Brunner and A.H. Meltzer, eds., *Understanding monetary regimes*. Amsterdam: North-Holland.

Tinbergen, J. (1952) *On the theory of economic policy*. Amsterdam: North-Holland.

Tinsley, P.A., H.T. Farr, G. Fries, B. Garrett and P. von zur Muehlen (1982a) 'Policy robustness: Specification and simulation of a monthly money market model', *Journal of Money, Credit, and Banking*, 14: 829–856.

Tinsley, P.A., P. von zur Muehlen and G. Fries (1982b) 'The short-run volatility of money stock targeting', *Journal of Monetary Economics*, 10: 215–237.

Tobin, J. (1970) 'Money and income: Post hoc ergo propter hoc?' *Quarterly Journal of Economics*, 84: 301–317.

Tobin, J. (1983) 'Monetary policy: Rules, targets, and shocks', *Journal of Money, Credit, and Banking*, 15: 506–518.

Turnovsky, S.J. (1987) 'Supply shocks and optimal monetary policy', *Oxford Economic Papers*, 39: 20–37.

Walsh, C.E. (1984) 'Interest rate volatility and monetary policy', *Journal of Money, Credit, and Banking*, 16: 133–150.

West, K.D. (1986) 'Targeting nominal income: A note', *Economic Journal*, 96: 1077–1083.

Chapter 23

MONETARY POLICY IN THE OPEN ECONOMY

RUDIGER DORNBUSCH

Massachusetts Institute of Technology and NBER

ALBERTO GIOVANNINI

Columbia University and NBER

Contents

Handbook of Monetary Economics, Volume II, Edited by B.M. Friedman and F.H. Hahn
© *Elsevier Science Publishers B.V., 1990*

1. Introduction

Monetary economics used to be oriented toward open economy issues until sometime in the interwar period. There was thought to be only very limited scope for national monetary policy except as an abrogation of the *automatic* mechanism associated with payments imbalances under fixed exchange rates. The rules of the gold standard, in its rigid form, meant that monetary policy was defined as sustaining gold convertibility. Openness of the economy and the linkage between the balance of payments and domestic prices and activity were the accepted frame of reference. This is clearly apparent in Keynes' Treatise but also in the 1920s central bank cooperation between Montague Norman of the Bank of England and Benjamin Strong of the New York Fed.

This central emphasis on open economy aspects of monetary policy was lost in industrial countries in the postwar period. The constraints remained the same as is made quite apparent from the attempts to cope with international capital mobility by "Operation Twist" in the 1960s, for example, or from capital controls, until very recently, in many European countries. But it took flexible exchange rates (and large exchange rate movements rather than sterilized gold flows) to make open economy aspects once again a central feature of the discussion of monetary policy. The experience with flexible exchange rates and the experiment in monetary integration in the European Monetary System have sharply livened the interest in open economy monetary issues, as has the high inflation experience of the early 1980s in many developing countries.

This chapter reviews international aspects of monetary policy, and is organized as follows. Section 2 sets out the classical model of the open economy. Here we emphasize the operation of the gold standard, the price–specie flow mechanism, purchasing power parity (PPP) and the monetary approach to the balance of payments. These are key ideas and mechanisms that remain essential ingredients in present-day discussion. Section 3 uses the Mundell–Fleming model which is an open economy version of the IS–LM model of monetary policy under conditions of short-run wage–price stickiness and capital mobility. We highlight the distinction between fixed and flexible exchange rates. In Section 4 we expand the macroeconomic model by drawing out the evidence on two central questions: the extent to which wages and prices are sticky and the international linkages among asset markets. Both issues are of central importance for the channels of transmission and the effectiveness of monetary policy.

Exchange rate regime choices and exchange rate oriented monetary policy are discussed in Section 5. We conclude with two sections dealing with special topics. In Section 6 we review the recent efforts at building up a new classical open economy economics, grounded in explicit and rigorous attention to maximization, attention to information structures and intertemporal optimization. This approach, although not far developed yet, is a promising and rich field of research. Section 7 deals with special issues in monetary policy issues in high inflation economies. Among the issues we discuss are the role of currency substitution, seigniorage and the place of exchange rate policy in stabilization.

2. Classical monetary economics, PPP and the monetary approach

This section introduces open economy monetary issues by laying out the classical model of the gold standard. The interest of that presentation is threefold. First to highlight the fact that under fixed exchange rates the money supply in the open economy is endogenous. This is the case as long as the "rules of the game" linking the balance of payments and the money supply are not suspended. Second, to show the real effects brought about by the monetary adjustment mechanism. Third, to highlight the policy implication that with full wage–price flexibility monetary changes or exchange rate changes have no sustained real effects.

Classical monetary economics deals with the linkages between money, spending and prices in the open economy. It is best represented by David Hume's price–specie flow mechanism. The simple model assumes full price flexibility and focuses on a money-goods economy with no non-monetary assets. Among the points of the model are the demonstration of a natural distribution of money in the world as well as the link between payments adjustment and price level movements.

2.1. The price–specie flow mechanism

The pure gold standard is the simplest rendition of classical monetary economics. In each country spending is linked to money (gold) holdings. Let G be the world stock of gold and the national money stocks are M and M^*, all measured in a common unit, say dollars.

The world money stock identity states:

$$G = M + M^*, \tag{1}$$

where M and M^* are the national money stocks. In this economy where money is the only asset, a link between money holdings and spending is posited. It takes the form of a constant expenditure velocity:[1]

$$A = VM , \qquad A^* = V^* M^* , \tag{2}$$

where A and A^* denote national nominal spending levels in the respective countries and V and V^* are the constant expenditure velocities. Note that because income and spending need not be equal in the open economy the proper velocity is defined relative to spending.

For the moment there is only one good in the world, the price of which is spatially arbitraged. The supply of output in the two countries is fixed at levels y and y^*, respectively. World goods market equilibrium then requires the balance of world income and spending:

$$P(y + y^*) = VM + V^* M^* = VG , \tag{3}$$

where we now assume, for the moment, the velocities are equal, $V = V^*$. The equilibrium price level in (3) is determined by the given world output and the world gold stock:

$$P = VG/(y + y^*) . \tag{3a}$$

The model is closed by an equation describing the balance of payments link to the money supply. The balance of payments surplus is equal to the trade surplus which, in market equilibrium, is equal to the excess of income over spending. Payments imbalances translate one for one into changes in the money supply. We can imagine this process as a reminting of coins from Maria Theresa Thalers into gold crowns, say:

$$\dot{M}_t = P_t y - VM_t = -\dot{M}_t^* , \tag{4}$$

which, using (3a) and (1), simplifies to:

$$\dot{M}_t = V(\alpha G - M_t) , \qquad \alpha = y/(y + y^*) , \tag{4a}$$

where α is the given home country share in world output.

The monetary adjustment mechanism in equation (4a) is the central equation of classical international monetary economics. It states that the distribution of the money supply, at any point in time, governs spending and the balance of payments. Payments imbalances redistribute money over time until the world

---

[1] We show below, in Section 6, that such a link between money and spending can be derived from a model of intertemporal optimization when money is an argument in the utility function.

economy converges on the natural distribution of specie. As is apparent from (4a), the process is stable. The natural distribution of specie defines the long-run share of the home country in the world money supply. This share depends only on relative size as measured by the output share, α.

Equation (4a) draws attention to two balance of payments results. First, economic growth, shown as an increase in the relative output share α, will improve the balance of payments of the growing country. Second, a monetary expansion occurring in one country (say gold discoveries in Australia) will lead to a balance of payments deficit which redistributes part of the increased money stock to the rest of the world.

2.1.1. Distribution effects

A central topic of open economy monetary economics is the role of distribution effects. In the model presented so far there are absolutely none. Money effects spending, but because of equal velocities and no other distribution effects the balance of payments adjustment process has no effect on the world price level. Several simple extensions bring in a variety of distribution effects. One extension recognizes the possibility that spending velocities might differ between countries. Another includes the possibility of fractional partial reserves against gold so that money expansion or contraction induced by the balance of payments could be a multiple of gold movements.

With these modifications the equilibrium price level [unlike in (3a)] now depends on the distribution of the world gold stock. Similarly, the balance of payments response to a maldistribution of gold now depends on the distribution of money as well as velocities and reserve ratios. But the stability of the specie flow mechanism is unaffected. Payments imbalances now lead to world price level movements because spending velocities and reserve ratios differ between countries.

2.1.2. Non-traded goods and PPP

A more significant extension of the analysis brings systematic variations of relative price levels into play. This extension is essential if monetary disturbances are to affect relative prices as is suggested by the expression price–specie flow mechanism.

We again assume identical velocities and a single traded good. But in addition there is in each country a non-traded or home good which is also in fixed supply. To keep the model tractable we assume that expenditure shares are constant and equal between countries. This model will determine equilibrium prices for traded and home goods (and hence their relative price) as well as the balance of payments. It is worth spelling out the details to show that with non-traded goods the international monetary adjustment process has systematic effects on absolute and relative prices. Although the model is highly simplified it captures the systematic relationship of payments imbalances and relative price levels which is one of the stylized facts of open economy macroeconomics.

Once again we use market equilibrium to derive equilibrium prices. These prices, in conjunction with the money-spending relation, yield the payments balance. We denote by subscripts T and N the variables of the traded and non-traded goods sectors, respectively. Equilibrium in the market for non-traded goods requires:

$$P_N y_N = \beta V M \,, \tag{5}$$

where β denotes the given expenditure share of home goods. The equilibrium price of home goods is higher the higher are money holdings relative to the supply of non-traded goods.

In the market for traded goods we have as equilibrium condition:

$$P_T(y_T + y_T^*) = (1 - \beta)VG \,. \tag{6}$$

The equilibrium price of traded goods (unlike the home goods price) depends on the *world* money stock, G. The balance of payments, when goods markets clear, is equal to the excess of income over spending. Using equilibrium prices from (5) and (6) this yields:

$$\dot{M} = P_T y_T - (1 - \beta)VM = (1 - \beta)V(\alpha_T G - M) \,, \tag{7}$$

where α_T is the share of the home country's output of traded goods in world output of traded goods. From (7) we observe that the balance of payments is affected by the presence of non-traded goods. The higher their share the more gradually the specie flow mechanism operates. But in the long run there is still an invariant distribution of money.

The dynamics of payments adjustment are shown in Figure 23.1 which highlights the determination of the relative price of home goods $p = P_N / P_T$ and the dynamics of the money stock or payments adjustment for a given world quantity of money. From (5) and (6) we obtain the relative price of non-traded goods as a function of the money stock. Figure 23.1 shows as NN the home goods market equilibrium schedule obtained from the ratio of (5) and (6). Given output the relative price can be written as $p = k M/G$, where k is a constant. Payments balance requires by (7) that the home money stock be equal to a fraction α_T of the world money stock and thus is shown as a vertical line. The equilibrium dynamics are indicated by the arrows. If our relative

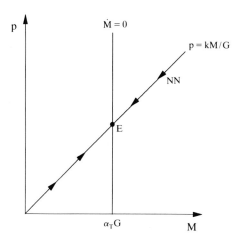

Figure 23.1. The monetary adjustment process.

money supply is low compared to the steady-state equilibrium at E, spending and hence the relative price of home goods will be low.

The home goods–traded goods model has strong implications for distribution effects. By definition the foreign propensity to spend on our non-traded goods is zero. Therefore monetary disturbances and payments imbalances affect relative prices at home and relative national price levels. The general price levels in each country, P and P^*, respectively, are expenditure-weighted, linear homogeneous functions of these sectoral prices. We want to briefly demonstrate the effect of monetary disturbances (given output) on relative price levels. Using the linear homogeneity of price levels and the expression for equilibrium relative price levels we can derive a simple formula:

$$P/P^* = c(M/M^*)^\beta ,$$ (8)

where c is a constant. Relative price levels thus depend only on the relative money supplies. With a low price of home goods the domestic price level is low. Abroad exactly the opposite conditions prevail. Spending is high and so are home goods prices and hence the price level. Thus, we conclude that in deficit countries prices are high. A redistribution of money toward one country will *transitorily* raise that country's relative price level until, via the balance of payments deficit, the initial distribution of money is restored.

This extended model describes the price–specie flow mechanism. It adds to the spending effects on the balance of payments the impact on absolute and relative prices and relative national price levels which stem from the impact of money-induced spending changes on non-traded goods prices. In the classical model, excepting trade barriers, perfect competition and spatial arbitrage ensure that the same good commands the same price (in any one currency). But even so national price levels need not move together. Consumer prices can show divergent movements, as we saw above, because of the divergence in home goods prices. In countries undergoing demand expansion inflation can, in the short run, exceed that abroad because the relative price of non-traded goods is rising. But this divergence, when it is related to demand expansion, is of necessity transitory since the resulting payments imbalance leads to correction. There is scope for a long-term departure from PPP which results from divergences in productivity growth rates.[2] Non-traded goods are essential for these divergences in national price levels.

2.1.3. More traded goods and elasticities

How does the monetary mechanism work when there is more than one traded good? And how vulnerable is the formulation once spending shares are no longer constant, as assumed above? In discussions of payments problems, price elasticities of trade flows appear commonly and the size of elasticities has a bearing on the stability of the monetary adjustment process. Price elasticities enter the discussion when there is more than one traded good and when expenditure shares are not constant, as we assumed so far.

We stay with the simple monetary model, dropping now home goods to see the issues and complications that emerge from the presence of an extra traded good and variable expenditure shares. Let the goods be indexed by 1 and 2, respectively, and let $\beta(p)$ be the expenditure share of good 1 with $p = P_1/P_2$ the relative price of good 1. World market equilibrium for the two goods requires:

$$P_1(y_1 + y_1^*) = \beta(p)VG , \qquad P_2(y_2 + y_2^*) = (1 - \beta(p))VG , \quad p = P_1/P_2 . \tag{9}$$

The equilibrium relative price is simply a function of output supplies and tastes. It is independent of the world money stock or its distribution. The latter result is due, once again, to the assumption of common tastes and expenditure velocities between countries and the absence of home goods.

Once again we are interested in links between monetary disturbances and the balance of payments. The balance of payments, when goods markets clear, is given by the excess of nominal income, Y, over spending:

$$\dot{M} = Y - VM , \tag{10}$$

[2]See, for example, Kravis and Lipsey (1984) and the review of PPP in Dornbusch (1988).

where Y denotes *nominal* income which depends on output supplies, tastes and world money.

So far there is no issue of elasticities. An excess of money translates into increased spending and a deficit. Thus, the monetary mechanism remains unchanged: increased money leads to deficits which are self-liquidating.

But real disturbances affect the payments balance in a manner that depends on their effect on nominal income. At this stage elasticities do enter the picture. Suppose, for example, that domestic output increases. The benchmark case of unit elasticities and hence constant expenditure is easy: an increase in output lowers price in proportion to the percentage increase in *world* supply. Since world supply grows proportionately less than the increase in domestic supply it is immediately clear that nominal income must rise and the balance of payments must improve.

We thus maintain the presumption that output growth leads to payments surpluses. But the result can be reversed, in principle, if demand for the good that is in increased supply is highly inelastic. In that case the price decline can be sufficiently large to reduce nominal income and bring about a worsening of the balance of payments.

At several points in the later discussion we will see extensions of the basic approach offered here. One set of questions deals with the money-spending link. What is the microeconomic function of money and how is this role reflected in the money-spending link? What role do expectations about future relative to current prices play in affecting the money-spending link as well as the allocation of spending between goods? How do these models extend to a world of less than full price flexibility? What happens when there are non-monetary assets? These questions are the menu for the reconstruction of international monetary economics that has come underway over the past decade and is discussed below. In the meantime we turn to some important implications of the simple monetary models studied so far.

2.2. The monetary approach

The monetary approach to the balance of payments is essentially a reincarnation of classical balance of payments and monetary economics. This approach was developed by Jacques Polak at the IMF and, especially, by Robert A. Mundell and Harry G. Johnson and their students at the University of Chicago.[3] It asserts that payments imbalances are a monetary phenomenon which, in the absence of sterilization, must be self-correcting. (It is said that

[3]See International Monetary Fund (1977), Mundell (1968, 1971), Johnson (1958, 1962, 1973a), Prais (1961) and Frenkel and Johnson (1976). See, too, Collery (1971) and Krueger (1971) as well as Hahn (1977).

without a central bank, there cannot be a balance of payments problem.)[4] The central idea of the monetary approach and its implications is the endogeneity of the money supply and the essential distinction between money and domestic credit.

2.2.1. The role of domestic credit

An important distinction in open economy discussions of monetary policy is between the monetary base and domestic credit. The difference between the two is the foreign exchange position of the central bank. Under fixed exchange rates, as we have seen above, the monetary base and hence the money supply are endogenous. Money demand determines the supply of money because support of the exchange rate involves buying or selling of domestic high-powered money for foreign exchange.

The central bank's credit policy determines whether the money growth is generated via payments surpluses or domestic credit creation. A program of balance of payments adjustment can therefore be organized by turning these relations around, targeting credit growth so as to secure a desired balance of payments result.

To simplify we focus on an economy with high-powered money only. Then the money stock is equal to foreign exchange reserves plus domestic credit on the sources side. But the balance of payments is equal to the change in foreign exchange reserves. Thus, targeting domestic credit, taking into account expected growth in money demand, implies targeting the balance of payments. We can formulate this as in (11) where we use the central bank balance sheet identity to write the change in foreign exchange reserves as equal to the change in money less the change in domestic credit.

$$\dot{R} = \dot{M} - \dot{C} . \tag{11}$$

This identity provides the framework for the discussion of targets on domestic credit as a means of controlling the balance of payments. Assuming equality of money demand and supply and a given path of nominal money demand, the tighter the limit on domestic credit creation the larger the increase in money that is generated by monetization of the payments surplus. Thus, targeting domestic credit means targeting the balance of payments. The lack of full wage–price flexibility does not impair the effectiveness of credit ceilings as a corset for the balance of payments. But it does imply, of course, that tight credit improves the trade balance in part by a decline in activity.

---

[4]For recent discussions see Khan et al. (1986) and Robichek (1986) and especially International Monetary Fund (1987).

2.2.2. Devaluation

A second implication of the monetary approach model is that devaluation under conditions of full wage–price flexibility will not have any *persistent* real effects. The reason is that devaluation achieves real effects only to the extent that it brings about a reduction in the real value of money. A reduction of real balances in turn reduces real spending relative to output and thus generates a trade surplus. But if, via the balance of payments, money is endogenous then there will not be persistent effects.

There is also the question of whether devaluation will in any way improve the trade balance, even if only transitorily.[5] It is readily shown that if goods are gross substitutes, devaluation must increase the price of all traded goods. Hence, it must raise nominal income relative to unchanged spending so that the trade balance is improved. This conclusion, in one form of another, emerges from the research of Kemp (1962), Hahn (1962) and Negishi (1965).

In the short run a depreciation raises the prices of traded goods in home currency, thus reducing real balances and hence real spending. But overall the resulting improvement in the trade balance leads to an increase in money and an increase in nominal spending. The process continues until the nominal money stock will have risen in the same proportion as the exchange rate. At that point home and traded goods prices will have increased in the same proportion, relative prices and real balances having returned to their pre-devaluation levels. With full wage–price flexibility devaluation is thus at best a policy to improve the central bank's reserve position.

It is immediately apparent that if a monetary expansion accompanies depreciation the real effects are immediately denied. Devaluation works, in this monetary model, only because it is equivalent to a tight monetary policy.

3. Capital flows, sticky prices and the monetary mechanism

We now turn from classical monetary economics, which emphasizes the determination of prices and the balance of payments under conditions of full employment, to a more macroeconomic framework where there is scope for policy. Since the early nineteenth century, if not much earlier, international capital flows were already thought an integral and even dominant part of the international monetary mechanism. Discount rate policy was not only seen as a means of protecting the Bank reserve against internal currency drain, but was particularly used to attract international capital flows and thus defend the

---

[5]In terms of the model set out above we can write world spending in home currency as $V(M + eM^*)$, where e is the exchange rate. Hence, depreciation, given nominal money supplies in each country, will raise world spending measured in home currency.

reserve. The role of international capital flows during the recurrent crises of the gold standard is well documented [see Morgenstern (1959) and Bloomfield (1959)].

The analysis of monetary policy does change significantly when we depart from the classical assumption of wage–price flexibility. The combination of capital mobility and wage–price stickiness modifies the operation of monetary policy dramatically from both classical analysis and from closed economy IS–LM models. We show how international capital mobility affects the monetary mechanism, limiting under fixed exchange rates the scope for independent monetary policy even in the short run. Under flexible exchange rates, by contrast, monetary policy is seen to be highly effective. This analysis originates with Mundell (1968) and Fleming (1962) whose discussion of the monetary mechanism remain essentially unaltered in present-day policy analysis.

Several extensions of the basic structure are entertained to highlight that they do not eliminate the basic effect, namely that under flexible exchange rates the money stock is exogenous and, hence, if prices are sticky in the short run the economy adjusts to the change in real balances. This is quite the opposite of the fixed exchange rate case where money adjusts to the economy.

3.1. The Mundell–Fleming model

The functioning of the monetary mechanism under conditions of international capital mobility has, until recently, focused on open economy extensions of the IS–LM model. The basic structure, especially in the fixed prices–flexible exchange rates version, is known as the Mundell–Fleming model. Of course, it has as its precursor Keynes' *Treatise* and James Meade's *The Balance of Payments* (1951).

The equations of the model are given in equations (12)–(14):

$$M/P = L(i, y) \,, \tag{12}$$

$$y = A(i, y) + T(y, y^*, eP^*/P) \,, \tag{13}$$

$$i = i^* \,, \tag{14}$$

where i and i^* are the home and foreign interest rates, respectively, T denotes net exports trade balance and eP^*/P is the real exchange rate which influences net exports. Under fixed exchange rates the exchange rate is given, but the money stock is endogenous. Under flexible exchange rates the money stock is determined by the central bank since there is no commitment to sustain the exchange rate by intervention. The model refers to a small country for which the world interest rate, i^*, foreign prices and foreign income are given.

The Mundell–Fleming model assumes that international capital mobility is perfect, meaning that home and foreign bonds are perfect substitutes. Hence, interest rates will be equalized continuously by incipient international reserve flows. Mundell has pushed furthest this kind of model to argue that under fixed exchange rates and perfect capital mobility the central bank of a *small* country cannot control the rate of interest. It can only control the composition of its portfolio between domestic credit and foreign exchange reserves.

An open market purchase of securities would lead to an incipient decline in interest rates. Because home and foreign securities are perfect substitutes asset holders shift out of home securities and toward foreign securities. The central bank, in supporting the exchange rate, loses reserves and hence the money stock contracts. The process continues (instantly) until the money stock is back to its initial level, the interest rate has returned to the international level and the only effect is a reserve loss offset by an increase in central bank holdings of securities.

In a two-country setting credit expansion by one country causes an increase in income in both, but reserve losses in the country originating the credit increase. Fiscal expansion, by contrast, increases the world interest rate and raises income in the expanding country. But it may lead to a contraction abroad. The potential for a negative transmission of fiscal expansion is due to the integration of the world capital market that spreads high interest rates abroad.

Under flexible exchange rates and perfect capital mobility the transmission of disturbances is the reverse. The key fact is that now money is no longer endogenous. But interest rates will still be equated internationally and hence now output and the exchange rate must adjust to accommodate monetary and fiscal disturbances. A monetary expansion leads to exchange rate depreciation and hence brings about a gain in competitiveness that sustains an expansion in output. The gain in competitiveness also implies that there will be a contraction abroad. Hence, the central result: negative transmission of monetary expansion. Fiscal expansion, by contrast, is shared worldwide.

An especially interesting issue concerns crowding out. The Mundell–Fleming model highlights that crowding out in response to fiscal expansion occurs not primarily via increased interest rates but also via deterioration in the external balance. Foreign lending finances part of the increased deficit or foreign resource transfers support the expansion in demand.

3.2. Price adjustment and expectations

An obvious extension of the Mundell–Fleming model allows for gradual price adjustment and expectations in asset markets. The introduction of dynamics and rational expectations in the Keynesian model is due to Dornbusch (1976).

The price level is assumed to adjust to excess demand: its rate of change is positive when demand exceeds output. Aggregate demand for domestic output is a function of the interest rate, output, fiscal policy and the real exchange rate. The equilibrium dynamics of the exchange rate are dictated by the requirement that domestic and foreign assets have the same rate of return. Equilibrium implies that the domestic-currency return on foreign assets be equal to that on domestic assets. Thus, the (forward-looking) rate of change in the exchange rate equals the differential between domestic and foreign interest rate:

$$i = i^* + \lambda , \tag{15}$$

where λ denotes the anticipated rate of depreciation. Under perfect foresight this will be equal to the actual rate of depreciation. The model is closed with a price adjustment whereby prices rise when the demand-determined level of output exceeds the full employment level, y_0. Let π denote the rate of inflation:

$$\pi = h(M/P, eP^*/P, y_0) . \tag{16}$$

An essential feature of this extended model is that the exchange rate is fully flexible, whereas prices can move only gradually.

The model predicts that a once-and-for-all increase in the money stock provokes immediately a nominal and real exchange rate depreciation. In the long run, after full price adjustment has occurred, prices, money and the exchange rate all increase in the same proportion. But in the short run the exchange rate overshoots the long-run equilibrium level. This occurs because the increase in the nominal and real money stock lowers the equilibrium home interest rate. The reduction in interest rates relative to those prevailing abroad is consistent with asset market equilibrium only if there is an offsetting expectation of appreciation. But for asset holders to expect appreciation the exchange rate must overshoot its new long-run level. Only if the exchange rate instantly overdepreciates can it be expected to subsequently appreciate.

The depreciation of the nominal and real exchange rates resulting from a monetary expansion, and the decline in home interest rates, lead to an increase in demand and output. The output expansion introduces an inflationary process which lasts until the initial real equilibrium is restored. In the manner of the Mundell–Fleming model this formulation highlights the impact of changes in nominal money on the real exchange rate, output and employment. But by adding expectations and long-run price flexibility the analysis brings out that monetary effects are transitory. Once again, though, the closed economy analysis of money is modified by showing that changes in the real exchange rate and in net exports are the central open economy channel of the monetary mechanism.

The formulation highlights the discrepancy between instant adjustment in interest rates and the exchange rate and the gradual adjustment in goods markets. But the discrepancy is bridged by forward-looking asset holders whose forecasts are based on the structure of the model.

Expectations thus play an important role in individuals' decision-making. As a result, systematic government policies will eventually be endogenized by the private sector. Important extensions of this approach by Mussa (1982a, 1982b) and Obstfeld and Rogoff (1984) confirm that the general results are sustained when some of the strict assumptions are relaxed. Wilson (1979) has enriched the analysis by drawing attention to the effects of anticipated future monetary and real disturbances. He showed that future monetary expansion brings about an immediate depreciation jump and continuing subsequent depreciation until the money increase occurs. At that time nominal and real appreciation restores the initial real equilibrium.

3.3. Portfolio substitution

The Mundell–Fleming model, and its immediate extensions, assume that domestic and foreign securities are perfect substitutes. Asset holders are indifferent between assets if the expected return, including adjustment for exchange depreciation, is equalized. A relaxation of this tight structure becomes possible if one allows for a risk premium due to portfolio diversification preferences. A risk premium will emerge if asset returns in different countries and currencies are not perfectly correlated *and* asset holders are not risk neutral. In this extension international interest rate linkages are given by equation (17):

$$i = i^* + \lambda + R ,\qquad (17)$$

where R is the risk premium.

The risk premium is commonly associated not with political risk but rather with the imperfect correlation of asset returns because of inflation and real exchange rate variability. The most obvious model of the risk premium is provided by the capital asset pricing model.[6] In this model risk averse wealth holders choose their optimal portfolio. Aggregating individuals (who have common information) and imposing market equilibrium yield an equation such

---

[6]See Kouri (1975), Kouri and Macedo (1978), Dornbusch (1983a), Frankel (1982), Krugman (1982), and Branson and Henderson (1985).

as (17) for the equilibrium real yield differential, or risk premium.[7] The determinants of the risk premium on assets denominated in a particular currency are the relative supply of outside assets denominated in a particular currency relative to the minimum variance portfolio. An increase in the relative supply of outside assets denominated in a particular currency reduces the desirable degree of diversification of the world portfolio. A compensating increase in the relative yield (or risk premium) is required to induce market participants to absorb these securities into their portfolio. Note that in this formulation the risk premium is associated with the relative *stock* supplies of *outside* assets. The current account plays no role.

Distribution effects will typically enter the determination of the premium. To the extent that consumption baskets differ between countries, the optimal (consumption-based) portfolio composition will differ. In that case the distribution of wealth which influences relative demands for the available assets will appear also as a determinant of the risk premium. The relatively wealthier country can now afford to have a relatively larger stock of its assets outstanding without affecting the risk premium since relative demand for these assets will be higher.

The portfolio model brings with it the possibility that asset returns adjusted for depreciation can differ internationally and that the differential itself can change as a result of changes in relative asset supplies. Let B and B^* be the outside asset supplies in home and foreign currencies. Then $B/(eB^* + B)$ represents the relative supply of domestic assets which, for a given stochastic structure of returns, determines the risk premium. An exchange depreciation reduces the relative supply of home assets in the world portfolio and, as a result, reduces the required risk premium. Hence, an exchange depreciation, other things equal, makes room for a lower home interest rate. Consider now the implications of the risk premium model, leaving aside for simplicity expectations and dynamics issues so that expected depreciation, δ, is assumed zero. Let output be demand determined in IS–LM fashion and domestic prices be given. Figure 23.2 shows the CC schedule along which capital market equilibrium prevails. Capital market equilibrium implies a combination of output levels, interest rates and the exchange rate such that the public willingly holds the existing stocks of domestic money and bonds, given the world interest rate. We summarize that condition in (18):

$$i(M/P, y) = i^* + R(B/(eB^* + B)) . \tag{18}$$

Exchange depreciation reduces the risk premium and thus lowers interest rates

---

[7]We discuss below, in Section 6, the alternative of a consumption based asset pricing mode. The analysis is also limited by imposing partial equilibrium of asset markets rather than intertemporal general equilibrium.

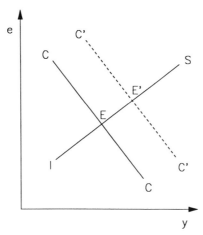

Figure 23.2. Monetary expansion, output and the exchange rate.

compatible with bond market equilibrium. The reduced interest rate creates an excess demand for money which requires, for money market equilibrium, a lower level of output.

Along IS the goods market clears. Exchange depreciation creates excess demand both by a gain in competitiveness and by the reduction in interest rates argued above. To eliminate the excess demand output must increase. Point *E* shows the determination of equilibrium output and the exchange rate, given prices, world interest rates and relative asset supplies.

An increase in the home money stock (shifting *CC* out and to the right) will lead to exchange depreciation and higher output. Fiscal expansion, by contrast, shifts IS out and to the right, raising output and appreciating the currency. The difference with the Mundell–Fleming model lies in the fact that home interest rates now can change and to that extent there is no longer full crowding out in the small country case.

An increase in the relative supply of domestic assets, say via budget deficits, increases the risk premium and hence interest rates. The new equilibrium will involve exchange depreciation and a higher level of output. The distribution of world wealth also affects the risk premium. A decline in relative domestic wealth, associated for example with a current account deficit, will reduce the demand for home outside assets and hence increase the risk premium. Again the exchange rate must depreciate. The interesting part of the prediction is the association between accumulation of domestic outside assets or a decline in relative wealth and the exchange depreciation.

We signal here two important issues taken up in more detail below. One has to do with the integration of money in the portfolio problem. Since money and short-term debt have the same stochastic return distribution, outside assets should include both public debt and high-powered money. The portfolio model only decides the allocation between assets denominated in different currencies, not the money–bond division. The latter requires a proper model of money demand to justify the holding of this return-dominated asset. In discussing the new classical economics we return to this problem.

The other question is to decide how successful this portfolio model is empirically. Frankel (1986) has argued that the effects of changes in relative asset supplies on risk premia should be quantitatively small. The reason is that the coefficient of relative asset supplies in the risk premium formula is the covariance of asset returns times the coefficient of risk aversion. The former, in all practical cases, will be the square of a small fraction. But he also offers empirical evidence suggesting that risk premia effects amount to a few basis points, not percentage points. This problem is taken up in the next subsection where we discuss empirical evidence on asset market linkages.

The stock market and the monetary mechanism

The money–bond model, even with imperfect substitution, is a very narrow structure by the standards of the real world. It is natural therefore to extend the framework to incorporate real assets in the form of capital. This has been done by Gavin (1989), Johnson (1986) and Branson, Fraga and Johnson (1985).

This analysis shows that because of the forward-looking nature of asset markets there are potentially conflicting impacts on asset values of increased output and increased interest rates. Because the stock market is forward looking, future disturbances will be immediately reflected in the value of the stock market, just as they would in long-term interest rates, and hence in wealth. The increased wealth spills over into higher spending and increased money demand. Thus, future disturbances will therefore have an immediate impact on output and on the exchange rate. Forward-looking models of exchange rates capture this effect to some extent. But this analysis shows extra channels through which future disturbances affect current spending decisions.

3.4. Evidence from econometric models

In Section 4 below we offer a more detailed analysis of the empirical evidence on price stickiness and asset market linkages. We conclude our analysis of the Mundell–Fleming model and its extensions with a brief look at the predictions of large macroeconometric models which are built around this paradigm. Frankel (1987) has reviewed the evidence from a comparison simulation of specified policy changes conducted with twelve econometric open economy macroeconomic models.[8] He asks: How do their predictions about the effects of monetary and fiscal policy compare to those of the simple Mundell–Fleming model? The finding is the following: a monetary expansion raises home output in each model while foreign output declines in eight of the models while increasing in four models. As to fiscal policy, each of the models predicts that fiscal expansion raises home output. All but two show a foreign increase in output. Thus, the majority of models confirms the Mundell–Fleming model. But where discrepancies do arise they can be explained by different treatment of capital mobility or by important effects of the exchange rate on the price level.

Table 23.1 shows the simulated effects of monetary contraction Federal Reserve Board Multi-country model. The table shows two simulations corresponding respectively to a 100 basis point increase in the U.S. T-bill rate alone and in the other case in the T-bill rate of the five main industrial countries, and of the United States. The table shows the percentage deviation of key variables from the baseline.

The simulation results are consistent with the Mundell–Fleming predictions of output contraction at home and currency appreciation. But, contrary to Mundell–Fleming, output abroad does not expand. The reason is that price effects associated with the foreign depreciation push up interest rates abroad and thus contain the expansion. In the United States the appreciation of the currency reduces the CPI. A joint monetary contraction of the industrial countries cuts output everywhere and reduces prices relative to the base line path. In the joint scenario there is some dollar appreciation.

Table 23.1
The effect of a monetary shock[a] (percentage deviation from the base line)

Years after shock:	Effect on U.S.			Effect on ROW		
	1	2	3	1	2	3
U.S. monetary shock						
GNP	−0.4	−1.0	−1.4	−0.0	−0.0	−0.0
Prices	−0.1	−0.2	−0.6	0.1	0.1	0.1
Exchange rate[b]				1.6	2.5	3.1
Joint monetary shock						
GNP	−0.4	−0.9	−1.3	−0.3	−0.6	−0.9
Prices	−0.0	−0.1	−0.4	0.0	−0.0	−0.2
Exchange rate[b]				−0.0	0.4	0.7

[a]Due to a 100 basis point increase in the T-bill rate in a model of the five main industrial countries.
[b]Units of foreign currency per dollar.
Source: Edison et al. (1986).

[8]See, too, Bryant et al. (1987) and Federal Reserve Bank of New York (1987).

Table 23.2
The effect of a fiscal shock[a] (percent deviation from baseline)

Years after shock:	Effect on the U.S.			Effect on foreign countries		
	1	2	3	1	2	3
	U.S. fiscal shock					
GNP	2.0	1.7	1.2	0.4	0.6	0.6
Prices	0.2	0.6	1.1	0.2	0.4	0.5
Exchange rate[b]				2.2	3.1	3.0
	Joint fiscal shock					
GNP	2.5	2.2	1.5	1.7	1.9	1.9
Prices	0.3	0.8	1.5	0.3	0.8	1.2
Exchange rate[b]				2.0	3.5	3.6

[a]Expansion of government purchases of 1% of GNP.
[b]Units of foreign currency per dollar.
Source: Edison et al. (1986).

Table 23.2 shows the impact of a fiscal shock equal to a 1 percent of GNP increase in government purchases. In these simulations M1 is held constant.

In line with Mundell–Fleming, fiscal expansion is positively transmitted to the rest of the world. The appreciation of the dollar likewise confirms the predictions of the simple model. Price effects are minor. An interesting finding in these simulations concerns the joint expansion. Here, too, the dollar appreciates – in fact by much the same as in the case of a U.S. expansion only. This result is explained by fact that the U.S. interest elasticity is significantly smaller than that abroad. Thus, an expansion pushes up U.S. interest rates relative to those abroad and therefore induces capital flows that bring about appreciation.

The review of the large econometric models highlights the key feature of open economy monetary economics today, namely the tight linkages of capital markets and their central role in the transmission of disturbances. The extent of transmission depends, of course, on whether governments have exchange rate targets, interest rate targets or targets for monetary aggregates. Not surprisingly, much of the policy discussion today is concerned with this issue of targeting.

We next turn to a review of the basic premise of the policy discussion. If money matters in the open economy this is so because wages and/or prices are less than fully flexible and because asset returns are linked internationally. We next review theory and evidence on these issues.

4. Empirical evidence on two key channels of transmission

The monetary mechanism in the open economy, portayed in the Mundell–Fleming model and its extensions, relies critically on two facts. First, wages and prices are sticky in the short run. If this is the case changes in the nominal money stock are changes in the real money stock which therefore lead to changes in equilibrium asset yields. Second, asset markets are linked internationally. Accordingly, nominal asset yields in one country cannot move apart from those abroad except to the extent allowed by variations in the risk premium or by anticipated movements in the exchange rate. In the Mundell–Fleming model these twin assumptions imply that changes in the quantity of money exert at least transitory effects on real interest rates, the real exchange rate, output and employment. In this section we investigate the evidence available on these two issues.

4.1. Evidence on sticky prices

Monetary shocks have different effects depending on whether or not goods prices adjust instantaneously and fully to new information, and whether goods markets clear continuously. The equilibrium models of the new classical economics leave little room for the stickiness of prices and persistent disequilibrium. Alternative approaches, by contrast, are built on these assumptions even if they have not developed a satisfactory and coherent explanation for this basic premise. Thus, one of the principal empirical questions in open economy monetary economics (just as in the closed economy, if there were such a thing) regards price dynamics.

The international evidence on price stickiness is of two types. On one side there is *indirect* evidence about the effects of changes in nominal exchange rates and changes in exchange rate regimes on relative prices of domestic and foreign goods. On the other side there are *structural* tests, based on specific models of the macro economy and of the transactions constraints faced by economic agents.[9]

4.1.1. Indirect evidence

Descriptive analysis of price and exchange rate movements represent a long and distinguished empirical tradition in open economy macroeconomics.[10] The benchmark theory is the purchasing power parity (PPP) hypothesis, according to which the same standard basket of goods trades at the same price all over

---

[9]Flood and Hodrick (1986) specify and offer some reduced-form evidence on an alternative model of price dynamics: the misperception model of Phelps (1969), Lucas (1972) and Barro (1980), which has been extended to the open economy also by Leiderman (1979), Saidi (1980), Harris and Purvis (1981), and Stockman and Koh (1986). While their vector autoregressions are less strongly supportive of the sticky-prices model than the data discussed above, they find no strong support to the misperception hypothesis, either.

[10]For a recent survey see Dornbusch (1987b, 1987c).

the world. The rationale for the PPP hypothesis is international goods arbitrage. The implicit assumption is that there are only negligible costs to international arbitrage, and therefore the same good is traded at the same price all over the world ("law of one price"). The ratio of national price levels measured in a common currency (assuming identical weights of different goods in these indices across countries) would therefore show almost no fluctuation. Certainly, fluctuations should not be correlated with movements in nominal exchange rates. Let R denote the ratio of U.S. to U.K. prices and E the exchange rate measured as dollars per pound:

$$R = P^{US}/EP^{UK} .$$ (19)

PPP theory in the strict form maintains that the ratio in (19) would be unity or, if transport costs are allowed, a constant. In a weaker form the theory makes concessions to various obstacles to trade. In practice, we expect transactions costs to play an essential role. Transactions costs make some goods only imperfectly arbitraged, and justify the presence of non-traded goods. The weak version of PPP would therefore hold that whatever the level of the relative price ratio, it should not exhibit significant and certainly not persistent fluctuations. Divergent inflation trends should be offset by movements in the exchange rate. Thus, the weak form of PPP implies a relation as in equation (19a):

$$\pi^{US} - \pi^{UK} - \lambda = 0 ,$$ (19a)

where π^{US} and π^{UK} denote rates of inflation and λ is the rate of depreciation of the nominal exchange rate. In reality, however, relative price levels measured in a common currency have fluctuated sharply and persistently, as we will see below.

The explanation for fluctuating real exchange rates (apart from the question of weights in the price index) must rely on product diversification combined with spatial discrimination or on non-traded goods. Transactions costs that prevent spatial arbitrage are an essential element in making these fluctuations possible. The fact that these ratios have fluctuated in response to *nominal* exchange rate changes can be interpreted as reflecting stickiness in wages or prices.

Deviations from PPP, i.e. fluctuations of real exchange rates, have been widely documented empirically.[11] This evidence, however, has little bearing on the question of whether goods prices are sticky per se. The ratio of national GNP deflators measured in a common currency, unlike in the case of consumer

[11]Tests of PPP are offered by Frenkel (1981), Krugman (1978), Hakkio (1984) and Davutyan and Pippenger (1985), among others.

price indices, can be expected to fluctuate. The reason is simply that different countries produce different baskets of goods so that fluctuations in the relative price level reflect changes in the relative price of different goods. Furthermore, fluctuations in the relative price of non-traded goods imply deviations from PPP, and need not be caused by nominal disturbances. Samuelson and Balassa have developed a theory of trend deviations from the law of one price based on differentials in productivity growth in the traded and non-traded goods sectors.[12] Furthermore, fluctuations of the real exchange rate might reflect the fluctuations of relative prices of traded goods, due to cost or demand disturbances. But even so there are limitations on the extent of fluctuations, especially among industrialized countries that have a great similarity in their production structure.

Evidence that is relevant for the question of price stickiness can be found, however, in the comparisons of patterns of deviations from PPP across different exchange rate regimes. The common result is that deviations are larger and more persistent during the flexible exchange rates period. Genberg (1978) measures the average absolute deviations of real effective exchange rates (defined as the ratio of the domestic price level relative to an aggregate rest-of-the-world price level expressed in terms of the same currency) from a constant time trend. Using data on industrialized countries, he finds that the magnitude of deviations from PPP increases steadily in the following three intervals: 1957–66 (very infrequent nominal exchange rates realignments); 1957–72 (includes the adjustable-peg period); and 1957–76 (includes flexible exchange rates period). Relatively poor performance by the standard of PPP for the 1970s is also reported by Frenkel (1981), who finds that deviations from PPP display a very high degree of persistence.

Mussa (1986) offers a comprehensive discussion, analyzing in detail the experience of several countries including Canada. The Canadian case is of special relevance since the country had a flexible exchange rate during 1950–62 while other countries were still on fixed rates, and floating again after 1970. Mussa offers convincing evidence that the different behavior of the real exchange rate has for the most part to be ascribed to the exchange rate regime, and not to the fact that the flexible exchange rates period is characterized by important real shocks, like the oil shocks of 1974 and 1979. The importance of his results is clearly apparent: if the stochastic properties of real shocks are not different across the two regimes, the different behavior of real exchange rates is only consistent with stickiness in the aggregate price levels. Mussa's findings

---

[12]The Samuelson–Balassa theory argues that productivity growth in the traded goods sector (manufacturing) is higher than in the non-traded goods sector (services). Productivity growth in the tradable goods sector translates into wage increases and that implies rising costs and prices of non-traded goods because in that sector productivity growth is small. As a result a country with rapid productivity growth will tend to experience trend real appreciation. This is, of course, strikingly the case for Japan.

are illustrated in Figures 23.3(a)–(d), which reproduce and update those reported by Cumby and Obstfeld (1984). The figures show monthly percentage changes in the real exchange rate of the United States relative to a number of industrial countries. The case of Canada highlights especially the absence of "nominal exchange regime neutrality" stressed by Mussa.

A more formal statistical analysis of the variability of the real exchange rate across exchange rate regimes is performed by Stockman (1983), who studies the annual volatility of the real exchange rate of 38 countries vis-à-vis the United States, in the 1957–79 period, using a fixed-effects model. The statistical model allows "country" effects and "year" effects to be controlled for: thus the higher variability of worldwide real shocks in the 1970s is controlled for. The results indicate that the regime of flexible rates is positively and highly significantly correlated with the volatility of the real exchange rates of the countries in the sample.[13]

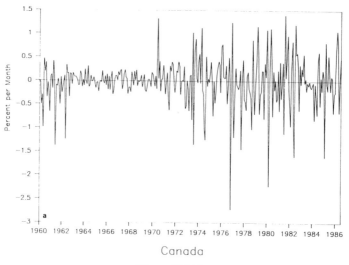

Canada

Figure 23.3(a)

[13]Stockman (1987a, 1987b) is reluctant to interpret these results as conclusive support of nominal stickiness models, but recognizes the importance and the potential uses of this empirical evidence to discriminate between equilibrium and sticky price models. See Baxter and Stockman (1989) for a further description of the statistical properties of macroeconomic variables under fixed and flexible exchange rate regimes. Stockman (1987a) explores the possibility that expectations about future capital controls and trade restrictions, through intertemporal substitution, have a stabilizing effect on relative prices under fixed exchange rates.

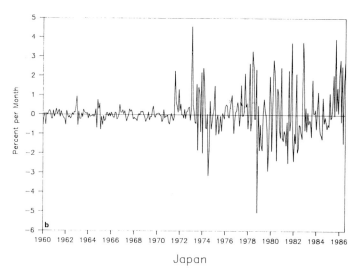

Japan

Figure 23.3(b)

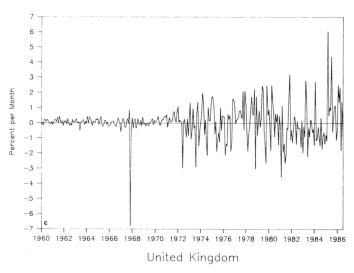

United Kingdom

Figure 23.3(c)

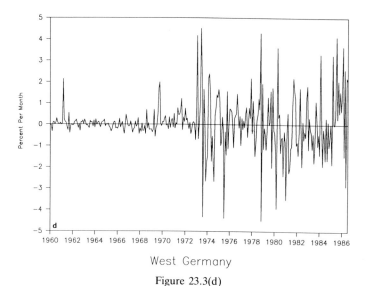

West Germany

Figure 23.3(d)

4.1.2. Direct evidence

Meese (1984) tests whether prices are predetermined in exchange rate models by estimating the covariance between innovations in an exchange rate equation and in a reduced-form price equation, which includes on the right-hand side lagged prices and lagged exchange rates. He used both a simple random walk model for the exchange rate, and a semi-reduced-form equation which assumes the exchange rate is determined by relative money supplies, relative output levels, and relative short-term and long-term interest rates. The hypothesis that innovations in the exchange rate are contemporaneously uncorrelated with innovations in the price level cannot be rejected for the dollar–yen, dollar–pound, and dollar–DM exchange rate models.

Meese's results, however, are limited by the maintained hypothesis that variables affecting the exchange rate contemporaneously do not affect the price level. While this hypothesis is consistent with backward-looking price-setting models, a number of models allow prices also to reflect current information. This is the case of overlapping wage–price setting, as for example in Phelps (1978) or Taylor (1980). We provide an illustration by using a discrete time version of the model of Calvo (1983).

Let P_t^n denote the index of *new* prices set every period to remain unchanged for a number of periods ahead. Expectations of demand and cost conditions in the future are incorporated in these new prices. Specifically, each item in P_t^n is a function of expectations of variables affecting costs and demand for the period during which the price remains preset. Let the proportion of prices that remains unchanged for at least i periods be $(1 - \gamma)\gamma^i$. This model gives rise to an expression for the aggregate price level as follows:

$$P_t = \gamma P_{t-1} + (1 - \gamma)P_t^n . \tag{20}$$

The aggregate price level is thus a linear combination of the lagged aggregate price level and the forward-looking new prices. Notice that in the case where prices are perfectly flexible ($\gamma = 0$) the whole of the aggregate price index is reset each period.

Under the assumptions of the model, a test that $\gamma = 0$ in equations (20) is a test that prices are perfectly flexible. Backus (1984) performs such a test using a Mundell–Fleming model with rational expectations and staggered wage setting applied to quarterly Canadian data from 1971 to 1982. His estimates of γ from the two equations are not significantly different, and imply a median wage–contract length of 5.4 quarters. The null hypothesis that $\gamma = 0$ is soundly rejected. Giovannini (1988a), using disaggregated data on Japanese domestic and export prices, also finds evidence of price staggering that is consistent with the model above.

The review of empirical work that seeks to establish wage–price stickiness in an open economy context indicates highly promising directions of research. There is certainly no indication here that the stickiness hypothesis is prima facie implausible.[14] On the contrary, the dramatic effects of nominal exchange rate movements on relative prices presses the conclusion that stickiness (for whatever reason) is an important part of the explanation. For the effectiveness of monetary policy there is accordingly support for the central pillar.

We next turn to the evidence on asset market linkages.

4.2. International capital mobility

International linkages among asset markets provided the second important consideration in judging the effectiveness and the channels of operation of monetary policy. Under fixed exchange rates tight linkages to the world capital market reduce a country's ability to move its interest rates significantly apart from the world level. Under flexible exchange rates (and stickiness) tight linkages to the world capital market imply major and almost instant effects on relative prices. The operation of monetary policy is thus dramatically affected by these open economy features. Indeed, the channels of operation are entirely different from what would be predicted in the closed economy. In this subsection we therefore review the empirical work on international capital mobility.

---

[14] See Giovannini (1988b) for macroeconomic evidence on price stickiness.

We address the issue of international capital mobility by reporting on three different approaches followed in empirical research. The first is represented by the estimates of the *offset coefficient*, which measures the extent to which domestic credit changes are neutralized (under fixed exchange rates) by international capital flows. The second approach attempts to explain the cross-country and cross-currency patterns of rates of return. These return relationships are interpreted in terms of a world capital market equilibrium, thus implicitly assuming perfect international integration and perfect international capital mobility. The third approach takes a much narrower view by identifying the arbitrage transactions that would link a country's capital markets with the rest of the world. This approach seeks to verify whether such transactions can be carried out, and whether available profit opportunities are exploited.[15]

In the conclusion of this subsection we will discuss the implication of the evidence on international capital mobility for the question of the effectiveness of foreign exchange market intervention.

Any practical discussion of international asset market integration must separate two concepts: one is international asset substitutability and the other is capital mobility. The former has to do with the response of desired portfolio composition to return differentials. In the limit, perfect substitution would imply that at depreciation adjusted yield differentials agents are indifferent between the securities of one country and another. Capital mobility has to do with the ability and fact of actually achieving the preferred portfolio composition. Informational obstacles, transactions costs and legal restrictions, specifically in the form of capital controls, limit the extent to which capital is mobile or the speed with which capital moves in response to changes in yield differentials. As a benchmark case, the Mundell–Fleming model assumes perfect capital mobility and perfect asset substitutability. In practice, it is difficult or even impossible to separately test these two aspects of international asset market integration.

4.2.1. The offset coefficient

Empirical work on the offset of domestic money innovations uses mostly data from the Bretton Woods period.[16] Most studies show that the short-term capital

---

[15]Feldstein and Horioka (1980) argue that correlations between savings and investment across countries test the international capital mobility hypothesis. Their approach has been criticized by several authors, see in particular Murphy (1984) and Obstfeld (1986b) who show that various patterns of correlations can be obtained in a world of perfect capital mobility, depending on the nature of the exogenous shocks.

[16]An exception is Cumby and Obstfeld (1984) who find that in the period from 1971 to 1979 monetary authorities retained substantial monetary independence in the short run, with the offset coefficient ranging from 0.3 to 0.5. See, too, Federal Reserve Bank of New York (1987).

account offset to monetary innovations is relatively small, suggesting that monetary policy is not as strongly constrained by international capital mobility in the short run.

This evidence is consistent both with low international capital mobility and with low substitutability between domestic and foreign assets. Kouri and Porter's (1974) estimates of the offset coefficient for Australia, Italy, and the Netherlands, which are biased towards 1 in the presence of systematic sterilization, range from 0.43 to 0.59. Herring and Marston's (1977) and Obstfeld's (1980) estimates for West Germany, which explicitly account for systematic sterilization of reserve flows, imply values of the offset coefficient as small as 0.1.

While the specification of several of the equations used for estimating the offset coefficient is questionable, the size of the empirical estimates is surprisingly small.[17] These results raise the question of the role of imperfect substitutability, which we take up next.

4.2.2. The risk premium

The presence of predictable rates of return differentials between assets denominated in different currencies is, in principle, consistent both with less than perfect international capital mobility, and with perfect capital mobility. Explaining observed rate-of-return differentials in terms of equilibrium capital asset pricing models would provide strong support to the perfect capital mobility hypothesis.

The typical test of the presence of predictable rates of return differentials relies on the following equation:

$$s_{t+1} - s_t = a + b(f_t - s_t) + u_t, \tag{21}$$

where s_t and f_t are the logs of the spot and the one-period forward rate, respectively. The null hypothesis to be tested in (21) is that $a = 0$ and $b = 1$. Note that forecast errors, u_t, are orthogonal to information available at the beginning of the period. Thus, the null is tested jointly with the rational expectations hypothesis.

Under the null hypothesis, equation (21) implies that the forward rate is an unbiased predictor of the future spot rate, or, alternatively, that there are no expected returns on uncovered forward foreign exchange contracts. In the

---

[17]The main difficulty is the assumption, with little theoretical justification, of partial adjustment dynamics (and with very small estimates of the partial adjustment parameters). Also, it is often implicitly assumed that a country's net external liabilities are determined by portfolio substitution on assets denominated in domestic and foreign currency (whereas a country's net liabilities could all be denominated in one currency).

absence of transactions costs, $f_t - s_t = i_t - i_t^*$, where i_t and i_t^* are the logs of one plus the domestic and the foreign interest rate, respectively. Therefore the null hypothesis is equivalent to the hypothesis that there are zero excess returns on foreign currency deposits relative to domestic currency deposits, i.e. that $i_t^* + E(s_{t+1} - s_t) = i_t$.

Rejections of the null hypothesis in (21) are reported by Hansen and Hodrick (1980), Frankel (1982), and Cumby and Obstfeld (1981). These tests are performed allowing for non-zero correlations of forecast errors across currencies, sampling periods shorter than the forward contract maturity, and heteroskedasticity in exchange-rate surprises. Cumby (1988) and Engel (1984) show that the rejection of the zero risk premium hypothesis is not due to the measurement of excess rates of return in nominal terms rather than in real terms.

The assumption of rational expectations also allows us to recover information about the stochastic properties of the risk premium, defined, as above, as the expected return differential between assets denominated in different currencies. The important results are that the risk premium is autocorrelated [see Cumby and Obstfeld (1981)], and correlated with interest rate differentials.[18] Fama (1984) shows that the risk premium displays a volatility that is at least as large as that of the forward premium. Frankel and Froot (1987, 1989), however, using survey evidence, question the validity of the rational expectations assumption.

The relevant empirical issue for the question of international capital mobility is what gives rise to these risk premia. Engel and Rodrigues (1987) and Giovannini and Jorion (1989) test the Sharpe–Lintner–Mossin capital asset pricing model, that is used to explain international rate-of-return differentials. According to that model, equilibrium return differentials are determined by the supply of outside assets denominated in different currencies.[19] The model has been statistically rejected by Engel and Rodrigues and by Giovannini and Jorion (1989). In particular, the model delivers implausible and insignificant estimates of the coefficient of relative risk aversion, and cannot explain the large measured variations in risk premia, either in terms of the volatility of asset supplies or in terms of the volatility of the conditional covariance matrix of returns.

An alternative explanation of the risk premium is provided by the intertemporal general equilibrium asset pricing model of Lucas (1978) and Grossman and Shiller (1981), which has been studied in the context of a two-country world by Lucas (1982). Risk premia for individual assets now arise not from the covariance of an asset with the portfolio, as in the CAPM, but rather from the underlying problem of maximizing the utility derived from consumption

---

[18]See Hansen and Hodrick (1983), Hodrick and Srivastava (1984), and Fama (1984).
[19]See Kouri (1975) and Dornbusch (1983a).

over time. Accordingly, risk premia are generated by the covariance individual assets' returns with the marginal utility of future consumption. Assets whose returns are more highly correlated with the marginal utility of future consumption command a lower expected return.

The return relations generated by the consumption-based asset pricing model are difficult to test since the marginal rate of substitution between present and future consumption is not directly observable. Hansen, Richard and Singleton (1981), however, show that these portfolio equilibrium conditions imply a special relationship among asset returns: the expected excess return of every asset relative to the nominal risk-free rate of interest is proportional to the expected excess rate of return of a benchmark portfolio over the nominal risk-free rate. The return on the benchmark portfolio is perfectly conditionally correlated with the intertemporal rate of substitution in consumption.

This condition has been estimated and tested by Hansen and Hodrick (1983) using data on dollar returns on Eurodeposits denominated in five major currencies, and assuming a linear projection equation for the unobserved benchmark portfolio risk premium. They are unable to reject the cross-asset proportionality constraints implied by the theory. Hodrick and Srivastava (1984) do, however, reject the model using the same currencies over a larger sample period.

The lack of empirical success of the portfolio models points to what is their most questionable feature. The models, just as the CAPM, assume a "representative agent" and in this way allow a perfect aggregation of individual countries' consumption baskets and asset portfolios. Only under this assumption does a unique world benchmark portfolio exist in either the static or dynamic CAPM. However, as Lucas (1982) noted, there is abundant evidence against the representative agent assumption: consumption baskets differ because of the presence of non-traded goods and portfolios differ greatly across countries. A pattern of national habitat is documented by Stulz (1983) who shows that residents of a country have a tendency to hold a relatively large share of national assets in their portfolio. This suggests that informational failures, transactions costs, and international capital controls are an important part of the world asset market equilibrium. We discuss transactions costs and capital controls in the next subsection.

4.2.3. Capital mobility and international arbitrage

The models surveyed above are typically estimated using data on Euromarket interest rates. These are rates paid on deposits and loans denominated in different currencies that are traded in countries other than those of their currency of denomination. The largest Eurodeposit market is in London. Thus, the empirical performance of the various portfolio models is more informative about the behavior of investors in the London Euromarket than about the phenomenon of capital flows across countries.

Information about cross-country flows can be obtained studying the arbitrage opportunities between domestic and "Euro" markets faced by investors.[20] Consider U.S. domestic certificates of deposit and Eurodollar deposits, for example. Both assets are issued by commercial banks and have very similar payoffs and risk characteristics. The chief difference between them is the location. It is possible, then, for a commercial bank to borrow in one market and lend in another. For that reason, with perfect international capital mobility the interest rate on dollar CDs should equal that on Eurodollar deposits, plus or minus transactions costs on an arbitrage operation.[21]

The evidence on return differentials is clear cut: when there are no outright restrictions on capital movements (as, for example, in the United States, the United Kingdom, or Canada) return differentials between onshore and offshore deposits can be fully accounted for by differential reserve requirements and other taxes. Kreicher (1982) has show that these data tend to confirm the hypothesis that there are no unexploited arbitrage opportunities, thus implying perfect international capital mobility.

But when there are restrictions on capital flows, as for example in the case of Italy or of France, return differentials between onshore and offshore deposits do arise. Moreover, on occasions where there are expectations of major exchange rate changes, and hence capital controls are tested as to their effectiveness in keeping residents locked into national-denominated assets, return differentials become strikingly large. This has been demonstrated in Giavazzi and Giovannini (1986) who draw attention to the implications of prospective realignments in the European Monetary System (EMS) for differentials. They show that the difference between the domestic and the offshore rate reaches 60 percent per annum during periods of particular pressure on the French franc. Thus, while asset substitutability would make for large portfolio shifts in response to return differentials, the data suggest that capital controls crucially affect international capital flows, and that they can substantially segment off the domestic capital market. This evidence runs counter to the popular view that capital controls can be easily bypassed and hence are always ineffective.

Frankel and MacArthur (1988) have attempted to measure capital mobility by separating out two factors: the political risk premium and the currency risk premium. They use national interest differentials in order to assess the extent

---

[20]See Jorion and Schwartz (1986) for evidence on the law of one price on stocks quoted in the U.S. and Canadian exchanges: their results also support the perfect capital mobility hypothesis.

[21]The transactions costs that are relevant in this case are the FDIC insurance premium, and the U.S. reserve requirement. Transactions costs differ depending on the institution involved in the arbitrage.

to which capital is mobile across national borders. Their decomposition is of

$$r - r^* = (i - i^* - fd) + (fd - \pi + \pi^*), \tag{22}$$

where $r - r^*$ denotes the real interest differential, f is the forward premium, and d denotes the expected rate of depreciation. The term $\pi - \pi^*$ denotes the inflation differential. In this decomposition the first bracket measures political risk; interest differentials in excess of the forward discount represent excess profits in a pure arbitrage situation. They arise from actual or prospective capital controls. The second bracket represents currency risk. They call it the real forward discount and it is equal to the differential between the forward premium and the inflation differential. Table 23.3 shows sample means for various countries relative to the Eurodollar U.S. rate.

Frankel and MacArthur conclude that among industrial countries the political risk (column 2) predominates even in those instances where there are important real interest differentials. The real interest differentials for these countries arises primarily from currency risk. Thus, they conclude (tentatively) that imperfections in the market for goods, in the sense of departures from strict PPP, rather than inefficiency in the market for financial assets predominate as sources of real interest differentials across countries. Table 23.3 also shows the large differential for countries like Mexico or Greece that are poorly integrated with the world capital market.

4.2.4. Effectiveness of foreign exchange market intervention

The central question about foreign exchange market intervention is whether it can work (other than in the very short term) if it does not involve a change in the money supply. The point is clarified by the distinction between *sterilized* and *unsterilized* intervention. When the monetary authorities intervene in the

Table 23.3
The Frankel–MacArthur decomposition of the risk premium: 1982–86 (sample mean, percentage points differential relative to U.S.)

	$r - r^*$	$(i - i^* - fd)$	$(fd - \pi + \pi^*)$
Canada	−0.27	−0.05	−0.23
U.K.	−0.26	−0.13	−0.15
Switzerland	−3.31	0.46	−3.80
Hong Kong	−2.77	0.11	−2.88
Greece	−9.51	−9.68	0.32
Mexico	−12.38	−16.80	4.10

Source: Frankel and MacArthur (1988).

foreign exchange market, for example by buying foreign exchange, they do so by creating in exchange high powered money. Sterilized intervention takes place when an offsetting open market operation is used to restore high powered money to its initial level; in which case the purchase of foreign exchange has been financed by a sale of domestic debt. Unsterilized intervention, by contrast, means that the domestic money supply has changed.[22] The distinction makes apparent that sterilized operations (if effective) would afford the monetary authority to independently pursue foreign exchange and money stock targets. Unsterilized intervention, however, might jeopardize the achievement of given monetary targets.

There is no disagreement, either theoretical or empirical, that non-sterilized foreign exchange intervention significantly affects the exchange rate. A non-sterilized foreign exchange operation amounts to a change in the domestic supply of money, and all models predict that changes in the stock of money affect the nominal exchange rate, both in the short run and in the steady state. The effectiveness of non-sterilized intervention is clearly evident in the empirical exchange rate models[23] and in the literature on the effects of monetary announcements on financial variables.[24] There is, however, no uniform prediction among theoretical models on the effects of sterilized foreign exchange market operations. If assets denominated in different currencies are perfect substitutes, sterilized intervention which changes their relative supplies should have no effect on portfolio equilibrium and hence on interest rates and on the exchange rate. Similarly, even if domestic and foreign assets were imperfect substitutes, changes in the relative supplies of inside assets denominated in different currencies can be ineffective.

The findings that risk premia exist and display significant variation does not imply that sterilized central bank intervention can affect the exchange rate per se. The effectiveness of open market operations is also determined by the extent to which the public internalizes the government budget constraint. Relevant factors are the length of private agents' horizons, the presence of liquidity or bequest constraints, and the difference between the discount rates used by the government and the public.[25]

Since existing empirical capital asset pricing models appear to be mis-specified, the only set of tests that might shed light on the question of sterilized intervention are reduced-form tests, or tests where the hypothesis of sub-

---

[22]The most recent survey of foreign exchange market operations by central banks is in Working Group on Exchange Market Intervention (1983), also called the Jurgensen Report.
[23]Among these, see in particular Driskill and Sheffrin (1981) and Frenkel (1981).
[24]See, for example, Edwards (1982) and Hardouvelis (1984).
[25]See Mundell (1960), Barro (1974), Stockman (1979) and Obstfeld (1982) for analyses of the effectiveness of open market operations when the public internalizes the government budget constraint.

stitutability is not embedded in a capital asset pricing model. Obstfeld (1983) and Rogoff (1984) provide two such examples. Obstfeld estimates a small aggregative model for Germany, with a reduced-form portfolio balance equation describing asset market equilibrium.[26] His simulations clearly suggest that sterilized intervention, unlike monetary intervention, has a negligible impact on the exchange rate. Rogoff attempts to explain the variation of ex ante risk premia in the foreign exchange market by the fluctuations of relative asset supplies in different currencies. He finds that asset supplies have no incremental explanatory power over a time trend in an equation explaining the rate of return differential between Canadian and U.S. assets.

In summary, despite the results on the offset coefficient, recent empirical analyses suggest that sterilized foreign exchange market intervention is very unlikely to affect the excange rate significantly. The reasons why sterilized intervention is ineffective remain open, however.[27] The evidence notwithstanding, governments do practice intervention. But it is increasingly clear that intervention is primarily used to smooth short-run fluctuations and reduce the abruptness with which misalignments are unravelled. The ability to perform this smoothing is itself becoming a research problem. If speculators know that ultimately an exchange rate will come down, how can the central bank slow down the descent? The answer might lie in the fact that speculation is shortsighted, but for the time being there is neither theory nor empirical evidence in support of such a hypothesis.

4.2.5. Concluding remarks

In summary we note from the empirical evidence reviewed in this section that two key ingredients for the operation of monetary policy in the open economy, along the lines of the Mundell–Fleming model, are broadly supported. There is evidence in support of price stickiness and there is evidence to support the view that there is significant substitutability between assets and capital mobility, except when limited by capital controls. These findings suggest that money supply changes will exert broadly the effects predicted by models of the extended Mundell–Fleming variety. And this leads to the next set of issues: given these facts about the way monetary policy operates, should its power be tamed by exchange-rate-oriented monetary policy or should it be enhanced by capital controls? These extremes have been suggested respectively by McKinnon (1988) and Tobin (1982). We now turn to this policy question.

---

[26]Obstfeld's assumption is that imperfect substitutability arises from political risk.
[27]An additional interesting question has to do with the reconciliation of the estimates of the offset coefficient with the current evidence on sterilized intervention.

5. Exchange rate regimes and policy coordination

The experience with flexible exchange rates since the early 1970s has been characterized both by a higher volatility and sustained misalignments of real exchange rates. The protracted dollar appreciation from 1980 to 1985, and the subsequent decline (shown in Figure 23.4), are commonly cited as the most striking example of misalignment to be associated with the current exchange rate regime.[28]

The volatility and possible misalignments of major exchange rates have further enhanced the popular appeal of proposals to limit exchange rate flexibility. Proponents of international monetary reforms often cite the lack of rules that characterize the present regime among the United States and the other industrialized countries as the central flaw of the current system. In particular, the IMF articles of agreement, sanctioning the principle of "exchange rate surveillance", according to which the IMF should monitor policies of individual countries that lead to excessively wide exchange rate fluctuations, have never been applied.

In this section we review four broad issues. The first is the general discussion about the relative merits of fixed versus flexible exchange rates. The second deals with proposals for exchange-rate-oriented monetary policy. The third topic is the growing literature on the gains from policy coordination. We

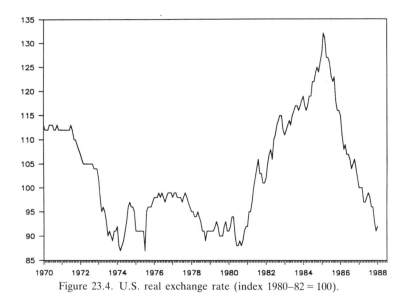

Figure 23.4. U.S. real exchange rate (index 1980–82 = 100).

[28]See, for example, Krugman (1985).

conclude by noting Tobin's recommendation to "throw some sand into the system" of international capital markets to increase the scope for national policy sovereignty.

5.1. Fixed versus flexible exchange rates

Many of the themes in assessing the merits of fixed versus flexible exchange rates go back to the Nurkse–Friedman discussion about lessons from the experience of France in the 1920s. Caves (1963) and Johnson (1973b) re-evaluate the arguments for flexible exchange rates.

The basic questions in the discussion are four: First, does the exchange rate system have a bearing on inflation performance? Second, are fixed or flexible exchange rates more conducive to discipline? Third, do fixed or flexible exchange rates provide a country more room for independent monetary policy? Fourth, do fixed or flexible rates represent a more efficient microeconomic system?

We review first the famous Nurkse–Friedman discussion on flexible exchange rates and the possibility of destabilizing speculation which centers on an evaluation of the French experience in the 1920s.

5.1.1. The French experience of the 1920s

Nurkse (1946, ch. 5), in evaluating reasons for the collapse of the French franc in the 1920s, claimed that it had been brought about by speculative capital outflows. Figure 23.5 shows an index of the French franc in the 1920s. Over the period from July 1925 to July 1926 the Franc depreciated by about 100 percent while prices had only risen 50 percent and the money stock (currency outstanding) by 23 percent. Nurkse concluded from this experience that a flexible exchange rate regime, by allowing the possibility of major exchange rate movements which would feed back to domestic prices and the budget, could exert a destabilizing influence.

> Depreciation set in again in 1921; and this time it was due increasingly to capital exports prompted by speculative anticipations of a continued fall in the exchange rate.
>
> Such anticipations are apt to bring about their own realization. Anticipatory purchases of foreign exchange tend to produce or at any rate to hasten the anticipated fall in the exchange value of the currency, and the actual fall; may set up or strengthen the expectation of a further fall. ... Exchange rates in such circumstances are bound to become highly unstable, and the influence of psychological factors may at times be overwhelming. French economists were so much impressed by this experience that they developed a

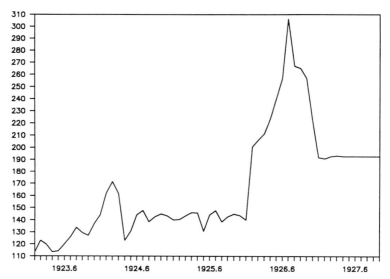

Figure 23.5. The French franc–dollar rate (index 1920–22 = 100).

special "psychological theory" of exchange fluctuations, stressing the indeterminate character of exchange rates when left to find their own level in a market swayed by speculative anticipation [Nurkse (1946, pp. 117–118)].

Friedman (1953) countered that speculators and capital flows react to macroeconomic policies and when they bring an exchange rate down it is because the prevailing policies do not support the level of the exchange rate. The issue, in Friedman's view, is not the exchange rate regime but the macroeconomic policies in place.

In retrospect it is clear that speculators were "right"; that forces were at work making for depreciation in the value of most European currencies relative to the dollar independently of speculative activity; that the speculative movements were anticipating this change; and hence, that there is at least as much reason to call them "stabilizing" as to call them "destabilizing" [Friedman (1953, p. 176)].

Friedman's view was that capital flight is the result of inappropriate policies and that these, not the exchange rate regime, were long accepted as the proper analysis. Sargent (1983b) accepts that conclusion in noting that the very symbolism of Poincare's appointment was enough to stabilize policy expectations and hence the franc.

Raymond Poincare was a fiscal conservative, who had raised taxes while Prime Minister in 1924 and was known to advocate a balanced budget and

France's return to gold. In 1926 he served as his own Finance Minister. As soon as he assumed control of the government, and even before his program was enacted by the legislature, the Franc recovered, and inflation stopped [Sargent (1983b, p. 61)].

But in light of recent theories of the interaction of government policies and public expectations it seems possible to give a more favorable reception to Nurkse's view. We now recognize that policies are not exogenous. Modern models of the interaction of the rational public and the policy-maker, for example in the mold of Barro and Gordon (1983), recognize the possibility of multiple equilibria. Clearly, if policy-makers can precommit themselves to stable policies – or are considered conservative – exchange speculation would be stabilizing. But if such a precommitment is impossible, then capital flight may well take the economy to a "bad" equilibrium. If macroeconomic policies are not strictly exogenous there is absolutely no assurance that capital flows under flexible exchange rates cannot "destabilize" a policy that is socially preferred.

We shall discuss in Section 7 reasons why the money supply may be highly responsive to exchange rate movements in a world where budget deficits are financed by money creations. The more money creation is endogenous the more nearly Nurkse's analysis correctly portrays events. That recognition has led to the question of whether exchange rate fixing can play an important role in inflation stabilization, as we shall discuss later in this chapter.

The Nurkse–Friedman debate covers the same ground as a much older discussion about the sources of inflation in the European extreme experiences of the 1920s. Two schools sought to interpret the origins of hyperinflation in the evolution of the exchange rate and the money supply. The former was called the "balance of payments school": the latter the "quantity theory school". Rist (1966), Angell (1986), and Bresciani-Turroni (1937) review the discussion. Modern analysis finds that the question is far from settled and may well favor the hypothesis that exchange rate movements can initiate a major inflation.[29]

Another way of looking at the Nurkse–Friedman debate involves the question of whether exchange speculation is guided by *long-run* fundamentals or follows a bandwagon dynamics. Friedman had dismissed the argument of bandwagon speculation by arguing that profitable speculation requires buying low and selling high. It is true that this is a recipe for success, but it has not dealt a fatal blow to the perception that financial markets may take too short a view. Focusing on capital gains can therefore affect not only the dynamics of the exchange rate, driving it away from fundamentals, but even fundamentals themselves. There is no firm evidence to support this view, but an increasing

---

[29]See Bruno et al. (1988), Dornbusch (1987a), and the discussion in Section 7 below.

interest in the excess volatility of asset markets has turned attention once again to this old problem.[30]

5.1.2. Fixed exchange rates and discipline

The exchange rate regime is also looked at in terms of the constraints it imposes on policies. In the early postwar discussion of flexible exchange rates the ability to conduct an independent monetary policy had been singled out as a critical advantage. It is clear today that there is independence, but that this comes at the expense of large and often unacceptable movements in the real exchange rate.

Do fixed or flexible exchange rates more nearly institute the kind of precommitment to non-inflationary policies that the Barro and Gordon analysis shows to be desirable? The literature on strategic monetary policy interactions initiated by the work of Canzoneri and Gray (1985) and Rogoff (1985) offers some useful insights. Their finding is that, under flexible exchange rates, the distortions associated with lack of cooperation among monetary authorities actually offset the inflationary biases associated with the lack of credibility of monetary authorities at home. Internationally, central bankers have an incentive to generate a real exchange rate appreciation in order to export some of the costs of a disinflation: thus the distortion from noncooperative behavior of central bankers is towards a monetary contraction. At home, however, central bankers would like to produce surprise inflation, to bring up domestic output: the distortion is towards monetary expansion. This general result can be used to evaluate, from the viewpoint of central bankers, alternative policy regimes. We return to this point in Section 6.[31]

Interestingly, on the independence argument the pendulum has swung in the other direction. Today fixed rates, as for example in the European Monetary System (EMS), are considered an advantage because they force governments who otherwise might inflate or accommodate inflationary pressures to pursue much more conservative inflation policies. Having to live with a fixed exchange rate forces denial of inflation accommodation that might otherwise be irresistible. The need to defend an exchange rate target thus allows monetary policy to become more exogenous to domestic politics.

Giavazzi and Pagano (1988) have offered a further argument. In a context where reputation matters, fixing one's exchange rate to a hard currency country is a means for a government to benefit from another country's

---

[30]See Keynes (1934, ch. 12), Grossman and Shiller (1981), Meese (1986) and the references cited in Dornbusch and Frankel (1987).

[31]Central bankers' objective functions, quadratic in the deviations of output from a target, and in the rate of inflation, do not necessarily correspond with private welfare in these models. See Subsection 6.3 below for a discussion of the welfare properties of alternative exchange rate regimes.

reputation for conservative monetary policy. This aspect, too, is thought to have been at work in the EMS, helping countries like Italy to reduce the costs of reducing inflation. This kind of precommitment to a fixed exchange rate with a hard currency country establishes credibility in a way suggested by the Barro and Gordon (1983) analysis, making up for the lack of reputation.[32] Of course, countries outside the EMS, such as the United Kingdom, Spain or Portugal, also reduced their inflation. In fact, some countries outside the EMS, the United Kingdom for example, reduced their inflation rate more than could be predicted by the experience of the 1970s. Thus the question of whether pegging the exchange rate unambiguously helps in a disinflation must be seen as still open. In particular, one issue that has not been yet resolved at the theoretical level regards the relative credibility of monetary versus exchange rate targets: only if exchange rate targets are perfectly credible does the imported discipline argument for exchange rate pegging follow. But what makes exchange rate targets more credible than monetary targets?

Against the view that fixed rates exert relatively more discipline, it is argued that under flexible exchange rates an inflation policy is instantly apparent in the depreciation of the exchange rate. Moreover, if the exchange rate over-depreciates and this process speeds up the inflationary effects of monetary expansion, flexible rates would make the pursuit of monetary policy more expensive. Of course, under fixed rates with high capital mobility and asset substitutability there would be no effects in the first place and hence the risk of an inflation policy might not arise. The exchange rate regime would seem to have an implication for the cost–benefit analysis of inflation policy and hence for the time-consistent inflation program. But even in this perspective there does not appear to be a decisive argument favoring one system or the other.

5.1.3. Independence under flexible rates

The third direction of discussion involves the independence conveyed by flexible exchange rates to conduct monetary policy. This argument is used in two directions. On one side it is argued that countries with a preference for low inflation, by comparison with the world trend, find in flexible rates a means to isolate their price level trend from that of other countries. This argument stands unchallenged.

But there is another view of the independence of monetary policy. This argument runs as follows. Since under flexible exchange rates the central bank is not committed to intervene in the exchange market, monetary policy is freed from the need to defend the exchange rate and becomes available to pursue domestic targets. It is true that the government can control the nominal money

[32]See Giavazzi and Giovannini (1988) on the EMS and alternative models of a fixed exchange rate system in the context of disinflation.

stock. But using monetary policy still runs into the problems posed by international interdependence. Monetary expansion that lowers interest rates also brings about depreciation. Monetary policy will be effective, but the integration of international asset markets directs the channels through which monetary policy will work. Moreover, world interest rate movements arising from monetary or fiscal policy changes in the rest of the world will still be transmitted through fluctuations in the real exchange rate.

Older literature focused on independence for monetary policy because that encompassed the interest of those who favored independence for short-run monetary policy and those who wanted independence for medium-term inflation policy. It is clear now that independence of monetary policy comes at the price of major movements in exchange rates, quite possibly accentuated by speculation. But long-run inflation independence remains as a definite advantage of flexible rates. Of course, that advantage could also be secured by a crawling peg exchange rate system.

5.1.4. Optimum currency areas

The choice of exchange rate regime has two aspects. One is whether fixed or flexible rates represent a more effective means of adjusting external imbalances without resort to protection. The other is which system enhances more the quality of money in the sense of yielding a higher level of welfare. Both have been addressed under the heading "optimum currency areas".

Friedman (1953) has argued that it is much easier to change one price, the exchange rate, rather than every single price and wage in the entire economy when there is a need for relative price changes. Moreover, when under fixed rates an external deficit calls for deflation there may instead be pressure to use protection. Flexible rates, by contrast, adjust the external balance "automatically" and hence dispense with the need for protection. But this view oversimplifies.

Since real exchange rate changes do not always move in the proper direction of adjusting the current account, flexible rates may actually aggravate the protectionist sentiment. A case in point is the U.S. experience with real appreciation under the impact of large capital inflows in the early 1980s. Whenever massive capital inflows bring about a real appreciation and create and finance large trade imbalances, flexible rates may well be the system most vulnerable to protectionist pressure. The system may also involve unnecessary variability in relative prices, although that would be largely the result of the policies rather than the system.

Mundell (1961) took the microeconomic adjustment question as the point of departure in asking: What is the optimum currency area? His point was that with inflexible wages there would be two means of adjustment: geographic mobility of labor, or movements in the nominal exchange rate which change wages relative to those prevailing in world markets. Mundell's optimum currency area thus is defined by the region over which labor mobility is substantial. The literature on optimum currency areas has grown significantly since the early contribution by Mundell. Other criteria [reviewed in Tower and Willett (1976), for example] have been added to those of Mundell. One important consideration which tends to enlarge the optimal monetary regime has to do with the quality of money. The wider the area over which a single currency can be used, or at least fixed rate prevail, the lower the information costs and the higher the usefulness of the monetary unit. Fixed rates, in this monetary theory perspective, are seen as a means of enhancing the quality of money.

5.2. Exchange-rate-oriented monetary policy

Under a gold standard the central bank is committed to the convertibility of the currency into gold. Within the limits of the gold reserve the commitment to defend the gold-par is the limitation on the use of domestic monetary policy. Should national and world monetary policy be once again operated in this fashion?

McKinnon (1974, 1984, 1988) has argued that monetary policy should be oriented toward defending exchange rates between the U.S. dollar, the yen and the DM within very narrow limits. We review his arguments since they present the most fully articulated position on *world monetarism*.

The McKinnon proposal

McKinnon has proposed a return to fixed exchange rates on the basis of an explicit world money supply target. In the McKinnon proposal, the United States, Germany, and Japan would enter an agreement on the desirable rate of expansion of the *world* quantity of money. Within this aggregate target each country would set its own rate of domestic credit expansion to be consistent with exchange rate stability. *Unsterilized* intervention would be used to ensure that exchange rates stay within narrow limits of the agreed part. Thus, each country effectively pursues an exchange-rate-oriented monetary policy.

This particular policy rule is advocated because of the belief that exchange rate volatility is primarily the source of money demand disturbances that go unaccommodated because governments follow *national* monetary targeting in a world where money demand shifts are *transnational*. The typical financial disturbance, in this view, is a shift in money demand from one currency denomination to another. When the demand for one country's money rises and that for another falls, interest rates rise in one country and fall in another and the exchange rate (nominal and real) appreciates. Thus, purely financial disturbances are shifted to the goods markets and spread internationally. If, instead, unsterilized invervention had kept the exchange rate fixed, the financial disturbance would have been fully accommodated in the manner suggested by Poole (1970). Undesirable and unnecessary real effects would have been avoided.

The chief difficulty with the prescription for exchange-rate-oriented monetary policy is that shifts in money demand from one denomination to another are not the typical disturbance. Portfolio shifts are predominantly between earning assets in one denomination and another. And when there is a shift between bonds, then sterilized, not unsterilized, intervention is the right policy response. In addition, of course, the argument runs into all the difficulties posed by monetary targeting per se.[33]

The case for world monetarism is not persuasive. But a role for exchange rates as one of the intermediate targets of monetary policy is, of course, warranted. Since the real exchange rate and the real interest rate are both affected in the short term by monetary policy, and since both influence aggregate demand and thus inflation, both nominal interest rates and the nominal exchange rate should be intermediate targets. But here it must be recognized that the exchange rate is a forward-looking asset price. A depreciation of the nominal exchange rate may signify the response to inflationary expectations or it may simply reflect a decline in the equilibrium relative price of domestic goods. Many of the problems in interpreting movements in the long-term interest rate also arise in explaining movements of the exchange rate. The joint behavior of long-term interest rates, short-term rates and the exchange rate may help better identify the stance of monetary policy. In this sense exchange rates are a useful part of indicators and intermediate target.

5.3. Policy coordination

The McKinnon proposal is based on crude monetarism with little concern for the fact that disturbances may be real or financial and, among the latter, may involve shifts in portfolio between bonds across currencies or monies. The simple rule of world money and exchange-rate-oriented monetary policy has no presumption of solving any policy optimization problem.

Miller and Williamson (1987) recognize this point explicitly and, in their proposal for international policy coordination, address the integration of policies over a wider range of instruments. Their concern, just like McKinnon's,

---

[33]For further discussion see Dornbusch (1988).

is to minimize real exchange rate volatility. The rules to combine a policy that supports and stabilizes growth while limiting fluctuations in the real exchange rate are as follows:

- The average level of *world* (real) short-term interest rates is set to achieve the target level of world *nominal* demand.
- Differences in short-term interest rates between countries and intervention in exchange markets are used to maintain exchange rates in their target range.
- National fiscal policies are set with a view to achieve the national target rates of growth of demand.

The key differences with a world monetarist conception are three. First, there is a focus on world nominal demand rather than world money. In this way velocity disturbances at the world level can be absorbed. Second, portfolio shifts in bond portfolios across currencies are automatically sterilized by the rules for interest rates and exchange intervention. Third, fiscal policy is recognized as part of the coordination problem.

The Miller–Williamson style proposal represents a natural outgrowth of the use of extended IS–LM style large econometric models of the world economy to the policy problem. Such an approach to policy is subject to two possible criticisms. One criticism, the new classical approach, which we consider in the next section, simply denies the possibility of manipulating economies on the basis of announced rules. The other criticisms focus on the setting in which policy choices are made. Adopting a game-theoretic optimization approach one can ask whether coordination of the kind prescribed by Williamson and Miller do in fact optimize national objectives. The game-theoretic approach to policy coordination that has flourished in the past ten years pursues this latter question.

Research on international policy coordination comes naturally out of the work of Mundell (1968) and Cooper (1969), where the question is posed in terms of dynamic stability or the assignment of targets and instruments. The modern approach, pioneered by Hamada (1985), places the discussion in a game-theoretic context. It asks what equilibrium results without cooperation and what the gains are if countries cooperate, recognizing the interdependence of performance and their implicit strategic interaction. The interdependence of performance emerges, for example, via spending linkages, interest rates, and the impact of exchange rate movements on inflation.

The central focus of the cooperation literature has been to note the difference between the non-cooperative Nash equilibrium which emerges from decentralized decision-making and the cooperative equilibrium. Work by Oudiz and Sachs (1985) reached the surprising conclusion that cooperation might only yield minor gains. Rogoff (1985) went further to show that cooperation might even make things worse. Bryant and Portes (1987) and

Buiter and Marston (1985) show the many possible directions of modelling the issue and Fischer (1988) presents a definitive survey.

An interesting direction of scepticism about policy coordination has emerged from very practical considerations. What happens if policy-makers use different models, if they do not agree on the true model of the world economy or if they have a different diagnosis of the state of their economies? Frankel, in a number of papers, has shown that in such a situation the gains from cooperation fall off sharply and may even be negative.[34]

5.4. Segmenting capital markets

The integration of international capital markets subordinates domestic policies to conditions in world asset markets. "Hot money" is seen as excessively mobile and thus limits the ability of any central bank to move interest rates away from world levels. Tobin (1982) notes:

> There are two ways to go. One is toward a common currency, common monetary and fiscal policy, and economic integration. The other is toward greater financial segmentation between nations or currency areas, permitting their central banks and governments greater autonomy . . . .

Specifically, Tobin has proposed a uniform, small tax to be levied worldwide on purchases of foreign exchange for any transaction. The transactions tax would limit the payoff that can be reaped on short duration round trips from one market to another, more so the shorter the trip. Therefore, short-term capital movements would be reduced to those that had only very large anticipated payoffs. Small differentials on short-term interest rates could easily be maintained without inducing massive capital flows or movements in exchange rates. At the same time the transactions tax would have virtually zero effect on the profitability of long-term investment.[35]

Where proposals like that of McKinnon (1988) seek to integrate the world economy by making monetary policies more interdependent, this proposal seeks to enhance the scope for independent monetary policies. It does so by limiting the allegedly unproductive short-term capital flows. Both proposals have in common that they see large exchange rate fluctuations as undesirable and disintegrating in the goods markets. The Tobin tax proposal runs counter to current trends of reducing the obstacles to international financial transaction

---

[34]See Canzoneri and Henderson (1988a), Bryant and Portes (1987), Buiter and Marston (1985) and the discussion and references in Dornbusch and Frankel (1987).

[35]It is interesting to note that Keynes (1936, ch. 12) already proposed a transfer tax on *all* financial transactions. Keynes writes: "The introduction of a substantial Government transfer tax on all transactions might prove the most serviceable reform available, with a view to mitigating the predominance of speculation over enterprise in the United States."

of any kind. There is a need for research to explore whether, in the presence of stabilizing speculation, such a tax would actually reduce the stability of the system. But if speculation could be shown to be destabilizing, short-sighted or uninformed the tax might well enhance the microeconomic efficiency of the international economy.[36]

Of course, the question of segmenting capital markets immediately raises the question of feasibility. Even if it were recognized that on efficiency grounds there is merit in a proposal to slow short-term capital movements, how can this be accomplished. For an individual country not only black markets but also offshore transactions present a formidable challenge. It would therefore be necessary to attack the problem on a common front by major financial centers. That seems unlikely.

After this review of monetary policy issues we return to two more specialized areas of discussion. One concerns recent research directions on the role of money in the open economy. The other deals with monetary policy issues in high inflation economies.

6. The new macroeconomics

The new classical macroeconomics, just as in the closed economy, is also seeking a reconstruction of open economy macroeconomics. The research program is to derive firm analytical support for behavioral relations and to construct equilibria that represent full maximization and rational use of information by all agents. In the light of the research program, the Mundell–Fleming model fails to meet the test. It is "ad hoc", meaning that the various behavioral equations are not obviously sculptured from a common, explicit maximization framework. Furthermore, the attempt to catch up with that task by patching up the model cannot improve much. The task of this part of our chapter is to describe the new views on the international transmission of monetary disturbances. We concentrate on the effects of monetary shocks on prices, exchange rates, interest rates, output, and asset accumulation.

The research program of the new classical approach is to rebuild open economy macroeconomics on the premise of rationality and optimization with explicit recognition of all relevant constraints.[37] While such an approach, in the end, may confirm much of the existing literature, it will also point much more sharply to implicit restrictions imposed on the underlying utility maximization. It certainly will highlight implications of budget constraints that are often entirely omitted. By highlighting the influence of constraints and forward-

---

[36]See Gros (1987) and Tornell (1988) for recent discussions of the capital control issue.
[37]For a statement of the research program see, for example, Stockman (1987b).

looking expectations this approach immediately cautions against a facile short-term analysis of essentially intertemporal problems. In that sense the recon-struction is far more than a rebuilding of foundations on a more solid ground.

Research in monetary economics has, for the past fifteen years, tried to uncover all important implications of the Friedman–Phelps expectations revo-lution and of the renewed emphasis on maximization. The research agenda has been profoundly affected by Lucas's contributions, which demonstrated the logical inconsistency of building models where behavioral relationships are assumed a priori, and where comparative statics are performed on the basis of these posited behavioral relationships, often across altogether different regimes. The work has focused on deriving individuals' decision rules from optimiza-tion problems conditional on a set of taste and technology parameters which are assumed to be more stable than the implied decision rules.

In international economics, more narrowly, the new classical research pro-gram has concentrated on three points. The first is the dynamics of macro adjustment to monetary shocks. The second deals with the implications of intertemporal optimization in a stochastic setting to derive jointly saving and portfolio rules. The role of intertemporal substitution on savings and the current account is particularly emphasized in this literature. The third problem deals with the indeterminacies that arise in a multiple currency world.

This research strategy naturally forces economists to face the issue of the role of money in a macroeconomy by explicitly describing the transactions costs or technological or natural constraints that allow money to coexist with assets dominating it in terms of real returns. Central to all the literature is to establish a theory of money. Unlike in the IS–LM model where the existence of a money demand function is simply posited, here it must be an explicit part of the taste and technology environment. Not surprisingly the particular role allowed for money totally dominates the manner in which money and monetary disturbances work themselves out. Two acceptable directions are money in the utility function or cash-in-advance constraints.

6.1. Money in the utility function

The money in the utility function approach has been explored among others by Kouri (1976), Obstfeld (1981) and Calvo (1981). Extending closed economy models, they ask how changes in the alternative cost of holding money affect the demand for real balances and the current account. The exchange rate and current account dynamics are studied with attention to the relevant inter-temporal tradeoffs, which affect both savings and the private-sector portfolio composition. Alternative monetary rules receive explicit attention.

The representative consumer (an infinitely-lived family) maximizes the present discounted value of future utility, under perfect foresight. In Calvo (1981) the consumer maximizes an intertemporal utility function with consumption and real balances as arguments and money is the only asset. Output or real income is given exogenously and so is the exchange rate rule. The authorities follow a rule of depreciating the currency at a given rate. With home prices determined by the exchange rate, the rate of currency depreciation sets the rate of inflation and hence the inflation tax. The inflation tax proceeds are redistributed in neutral lump-sum form. The model can be used to answer two questions: What is the effect of a once and for fall depreciation? What is the effect of an increase in the rate of depreciation?

Individual maximization leads to the first-order condition:[38]

$$\phi(c/m) = \pi + \delta , \tag{23}$$

where $\phi(\cdot)$ denotes the ratio of the marginal utility of money to the marginal utility of consumption. By the assumption of homotheticity this ratio is an increasing function of the ratio of consumption to real balances, c/m. The term δ is the rate of time preference and π the rate of inflation and depreciation. In Figure 23.6 we show the typical indifference curve and the ray OR shows the locus along which (23) is satisfied for the initial rate of inflation. Consumption for any given level of real balances is indicated by the corresponding point on OR. Output is indicated by the line yy. Over time the household converges to

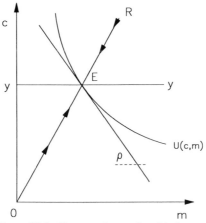

Figure 23.6. Consumption and real balances.

[38]Without loss of generality we concentrate for expository ease on the case of a homothetic utility function. See Dornbusch and Mussa (1975).

the steady-state level of consumption and real balances indicated by point E. It is interesting to note that the opimal rate of adjustment takes the form:

$$\dot{m} \sim v(m' - m), \tag{24}$$

where m' is the steady-state level of real balances. The speed of adjustment, v, is an increasing function of the alternative cost of holding money. Thus, the higher the rate of inflation the more rapid the adjustment of real balances.

Consider first a depreciation of the exchange rate (and hence an increase in the price level), for a given nominal money stock. Real money balances fall and consumption therefore declines and the trade balance improves as consumption declines below the level of income. Over time real balances are rebuilt through the trade surplus until the economy returns to point E. This adjustment process is, of course, exactly the monetary approach as seen before.

The second experiment is a sustained increase in the rate of depreciation. By (23) the desired ratio of real balances to consumption falls, as shown by a rotation of OR to OR' in Figure 23.7. At the initial level of real balances, m_0, consumption increases. The resulting trade deficit leads to decumulation of real balances until point E' is reached. This short-run adjustment of consumption and the trade balance to increased inflation is a systematic part of open economy inflation models. Note that because money is the only asset the "flight from money" here is of necessity into consumption. The diminishing marginal utility of consumption ensures that the adjustment process of running down real balances is drawn out in time.

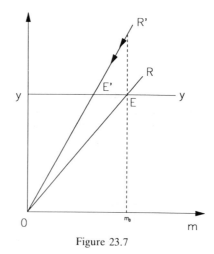

Figure 23.7

It is immediately apparent that when there are in addition to traded goods also non-traded goods the adjustment process to increased inflation will involve transitory real exchange rate movements. As consumption rises, initially part of the increased consumption falls on non-traded goods and hence leads to an increase in their relative price. Over time, as consumption declines back to the level of income, the real exchange rate depreciates until the initial real equilibrium is reattained.

6.1.1. Currency substitution

A critical feature of the model discussed so far is that money here is the only asset. This makes it impossible to consider portfolio shifts. Any flight from money is a flight into consumption which occurs only over time because of the diminishing marginal utility of consumption. The model is enriched, therefore, when alternative assets are introduced.

One possibility, explored by Calvo (1985) among others, introduces foreign assets and treats them in a symmetric way with domestic money. In this approach, called "currency substitution", home and foreign money are combined to yield liquidity services which in turn generate utility. Both monies are inputs in a production function for liquidity which is valued by the consumer. Let z denote the index of liquidity and assume the production function for z is linear homogeneous in home- and foreign-currency-denominated real balances. The consumer then solves two problems. One is to find, for a given level of assets, the lowest cost means of generating liquidity services. This yields the preferred ratio of home to foreign currency real balances, which will be a declining function of the rate of depreciation. The other is to determine the optimal part of consumption which depends on the alternative cost of holding liquidity.

The presence of alternative assets introduces the possibility of portfolio shifts. Now an increased rate of depreciation immediately reduces the desired ratio of home money to foreign-currency-denominated real balances. There is thus an instant portfolio shift. There are additional effects that stem from the impact of increased depreciation on the marginal rate of substitution between consumption and liquidity. The increased alternative cost of holding liquidity, although mitigated by currency substitution, reduces the desired ratio of liquidity to consumption. Accordingly, consumption initially rises and over time the trade deficit reduces assets.

Calvo and Rodriguez (1977) and Liviatan (1981) investigate the case of a small country under flexible exchange rates. The principal effect of changes in the rate of credit creation centers on the time path of relative prices between home goods and traded goods and on the current account. The current account is the channel through which the country acquires increased stocks of foreign assets over time. A shift to a higher rate of credit creation, under flexible exchange rates, leads to an immediate shift out of domestic money. But because the exchange rate is flexible and hence the central bank does not accommodate the portfolio shift, the result is a depreciation of the exchange rate and a decline in the real value of assets. Saving increases, the real price of home goods declines and the current account improves. Over time external assets are accumulated. The impact on the long-run real exchange rate, as Liviatan (1981) and Calvo (1985) have shown, depends in a maximizing framework on the manner in which money enters the utility function.

6.1.2. External interest-bearing assets

A different modelling of alternative assets in a maximizing framework has been proposed by Obstfeld (1981). Specifically assume that there is a foreign interest yielding asset which is held as a store of value. Domestic money continues to be an argument in the utility function. The portfolio choice between domestic money and foreign assets, given wealth, is now determined by the alternative cost of holding money (rather than foreign assets), which is the foreign interest rate plus the rate of depreciation, λ:

$$\phi(m/c) = i^* + \lambda , \tag{25}$$

where λ is the rate of inflation and depreciation. Inverting equation (25) we arrive at the equilibrium level of real balances, given consumption and the alternative cost of holding money:

$$m = \phi^{-1}(i^* + \lambda)c. \tag{25a}$$

The consumption rule specifies the optimal rate of increase of consumption as a function of the discrepancy between the discount rate and the interest rate on external assets. The discount rate is an increasing declining function of the level of utility. With this specification the steady-state level of utility is such that the discount rate equals the foreign interest rate. This condition, combined with (24), defines the steady-state level of consumption and of real balances.

In this approach an increased rate of depreciation exerts its effects through a number of channels. There is an immediate portfolio shift out of home currency into foreign assets. This portfolio shift, even though it raises interest earnings from abroad, leaves disposable income unaffected because there is a compensating reduction in transfers as the central banks' holdings of foreign assets are reduced. But the decline in real balances reduces utility and hence lowers the discount rate. The initial level of consumption declines and the country runs a current account surplus, adding to external assets. Over time consumption and real balances rise and external assets and hence disposable income also rise. A new steady state is ultimately reached with a higher level of consumption and a higher ratio of consumption to real balances. The new steady state level of real balances is, of course, lower.

Models of money in the utility function offer an attractive conceptual framework for the discussion of private sector adjustment to shifts in the expected rate of inflation and depreciation. We return to these ideas in Section 7 below when we discuss the empirical evidence on, and issues raised by, currency substitution. In the meantime we pursue the question of recent approaches by looking at the alternative model of money which is based on transactions requirements in the cash-in-advance tradition.

6.2. Cash-in-advance economies

A critical feature of models with money in the utility function is the responsiveness of velocity to the anticipated cost of holding money. In this respect there is an important difference, at least with the simpler versions of cash-in-advance models, where technology determines fixed transactions requirements.

6.2.1. Non-stochastic models

Helpman (1981) offers an example of this point. He studies a two-country world where, as in the case discussed above, output flows are exogenously given, and individuals maximize over the infinite horizon the present discounted value of future utility. In Helpman's model, however, money is introduced through a transactions constraint which requires that the currency of a given country be used to purchase the output of that country both in the traded and the non-traded goods sectors. With perfect foresight the transactions constraint implies a unit-velocity money demand equation, which period by period determines the price level.

In this world money is superneutral. The velocity of circulation is constant, and anticipated future money shocks are reflected in nominal interest rates. Real interest rates and intertemporal substitution are unaffected. But there are distribution effects of monetary shocks which arise from the presence of nominal debt contracts. Although anticipated monetary shocks are fully reflected in the nominal interest rate, unanticipated monetary increases do have distributional effects between domestic and foreign residents the nature of which depends on the foreign indebtedness of each country and its currency of denomination. If domestic residents' indebtedness in domestic currency is positive, an unanticipated increase in domestic money increases domestic residents' wealth and their spending. The relative price of domestic non-traded goods tends to increase (foreigners decrease their demand of traded goods as they see the incipient price rise, and because their wealth has decreased): thus the domestic price level increases relative to that abroad and the domestic real exchange rate appreciates. This implies that the domestic monetary expansion is not fully reflected in the domestic price level and nominal exchange rate.

6.2.2. Stochastic models

A parallel line of research deals with the integration of international financial issues – pricing of international assets, and the determination of equilibrium rates of return – with monetary theory. One task of this analysis is to derive asset pricing equations and demand for output functions from a common general equilibrium formulation. The stochastic, general equilibrium approach is bound to offer consistent answers to questions such as the effects of monetary disturbances and changes in monetary regimes on equilibrium rates of return on domestic and foreign assets. Other questions include the interactions between domestic money markets and international financial markets, and issues that are addressed also by perfect foresight models, like the correlation between the capital account, the exchange rate, and nominal interest rates.

The basic structure of these models is as follows. At the beginning of each period, agents learn the realizations of exogenous shocks to the economy. These shocks are commonly monetary injections and productivity disturbances. Then they engage in transactions in the goods and assets markets. Transactions in the goods markets are subject to a liquidity constraint, which typically requires that the goods produced in any given country be purchased exclusively with the country's currency.[39] The timing of transactions within each period is crucial, since it determines the liquidity properties of money and the way in which monetary disturbances affect real variables. We consider here the model proposed by Svensson (1985b). There are two types of stochastic shocks in the world economy: real disturbances, representing payoffs on claims on the domestic and foreign capital stock, and nominal disturbances, representing increases in the stocks of domestic and foreign money. Domestic and foreign output is produced costlessly from the domestic and foreign (non-depreciating) capital stocks. At the beginning of each period agents learn the realizations of all stochastic shocks. They require money for goods transactions but cannot acquire money balances at the time goods are traded. Since goods markets open first, agents start each period with predetermined nominal money balances. At the opening of the asset market, agents' money demand is determined by the expectations of future liquidity services of money. This formulation gives rise to a precautionary money demand and a variable

---

[39] See Helpman and Razin (1984) for an analysis of the effects of alternative international payments arrangements.

velocity function. Now it is possible to ask questions about the effects of endowment and monetary shocks on relative prices.

Expected utility maximization yields a set of marginal conditions that are used for pricing assets. The interesting point of these models is to suggest that the liquidity constraint associated with goods transactions affects the pricing of assets. An open economy version of this model is developed by exploiting the pooled equilibrium assumption by simply introducing a second good, with its own specific money transaction requirement. Now it is possible to ask questions about the effects of endowment and monetary shocks on relative prices and an exchange rate. These effects will depend on whether the liquidity constraint is binding for one or the other of the two goods or for neither.

When liquidity constraints are not binding, real exchange rate fluctuations are only driven by fluctuations in the exogenous endowments. The real exchange rate might be correlated with monetary innovations to the extent that the latter are correlated with endowment shocks. But when the liquidity constraint is binding, monetary shocks affect the real exchange rate. Consider the case of a home monetary increase. At the beginning of the period, when agents learn about the increase of the money stock, they cannot increase their demand for domestic goods, since the goods markets close before monetary transfers are received. Thus nominal goods prices are unaffected by the increase in the domestic money stock. When asset markets open, the higher domestic money stock brings about a fall in its relative price – the nominal exchange rate. Thus, when agents are liquidity constrained, the monetary expansion generates a depreciation of both the real and the nominal exchange rate, and leaves nominal goods prices unaffected. This result arises from the specific timing of transactions where current monetary injections can only be traded for assets, not goods today.

This effect is present also in Svensson and van Wijnbergen (1986). In that model money balances are available immediately for use in the goods market, but prices are sticky. There is still a precautionary demand for money balances, since the lack of adjustment of goods prices to current information may still make existing nominal balances insufficient relative to planned expenditures. With sticky prices and flexible exchange rates, innovations in the nominal exchange rate are reflected one-to-one into real exchange rate changes. We now turn to the analysis of international transmission of monetary disturbances in this model, which contains two of the important ingredients of the Mundell–Fleming model: international capital mobility and sticky goods prices.

6.3. Choice of exchange rate regime

The international transmission of monetary disturbances crucially depends on the regime where the domestic and foreign goods markets find themselves.

With sticky prices consumption determines the level of activity up to the point where the capacity constraint binds. Similarly, monetary innovations affect consumption differently, depending on whether the liquidity constraint is binding or not. When the capacity constraint is binding, consumption is determined by the given capacity level. A domestic money shock increases consumption of domestic output by both domestic and foreign residents if the capacity constraint is not binding. Domestic output increases. How does the increase in domestic output get transmitted to foreign production? Foreign output can increase as a result of the domestic monetary expansion only if consumers are neither liquidity not capacity constrained in the foreign good's market. The channel through which foreign output increases is the world representative consumer's utility function: if an increase in consumption of the domestic good increases the marginal utility of the foreign good there is an incipient increase in foreign good consumption, which translates into higher foreign output if liquidity and capacity constraints are not binding in the foreign good market.

We conclude by noting four other directions of research that are being explored in the new classical approach. One strand, initiated by Kareken and Wallace (1981), develops an open economy model on maximizing foundations in the context of an overlapping generations model. Sargent (1983a) has explored this structure in a discussion of the indeterminacy of exchange rates. Miller and Wallace (1985) use an overlapping generations structure to explore the issue of coordination and the response of key variables like interest rates and the exchange rate to shifts in monetary and budget rules.

The second direction is suggested by the work of Greenwood and Williamson (1989). They explore the implications of financial intermediation via credit markets for the international transmission of shocks. With differential scope for intermediation within and across countries financial intermediation becomes an essential aspect of the international transmission of the business cycle.

Another direction, particularly successful in the work of Adams and Greenwood (1985) and Tornell (1988), explores the implications of capital controls and dual exchange rates in a maximizing context. A final direction of research to be mentioned here considers the welfare aspects of exchange regimes. Helpman and Razin (1979, 1982, 1987) in a number of papers have opened this discussion. Alternative exchange rate regimes do not affect welfare differently with perfect goods and assets markets. Thus, welfare anlysis of alternative exchange regimes has been recently carried out in the context of second-best situations. Hsieh (1984), Helpman and Razin (1982, 1987), and Persson and Svensson (1987) concentrate on incomplete markets. Hsieh challenges the argument that, in the absence of an insurance market, fixed exchange rates are desirable because they provide risk sharing, thus partially replacing the missing insurance market. Persson and Svensson similarly question whether policies aimed at stabilizing the exchange rate can produce higher welfare.

Concluding remark

The new classical approach has produced an overriding challenge to traditional open economy macroeconomics, namely that most of the policy discussion proceeds without support, neither theoretically nor empirically. Equilibrium theory asserts that monetary policy simply has no effects except as a result of illiquidity effects.

The claim of the new classical approach that for empirical purposes the assumption of market clearing and full wage–price flexibility best characterizes the economy, remains to be established. The belief that monetary policy does not affect the exchange rate in a lasting fashion and that persistent real disturbances predominate is at best a working hypothesis; so far it certainly has no empirical support. But it would be a grave error to dismiss the new classical approach in the open economy. No doubt in a decade the ruling paradigm will be three quarters new classical with just enough remnants of Mundell–Fleming to justify the term macroeconomics. That tendency is clear in the increasing grouping of the new classical approach for bringing back some nominal fixity, albeit on grounds of optimality.

7. Money in high-inflation economies

In this section we investigate several monetary issues of the open economy particulary relevant to high-inflation economies. We first look at empirical issues raised by currency substitution. Next we explore the question of seigniorage, and finally we look at the contribution of exchange rates and monetary policy in stopping high inflation.

7.1. Issues raised by currency substitution

In this subsection we report on the empirical issues raised by currency substitution which we discussed in Section 5 above. In high-inflation economies, particularly in the experience of Israel and Latin America, substitution from domestic money to dollars has been pervasive. This substitution limits the room for policy mistakes. But it also has implications for public finance because it affects the revenue from money creation or seigniorage.

Empirical evidence

Currency substitution can take a number of forms. In some instances, as for example in Mexico until 1982 or in Israel, the government allowed the domestic banking system to offer foreign currency denominated deposits. More generally, residents in high-inflation countries will hold U.S. dollars in the form of actual currency or in deposits abroad. There are no precise dates available on holdings of U.S. currency abroad and there is even less information on the motivation, i.e. drug-trade-related holdings, tax evasion, or financial instability.

New data on liabilities by banks in the industrial countries to nonbank nonresidents give an indication of the substantial quantitative importance of external deposit holdings. Table 23.4 shows these data for recent years for several regions and groups of countries. To have some benchmark against which to judge the external deposits of various countries we have included Korea and Japan for comparison. By comparison, France and Italy are the European countries most associated with financial instability and tax evasion. But even by comparison with these much richer European countries the Latin American countries show impressive evidence of a pattern of external deposit holdings motivated by financial instability.

There is more detailed evidence on the experience of individual countries. Ortiz (1983) has studied the determinants of dollar-denominated deposits in Mexico, the so-called Mex-dollar deposits. Empirical evidence strongly confirms the theoretical proposition that anticipated depreciation is a major determinant of the extent of dollarization. The fluctuations in the ratio of foreign to domestic deposits coincide with major shifts in the expectations of depreciation. Ramirez-Rojas (1985) studied currency substitution in the cases of Argentina, Mexico, and Uruguay. Figure 23.8 shows the ratio of dollar to peso deposits reported by Ramirez-Rojas for Mexico in the period 1970 to 1982. Note the peaks in the ratio prior to the major exchange rate crises of 1976 and 1982. Ramirez-Rojas interestingly concludes that dollarization appears to be irreversible.

Table 23.4
Cross-border bank deposits of non-banks by residence of depositor
(billion $U.S., end of year)

	1981	1983	1985	1986	1986 per capita
Argentina	6.4	7.9	8.5	8.6	277
Brazil	3.5	8.1	9.8	10.5	77
Mexico	9.4	12.7	16.1	16.1	205
Venezuela	15.6	10.9	14.0	13.1	734
Korea	0.3	0.3	0.7	0.7	17
Italy	12.0	10.6	10.9	11.2	195
France	12.7	11.8	11.0	13.3	240
Japan	1.9	2.0	4.4	7.1	59

Source: IMF Banking Statistics.

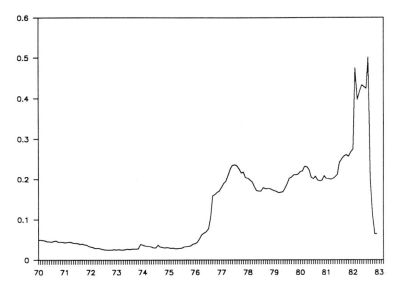

Figure 23.8. Coefficient of dollarization (dollar deposits as percent of all deposits).

Marquez (1987) reports pervasive evidence on currency substitution for the case of Venezuela. Expected depreciation, just as in the cases of Argentina, Mexico, and Uruguay, appears as a significant determinant of relative holdings of domestic and foreign currencies. In these empirical formulations an important issue is how to formulate the expected rate of depreciation. In a situation where the exchange rate is often allowed to become overvalued, the task is to find how the public predicts the devaluation that ultimately must occur. The evidence is that a range of variables, including foreign exchange reserves and political dummies, help predict devaluation and hence the demand for foreign assets.

Other evidence on dollarization comes from studies of black markets for foreign exchange and capital flight. Cuddington (1986) finds that capital flight (including flight into dollar deposits and other external assets) from Latin America can be explained in terms of inflation and depreciation variables in Latin America.[40] In Dornbusch et al. (1983) the black market premium for dollars in Brazil is explained by inflation differentials between dollar and cruzeiro assets. All this evidence supports the view that whether or not countries practice exchange controls and whether or not they allow domestic banks to offer foreign currency deposits, there is a significant extent of

---

[40]See, too, the papers in Lessard and Williamson (1987) that report on the capital flight experience in a number of Latin American countries.

dollarization, more so the higher the instability as measured by anticipated depreciation.

7.2. Seigniorage

The evidence on dollarization and its responsiveness to the alternative cost of holding domestic money introduces the issue of the revenue from money creation. The seigniorage question is important because the choice of inflation and exchange rate policy affects the revenue from money creation and hence the financing of the budget. Two separate questions emerge. First, should a government have its own money? Secondly, what are the problems involved in choosing too high or too low a rate of inflation?

7.2.1. Costs and benefits of national monies

Fischer (1982) addresses the question of the benefit of national monies. The case for a national money arises from the resource saving: rather than earn foreign exchange to build up a national money supply the country can manufacture its own at a small resource cost. The two counter-arguments are concerned with the cost of money changing that comes with a national money and the issues of discipline and credibility already raised earlier in the discussion of the EMS.

The question of using domestic or foreign monies is relevant since some countries use foreign currencies, specifically the U.S. dollar, as their national money. In other cases local money is confined to coin, and in yet other instances a local money circulates on an institutionalized parallel footing with a foreign currency.

The argument for a national money concerns seigniorage. In issuing its own money the government collects seigniorage. Thus, some resources can be collected to finance the budget without the need to resort to distortionary taxation. Of course, the ability to print money and give it legal tender also creates the possibility of inflationary taxation. But, as Phelps (1973) has shown, the inflation tax is part of an efficient tax system. It is therefore a case-by-case question to know what the optimal inflation tax is.

A national money does involve two possible costs. There are transactions costs that arise from the calculations needed to convert prices quoted in foreign exchanges into home currency. The other cost arises from the uncertainty about an economy that may arise from a government's discretionary use of monetary policy. Fixed exchange rates may not be enough to achieve the requisite degree of precommitment. Interestingly, in the stabilizations of countries in Central America, notably in the case of the Dominican Republic, a one-to-one fixed exchange rate was made a provision of the consitution. And even that was not enough to stop fiscal and monetary policies ultimately inconsistent with the fixed exchange rate. But using a foreign money outright, with no domestic money at all, establishes a very substantial protection against an independent potentially very unstable monetary experience. Of course this is not enough to rule out financial instability. For that to happen there would need to be, in addition, control of the budget.

The amount of seigniorage collected by governments is in fact quite significant. Fischer (1982) reports that industrial countries in the period 1960–73 collected an (unweighted) average 1.1 percent of GNP as revenue from creating high-powered money. The extent of gains from seigniorage will depend on financial institutions, on the rate of inflation, and on the growth rate of real income. Thus, for a number of countries seigniorage gains were, in some cases, much higher. Italy and Portugal, for example collected about 4 percent of GNP in this form. For developing countries the ratio of creation of high-powered money to GNP averages more than 2 percent. In countries with substantial inflation it reaches as much as 6 percent.

7.2.2. Inflation policy and financial instability

In countries where budget deficits are difficult to finance by extra explicit taxation or by expenditure cuts, there is a difficult choice to be made between inflation and borrowing as alternatives. An excessive reliance on foreign borrowing in preference to an inflation policy may build up its own problem by debt accumulation which leads to ultimate insolvency.

This point can be appreciated by deriving from the budget constraint an expression for the growth in the ratio of debt to GNP. The ratio of debt to GNP rises at a rate equal to:

$$\dot{b} = (r - x)b + (g - s),\tag{26}$$

where b is the ratio of debt to GNP, r and x are the real interest rate and the growth rate of output, respectively, and g and s denote the non-interest budget deficit and seigniorage, respectively, each expressed as a fraction of GNP. Thus, reduced use of seigniorage implies, other things equal, an increased reliance on debt accumulation. Thus choosing a lower rate of inflation, when money demand is inelastic with respect to interest rates, means sacrificing seigniorage. If there is no means to correct the non-interest budget, and if growth is low, there is a possibility of serious fiscal imbalances ahead. This kind of dilemma poses itself not only for developing countries but it is even an issue for countries like Italy, Spain or Portugal as they reduce their inflation rates in the context of the European monetary system.

The link between inflation policy and the budget also comes in another form. Dollarization and financial liberalization introduce alternatives to holding domestic money which are of particular interest when inflation runs high. But when inflation is high there is pressure to allow for financial deregulation that makes it possible to offer interest-bearing near monies. If the government yields to these pressures, there is a reduction in the inflation-tax base and hence an increase in the inflation rate required to finance the budget. The point can be shown readily by looking at the steady-state link between money creation, inflation and the budget. Suppose the entire budget is financed by money creation. Hence, the growth rate of money is equal to the deficit/GNP ratio times the income velocity of money denoted by V. Since the steady-state rate of inflation is equal to the growth rate of nominal money less the rate of output growth, we have:[41] $\pi = gV - x$, where g is the budget deficit as a fraction of GNP. Assuming monetary equilibrium and letting velocity be a linear function of the rate of inflation, $V = \alpha + \beta\pi$, we derive the steady-state rate of inflation:

$$\pi = (\alpha g - x)/(1 - \beta g) . \tag{27}$$

We can think of official sanctioning of dollarization and of financial liberalization as measures that increase the non-inflationary level of velocity captured by the term α, or as increasing the responsiveness of velocity to inflation. As (27) shows, for a given deficit ratio an increase in dollarization or liberalization would accordingly raise the rate of inflation. This points to the need to combine changes in the financial structure with a budget reform to avoid the emergence of an unwelcome and surprising fiscal problem.

7.3. Speculative attacks and collapsing exchange rate regimes

Policies of domestic credit expansion that are inconsistent with a fixed exchange rate lead to continuing reserve decumulation. Ultimately the government will run out of reserves with which to sustain the exchange rate. This recognition leads the public to mount a speculative attack to avail themselves of foreign exchange reserves before the inevitable shift in regime to devaluation or a floating rate. Salant and Henderson (1978), in a seminal article on the gold market, explored this problem and Krugman (1979) adapted it to the balance of payments problem. Work by Flood and Garber (1984), Obstfeld (1984), Buiter (1987), and Penati and Pennacchi (1989) extended these ideas to a stochastic credit policy setting.

The key idea in these models is that when the government no longer has reserves to support the exchange rate there will be a transition from fixed to

---

[41]Without loss of generality we assume here a unit income elasticity.

floating rates. Moreover, given the (assumed unchanged) growth rate of domestic credit the exchange rate now will be depreciating at the rate of credit creation. Because under flexible rates there is now inflation, the demand for real balances declines. Thus, in the shift from fixed to flexible exchange rates real money demand falls. Speculators anticipate that this decline in real money demand implies a jump in the exchange rate at the time of transition. The only way for this jump not to occur is for a speculative attack that takes place exactly at a time where the central bank possesses sufficient reserves to accommodate the portfolio shift at the fixed rate. The characteristic of perfect foresight transitions, therefore, is that they occur while reserves are finite and without any jump in the exchange rate.

In stochastic models the reserve depletion does not occur in the form of a speculative attack but rather as a steady and accelerating depletion. While reserves are plentiful the depletion is on a one-to-one basis with increases in credit. But as reserves decline a positive probability develops that the next realization of credit growth could bring about the transition to floating. The expected inflation and depreciation now becomes positive and increases with successive realizations of credit growth. As a result reserves fall on a more than one-to-one basis since real money demand now falls.

The models of speculative attack offer an important extension of the monetary approach to the balance of payments. They help explain why interest rates can exceed world levels even under (for the time being) fixed exchange rates. They also explain why reserve movements can exceed increases in domestic credit. Their empirical relevance has been documented in a number of papers, especially by Lizondo (1983) as well as Blanco and Garber (1986).

The regime change idea is also central to a number of important papers by Calvo (1986b). He seeks to explain the behavior of optimizing agents as they view prospective, possibly unsustainable, stabilization programs. The interest of the analysis is to explain the behavior of relative prices and other variables in the context of failed policy reforms. Increasingly research is setting out models where governments interact actively with the public in selecting the path of inflation and depreciation, and of taxation, which finances the budget. Multiple equilibria in such situations are common, as for example in Obstfeld (1988), and call for a link with an explicit optimizing framework that allows a welfare-theoretic evaluation of optimal policies.

7.4. Stopping high inflation

An important area of disagreement in open economy macroeconomics concerns the question of how best to stop high inflation. Sargent (1983b), in his seminal paper on the end of hyperinflations, made much of the argument that a credible fiscal reform would in and of itself lead to an immediate and near-costless end of inflation. The experience of stopping inflation in the 1920s served as a demonstration of that claim. More recent work on these stabilizations throws doubt on these assertions.[42] The doubts concern not only the question of whether stabilization was near costless but also, in a more basic way, the mechanics of stabilization. The fundamental point is that governments have really no way of precommitting their policies. Accordingly, some reforms may "look" better than others but anyone may be abandoned should it prove politically too difficult to execute. Indeed, the experience of many countries has been that stabilization is attempted a number of times before it ultimately succeeds. Moreover, the all-important change in fundamentals often occurs on the strength of having stopped inflation temporarily rather than as a move prior to stabilization.

The recent experience of Israel, Argentina, and Brazil has a bearing on this question. In these episodes inflation was stopped (at least transitorily) by programs of wage, price and exchange rate freezing. Thus, the end of inflation was mandated rather than achieved as a result of policy changes. The divergent experience of the three countries documents that success at stopping inflation cannot be expected unless the fundamental changes in fiscal policy (and hence in credit expansion) also occur in time. That was the case in Israel, and to a lesser extent in Argentina. In Brazil, where policy sought to use the freeze to seek a dramatic expansion, the freeze predictably failed. But these experiences raise the question of whether a freeze of the exchange rate, wages and prices is also an essential step if a recession is to be avoided. Of course, the counter-argument to the freeze approach is that relative prices might become distorted. That is almost certainly the case, but there is, so far at least, welfare economic demonstration that recession is preferable to relative price distortions.

In a hyperinflation, pricing converges on the exchange rate. In the acute stages of a hyperinflation all wages and prices tend to be set by reference to the exchange rate on a daily basis. Hence, a policy of stopping exchange depreciation by a commitment to support a fixed rate will immediately stop inflation. If reserves are adequate and policy reforms come about in time, then the fixed exchange rate can be supported and stabilization is achieved. If policy reforms do not occur, then the exchange rate regime soon becomes unsustainable, reserve losses will grow, and ultimately the fixed exchange rate has to be abandoned in the face of speculative attacks. The research agenda today certainly includes the question of whether a policy of stopping an extreme inflation is more easily achieved by announcing a new monetary program or by fixing the exchange rate accompanied, or soon followed, by a new monetary and fiscal program.

---

[42]See Wicker (1986), Dornbusch and Fischer (1986), Dornbusch (1987a), Kiguel and Liviatan (1987) and Blejer and Liviatan (1987) as well as the papers in Bruno et al. (1988).

The new policy experiments open an important direction of research for the cases of less extreme inflation. When synchronization of pricing and exchange depreciation is not complete, and certainly when there are contracts of a duration of a few months, stopping inflation involves important coordination problems that may not be solved easily by just implementing a new monetary and fiscal policy. Expectations and contracts would stand in the way of an instant resetting of all prices to levels consistent with changed policies. As Simonsen (1987) has argued, a game-theoretic problem is involved and a freeze may solve this coordination problem in a better way than a sharp deceleration of money growth taken by itself. This assertion is developed in a number of case studies in Bruno et al. (1988). Of course, adherents of an equilibrium view will differ because they do not accept the premise that contracts are an overriding obstacle to stabilization that uses only changes in fundamentals. But other than the question of inflation inertia, these new programs also force a deeper discussion of policy. Recent experiences suggest that there are political economy aspects of stabilization that have received insufficient attention. Stabilizations that are costly in terms of output lost are for that reason politically vulnerable to the temptation of abandoning them in midstream. Because they are vulnerable they are likely to be attacked and hence are more likely to fail. Programs that build a strong support (as wage–price controls always do with the broad public) may generate a stronger potential for basic policy reform and hence for ultimately achieving the changes in fundamentals that warrant lower inflation.

References

Adam, C. and J. Greenwood (1985) 'Dual exchange rate systems and capital controls. An investigation.' *Journal of International Economics*, 18: 43–64.

Angell, J.W. (1986) *The theory of international prices*. New York: Augustus Kelley.

Backus, D. (1984) 'Exchange rate dynamics with staggered wage contracts', mimeo.

Backus, D. and J. Driffill (1985) 'Credibility and commitment in economic policy', Center for Economic Policy Research, London, mimeo.

Barro, R. (1974) 'Are government bonds net wealth?', *Journal of Political Economy*, 82: 1095–1118.

Barro, R. (1980) 'A capital market in an equilibrium business cycle model', *Econometrica*, 48: 1393–1417.

Barro, R. and D. Gordon (1983) 'A positive theory of monetary policy in a natural rate model', *Journal of Political Economy*, 91: 589–610.

Baxter, M. and A. Stockman (1989) 'Business cycles and the exchange rate regime: An empirical investigation', *Journal of Monetary Economics*, 23: 377–400.

Bilson, J.F.O. (1981) 'The "speculative efficiency" hypothesis', *Journal of Business*, 54: 435–452.

Blanco, H. and P. Garber, (1986) 'Recurrent devaluation and speculative attacks on the Mexican Peso', *Journal of Political Economy*, 1: 148–166.

Blejer, M. and N. Liviatan (1987) 'Fighting hyperinflation. Stabilization strategies in Argentina and Israel', *IMF Staff Papers*, 34: 409–438.

Bloomfield, A. (1959) *Monetary policy under the international gold standard*. New York: Federal Reserve Bank of New York.

Borensztein, E. and M. Dooley (1987) 'Options on foreign exchange and exchange rate expectations', *International Monetary Fund Staff Papers*, 34: 643–680.

Branson, W. and D. Henderson (1985) 'The specification and influence of asset markets', in: R. Jones and P. Kenen, eds., *Handbook of international economics*, Vol. 2. Amsterdam: North-Holland.

Branson, W., A. Fraga and R. Johnson (1985) 'Expected fiscal policy and the recession of 1982', Board of Governors of Federal Reserve, Washington, International Finance Discussion Paper 272.

Bresciani-Turroni, C. (1937) *The economics of inflation*. London: Allen & Unwin.

Bruno, M., G. diTella, R. Dornbusch and S. Fischer, eds. (1988) *Stopping high inflation*. Cambridge: M.I.T. Press.

Bryant, R., (1987) *International financial intermediation*. Washington: Brookings Institution.

Bryant, R. and R. Portes, eds. (1987) *Global macroeconomics*. London: Macmillan.

Bryant, R. and G. Holtham and P. Hooper (1987) *External deficits and the dollar*. Washington: Brookings Institution.

Buiter, W. (1987) 'Borrowing to defend the exchange rate and the timing and magnitude of speculative attacks', *Journal of International Economics*, 23: 221–240.

Buiter, W. and R. Marston, eds. (1985) *International economic policy coordination*. Cambridge: Cambridge University Press.

Calvo, G.A. (1981) 'Devaluation: Level versus rates', *Journal of International Economics*, 11: 165–172.

Calvo, G.A. (1983) 'Staggered contracts and exchange rate policy', in: J.A. Frenkel, ed., *Exchange rates and international macroeconomics*. Chicago: University of Chicago Press.

Calvo, G.A. (1985) 'Currency substitution and the real exchange rate: The utility maximization approach', *Journal of International Money and Finance*, 2: 175–188.

Calvo, G.A. (1986a) 'Incredible reforms', University of Pennsylvania, mimeo.

Calvo, G.A. (1986b) 'Temporary stabilization: Predetermined exchange rates', *Journal of Political Economy*, 94: 1319–1329.

Calvo, G.A. (1987) 'Notes on credibility and economic policy', University of Pennsylvania, mimeo.

Calvo, G.A. and C.A. Rodriguez (1977) 'A model of exchange rate determination and currency substitution and rational expectations', *Journal of Political Economy*, 85: 617–625.

Canzoneri, M.B. and J. Gray (1985) 'Monetary policy games and the consequences of non-cooperative behavior', *International Economic Review*, 26: 547–564.

Canzoneri, M. and D. Henderson (1988a) 'Is sovereign policymaking bad?', *Cornegie-Rochester Conference Series*, 28: 93–140.

Canzoneri, M. and D. Henderson (1988b) *Noncooperative monetary policies in interdependent economies*, forthcoming.

Caves, R. (1963) 'Flexible exchange rates', *American Economic Review*, 53: 120–129.

Collery, A. (1971) *International adjustment, open economies and the quantity theory of money*, Princeton Studies in International Finance. Princeton: Princeton University Press.

Cooper, R.N. (1969) 'Macroeconomic policy adjustment in interdependent economies', *Quarterly Journal of Economics*, 83: 1–29.

Cuddington, J. (1986) 'Capital flight: Estimates, issues and explanations', *International Studies in International Finance 58*.

Cumby, R. (1988) 'Is it risk?' *Journal of Monetary Economics*, 22: 279–300.

Cumby, R.E. and M. Obstfeld (1981) 'A note on exchange-rate expectations and nominal interest differentials: A test of the Fisher hypothesis', *Journal of Finance*, 36: 697–704.

Cumby, R.E. and M. Obstfeld (1984) 'International interest rate and price level linkages under flexible exchange rates: A review of recent evidence', in: J.F.O. Bilson and R.C. Marston, eds., *Exchange rate theory and practice*. Chicago: University of Chicago Press.

Davutyan, N. and J. Pippenger (1985) 'Purchasing power parity did not collapse during the 1970s', *American Economic Review*, 75: 1151–1158.

Dornbusch, R. (1976) 'Expectations and exchange rate dynamics', *Journal of Political Economy'*, 84: 1161–1176.

Dornbusch, R. (1983a) 'Exchange rate risk and the macroeconomics of exchange rate determination', in: R. Hawkins et al., eds., *The internationalization of financial markets and national economic policy*. New York: JAI Press.

Dornbusch, R. (1987a) 'Lessons from the German inflation experience of the 1920s', in: S. Fischer et al., eds., *Macroeconomics and finance*. Cambridge, Mass.: M.I.T. Press.

Dornbusch, R. (1987b) 'Exchange rate economics 1987', *Economic Journal*, 97: 1–18.

Dornbusch, R. (1987c) 'Purchasing power parity', *The new Palgrave's dictionary of economics*. London: Macmillan.

Dornbusch, R. (1988) 'Some doubts about the McKinnon standard', *Economic Perspectives*, 2: 105–112.

Dornbusch, R. and M. Mussa (1975) 'Consumption, real balances and the hoarding function', *International Economic Review*, 16: 415–421.

Dornbusch, R. and R. Fisher (1986) 'Stopping hyperinflation: Past and present', *Weltwirtschaftliches Archiv*, 122: 1–47.

Dornbusch, R. and J. Frankel (1987) 'The flexible exchange rate system. Experience and alternatives', in: S. Borner, ed., *International finance and trade in a polycentric world*. London: Macmillan, pp. 151–197.

Dornbusch, R. et al. (1983) 'The black market for dollars in Brazil', *Quarterly Journal of Economics*, 98: 25–40.

Drazen, A. and E. Helpman (1987) 'Stabilization with exchange rate management', *Quarterly Journal of Economics*, 102: 835–855.

Driskill, R.A. and S.M. Sheffrin (1981) 'On the mark: Comment', *American Economic Review*, 71: 1068–1074.

Edison, H. et al. (1986) 'An empirical analysis of policy coordination in the United States, Japan and Europe', Board of Governors of the Federal Reserve, International Finance Discussion Paper 286.

Edwards, S. (1982) 'Exchange rates and news: A multi-currency approach', *Journal of International Money and Finance*, 1: 211–224.

Engel, C.M. (1984) 'Testing for the absence of expected real profit from forward market speculation', *Journal of International Economics*, 17: 299–308.

Engel, C.M. (1985) 'Reliability of policy announcements and the effects of monetary policy', *European Economic Review*, 29: 137–155.

Engel, C.M. and A. Rodrigues (1987) 'Test of international CAPM with time varying covariances', University of Virginia, mimeo.

Fama, E.F. (1984) 'Forward and spot exchange rates,' *Journal of Monetary Economics*, 14: 319–338.

Federal Reserve Bank of New York (1987) 'International integration of financial markets and U.S. monetary policy', mimeo.

Feldstein, M. and C. Horioka (1980) 'Domestic savings and international capital flow', *The Economic Journal*, 90: 314–329.

Fischer, S. (1982) 'Seigniorage and the case for a national money' *Journal of Political Economy*, 90: 295–313.

Fischer, S. (1986) 'Comment: Panel on flexible exchange rate', *Brookings Papers on Economic Activity*, 1986-2: 227–232.

Fischer, S. (1988) 'International macroeconomic policy coordination', in: M. Feldstein, ed., *International economic cooperation*. Chicago: University of Chicago Press.

Fleming, M. (1962) 'Domestic financial policy under fixed and under floating exchange rates', *International Monetary Fund Staff Papers*, 9: 369–379.

Flood, R.P. and P. Garber (1984) 'Collapsing exchange rate regimes. Some linear examples', *Journal of International Economics*, 17: 1–13.

Flood, R.P. and R.J. Hodrick (1986) 'Money and the open economy business cycle, a flexible approach', NBER Working Paper 1967.

Frankel, J. (1979) 'On the mark: A theory of floating exchange rates based on interest differentials', *American Economic Review*, 69: 61–622.

Frankel, J. (1982) 'In search of the exchange risk premium: A six-currency test assuming mean–variance optimization', *Journal of International Money and Finance*, 1: 255–274.

Frankel, J. (1986) 'The implications of mean–variance optimization for four questions in international macroeconomics', *Journal of International Money and Finace*, 5: 553–575.

Frankel, J. (1987) 'The sources of disagreement among international macro models, and implications for policy coordination', University of California, Berkeley, mimeo.

Frankel, J. and K. Froot (1987) 'Using survey data to test standard propositions regarding exchange rate expectations', *American Economic Review*, 77: 133–153.

Frankel, J. and K. Froot (1989) 'Forward discount bias: Is it an exchange risk premium?', *Quarterly Journal of Economics*, 104: 139–162.

Frankel, J. and A. MacArthur (1988) 'Political vs. currency premia in international real interest rate differentials', *European Economic Review*, 32: 1083–1114.

Frankel, J. and R. Meese (1987) 'Are exchange rates excessively variable?', in: S. Fischer, ed., *NBER macoreconomcs annual*. Cambridge, Mass.: M.I.T. Press.

Frenkel, J.A. (1981) 'A collapse of PPP during the 1970s', *European Economic Review*, 16: 145–165.

Frenkel, J., ed. (1987) *Exchange rates and international macroeconomics*. Chicago: University of Chicago Press.

Frenkel, J. and H.G. Johnson, eds. (1975) *Flexible exchange rates*. Reading, Mass.: Addison-Wesley.

Frenkel, J. and H.G. Johnson, eds. (1976) *The monetary approach to the balance of payments*. London: Allen & Unwin.

Friedman, B. (1987) 'The substitutability of international assets', Harvard University, mimeo.

Friedman, M. (1953) *Essays in positive economics*. Chicago: University of Chicago Press.

Gavin, M. (1989) 'The stock market and exchange rate dynamics', *Journal of International Money and Finance*, 8: 181–200.

Genberg, H. (1978) 'Purchasing power parity under fixed and flexible exchange rates', *Journal of International Economics*, 8: 247–276.

Giavazzi, F. and M. Pagano (1988) 'The advantage of tying one's hands: EMS discipline and central bank credibility', *European Economic Review*, 32: 1055–1074.

Giavazzi, F. and A. Giovannini, (1986) 'The EMS and the dollar', *Economic Policy*, 1: 455–478.

Giavazzi, F. and A. Giovannini, (1987) 'Models of the EMS: Is Europe a greater deutsche mark area?', in: R. Bryant and R. Portes, eds. *Global macroeconomics*. London: Macmillan, pp. 237–272.

Giavazzi, F. and A. Giovannini, (1988) *The European monetary system*. Cambridge, Mass.: M.I.T. Press.

Giovannini, A. (1988a) 'Exchange rate and traded goods prices', *Journal of International Economics*, 24: 45–68.

Giovannini, A. (1988b) 'The macroeconomics of exchange rate and price-level interactions: Empirical evidence for West Germany', Columbia University, mimeo.

Giovannini, A. and P. Jorion (1989) 'The time-varying risk and return in the markets for foreign exchange and stocks', *Journal of Finance*, 44: 307–325.

Greenwood, J. and S. Williamson (1989) 'International financial intermediation and aggregate fluctuations under alternative exchange rate regimes', *Journal of Monetary Economics*, 23: 401–432.

Gros, D. (1987) 'The effectiveness of capital controls: Implications for monetary autonomy in the presence of incomplete market segmentation', *International Monetary Fund Staff Papers*, 34: 621–642.

Grossman, S.J. and R.J. Shiller (1981) 'The determinants of the variability of the stock market prices', *American Economic Review*, 71: 222–227.

Hahn, F. (1962) 'The balance of payments in a monetary economy', *Review of Economic Studies*, 25, 110–125.

Hahn, F. (1977) 'The monetary approach to the balance of payments', *Journal of International Economics*, 7: 231–250.

Hakkio, C.S. (1984) 'A re-examination of purchasing power parity', *Journal of International Economics*, 17: 265–277.

Hamada, K. (1985) *The political economy of international monetary interdependence*. Cambridge, Mass.: M.I.T. Press.

Hansen, L.P. and R.J. Hodrick (1980) 'Forward exchange rates as optimal predictors of future spot rates: An econometric analysis', *Journal of Political Economy*, 88: 829–853.

Hansen, L.P. and R.J. Hodrick (1983) 'Risk averse speculation in the forward foreign exchange market: An econometric analysis of linear models', in: J.A. Frenkel, ed., *Exchange rates and international macroeconomics*. Chicago: University of Chicago Press.

Hansen, L.P., S. Richard and K.J. Singleton (1981) 'Econometric implications of the intertemporal asset pricing model', mimeo.

Hardouvelis, G.A. (1984) 'Market perceptions of Federal Reserve policy and the weekly monetary announcements', *Journal of Monetary Economics*, 14: 225–240.

Harris, R.G. and D.D. Purvis (1981) 'Diverse information and market efficiency in a monetary model of the exchange rate', *The Economic Journal*, 91: 829–847.

Helpman, E. (1981) 'An exploration in the theory of exchange rates', *Journal of Political Economy*, 89: 865–890.

Helpman, E. and A. Razin (1979) 'A consistent comparison of alternative exchange rate regimes', *Canadian Journal of Economics*, 12: 394–409.

Helpman, E. and A. Razin (1982) 'A comparison of exchange rate regimes in the presence of imperfect capital markets', *International Economic Review*, 23: 365–388.

Helpman, E. and A. Razin (1984) 'The role of saving and investment in exchange rate determination under alternative monetary mechanisms', *Journal of Monetary Economics*, 13: 307–325.

Helpman, E. and A. Razin (1987) 'Exchange rate management: Intertemporal tradeoffs', *American Economic Review*, 77: 107–123.

Herring, R.J. and R.C. Marston (1977) *National monetary policy and international financial markets*. Amsterdam: North-Holland.

Hodrick, R.J. and S. Srivastava (1984) 'An investigation of risk and return in forward foreign exchange', *Journal of International Money and Finance*, 3: 5–29.

Hsieh, D.A. (1984) 'International risk sharing and the choice of exchange-rate regime', *Journal of International Money and Finance*, 3: 141–151.

International Monetary Fund (1977) *The monetary approach to the balance of payments*. Washington: International Monetary Fund.

International Monetary Fund (1987) *Theoretical aspects of the design Fund-supported adjustment programs*, Occasional Paper 55. Washington: International Monetary Fund.

Johnson, H.C. (1958) 'Toward a general theory of the balance of payments', in: H.G. Johnson, *International trade and economic growth*. London: Unwin University Books.

Johnson, H.C. (1962) 'The balance of payments', in: *Money trade and economic growth*. Cambridge, Mass.: Harvard University Press.

Johnson, H.G. (1973a) 'The monetary approach to balance of payments theory', in: H.G. Johnson, *Further essays in monetary economics*. Cambridge, Mass.: Harvard University Press.

Johnson, H.G. (1973b) 'The case for flexible exchange rates 1969', in: H.G. Johnson, *Further essays in monetary economics*. Cambridge, Mass.: Harvard University Press.

Johnson, R.A. (1986) 'Anticipated fiscal contraction: The economic consequences of the announcement of Gramm–Rudman–Hollings', International Finance Discussion Papers 291.

Jorion, P. and E. Schwartz (1986) 'Integration vs. segmentation in the Canadian stock market', *Journal of Finance*, 41: 603–613.

Jurgensen, P. (Chairman) (1983) 'Report of the Working Group on Exchange Market Intervention', Board of Governors of the Federal Reserve.

Kareken, J. and N. Wallace (1981) 'On the indeterminacy of equilibrium exchange rates', *The Quarterly Journal of Economics*, 156: 207–222.

Keynes, J.M. (1936) *The general theory of employment, interest and money*. London: Macmillan.

Kemp, M. (1962) 'The rate of exchange, the terms of trade and the balance of payments in a fully employed economy', *International Economic Review*, 3: 314–327.

Khan, M. et al. (1986) 'Adjustment with growth: Relating the analytical approaches of the World Bank and the IMF', The World Bank Discussion Paper: Development Policy Issues Series.

Kiguel, M. and N. Liviatan (1987) 'Inflationary rigidities and orthodox stabilization policies. Lessons from Latin America', *World Bank Economic Review*, 2: 273–298.

Kouri, P.J.K. (1975) 'Essays on the theory of flexible exchange rates', Unpublished M.I.T. dissertation.

Kouri, P.J.K. (1976) 'The exchange rate and the balance of payments in the short run and in the long run. A monetary approach', *Scandinavian Journal of Economics*, 78: 280–304.

Kouri, P.J.K. and J. de Macedo (1978) 'Exchange rates and the international adjustment process', *Brookings Papers on Economic Activity*, 1978-1: 11–50.

Kouri, P.J.K. and M.G. Porter (1974) 'International capital flows and portfolio equilibrium', *Journal of Political Economy*, 82: 443–467.

Kravis, I.B. and R. Lipsey (1984) 'Toward an explanation of national price levels', Princeton Studies in International Finance 52, International Finance Section, Princeton University.

Kreicher, L.L. (1982) 'Eurodollar arbitrage', *Federal Reserve Bank of New York Quarterly Review*, 7: 10–22.

Krueger, A. (1971) 'Balance of payments theory', *Journal of Economic Literature*, 7: 1–26.

Krugman, P., (1978) 'Purchasing power parity and exchange rates: Another look at the evidence', *Journal of International Economics*, 8: 397–407.

Krugman, P., (1979) 'A model of balance of payments crises', *Journal of Money, Credit and Banking*, 3: 311–325.

Krugman, P. (1982) 'Consumption preferences and the risk premium', Massachusetts Institute of Technology, mimeo.

Krugman, P. (1985) 'Is the strong dollar sustainable?', in: Federal Reserve Bank of Kansas, *The U.S. dollar – recent developments*. Kansas, pp. 103–132.

Leiderman, L. (1979) 'Expectation and output–inflation tradeoff in a fixed-exchange-rate economy', *Journal of Political Economy*, 87: 1285–1306.

Lessard, D. and J. Williamson, eds. (1987) *Capital flight and Third World debt*. Washington: Institute for International Economics.

Liviatan, N. (1981) 'Monetary expansion and real exchange rate dynamics', *Journal of Political Economy*, 89: 1218–1227.

Lizondo, J.S. (1983) 'Foreign exchange futures prices under fixed exchange rates', *Journal of International Economics*, 14: 69–84.

Lucas, R. (1972) 'Expectations and the neutrality of money', *Journal of Economic Theory*, 4: 103–124.

Lucas, R. (1978) 'Assets prices in an exchange economy', *Econometrica*, 46: 1429–1445.

Lucas, R. (1982) 'Interest rates and currency prices in a two-country world', *Journal of Monetary Economics*, 10: 335–360.

Lyons, R. (1987) 'Exchange dynamics with monetary policy uncertainty', Unpublished Ph.D. dissertation, M.I.T.

Marquez, J. (1987) 'Money demand in open economies: A currency substitution model for Venezuela', *Journal of International Money and Finance*, 6: 167–178.

McKinnon, R. (1974) *A new tripartite monetary system or a limping dollar standard*, Essays in International Finance 106. Princeton: International Finance Section, Princeton University.

McKinnon, (1982) 'Currency substitution and instability in the world dollar standard', *American Economic Review*, 72: 320–333.

McKinnon, R. (1984) *An international standard for monetary stabilization*, Policy Analyses in International Economics 8. Institute for International Economics.

McKinnon, R. (1988) 'Monetary and exchange rate policies for international financial stability: A proposal', *Economic Perspectives*, 2: 83–104.

Meade, J.E. (1951) *The balance of payments*. London: Oxford University Press.

Meese, R.A. (1984) 'Is the sticky price assumption reasonable for exchange rate models?', *Journal of International Money and Finance*, 3: 247–260.

Meese, R.A. (1986) 'Testing for bubbles in exchange markets. A case of sparking rates?', *Journal of Political Economy*, 94: 345–373.

Miller, P.J. and N. Wallace (1985) 'International coordination of macroeconomic policies: A welfare analysis', *Federal Reserve Bank of Minneapolis Quarterly Review*, 9: 14–32.

Miller, M. and J. Williamson (1987) 'The international monetary system: An analysis of alternative regimes', Institute for International Economics, mimeo.

Morgenstern, O. (1959) *International financial transactions and business cycles*. Princeton: Princeton University Press.

Mundell, R.A. (1960) 'The public debt, corporate income taxes and the rate of interest', *Journal of Political Economy*, 68: 622–626.

Mundell, R.A. (1961) 'A theory of optimum currency areas', *American Economic Review*, 51: 651–667.

Mundell, R.A. (1968) *International economics*. New York and Toronto: Macmillan.

Mundell, R.A. (1971) *Monetary theory*. Pacific Palisades: Goodyear Publishing Company.

Murphy, R.G. (1984) 'Capital mobility and the relationship between savings and investment in OECD countries', *Journal of International Money and Finance*, 3: 327–342.

Mussa, M. (1976) 'The exchange rate, the balance of payments and monetary and fiscal policy under a regime of controlled floating', *Scandinavian Journal of Economics*, 78, 229–248.

Mussa, M. (1982a) 'A model of exchange rate dynamics', *Journal of Political Economy*, 90: 74–101.

Mussa, M. (1982b) 'The theory of exchange rate determination', in: J. Bilson and R. Marston, eds., *Exchange rate theory*. Chicago: University of Chicago Press.

Mussa, M. (1986) 'Nominal exchange rate regimes and the behavior of real exchange rates: Evidence and implications', *Carnegie-Rochester Conference Series on Public Policy*, 25: 117–214.

Negishi, T. (1965) 'Approaches to the analysis of devaluation', *International Economic Review*, 9: 218–227.

Nurkse, R. (1946) *International currency experience in the interwar period*. Geneva: League of Nations. Reprinted by Arno Press.

Obstfeld, M. (1980) 'Sterilization and offsetting capital movement: Evidence from West Germany, 1960–1970', NBER Working Paper 494.

Obstfeld, M. (1981) 'Macroeconomic policy, exchange-rate dynamics, and optimal asset accumulation', *Journal of Political Economy*, 89: 1142–1161.

Obstfeld, M. (1982) 'The capitalization of income stream and the effects of open-market policy under fixed exchange rate', *Journal of Monetary Economics*, 9: 87–98.

Obstfeld, M. (1983) 'Exchange-rate, inflation and the sterilization problems: Germany, 1975–81', *European Economic Review*, 21: 161–189.

Obstfeld, M. (1984) 'Balance of payments crises and devaluation', *Journal of Money, Credit and Banking*, 16: 311–325.

Obstfeld, M. (1986a) 'Capital controls, the dual exchange rate and devaluation', *Journal of International Economics*, 20: 1–20.

Obstfeld, M. (1986b) 'Capital mobility in the world economy: Theory and measurement', *Carnegie-Rochester Conference Series on Public Policy*, 24: 55–104.

Obstfeld, M. (1988) 'A theory of capital flight and currency depreciation', National Bureau of Economic Research, mimeo.

Obstfeld, M. and K. Rogoff (1984) 'International exchange dynamics with sluggish prices under alternative price adjustment rules', *International Economic Review*, 25: 1–15.

Ortiz, G. (1983) 'Dollarization in Mexico: Causes and consequences', in: P. Aspe et al., eds., *Financial policies and the world capital market: The problem of Latin American countries*. Chicago: Chicago University Press.

Oudiz, G. and J. Sachs (1985) 'International policy coordination in dynamic macroeconomic models', in: W. Buiter and R. Marston, eds., *International economic policy coordination*. Cambridge: Cambridge University Press.

Penati, A. and G. Pennacchi (1989) 'Optimal portfolio choice and the collapse of a fixed exchange rate regime', *Journal of International Economics*, 27: 1–24.

Persson, T. and L.O. Svensson (1987) 'Exchange rate variability and asset trade', mimeo.

Phelps, E.S. (1969) *Microeconomic foundations of employment and inflation theory*. New York: Norton.

Phelps, E.S. (1973) 'Inflation in the theory of public finance', *Swedish Journal of Economics*, 75: 66–82.

Phelps, E.S. (1978) 'Disinflation without recession: Adaptive guideposts and monetary policy', in: E.S. Phelps, ed., *Studies in macroeconomic theory*. New York: Academic Press.

Polak, J. (1957) 'Monetary analysis of payments problems and income formation', *International Monetary Fund Staff Papers*, 5: 1–50.

Poole, W. (1970) 'Optimal choice of monetary policy instruments in a simple stochastic macro model', *Quarterly Journal of Economics*, 134: 197–216.

Prais, S. (1961) 'Some mathematical notes on the quantity of money in the open economy', *International Monetary Fund Staff Papers*, 9: 212–226.

Ramirez-Rojas, C.L. (1985) 'Currency substitution in Argentina, Mexico and Uruguay', *International Monetary Fund Staff Papers*, 32: 629–667.

Rist, C. (1966) *Monetary and credit theory* (Reprints of Economic Classics). New York: Augustus Kelley.

Robichek, W. (1986) 'Financial programming as practiced by the IMF', World Bank, mimeo.

Rogoff, K. (1984) 'On the effects of sterilized intervention: An analysis of weekly data', *Journal of Monetary Economics*, 14: 133–150.

Rogoff, K. (1985) 'Can international monetary cooperation be counterproductive?', *Journal of International Economics*, 18: 199–217.

Saidi, N.H. (1980) 'Fluctuating exchange-rate and the international transmission of economic disturbances', *Journal of Money, Credit and Banking*, 12: 575–591.

Salant, S.W. and D.W. Henderson (1978) 'Market anticipations of government policies and the price of gold', *Journal of Political Economy*, 86: 627–648.

Sargent, T.J. (1983a) 'Comment', in: P. Aspe, R. Dornbusch and M. Obstfeld, eds., *Financial policies and the world capital market: The problem of Latin American countries*. Chicago: Chicago University Press.

Sargent, T.J. (1983b) 'Stopping moderate inflation: The methods of Poincare and Thatcher', in: R. Dornbusch and M. Simonsen, eds., *Inflation, debt and indexation*. Cambridge, Mass.: M.I.T. Press.

Sargent, T.J. (1983c) 'The end of four big inflations', in: R. Hall, ed., *Inflation*. Chicago: University of Chicago Press.

Simonsen, M. (1987) 'Incomes policy, game theory and rational expectations', Getulio Vargas Foundation, mimeo.

Stockman, A.C. (1979) 'Monetary control and sterilization under pegged exchange rates', University of Rochester, mimeo.

Stockman, A.C. (1980) 'A theory of exchange rate determination', *Journal of Political Economy*, 88: 673–698.

Stockman, A.C. (1983) 'Real exchange rate under alternative nominal exchange rate systems', *Journal of International Money and Finance*, 2: 147–166.

Stockman, A.C. (1987a) 'Exchange rate systems and relative prices', *Journal of Policy Modelling*, 9: 245–256.

Stockman, A.C. (1987b) 'The equilibrium approach to exchange rates', *Federal Reserve Bank of Richmond Economic Review*, 16: 12–30.

Stockman, A.C. and A.T. Koh (1986) 'Open-economy implication of two models of business fluctuation', *Canadian Journal of Economics*, 29: 23–34.

Stulz, R.M. (1983) 'Currency preferences, purchasing power risks and determination of exchange rates in an optimization model', mimeo.

Svensson, L.E.O. (1985a) 'Money and asset prices in a cash-in-advance economy', *Journal of Political Economy*, 93: 919–944.

Svensson, L.E.O. (1985b) 'Currency prices, terms of trade, and interest rates', *Journal of International Economics*, 18: 17–41.

Svensson, L.E.O. and S. van Wijnbergen (1986) 'International transmission of monetary policy', Seminar Paper 362, University of Stockholm, Institute for International Economic Studies.

Taylor, J.B. (1980) 'Aggregate dynamics and staggered contracts', *Journal of Political Economy*, 8: 1–17.

Tobin, J. (1982) 'A proposal of international monetary reform', in: *Essays in economics: Theory and policy*. Cambridge, Mass.: M.I.T. Press.

Tornell, A. (1988) 'Insulating properties of dual exchange rates. A new-classical approach', Discussion Paper series 380, Columbia University.

Tower, E. and T. Willett (1976) *The theory of optimum currency areas and exchange rate flexibility*, Special Papers in International Economics, International Finance Section. Princeton: Princeton University Press.

Wicker, E. (1986) 'Terminating hyperinflation in the dismembered Habsburg monarchy', *American Economic Review*, 76: 350–364.

Wilson, C. (1979) 'Exchange rate dynamics and anticipated disturbances', *Journal of Political Economy*, 87: 639–647.

INDEX